SPURGEON'S
PROVERBS and SAYINGS
WITH NOTES

SPURGEON'S
PROVERBS and SAYINGS
WITH NOTES

VOL. I — A to L

C. H. SPURGEON

BAKER BOOK HOUSE
Grand Rapids, Michigan

Formerly published under the title,
The Salt-Cellars, Volumes I and II

Reprinted 1975 by
Baker Book House Company
ISBN: 0-8010-8052-5

PHOTOLITHOPRINTED BY CUSHING - MALLOY, INC.
ANN ARBOR, MICHIGAN, UNITED STATES OF AMERICA
1975

PREFACE

FOR many years I have published a Sheet Almanack, intended to be hung up in workshops and kitchens. This has been known as " John Ploughman's Almanack," and has had a large sale. It has promoted temperance, thrift, kindness to animals, and a regard for religion, among working people. The placing of a proverb for every day for twenty years has cost me great labour, and I feel that I cannot afford to lose the large collection of sentences which I have thus brought together : yet lost they would be, if left to die with the ephemeral sheet. Hence these two volumes. They do not profess to be a complete collection of proverbs, but only a few out of many thousands.

The salt of proverbs is of great service if discreetly used in sermons and addresses; and I have hope that these SALT-CELLARS of mine may be resorted to by teachers and speakers, and that they may find them helpful. There are many proverb books, but none exactly like these. I have not followed any one of the other collections, although, of necessity, the most of the quaint sayings are the same as will be found in them. Some of my sentences are quite new, and more are put into a fresh form. The careful omission of all that are questionable as to purity has been my aim; but should any one of them, unknown to me, have another meaning than I have seen in it, I cannot help it, and must trust the reader to accept the best and purest sense which it bears; for that is what it meant *to me.* It is a pity that the salt of a proverb should ever be unsavoury; but, beyond doubt, in several of the best collections, there are very questionable ones, which ought to be forgotten. It is better to *select* than indiscriminately to *collect.* An old saying which is not clean ought not to be preserved because of its age; but it should, for that reason, be the more readily dropped, since it must have done harm enough already, and the sooner the old rottenness is buried the better.

My homely notes are made up, as a rule, of other proverbial expressions. They are intended to give hints as to how the proverbs may be used by those who are willing to flavour their speech with them. I may not, in every case, have hit upon the first meaning of the maxims: possibly, in some instances, the sense which I have put upon them may not be the general one; but the meanings given are such as they may bear without a twist, and such as commended themselves to me for general usefulness. The antiquary has not been the guide in this case; but the moralist and the Christian.

From what sources I have gleaned these proverbs it is impossible for me to tell. They have been jotted down as they were met with. Having become common property, it is not easy to find out their original proprietors. If I knew where I found a pithy sentence, I would acknowledge the source most freely; but the gleanings of years, in innumerable fields, cannot now be traced to this literary estate or to that. In the mass, I confess that almost everything in these books is borrowed—from cyclopædias of proverbs, "garlands," almanacks, books, newspapers, magazines—from anywhere and everywhere. A few proverbs I may myself have made, though even this is difficult; but, from the necessity of the case, sentences which have become proverbs are things to be quoted, and not to be invented.

Lists of proverb-books are common enough, and there is no need to present another in this short preface; but I believe I have read them all, and the most of them year after year, till their contents dwell in my memory, and are repeated by a use which has become a second nature, almost without the thought of their having been the sayings of men of old time.

One who has written many books upon solid subjects may well be excused for finding relief and recreation in lighter forms of literature. If even the inspired Scripture affords space for " the words of the wise, and their dark sayings," there would seem to be allowance, if not example, for the ordinary teacher supplementing his Psalms with proverbs, and his Ecclesiastes with selections from the wisdom of the ancients. I have never lost sight of my one aim in a page which I have written, whether the manner has been grave or gay; and that one aim has been the spiritual good of my readers. A line may strike where a discourse may miss. Godly sentiments sandwiched in between slices of wit and common-sense, may become nutriment for the soul, although they may be almost unconsciously received. Pills when gilded may be none the less health-giving. Under this belief, I have therefore placed, not only moral precepts, but Gospel instructions in the midst of these common maxims. Thus has the salt itself been salted. The good hope abides with me that I may lure to better things by things which are themselves good. " Stepping-stones of our dead selves " may be a pretty poetical phrase; but, practically, stepping-stones to the highest attainments are better found among common-sense sayings applicable to everyday life, which lead up to a high morality, and then charm us on to that which mere morals can never teach. Perchance, while amused with the wit and wisdom of men, some reader may perceive the glow of a diviner light, and may be led to seek after its clearer illumination. This is the innermost design of my work. If the occupation of hours in which it was imperative upon me to find rest by ceasing from more weighty themes will only lead to this, I shall be happy indeed.

Books of illustration are admirable helps to teachers; but it seems to me that in proverbs they will find suggestions of the very best illustrations. Those short sentences are often summaries of discourse, verdicts given after the hearing of the case, or else briefs for the pleaders on the one side or the other of a disputed question. When wisely quoted they arouse attention, and in some cases carry conviction. Sermons would seldom be dull if they were more alive with aphorisms and epigrams. These are not the point of the shaft, but they may be the feathers of the arrow. Comparatively they are trifles; but nothing is trifling by which serious truth can be brought home to careless minds. Our age is restless, and we must not be prosy; men are ever seeking some new thing, and therefore we must not, by our dulness, increase their weariness of the old. We must regard the words of Holy Writ, and remember that it is written :—

"𝔐oreover, because the preacher was wise, he still taught the people knowledge; yea, he gave good heed, and sought out, and set in order many proverbs."

Proverbs and Quaint Sayings.

 BAD bank-note is sure to come back.

> Some say, "A bad penny comes home." Anything evil will come back to the man who sent it out.

A bad book is a big thief,

For it robs a man of his time, and of his good principles. Many young people have been ruined by the vile literature which is now so common. A German writer says, "Such books rob the public of time, money, and the attention which ought properly to belong to good literature with noble aims. Of bad books we can never read too little; of the good never too much."

> Books should to one of these four ends conduce:
> For wisdom, piety, delight, or use.

A bad dog does not see the thief.

We have plenty of such dogs nowadays. Ministers will not see the error which abounds; statesmen wink hard at vice; and religious people sleep while Satan plunders the church.

A bad dog may get a good bone.

Often very unworthy men gain fortunes, offices, and honours. This world is not *the* place of rewards and punishments, and so it happens that Satan's bullocks often feed in the fattest pastures

A bad excuse is worse than none.

A bad horse eats as much as a good one.

A reason for keeping good cattle, and employing efficient persons.

A bad husband cannot be a good man.

He fails in the tenderest duties, and must be bad at heart.

A bad motive makes a good action bad.

What appeared good enough in itself has often been polluted by the motive. It might be well to kiss the Lord Jesus, but the motive of Judas made his kiss a crime.

A bad padlock invites a picklock.

Carelessness on the part of owners may prove a temptation to servants and others. We should not put theft into their minds by want of proper care.

A bad reaper blames the sickle.

Every bad workman finds fault with his tools. The Chinese say :—

> " All unskilful fools
> Quarrel with their tools."

A bad servant will not make a good master.

Observation proves this. He who does not shine in one position will not shine in another. Yet a good servant does not always make a good master; for he may not have brain enough to go first, though he may have all the virtues which enable him to be a good second.

A bad wife likes her husband's heel to be towards home.

She is very different from her who so sweetly sang—

> " Sae sweet his voice, sae smooth his tongue,
>   His breath's like caller air ;
> His very foot has music in't
>   As he comes up the stair.

> " There's nae luck about the house,
>   There's nae luck at a' ;
> There's little pleasure in the house
>   When our gudeman's awa'."

A bargain is a bargain.

See what is said of the just man in Ps. xv. 4 : " He sweareth to his own hurt, and changeth not."

A bird in hand is better far
Than two which in the bushes are.

> This proverb turns up in several forms, but it always means that we are to prefer that which we have to that which we only expect. It is a proverb of this world only, and is not true on the broad field of eternal things. There our bird in the bush is worth all the birds that ever were in mortal hand.

A bird is known by his note, and a man by his talk.

> "By thy words thou shalt be justified, and by thy words thou shalt be condemned."—Matt. xii. 37.

A bird that cannot be shot may be snared.

> Dispositions vary, and Satan knows how to fit his temptation to our temperament. He who will not fall into open sin may be seduced into secret unbelief or pride.

A bitten child is afraid of a stuffed dog.

> The same sense as "A burnt child dreads the fire," or "A scalded cat dreads cold water." It were well if more who have suffered from sin would have a solemn fear of it, and henceforth shun it.

A black hen lays a white egg.

> Black sorrows bring us joyous results.

A blind man does not see himself in a looking-glass.

> Neither do the spiritually blind see themselves in the Word of God, although it is a perfect mirror of truth and character.

A blind man gets small good of a lantern.

> All the illumination in the world will not make a man see spiritual things unless the Holy Spirit opens his eyes. *Miss Cobbe* asks, "What shall it profit a man if he finds the origin of species, and knows exactly how earth-worms and sun-dews conduct themselves, if all the while he grows blind to the loveliness of nature, and is as unable to lift his soul to the Divine and Eternal as were the primæval apes?"

A blind man is no judge of colours.

> When persons profess to criticize things which they know nothing about, this proverb may be applied to them.

A blithe heart makes a blooming face.

> A blooming face is an attraction to a shop or to a place of worship. We should endeavour to be cheerful in our manner, but this will be best secured by having a happy heart within our bosom. A merry heart makes music wherever it goes. The light within the soul shines out through the windows of the eyes.

A blustering fellow is always a coward.

> This observation has come down through long ages of observers. It is a rule to which there are very few exceptions. Mr. Bluster is soon in a fluster.

A boaster and a fool are two of a school.

A boaster and a liar are first cousins.

A boaster and a liar are much about the same thing.

> These three proverbs are but specimens of many just observations upon the vice of bragging. It would be hard to tell where a boast ends and a lie begins : it is like the distinction between a snake and its tail. Boasters are hardly conscious of their own falsehoods, for they have talked themselves into believing their own bombast.

A borrower is another name for a beggar.

A boy is a boy; two boys are half a boy; three boys are no boy at all.

> One may do something ; two will waste time ; three will do nothing. The Chinese say, "One man will carry two buckets of water for his own use; two men will carry one for their joint use ; but three will carry none for anybody's use."

A boy untaught will be taught by the devil.

A braying donkey may spoil a grazing donkey's business.

> A noisy person may prevent a neighbour from following his work with success, and may even cause a prejudice against others in the same line who are quiet and unassuming.

A brazen face and a broken heart
Are things you'll find are far apart.

> The manner of the penitent is very different from that of the person who is bold and impudent in evil. Holy bashfulness goes with penitence. A blushing face and a broken heart are beautiful in the sight of heaven.

A bridle for the tongue is a fine piece of harness.

> And all the more so because when this is secured all is right, for the whole man is harnessed when the tongue is under due command.

A cake in peace is worth a loaf in trouble.

A calf seems a big beast till you see a cow.

> A beginner claims your admiration till you see one who is fully instructed in the art.

A calf will not be a cow in a year.

> We must have patience with young people and learners, who will grow to something if we give them time.

A careless watchman invites thieves.

A carnal heart cannot like truth, because it is not like to truth.

A cat may look at a king.

> Surely there's no harm in looking; but no one should stare in a rude manner either at kings or clowns. No doubt a cat would sooner see a mouse than a monarch.

A cat must not always keep her back up.

> If now and then a man has to assert himself, and be on the war-path, let him come to his usual level as soon as possible.

A cat on hot bricks is all in a hurry.

> And so is a person when he is out of his element. Many a man at church, or in court, or at a prayer-meeting, or by a dying-bed is very much in this unhappy condition.

A cat with a silver collar is none the better mouser.

> Fine dress, learned degrees, high titles, and grand offices do not give ability. We have heard of doctors of divinity who were duller preachers than the generality of the clergy.

A cheerful spirit moveth quick;
A grumbler in the mud will stick.

A cheerful wife is the joy of life.

A child is a burden as well as a blessing.

A clear conscience gives sound sleep.

A clear conscience is a coat of mail.

A clear conscience is a good pillow.

> One said that he had a conscience which was as good as new, for he had never used it ; and he is the representative of many. It would be a great blessing if some men were a little more troubled by conscience At the same time, a conscience void of offence is a quietus for fear : we are afraid of meeting neither God nor man when conscience is cleansed.

A clear head is desirable ; but a clean heart is essential.

A clear understanding saves much quarrelling.

> When a bargain is not plainly put, the loser is sure to raise questions in after days, and a bitter spirit is likely to be engendered. Care should be taken in this matter when the dealings are between relatives and friends, for families have often been divided through agreements which created disagreements, because they were not clearly worded and fully understood.

A clever head is all the better for a close mouth.

> Then the man will *act* rather than gossip; and he will not disclose his plans before the proper time for carrying them out.

A cloudy morning may bring a clear day.

> We may begin a work with trouble, and yet the business may bring us great joy as it proceeds.

A club at a " pub " is a dangerous weapon.

> No doubt many are injured and even killed by the drink, which comes in the way of the club at its meetings. There is not much profit in joining a club where you spend sixpence a week to save a shilling a month.

A cock often crows without a victory.

> Silly bird ! Sillier men who imitate him !

A cold which comes sneezing
Goes off in short season.

> Whether this is medically true or not I cannot say, but I have heard the saying in Essex.

A contented mind has a continual feast.

A cow does not know what her tail is worth till she has lost it.

Neither do any of us value our mercies till we lose them.

A cow in a parlour does best when it makes for the door.

When one gets into the wrong place it is his wisdom to get out of it quickly.

A cow is not ashamed because it cannot fly.

Let no man blush because he cannot do what he was never made for. The coachman on the Bath coach could not tell the names of the gentry who owned the mansions along the road, but he gave a fine answer to the angry passenger who asked, "What do you know?" when he replied, "I know how to drive this coach to Bath."

A cow stares at a new gate.

Novelties arrest the attention of many, although there may be nothing in them worth a moment's thought. *Martin Luther* used this expression in reference to the sectaries of his time who were carried away with the last new opinion : he said that they stared at a doctrine like a cow at a new gate.

A cow's tail droops down, yet never drops off.

Many institutions look as if they would fall, but they have not done so yet, and they will not do so for many a year.

A cracked bell can never sound well.

A cracked bell is sure to be heard.

Everyone notices a foolish speech, though they will forget sound teaching.

A cracked bell should not be rung.

It would be well if we could keep foolish persons quiet. But who can? If they were not cracked you might quiet them, but they have not wit enough to hold their tongues.

A cracked plate will last long if handled with care.

Invalids may hold out if they are careful. Good work may be done by feeble persons, if they are prudent and prayerful.

A creaking door hangs long on its hinges.

Persons who are usually ill often live on for many years, while robust persons die suddenly. This may comfort the invalid, and be a warning to the strong.

A cripple in the right road is better than a racer in the wrong.

A cunning man is not a canny man.

One had better keep clear of him : he is too clever for the most of us—too crafty to be honest.

A day's playing is as hard work as a day's ploughing.

See the working-man carrying a child and a basket, steaming and sweating as he drags along. See how hard he works when he calls it holiday ! The illustrations are superabundant.

A dirty tale should neither be told nor heard.

How we wish that this were carried out ! If it were not told, it could not be heard ; and if it were not heard, it would not be told.

A doctor and a ploughman know more than a doctor alone.

A dog may look at a doctor.

But he must not dogmatize with him.

A donkey brays when he likes, because he is a donkey.

Uncouth, uneducated persons talk, and make noises without regard to others, simply because they are uncivilized beings.

A donkey may grow, but he will never be an elephant.

It is not in some men, advance as they may, to grow out of their natural folly, and arrive at any measure of sagacity.

A drinking dame :
A sight of shame !

Yet, how sadly common is such a horrible spectacle ! A lady drunk ! A wife and mother tippling ! The vice is equally wicked in men, but in women it wears a special shame. What heart-break this evil is making in many a house !

A drinking man is on the road to Needham.

He will soon have need in his purse, and need in his house : his way to Needham will be short and sure.

A drop of gin is a drop too much.

> We can only say, " Drop it."

A drowning man will catch at razors.

> A man who is losing money will gamble, or speculate, or try the most shameful trick to save himself. Thus he hurts himself still more, and makes his ruin and wretchedness sure.

A drunkard's mouth dries up his pocket.

> All his money runs into the hole just below his nose.

A duck of a child grows up a goose of a man.

> He is fondled and spoiled, coddled and made a fool of.

A dull morning follows a drunken night.

> The poor creature has headache and general lowness of spirits, and he tries to " get his spirits up by pouring spirits down." He must have " a hair of the dog that bit him." He hastens to his cups again, because he feels a cup too low. To use the popular pun : " It is champagne at night and real pain in the morning."

A fair face may be a foul bargain.

> Young men should not be carried away with mere beauty, but look to character and disposition. One who marries a woman for her beauty alone is as foolish as the man who ate a bird because it sang so sweetly.

A faithful friend is hard to find
Among ten thousand of mankind.

A faithful friend loves to the end.

> Where there comes an unhappy end to friendship there never was any friendship worthy of the name.

A faithful preacher is a rare creature.

> And, like a diamond, as precious as he is rare.

A false promise thou must shun,
'Tis a lie and theft in one.

A false tale is a nimble footman.

> It runs everywhere, and knocks at everybody's door long before the truth is out of bed.

A fault confessed is half redressed.

By the confession of it, the man has begun to undo the mischief of his action. Let us hope he will redress the other half.

A fault-mender is better than a fault-finder.

A fault once excused is twice committed.

By the excuse you try to justify the wrong, and so you do it again. By the fault you commit a trespass, but by an excuse you set up a sort of claim to a right of way; and this is a worse injury than the first offence.

A fine bonnet may cover an empty head.

When very fine and tawdry there is no doubt about it.

A fine woman can do without fine clothes.

Do women dress heavily when they are ugly? They know best how much they need to set them off.

A fog will not be driven away with a fan.

Trifling acts cannot accomplish great results.

A fool and his money are soon parted.

We have heard it neatly put, "There is a proverb about a certain class of persons and their cash."

A fool and his words are soon parted.

"For so," says *Shenstone,* "should the proverb run."

A fool calls others fools.

He ought to be a judge of fools, since he is in that line himself. Perhaps he unconsciously hopes that he may turn upon others the contempt which he half suspects is due to himself.

A fool frets to flourish full in front.

He must be seen and noticed or he is unhappy.

A fool, if he saith he will have a crab, will not accept an apple instead.

So obstinate is he that he will not change to his own profit.

A fool in a gown is none the wiser.

The same is true of any member of All Fools' College when he wears a square cap.

A fool in his own house will not be wise in mine.

If he does not know his own business he will not be likely to know mine one half so well. It is idle to seek or accept counsel from one who has already failed in the management of his own concerns.

A fool is a man who is wise too late.

This is a sententious and instructive definition. Alas, how many are in that condition on a dying bed!

A fool is happier thinking well of himself, than a wise man is in others thinking well of him.

No doubt a good conceit of one's self is a primary element of the fool's paradise in which some live. It might be a pity to undeceive some men, for they would be very unhappy, and perhaps lose some of the energy with which they get through life at present.

A fool is never wrong.

If he were not a fool he would own that he sometimes makes a mistake, but he is not sensible enough for that. Someone advertises "Sensible Boots"; would even these furnish a fool with a good understanding? Even if he should wear a wide-awake, would he get out of the dream of his personal infallibility?

A fool lingers long, but time hurries on.

Oh, that men would be prompt to seek salvation while it is called to-day!

A fool says, "I can't"; a wise man says, "I'll try."

John Ploughman says ·—

"Once let every man say *Try*,
Very few on straw would lie,
Fewer still of want would die;
Pans would all have fish to fry;
Pigs would fill the poor man's sty;
Want would cease, and need would fly;
Wives and children cease to cry;
Poor rates would not swell so high:
Things wouldn't go so much awry—
You'd be glad, and so would I."

A fool is none the wiser for having a learned grandfather.

The boast of pedigree is common, but silly.

A fool with wisdom is like a cow with a nutmeg.

He does not know what to do with it : he does not like the flavour of it : before long he drops it.   But we had need be chary of what we say about fools, lest someone should reckon us among them. There is a passage which is very hard on proverb collectors—

"This formal fool, your man, speaks nought but proverbs ;
And speak men what they can to him he'll answer
With some rhyme-rotten sentence, or old saying,
Such spokes as the ancients of the parish use."

A fool's fortune is his misfortune.

He rushes into all the more extravagance and vice because he has the means of paying for his pleasures.   Nothing is a greater misfortune to some young men than to be born rich.   Yet many fathers are hoarding that they may ruin their heirs.   If a young man is to be burned, it is a pity that his father should slave to gather the faggots.

A fool's gun is soon fired.

He has little to say, but he is in a desperate hurry to say it.   In olden times they said " A fool's bolt is soon shot."

A fool's heart dances on his lips.

Especially if he is what the French call "a fool of 25 carats " (the finest gold is 24 carats).   Such a special, particular fool must tell out all his silly soul.

A foolish man diligently advertises his own folly.

He will talk, and talk most upon that which he should never mention for his credit's sake.

A foolish man is generally a proud man.

A foolish woman is known by her finery.

A free-thinker is Satan's bondsman.

A friend is easier lost than found.

A friend must bear with a friend's infirmities.

David did not slight Mephibosheth because he was lame.   Mental weaknesses, such as quick temper, fancies, peculiarities, and odd habits must be borne with if friendship is to last.

A full cup needs a steady hand.

> Prosperity is not easily endured. Many make a sad spill.

A full grate should make us grateful.

A gardener is known by his garden ;

> Or, "As the garden so is the gardener." Every man's character may be seen in his work.

A garment of sanctity is better than a gown of satin.

> The beauty of holiness is a far fairer adornment than all that rich raiment can supply.

A glutton buries himself in pudding.

> And when he does so, we may call him "a toad in a hole."

A good book is the best companion.

> It will speak or be quiet, and it neither talks nonsense nor perpetrates folly.
>
> > If love, joy, laughter, sorrow please my mind,
> > Love, joy, grief, laughter in my books I find.

A good cat should have a good rat.

> And so she will if she catches it herself. God helps those who help themselves. We all wish well to him who works well. "May the best man win!"

A good character is an estate.

> Those who have lost it know what poverty it brings : they cannot even obtain a situation in which to earn their daily bread. Some are like the Irishman who, on applying for a situation, was asked for his character. "Well, sir," said he, "my last master said he thought I should do better without my character. He was afraid it would hinder my getting a place!"

A good conscience hath good confidence.

A good conscience is a choice companion.

> When others forsake and condemn, its verdict sustains the spirit.

A good example is a powerful sermon.

A good farthing is better than a bad sovereign.

A good education is the best dowry.

A young man may lose his estate, but knowledge will stick by him, according to the old saw—

"When land is gone and money's spent,
Then learning is most excellent."

To this *Dickens* added—

"Though house and land he never got,
Learning will give what they cannot."

A good friend is better than a near relation.

The relation may do nothing to help you, but the friend will assist if he be indeed a good friend.

A good gaper makes two gapers.

It is curious how gaping is taken up by all when one begins. Like many other things, the example is infectious, though one can hardly say why.

A good goose may have an ill gosling.

Sadly true. Good men and women may have wicked sons. David was the father of Absalom.

A good head will get itself hats.

A good head will save the feet.

A sensible person takes a practical view of things, uses a little foresight, and does two or three things at the same time, thus saving future journeys.

A good horse cannot be of a bad colour.

Neither can a good man or woman be of a wrong colour, family, nation, or appearance.

A good horse never lacks a saddle.

Somebody or other will employ the man of ability, character, and tact. The man needs his place, but the place also needs the man.

A good husband makes a good wife.

A gracious disposition in the one influences the other, and little faults are almost insensibly cured. The proverb is equally true in reference to the wife, but she has harder material to work upon, and sometimes she fails to make her husband what he should be.

A good layer-up should be a good layer-out.

Hoarding is a vulgar thing which any fool may accomplish ; but it needs a wise man to expend judiciously what has been saved carefully.

A good name is better than a girdle of gold.

It is more useful, more to be valued, and more ornamental.

A good recorder sets all in order.

Good accounts should be kept. Where books are neglected, affairs get into such a muddle that a man's character for honesty can hardly be maintained, though he may have no idea of robbing any one. Remember the old saying, "If you throw all your money into the sea, yet count it before you let it go."

A good seaman is known in bad weather.

A good thing, if thou know it—do it.

Remember the text " To him that knoweth to do good, and doeth it not, to him it is sin."—James iv. 17.

A good thing is all the sweeter when won with pains.

A good thing is soon snatched up.

Be it a tool, a servant, a house, or a wife, there are sensible people abroad who perceive, value, and hasten to appropriate it.

A good wife and health are a man's best wealth.

A good word is as easily said as a bad one.

A good worker should have good wages.

He deserves them, and it will be to his employer's interest to see that he has them. Never lose a good servant through bad pay.

A good-for-nothing lazy lout,
Wicked within and ragged without,
Who can bear to have him about?
Turn him out! Turn him out!

A goose on a common is nothing uncommon.

But it soon will be unless something is done to save our commons from enclosers. Well is it said :—

"The law is hard on man or woman
Who steals the goose from off the common,
But lets the greater sinner loose
Who steals the common from the goose."

A gossip and a liar are as like as two peas.

A gossip and a liar;
Like as bramble and briar.

A gossip in a village is like a viper in a bed.

A gossip is the lucifer match of the village.

> She is for ever setting it on a blaze with her tongue, which is like the tongue mentioned by the apostle James, "set on fire of hell." There is no end to the evil of an evil tongue.

A gracious eye
Will soon espy
God's hand as nigh.

> "He who notices providences," says *Flavel,* "will not be long without a providence to notice."

A grain of grace is better than a mint of gold.

A grateful man is a rare bird.

> Yes, he is almost as rare as a phœnix. How often does charity receive an ungrateful return! But we must not be discouraged, for we are bound to give our alms for Christ's sake, and not to purchase thanks.

A great cage does not make a bird sing.

> Large possessions bring great cares, and these too often silence songs of praise

A great city is a great wilderness.

> There is no such absolute loneliness as that which many have felt in London. It is "a great and terrible wilderness" to those who have not found friends. All Christians should remember this, and make holy homes for strangers.

A great man's blunders are great blunders.

> When a whale makes a splash it is a great splash. A man of distinguished capacity and position does everything right or wrong upon a large scale.

A guilty conscience needs no accusing.

A half-paid servant is not half a servant.

> He is tempted to steal to make up his wages, and he has no heart or spirit for his work, because he feels himself injured.

A hammer of gold will not open the gate of heaven.

Money opens many of the gates of earth, for bribery is rife ; but it has no power in the world to come. Money is more eloquent than ten members of parliament, but it cannot prevail with the Great Judge.

A handful of common-sense is worth a heap of learning.

Learning of a certain kind, which does not really cultivate the man, may make its possessor magnificently ridiculous, so that the simplest ploughman may perceive his shortness of wit. *Hazlitt* says, "Learning is the knowledge of that which is not generally known to others, and which we can only derive at second hand from books or other artificial sources. The knowledge of that which is before us, or about us, which appeals to our experience, passions, and pursuits, to the bosoms and businesses of men, is not learning. Learning is the knowledge of that which none but the learned know. The learned man prides himself in the knowledge of names and dates, not of men or things. He thinks and cares nothing about his next door neighbours, but he is deeply read in the tribes and castes of the Hindoos and Calmuc Tartars. He can hardly find his way into the next street, though he is acquainted with the exact dimensions of Constantinople and Pekin."

A handful of holy life is worth a ton of tall talk.

This may with advantage be remembered by very pious persons whose godliness is from the lips outwards. "Dr. Lathrop was a man of generous piety, but much opposed to the noisy zeal that seeketh the praise of man. A young divine, who was much given to enthusiastic cant, one day said to him, 'Do you suppose you have any *real religion?*' 'None *to speak of,*' was the excellent reply."

A handsome woman is soon dressed.

She does not require such careful setting off. She is "most adorned when unadorned the most."

A happy breast is better than a full purse.

A happy new heart brings a happy new year.

A headless army will win no victories.

It will be divided and dispirited. There must be a captain. How well it is that God has sent one to be "a Leader and a Commander to the people"! The church conquers when she keeps to Jesus as her Captain and King.

A hasty man is seldom out of trouble.

He is constantly offending some one or other, and picking quarrels right and left. He boils over, and scalds himself.

A healthy size for a man is exercise.

A heavy shower is soon over.

We may in this way derive comfort from the severity of our troubles, and even from the abundance of the opposition which we encounter. Men who are very furious in their anger are often persons whose passion subsides as quickly as it rises.

A hedge-hog is a poor bed-fellow.

And so are bad tempered people, especially Mrs. Caudle.

A hen with one chick seems mighty busy.

Some persons make as much fuss about little as others do who have ten times their work.

A hog in a parlour thinks himself in a sty.

A man taken from low society behaves himself according to his upbringings.

A hog in a silk waistcoat is still a hog.

Circumstances do not alter a man's nature, nor even his manners.

A hog is always thinking of wash.

Low-minded men think of nothing but their base pursuits and sordid gains. Another form of this proverb is—

" The little pig is thinking
Of eating and drinking."

A hog upon trust grunts till he is paid for.

I wish he did. Some people can stand a lot of grunting before they will pay for the pig. Debtors would seem to be deaf as posts.

A hogshead of wine turns men into swine.

And so will less than a hogshead turn many hogs' heads.

A holy man is a whole man.

Holiness is another word for wholeness of soul and life.

A holy Sunday brings a happy Monday.

A horse may have firm feet, and yet stumble.

> There is no wonder that men stumble if horses do, for we have only two feet to keep us up.

A horse may stumble badly, and yet he may not fall.

> Truly good and upright men may be tempted. "As for me," said David, "my feet were almost gone; my steps had well nigh slipped."

A horse will not attempt to fly ;
It knows its powers, and so should I.

> This would keep many out of the pulpit who are now as much out of place in it as if a salmon should climb a tree.

A hundred years hence we shall all be bald.

> Our skull will be bare as the palm of our hand when it has lain a little while in the grave. What's the use of making much of trifles which will soon come to an end? So also we may see the folly of those who glory in their luxuriant tresses.

A hundred years of regret
Pay not a farthing of debt.

> Yet people say—they are sorry that they cannot pay. What's the good of that? Why did they take the goods when they knew they could not pay for them ?

A hungry belly has no ears.

> There is no reasoning with a starving creature ; feed him. Appeal to his stomach first, and then deal with his conscience.

A hungry horse makes a clean manger.

> Boys eat without daintiness when they really need food. Persons who are spiritually hungry are good hearers, and feed with delight upon what they hear.

A hungry man is an angry man.

> Never collect subscriptions before dinner, for you will get nothing.

A jealous man puts nettles in his own bed.

A journey of a thousand miles is begun with a step.

Beware of despising small beginnings. Some men never arrive at usefulness because they are not satisfied to begin in a small way, and proceed by a step at a time.

A kind face is a beautiful face.

Even a plain countenance is made absolutely charming when a kind disposition lights it up.

A lad who is not taught to work is trained to steal.

A lame foot may tread the right road.

Many a feeble-minded one is following Christ as best he can, and he shall be found safe at the last.

A lark paid for is better than a turkey on tick.

When will the system of taking credit come to an end? It is the parent of many evils. It ought to be most of all distasteful to those who remember the score behind the door, or the long account in the tradesman's books. A little that is my own is better than great things which belong to my tailor, or my furniture-dealer, and not to me.

A lawyer is a cat that is called in to help mice to settle their quarrels.

We cannot resist the suggestion to insert the old, well-worn story. We take it from *Legal Facetiæ*, but we have seen it elsewhere. An opulent farmer applied about a law-suit to an attorney, who told him he could not undertake it, being already engaged on the other side. At the same time, he said that he would give him a letter of recommendation to a professional friend, which he did. The farmer, out of curiosity, opened it, and read as follows:—

" Here are two fat wethers fallen out together,
If you'll fleece one, I'll fleece the other,
And make 'em agree like brother and brother."

The farmer carried this epistle to the person with whom he was at variance. Its perusal cured both parties, and terminated the dispute.

A lazy boy and a warm bed are hard to part.

Solomon describes the sluggard as begging for a little more sleep. Very unpleasant on a frosty morning was the cry, " Now, you boys, get up ! "

A lazy man is the devil's footman.

> He is prepared to commit any evil which may come in his way; he is waiting for Satan's orders, and is wearing his livery.

A lazy man is the thief's brother.

A lazy man is tinder for the sparks of temptation.

A lazy man makes himself more work by his laziness.

> He adopts shifts to save himself trouble; and as these do not answer, it costs him ten times more to do the thing than if he had set about it in the right way at first.

A lazy man shall not be my lady's man.

> She will be very unwise to favour such a worthless body, however fair his looks may be. The only time in which laziness was had in honour was in the three hundredth year of the reign of Queen Dick.

A lazy man tempts Satan to tempt him.

A lazy spirit is a losing spirit.

> It loses time, profit, reputation, everything. It would seem that the lazy man also loses his soul, for old *Dr. Dwight* said:—" Among all those, who, within my knowledge, have appeared to become sincerely penitent and reformed, I recollect only a single lazy man; and this man became industrious from the moment of his apparent, and, I doubt not, real conversion."

A leaden sword in an ivory scabbard is still lead.

> You cannot make a man of one who is no man, though you may make him a magistrate, or a minister, or an emperor.

A lean compromise is better than a fat law-suit.

> You will lose less by it, and have less worry and care. Remember the quaint old parable of the two people who went to law over an oyster. The Court awarded them a shell each, and the lawyers ate the oyster. The litigants would have been gainers if they had each eaten half of the oyster; that is to say, *if it was fresh.*

A liar is not believed when he speaks the truth.

A liar is sooner caught than a cripple.

> He trips himself up. The further he goes, the more sure is he to throw himself down by self-contradiction.

A liar never believes other people.

Of course he does not, for he judges them by himself.

A lie has no legs, and cannot stand; but it has broad wings, and flies far.

A lie is a lie, whatever name you call it by.

An untruth a day old is called a lie, a year old it is called a falsehood, a century old it is called a legend : but the nature of a false statement is not altered by age.

A lie which is half true is doubly a lie.

It has more power to deceive people than if it were altogether false. Crafty slanderers never make their libels smell too strongly of lies, for then they would be known at once to be false. The devil likes to lay his lies asoak for a while in the oil of truth, for this gives them a savour of probability.

A light heart can bear heavy burdens.

A light heart lives long, but a new heart lives for ever.

A little bird only wants a little nest.

If we were not so great in our own esteem, contentment would be easier work ; for we should be the little bird with its little nest. *Goldsmith* was right when he wrote :—

"Man wants but little here below,
Nor wants that little long."

A " little drop " may lead to a great fall.

Why do men always say they took " just a drop " ? What a drop in their character and circumstances that drop has often caused ! In fact it is " the little drop " which leads on to the fatal drop : many would never have been murderers if it had not been for the drink.

A little each day is much in a year.

A little explained, a little endured,
A little forgiven, the quarrel is cured.

A little fore-talk may save much after-talk.

Let the bargain, or agreement, be clearly understood, that there may be no after contention. Let counsel be carefully taken that there may be no need for regret. Better meet thrice for consultation than once for lamentation.

A little gall spoils a great deal of honey.

A few angry words have embittered the friendship of a life. A few bitter sentences have destroyed the usefulness of a sweet sermon, and even of a sweet life.

A little help is worth a deal of pity.

"Ah, thank 'ee, neighbour," said a perspiring sheep-driver the other day, to one who hooted away his flock from going down a wrong road, — "Thank 'ee—a little help is worth a deal o' pity!"

A little leak may sink a great ship.

A little love is better than a lump of learning.

A little man may cast a long shadow.

Though his talents are small, his influence may be great. A holy life may tell upon a wide circle, and prove a blessing to many generations.

A little mouse can creep into a great stack.

Yes, we may feed upon the great promises of God, and the great doctrines of grace.

A little mouse can help a great lion.

How often have the champions of the gospel been cheered by lowly believers!

A little oil may save a deal of friction.

Just a kind word and a yielding manner, and anger and complaining will be avoided.

A little pack serves a little pedlar.

Small possessions and humble positions should satisfy us.

A little pot is soon hot.

Small minds are quickly in a passion. A good woman, troubled by a quick temper, was helped to overcome the evil by reading this proverb in "John Ploughman's Almanack." She said that it was like a text of Scripture to her, for often she heard in her ear the words "Little pot, soon hot"; she grew ashamed of her irritability, and conquered it.

A little sin is a great folly.

A little spark shines in the dark,

A little stone in the shoe may lame the pilgrim.

A small scruple of conscience may render life sadly uneasy. If we are not quite sure that a thing is right, we should have nothing to do with it. It may seem a trifle, but conscience does not trifle with trifles ; or if it does, it is greatly hurt thereby.

A little too late is too much too late.

Punctuality is an important duty, and we ought to be ashamed if we are five minutes behind the promised time.

A little wariness may save great weariness.

By forethought, contrivance, and arrangement much care and labour may be saved.

A living rabbit is better than a dead elephant.

Another form of the proverb, "A living dog is better than a dead lion." The least life is preferable to the most bulky form of death.

A Loan Society is mostly a fool-trap. Do not be caught in it.

A Loan Society: let it alone.

These advices arise out of our own observation. We have seen too often the wretched end of a loan which, like Napoleon's war with Germany, was taken up with a light heart, but ended in disappointment and ruin. A loan of this sort has often proved a mill-stone about the borrower's neck.

A lock stops a thief; but what can stop a liar?

What indeed but a shovelful of grave-digger's earth? David says: "The mouth of them that speak lies shall be stopped." Ps. lxiii. 11. The sooner the better.

A loose tooth and a fickle friend are two evils.

The sooner we are clear of them the better: but who likes the wrench ?

A loud horn may play a poor tune.

It generally does. Loudness is a foe to melody. He who blows his own trumpet with great vehemence is almost always a fraud,

A loveless life is a living death.

For to love is to live. Our laureate says :—

" 'Tis better to have loved and lost,
Than never to have loved at all."

A mad parson makes a mad parish.

For good or for bad the shepherd affects the flock. One wonders if that clergyman was of this kind of whom we read that a thief stole his linen, and he offered a reward for the discovery of the offender, whereupon the following verse was written at the bottom of one of the bills : —

" Some thief has stolen the parson's shirts
To skin nought could be nearer :
The parish will give five hundred pounds
To him who steals the wearer."

A man beyond his line is never like to shine.

When the cobbler leaves his last he also quits his awl, and is all at sea. What can a man do well when he quits his own business, and takes to an occupation of which he knows nothing ?

A man brings the stones, but the woman builds them into the wall.

A man cannot prosper till he gets his wife's leave.

She must practise economy, or all his earnings will insensibly melt away.

" A man may spare,
And still be bare,
If his wife be nowt, if his wife be nowt ;
But a man may spend,
And have money to lend,
If his wife be owt, if his wife be owt."

A man had better have his hands in his own pockets than in other people's.

Persons usually put their hands into their pockets because there is nothing else there, and nature abhors a vacuum ; but hands in another man's pocket are engaged in creating a vacuum, and that is a crime against both natural and national law.

A man had need be a great philosopher to bear toothache patiently.

A man in debt is caught in a net.

Some never get out of it : they do not pay any one, and yet they live on, like Tom Farbehind, of whom we read :—

> " His last debt paid, poor Tom's no more.
> Last debt ! Tom never paid a debt before."

A man is known by the company he shuns,

Quite as much as by the company he keeps.

A man is not bad because a viper bites him.

Excellent persons are liable to be assailed by malicious slanderers, who, because of their serpent nature, take delight in attacking the good.   An apostle once had a viper fasten upon his hand, but he shook it off into the fire, and it did him no harm.

A man is only the head, a good wife is the crown.

Solomon is our authority for this.—Prov. xii. 4.

A man may be a fool and not know it.

Indeed it is generally the case that he is not aware of his own folly.   If he did know it, he would not be a fool any longer.

A man may be a great divine and yet have no religion.

A man may dig his grave with his teeth.

Gluttons, *bons vivants*, and even careless eaters may commit suicide while eating.

A man may drown himself in a quart pot.

Have you not seen it done ?

A man may tell a lie till he believes it.

And this is often done.   We have heard persons tell tales which we are sure are not true.   Those stories have altered year after year to our knowledge, but the narrators are quite sure of their accuracy.   They have told the story so often that they have persuaded themselves into a firm faith in it.

A man may threaten and yet be afraid,

A man may wear out a suit of clothes, but a suit at law may wear a man out.

Such is the law's delay that the Court of Chancery is as great a trier of patience as was Satan in the case of Job. Among the Jews, judgment-seats were placed at the gates of cities, intimating quick despatch, that causes should not wait so long as to become old and grey-headed, nor the client be forced to say to his lawyer what Balaam's ass said to his master : " Am not I thine ass, upon which thou hast ridden ever since I was thine unto this day ? "

A man of kindness, to his beast is kind,
A brutal action shows a brutish mind.

A man of many professions has but few profits.

A man of many trades begs his bread on Sunday.

A man of many trades lives on short commons.

He is so deficient and inefficient that he never gets on. Being Jack-of-all-trades he is master of none, and can do nothing properly. As soon as he is known his customers are gone.

A man of prayer is a man of power.

But he must not be of the same kind as the Berkshire farmer who said, "It was no use praying for rain as long as the wind was in the north."

A man of silence is a man of sense.

Even if he has no other sense he acts sensibly when he keeps quiet. He has at least sense enough to conceal his want of it.

A man of snow is soon dissolved, and so is a man of flesh.

Such is our mortality, that flesh is like snow. *Erskine*, in comparing himself to his pipe, says :—

" Thou'rt even such,
Gone with a touch."

A man of words and not of deeds
Is like a garden full of weeds.

A man who can do everything can do nothing.

" I'm of no trade, but I can turn my hand to anything," is a remark we often hear ; and those who talk so are of no manner of use to anybody. There are exceptions enough to prove the rule.

A man who does nothing never has time to do anything.

If you want work done, go to the man who is already fully occupied. This is unkind advice so far as he is concerned, but sound for all that. Of what use will it be to seek help from a man who has nothing to do? He for certain will continue to do nothing.

A man who is never spoken of is never abused.

This is one of the sweet uses of obscurity: it helps one to a quiet life. An eminent person saved his life during the French revolution by keeping in the background. The proverb also implies that everybody is abused more or less. Like rain, it falls on everybody's field, sooner or later.

A man who will not flee will make his foes flee.

He only will move the world who will not let the world move him. Stand against those whom you withstand, and in a short time they will not stand against you.

A man will never change his mind if he has no mind to change.

There are plenty of the latter sort, whose minds, if they had a hundred of them, could all dance on the point of a needle; and these must for ever do what their grandfather's grandmother did. As it was in the beginning, it ever shall be with them.

A man with long curls we reckon with girls.

We look upon him as effeminate, and rightly so.

A man without courage is a knife without an edge.

He will never cut his way to success.

A man without manners is a bear in boots.

We have seen the sign of the "Goat in Boots," and could never make out its meaning. We have seen the "Bear in Boots," and we have no desire to renew our acquaintance with the animal.

A man you'll find whom none have said a fault on,
When you on swallows' tails have laid the salt on.

A man's best fortune, or his worst, is his wife.

A man's purse will never be bare,
If he knows when to buy, to spend, and to spare.

A man's tongue should never be larger than his hand.

>He should not say more than he can do, nor promise more than he can perform.

A man's wife is either his crown or his cross.

>" Of earthly good, the best is a good wife,
>   A bad—the bitterest curse of human life."

A mask is an instrument of torture to a true man.

>He hates all disguise. He wishes to be known and read of all men.

A merry heart goes all the day,
Your sad tires in a mile a'.

A mewing cat is a bad mouser.

>Talkers are seldom doers. It is a catastrophe when a cat forsakes his proper calling to become a vocalist. This is the sort of gentleman of whom the muse has mewed or sung—

>>" He never caught a rat or mouse,
>>   But practised all the long night through,
>>To walk about from house to house
>>   And see what woe his wail could do."

A mischievous dog must be tied short.

>Persons who injure others must have their power limited.

A miser hoards much, but it comes to nothing.

>Thus the Chinese say :—

>"He hoards to-day; he hoards to-morrow; does nothing else
>   but hoard :
>At length he has enough a new umbrella to afford ;
>When all at once he is assailed—a wind arises quick,
>And both his hands grasp nothing but a new umbrella stick."

A miser is a rich pauper.

>Such men as Dancer and Elwes were much worse off than common beggars. One said of a miser :—

>>" They call'd thee rich, I deem'd thee poor,
>>   Since if thou dared'st not use thy store ;
>>But saved it only for thy heirs,
>>   The treasure was not thine, but theirs."

A miser is like a hog, of no use till he is dead.

Many are hoping that he will cut up well. Our societies could do very well with a side of such bacon.

A miser lives poor that he may die rich.

A mother, I ween,
Is at home a queen.

A mother's breath is always sweet.

In life she is a man's best comforter. When she is gone, her memory is fragrant.

A mother's mission lies at home.

If she remembers this she will not roam.

A new broom is good for three days.

Admirers are fickle : they want a change continually. The best only suit them for nine days at the outside.

A new gospel is no gospel.

For what is true is not new, and what is new in theology is not true.
"Tell me the old, old story."

A new heart creates a new life.

And nothing else will do it thoroughly and permanently.

A new lip without a new life is little worth.

Affectations of pious talk are worse than useless.

A new net does not tempt an old bird.

But it catches a good many young ones, and even old ones are only safe because they are aware of the danger.

A nice dog can give a nasty bite.

Very sweet-spoken men can say slanderous things. You fancy that butter would not melt in their mouths; but you soon find that in proportion to the softness of their oil is the sharpness of their sword.

A nimble ninepence beats a slow shilling.

Quickness in trade is a great thing. The oftener the capital is turned over, the better. "Small profits and quick returns" is a good motto.

A nine days' wonder, and then kick'd under.

"He went up like a rocket, and came down like a stick." Puffed and advertised for a time, and then despised and ridiculed.

"This is the fate of not a few :
Will they do the same with you?"

A nip now, and a nip then, will be the death of many men.

We have many such *nippers* in London, who are always at it, and are earning themselves a drunkard's guilt and a drunkard's grave.

A noble animal—a pig in a poor man's sty.

What would Paddy do without him? In this country the black pig is a far nobler animal than the Red Lion.

A nod from a lord is a breakfast for a fool.

Flunkeyism is enough to make one sick ; yet there's plenty of it. I remember a good man who never made a speech without bringing in "the noble earl." One gloried that he was once spoken to by a prince. "And what did he say?" He shouted to me, "Out of the way there !"

A nod is as good as a wink to a blind horse.

As he can see nothing at all it matters not how you try to direct him. Plenty of men are equally hard to guide.

A northern air
Brings weather fair.

The north wind may be cold, but it driveth away rain, and so it hath its virtues for dwellers in towns.

A nose that can smell a rat
Should be found on every cat.

And every man should have enough power of discrimination to know when deadly error is being preached, or a trick is being played by statesmen, or a cheat is attempted by tradesmen.

A pack of cards is the devil's Prayer-book.

A parliament of dogs breaks up with a fight.

In some human parliaments the same result is nearly realized.

A parson should not drive a grey horse.

Because the hair comes off and shows on his black coat. Our company and our pursuits should be congruous to our calling.

A pearl among pebbles is still a pearl.

Good people found among the lowest of the low are none the worse because of the adversity which brought them there. Joseph in Egypt still enjoyed the favour of God.

A peck of March dust is worth a king's ransom.

It would seem to be good for the crops that this month should be dry. The old saw puts it—

"March dust is a thing
Worth ransom of a king."

A pendulum travels much, but it only goes a tick at a time.

Much comfort is in this. We may yet survive for fifty years, but we shall only have to live a day at a time, and therefore we need not forestall the future, but "do the next thing."

A penny is a debt as true
As if ten thousand pounds were due.

Little sums are apt to be forgotten, but the principle involved in leaving them unpaid is the same as knavery in larger amounts.

A penny-weight of love is better than a hundred-weight of law.

Try it if there is a feud in your family.

A place for everything and everything in its place.

A capital motto to put up in places of business. Have it printed on a card, and hang it on the wall.

A ploughman doesn't stick for a little mud.

Neither should a Christian worker give up work because his finer feelings are hurt, or because some one abuses him.

A ploughman is known by his furrow.

His work shows what kind of ploughman he is.

A poor man's debt makes a great noise.

> Tens of thousands due from nobility are scarcely mentioned, but a labourer's score is chatted about among his neighbours.

A pound of idleness weighs twenty ounces.

> That is to say, it is more heavy and burdensome than anything else. Doing nothing is hard work.

A pound of pluck is worth a ton of luck.

> Resolution will bring the success which the believer in luck gapes for in vain.

A prejudiced man puts out his own eyes.

> He refuses to see the other side of the question. His judgment is blinded by his own wilfulness, and this is the worst of blindness.

A priest in the confessional is a fox with a goose.

A promise is a debt that we may not forget.

A proud heart in a poor breast
Gives its owner little rest.

> Especially when the poor but dishonest one is "rustling in unpaid-for silks." Better poor and pious than poor and proud.

A proud man is always a foolish man.

> For there is really no justifiable cause for the conceited feelings which he indulges. He needs to listen to *Cowper's* advice :—
>
> > "Beware of too sublime a sense
> > Of your own worth and consequence."

A purse with piece or two of gold
Makes a man in dealing bold.

> He has ready money to pay with, and is not forced to give way to the exactions of those who think him needy.

A quarrelsome man never lacks words.

> He turns the answers of his opponents into fresh texts, upon which he preaches disputation. He nags, and nags, and nags.

A ragged colt may make a good horse.

> Let us hope well for some of the ragged colts in our streets and lanes : there are enough of them, and they are ragged enough.

A ready penny is as good a friend as any.

A red nose is a danger signal.

> Have you not heard of the inn with the sign of "The Mortal Man"? It was once kept by Mrs. Sarah Burton, and it had on the one side the question—
>
>> "O mortal man, that liv'st by bread,
>> What makes thy nose and cheeks so red?"
>
> On the other side was the answer—
>
>> "Thou silly man, that looks so pale,
>> It's drinking Sally Burton's ale."
>
> Just so. The victims rejoice in signs which mark mischief. Their noses seem to be beautiful to themselves, when to others they are sorrowful signs that the mortal man is hastening on his mortality.

A red nose oft looks down on ragged clothes.

>> "What pearls and rubies does the drink disclose!
>> How poor the *purse!* But, oh, how rich the *nose!*"

A rich man may make a poor husband.

> Better to have a treasure *in* the man than *with* the man.

A rolling stone gathers no moss.

> This is the home-lover's reason for stopping for ever in his native village. There is some reason in it, for frequent and freakish changes hinder prosperity.

A rose among nettles is none the less a rose.

A rotten apple spoils its neighbour.

> Such is the power of evil example.
>
>> "One sickly sheep infects the flock,
>> And poisons all the rest."

A Sabbath's rest blesses the rest of the week.

A scolding wife and crowing hen,
I could not wish to hear again.

A scold's tongue is a razor which sharpens by use.

A Scotch mist will wet an Englishman to the skin.

> What is sport to one may be death to another, as the frogs said when the boys pelted them with stones. We have often heard the weather in the Highlands spoken of as "a little soft" when we thought it was pouring with rain. When you once get used to a thing you hardly notice it.

A servant is best discovered by his master's absence.

> That is to say, he is found out by what he does when his master goes out, and leaves him to himself. Then you see whether he is honest and industrious, or the reverse.

A sheep may get fat in a small meadow.

> A tradesman may grow rich in a little shop.

A sheep should not tire of carrying its own wool.

> He is a lazy man who complains of the weight of his clothes, the toils of his trade, or the natural care of his own family.

A shilling is well spent to save a pound.

A ship with no captain will reach no port.

> Somebody must be at the head, or everything will be a failure.

A ship with two captains is soon wrecked.

> Divided authority is nearly as bad as none at all.

A short cut is often the longest way.

> *Experientia docet!* When over the shoes in mud down some wonderful lane, which was warranted to be a short cut, how one has wished that he had kept to the roundabout road!

A shower in July, when the corn begins to fill,
Is worth a yoke of oxen and all that goes there till.

A silent man's words cannot be quoted against him.

A silver hammer breaks an iron door.

> Men everywhere seem open to bribes, and tips, and gifts. Miserable sign of the times!

A silver sofa cannot cure the sick.

> Wealth cannot purchase ease or health.

A single penny fairly got
Is worth a thousand that are not.

A sitting hen gets no barley.

> This is the Australian's answer to those who speak against emigration. If you want a living, you must go after it.

A slanderer is a cur that will bite to the bone.

> Like a mad dog, he leaves venom in the wound which may drive the sufferer to madness.

A slothful hand makes a slender estate.

A slothful man is the beggar's brother.

> And the beggar will hardly own him until it is time to go to bed.

A slovenly farmer's hedge is full of gaps.

> So is it with all poor work: it is useless because it is so imperfect that it does not answer its purpose.

A small horse is all the easier groomed.

> If we have little, we have the less to take care of.

A small house is big enough for love.

> In great mansions form and state tend to damp the warmth of affection. I have seen over a little house in Italy the inscription, DOMUS PARVA, QUIES MAGNA—A little house and great quiet.

A smoky house and a scolding wife
Are the two worst evils of our life.

> "All the injuries of the heavens, of the sun's heat, of the wind's blowing, of the snow's coldness, of the rain's wetting, are rather to be endured than the fiery-scorching, fierce-blowing, cold-biting, loud-thundering showers of this terrestrial dog-star."—*Jermin.*

A soft heart needs a hard head.

> Otherwise sympathy will run away with a man, and lead him into foolish actions. Judgment must sway the feelings, and keep them in their right place, or harm will be done where good was intended.

A sore-eyed person should never be an oculist.

> He will not recommend his business, nor be likely to do what is needed with the eyes of others.

A sore horse does not like to be curried.

> Men who are wrong do not wish to be reproved.

A sparrow in the hand is better than a pigeon on the wing.

A sparrow may fly as high as it will,
But it must remain a sparrow still.

So a person may soar aloft in outward show, and in high pretence, but it makes no difference to the man's real self.

A spoonful of vinegar will sour much sweet milk.

Don't supply that vinegar. Believe John Ploughman, and don't test his statement.

A stiff breeze sweeps the cobwebs out of the sky.

Much of stagnant mischief is removed by great stirs among mankind. Theological and political breezes are as healthy as storms in the natural world.

A stitch in time saves ninety-nine.

A stone that is fit for the wall will not long be left in the way.

A place will soon be found for a person who is fit for it.

A story and a ball of snow
Gather substance as they go.

The narrative which follows may not be literally true, but it may serve as a specimen of the evolution of a sensational story :—

" The servant of No. 1 told the servant of No. 2 that her master expected his old friends, the Baileys, to pay him a visit shortly ; and No. 2 told No. 3 that No. 1 expected to have the Baileys in the house every day ; and No. 3 told No. 4 that it was all up with No. 1, for they could not keep the bailiffs out : whereupon No. 4 told No. 5 that the officers were after No. 1, and it was as much as he could do to prevent himself being taken in execution, and that it was nearly killing his poor dear wife ; and so it went on increasing and increasing till it got to No. 32, who confidently assured the last, No. 33, that the Bow Street officers had taken up the gentleman who lived at No. 1 for killing his poor dear wife with arsenic, and it was confidently hoped and expected that he would be executed ! "

A strong-minded woman should not be a wrong-minded woman.

Surely this is the sort of woman of whom it was written upon the Dane John Monument at Canterbury :—

" Where is the man who has the power and skill
    To stem the torrent of a woman's will ?
For if she will, she will, you may depend on't ;
    And if she won't, she won't, and there's an end on't."

A strong will walks through a wall.

> No difficulty can hinder the man of firm resolution.

A swallow comes and a swallow flies,
Our summer friend the winter tries.

A swarm of bees in May is worth a load of hay.

> The earlier in the season the bees gather together, the more time they will have for collecting a good supply of honey.

A tale-hearer is brother to a tale-bearer.

> Indeed, if there were no hearers of tales, none would bear them. The receiver is as bad as the gossip.

A tame tiger is still a tiger.

> If nature is restrained and not renewed, its sinful propensities will break out sooner or later.

A tame tongue is a rare bird.

> One wishes these birds would multiply till they were as numerous as sparrows.

A thief thinks every man steals.

A thorn in the bush is worth two in the hand.

> We should think so. Who wants thorns in the hand? Some fret a good deal over troubles which have not yet happened to them, and may never do so.

A thousand probabilities do not make one truth.

A thrifty wife is better than a great income.

A thriving cheat 'tis rare to meet.

> Somehow or other, money badly gotten does not come to much, nor make the getter rich for long.

A ton of clack won't fill a sack.

A tradesman must be self-made or never made.

> He must stick to his business, and get on by his own energy, or he will not prosper for any length of time.

A tree that is often transplanted bears little fruit.

> A good argument against needless changes.

A velvet slipper cannot cure the gout.

> Another version of "A silver sofa cannot cure the sick." Wealth cannot purchase immunity from disease. Remember the painful case of the late German Emperor Frederick.

A virtuous woman is a splendid prize;
A bad—the greatest curse beneath the skies.

A wager is a fool's argument.

> He does not pretend to prove his statements, but bawls out, "I'll bet you a pound on it," which is neither sense nor reason.

A watched pot boileth not.

> It is noticeably so that, if we long for a thing, and watch for it with anxiety, it seems all the longer in coming.

A weather-cock is a poor chicken.

> He who changes his opinions to suit the prevailing current is a being of small value. In fact, a weather-cock is not a cock at all, but a mere creature of the wind, the obedient slave of every wandering breeze.

A whispered lie is just as wrong
As one that thunders loud and long.

> In fact, the meanness of the whispering adds to its wickedness.

A white devil does double mischief. Beware!

> Putting on the form of an angel of light, the prince of darkness gets advantage over men. Error is terrible when it professes to be a purer form of Christianity.

A white glove often hides a dirty hand.

> Deceitful professions are used to conceal base actions.

A wife, domestic, good, and pure,
Like snail should keep within her door;
But not, like snail, with silver track,
Place all her wealth upon her back.

A wife should husband her husband's money.

> He brings the money home, but she must lay it out, or lay it up.

A wilful man had need be a wise man.

> Otherwise he is sure to do many rash things, and bring harm upon himself and others.

A willing mind makes a light foot.

A willing soldier will soon find a sword.

> Where there's a will there's a weapon.

A wise head makes a still tongue.

A wise man knows his own want of wisdom.

> This is a sure token of his wisdom.

A wise man may often learn from a fool.

> The ignorant man often blunders out absurdities which suggest new views, and on some one point he may happen to be better informed than the cultured man.

A wise man thinks twice before he speaks once.

> And, after the twice thinking, it often happens that he does not speak the once.

A woman jumps at conclusions where a man limps towards them.

> She may not be always right; but when you go against your wife's opinion, you will generally be wrong. Woman has a quick instinct in many things in which man has a slow reasoning.

A woman strong in flounces is weak in brains.

A word once out flies much about.

> Words are like thistle-down, and no one knows where they will go, and what will grow of them. "Keep the door of thy mouth."

A word whispered is heard afar.

A wound to be healed must be little handled.

> A quarrel which you wish to end should be little talked about.

A year begins well if we begin it with God.

A young man idle is an old man needy.

> All chance of making provision for old age was thrown away, and so he sits in the workhouse, and talks of his hard fate.

A YY man will beware of the three vowels, I O U.

If all men were wise enough to avoid such bits of paper it would save much trouble.

A Y Z may wear a C D hat.

Nobody objects to any hat which covers a wise head; but the owner of such a *caput* seldom cares to wear anything which is objectionable.

Absence of body is sometimes better than presence of mind.

As, for instance, in a railway accident.

Adam's ale is the best brew.

Water as a drink hurts no one. Try it!
'Tis the drink that never makes drunkards,
'Tis the cup that never makes sad;
The friend and the help of the toiler—
It makes every humble home glad.

Acquaint yourselves with yourselves.

Yet is the command better, "Acquaint now thyself with God, and be at peace."—Job xxii. 21.

Add pence to pence, for wealth comes hence.

Add odd to odd, and it makes even.

The net result of many trials may be our lasting benefit. Losses added to losses may leave a clear gain as the result.

Adversity has slain her thousands; prosperity her ten thousands.

Advice to a thirsty soul. Try Coffee.

Advice to persons about to fight. Don't!

Advice when most needed is least heeded.

Persons usually come for it when their minds are made up, and some even think you their enemy if you suggest that their way is not the best. A French *curé* was wont to tell persons who came for advice about marriage to listen to the bells. Of course the bells said, "Make haste and get married." Some months after, when the spouse had turned out a shrew, the husband came to upbraid the priest for leading him into trouble. But the priest bade him give more attention, for he had misunderstood the bells. The man listened, and heard the bells distinctly say, "Never get married." So is it, that people take only such advice as suits their inclinations.

Advise none to marry, or to go to law.

As to marriage, it is as the case may be; but as for law, it is said to be to the litigant what the poulterer is to the goose: it plucks him, and it draws him. Here the simile ends, for the litigant, unlike the goose, never gets trust (trussed), although he may be roasted and dished.—*Legal Faceti*æ, *by John Willock.*

Advise with your pillow.

Don't be in a hurry. Turn the business over, and look at it from all points. When you are cool, you will judge better than in the heat of anxiety. The placing of your head on the pillow, and there considering the ins and outs of a matter, may save you from being feather-brained.

Affection has its share of affliction.

A tender heart is sure to endure pain. The French say, "*Aimer n'est pas sans amer.*"—"Love is not without its bitterness." Even the highest form of affection—love to God and holiness—involves a measure of suffering.

After a tempest comes a calm; After a feast full often harm.

After rain sunshine; after sunshine rain, The same thing over and over again.

Thus life is made up of many changes; and no state, be it bright or clouded, will always continue.

After the cup of affliction comes the cup of consolation.

After the Lord Mayor's coach comes the dust-cart.

So after a fine speech comes a lot of twaddle. How often, after a great life, comes a miserable falling off!

Against threescore have something in store.

This is not the taking thought for to-morrow which is forbidden, but a wise forethought, of which God himself sets us an example in the provision which he makes for the wants of his creatures, giving them in summer supplies for the coming winter.

Alas! Alas! Wise men pass a dressy lass.

The Alas! is for the dressy lass who hoped to catch a husband by her fine array, and saw all the men worth having turning away from her.

All are not friends that speak thee fair.

No : flatterers are abroad who make a market of vain minds.

All are not hunters that blow the horn.

They would like to be thought so, but we know better.

All are not merry that dance lightly.

Heavy hearts are often concealed beneath the pretence of gaiety.

" Almost " never shoots a cock-sparrow.

The half-hearted man does nothing. He is always going to do much, but it ends in mere proposing, and comes to nothing. A life which lingers on the verge of something, but never comes to anything, is most ridiculous.

Almost saved will be altogether lost.

It must be so, for, as *Henry Smith* says in his sermon, "*Almost* a son, is a bastard ; *almost* sweet, is unsavoury ; *almost* hot, is lukewarm, which God spueth out of his mouth (Rev. iii. 16). He which believeth almost, believeth not, but doubteth. Can the door which is but almost shut keep out the thief ? Can the cup which is but almost whole hold any wine ? Can the ship which is but almost sound keep out water ? The soldier which doth but almost fight is a coward. The servant which doth but almost labour is a loiterer. Believest thou almost ? ' Be it unto thee,' saith Christ, ' as thou believest.' Therefore, if thou believest, thou shalt be saved ; if thou believest almost, thou shalt be saved almost."

Almsgiving harms no living ; yet charity is a rarity.

"Always at it " wins the day.

Perseverance conquers every difficulty by its dogged determination. He that will not be beaten cannot be beaten. He who keeps on pegging away will do it sooner or later.

Always do your best ; angels do no more.

Always drinking, always dry.

It is evident that thirst is not quenched by drinking beer and spirits. Drinking men have a spark in their throats which barrels of beer could not put out. Like snipes they live by suction. They have always a reason for another pint.

> Some drink because they're wet,
> And some because they're dry ;
> Some drink another glass
> To wet the other eye,

Always help a lame dog over a stile.

Always in a hurry, always behind.

> A little punctuality would save life from being a worry, a flurry, a hurry, a scurry. Half the ease of life oozes away through the leaks of unpunctuality.

Always leave a little coal for the next day's fire.

> Don't say all on a subject, nor spend all on a feast.

All are not asleep who have their eyes shut.

> Therefore do not presume upon their not hearing you.

All are not saints that go to church.

> Nor to chapel either.

All are not soldiers that wear red coats.

All are not thieves that dogs bark at.

> On the contrary, slander dogs the heels of the best. The shadow of detraction attends the substance of merit. When we hear a howl against a man we should be slow to accept the vulgar verdict, lest we do injustice to one who deserves sympathy.

All between cradle and coffin is uncertain.

> " Nothing is certain " except that nothing is certain.

All birds will not sing the same note.

> It would be a sad pity that they should. Variety is charming, uniformity would be most wearisome.

All bread is not baked in one oven.

> No one man, or society, or denomination, or section of the community, can do all the good work that is needed in this poor world.

All cats do not make music under the same window.

> Yet in London we are driven to think they do. We are apt to exaggerate and say:
>> "A hundred and fifty cats or more
>> Arched their backs, and howled and swore."
>
> But cats are everywhere, from Dan to Beersheba, and night is made hideous all over this Babylon. Other nuisances are also pretty equally distributed, and we have not a monopoly of them, as we sometimes imagine.

All death is sudden to the unprepared.

All feet cannot wear one shoe.

It would be great folly to have only one last for men, women, and children. Uniformity of opinion will never be reached, and is not desirable.

All flowers are not in one garland.

It would be a pity that they should be. God distributes gifts and graces, and allows no one to monopolize his good things.

All have tongues, but few hold them.

"And 'tis remarkable that they
Talk most who have the least to say."

All is fine that is fit.

If a thing is suitable it is admirable; but if unfit for its purpose it is often unendurable, however grand may be the look of it.

All powder and no shot
Maketh noise but killeth not.

Zeal without knowledge has the same barren result. Many hear the excited preacher, but few feel the power of true religion through his ravings, because there is no solid teaching in what he says.

All praise and no pudding starved the parson.

Many are in this danger. No, not quite: they do not get "all praise," they get enough fault-finding to keep them from being cloyed with the honey of admiration.

All relations are not friends.

All sunshine, and nothing else, makes a desert.

If we had nothing but prosperity, we should be burnt up with worldliness. We may be thankful that there is no fear of this.

All take and never give,
Better die than thus to live.

Some men are like the old earthenware money-boxes, which must be broken before anything can be got out of them, though they will receive all you may bring.

All taking out and no putting in,
Soon squanders all our little tin.

> This is the complement of the former proverb. We must look to our comings-in as well as to our goings-out.

All talk, but few think.

All that self spins will be unravelled.

> Salvation is of the Lord; consequently, that which is of man is deception, and not salvation, and it will come to nothing.

All the joys of earthly life
Are but toys, and noise, and strife.

All the keys in the world are not on your ring.

> You have not all power, knowledge, and influence. Is it likely?

All the speed is not in the spurs.

> Strength is wanted as well as stimulus. Comfortable instruction is as needful as earnest exhortation.

All wit is not wisdom.

All women are angels, but there are two sorts of angels.

All women are good; but some are good *for nothing.*

All work and no play makes Jack a dull boy;
All play and no work makes Jack a sad shirk.

All's well that ends well.

An angry man is a man in a fever.

An angry man suffers temporary insanity.

> " Madness and anger differ but in this,
>   This is short madness, that long anger is."

> For this reason it is best to do nothing while angry, but wait till the steam is blown off; for who would wish to act insanely?

An ape is an ape, though dressed in a cape.

> No garments can long conceal character. The man comes out sooner or later. Let nine tailors do their best, a fop is not a man for all that.

An ass may think he's Solomon ; but he isn't.

"If a man think himself to be something, when he is nothing, he deceiveth himself."—Gal. vi. 3.

An early start makes easy stages.

To begin promptly causes work to go pleasantly ; whereas delay keeps one in a perpetual heat.

An easy fool
Is a knave's tool.

And he will handle him for his own purposes, laughing in his sleeve all the while.

An empty man is full of himself.

An empty purse makes a bashful buyer.

He is afraid that his bid will be taken, and then he will be in a fix for want of money to pay what he offered. If he must have a thing, and yet cannot pay for it, he knows that he must agree to any demand, and so he does not stand out for a lower price.

An envious man throws away mutton because his neighbour has venison.

An evil eye can see no good.

An honest darn is better than debt.

An honest man is a fine sight for sore eyes.

They say, "An honest man is the noblest work of God" ; but we can scarcely go that length. Others think that integrity is so rare that an honest man is a *non est* man ; but we go much further than that. Honesty has a beauty all its own, and to see it is to admire it. Father Honest is a choice companion.

An hour of care should be an hour of prayer.

An ill calf may come of a good cow.

We cannot depend upon parentage. Grace does not run in the blood. The best of men have had the worst of children.

An ill cow may have a good calf.

Sovereign grace so arranges it that some of the best are born of the worst ; as, for instance, Jonathan of Saul.

An ill calf sucked two cows, and was never the fatter.

We know a gentleman who went to two colleges, and was not much the wiser.

An ill life brings an ill death.

An inch is a good deal on a man's nose.

Minute accuracy may be of vital importance in some matters, for a little mistake may prove a great one. It is always vitally important to ourselves to be scrupulously true, whether we speak of noses or anything else.

An inch of love is better than a mile of strife.

An iron key may open a golden box.

Yes ; poor illiterate preachers have reached the hearts of men of learning and talent. Our unworthy prayers may open the treasures of divine grace.

An obedient wife commands her husband.

By her love the good man is conquered, so that he delights to give her pleasure.

An old and useful horse works very light of course.

You have had his strength ; be patient with his weakness. If you can afford it, give him the run of your pastures for the rest of his career. Should not some provision be made for old ministers and old servants, or should they all be shot ? Better this than let them starve.

An old dog does not bark for nothing.

Warnings from men of years and experience ought to be respected ; though, alas ! they are not.

An old dog must bark in his own way.

There must be much indulgence shown to age, and long established habit.

An old house eats up the tenant.

So much is required for repairs, that though the buyer gets it cheap, it will turn out dear in the end.

An old maid always knows how to bring up children.

Most people think they can do what they have never attempted to do far better than those whose duty and habit it is to do it

An old score is an old sore.

This kind of chalk deposit should be stopped at once. Let the score be paid, and the sore be healed.

An old tub is apt to leak.

Memory fails when age creeps on.

An open hand shall have something in it.

If we give freely, God will see that we have something still to give. God's hand is open for those whose hands are open.

An open mouth shows an empty head.

When persons are so exceedingly ready to chatter, it is soon discovered that they know nothing. If there had been anything in the box, the owner would have had some kind of fastening for it.

An ounce of debt spoils a pound of credit.

Before a man knows it, his reputation in the business-world may be sinking because of his not clearing-up an account which he thinks is too small to hurt him. Trust dies because Bad-pay poisons him.

An ounce of patience contains a pound of wisdom.

An owl will never teach an eaglet to look at the sun.

Tutors of doubtful character and irreligious principles can never instruct young people in the ways of godliness.

An untried friend is like an uncracked nut.

You cannot tell whether there is the kernel of sincerity in him till he is tried. He may be rotten. A Frenchman wrote:

" Friends are like melons, shall I tell you why ?
To find one good you must a hundred try."

Let us hope that things are not quite so bad in England.

Anger at an injury causes more injury than the injury itself.

In many cases anger is a serious injury to the bodily health. Passion is as perilous as having a fit. Persons whose hearts are diseased should carefully abstain from it. Who can be quite sure that his heart is not a little affected ?

Anger is dangerous in hot weather:
Subdue your temper altogether.

Anger is short-lived where saving grace has thrived.

"Another pot." Try the tea-pot.

> No. They crave some headier, heavier beverage, and so they go to pot, through the pot coming to them.

Answer him not, lest he grow more hot.

Answer him well, lest his pride should swell.

Answers are honours to a scold,
And make her spirit still more bold.

> "Where no wood is, the fire goeth out." If silence is tried with a passionate person, it will be found to have a most powerful effect.

Any boy or girl you see
Can leap o'er a fallen tree.

> As soon as the man is down, there are plenty to triumph over him. A hare can sport with the beard of a dead lion. In fact, some spirits take peculiar delight in pouring contempt upon the great in the day of their calamity.

Any temptation will prove too strong for the man who
thinks himself too strong for any temptation.

Any time means no time.

> When a work has no appointed season, it is put off from day to day, and in all probability is forgotten and neglected altogether.

Anything is better
Than being a debtor.

April showers bring forth May flowers.

> So sorrows and tears produce joyful results.

Ardent spirits are evil spirits.

> You know where they are retailed. Keep clear both of them and their tails.

As an earthen pot is tried by the sound, so is a man by
his words.

As deep drinks the goose as the gander.

> The more's the pity, but drunkenness among women is fearfully common. The fairer the image the more sad it is to see it thrown into the mire; and hence a woman rolling in liquor is one stage worse than a man in like condition.

As easy as an old shoe, and of as little value too.

> Many are without spirit, and for that reason are very agreeable to others, but are worth nothing for practical service.

As for thy wife, love her as thy life:
As thou lovest life, cease thou from strife.

As good never a whit as never the better.

> If we do not improve by what we do, why are we doing it?

As long as we live we may learn.

> Living and learning should go together. We do not know everything, and therefore we may learn; we may need all sorts of learning, and therefore we should learn. Yet we must not be rudely inquisitive, lest *Chaucer's* lines describe us truly—
>
> > " As prate and prying as a wood-pecker,
> > And ever enquiring upon everything."

As soon as a man is born he begins to die.

> *Withers* rhymes it,—
>
> > " As soon as we to be begun
> > We did begin to be undone."

As soon as you're up, pull off blanket and sheet;
And open the window to make the room sweet.

As the corn is, such will the flour be.

As the corn is, such will the walk be.

> This last is not corn in the field, but corn on the foot. Corns and bunions do not contribute to a pilgrim's progress.

As the day lengthens, the cold strengthens.

> This is true in the early months of the year when the long nights still add to the cold. It is also true in the heart, where it sometimes happens that as we make real advances towards the summer of joy, we also feel more and more of distress on account of the sin which dwelleth in us,

As the diamond to the ring, so is grace to the soul.

It is its glory and preciousness.

As the good man saith, so say we ;
But as the good wife saith, so it must be.

Cunning servants will approve of what the master says, and yet
feel sure that the mistress will have her own way. As they are
much in the house and observe how matters go, they come as a rule
to a true conclusion when they reckon that the lady of the house
will practically carry her point. Well, it is best it should be so.
The house is the woman's dominion, and her husband should let
her reign, saying, "Only in the throne will I be greater than thou."
He will be wise seldom to sit on that throne.

As the man lives, so will he die ;
As the tree falls, so will it lie ;
As the man dies, so must he be
Throughout a whole eternity.

As the mother, such the daughter ;
Look to this before you court her.

As the old birds sing the young birds twitter.

As the old cock crows the young cock learns.

Children imitate their parents' examples. Nature goes for much,
and example for more.

> To fix a good or evil course,
> Example is of potent force ;
> And they who wish the young to teach
> Must practise ever what they preach.

As the tree, so the fruit.

As they must dig who gather ore,
So they must dig who gather lore.

The notion with many is that reading and studying are mere
amusements ; but if they would try for themselves, they would find
that head-work is more tiring than hand-work.

As well be blind as see too much.

No doubt an over-sensitiveness causes great misery both to the
person, and to those around him. Solomon's advice is most excellent : "Take no heed unto all words that are spoken ; lest thou
hear thy servant curse thee."—Eccles. vii. 21.

As you bake, such your cake.

As you brew, such your beer.

As you build, such your house.

> All these proverbs indicate that a man must abide by the results of his conduct. If we sow the wind, we shall reap the whirlwind. Both Scripture and history prove this truth.

As you get whiter, try to get wiser.

> Our growing years should teach us;
> They are the best of preachers.

As you give love, you will have love.

> This is generally true; at least, the price of love is love. Those who love everybody will win love, or, better still, they will deserve it.

As you make your bed, so you must lie on it.

> If young people will choose unfit partners in life, they must take the consequences. If they choose poverty or vice, they must abide by their choice. The old saw says—
> > "Who makes his bed of briar and thorn,
> > Must be content to lie forlorn."

As you sow you must reap.

> Read Galatians vi. 7, 8.

As you think of others, others will think of you.

> This is strangely true: but then our Lord said it would be so.—
> "With what judgment ye judge, ye shall be judged."—Matt. vii. 2.

As you wend, such your end.

Ask your purse what you should buy,
And oftentimes your whims deny.

Asses carry the oats, and horses eat them.

> So it comes to pass that mere labour gets little compared with the more skilled form of work. The proverb indicates a grievance, but hints at the only way of escaping it.

At the sign of the Angel, beware of the Devil.

> In Vanity Fair this is the tavern that Diabolus always patronizes.

Avarice is a mad vice.

> The miser is called by a French wit, "The treasurer of his heir."
> Poor idiot!

Avoid extremes, and bubble schemes.

> Avoid that which makes a void in your pocket.

Avoid the Queen's Head, and comfort ycur wife's heart.

Sayings of a more Spiritual Sort.

A calm hour with God is worth a lifetime with man.

A child in arms may be heir to a crown.

> A young believer has the promise of eternal life and glory. His
> being so young does not disturb his heavenly heirship. The Prince
> of Wales was heir to the throne as soon as he was born, and every
> child of God is an heir of heaven. "If children, then heirs."

A child of light may walk in darkness, and a child of
darkness may walk in light.

> See Isa. 1. 10. The light of the ungodly man comes from the
> dying sparks of his own fire; the light of the righteous is a sun
> which may be under a cloud, but is ever shining. *Bunyan's* ditty
> is worth quoting: he describes his pilgrim in the valley of the
> shadow of death, and says to him—
>
> > "Poor man! where art thou now? thy day is night.
> > Good man! be not cast down, thou yet art right.
> > The way to heaven lies by the gates of hell;
> > Cheer up; hold out, and all things shall go well."

A Christian should be a lamp, and not a damp.

> He should cheer and enlighten his brethren, and never act as a
> wet blanket to their zeal.

A Christian's growing depends on Christ's watering.

A Christless soul is a strengthless soul.

> Paul said, "I can do all things through Christ that strengtheneth
> me;" but Jesus himself said, "Without me ye can do nothing."

A Christless sermon is a worthless sermon.

It is like bread made without flour : the essential element is lacking. Of such a sermon we may say—"They have taken away my Lord, and I know not where they have laid him." The writer is of the same mind as *John Berridge*, who wrote,—

> " Some fast by Calvin hold,
> Some for Arminius fight,
> And each is mighty bold,
> And seemeth surely right :
> Well, though with Calvin I agree,
> Yet Christ is all in all to me.''

A gill of faith is worth a gallon of tears.

Tears may come from mere excitement ; faith leads to Christ, and so to salvation.

> "Not rivers of tears, though a deluge appears,
> Could wash out a sin in a million of years."

A godly woman sure should be
A Sarah to her lord,
A Martha to her company,
A Mary to the Word.

A gracious eye beholds God's gracious hand.

A little saint may enjoy a great promise.

A little will serve a man who is strong in grace ·
Much will not serve him who is weak in grace ;
Nothing will do for him who is void of grace.

A little with God's love is a great estate.

A man finds grace when grace finds him.

This is a bit of sound doctrine and sure experience. Do you understand it ?

A man may be a member of *a* church, but not of *the* church.

A man may hide God from himself, but not himself from God.

A new heart better suits the Sabbath than a new suit.

A prayerless soul is a Christless soul, and a Christless soul is a graceless soul.

A Sabbath broken is an evil token.

It is the sign of a disobedient spirit, and of carelessness as to the blessings of salvation.   When we see how the holy day is profaned, we do not wonder at the godly Scotchwoman's lament—

> "There's nae Sabbath noo, lassie,
>   There's nae Sabbath noo :
> The holy day our fathers loved
>   Is a' broken through."

A Sabbath well spent
Brings a week of content.

A saint is often under a cross, but never under a curse.

Sweet comfort this to the afflicted believer.   In a sea of sorrow there is not a drop of wrath to the man who is in Christ Jesus.

A sermon's length is not its strength.

It may be very much its weakness.   In this case brevity is a virtue.   It is a pity to weary the head when we should win the heart.   Some divines are long in their sermons because they are short in their studies.

A sheep must be fed on the ground.

We must preach according to the capacity of our hearers.   The Lord Jesus did not say "Feed my giraffes," but "Feed my sheep." We must not put the fodder on a high rack by our fine language, but use great plainness of speech.

A small cloud may hide the sun.

A little shortcoming, or an unnoticed transgression, may deprive us of joyous communion with God.

A soul-winner must be a soul-lover.

We can never save a sinner whom we do not love.

A true believer converses in heaven while he sojourns on earth.

A true believer loves not the world, and yet he loves all the world.

A true Christian is both a beggar and an heir.

A walking Christian is better than a talking Christian.

A weak believer hath a mighty Helper.

Above the clouds the sky is blue.

> God's love is not altered by the circumstances of this mortal life.
>
>> " Be still, sad heart, and cease repining;
>> Behind the clouds the sun's still shining.
>> Thy fate is the common lot of all;
>> Into each life some rain must fall."

Abraham left off asking before God left off giving.

> See Gen. xviii. 32.

Abraham's faith was tried, but not tired.

Affliction is not toothsome, but it is wholesome.

Affliction is the good Shepherd's black dog to fetch in his stray sheep.

> David said, " Before I was afflicted I went astray."—Ps. cxix. 67.

Affliction is the school of faith.

> The black-letter lore which we acquire therein is of infinitely more value than all the philosophy of the world.

Affliction is the shadow of God's wings.

Affliction scours the rust from faith.

Afflictions are flails to thresh off our husks.

All sinners are Satan's slaves.

> And like many slaves, they have lost the desire for freedom, and almost the capacity for it. Only a divine power can emancipate minds enslaved by the love of sin.

All thy powers and all thy hours
Give God on his own day.

All-sufficiency destroys self-sufficiency.

> God realized soon makes us forget our self-glorying. Faith in the infinite God weans us from confidence in ourselves.

Almost persuaded was never persuaded.

> See the story of Agrippa in Acts xxvi. We have no reason to believe that Agrippa ever took another step towards Christ.

An ounce of revelation outweighs a mountain of speculation.

Are you discouraged? Pray! It will comfort you.
Are you peaceful? Pray! It will confirm you.
Are you tempted? Pray! It will uphold you.
Are you fallen? Pray! It will uplift you.

> We should pray when we are in a praying mood, for it would be
> sinful to neglect so fair an opportunity. We should pray when we
> are not in a proper mood, for it would be dangerous to remain in so
> unhealthy a condition. Prayer is as suitable for any spot on earth
> as praise is suitable for any place in heaven.

As grace lives sin dies.

As we get up to God we get down to our people.

> It is really so, that when our fellowship with God is nearest, we
> obtain a fuller communion with poor lost humanity.

As well hope to climb to the stars on a treadmill as to
reach heaven by your own works.

As you hope for mercy, show mercy.

> "Blessed are the merciful; for they shall obtain mercy."—
> Matt. v. 7.

As you live you'll die, and as you die you'll live for ever.

> Carefully study 2 Cor. v. 10.

Assurance is lovely, but Christ is altogether lovely.

Assurance is the cream of faith.

> The milk comes first; and when it is settled, the cream follows.

At six days' work be at your best,
But on the Sabbath take your rest.

ACCHUS, well his sheep he knows,
For he marks them on the nose.

Babble will not boil the kettle.

Or as the Persians say, " I hear the sound of the mill-stones, but see no meal." Mere words do nothing abroad or at home.

" Oh, that the tongue would quiet stay,
And let the hand its power display."

Bad beef will never make good broth.

Several meanings may be given to this proverb. You cannot get good influences out of bad doctrine. Ill-gotten money brings no blessing in its use. Bad schemes cannot lead to good results.

Bad companions are the devil's decoy ducks.

In the old poem of " The Plain-Dealing Man " (1609), we read :—

" In the first place, I'd wish you beware
What company you may come in,
For those that are wicked themselves
Will quickly tempt others to sin."

Bad company is the devil's net.

Thousands are every year drawn to destruction through association with the vicious. " Evil communications corrupt good manners." If coals do not burn they blacken : evil company hurts reputation if it does not deprave character, and therefore it ought to be earnestly avoided.

Bad customs are not binding.

In fact, it is our duty to break through them, and set up new and righteous customs. Let us create precedents pure and honest.

Bad lessons are soon learned and long remembered.

Fuller wrote : " Almost twenty years since I heard a profane jest, and still remember it. How many pious passages of far later date have I forgotten ! It seems my soul is like a filthy pond, wherein fish die soon, and frogs live long."

Bad wares are never cheap.

Yet they catch a crowd of customers. The reason for this lies in *Carlyle's* remark, that the United Kingdom contains so many millions of inhabitants, *mostly fools*.

Bad words better no one.

Bad work is never worth doing.

> It will only need undoing, or if it be left as it is, it will be a perpetual abomination. Work thou thy best, or let it rest !

Badly won is soon wasted.

> The man is unable to make good use of what he has gained ; for he has injured his own mind in the process of getting it, and made himself incapable of making the best of his gains. Moreover, a sort of fatality goes with ill-won wealth, and it soon melts away.

Bairns must creep before they walk.

Bald men have all the less to brush.

> Men without property have all the less to take care of.

Bare-footed folk should not tread on thorns.

> Those who are peculiarly sensitive in any direction should keep out of the way of the evil they dread.

Bare walls make gadding wives.

> When the rooms are unfurnished, and there is really no home, does anybody wonder that the wife goes abroad to spend her weary hours ? How much of misery the wives of drinking men have to bear, is known to him who will not let their tears fall to the ground without making enquiry of the wrong-doer.

Bashful dogs get little meat :
Bravely take thy proper seat.

> Some spoil their prospects by being too shy. Modesty is beautiful, but one may have so much of it that the beauty is likely to turn to skin and bone. Let the timid reader think of this couplet, and pluck up courage to do what he has a right to do, and to claim his own. We know some who will never suffer from any excess of bashfulness ; but we need not introduce them, for they will speak for themselves.

Be a little fish if you have but little water.

> Accommodate yourself to your condition.

Be a man, and not a masher.

> Don't want to know what this means: the subject is too insignificant.

Be a man, and not a mouse.

Latimer said : " When I live in a settled and steadfast assurance about the state of my soul, methinks I am as bold as a lion. I can laugh at all trouble ; no affliction daunts me. But when I am eclipsed in my comforts, I am of so fearful a spirit that I could run into a mouse-hole."

Be a man, and not a clothes-horse.

Be not a mere thing to hang clothes on. Though *Teufelsdröckh* asserts that "man's earthly interests are all hooked and buttoned together, and held up by clothes," we like something inside the clothes.

> " We little care for coat and vest,
> For trousers, hat, and all the rest.
> In tailor's dummy we can see
> Just such a man as mashers be."

Be a man before your mother.

Some do not seem as if they would be. The mere dandy is like his mother in this only—she will never be a man, nor will he.

Be always ahead of your work.

Then you will be comfortable. If you are behind-hand, you will be constantly whipped at the cart's tail of hurry.

Be always as cheerful as ever you can,
For few will delight in a sorrowful man.

Hood, visited by a clergyman whose features, as well as language, were lugubrious, looked up at him compassionately and said, " My dear sir, I'm afraid your religion doesn't agree with you." The same remark might be made to others who seem to have just religion enough to make them miserable. They forget the precept " Rejoice in the Lord."

Be always in time ; too late is a crime.

This is putting it rather strong ; but I would talk to an un-punctual man like a Dutch uncle, and give him the rough side of my tongue.

Be always valorous, but seldom venturous.

We are to be ready for all that comes, but we are not to seek conflict. Face a lion if you must, but don't go down to the circus and get into a cage with him of your own accord.

Be angry with self and sin, for such anger is no sin.

It is a case of "Be ye angry, and sin not." He who cannot be angry at evil has no love for goodness. He may be truly called, in Dr. Johnson's phrase, "a good hater" who hates only that which is morally hateful.

Be as firm as a rock when tempted to sin,
And as calm as a clock when troubles begin.

Be as loving as a dove, and as cheerful as a cricket.

Be as neat as a pin, and as brisk as a bee.

Appearance and deportment may seem little things, but they greatly affect success in life. Employers like to have about them persons who are neat in attire and quick in their movements. Nobody wants to have a bundle of old rags rolling about his shop.

Be as prompt to pay as to receive payment.

Be bold, but not too bold; strong, but not head-strong.

Be bound for your friend, and your friendship will end.

You will have to pay the amount for which you are surety, and then your friend will keep out of your way, and you will be glad that he should.

Be careful, but not full of care.

It has been well said that our anxiety does not empty to-morrow of its sorrows, but only empties to-day of its strength.

Be careful with asses, and lasses, and glasses.

These are three different but dangerous things. We place them in order, in the positive, comparative, and superlative degree.

Be chaste as a lily.

Never was this exhortation more needed than now, when men are trying to legalize impurity. Young men, shun all unchastity!

Be clean if you can't be clever.

Many fail not from want of genius, but from want of soap and water, clothes-brush and tooth-brush. It is a pity that no one tells them of it.

Be deaf to furious quarrels, and dumb to foolish questions.

The less you have to do with either the one or the other, the better for your peace of mind.

Be deaf with one ear, and blind with one eye.

Some things it is well neither to hear nor see. Discretion will tell us when to be observantly blind, and forgetfully deaf.

Be good, and then *do* good.

You cannot really do more than you are.

Be good, get good, and do good.

Do all the good you can; to all the people you can; in all the ways you can; as often as you can; and as long as you can.

Be good, or it will not be good to be.

Without grace in the heart, it were better for that man that he had never been born. Even for this world he who does no good dies "much unlamented."

Be good within; do good without.

When a candle is alight within a lantern it sheds a light all around: but if the lantern be dark within it is of no use to those outside. It is the same with men. Have light in yourselves.

Be hardy, but not hard.

Endure hardship yourself; but do not become unkind to others because you are strong and can rough it. A hardy man with a tender heart is a beautiful character; but an unfeeling tyrant is a curse to his household.

Be honest, and thus outwit the rogues.

Honesty perplexes the cunning. They think you are practising some deep policy, and they are baffled.

Be hospitable, but take nobody in.

In other words—Receive many, but deceive none.

Be humble, or you'll stumble.

"Pride goeth before destruction, and a haughty spirit before a fall."—Prov. xvi. 18.

Be in good spirits without ardent spirits.

Be in the mill and expect to have flour on your coat.

Your associations in business and friendship will tell upon your reputation and character.

Be in the right way, but be in nobody's way.

Be it weal, or be it woe,
It will not evermore be so.

> Our condition will change; and this is a good reason why we should neither presume on the present, nor despair concerning it.
>> " The world goes up, and the world goes down,
>> And the sunshine follows the rain ;
>> And yesterday's sneer, and yesterday's frown,
>> Can never come over again."—*C. Kingsley.*

Be just to all, but trust not all.

> It would be unjust not to trust some : it would be unwise to trust many.

Be kind to mankind.

> We are all of a kind, all of kin, or say, all kinned, and therefore we should be kind to each other.

Be kind to your horse, for it cannot complain :
Be tender when using the whip or the rein.

> There is a special venom in cruelty to dumb animals. Their silence should be eloquent with every heart.

Be low in humility and high in hope.

> He who will not bend his head in humility will run against a beam : he that will not hold up his head in hopefulness will not be cheered by an early sight of the good which is waiting for him.

Be low, or you will be sent below.

> Many have had " with shame to take the lowest room," because they would push themselves forward where they had no right to be.
>> " Who wrongly takes the highest place
>> Shall be sent down with much disgrace."

Be merrily wise and wisely merry.

> It is to be done, though it will need prudence and prayer.

Be neither careworn nor careless.

Be no time-server, and yet serve your times.

> As David served his generation by the will of God, so should we ; but this is a very different thing from standing cap in hand to curry favour with those who for a while are in power.

Be not a baker if your brow is butter.

Don't undertake works and offices for which you are peculiarly unfit. If you have a special weakness, do not expose it by attempting to do things which will bring it out. He who has no voice should not be a public speaker : he who cannot make the worse appear the better reason should not be a statesman.

Be not all abroad when you are abroad.

If you are so, you will find many who will prey upon you.

Be not all rake, nor all fork;
Be not all screw, nor all cork.

Neither spend all, nor grasp all; neither draw all out, nor keep all in. Follow wisdom in all her ways.

Be not, and believe not, a tale-bearer.

It is announced that the ladies of a certain place are forming an Anti-speak-evil-of-your-neighbour Society, and it is generally understood that auxiliaries are needed elsewhere.

Be not eagles abroad and moles at home.

Seeing great beauties in foreign scenery, and none in our own fairest of lands, is the folly of shallow minds. The same kind of blindness to things near shows itself in other ways.

Be not ever and over touchy.

Too much sensitiveness will be avoided by a sensible man. Persons who are easily aggrieved will have a sad time of it in this rough-and-tumble world.

Be not everybody's dog that whistles you.

Have a mind of your own, and do not follow first one leader, and then another.

Be not cast down when thou art poor,
But stir thy hand, and work for more.

A wit observes that we ought not to be down when it seems to be all up with us. Remember *Robert Bruce's* spider, and begin to spin again.

Be not fast to feast, and loth to labour.

A good trencher-man should be good at other tools besides his knife and fork.

Be not first to quarrel, nor last to make it up.

> Generally the first to fall out is the last to make peace. We may often know who is in the right by seeing who is most ready to set matters right. A quarrel is always well ended, when truly ended; but it is never well begun, for it should never begin.

Be not honey abroad and wormwood at home.

> Do not spend all your good humour on strangers, and then sulk and scold in your own house. Some read it, "Be not an angel abroad and a devil at home." Who but a hypocrite will bring himself under the censure of this proverb?

Be not little and loud, nor long and lazy.

Be not only good, but good at something.

> Have a *spécialité*, a work at which you are at home. The worst of many is that their goodness is distributed rather than concentrated. They are like a sheet of water, instead of being like a running stream, which can be used to turn a wheel.

Be not proud of race, face, place, or grace.

Be not the first by whom the new is tried,
Nor yet the last to lay the old aside.

> *Pope* has given us this and a vast number of equally wise aphorisms. Here we have a man of Conservative-Radical opinions, and in the long run these are what wise men run to.

Be not YY in your own II.

> For if so, you will not be wise in the eyes of anyone else.

Be old when young, that you may be young when old.

> Prudence, sobriety, and true godliness are supposed to be appropriate to the aged; but we should possess them in our youth. So may we hope to be preserved in health and vigour when years have multiplied upon us.

Be old young, and old long.

> Doubtless prudence in youth, by keeping men back from vice, tends to lengthen their lives.

Be quick to work thy neighbour's weal,
And for his sorrows kindly feel.

> "That charity is valueless which, like the blood of St. Januarius, liquefies but once a year."

Be quick at work, and slow to talk.

Especially be quick in holy service ; but be slow to speak unless you have something worth saying. When folks were quarrelling round the table, the Dutchman said : "I says notings—I eats." So let every man who loves peace keep out of harm's way, and whisper to himself : "I says notings—I works."

Be quiet : walls have ears.

Nobody knows who may be listening ; say nothing which you would not wish put in the daily paper.

Be ready *for* work and steady *at* work.

> In a laborious husbandman you see,
> What all true Christians are, or ought to be.

Be rough and ready rather than fine and faddy.

Be slow enough to be sure.

Don't shut your eyes and go at it like a bull; but see your way, and then make a way.

Be slow in choosing, slower in changing.

Especially with regard to wife or husband. *Ovid* says :—

> "Before your youth with marriage is oppressed,
> Make choice of one who suits your humour best ;
> Such choicest damsel drops not from the sky,
> She must be sought for with a studious eye."

Be solid, not sad ; be merry, not mad.

There's a medium in thoughtfulness and gaiety ; find it out, and keep to it. The middle way in this matter is the safe way.

Be spare of diet, sparer of words, sparest of time.

Be sure you know your own know.

Don't pretend to knowledge, and then break down under a question or two. Also, be quite sure of what you know, and let nobody beat you from your belief.

Be sure you possess what you profess.

Because so many are mere professors, religion is not in the repute it should be. The profession of riches without their possession leads to the worst form of poverty. None is so wretched as the poor man who maintains the semblance of wealth. It must be hard to pay the Income Tax of "keeping up appearances" when he is well nigh penniless.

Be surety?   Of a surety, no!

Yet again and again men are sureties for more than they can spare, and bring misery upon their families.   I have known men's wives and children brought to absolute want through the father's "just putting his name to a bill," of which he was solemnly assured that he would never hear again, and just the use of his name would save his friend from going to the dogs!   Alas, he did hear of it again, and was compelled to impoverish his wife and children to pay another man's debt!

Be swift to console, and slow to condemn.

Be thou gentle every way,
So thy peace shall with thee stay.

A quiet spirit, which never yields to passion, is one of the happiest possessions outside of heaven.   Happy is he who is ever tender in heart, and tone, and spirit!   The gentle man is the true gentleman.

Be true as steel, come woe or weal.

Be very slow a pledge to make,
But slower still your word to break.

Dr. Johnson spoke of one who was no genius, but so true to his pledge, that if he promised you an acorn, and none grew in England that year, he would send to Denmark to get one rather than let his promise fail.

Be wary whereso'er thou be,
For from deceit no place is free.

Be willing to want that which God is not willing to give.

"I find the best way to have my own will is to resign myself to thy will, and to say Amen to thy Amen."—*T. Brooks.*

Be wisely worldly, but not worldly wise.

We must be prudent in our dealings, but not with the wisdom of this world!   *Bunyan's* rhyme is a good one :—

"When Christians unto carnal men gave ear,
Out of their way they go and pay for't dear;
For Master Worldly Wiseman can but show
A saint the way to bondage and to woe."

Be with the bad, and bad you will be.

Sleep in the soot, and you will be black.

Be your own most useful friend;
Cease on others to depend.

An ancient philosopher once said, "I am the only one of my friends that I can rely upon." A friend may help you over a stile, but he cannot be expected to carry you on his back.

Bear and forbear, and bear again:
Let four bears with you remain.

Bear the hen's cackle for the sake of the eggs.

Little annoyances must be put up with because of great advantages. The rattle of machinery, and the noise of traffic must be endured for the sake of the business.

Beauty doth bind all but the blind.

Beauty is a fair but fading flower.

Beauty is best when plainly drest.

Hannah More without a jewel shone like a star amid fine ladies.

Beauty is but skin deep.

A lady who had nothing attractive in her appearance was wont to say sharply to a young lady, "Beauty is only skin deep." That lady, who was fair to look upon, replied, "And so is ugliness." All quarrels about looks may well end, for we have something better to care about. Socrates wisely said: "I pray thee, O God, that I may be beautiful within!"

Beauty turns to ashes at last.

Hence the higher value of beauty of character.

"Beautiful hands are those that do
Work that is earnest, brave and true,
Moment by moment the whole day through."

Such hands will not be lost in the grave, but remembered by what they have done.

Beauty wins, but bounty holds.

The eye is charmed by an elegant appearance, but the actual receipt of kindness is that which retains the heart.

Beauty without grace is a violet without scent.

Beauty with wickedness is Satan's baited hook.

Beer brings many to their bier.

He who made this pun would no doubt pick a pocket of hops rather than drink a drop of the bitter.

Beer is never so flat as those who drink it.

Bees gather sweet honey from bitter herbs.

Gracious men are taught to take pleasure in infirmities and trials; and they also make accidents and calamities occasions for doing good.

Before a fool handles a whip he ought to feel it on his own back.

Not meant to be a cruel observation, but to prevent much of that cruelty which arises from ignorance of the pain which the lash is causing.

Before ill chances men are ever merry,
But heaviness foreruns the good event.

This observation has been made by many; and one of our hymn-writers has embalmed the prognostic in a verse which ends:—

"We should suspect some danger nigh
When we perceive too much delight."

Before you call a man your friend eat a bushel of salt with him.

Know him, and try him. Be not in a hurry to trust one of whom you have no experience. The costermongers say, " Crack and try, before you buy," and that is only about a walnut. Eating with a man is a good test, lodging with him is better, but travelling with him is best of all.

Before you decide
Hear the other side.

This is sensible advice, but many persist in the neglect of it.

Before you doctor others, try your own physic.

Especially if you try to teach the gospel. Never preach beyond your experience.

Before you hang up your hat look at the peg.

See what sort of family you will be connected with by the marriage. Observe well your mother-in-law !

Before you get a bird provide a cage.

Or, in other words,

" Before you marry
Have a house wherein to tarry."

One would think this advice unnecessary, but people are reckless nowadays. We hope our readers will not begin housekeeping with furniture on credit : it is not creditable.

Before you keep your carriage, be sure that you can keep your legs.

Don't rush into a large expenditure before you are certain that you can keep up your ordinary business standing.

Before you mount look to your girth.

Applicable to many mounts beside those upon a horse's back. Many men accept offices which they cannot fulfil, and enter upon positions which they cannot maintain.

Before you put on your new clothes take off the old.

You must repent and leave off old sins before you can hope to exhibit the graces of the Christian life. Put off the old man and put on the new man.—Col. iii. 9, 10.

Before you rectify another, be right yourself.

It is an evil for rebuke and blame,
A vice to reprehend, and do the same.

Before you run in double harness, look well at the other horse.

Before you spend elevenpence, earn a shilling.

Before you trust the cat, put the cream out of reach.

Remove temptation even from those in whom you have confidence. He who bids you pray, " Lead us not into temptation," would not have you lead others into it.

**Before your pocket has gone to the socket,
Either new stock it, or totally block it.**

Begin as you mean to go on.

Do not yield everything at first. Do not make the new-comer think that there are seven Sundays in the week in your house. Don't spend all in the honeymoon, &c., &c.

Beggars must not be choosers.

Take gratefully what is given thee, O man, for what art thou but a mendicant at the gate of mercy ?

Begin on porridge, that you may end with chicken.

This is the Scotch form of very good advice, and it means—Live at first with great frugality, that you may rise in the world, and have easy times later on. It is to be feared that many begin with the chicken, and what they will end with we can easily guess. In England we say, "Eat your brown bread first." While a young man is single let him live hard, that in after years he may not be forced to keep to "bread and pull it "; but may have pullet with his bread.

Begin only what you can hope to finish.

Believe not all, doubt not all.

Have a judicious mind towards men, and neither fall into credulity nor suspicion.

" I rather would, because it seemeth just,
Deceivèd be, than causelessly distrust."

Believe not half you hear, and repeat not half you believe.

My uncle used to say, "When you hear an ill report of any one, halve it, and then quarter it, and then say nothing about the rest."

Believe nothing ill of an old friend.

Bend the boy's neck, or he'll be a stiffnecked man.

Want of training to obedience in youth is the cause of much of the disorder and love of anarchy which we see in certain classes of society. The child is getting to be the father of the man with a vengeance, and the father is coming to be the son's slave.

Bended knees save broken bones.

Yield to God's word and will, and you will escape many a calamity. Prayer will be your safeguard.

Better a blush on the face than a stain on the heart.

Better a bridle on the tongue than a lash upon the conscience.

If we are not careful what we say, we may have to smart in conscience over evils which we cannot undo, which were wrought by our unbridled tongues.

Better a blind horse than an empty stall.

Better a fortune *in* a wife than a fortune *with* a wife.

Better a friendly " No," than a grudging " Yes."

Better a full barrow than an empty waggon.

A little man doing his best is to be preferred to a greater man of whom nothing comes.

Better a good groat than a bad bank-note.

Sincerity makes the least man to be of more value than the most talented hypocrite.

Better a little loss than a long sorrow.

Better a low house than no house.

Better a patch than a hole.

Better a purse empty than full of other men's money.

Gaining riches by chicanery is drawing down a curse upon ourselves. Honourable poverty is infinitely to be preferred to dishonest wealth, or to large indebtedness. In the Telugu we read : " A cupful of rice-water without debt is enough."

Better a salt tongue than an oily one.

Sensible persons prefer a little sharp honesty to glib deceit. We say, " Speak truth, and shame the devil," but we know some who warp the truth, and please the devil.

I heartily hate
All plausible prate.

Better a small nose than no nose at all.

Thus may those who are ridiculed as to their features readily comfort themselves.

Better a spur *in* the brain than *on* the heel.

Activity of mind is the great thing : the mere show of speed is nothing. Or we may understand that a man of sense can make matters go on better by the use of his brain, than by any mere force or cruelty.

Better a tooth out than aching.

Or as some put it, " Better an empty house than a bad tenant."

Better a tough rabbit than a tender cat.

> One can be eaten, and the other cannot. So there are characters of whom the best is not so good as the worst of another sort. Yet have we no liking for tough rabbits though we thus speak.

Better a true enemy than a false friend.

> We know what to do with an open foe, and are not disappointed in him.

Better a witty fool, than a foolish wit.

> Wit is a razor, and if it be in unwise hands it may injure men. It needs great sense to play the fool, and a man who attempts wit should have all his wits about him.

Better absent from a feast than present at a fray.

Better alone than in bad company.

Better an ass that carries you than a horse that throws you.

Better ask the way than go astray.

> An Eastern philosopher was asked how he had acquired so much knowledge, and his answer was : " I never was prevented by pride or by shame from asking questions." A coachman completely lost himself in London because he was too conceited to enquire the way, and many will thus miss their way to heaven.

Better ask the way twice than wander once.

Better be a living dog than a dead lion.

> This is Solomon's proverb, and it may be applied in many ways. The poorest genuine Christian is to be preferred to the most pretentious hypocrite.

Better be a lean bird in a wood than a fat one in a cage.

> The sweets of liberty are worth paying for. The Creoles say that " Fat has no feeling," hence the fat bird does not fret about the cage.

Better be good and have good than hear of good.

> The mere report will tantalize ; but to have and enjoy is a great privilege. He knew little of sweet who is mentioned in the Singhalese story, but there are many like him : he said that sugar-candy was sweet. When asked if he had tasted it, he answered, " No : my brother told me." Being further questioned, " Has your brother tasted it ? " He replied, " No ; but a man at Colombo told him so." Personal experience is better far than hearsay.

Better be half-an-hour too soon than a minute too late.

Then you only lose your own time, but in the other case you are wasting the time of others. If you keep four persons waiting a quarter of an hour, you have stolen an hour of their time.

Better be last among saints than first among sinners

Better be little in Israel than great in Babylon.

Better be mute than mutter.

Silent patience is better than murmuring against God.

Better be rich in good than rich in goods.

Better be the Lord's dog than the devil's darling.

The most despised and afflicted saint is to be preferred to the most prosperous and honoured of the wicked.—Ps. lxxxiv. 10.

Better be unknown than ill-known.

Better be untaught than ill-taught.

What we learn incorrectly has to be unlearned. He that learned French "after the manner of Stratford-at-Bow" found, when he went to Paris, that the French did not understand their own language; at least, not as he spoke it. In religion, science, and everything else, it is the false which hinders the true knowledge.

Better be well and lean than ill and fat.

Better bend than break : giving way makes way.

Better bend the neck than break the brow.

Better birds' song
Than lordly throng.

The joys of a country life far surpass those of town and court.

Better bread in the lap
Than feather in the cap.

A supply for necessities is better than mere honour or the pretence of it. "Rag and famish" is a poor motto.

Better break your leg than your neck.

Undoubtedly the one is a sad accident, but to lose life itself is worse. In all matters prefer the less evil to the greater, and solace yourself under any ill with the reflection that it might be worse. The wicked old woman when she lost her old man said, "Well, it might have been worse. The cow might have died."

Better buy than borrow : better give than lend.

Better catch small fish than come home with empty dish.

Better come from the barn than from the band-box.

> Common-sense working men are worth a dozen dandies. " He looks as if he had just stepped out of a bandbox " is not a compliment to any man.

Better die than lie ; better suffer than sin.

Better do than dream ;
Better be than seem.

Better do what you like not than what you ought not.

Better dove without serpent than serpent without dove.

> Simplicity without prudence is better than subtlety without sincerity. Yet when a fellow will not do right when softly persuaded by your dove, it may be wise to set your serpent at him.

Better eat humble pie than no pie at all.

> Some throw themselves out of situation sooner than apologize for a fault or put up with a rebuke. This is extreme folly.

Better enquire and enquire than flounder in the mire.

Better face a danger than be always in fear.

Better fare poorly than feel proudly.

Better fast than be scolded all dinner-time.

> Solomon saith : " Better is a dry morsel, and quietness therewith, than an house full of sacrifices with strife."—Prov. xvii. 1.

Better fear God than fear ghosts.

> Strange that some who do not yield homage to the true God are yet afraid of the silly inventions of superstition.

Better give a shilling than lend half-a-crown.

> You will save eighteenpence by the transaction.

Better go barefoot than wear a pinching shoe.

> Thus the bachelor justifies his preference to being without a wife rather than having a bad one.

Better God than gold;
Better give than hold.

Better go round about than fall into the ditch.

Better go round than be drowned.

Better go to heaven in rags than to hell in robes.

Better half a loaf than no bread at all.

> If wages be not so high as we could wish, yet if we are out of work for a single week it will take months to recover the loss. Strikes hurt the strikers, even if they win.

Better half an egg than an empty shell.

Better have a slow repast
Than choke yourself by eating fast.

> Haste, in other matters beside eating and drinking, is the cause of much evil. "He that hasteth to be rich shall not be innocent."

Better keep peace than make pence.

> What are small gains compared with the pearl of peace?

Better keep Satan out than get him out.

> Well worth remembering. It is a simpler and easier thing to fasten the doors and keep out thieves, than it is to fight with burglars when they are once indoors. It is easier to prevent a quarrel than to bring it to a happy end when once begun. It is better not to form any bad habit than to overcome it.

Better hermit's desert cell
Than with brawling wife to dwell.

Better late than never, but better never late.

> It is a sad thing when true religion has been left till late in life, but yet a mercy if a man finds it at all. Mr. Bunyan makes Christian sing:—
>
>> "'Tis true, 'twas long ere I began
>> To seek to live for ever;
>> But now I run fast as I can;
>> 'Tis better late than never."

Better leave undone than have to undo.

> When a case is doubtful, it is best to do nothing till you see what to do; for if we do the wrong thing it may make bad worse.

Better limp to heaven than leap to hell.

Better little man for friend than great man for foe.

Better live on a little than outlive a great deal.

> Economy must be strictly practised when a business is in peril; for the greatest pinching will be better than losing the chance of a livelihood. Cultivate forethought upon a little oatmeal. Do not by extravagance kill the goose which lays the golden eggs.

Better long little than soon nothing.

> To remember this will check hasty and excessive expenditure.

Better lose much than lose more.

Better lose the wool than the sheep.

> Let go a little to keep the larger part: lose the interest to save the capital. Let the salary go if the church can be kept right. But in this last case some would let the sheep go if the wool would remain for their portion.

Better miss a dinner than make work for a doctor.

> Is not a little fasting the best medicine? Are not "little dinners" a great risk to weak stomachs?

Better one's house be too little one day than too big all the year round.

> For a house which is too large involves daily trouble and expense, and tends to the impoverishment of the inhabitant.

Better preserved in brine than perished in honey.

> To be kept right by trouble is to be desired rather than to be led astray by pleasure.

Better out of fashion than out of credit.

> Some spend so much to be fashionable that they get into debt, and lose credit with neighbours. "You must be in the fashion" is the utterance of weak-headed mortals.

Better poverty and truth than prosperity with falsehood.

> For wealth gained by falsehood yields no rest. It would be wise at once to get out of a false position.

> > By seeming other than thou art,
> > Thou dost perform a foolish part.

Better rub away than rust away.

Better run a mile-than pick a quarrel.

Better serve God in a city than in a cell.

Because there is more opportunity for doing good among the masses. Lonely service may be good for me ; but what is to become of perishing millions ?

Better serve God in solitude than sin with the multitude.

Better short of pence than short of sense.

A philosopher has said, "A man without money is poor, yet a man with nothing but money is poorer."

Better sit still than rise to fall.

Many were once doing well in business ; but they tried to do too much, and did it. "Vaulting ambition doth o'erleap herself." A courtier wrote on a pane of glass,
"Fain would I climb but that I fear to fall."
Queen Elizabeth wisely wrote under it,
"If thy heart fail thee, do not climb at all."

Better sing than sigh ; but better sigh than sin.

Better slip with foot than slip with tongue.

Better sober silence than sottish song.

Better slow in the road than quick in by-path meadow.

Better some of a dumpling than none of a pudding.

The Knight, in Don Quixote, wisely said : "Since we have a good loaf let us not look for cheese-cakes."

Better stint than run in debt.

Indeed this is a duty. What we cannot pay for we must wait for.

Better suffer a great wrong than do a little one.

The bulk of men would reverse this, and do great wrongs to escape from slight sufferings.

Better suffer without cause than cause suffering.

Better than star on the breast is a conscience at rest.

"Bless my stars and garters ! " is a common exclamation · but a quiet conscience is blest already.

Better the child cry than the father sigh.

Fuller said : "He that will not use the rod on his child, his child shall be used as a rod on him."

Better the error of love than the love of error.

The error of love is sincere, and may lead to fanaticism ; but the love of error is of the devil altogether.

Better the ills we know than those we know not.

It is perilous work to change our crosses ; for our shoulders are growing accustomed to those we have. Some even bid us be careful in brushing off a mosquito, for that particular tormentor is getting satisfied, and a new-comer will be more hungry, and therefore bite you all the worse. The element of uncertainty should make us slow to change our trials, even if we had the power to do so.

Better to bed without supper than rise in debt.

Better to starve in honesty than to fatten in roguery.

Better trust an unbroken horse than an unbridled tongue.

Both will run away with you ; but the tongue will take you into the greatest danger.

Better wait than burn your mouth.

Better wear out shoes than sheets.

Industry is much to be preferred to indolent self-indulgence. Better trudge along the road to success than doze one's self into failure.

Better wear on than rust out.

This is an improvement upon the old saying, "Better wear *out* than rust out !" When a man works on fairly, he does not wear out, but the work does him good.

Better wear the blue than bear the blues.

The Blue Ribbon is the ensign of Temperance, but the blues are the melancholy which grows out of excess.

Better wee fire to warm than big fire to burn.

Better work for nothing than become lazy.

It is really so. Gentlemen who have retired from business often take up an unpaid occupation to keep themselves from absolute weariness of life.

Between right and wrong there is no middle path.

> Though a great many try to make one, they can never **succeed.**
>> There is a right way and a wrong,
>> You cannot travel both along.
>> Choose this or that without delay,
>> But don't pretend a middle way.

Between *said* and *done* a race may be run.

> It is greatly desired that they may very nearly keep pace with each other. *Said* will be a little ahead, but *Done* should follow at his heel.

Between two fires one finds it too hot.

> Two to one is no fun. We may answer one questioner, but two brow-beaters beat us altogether.

Between two liars the truth comes out.

Between two stools we come to the ground.

Beware of a dog that barks little, but makes his teeth meet.

Beware of a man of two faces.

Beware of a man who has quitted his friend,
His friendship with you will soon come to an end.

Beware of a man who has nothing to lose.

> He is reckless, and raves like a mad dog.

Beware of a woman who says she " hates gossip."

> She is pretty sure to be up to her neck in it.

Beware of bees in your bonnet.

> Some call them "hobbies," "maggots," or "fads." See " Beware of crotchets in your crown."

Beware of brawlers and crawlers.

> Men who, either by noise or by craft, try to make something for themselves are to be avoided.

Beware of building speculators and buildings' peculators.

> We saw a misprint in the newspapers, and copied it into this sentence. It is wonderful how we sometimes stumble on the truth by accident.

Beware of crotchets in your crown.

Persons who have them become a nuisance.   One man of my acquaintance never finished a conversation without recommending Morrison's pills, another drags in Anglo-Israelism, and a third is of horses horsey.   Nothing in the world is half so important as our friend's one craze :

> " As Paganini played one string,
> This other ninny harps one thing."

Beware of daggers of gold.

These stab at honesty.   Many a character has been slaughtered by bribes.   Love of gold may stab our piety.

Beware of error sugared with truth.

Nothing is more likely to impose upon you than false doctrine disguised with a smattering of truth.

Beware of gifts that God never gave.

Touch not things which have been gained by knavery ; pretend not to talents which you do not really possess.

Beware of having more notion than motion.

We see everywhere persons who know more than they practise, and have more conceit than industry, more doctrine in the head than holiness in the life.   Let such men serve us as beacons.

Beware of having sticky fingers.

In handling public money, some have need to hear this warning. In such matters care must be extreme.   Here Cæsar's wife must not only be innocent, but beyond suspicion.

Beware of "heavy wet"!   Carry an umbrella.

Yet the "heavy wet" we mean cannot be kept off by an umbrella, for it falls inside the man.   Let him shut his mouth against it.

Beware of idols and idlers.

Beware of men made of molasses.

Persons who are very plausible and excessively polite have generally some design upon you, as also religionists who call you "dear" the first time they see you, and are for ever prating of a love which lies only on their lips, and *lies* even there.

Beware of mettle in a blind horse.

He is apt to dash into danger. He must go, and he does not see where. Many zealots are so ignorant that they come under this proverb: they are dangerous when they are not well guided.

Beware of rolls from the brewer's basket.

Nasty rolls they are which come of swimming heads and staggering legs.

Beware of spooning and mooning.

What's the use of giving such advice? One after another the young people come under these lunar influences, as their parents did before them.

Beware of sun-strokes and beer-strokes.

They are great dangers. When a man is said to have "been in the sun" we know what it means.

Beware of the angler with the golden hook.

Money will bribe the most honest. If they do not look well to their dealings, men will find themselves bought and sold before they are well aware of it. Beware of palm-oil!

Beware of the love which has an eye to the larder.

Suspicion that love is selfish should put an end to the acquaintance. One is reported to have said, "Leave you, dear girl? Never! So long as you have a shilling." Cold mutton has enticed many men into the kitchen who were supposed to come there for a certain lamb.

Beware of the mass. Remember the massacre.

St. Bartholomew should be an eternal warning to weak-kneed Protestants.

"Beware of the paint," whether on walls or on women.

Mrs. Partington was right when she would have nothing to do with Beautifiers of the complexion. "Well," said she, "they may get up ever so many of their rostrums, but, depend upon it, the less people have to do with bottles for it the better. My neighbour, Mrs. Blotch, has been using a bottle a good many years for her complexion, and her nose looks like a ruption of Mount Vociferous, with the burning lather running all over the contagious territory." Beware of such paint, whether it be for external or internal application!

Beware of the pottage which colours the nose.

> Keep clear of the pots in which it is brought :
> Pewter's a metal of dubious sort.

Beware of the stone thou stumbledst at before.

> We shall be doubly guilty if we do not learn to avoid in future that which has already proved an occasion of sin to us.

Beware of the sweet meat which will be followed by sour sauce.

> Certain sins are of that sort even in this life.

Beware of those who are good-looking, but not good.

Beware of two black eyes.

> Whether in your own head, or in the lovely face of a doubtful woman.

Big mouthfuls are apt to choke.

> When men boast, or over-promise themselves, they expose themselves to peril. When men go in for great speculations, or large ambitions, they run heavy risks.

Big words from a weak stomach are poor things.

Bills look best receipted.

> The Queen's likeness on a receipt stamp is a cheering work of art when seen at the foot of an account.

Bills of accommodation are ills of abomination.

> May our uninitiated readers never know what this means.

Bind fast, and find fast,
> Keep ye tryst ever ;
Strive weel, and thrive weel,
> Falter ye never.

Birds of a feather flock together.

> "Being let go, they went to their own company."—Acts iv. 23.

Birds sing on a bare bough :
O believer, canst not thou ?

Birds that keep aloft escape the net.

> Hearts kept near to God are spared many temptations.

Birds when full fledged must fly away :
Young men should not on parents prey.

> The ill effects of young men loafing about in the old home are
> manifest to all. They grow dissatisfied with what their parents do
> for them, while their parents feel that they are a burden to them.
> They are in the worst state of dependence, are unfitted for future
> life, and take liberties which they will find it hard to give up when
> they are forced to go elsewhere.

Bitter pills cure bitter ills.

Bitter truth should be sweetly spoken.

> We should be anxious to cause no more offence than naturally
> goes with the truth itself. Coat your pills with sugar.

Biters in their turn are bitten ;
So expect, for so it's written.

Black care makes grey hair.

> Why do we indulge it when we are bidden to be careful for
> nothing ? Are we so eager to make ourselves old ?

Black clouds yield silver showers.

> "Ye fearful saints, fresh courage take ;
> The clouds ye so much dread
> Are big with mercy, and shall break
> In blessings on your head."

Black earth yields white bread.

Black soils grow bright flowers.

> Adversity produces spiritual prosperity when sanctified by grace.

Black will take no other colour.

> Yet the grace of God can remove the blackness of sin, and make
> us whiter than the snow.

Blend serpent and dove : have both wisdom and love.

Blow the wind never so fast,
It will lower at last.

> Hope, therefore, that time will bring calm after tempest, joy
> after sorrow, rest after trouble.

Blue is blue, but there may be better blue.

True and faithful, good and generous as a man may be, there may be others quite as good, if not better.

Blue ribbon is better than blue ruin.

Recommend Gospel Temperance everywhere, and specially recommend it by your own practice of it.

Boast not of what thou hast : let God be magnified.
Boast not what thou hast not, lest men thy brags deride.

Boast not your wisdom : Satan knows more than you.

Boil stones in butter, and you lose your pains.

They will neither be soft nor palatable. Certain persons seem none the better for all the kindness you can do them.

Borrowed pots are apt to leak.

They are a miserable makeshift and usually go home cracked.

Borrowing may be tried once, but only once.

Sudden need may come to any one, but *the habit* of running to others should not be formed, much less continued in.

Both folly and wisdom grow with our years.

Too often they seem to grow side by side. Some know better and do worse. Time makes some mellow, and others rotten.

Both God and man hate pride.

Even the man who is proud as Lucifer himself detests pride in others.

Boughs that most with fruit abound,
Bow themselves towards the ground.

Fruitfulness fosters humility.

Bought wit is better than short wit.

Bought wit is not always worth what it costs.

No. You can be so wounded by experience of your own folly that no prudence throughout the future will ever heal it. It is far wiser to learn from the Word of God, and the Spirit of God, than to need the painful teaching of sorrow.

Bought wit lasts longest.

It makes a deep impression on the memory, and usually remains for life. Its serious price helps its preservation.

Bounce is the language of folly.

Loud braying reveals a certain creature by no means famed for wisdom.

Boundless misery is met by boundless mercy.

This is the essence of gospel truth. Let the miserable try it.

Boys will be boys.

Yet it is well for us and for them to remember that "boys will be men"; and that—

> The boy who best learns all he can,
> Will best succeed when he's a man.

Brag and Bounce don't weigh an ounce.

Brag is a good dog, but Holdfast is better.

Bragging sportsmen bag few birds.

Bread baked must be eaten.

Either by ourselves or somebody. Our conduct has results, and very sad ones, too, in some cases.

Break the egg, and no bad bird will come of it.

End the matter while yet the evil is only in thought and plan, lest it become an overt act of wrong.

Break up family jars, and cover old scars.

Brevity is a fine thing in a speech.

Want of study, and want of really knowing what one is driving at, must bear the blame of many a long and weary talk. Hence a short speech is usually of better quality than a long one; and if it is not, it is all the better that it is short.

Bribes throw dust into eyes
Of men who else were wise.

This bribing takes a thousand shapes, and operates on men who would scorn the influence if they were aware of its operation.

Brick by brick houses are built.

Steady plodding will accomplish anything.
By many strokes the work is done,
Which cannot be performed at one.

Bridesmaids may soon be made brides.

One wedding usually brings on another, "and so the world wags." Those who play second fiddle well, will one day rise to be principal performers.

Bring up a raven, and it pecks out your eyes.

Alas, that ingratitude should be so common as to have produced and justified this proverb ! Ingratitude is ravenous cruelty.

Bring up your boy to nothing, and he'll be a rogue.

He will have nothing to do, and he will do it diligently. Of course he will run into bad company, and wicked men and the devil together will soon make a tool of him.

Broken eggs can never be mended.

So is it with many a broken vow, a plighted troth, a spotless character, a hopeful usefulness.

Broken friendship may be soldered, but it is seldom sound.

Brotherly love is the livery of God's servants.

"We know that we have passed from death unto life, because we love the brethren."—1 John iii. 14.

Busy tongues make idle hands.

It's woful to have a house full of cacklers, and never an egg from the whole of them. While they talk about everything, they do nothing.

Buttons all right are husbands' delight.

What vexation may be caused by neglect of such a little thing as a button ! Let wives think nothing trivial which tends to peace.

Buy a bit of flannel, never mind ribbons.

Buy at market, but sell at home.

One is not sure of the wisdom of this ; but we suppose there is something in it, or it would not be a proverb. Very much must depend upon whether you can find purchasers near home.

Buy not on trust; down with the dust.

A shopkeeper's sign in China bore the inscription : "No credit—we have learned wisdom from former customers."

Buy one fine thing, and you must buy ten more.

Thus the piano on the hire system leads to no end of purchases, and the family is impoverished. To make things all of a piece they go to pieces. They have a hole, and so they are bound to have a mouse, and having a mouse they must have a cat : of course, the cat has kittens, &c., &c.

Buy sixpenny-worth of stick-to-it.

Application and perseverance are necessary. Some persons are everything by turns and nothing long, and therefore they never succeed in anything.

Buy the best : things may cost less, and be worthless.

Horrible cheapness is ruining both buyer, seller, and producer. If we get things for less money, there is less material or less work in them, and they are soon worn out.

By digging and digging the truth is discovered.

By doing nothing we do ill.

By drops and wets Jack's money sweats.

By everyone minding his own business work is done.

By frequent trying Troy was won,
All things by trying may be done.

By loaning and squabbling one loseth one's friend,
But squaring and settling keep peace to the end.

By losing present time we lose all time.

Since we have in truth no time but time present.

By our own toothache we learn
To pity others in our turn.

"A fellow feeling makes us wondrous kind."

By perseverance the snail reached the ark.

No doubt the snails started early, and by keeping on they entered the ark, and were saved as surely as the greyhounds. *Wither* says in his couplet :—

"They who but slowly pacèd are
By plodding on may travel far."

By saying nothing you may pass for wise.

Who is to know to the contrary? "Mother," said the girl, "if I hold my tongue at the party they will think I am a fool." "Never mind, child," said the old lady, "if you are quiet they will only *think* you a fool; but if you begin talking they will *know* you are. So hold your tongue."

By staring at the moon men stumble into the ditch.

Great questions and speculations lead men into errors, both doctrinal and practical. It would be better if these superior persons would have sense enough to mind the more common truths and the more practical duties. We are afraid that it cannot be said of certain of them—

> "He knew what's what, and that's as high
> As metaphysic wit can fly."

By the street of By-and-by we come to the house of Never.

> Then shun the road, my youthful friends;
>   Work on yet while you may;
> Let not old age o'ertake you as you slothfully delay,
> Lest you should gaze around you, and discover with a sigh,
> *You* have reached the house of "Never" by the street of "By-and-by."

By the thread we unwind the skein.

Get the thread of the matter and follow it up, and it will be all straight before you. For instance, know the love of God, and then all that he does will be explainable.

By timely mending save much spending.

Sayings of a more Spiritual Sort.

Be all for Christ, since he is all for thee.

> Welcome, great guest, this house, mine heart,
>   Shall all be thine;
>   I will resign
> Mine interest in every part.
> Only be pleased to use it as thine own
> For ever, and inhabit it alone.

Be ballasted with grace, that you be not blown over with temptation.

Be holy in commerce and converse.

> *Luther* says, "Holiness consisteth not in a cowl, nor in a garment of grey. When God purifies the heart by faith, the market is sacred as well as the sanctuary."

Be holy, kind and true always,
If you would live an angel's days.

Be jealous for God; for he is a jealous God.

> "I the Lord thy God am a jealous God."—Ex. xx. 5. "I have been very jealous for the Lord God of hosts."—1 Kings xix. 14.

Be not hot in prayer and cold in praise.

Be not idle in the means, nor make an idol of the means.

> That is to say, neither neglect public worship and Christian ordinances, nor so put your trust in them as to forget that they are nothing without God.

Be sick *of* self and sick *for* Christ.

> O happy sickness, where the infirmity is not to death, but to life, that God may be glorified by it ! "—*Quarles.*

Beauty and bounty unite in Christ Jesus.

> Happy combination ! All that enraptures, and all that enriches.

Begin praying, continue watching, and you will end with praising.

> Take care of prayer, and prayer will take care of everything else.

Begin the web, and God will send you thread.

> If it is a holy or charitable work, seek the divine help, and begin at once in confidence that he will supply the need of his own cause.

Begin the year with godly fear.

Behind a frowning providence God hides a smiling face.

Believe God's promise, and he will receive thy prayer.

> If we will not give God credit for being true, we cannot expect him to give credit to our prayers for being sincere.

Believe and live.

This is the message of the gospel. It should be a proverb in every land. *Cowper* has said of it:—

" Oh how unlike the complex works of man,
    Heaven's easy, artless, unencumbered plan !
No meretricious graces to beguile,
No clustering ornaments to clog the pile ;
From ostentation as from weakness free,
It stands like the cerulean arch we see,
Majestic in its own simplicity.
Inscribed above the portal from afar,
Conspicuous as the brightness of a star,
Legible only by the light they give,
Stand the soul-quickening words—' BELIEVE AND LIVE.' "

Believers are Christ's own, and he is their own.

Believers are not free *from* sin, that is their burden; but they are not free *to* sin, that is their blessing.

Believers are worthies of whom the world is not worthy.

Believers in Jesus are receivers from Jesus.

Matthew Henry says:—This excludes proud boasting, that we have nothing but we *have received it;* and silences perplexing fears, that we want nothing but we *may receive* it.

Believers sin less, but they are not sinless.

Yet faith will ultimately kill sin. The evil it has driven out of us should be viewed as a pledge that it will conquer evil altogether.

Believing in Christ should not exclude sorrow for sin, nor sorrow for sin exclude believing in Christ.

Faith and repentance all must find ;
    But yet we daily see
They differ in their time and kind,
    In manner and degree.

But, be our conflicts short or long,
    This commonly is true,
That wheresoever faith is strong,
    Repentance is so too.—*Joseph Hart.*

Better be a poor man and a rich Christian than a rich man and a poor Christian.

Better be new-born than high-born.

The regenerate possess a nobler nature than the proudest of earth's nobility if they are not born from above.

Better be than seem.

> Yet, Lord, the double grace impart :
> Give me the open, upright heart,
> Then shall I *seem* to live to thee,
> And *be* all that I *seem* to be.

Better be troubled *for* sin than *by* sin.

Conscience troubled for sin may lead to repentance and salvation , but the results of sin are terrible.

Better beg one's bread with Lazarus here, than one's water with Dives hereafter.

True, but how terrible to have Lazarus' miseries in this life, and the rich man's woes in the next !   Let me not be a poor, bad man !

Better holiness without comfort than comfort without holiness.

Better nail your heart to the cross than your ears to the pulpit.

That is to say, true love to Jesus is better than slavishly following any human preacher, and accepting all that he may say.

Better the least in Christ than the greatest out of him.

Better unborn than unsaved.

" I wish," said *Voltaire*, " I had never been born."
" O blessed be God," cried *Hallyburton*, " that ever I was born."

Better walk by faith than talk of faith.

Better walk with God than talk with kings.

Beware of hidings of heavenly tidings.

Beware of the time when "the door is shut."

Great solemnity should attend the thoughts of that hour: for "when once the Master of the house has risen up, and hath shut to the door ; " all knocking will be in vain.

Bless God for your afflictions, and your afflictions will be your greatest blessings.

> Amid my list of blessings infinite,
> Stands this the foremost, " That my heart has bled."— *Young.*

Bless God heartily though he afflicts thee heavily.

> Very wisely *French* enquires :—
> " When thou hast thanked thy God for every blessing sent,
> What time will then remain for murmurs or lament ? "

Bless the Lord to-day ; he blesses you every day.

Broken-hearted penitents and whole-hearted seekers please God well.

Brown bread with the gospel is good fare.

> So she thought who had nothing but bread and water, and yet exclaimed, "What ! all this and Christ too ? "

Build on the rock and fear no shock.

> How firmly they stand,
> Who, piercing the sand,
> Have reached and have built on the durable rock!
> The wind and the wave,
> However they rave,
> Shall assault them in vain with impetuous shock.

By nature we are vessels of wrath and vassals of sin.

By prayer prevail, if strength should fail.

ACKLING is not laying, and promising is not paying.

Creditors who have waited long for their money are well aware of this, and their patience grows feeble as the false promise is repeated. *Thomas Fuller* says, "Creditors have better memories than debtors, and are great observers of days and times."

Call me, and I'll call thee.

Puff me, and I'll puff thee. Mutual-admiration societies are very common. Some seem to be in league to support each other's falsehoods: the Indians represent one man as saying, "There's a tiger!" whereupon the other backs him up by saying, "There's his tail!" This joining of hand with hand will not save the guilty.

Call me cousin, but cozen me not.

Don't use your relationship as scissors to shear me with. Don't try to creep up my sleeve.

Call me not Olive till you see me gathered.

So uncertain is human life, that we cannot judge it to be either happy or good till we reach the end of it.

Call me what you like, but don't call me too late for dinner.

Most people take a great interest in feeding time. However, it is an animal business.

Call me wise, and I will allow you to be a judge.

Of course you will; but in this case there will be two of us who are not wise, and by no means good judges.

Camomile—the more you tread it the more you spread it.

In this it is like a persecuted opinion, or grace in the heart. The more the true Israelites are afflicted, the more they multiply.

"Candidly but cautiously," said the wise man.

So should we always speak. The truth by all means, but that truth with caution; for there are so many lying upon the catch, that one has need to look at his words twice before he speaks them.

Candles in the daytime are the light of folly.

Yes, and the height of folly too. Yet how commonly are they seen in churches nowadays ! We wax wroth at the sight.

**Candles on altars are a mark
That the parson's in the dark.**

His Roman candles will not help him : the poor man is blind.

**Candles on the altar
Prove Protestants falter.**

Many other signs there are of this faltering. Men put up with anything nowadays. Even in Scotland, the modern backbone is not so firm as the ancient. Sometimes we say to ourselves, when we see Popish ornaments—

" Oh, were John Knox but here
To clear out all this gear ! "

Can't I be your friend without being your fool ?

Must I carry out your silly notions in order to be on good terms with you ?

**Care brings us clouds which bring no rain,
It veils the sun, but all in vain.**

Beecher said, " And yet men love to nurse their cares, and seem as uneasy without some fret as an old friar would be without his hair girdle."

Care is no cure, and covet is not have it.

Care killed the cat, but sobered the kit.

Young people are the better for a little care, but older folks are apt to be overcome by it.

Care will kill a cat though she has nine lives.

Men are killed by worry, not by work. Let us turn an old song to better account, and sing :—

" Begone, dull care !
I pray thee begone from me ,
Begone, dull care !
By faith I will banish thee.
Long time thou hast been tarrying here ;
And fain thou wouldst me kill ;
But now I have learned to trust in God
Thou never shalt have thy will."

Careless prayers ask a denial.

Certainly they will get it. How can we expect God to answer us when our own heart does not answer to our words?

Carry an umbrella when it's dry; do as you like when it's wet.

A few eccentric persons always carry their ginghams; but the most of us care rather for the spirit of this proverb, and try to be prepared for danger when none is yet visible.

Carry no sticks to the wood : add no mire to the slough.

There is sin enough in the world without our increasing it. There are sticks enough in the world's wood, and there is mire enough in the world's slough; why add thereto? May grace be given us to diminish evil, burn the sticks, and drain the slough!

Carry not fire in one hand, and water in the other.

Let not your conduct be self-contradictory. Do not preach the gospel in words, and deny it in works.

Carry your eyes in your own head.

Judge for yourself. Don't make another your guide.

Casks are soon set rolling.

Some men are always ready to change. *Oldham* says of one of these for-ever-rolling folks—

" More changing than the weather-cock, his head
Ne'er wakes with the same thoughts he took to bed."

Cast not a clout till May is out.

It will be found by experience that one had better keep on winter clothing till June, for our weather is so treacherous.

Cast not dirt into the well which gives you water.

Find not fault with those who feed you, nor with the trade which supports you, nor with the Lord who gives you all things.

Cast up your books, or your books will cast up you.

Bankrupts are afraid to look to their accounts, and so everything gets into a muddle, and goes to ruin.

Catch the hare before you sell her skin.

Catch the squirrel before you sell its tail.

> These two proverbs forbid our making too sure of our hopes. The man who sold the bear's skin before he had killed it, was eaten by that bear, skin and all.

Cats always fall on their feet.

> So do some men seem to prosper under all circumstances. Like the three legs of the Manx penny, they are always standing.

Cats are honest when the meat is out of reach

> Many who are not cats come under this category.

Cats can't catch fish if they won't wet their feet.

> We must consent to some discomfort if we are to get on in the world, or hope to accomplish any useful design. This proverb is thus rhymed :—
>> " Fain the cat would fishes eat,
>> But she's loth to wet her feet."

Cats in mittens catch no mice.

> Persons who are fastidious in dress seldom accomplish much. A minister who preaches in gloves is usually too fine a gentleman to move men's consciences.

Cats know the ways of cats.

> Certain classes of people know one another's ways, which cannot be comprehended by strangers.

Cause not thy weaker brother to offend;
But to the needy helpful succour send.

Caution is the parent of safety.

Cease from dispute which causeth ill blood.

> *Plutarch* says :—
>> "Where two discourse, if the one's anger rise,
>> The man who lets the contest fall is wise."

Cease not loving because of hasty words.

> Forget them, and begin again.

Cease not to pray, and hammer away.

> Mix efforts with prayer. Cease neither from action nor supplication. " Trust in God, and mind your own business."

Cease play when it ceases to be play.

When bad temper creeps in because the weaker does not like to be beaten, drop the game. It is meant for pleasure ; end it when it causes pain.

Censure from the bad is true praise.

When *Agesilaus* heard any persons praised or censured, he remarked that it was as necessary to know the characters of the critics as the character of the person of whom they spoke. Slander is the homage which vice pays to virtue. If the wicked praised us, we should have to ask with the Stoic, " What have I done wrong, that these fellows should speak well of me ? "

Change of weather is the discourse of fools.

" In England, if two are conversing together,
The subject begins with the state of the weather ;
And 'tis ever the same, both with young and with old,
'Tis sure to be either too hot or too cold.
'Tis either too wet, or else 'tis too dry ;
The glass is too low, or else 'tis too high :
But if all had their wishes once jumbled together,
Pray who upon earth could live in *such* weather?
It seemeth to me that it's best as it be,
And one thing is sure, they would never agree.
There's corn in the markets, there's hay in the mangers,
And that's more than there'd be if men were the rangers.
Jack would dry up the wheat to get in his hay ;
We should have no more turnips if Tom had his way :
But thanks to the goodness that rules altogether,
Say whatever they like they can't alter the weather."

Character is a man's best capital.

It is the backbone of success, especially with those employed by others. Young man, see that you do not impoverish yourself by wasting this precious stock-in-trade of life.

Charge at your pleasure, but give me good measure.

Cheap or dear, fill to the brim.

> False weights, and measures short eschew,
> And give to every man his due.

Charity bread has hard crusts : bread of your own earning tastes sweet.

Charity gives itself rich, covetousness hoards itself poor.

> "There was a man, though some did count him mad,
> The more he gave away the more he had."

Charity is never so angelic as when its hand is hidden by its wing.

Charity is the salt of riches.

> Sprinkle a good deal of it over your income. Be not one of those of whom *Sidney Smith* said that they were "ready to act the good Samaritan, without the oil and the twopence."

Charity lives at home, but walks abroad.

Charity should be warmest when the season is coldest.

> Then is the time for coals and blankets, and the more the merrier. It will warm your hearts to warm poor people's bodies.

Charity to the soul is the very soul of charity.

Cheerfulness is the sunshine of the heart.

> It is the fine weather of the soul, and makes the face to shine. Oh, for more of it!

Cheerfulness smoothes the road of life.

> It either gathers out the stones, or else trips so lightly over them that they are not noticed.

Chide thy friend in private, praise him in public.

> The first will prove that thy faithfulness is full of love, and the second that thy love is not ashamed to own itself. This is what thou wouldst expect of him, therefore so act towards him.

Children and chicken, must ever be picking.

> "Little and often" is said to be the rule; but some children prefer a good deal and often. It is cruelty to keep growing children without their meals, or even to delay them very long beyond the proper hour. Boys can eat anything, and any quantity. It has been tartly observed, that a boy's appetite is always in apple-pie order.

Children and dogs love lovable people.

> By a strange instinct, the young dogs find out kind folk. Men with whom children and dogs make friends are seldom bad-natured.

Children are certain cares, but uncertain comforts.

Children have wide ears and long tongues.

> So with the child who looked sharply at a visitor, and being asked what he meant by it, replied, " I wanted to see if you had a drop in your eye; I heard mother say you had frequently."

Children may make a rich man poor, but they make a poor man rich.

> Was not this the saying of *Bishop Hall*, when at Waltham Abbey? One who saw his large family observed, "These are they that make a rich man poor." "Nay," said *Hall*, "these are they that make a poor man rich."

Children never tell what they don't know.

> They are best sent out of the way when things are talked of which you do not wish reported.

Children speak words; men should speak things.

> It is to be feared that we have many old children about, and very few well-grown men. Words are many, and works are few.

Chins without beards are better than heads without brains.

> Young men, when wise, are to be preferred to those without sense, who have not even youth to excuse their folly. When Queen Elizabeth had sent a somewhat young ambassador to a foreign court, and the king complained of it, the ambassador replied, " If Her Majesty had known that you measure wisdom by beards, she would have sent you a goat."

Choice flowers bloom in the garden of affliction.

> Some of us have there gathered such roses and lilies as grow nowhere else. Sweet herbs of sage, and balm, and a thousand others grow in this garden, whose hedge is of thorns.
>
> > He that enjoys a patient mind
> > Can pleasures in affliction find.

Choose a kit from a good cat.

> Daughters will probably be like their mothers; therefore the mother is a good guide for a young man in selecting a wife.

Choose not alone a proper mate,
But proper time to marry.

> Marriage too early or too late will prove a calamity.

Choose your friends with care, that you may have choice
  friends.

> The Burmese bid us avoid sluggards, grumblers, the ungrateful,
> and the men who are always timorous.

> > "A sleepy head, and discontented mind,
> >   The pilgrims wisely quit and leave behind :
> > So, too, th' ungrateful, and the slave of fear,
> >   We hurry on and drop them in the rear."

Choose your love, and then love your choice.

Choose your wife from the wash-tub rather than the piano.

Choose your wife on Saturday rather than on Sunday.

> When she is in her work-day clothes, and you can better see what
> she will be in common, every-day life.   The same advice is put in
> another form, as follows :

> > "When you would select a wife,
> >   Do not call on Sunday ;
> > If you'd know her as she is,
> >   Better seek on Monday."

Chop, and there will be chips.

> Of course, if you attack any evil, there will be angry words and
> fierce replies , but no true woodsman puts up his axe because he is
> afraid of the chips.

Circumstances alter cases, and faces, and paces.

> By the omission of a single circumstance a whole *case* may be
> made to seem other than it is.   Change will soon affect the *faces* of
> men towards us, and alter their *pace* in journeying.   This saying
> has also been used in legal matters.   See the old story in *Merry
> Tales and Quick Answers :*—"A husbandman in Zealand came
> before the chief ruler of the country, whose bull had killed the
> poor man's cow, and after he had leave to speak, he said, 'My bull,
> leaping over the ditch, hath killed your cow; what is the law?'
> The ruler, suspecting no deceit, answered, 'Thou must pay for her.'
> Then the poor man said, 'Sir, I failed in my tale, your bull hath
> killed my cow.'   The ruler, being a little taken back, said, 'This
> is another matter,' but the poor man answered, 'Verily, it is all one
> thing, and you have truly judged.'"

Clean hands are better than clever hands.

> Much is made of cleverness nowadays ; but the devil is the
> cleverest of all, and yet he is the most wicked.

Clean hands need no rings.

Clean your own windows ; don't break other people's.

Clean your tongue as well as your teeth.

> This is easier said than done.

Cleanliness is a fine life-preserver.

> Both as to body, food, air, and dwelling-place, this proverb holds; for "cleanliness is the seed of healthiness."

Close clipping makes thick hedges.

> So the carrying out of the law tends to make it a greater defence to righteousness. Or the proverb may mean, that when expenses are cut down, an estate grows to solid wealth.

Close mouth and open eyes,
Marks of men truly wise.

Coaxing is better than scratching.

> Gentle behaviour is greatly to be preferred to rough ways.

Cobbler, stick to your last.

> Parson, keep to your text. Tradesman, mind your business.
>
> > "Ring your bell, your crumpets vend ;
> > Each must to his trade attend."

Cockneys on the spree are lunatics at large.

> One has only to see their conduct to feel that this is a very mild censure. "'Arry and 'Arriet go on any how."

Cold love soon grows colder.

Comb a dog, and curl a dog ; still a dog is but a dog.

> Do what you will with some people, they are what they always were. Combing and curling only make dogs snarl the more.

Come, Five-and-twenty ! Don't work to the tune of " Old Hundredth " !

> Let not the young man copy the aged in the slowness which the infirmity of age necessarily engenders.

"Committee" is a noun of multitude, signifying many, but not signifying much.

> This is not yet a proverb in language, but its sense is generally admitted by all who have dealings with committees. How often committees commit themselves is equally well known.

Common fame is much to blame.

> They say also, "Common fame is a common liar"; yet often "where there's smoke there's fire"; while another proverb saith, "Common fame is seldom to blame." The truth lies between the two sayings: general repute has usually a foundation in fact.

Compassion is of God, but passion is of the devil.

Compassion will do more than passion.

> The kindly warmth of the sun made the traveller take off his cloak, while the cutting wind could not tear it off, but made him bind it close about him; so love does more than wrath.

Confess that you were wrong yesterday; it will show that you are wiser to-day.

> A very learned man has said, "The three hardest words to pronounce in the English language are, 'I was mistaken'"; and when Frederic the Great wrote his letter to the Senate, "I have just lost a great battle, and it was entirely my own fault"—*Goldsmith* says, "This confession displayed more greatness than all his victories."

Conquer a dog before you contend with a lion.

> Better always accomplish the easier before you enter upon the harder task. Overcome your fellow mortal before warring with God.

Consider well, I beg you so,
Who you are, and what you do,
Whence you come, and whither you go.

> If men would only think, they would be far more likely to go right. Surely it must be the first duty of an intelligent being to consider his own position towards God.

Constant dropping wears the stone.

> Perseverance and importunity conquer. It is rhymed thus:—
>
> > Of all the proverbs none is better known
> > Than "Constant dropping wears away a stone."

Constant occupation removes temptation.

In a great measure it does so. David sinned with Bathsheba when he stayed at home from battle, and was resting on his bed in the day-time.

Content is health to the sick, and riches to the poor.

That is to say, it makes the sick man's mind well, and gives the poor man satisfaction in the little which he possesses. One says, " I do not love suffering, and yet I love to suffer when God wills it. I am not fond of the burden which I carry, and yet I am fond of carrying it when the Lord would have me do so."

Content thyself with knowing what is boiling in thine own pot.

Contentment comes of the heart, not of the house.

Isaac Walton, himself a man of a very cheerful, contented spirit, relates the following anecdote : " I knew a man who had health and riches, and several houses, all beautiful and well-furnished, who often troubled himself and his family to remove from one to another of them. On being asked by a friend why he removed so often from one house to another, he replied that it was in order to find content in some of them. But his friend, knowing his temper, told him that, if he would find content in any of his houses, he must leave himself behind, for content can never dwell but with a meek and quiet soul."

Contentment makes a fast a feast.

Contentment makes much of little; greed makes little of much.

Contentment, says *Fuller,* consisteth not in heaping more fuel, but in taking away some fire. Contentment finds *multum in parvo :* it hath a quick eye with which to spy out benefits.

> Contentment from a little gift
> A heap of precious joy will sift.

Cool head and warm heart :
These should never be apart.

Lest we should be carried away by excitement, and lose our balance of mind.

Cool ovens bake no biscuits.

Men without zeal accomplish little.

Copy the cows, and think more than you say.

They chew the cud, and hold their peace. Many would be better men if they gave less bellow, and more butter.

Coughing is catching.

When November comes, all the members of the family go down to Barking. At church the minister's "Let us pray" is understood to mean "Let us cough." Some part of the coughing might be suppressed—this we condemn ; a part is real affliction—this we pity.

"Couldn't help it" doesn't mend it.

Frequent is the excuse, "I couldn't help it." It does not comfort the injured party, and it is seldom true. The Creoles very wisely say, "Asking my pardon does not cure the bump you made on my forehead."

Counsel must be followed as well as praised.

There is no use in hearing the gospel and admiring the sermon, unless we put it in practice.

Counsel over cups is crazy.

Drunkards are never good advisers.

Count money after your own kin.

In trade transactions deal with relatives as you would with strangers, so far as methods of business are concerned. This rule is a wise one, and promotes love.

Count not your chickens before they are hatched.

We have known some not only count them, but sell them, and spend the money ; and pretty fowls they looked when the time came to deliver the birds, and they had none! We found in a small collection of Singhalese proverbs the following tale, which reminds us of the milkmaid and her eggs : "A person who had a drum-stick tree in his garden, when he saw the first blossoms on it, fell to thinking about the way the drum-sticks they would produce should be tied into bundles ; from that he passed on to a speculation about the profits that would accrue to him by selling them, and the trade he could carry on with this money, and the extensive trade which, in course of time, he would be able to carry on with foreign countries with ships of his own ; and the store-houses that should be built for foreign goods ; and as the drum-stick tree seemed to obstruct the way to the store-houses, he cut it down."

Courage is the salt of character: put your fears in this brine.

Courage needs eyes as well as arms.

We must not blindly rush into danger. Fearless need not be heedless. True courage is not cousin to rashness.

Courageous foe is more to be admired than cowardly friend.

Courtesy costs little, but buys much.

When old *Zechariah Fox*, the great merchant of Liverpool, was asked by what means he contrived to realize so large a fortune as he possessed, his reply was, "Friend, by one article alone, in which thou mayest deal too, if thou pleasest—civility."

Covetousness is the punishment of the rich.

But the poor may suffer from it too. Covetousness is the hunger which comes from eating.

Cowards dread a pigmy's blows ;
Heroes conquer giant foes.

Cowards should stop in their castles.

Then they can brag without testing their boasts.

Cows forget that they were calves.

Elderly persons fail to remember that they were once young themselves, and so they do not make allowance for the juveniles around them.

Creaking waggons are long on the road.

The proverb means the same as that which says, "Creaking doors keep long upon their hinges." Feeble lives are often long ones.

Credit won by lying is quick in dying.

For very soon the falsehood is found out. Truth is like a cuckoo, you cannot hedge it in, nor prevent its voice being heard.

Crest or no crest, do your best.

He is noble who does nobly. Shirt sleeves, or arms without a coat, make a capital coat of arms.

Crooked Lane is a dirty road.

Policy, trickiness, duplicity, these are all foul ways.

Crooked questions ask for crooked answers.

Crow and corn should not be in the same field.

We should endeavour to keep our holy work free from evil influences. This is hard work, for crows fly over hedges; yet we can keep the clappers going by entering our protest.

Crow not; croak not.

Be neither a boaster, nor a grumbler.

Crows have no cause to blame rooks for being black.

Yet black hates black, and here's the tug of war. The poker rails at the tongs, and the frying pan calls the tea-kettle smutty.

Crow-bars swallowed strengthen the back.

Hard things, when patiently endured, tend to increase our mental and spiritual strength. An old friend of mine told me in my youth that I should have to swallow many bush-fagots cross-ways. I have done so, and have found the process of great service in clearing the throat.

Cultivate your roses, but not on your noses.

Roses on noses grow without watering, but readily come from vinous and beery liquidation. A seedy-looking individual said to one of his companions, "I have just seen a picture, only a few inches square, for which the owner paid a great sum of money. I should be sorry to spend my money like that." Some one who stood by, answered, "You have paid more for a smaller picture than that." "I have? Where is it?" "On the tip of your nose."

Curiosity is ill-manners in another's house.

Nobody likes a guest to be prying and poking his nose into private affairs.

Of Paul Pry we fight shy.

Curses and chickens come home to roost.

What a full hen-house some men will have!

Cursing men are cursed men.

For curses are like processions, which go their round and come home again.

Curved is the line of beauty;
Straight is the line of duty.
Walk in the last, and thou shalt see
The former ever follow thee.

Custom in sin kills conscience of sin.

> Wrong can be so often done that the doer thinks he is right.

Custom is the plague of wise men, the idol of fools.

Cut no more than you can eat.

> Specially referring to your finger, or your hand.

Cut the loaf fair if you eat it all.

> Housekeepers don't like to see food carved unfairly : only selfish and rude persons would be guilty of such conduct. But fools and clowns are not all gone to Gotham.

Cut your coat according to your cloth.

> Longer or shorter according to the measure of the stuff. Outgoings must be regulated by incomings.

Cut your wisdom teeth as early as you can.

> Have as little as possible sown in the field of folly, for it is bad harvesting. He is wise truly who is wise early.

Cutting off a mule's ear won't make him a horse.

> Mere change of appearances is of little value. To take away some one glaring folly will not change a man's nature. The proverb is Creole. The Italians say, "Cut off the dog's tail, and he remains a dog."

Sayings of a more Spiritual Sort.

Can pride and grace
Dwell in one place?

> They squeeze in somehow, but they can never agree.

Carnal joys breed sorrow, but spiritual sorrows breed joy.

> Earth's entertainments are like those of Jael :
> Her left hand brings me milk; her right a nail.

Carnal men love the God that *they* make, but not the God that made *them.*

Carnal minds may hear and wonder;
Gracious souls will hear and ponder.

Carry an appetite to God's house, and you will be fed.

> A notable preacher said : "The hearer sometimes complains, 'There was no food for my soul,' when the truth is, there was no soul for the food."

Change not thy faith with changing times.

> The gospel never alters; alter not in thy belief of it. These are ill times. Not without cause does the Scotch believer cry :—

> "There's nae gospel noo, lassie,
>   There's nae covenant blood :
> There's nae altar noo, lassie,
>   There's nae Lamb o' God.

> "There's nae Chalmers noo, lassie,
>   There's nae gude M'Cheyne ;
> And the dear, dear cross they preached, lassie,
>   The dear, dear cross is gane.

> "Folks dinna want the cross, lassie,
>   They've cutten down the tree ;
> And naebody believes in it
>   But fules like you and me."

Christ and a crust is heaven below.

Christ became a man for you ; be a man for Christ.

> That was an instructive epitaph which was placed on the grave of a converted soldier : —

> "When I was young, in wars I shed my blood,
> Both for my king, and for my country's good ;
> In older years my care was chief to be
> Soldier to him that shed his blood for me."

Christ bore our curse, and we may well bear his cross.

Christ chooses us that we may choose him.

Christ died that sinners might live.

> "O boundless depth ! O love beyond degree !
> The offended dies to set the offender free !"

Christ has come to us, that we might come to him.

Christ has cords of love; but he has also a rod of iron.

Christ has many joint heirs, but no successors.

Christ in the heart is better than corn in the barn.

Christ in the heart is heaven on earth.

Christ is a great Saviour for great sinners.

Christ is a physician who asks no fees

Christ is all in all to all his people.

> " My Christ, he is the heaven of heavens :
> My Christ what shall I call ?
> My Christ is first, my Christ is last,
> My Christ is all in all."—*Mason.*

Christ is better with his cross than the world with its crown.

> *Rutherford* wrote : "I know his sackcloth and ashes are better than the fool's laughter."

Christ is gone from our eyes, but abides in our hearts.

Christ is in all believers, and all believers are in Christ.

Christ is not loved at all if not loved above all.

Christ is our adornment as well as our atonement.

Christ is our hope of glory, and the glory of our hope.

Christ is our mercy and our merit, our myrrh and our mirror.

Christ is our patron and our pattern.

> He spent his life for us, and now he reproduces his life in us. *Toplady* has the idea in his verse—
>
> > " Let thy Cross my will control ;
> > Conform me to my Guide ;
> > In the Manger lay my soul,
> > And Crucify my pride."

Christ is preparing saints for heaven, and heaven for saints.

Christ is the soul's sole solace.

> " I have heard the voice of Jesus,
> Tell me not of aught beside ;
> I have seen the face of Jesus,
> All my soul is satisfied."

Christ is now with us, but soon we shall be with Christ.

Christ keeps no servants merely to wear a livery.

> They have each an appointed service, and let them fulfil it.

Christ lives *for* believers and *in* believers.

Christ may wait long, but he will not wait for ever.

Christ not only gives life to repentance, but he gives repentance unto life.

Christ pleads for us above; let us plead for him below.

Christ receives the Devil's castaways.

> In *Mr. Whitefield's* Memoir a memorable instance is recorded of a wretched woman who was led to hope in Christ Jesus by hearing the preacher say that Christ was willing to receive even the devil's castaways. How gloriously true is the expression !

Christ sends none away empty but those who are full of themselves.

> " He hath filled the hungry with good things ; and the rich he hath sent empty away."—Luke i. 53.

Christ sweetens our comforts and sanctifies our crosses.

Christ takes possession *of* us on earth, and *for* us in heaven.

Christ was born *for* us that he might be born *in* us.

> " If he had not lived for thee,
> Thou hadst died most wretchedly ;
> And two deaths had been thy fee."—*Herbert.*

Christ was born a man that we might be born again.

Christ was delivered *for* our sins that we might be delivered *from* our sins.

> " If he had not died for thee,
> Thou hadst lived in misery,
> Two lives worse than ten deaths be."—*Herbert.*

Christian names are everywhere ;
Christian men are very rare.

Christians may sin most when least tempted, and sin least when most tempted.

Christ's actions are our patterns.

Christ's crimson blood cleanses crimson sin.

Christ's cross is a happy burden.

> "Christ's cross is the sweetest burden that ever I bore; it is such a burden as wings are to a bird, or sails to a ship, to carry me forward to my harbour."—*Rutherford.*

Christ's cross sweetens our crosses.

Christ's merit covers our demerit.

> "Cover" is the Old Testament word for expiation and propitiation, and we rejoice in it, notwithstanding the opposition of "philosophy falsely so called." Yet let no man wickedly say that "imputed righteousness is a clean glove which covers a foul hand" for whom the Lord Jesus covers he also cleanses.

Christ's name on your heart proves that your name is on Christ's heart.

> "We love him, because he first loved us." Our love to him is the sure token of his peculiar love to us.

Christ's riches are prepared for the poor.

> Read Psalm lxviii. 10. "Thy congregation hath dwelt therein: thou, O God, hast prepared of thy goodness for the poor."

Christ's school is a free school.

> The penniless scholar is free to all his teaching. It must be without price, for it is priceless.

Christ's soldiers fight best on their knees.

> The praying legion is the thundering legion, and chases the enemy before it.

Clocks need weights, and men need troubles.

> Afflictions by God's grace set our graces going.

Cold prayers are called prayers, but are no prayers.

> They are prayers in name only. Their manner asks for a denial, and a denial will be given them.

Cold preachers make bold sinners.

> Imagining that there is no truth in religion preached so feebly, the ungodly take liberty to sin.

Come over to Him whom you cannot overcome.

> Even to the Lord, against whom resistance is vain.

Comfort of the promises comes to those who make conscience of the precepts.

The promises often lose their sweetness because we have been eating the grapes of Sodom. Obedient children receive the kiss.

Confession must be salted with contrition.

Otherwise it is a mere form, and may be even an aggravation of the fault.

Conformists to Christ are nonconformists to the world.

"Those who are bound for heaven must be willing to swim against the stream."—*Matthew Henry.*

Conscience cannot speak peace till God speaks pardon.

How can we be at peace with ourselves till we have reason to believe that God is at peace with us?

**Consciences and souls were made
To be the Lord's alone.**

It was a saying of *Napoleon's,* "My dominion ends where that of conscience begins."

Conviction may be without conversion, but there is no conversion without conviction.

Corn is cleansed with wind, and the soul with chastenings.

The Lord uses trouble as a means, but he himself is the real purifier. "I have chosen thee in the furnace of affliction."

Count upon trials, or you count amiss.

"Whom the Lord loveth he chasteneth." "Man is born unto trouble, as the sparks fly upward." It is as *Master Bunyan* saith:
"A Christian man is never long at ease;
When one grief's gone, another doth him seize."

Corruptions may slumber, but godliness must watch.

So long as we live, the corruptions of the old nature will be ready to rise in rebellion, and they must be held down by divine grace working in us continual care. Quaint *Berridge* wisely says:—
"And if the monsters round thy head
Lay harmless down, like sheep,
Yet never once surmise them dead,
They have but dropped asleep."

ARE to be true, nothing can need a lie,
The fault that needs it most grows two thereby.

Bacon has well said, "A liar is a bravado towards God, and a coward towards man." To escape the censure of his fellows he insults his God. To deny a fault is to double it, and even to increase it a hundred times. Yet so commonly do children fall into the evil, that one friend of ours, having the picture of a boy in his garden, said to a child, "Come with me, and I will show you a boy that never told a lie." To this the child answered, "Then I am sure he is not alive."

Daub yourself with honey, and you will never want flies.

The name of being very kind and generous will gather around you a swarm of loafers, who will come for what they can get. In Italy we had only to give a beggar a copper, and we were surrounded by a crowd of mendicants whom nothing could keep off.

Day by day life glides away.

Each day that's lived a mortal gains,
Yet just so much the less remains ;
Say, are we gaining life each day ?
Or are we losing every way ?

Day of rest, of days the best.

A poet calls the Sabbath, "Heaven once a week."

Daylight will come, though the cock should not crow.

Even if no one should proclaim it, God's word will be fulfilled.

Viewing the proverb from another point of view, it reminds us that conceited persons are apt to think that the world depends upon *them;* and it does so, just as much as the day depends on the cock. The earth will revolve upon its own axis even when we are dead, and society will go on much the same as it did when we mingled in it.

Daylight will peep through a very small hole.

Secrets are made known by very simple circumstances. Truth is disseminated by the weakest means.

Dead men shall live, and living men shall die.

Deaf people lose less than they think.

Common talk is seldom worthy of being heard.   Oh for cotton in one's ears when certain clackers are near !   Yet in all soberness it is a serious trial to be deaf, and the thought of it brings to mind the epigram of our late friend, Sir John Burgoyne—

> " You wish me a happy new year as a toast,
> And a kindly good act it appears ;
> But when you perceive I'm as deaf as a post
> You should wish me two happy new ears."

Deal tenderly with a fresh wound.

A new sorrow calls for tender sympathy.

Deal with the master rather than with the man.

You may come to a more gainful conclusion, and you will know better where you are.   Go to God rather than to his ministers.

Dear is often cheap, and cheap is often dear.

Indeed, it is generally so in these days.   But the word "dear" is hardly correct, it should be "high-priced."

Death devours lambs as well as sheep.

The young die as well as the old.   *Sir Richard Baker* says :—

> " Think not thyself from death secure to rest
> For being young , death loves the green fruit best."

Death is a great leveller.

> " ' Earth to earth, and dust to dust ! '
> Here the evil and the just,
> Here the youthful and the old,
> Here the fearful and the bold,
> Here the matron and the maid,
> In one silent bed are laid ;
> Here the vassal and the king
> Side by side lie withering ;
> Here the sword and sceptre rust—
> ' Earth to earth and dust to dust ! ' "

Death is still in the pot.

It was the big pot on the prophets' fire of which it was first said, "There is death in the pot" ; but now it is the pewter pot which has become the chosen shrine of death.   What else is in the pot this deponent knoweth not ; but poverty, crime, and death certainly come cut of it.

Debt makes fret.

That is to say, when a man is honest; but many seem quite comfortable under it. Alas, for their stupefied consciences! "Once upon a time," says *Bacon*, "a merchant died that was very far in debt. His goods and household stuff were set forth to sale. A stranger would needs buy a pillow there, saying, 'This pillow, sure, is good to sleep on, since he could sleep on it that owed so many debts.'"

Debts and sins are more than we think them.

They accumulate insensibly, and we are willing to forget them.

Delay is dangerous; promptness is prudent.

> Don't tell me of to-morrow :
> Give me the man who'll say,
> When any good deed's to be done,
> "Let's do the thing to-day."

Depart from them that depart from God.

He who is God's enemy should not be your friend.

Desire for more property is the rich man's poverty.

> He that needs five thousand pounds to live
> Is full as poor as he that needs but five.

Desire to shine out thyself, not to outshine others.

It is written, "Let your light shine," but not, "Let your light outshine."

Despair of none
While shines the sun.

Saul became Paul; and he is the pattern of God's work in grace.

Despair will make a coward brave.

He is like an animal at bay, which forgets its timidity, and fights to the death.

Despise none : a tinker taught the world.

O rare John Bunyan, thou didst tinker to purpose when thou didst compose the "Pilgrim's Progress"! We ought, henceforth, to count no man common or unclean. The Easterns say :—
"A jewel is a jewel still, though lying in the dust;
And sand is only sand, though up to heaven by tempest thrust."

Despise your enemy, and you'll soon be beaten.

This has been the reason for many a warrior's failure ; let us not fall into it in reference to our spiritual enemies.

Diamond cut diamond.

In unholy things rogues meet rogues.   In holy things Scripture explains Scripture.

Difficulty is the spur of diligence.

Dig a well before you're thirsty.

Provide for wants before they fall upon you.

Diligence is the mother of good luck.

For the most part the man who prospers is capable, industrious, and persevering.   It is not invariably so ; but the exceptions are not very many.   On the other hand the absence of diligence is fatal.

What heart can think or tongue express
The harm that comes of idleness?

Dinner late is trial great.

A writer very feelingly says :—

" How sad it is to sit and pine
The long half-hour before we dine !
Upon our watches oft to look,
Then wonder at the clock and cook ;
And cast as long as we are able
Desponding looks across the table."

Surely no Christian hostess will put her guests to this great strain upon their tempers.   Which tries the temper most, for a man to come home and find no dinner ready, or for the wife to prepare the dinner and find that her husband does not come home?

Dip the pen of the tongue in the ink of the heart.

Dirt cheap is generally dear dirt.

We pay less and get less.   Modern cheap things are often mere rubbish, "made to sell," or stained with the blood of the poor worker.

Dirtiness is next to wretchedness.

To decent people it would be wretchedness itself.   Others, who seem to like it, must be strangers to all idea of comfort.   Yet they make excuses for filthy clothes on the score of economy, and there is even a rusty old saw which grates as follows :—

" Linen often to water
Soon to tatter."

Dirty linen should be washed at home.

Family quarrels should not be made public. Almost any degree of suffering is better than the public exposure of private wrongs and personal bickerings.

Dirty paws and poor jewellery fit each other.

Often a sloven is also a lover of gaudy finery.

Dirty water will not wash clean.

Teaching which is not true will not overcome sin in the hearers.

Dirty wives make drunken husbands.

Doubtless if the house or the room were kept more clean and comfortable, the man would have less temptation to spend his evenings in drinking company.

Disease known is half cured.

It is certainly so in the case of the disease of sin : when free grace reveals the ruin, we soon find the remedy.

Do a fair day's work for a fair day's wage.

Some will work by the piece, but they play when it is by the day. Yet it is wise not to make remarks on a man's work when it is not your business. A person, noticing a man moving slowly, observed to him, "I should think you work by the day!" "Well," said the other, "would you have me work by the night?" (Collapse of intrusive individual.)

Do a thing at once, and you won't forget it.

Very sage counsel. Some of us have very poor memories ; let us not trust to them, but get things off our mind by getting them done.

Do a thing well, or let it alone.

It is the thorough doing of everything which wins commendation. Not the slurring of great things, but the perfection of little things, makes up excellence.

> Circles are praised, not that abound
> In largeness, but th' exactly round ;
> So life we praise that does excel
> Not in much time, but acting well.

Do a thing yourself, and then you know it is done.

Do all you can ; Samson could do no more.

"Do! Do!" says the wood-pigeon, but it builds a very poor nest.

> This has often been repeated from the pulpit in sermons which are aimed against Popish notions of salvation by works.

Do good to them that do ill to you.

Do good with your money, or it will do you no good.

> There is no power in it of itself to do real good to you. It may even do you evil ; but, if used for God and his cause, and the poor, it will bless yourself.

Do is well, but *overdo* is ill.

Do just as you please, if you please to be just.

Do more good, and talk less of it.

Do not always shake the same apple-tree.

> Run not perpetually to the same friend for help. Do not talk always on the same subject.

Do not brag with the Pharisee, but beg with the Publican.

Do not call a fly an elephant.

> Avoid exaggeration, that you may keep clear of lying.

Do not carry the dust of this year into the next.

> If sufficient unto the day is the evil thereof, much more must be so with the year.

Do not growl, lest you be taken for a dog.

> Certain persons can never be pleased. They are cynics, and prove their right to the name by their dogged complaints.

Do not hurry, do not flurry!
Nothing good is got by worry.

Do not in the darkest night,
What you'd shun in broad daylight.

Do not look great things, but live them.

Do not make a butt of another.

> How would you like to be jested at yourself?

Do not play when thou shouldst pray.

Do not ride a free horse to death.

> A willing man is called for here, there, and everywhere; every one does his best to wear him out, and yet each one says, "He is doing too much, and will kill himself."

Do not show all you know
At the very first go.

> For then you will have no reserve force, and will not fulfil expectations which you have raised. Save your master-stroke till it will best serve you.

Do not thou forget
That a promise is a debt.

Do not thou thy manhood drown,
By drinking at the "Rose and Crown."

> A tavern is said to be "a place where madness is sold by the bottle." Let it have no patronage from you, for that article.

Do not to-day what will grieve thee to-morrow.

> It is a pity to spend your strength in earning regret.

Do not trouble, do not trouble!
Heavy hearts make toiling double.

Do not turn friends into enemies, but turn enemies into friends.

Do nothing rashly.

> Beware of desperate steps. The darkest day,
> Live till to-morrow, will have passed away.

Do on the hill as you'd do in the hall.

> When you are away from eye-witnesses do not take liberty to do evil, for God is there if no one else.

Do the best; hope the best; and have the best.

Do the duty that lies nearest thee.

> "Whatsoever thy hand findeth," said Solomon, "do it with thy might." *Carlyle* says: "Our grand business is not to *see* what lies dimly at a distance, but to *do* what lies clearly at hand." Do the next thing.

Do to others as you would that they should do to you.

The golden rule; but not the rule by which to get gold. It is much admired in church; but if it were to wander into the Exchange, or the market, it would be locked up by the beadle. The world's golden rule is, "Do others, or others will do you."

Do what you do.

Age quod agis, says the Latin. Be in earnest, and do not trifle.

Do you ride slowly? Then start early.

He who is by nature somewhat slow in his work should be the more prompt at beginning.

Do you think yourself wise? Then there's a donkey inside your waistcoat.

A polite way of saying that you are not wise, but otherwise.

Do you want to be cheated? Then buy a horse.

Generally a man either is cheated in horse-dealing, or thinks himself so. We incline to a very lenient view of the matter, for an honest man may sell a very bad nag, and think it all right. Who is to know all the faults or infirmities of either horse or man?

Dog with bone pray let alone.

He knows no friend at that time. In this he is like a man possessed with one notion, who cannot bear contradiction.

> With a man of one idea
> Never dare to interfere.

Dogs bark as they are bred.

Men act according to their birth and education.

Dogs have nothing to do, and no time of rest.

So says the *Tamil.* Many men are in like condition, no business, and yet busybodies.

Dogs that put up many hares will catch none.

Individuals who can do a little of everything, can usually do nothing well. Scheming this and scheming that, they accomplish nothing. Full often clever inventors find others running away with the practical results of their brain-work. Rich manufacturers thus catch the hares which poor inventors start.

Doing not_ing is doing evil.

> Omission of duty is commission of sin.

Don't accuse the times to excuse yourself.

> The times are good enough for men who are good enough. If times are hard, we must work harder.

Don't advertise it : tell it to a gossip.

> She will make it known where no advertisement would have carried the news. " The Tatler " has a wide circulation.

Don't always harp on one string.

> No mortal can bear incessant repetition : have a little variety ; and if you cannot change the subject allow an interval of silence.

Don't bale a boat that does not leak.

> That is to say, among other things,—do not try to prove a doctrine which nobody doubts, or defend that which is quite beyond attack, or vindicate a man for doing what is clearly right.

Don't be above your business, nor below it.

> To be too proud to attend to your work, or too uneducated to do it thoroughly, will be equally injurious. There is an honour in hard work. The French rule is " Respect the burden ", and every burden of labour is respectable.

Don't be drinking at the " Harrow " when you should be driving the plough.

> One of the evils of the beerhouse is the shocking waste of time by labourers and tradesmen who sit and booze there. They say that "time was made for slaves," surely a good deal of it falls to the lot of these slaves of Bacchus.

Don't be first in a quarrel, *nor second.*

Don't be fooled by pretty face ;
Look for character and grace.

> Mere bodily beauty is like an almanack : if it last a year it is well. This is too fleeting a reason for marriage.

Don't be like a bell which answers every pull.

> Have a mind of your own, and mind that you use it.

Don't be in a hurry to tie what you cannot untie.

Marriage is one of these things. Be careful!

> In choice of a friend
> One may often amend
> When he finds his affection misspent;
> But in choosing a wife
> A close partner for life,
> There is left us no room to repent.

Don't be loud as a bull's roar, and weak as a bulrush.

Don't be the family magpie.

We know some who are this, and terribly noisy and mischievous birds they are. The worst pie at table is magpie.

Don't be the first on the ice, nor the last off.

To be taken literally. Very safe rule to follow. It will also apply to speculations, both monetary and mental.

Don't be weak of brain, and strong of lung.

Strength of lung is a talent, but without knowledge and discretion to use it aright, it may make a man a nuisance. When Stentor is a Mentor it is well. When a man has nothing to say, the more he bawls, and the sooner people are weary of him.

Don't be yoked to one who refuses the yoke of Christ.

Paul saith, "Be ye not unequally yoked together with unbelievers."—2 Cor. vi. 14.

Don't bet even a farthing cake.

This was the very largest wager of an old friend of ours, and then he always stipulated that he should himself have the first bite, whether he won or not. We don't recommend even this.

Don't be like a bunch of nettles,
Nor all hot, like boiling kettles.

Don't blame it, but better it.

And if you cannot better it, shame it by your own example.

Don't blow the broth which does not burn you.

If there's no real fault, don't blame a man. Never grumble without cause. If it's no concern of yours, let it alone.

Don't bray ; eat your hay.

> Hold your tongue, feed your mind, fill your pocket.

Don't break your head for the sake of trying a plaster.

> To sin because there is forgiveness is wickedness.   To indulge at table because there is medicine is folly.

Don't bring a hornet's nest about your own ears.

> Sometimes you will have to do it for righteousness' sake, but never do it wantonly.   When hornets are quiet don't arouse them, for you can't send them to sleep again.   Never wake sleeping wasps.

Don't burn out a candle in search of a pin.

> Pins would be dearly bought if they cost a candle each.

Don't burn your candle at both ends.

> It will go fast enough at one.   Don't lose your wages in holidays, and at the same time spend your money in your frolics.

Don't burn your finger at the grate,
And then cry out "It was my fate."

> Persons bring sorrow upon themselves by their folly, and then lay the evil at the door of Providence·   This is both foolish and wicked : indeed, it is a sort of practical blasphemy.

Don't burn your house to kill a mouse.

Don't burn your lips with other men's broth.

> If you get sipping a little with them, and mixing up with their affairs, you will come in for a share of their trouble when it is served out hot to them.

Don't buy a whale till you've paid for your sprats.

Don't carry fir trees to Norway,

> Nor water to the sea, nor coals to Newcastle, nor noise to the Salvation Army, nor your own merits to Christ

Don't carve another man's leg of mutton.

> Some are very pleased when they are eating and drinking at other people's expense; but it never pays with men of honour, for they feel bound to make a return, and they will be called on to do it.

Don't change a one-eyed horse for a blind one.

It will be improving the wrong way. Never go from bad to worse, but mend a little.

Don't colour your nose with publican's paint.

Don't come a day after the fair, like Tom Long the carrier.

We don't know who Tom Long may have been, but he was evidently long on the road, and perhaps he watered his horse, and portered himself so often that he did not arrive in time. Many persons are always a little too late with their projects. They arrive just as the fair is over.

Don't crawl all day over one cabbage leaf.

The movements of some parties are so slow that this admonition might be fairly addressed to them. A master once asked his gardener, "John, did you ever see a snail?" "Yes, sir." "Then," said the master, "I am sure you met it; for you would never have overtaken it."

Don't cross the bridge till you come to it,
Proverb old and of excellent wit.

Don't cry before you are hurt.

And when you are hurt, crying heals no bruises.

Don't cry herrings till they are in the net.

Don't cry over spilt milk.

What's the use? you can't gather it up. When the thing's done, why sit down and cry? Cry before your milk is spilt, if crying will do any good. But why cry even then if you have nothing to sell?

Don't cut down an oak to plant a thistle.

To destroy an old institution for some new nonsense is not wise.

Don't cut off your nose to spite your face.

Proverbs of a like kind are, "Don't cut off your head because it aches." "Set not your house on fire to spite the moon." To injure yourself because you are out of temper is a freak of madness. Dick vexed his master, and because he was spoken to, he threw himself out of his work, and left his wife and family to starve all through the winter.

Don't dance to every man's whistle.

Don't dig your grave with your knife and fork.

Don't drive a second nail till you've clenched the first.

> One thing at a time, and that done well,
> Is a very good rule, as many can tell.

Don't drop into the water to grasp the foam.

Don't drop the meat to catch the shadow.

> Æsop's fable of the dog and the meat is the best explanation. Greed risks what it has to get more, and usually misses its aim. Many in these days give up the substance of the Gospel for the shadow of "Modern Thought." May they learn better very soon!

Don't drown the man who taught you to swim.

> If you learned your trade or profession of the man, do not set up in opposition to him. Do not kick down the ladder by which you climbed. Yet this unnatural course of action seems natural to some, *as we know right well.*

Don't expect sense from a man in love.

> He is too excited: his heart has mastered his head. They say that love gives wit to fools, but it often takes wit away from wise men. Love is blind, and it blinds lovers in many ways.

Don't expect to be rich
As easy as you jump a ditch.

Don't expect to find ostrich feathers on a gander.

> Nor look for wisdom from one who has neither sense nor education.

Don't expect to find otto of roses in a dog-kennel.

> Nor moral sense in clubs of godless men.

Don't fight for the shell, and lose the kernel.

> This is done when mere words are the ground of contention, and the essential doctrine is overlooked.

Don't fight over a cheese-mite.

> It is a pity to contend over a great matter, but to quarrel for a mere trifle is never justifiable.

Don't find fault with what you don't understand.

Don't find fault with my shoes unless you'll pay my cobbler to mend them.

Don't fire a gun at a blue-bottle.

> Nor a cannon at a cock-sparrow, nor a furious speech at a poor child, nor a big book at a silly opinion.

Don't fish for sprats with golden hooks.

> The hook would be worth more than you could catch with it. How often are abilities and energies laid out upon objects which are quite unworthy of them!

Don't fly higher than you can roost.

> It is unwise to begin a style of living which you cannot keep up. It is unwise to display a high degree of ability at first, and then decline because you cannot do so well as a general rule.

Don't fly if you have no wings,

> Or till your wings are feathered. If you are not wealthy, don't spend as if you had ample means.

Don't fret yourself lean because another man is fat.

> Envy is apt to do this, and there is plenty of it abroad. Should we not all rejoice if others are more happy than ourselves? Pity in most cases would be more fitting than envy.
>> "If every man's internal care
>> Were written on his brow,
>> How many would our pity share,
>> Who raise our envy now!"

Don't gaze at the stars, and fall into the ditch.

> *Diogenes Laertius* writes that Thales the Milesian on one occasion went out of his house to behold the stars, and he walked so far backward that he fell plump into a ditch. Whereupon, an old woman, who kept his house, laughed at him, and said to him in derision:—"O Thales, how shouldest thou have knowledge in heavenly things above, and knowest not what is here below under thy feet?"

Don't give a good pail of milk, and then put your foot in it.

> Cows sometimes do this; but it is by no means a pleasure to the farmer. Don't do a good action, and spoil it by your after-conduct; nor preach a good sermon and contradict it. As a rule, do not "put your foot in it" in any sense. An Irishman observed that whenever he opened his mouth he put his foot in it. Don't imitate him.

Don't go out woolly, and come home shorn.

Plenty do this who would have been more sensible had they stayed at home: they leave the old faith for something more attractive, and lose their comfort, if not their character.

Don't go to church to see the fashions.

"Was Mrs. Green at church this morning with her new bonnet?" was the question put to a plain Christian woman. Her answer was, "I didn't go to church to see who was there, or what clothes they had on."

Don't go to law for the wagging of a straw.

But keep out of it even at a loss. The law has improved of late, but when this proverb was written, "a certain learned Judge, being asked what he would do if a man owed him £10, and refused to pay him," replied, "Rather than bring an action, with its costs and uncertainty, I would send him a receipt in full of all demands. Ay," said he, recollecting himself, "and I would, moreover, send him £5 to cover all possible costs."

Don't go to sea in an egg-chest.

Trust only in that which is worthy of trust: do not risk your money on a bubble scheme, nor your soul on a novel doctrine.

Don't go under the spout to get out of the rain.

Be not so foolish as to go to the worse to escape from that which is bad. To do wrong to escape trouble is just this. To engage in speculation to retrieve a loss is another case in point.

Don't grab at every red-hot poker you see.

Do not rush into controversy, nor take up quarrels needlessly. You have something better to do than to burn your fingers with that which does not concern you.

Don't hang a dead dog.

When a fellow has been punished and his fault is forgotten, why raise the case again?

Don't hang a man first, and try him afterwards.

Hasty judgments act in this fashion :—

"First hang and draw,
Then hear the cause by Lydford law."

Don't hang your hat on two pegs at once.

Mr. Flirt does this, and he will get into trouble before long.

Don't hold with the hare and run with the hounds.

Jack-o'-both-sides generally catches it from both parties before long.   Don't play the game of Double-shuffle.

Don't howl before you are hit.

In the Telugu, a proverb represents a boy as crying, and a friend asks, "Why do you cry, my boy?"   He replies, "Because my father is going to beat me the day after to-morrow."   It will be wise to let to-morrow take care of the things of itself.

Don't hunt a dead rat.

When it was alive it was worthless, and now it is dead it is not worth a thought.   So certain silly doctrines which were long ago quite disproved need not be further discussed.

Don't jump into the river to get out of the rain.

Unwise persons rush from bad to worse: from small wages to none at all, from trifling inconveniences into real hardships.

Don't kick the bucket out of which you drank.

The very appearance of ingratitude is hateful.

Don't kill a pig to save a chicken.

Don't kill the goose that lays the golden eggs.

Be careful not to injure the business which brings you your income, nor to anger the man on whom you depend.

Don't knock a man down and kick him for falling.

Don't let the public-house live on your private house.

Don't let the rain damp your devotion.

Weather which does not keep men from market will often prevent their going to the public worship of God.   In this case it is a great damper upon devotion.

Don't let your feet run faster than your shoes.

It is unwise to go faster than you can do with safety and comfort. Many have brought their bare feet to the ground by spending more than their income could provide.

Don't let your heart sink into your hose.

Fear makes the heart go down into the stockings. But heart in hose is out of place. Why fear if you are right?

Don't lie in bed and addle your head.

No doubt sluggards grow dull and stupid. Too much sleep is injurious. A fellow who comes down late, and then loafs about the room, might almost as well have kept his head in his feather-bed.

Don't light a fire which you cannot put out.

You can start a story which you cannot recall, or commence a quarrel which you cannot end ; but how can you tell the result?

Don't live in Idleburgh.

In other words, let no one number you with the slothful.

> Oh, now, while health and vigour still remain,
> Toil, toil, my lads, to purchase honest gain !
> Shun idleness ! shun pleasure's tempting snare !
> A youth of revels breeds an age of care.

Don't look as dark as thunder.

Don't lose half your cheese in parings.

Waste is a worse tax than the income tax.

Don't make a long harvest of little corn.

Get through with it, and have done. Don't talk long when you have little to say. Don't weary us with waiting for nothing.

Don't make a rod for your own back.

Don't make fish of one and flesh of the other.

Treat people alike, so far as justice demands.

Don't make mountains of molehills.

Don't make one hole to stop another.

It is small gain to make a new enemy to conquer an old one. So also to get a new loan to pay an old debt is a sorry course of action.

Don't make three rents while you mend one.

A foolish attempt to patch up a private feud ended in a public wrangle, and illustrated this sage sentence.

Don't make three voyages for one biscuit.

"Much ado about nothing" is unwise.

Don't make two bites of a cherry.

In the Sanscrit it runs, "Don't make nineteen bites of a bilberry." Do not waste time and effort over a trifling affair.

Don't make your face as long as a fiddle.

After all, life is not a funeral. There is a medical power about mirth, and it is by no means to be abjured so long as it is timely, clean, and moderate.

> "A little nonsense now and then
> Is relished by the wisest men."

Don't make your nose blush for the sins of your mouth.

Which it does when it becomes red through drink. Of old, the topers tried to lay the roses of their noses at the door of the spices in their drink ; so we read—

> Nose, nose, nose, nose,
> " And who gave thee that jolly red nose ? "
> Cinnamon, ginger, nutmegs, and cloves,
> And that gave me my jolly red nose.

Don't make your promises like pie crust, which goes to be broken.

Yet some pervert this proverb, and speak as if promises might as readily be broken as the crust of a penny pie. We heard it said of one, " He is a promising young man." " Yes," said another, " but he is a poor performer."

Don't make your wheat so long in the straw.

Have not so much talk about what you are doing.

Don't meddle, or you'll muddle.

Is it not generally the case, that those who interfere do more harm than good ? These amateur cooks spoil the broths.

Don't meddle with to-morrow's trouble.

"Sufficient to the day is the evil thereof."—Matt. vi. 34.

Don't mutter at cold mutton.

Cold mutton is thought to be rather tasteless; and when it appears again and again husbands are not in ecstasies. But in truth, there is nothing to murmur at so long as hunger is supplied. " This meat is hard," cried one ; but his companion wisely answered, " It is harder where there's none."

Don't open the door when the devil looks in at the window.

Far better to fasten the bolts, turn the key, and put the chain up.

Don't pick a man up before he is down.

Don't correct him before he has made a mistake.

Don't pitch too high, or you won't get through the tune.

Expenditure which begins at a great rate often comes to a sudden end by bankruptcy. Begin so that you can keep on, and even rise higher. Orators should beware of splendid openings, for it will never do to drop ; and it will be hard to keep up the big style to the end.

Don't pity me, but help me.

Yet you may pity me if you will therefore help me, but not else.

Don't play with bears if you're afraid of being bitten.

Don't please your eye, and plague your heart.

Lightly have many done this by a marriage made only for beauty.

Don't pour water on a drowned mouse.

When a man is going down, don't increase his troubles ; when everybody is blaming him, do not swell the chorus of censure.

Don't promise pounds and pay pence.

Don't pull down your house to build a pig-sty with the materials.

We have seen people destroy a grand work for the sake of a paltry object.

Don't pull so hard as to break the rope.

Don't worry a person till he will bear it no longer, nor use a friend till he feels that you impose upon him, nor work your own brain till it gives way.

> Pull somewhat less than rope will bear,
> And when it straineth quickly spare.

Don't put all your eggs into one basket.

It is unwise to risk all that you have in any one concern. If you have any savings, put them in several places. The marine form of this saying is: "Do not ship all your goods in one vessel."

Don't put all your plums into one pudding.

He who says all he can say in one speech has acted very unwisely. The proverb has many other applications.

Don't put on a dry shirt till you're out of the water.

Don't congratulate yourself upon your deliverance, and begin to make yourself too secure before the trial is quite over.

Don't put on so much coal as to put out the fire.

You can lay so many books on the brain as to bury it, and teach children so much that they learn nothing, and preach so long that the people forget all that is said.

Don't put out the candle because of its snuff.

A good work is not to be stopped because of some fault in the way of carrying it on.

Don't put more corn in the mill than you can grind.

Undertaking more than we can carry through is very unwise.

Don't put yourself out, but put the devil out.

Be not angry, but conquer passion.

Don't rely too much on labels,
For too often they are fables.

Do not take a label to be true either as to the quality or the quantity of the article. One would think this saying had been newly invented, but the first line is an old proverb. He who buys the sack which is labelled "*pig*," may find nothing but a rat in it when he gets home.

Don't rip open old sores.

Forget past injuries and disputes; to mention them will cause pain, and prove mischievous. Let bygones be bygones,

Don't roast the duck till you've got it,

Don't rob Mary to pay Maggie.

Favouritism, and the injustice which comes of it, should be carefully avoided.

Don't roll in tne mire to please the pigs.

Do nothing wrong to please those who take delight in evil.

Don't saw off the branch you're sitting on.

It would be foolish to destroy the business by which you get a living, or to injure the person upon whom you depend, or to cast doubt upon the truth on which your salvation rests.

Don't say you found what was never lost.

Some people are rather too apt to think findings are keepings, and to call it finding when it is very like stealing. A person who found a gold watch on the mantel-shelf of a house at which he called, was ultimately found guilty of theft.

Don't say too much lest you say too little.

Like the Irish patriot who says, "The cup of Ireland's miseries has long been overflowing, and even yet it is not filled."

Don't seek profit from the misfortunes of others.

The Turk said : "If my beard were burning, others would try to light their pipes at it." So they would in England ; ay, and set his beard on fire on purpose to get a light for their cigarettes.

Don't send a cat to fetch milk.

The employment of dishonest persons in money matters is very dangerous.

Don't share the spoil before you gain the victory.

Don't shiver with last winter's cold.

Let not past sorrows be renewed. If the memory of them awakens gratitude—well and good ; but if they renew your pain, it is foolish to raise them from the grave of the past.

Don't shout till you're out of the wood.

Don't sit up by moonlight, and lie in bed in the sun.

Night-work is undesirable. "Man goeth forth unto his work and to his labour until the evening."—Ps. civ. 23.

Don't snap ; you're not a trap.

Snappishness is a sad disease, and frightens people from you. Nobody wants to have his head bitten off.

Don't sniff at a bottle which had gin in it a year ago.

That is to say, if you would avoid the temptation to drink, keep clear of it most carefully.

Don't sow your wild oats ; they're bad reaping.

Many talk as if young people ought to be vicious for a time, or as if it was a very excusable thing for a young man to be impure in his behaviour. This opinion is very pernicious. Alas ! throughout life men have had to feel in their bones the sins of their youth.

Don't spend a penny till you have twopence.

Don't spend money till you've got it.

Not even if tempted by " the Hire System."

Don't spend other people's money.

This is too often done. Expenditure upon credit, tampering with trusts, and many other matters come under the lash of this sentence.

Don't spend sixpence if you only have fourpence.

**Don't spend ten precious pounds in court
To get by law a paltry groat.**

Don't spread a grain of butter over fifty yards of bread.

By attempting to cover a great surface of work when you have little ability and less grace, you will only court a wider failure. " Vauxhall Slices " became the common jest of Londoners because the ham of the sandwiches sold at Vauxhall was so marvellously thin. We have known persons who have attempted so much that their work grew thinner and thinner, and nobody was the better for it.

Don't stand like a cat on a cross-wall.

The other form of it is, " Don't keep sitting on the fence." Certain fellows do not know which side to take, and so they hesitate. When they see which way the cat jumps, they will follow suit.

Don't steal sheep and give away the trotters in charity.

Instances of this kind turn up : the trotters are meant to get the wretch good enough repute to let him steal the sheep without being suspected.

Don't stop sowing because of the birds.

If evil persons injure your good work, or Satan himself hinders it, do not therefore slacken your diligence.

Don't stop the plough to kill a mouse.

Do not hinder important business for the discussion of a trifle.

Don't strain at a fly and swallow a spider.

Don't strike against your bread and butter.

Very seldom does a strike really benefit the workman. The money lost while doing nothing is hardly ever made up, even if the wages are advanced.

Don't strut like a crow in a gutter.

Those who have observed a crow in that position will see the peculiar fitness of the figure.

Don't take a helpmeet till you've meat to help.

Don't take off your clothes before you go to bed.

Do not hand over your property to your children while you are yet alive, and need it yourself. Remember how possible it is for ingratitude to show itself when you become a burden, because no more is to be got out of you.

Don't talk all the talk, nor eat all the meat.

It would be exceedingly bad manners to invite friends to dinner, and then eat all yourself; but it is equally bad to talk without ceasing, and give no one a chance of being heard. *Sydney Smith* said, "Never talk more than half a minute without pausing and giving others an opportunity to strike in."

Don't talk of my debts unless you mean to pay them.

Don't teach your grandfather to cough.

Don't teach your grandmother to suck eggs.

Don't threaten war and then tremble at your own words.

Threatening should be very rarely resorted to, and it must never be mere pretence : the Chinese call a blusterer "a paper tiger."

Don't toast your cheese till there is a fire.

Hurry to act upon mere hopes is extremely foolish, for the hopes may never be fulfilled.

Don't throw away dirty water till you have clean.

Do not leave a poor situation till you have found a better. Another form of the saying is, "Don't throw away your old shoes till you have got new ones."

Don't throw good money after bad.

It is useless to spend your money in going to law with a person who will not or cannot pay. If you sue a beggar you know what you will get, and that fact should make you forbear.

Don't touch a man on his sore heel.

It is cruel to play upon a man's weakness. If anything annoys a neighbour don't touch upon it.

Don't tread on a worm wantonly.

Cowper wrote :—

"I would not enter on my list of friends
(Though graced with polished manners and fine sense,
Yet wanting sensibility) the man
Who needlessly sets foot upon a worm."

Don't tread on other men's corns, nor on their wheats either.

Do no injury to any man through want of thought.

Don't trust a rickety chair or a tricky man,

For if you do, you may get an ugly fall, or find yourself deceived. It is risky to ride broken-kneed horses, or to trust men who have already failed, and fellows who have once deceived you.

Don't try to do that which is worth no man's doing.

Foolhardy feats should not be attempted. When a man had gone to the top of a steeple, and had there stood on his head, he sought a reward of King James. The King gave him no money, but offered him a patent by which he was to have the sole monopoly of the right to make a fool of himself in that risky way. A fit reward for such folly.

Don't try to walk on both sides of the hedge.

Decide for the right side, and keep to it bravely.

Don't turn recreation into degradation.

Those do this who make their play the occasion of sin, and act as if their outings were meant to be innings for the devil.

Don't wade where you cannot see the bottom.

If you like, you may risk money which you can afford to lose, but speculate no further. Many try to do too much, and do it. I knew a builder who would never tender for work under water, because he could not see what he might have to do. He was a sensible man, and avoided many a loss.

Don't wait for windfalls; gather your own apples.

Whether the legacy comes or not, the way of self-help is always to be followed. Windfalls are seldom fit for keeping.

Don't wait for something to turn up, but turn it up yourselves.

> Inactive wishes are but waste of time,
> And, without effort, prayers themselves a crime:
> Vain are their hopes who miracles expect,
> And ask from heaven what they themselves neglect.

**Don't walk in in state
If you go to church late.**

Why, they stalk up the church as if they were the Lord of the Isles! Hear how their boots squeak! They ought to hold their heads down with shame for disturbing the devotions of so many. Let it be part of your religion not to disturb the religion of others.

Dr. Diet and Dr. Quiet are fine physicians.

Draw not your bow till your aim is fixed.

Know what you are going to do before you begin work.

Drawn wells have the sweetest waters.

Those who give enjoy their money. Those who preach most of Jesus preach best about him. Those who are at work are happy.

Dread a blow from a frying-pan, for, if it does not hurt, it smuts.

Dread an action at law as you would a lion's paw.

Dress your soul as well as your body.

Only take much more pains with the soul than with the outward appearance. As you do not go abroad without your garments, so do not live without the robe of righteousness and the garments of salvation. Carefully see yourself arrayed in the beauty of holiness,

Drink first dims, then darkens, then deadens, then damns.

> Drink ! Drink ! this terrible drink !
> Causing more sorrow than any can think !

Drink injures a man externally, internally and eternally.

> I think I have read of a temperance lecture by *Barnum*, after which he was asked, "Does drink injure a man externally or internally ? " His prompt answer was, "Eternally and infernally."

Drink like a fish—water only.

> Drinking water neither makes a man sick, nor in debt, nor his wife a widow. But some men are like the drunken Parisian, who declared that in his childhood he had been bitten by a mad dog, and consequently had a horror of water.

Drink no wine, and you'll not drink too much.

Drink won't hurt you if you don't drink it.

> It's not the liquor, but the liquorish man that is to be blamed. Keep the cork in the bottle, and no evil spirits will carry you off your legs. "Whiskey," said the Highlander, "is a bad thing. Especially bad whiskey." Good or bad, it will do no harm if it never comes into the house, much less into the mouth.

Drinking and stuffing makes a man a ragamuffin.

> Yet drink they will if their backs go bare. The old saw says :—
>
> > " Money we want and cannot borrow,
> > But drink we must to drown our sorrow."

Drive gently over the stones.

> When anything occurs about which you are likely to disagree, keep your temper and be very calm.

Drive one plough at a time.

> Turn all your strength in one direction. Divided energies threaten failure. " One thing I do " is a good motto.

Drive the nail that will go.

> Work most at that part of your trade which most prospers.

Drive thy work lest it drive thee.

Drop by drop the tub is filled.

> Things to their best perfection come,
> Not all at once, but some and some.

Drought never bred dearth in England.

> Our forefathers preferred a dry season to a wet one. It is thought to be best for corn, though it is by no means so good for roots and grass. All districts are not in the same condition, and varying seasons tend to make a more equal distribution of the precious fruits of the earth. On the whole, England likes dry weather.

Drunkards drown themselves on dry land.

Dry bread at home is better than roast meat abroad.

> That is to say, as a general rule. One does not turn up his nose at roast or boiled when one is at a friend's house, or sojourning by the sea, or wandering among the Alps. Still there's no table, no bed, no fireside, no home, no wife like our own.

Dry wood makes a quick fire.

> Our evil hearts and headlong passions yield readily enough to temptation. Oh, that grace may continually moisten our souls, and thus preserve them from Satan's sparks !

Ducks lay eggs ; geese lay wagers.

> Such geese are very common near our common, especially towards Derby Day. Where is the sense of this mania for gambling ? We need not ask where is the morality of it ?

Ducks will not always dabble in the same gutter.

> So we find. Men change their follies.

Dutiful daughters make suitable wives.

Duty by habit is to pleasure turned :
He is content, who to obey has learned.

> But in this age nobody cares to obey. Everybody would be captain, and nobody is willing to be common sailor. "England expects every man to do his duty." England will not get all it expects. Every man will do his duty *if he likes.*

Sayings of a more Spiritual Sort.

Dare to do right ; and walk in the light.

> Beware of that "bold bashfulness," as *Fuller* calls it, which
> dares to offend God while it fears to offend man.

Darkness is the devil's element and the sinner's punishment.

Dead devotion is living mockery.

> Have we not had too much of this thing ?   No, I don't refer to
> our neighbours, but to ourselves, John Ploughman, and you Mr., or
> Mrs., or Miss Reader.

Dead men cannot speak, yet Abel, being dead, yet speaketh.

Death cuts the saints down, but it cannot keep them down.

> Say, rather, they rise the higher.   We have heard of a tomb-
> stone which bore the inscription, "Lifted higher."   The dying
> request of the tenant of that tomb had been, as she pointed to the
> skies, "Lift me higher, lift me higher !"

Death died when Christ rose.

> By death, he death's dark king defeated,
>   And overcame the grave ;
> Rising, the triumph he completed ;
>   He lives, he reigns to save.

Death mows down the fairest lilies, as well as the foulest
thistles.

Death *shortens* our way to heaven, but grace *sweetens* our
way to heaven.

Delays in answering prayers are not denials.

Delight in the Sabbath, and it will be a delight.

Delight thyself in the Lord, that the Lord may delight in
thee.

> The disciple whom "Jesus loved" was the disciple whose love
> to Jesus was pre-eminent.

Deny yourself, or Christ will deny you.

> "Whosoever shall deny me before men, him will I also deny
> before my Father which is in heaven."—Matt. x. 33.

Despair not, for thou hast a God; presume not, for thou art a man.

Devotion, when lukewarm, is undevout.

Where God's glory is concerned it is a true rule; *Non amat qui non zelat.* He loves not who has no zeal.

Dispose thyself to patience rather than to comfort, and to the bearing of the Cross rather than to gladness of heart.

This was the saying of an ancient saint, *Thomas à Kempis;* and we may compare with it the saying of a modern sage, *Thomas Carlyle,* "There is in man a higher than love of happiness; he can do without happiness, and instead thereof find blessedness."

Divine knowledge is not as the light of the moon, to sleep by; but as the light of the sun, to work by.

Do not pray *by* heart, but with the heart.

Repeating words without feeling is not prayer . the heart can even pray without words.

Do not wrest the Scriptures, nor rest without the Scriptures.

Benjamin Franklin advised Tom Paine not to print his "Age of Reason," "For," said he, "if men are so bad with the Bible, what would they be without it?"

Do thy little, though it be
Dreariness and drudgery:
They, whom Christ apostles made,
"Gathered fragments" when he bade.

Don't bolt the door till all the children are in.

Those do this who despair of those outside, who will yet come to Jesus.

Don't cut away the roots and water the branches.

To preach works and decry faith is absurd.

Don't go to hear Dr. Smoothaway.

He preaches down at St. Judas's Church, and a brother of his is minister at the Modern Thought Chapel. "Salvation made worldly" might be the motto of both the brothers.

Don't hear all your sheep a-bleating,
While you're sitting in the meeting.

> Keep your thoughts on heavenly things, and let the flock wait till you have yourself been fed by the Good Shepherd.

Don't hope for the shadow without the tree.

> Expect not the moral influence of religion when that religion is denied and despised.

Don't leave your heart at home when you go to worship.

> It is to be feared that we often get the chrysalis case of the man, but he himself is not truly at worship.

Don't parley with sin, or you'll surrender.

> If mother Eve had not listened to the serpent's insinuating speech, she would not have consented to touch of the forbidden tree. You are half conquered when you begin to consider the devil's question.

Don't pray cream and live skim milk.

> A weighty word. Very applicable to some who have more of the gift of prayer than of the grace of prayer.

Don't put an empty spoon in people's mouths.

> Preachers do so who give their hearers no gospel.

Don't worship your broom, but keep your house clean.

> Methods and theories of sanctification can be too much admired; the more important thing is to be really sanctified.

Drops of praise are poor acknowledgments for oceans of mercy.

> "O that within us hearts had propagation,
> Since many gifts do challenge many hearts!"—*Herbert.*

Duty should be delight.

> Don't do right unwillingly,
> And stop to plan and measure;
> 'Tis working with the heart and soul,
> That makes our duty pleasure.

ACH bird whistles its own note.

What a loss it would be to the harmonies of nature if all sang alike! The charm of creation lies very much in its variety. Let each man, like each bird, praise God in his own way.

Each blade of grass has its own drop of dew.

Nothing is forgotten in the economy of providence, or in that of grace. The Lord will not pass by "even me."

Each day bringeth its own tears :
Add not to them by thy fears.

Go on, bravely hoping for better things. Forebodings are but superfluous loadings.

Do your best,
And leave the rest.

Each day has its care ; but each care has its day.

It will not last for ever. If joy be fleeting, so is grief.

Each New Year brings death more near.

For we grow older and weaker, and
Time fleeth away
Without delay.

Early risers gain the dew of the day.

One of the most beautiful sights is the rising sun, and one of the most delicious sensations is to feel the morning's freshness ; but those who prefer longer sleep say that at an early hour the world is not properly aired, and the chill is not taken off the air. When early worms are being caught, those which are not yet up are out of harm's way.

Early up, and never the nearer.

A man might as well keep in bed if he does not rightly use his time after he has risen. The main matter is not rising early, but well spending the day.

Early winter, surly winter.

Of the truth of this maxim I can say nothing ; but there is always more or less of truth in these old adages.

Early to bed and early to rise,
Makes a man healthy, wealthy, and wise.

This saying must stand against all cavil : it is the teaching of ancient wisdom, and of modern observation. Yet there may be some truth in Archbishop Whately's jocose remark, that he should not get up early ; for when he once did so, he was proud all the morning, and sleepy all the afternoon. There's a happy medium in this matter. Too little sleep is quite as bad as too much. That is a merry verse in which some lie-a-bed protests against getting up early :—

> " Blessed be he who first invented sleep ! "
> Said Sancho Panza, and I, too, would heap
> Blessings unnumbered on his honoured head,
> If by some happy chance he were not dead.
>
> Blessings on him, and honoured be his name,
> Peaceful his rest, eternal be his fame ;
> But hang the other chap, whose taste surprising
> Made him invent the art of early rising.

Earn all you can ; save all you can ; give all you can.

This, I think, was John Wesley's saying. It embodies much of his shrewd sense and consecration. Some take firstly and secondly ; but thirdly is too much for them : giving goes against their grain.

Earth knows no joy without alloy.

Show me a land which has mountains without valleys, and I will show you a life which has joys without sorrows.

Earthly riches are full of poverty.

There is nothing in them to enrich our nobler part ; but much which causes the spirit to feel impoverishment.

Ease and honour are seldom bed-fellows.

" Peace with Honour " was a pretty motto ; but ease and honour are by no means Siamese twins. In the end of life a man may look for *otium cum dignitate*, but in earlier days he must forego ease for the dignity of labour. A work that is as easy to be done as 'tis to say Jack Robinson, brings no great honour to the doer.

East or west, home is best.

Foreign travel pleases for a season, but the heart turns to home as the needle to the pole. He has no home who does not love it dearly.

Easy come, easy go.

Those who get money in heaps, without labour, are apt to use it recklessly. Labour in gaining it teaches the value of property.

Easy to say, but hard to do.

Jaw-work is a deal easier than life-work. You may say, "Snuff the moon," but it would need a long arm to do it.

Eat not mustard only, but try a little beef

Advice to those who want to hear constant denunciations of error, but care not for a clear exposition of gospel truth.

Eat thy food at leisure;
Drink thy drink by measure.

Hurried eating creates indigestion, and excessive drinking is even worse, whatever the drink may be.

Eaten bread is soon forgotten.

But it should not be so. Gratitude should be natural to us, and abiding with us; but, alas! at God's hand we have received life itself, and yet we forget him. Let us not live like hogs under the oak, which eat the acorns, but thank not the tree.

Eating little, and talking little, harm but little.

Economy makes much out of little.

> A penny saved is twopence clear;
> A pin a day's a groat a year.

Edged tools, and sacred things, are dangerous playthings.

He must be short of wit who makes fun of holy texts. It is like Belshazzar drinking wine out of the vessels of God's sanctuary.

Elbow grease makes wealth increase.

Elbow polish makes old chairs new.

This said elbow polish, or elbow grease, is a fine article in a household, and beats bear's grease and goose grease into fits.

Employment brings enjoyment.

Laziness is misery. Stagnant pools breed foul creatures.

Empty tubs are easily rolled.

When there is nothing in a man he has no stability, but is easily persuaded and deluded. A drunkard said he was sure the world was round, for he rolled about so ; and certain others have a sort of mental reeling which can only come of emptiness.

Empty vessels make the most noise.

> He who ought to be quiet
> Is the man for a riot.

End a quarrel before it begins.

Put out the fire of strife before it fairly burns.

Enjoyment needeth not excess.

Enough is a feast, if thou be not a beast.

And many beasts will leave off as soon as they are supplied. Men, alas ! are to be found who glory in gluttony, and dote on drunkenness. These are not men, but walking swill-tubs. Let us not even laugh at them, for they take that as a sort of encouragement.

Enough is as good as a cartload.

So long as we have food and raiment, we may be well content to be without the care of riches. *Bunyan* saith—

> " Fulness to such a burden is
> That go on pilgrimage ;
> Here little, and hereafter much,
> Is best from age to age."

Enough, with most people, means a little more than they have.

A highly respectable and wealthy farmer in Connecticut gives the following as his own experience :—When I first came here to settle, about forty years ago, I told my wife I wanted to be rich. She said she did not want to be rich, all she wanted was enough to make her comfortable. I went to work and cleared up my land. I've worked hard ever since, and got rich—as rich as I want to be. Most of my children have settled about me, and they have all got farms—and my wife ain't comfortable yet !

Envy is pained by the pleasure of others.

It is a sickness which is produced by another man's health, a poverty created by a neighbour's wealth. Sometimes it grows out of being superseded : old Tinder Boxes sneer at young Lucifer Matches.

Envy shoots at others, but hits itself.

" The envious man is his own tormentor. He feeds and cherishes a viper, which preys upon his own soul. He has to bear both his personal disasters and calamities, and the pain of witnessing the successes and comforts enjoyed by his neighbours. Hence *Bion*, seeing a man of this character who appeared gloomy and depressed, wittily said : ' I am sure he has either met with some misfortune himself, or some favourable event has happened to another.' "

Equivocation is half-way to lying, and lying is the whole way to hell.

The first part of this saying is by far too moderate. A writer has truly said that " A sudden lie may be only the manslaughter of truth, but by a carefully constructed equivocation truth is murdered."

Ere thou leap see where thou land.

And if thou canst not be sure of a safe and clean landing, don't leap at all.

Error in the pulpit is like fire in a hayloft.

It is where it is sure to spread and do mischief.

Even a fool speaks a wise word sometimes.

According to the law of chances he should do so ; but it is so seldom, that it will not pay to catch cold while waiting for it.

Even a ploughman can see who is a true gentleman.

An indescribable something in tone, manner, and spirit will cause the most uncultured mind to see who is the true gentleman, and who is the mere pretender.

Even a spark is fire.

A little grace is grace. A sinful desire is sin.

"Think, and be careful what thou art within,
  For there is sin in the desire of sin :
Think, and be thankful, in a different case,
  For there is grace in the desire of grace."—*Byrom.*

Even among apostles there was a Judas.

In every company we may expect to find one false heart, if not more ; nor are we worse off than our Lord.

Even an ant can be angry.

Very little men can have very lively tempers.

Even if a pig does fly, it is a queer bird.

Saul among the prophets is unprofitable. Some men are awkward at anything good, great, or generous: their nature cannot rise to it.

Even if you eat the pudding, don't swallow the bag.

Set some limit to your credulity: don't believe every detail of a romantic story. Or the proverb may mean—Don't go the whole hog. Draw a line somewhere. Be not a thick and thin supporter of a doubtful cause. Do not vote black white to serve your party.

Even inconsistent men praise consistency.

By some ingenious theory they try to prove that their own circle is "a square with a circumbendibus"; but they admire the square which does not need such squaring.

Even Solomon was not always wise.

Indeed he was the greatest fool of his time. He was always the most knowing, but not always the wisest man.

Even white lies are black.

A lie of any sort is evil. Lying in jest is sinning in earnest.

Evening red and morning grey,
Hopeful signs of a fine day.

These weather signs depend upon locality, and it is the height of folly to apply to India, or even to Italy, the proverbs of Great Britain. Every land has its own weather-wise men.

Every ass thinks itself worthy to stand with the King's horses.

But thinking does not make it so. Poor ass!

Every bean has its black.

Every man has his faults as surely as the bean has its black eye.

Every bird favours its own nest.

Of course it does. There's no place like home, even though it be a palace. He who loves not home deserves to be homeless

Every bullet hath its billet.

There are no chance-shots. An overruling providence arranges even the hurly-burly of battle. The arrow which pierces between the joints of the harness bears a message from God.

Every cat should mind its own kittens.

It is to be hoped that there are very few women like that minister's wife, whose children were allowed to go to ruin while their mother was presiding at sewing societies, where the ladies made knickerbockers for nigger-boys.

Every cock may crow on his own dunghill.

But he had better confine his crowing to his own dominions. A certain man's motto was, "While I live I'll crow"; but he did not live by his crowing.

Every cook bastes the fat joint, and the lean one burns.

If it is not so in the kitchen, it is so in the world. Anyone would make a present to the Queen, but how many will help poor Jack? So long as you need nothing, friends are liberal; when it comes to downright want, you are fortunate if anyone notices you.

Every cook praises his own broth.

But perhaps everyone else is blowing upon it.

Every dog has his day.

And every day has its dog; but the day is not much the better for the dog, nor is the dog the better for his day. When a swaggering fellow is to the front, the comfort is that his day is only a day. But the dog-days are long ones. It is not insulting to call men dogs, for that learned pundit *Tom Hood* says:—

> "Most doggedly I do maintain,
>   And hold the dogma true—
> That four-legged dogs although we see,
>   We've some that walk on two."

Every dog may bark before his own kennel.

It would be well for the quiet of the neighbourhood if he would not bark anywhere else. Some dogs bark indiscriminately, so that *Hood* said:—

> "I've heard of physic thrown to dogs,
>   And very much incline
> To think it true; for we've a pack
>   Who only bark and w(h)ine."

Every donkey likes to hear himself bray.

He has a great ear for his own music, and, therefore, he lifts up his voice with confidence.

Every drop helps to make the ocean.

" Little drops of water,
  Little grains of sand,
Make the mighty ocean,
  And the beauteous land :
And the little moments,
  Humble though they be,
Make the mighty ages
  Of eternity."

Every fool will give advice, but few of them will take it.

Indeed it needs much good sense to be willing to be advised. The humility and self-diffidence which will submit to be led by the wisdom of the really prudent are rarer than we think.

Every gardener should kill his own weeds.

This, however, many fail to do, because they are hard at work over the road in other people's grounds, where they are not wanted. Hunt your own dandelions, and dig your own docks.

Every generation needs regeneration.

None needs it more than the present.

Every girl can keep house better than her mother till she tries.

This is the fault of many young folk : they know nothing about a matter, but yet feel that they could do the business in first-rate style. The proof of the pudding is in the eating, and the proof of the work is in the doing and the lasting.

Every goat must graze where he is tied.

A man must live where providence has placed him.

Every heart hath its own ache.

There's a skeleton in every house, a crook in every lot.

Every herring must hang by its own head.

" Every man must bear his own burden." We must personally answer for our own actions.

Every ladder has a top round to it, and few are on it.

There's always room at the top. Mediocrity has its crowd, but excellence has a small company. Competition grows less the more first-class the workman becomes.

Every lamb knows its dam.

Yes, and every dam knows its lamb. See how soon they find each other out when mixed up in a field !

Every little fish expects to be a whale.

But it will not be. If all fish were whales, the sea would want enlarging. What would the streams and brooklets do for fish ?

Every man can be handled if you find out his handle.

There's a joint in the harness of the invulnerable, and a soft place in the man of iron.

> " So in the hardest human heart
> One little well appears,
> A fountain in some hidden part,
> Brimful of gentle tears.
> It only needs the master touch
> Of love's or pity's hand,
> And lo ! the rock with water bursts,
> And gushes o'er the land."

Every man cannot be Bishop of London.

What would Littleton-in-the-Marsh do for a curate if all were bishops? Where would the cash come from to support their dignity?

Every man cannot be purveyor of cat's-meat to Her Majesty.

Such eminence only awaits a mere handful of sublime officials.

Every man cannot do everything.

The men of the Encyclopædia were wonderful persons, but they disproved their own hopes. They aimed at knowing everything, but never reached it. No man can be good in every department. The law of division of labour is correct, and the divine plan of division of talents is the best for all concerned.

Every man carries an enemy inside his own waistcoat.

He had better watch that fellow well, or he will be stabbing at his heart, or tampering with his conscience.

Every man is a volume, if you know how to read him.

Some seem like Hebrew, which needs to be taken backwards; and many are in too small print to be read at all. In all we find errata, and in some a sheet left out: but there's something to be learned from all; although some men are such books as Charles Lamb spoke of—"things in book's clothing," not much above the level of draught-boards bound and lettered on the back.

Every man is after all *the* man.

> There's but one wise man in the world,
> And who do you think it be?
> 'Tis this man, that man, t'other man:
> Every man thinks 'tis he.

Every man is either a fool or a physician at forty.

He ought by then to be able to doctor and diet himself. We know some friends who are fifty, who are neither fools nor physicians, but a little of both.

Every man is the best interpreter of his own words.

Let him, therefore, be understood in his own sense, and much wrangling will be avoided.

Every man knows his own business best.

Or at least he should do so, and he will not like your interfering. He who tried to teach a dog how to gnaw bones learned something himself which he would like to forget.

Every man knows where his own shoe pinches.

It will be needless for him to tell anyone else, for that will not help him, and probably no one will understand him. Every shoe pinches more or less, but it's usually the fault of the foot.

Every man's garden has a weak spot in the fence.

The foxes, big and little, will get in where the wall is broken down. Let us watch with double diligence over those points of character in which we are feeblest; *and there are such.*

Every " may-be " hath a " may-not-be."

Therefore let us not be too sure. The reader may be Lord Mayor, but he may not be. This book may sell, and it may not sell.

Every misery spared is a mercy bestowed.

Every monkey has his tricks.

Spoken of larkish fellows who annoy people with their follies.

Every one feels the cold according as he is clad.

Where the garments of faith and patience are worn, the Arctic winter of poverty is endured without harm; but trying circumstances freeze the life out of some men, because their religion is a dreadfully thin and flimsy fabric.

Every one for himself is the pig's doctrine.

And there are a great many believers in it. The worshippers of Number One are numerous, and enthusiastic. Self is the man!

As I walked by myself, I said to myself,
And myself said again unto me :
"Look to thyself, take care of thyself,
For nobody cares for thee."

Every one is wise after the business is over.

This is the especial wisdom of the unwise. Yet we could all do much better if we had to do it over again : at least, we think so. We are fools enough to imagine that we should not be fools again!

Every one must row with the oars he has.

This is wisdom. Instead of quarrelling with our tools, let us do our best with them. Paddle your own canoe with such paddles as come to hand.

Every one takes his pleasure where he finds it.

Hence a man's pleasures become the index of his character. If he takes pleasure in sin, it is because he loves it. If he frequents the pit, it is because he is going there.

Every one thinks he could have done better.

Had he been consulted, mistakes would have been avoided, and grander results would have been obtained. Others may be all very well ; but *we* live at Nonsuch House, in the parish of Nonpareil.

Every one to his liking, as the man said when he kissed his cow.

Happily, in this case, the kissing would neither involve an action for assault, nor excite another man's jealousy concerning the lady. There is no accounting for tastes.

Every one thinks his own sack to be the heaviest.

> Each one thinks his lot the worst; but he is mistaken. If he thought himself the worst of the lot he might be right.

Every one will be thy friend,
Whilst thou hast wherewith to spend;
But if store of crowns be scant,
No man will supply thy want.

> We fear this is too often the fact; but assuredly it is not always so, nor is it often so with gracious men.

Every path hath its puddle.

> No man's life is quite beyond rebuke : no man's course is without its difficulties and sorrows.

Every pea helps to fill the sack.

> Every worshipper increases the congregation, every member helps to make up the church, every penny enlarges the collection

Every pedlar sells the very best pins.

> At least he says so, and he ought to know.

Every pig can grunt.

> It needs no genius to grumble and find fault. He who can do nothing else is often great in this art. Let the creature grunt.

Every poor man is a fool in the judgment of a fool.

> The same fool considers every wealthy person to be a paragon of wisdom. The poorest twaddle is eloquence when it comes from a nobleman's mouth. Lord Fitznoodle is the patron saint of fools.

Every potter praises his own pot.

> If he does not do so, who will? Potters cannot afford to keep trumpeters, and therefore they praise their own ware. We all do so, more or less. This proverb often runs, " Every potter praises his own pot, *and all the more if it is cracked*." Does not self-praise imply a crack somewhere?

Every question is not for me to answer.

> If I attempt to do so I shall show my ignorance. " Teach thy tongue to say ' I do not know,' " is a Talmudic proverb.

Every smith should shoe his own mare.

We should take care that our own household is not neglected, because we are looking after others. Note the lament of the spouse: "They made me the keeper of the vineyards; but mine own vineyard have I not kept."—Cant. i. 6.

Every sot will go to pot.

First for a drain, and then to be drained dry by his expenditure.

Every sprat nowadays styles itself a herring.

John Foster declares that two of the most egotistic persons he ever met with were a chimney-sweep and a breaker of stones on the highway.

Every time the sheep bleats it loses a mouthful.

Solid profit is lost when time is wasted in idle talk.

Every tub must stand on its own bottom.

We are individually accountable, and no one can hide behind another, so as to justify himself.

Every vine must have its stake.

Each one needs some support, as the vine does.

Every why hath its wherefore.

The toughest question can be answered by some one, though we cannot handle it, and need not wish to do so. Practical questions are easily met. "One of my friends observed yesterday that it was a difficulty in many cases to know *wherefore* God contended with us. But, I thought, that it was no difficulty with me."— So wrote *Andrew Fuller.*

Everybody cannot be first.

Everybody would like to be. If we would become candidates for the lowest place we should gain the election without opposition.

Everybody is glad when the smiter is smitten.

Or when "the biter is bitten." The natural instinct of justice is gratified by seeing the *lex talionis* in operation.

Everybody lays the load on the willing horse.

But it is a very thoughtless and shameless thing to do so.

Everybody wears out one pair of green slippers.

And he is a wise man if he soon throws them away, and afterwards
wears the shoes of common sense, or the boots of prudence.

Everybody who carries a horsewhip is not a horseman.

Yet he would like us to think so. He used to be known as " a
gent." The proverb applies to all who have the outward sign of a
craft, a profession, or a proficiency, but have not the thing itself.

Everybody's friend is everybody's fool.

He is so easy that people think him soft, and ridicule him behind
his back ; while he thinks himself immensely popular.

Everybody's friend is nobody's friend.

His universal generosity lies all in talk. He is not to be depended
on. He is always helping so many that he cannot come to your aid.

Everybody's work is nobody's work.

A horse would starve if it had twenty grooms to feed it ; for each
groom would leave it to the rest. The people who projected the
tower of Babel said, " Let us build " ; but as they were all builders,
the works have not yet been completed. Noah built the ark, for
he was one man ; but all the men in the world, when formed into
a committee, could not finish a tower.

Everything comes to the man who can wait.

It is only a matter of time. Patience beholds great wonders. In
spiritual things, if we watch and wait, we shall see glorious things.

Everything is hard at first.

The simplest trade is difficult to the beginner; but the most
difficult art becomes quite easy by practice.

Everything may be repaired except the neck-bone.

While there's life there's hope. After the rope there's no hope.

Everything that happens is but a link in a chain.

Like texts of Scripture, facts should be viewed in their connection,
and this often corrects our view of them. One thing draws on
another, and often accounts for, and justifies it.

Evil cannot be conquered by evil.

Satan will not cast out Satan : we must overcome evil by good Anger is not to be met with anger, nor cunning with cunning.

Evil communications divide near relations.

Wicked tittle-tattle, exaggeration, and insinuation have parted very friends, and rent families with enmity. No quarrel is so bitter as a family quarrel. Home-made wine makes sharp vinegar.

Evil deeds are evil seeds.

What will come of them will be a harvest which will crush the reapers. *Joseph Cook* calls sin "an eternal mother."

Evil for good is devil-like.
Evil for evil is beast-like.
Good for good is man-like.
Good for evil is God-like.

There is much sense in these four lines. I well remember learning them as a child, and I know the good effect which they had upon my moral judgment. Let your son and heir get them by heart.

Evil reports find willing ears.

Sad fact that it is so ; but assuredly there is everywhere a fine market for rotten cheese. What better sport can be found for many than ferreting out the rats in a friend's character !

Evil words cut worse than swords.

Evils for which we must blame ourselves are hard to bear.

They have a sting in them, because conscience condemns.

Ewes dressed like lambs are silly shams.

Elderly women who trick themselves out like girls are commonly called, " Old ewes dressed lamb-fashion." Are they aware of this ? Why do they provoke such remarks ?

Exalt wisdom, and she will exalt thee.

Example draws where precept fails ;
And sermons are less read than tales.

If the words of the wise are "as nails," their examples are as hammers. What's the use of a nail if you cannot drive it in ?

Example is the school of mankind; and they will learn at no other

Examples preach to the eye, and leave a deeper impress than counsel addressed to the ear. As children like pictures better than letterpress, so do men prefer example to precept. There is no doubt about the truth of this proverb, so far as *evil* examples are concerned, but, of *good* examples, it has been said that, "They would indeed be excellent things, were not people so modest that none will set them, and so vain that none will follow them."

Exchange is no robbery, but on it there is jobbery.

So we have heard; but the information has come from those who have lost money by speculation, and theirs is hardly an impartial report. We guess that if they had made a profit they would have thought the exchange to be the Temple of Honesty. Exchange may be robbery, as when a man knowingly takes a better hat or umbrella than his own.

Exercise is the best fire for cold limbs.

So father Hodge would not let the boys stand shivering over the fire, but drove them out hedging and ditching, or ploughing, and then they came in warm as a toast.

Expand your chest by enlarging your heart.

Many a man has found his chest enlarge, or rather his estate increased, when he has begun to use his substance for the good of others.

Expect from the world more kicks than half-pence.

This is called "monkey's allowance", but it usually falls to the lot of good men.

Expect nothing from those who promise a great deal.

Their readiness to promise should make you more than a little suspicious. They would not issue so many bank-notes if they had to keep enough gold in the cellar to meet them.

Expect soot from a sweep.

If a man blackens you by abuse, but is himself of evil character, never mind it; above all do not follow soot.

Expect to be disappointed, and you will be.

For, even if no disappointment comes, you will be disappointed in the expectation which is herein recommended.

Expectation is the fool's income.

He is always looking for something which has never yet occurred, and never will occur in his time. His ship is to come home ; but as yet it is not launched. He has an estate some-where, which is to come to him when we have a week all Sundays, but at present the rightful owner is depriving him of it.

Expensive wife makes pensive husband.

When the draper's bill drains his pocket, the poor man thinks more than he dares to say. The arithmetic of a good wife is very different. She *adds* to his happiness, *subtracts* from his cares, *multiplies* his joys, *divides* his sorrows, and practises *reduction* in the expenditure of his household.

Experience teaches nothing to a simpleton, not even that fire burns.

We have known foolish persons injured by vice, and yet they have returned to it as speedily as they could ; and we have met with persons who have lost their money by gambling go to it again as soon as they could scrape together another pound. The moth will not learn from its singed wings.

Extravagance is the common disease of the times.

Is it not so ? Does not every one live at a rate which would have frightened his father ? Is this the way to promote national wealth ?

Extremes meet, but extremes are not meet.

> Do not the golden mean exceed,
> In word, in passion, or in deed.

Eye-servants are eye-sores.

One cannot bear to see them hard at work in your presence, when you know that the moment your back is turned they will be wasting their time. We must mind that we do not become eye-servants ourselves. We must remember the couplet—

> Live not only to the eye,
> Sin is sin though none be nigh.

Sayings of a more Spiritual Sort.

Early piety leads to eminent piety.

> It will be found, upon investigation, that the most of those who become notable for godliness are those who from childhood have feared the Lord. Beginning early, they have time to ripen.

Earth is our inn : heaven is our home.

> We may well put up with discomfort in this world, for we shall soon be away from it; it is only for a few days that we accept its hospitality. *Archbishop Leighton* often said that if he were to choose a place to die in, he would choose an inn ; for it looked like a pilgrim going home, to whom this world was all as an inn, and who was weary of the noise and confusion in it. He had his desire, for he died at the Bell Inn, in Warwick Lane.

Earth's sorrows are soothed by heaven's sympathy.

E'er since I knew the Lord aright,
I'd dwell with him from morn till night.

> Experience of God's goodness breeds an intense longing to abide in constant communion with him.

Empty your bucket before you draw from the well.

> Feel your own need, and your inability to supply it, before you go to the fulness of Christ for the supplies which are treasured up in him. He wants nothing from you but your necessity.

Enthusiasm is essential to the triumph of truth.

> It is not true that truth is mighty, and will prevail, if it be left to lie on the shelf neglected, or if it be only taught by frozen lips. Truth set on fire will burn its way, like flame on the prairie ; but the fire of enthusiasm is absolutely needful.

Eternity is the lifetime of the Almighty.

Even apostles would be apostates did not grace prevent.

Even in light matters get light from heaven.

> We mostly make our worst mistake where mistake seems impossible. We stumble most on level ground. How plain seemed the case of the Gibeonites to Israel, but Israel erred !

Even in small things there is a great providence.

Or if there were not, we should be in great trouble before long, for the great things would go away. The small things are the pivots of history, the hinges of change, the linch-pins of continuance.

Every lock of sorrow has a key of promise to fit it.

Every man in Christ is not a man in Christ.

He may not yet have come to ripeness of spiritual manhood, even though, as a man, he is in Christ by living faith.

Every man is born a Pharisee.

Human nature is proud, self-righteous, and disdainful of others.

Every member of Christ hath the whole of Christ.

Christ's whole person and work belong to each individual believer, as truly as if there were none besides himself to enjoy it.

Every road leads to London.

This saying was used right well by an old minister in instructing a younger one. "Every sermon," said he, "must have Christ in it. The way to preach is to find out the way from your text to the Lord Jesus, and then travel along the road. As every little hamlet has a road to London, so every Scriptural subject leads to Jesus." "But," said the young beginner, "suppose there is no road from my text to Christ; what then?" "My friend," replied the elder man, "you must not suppose anything of the sort, for it would not be true; but even if it were true, you must make a road; or even go over hedge and ditch, for you must get to Jesus before you have done."

Evil society is the death of piety.

He cannot smell sweetly who sleeps in a bed of garlic.

Exalt him who has exalted you.

> I will exalt thee, Lord of hosts,
>   For thou'st exalted me;
> Since thou hast silenced Satan's boasts,
>   I'll therefore boast in thee.

Expect much from the Creator, and little from the creature.

Experience and instruction are the way to perfection.

ACE to face clears many a case.

> Quarrels are fomented by hearsay statements and reports. Bring the parties together, and let the truth come out.

Failures daunt a dastard, but make a man.

A real man gathers up his strength for persevering attempts, and so by difficulties his force and character are developed and increased. Cowardice adds to the natural difficulties those inherent in itself; as says the old rhyme :—

> " The wind blows east, and the wind blows west;
>   We shall know a tree by its fruit;
> The world, they say, is worst to the best;
>   But a dastard has evil to boot."

Faint heart never won fair lady.

Faint heart sees dangers where there are none, and so avoids attempts which might succeed. Doubtless even in the tender business of courtship this operates to the young man's injury. If *he* is afraid to propose, he can hardly expect *her* to do so.

Faint praise is often strong censure.

It is a way the courteous use of suggesting more than they express.

> Willing to wound, and yet afraid to strike,
> Just hint a fault, and hesitate dislike.

Fair and softly goes far in a day.

Hurry exhausts itself; a judicious pace is best for travelling and working. Begin as you hope to go on, and then go on, and on, and on, till your sun goes down.

Fair faces need no paint.

Leave that to Jezebel.

Fair words butter no parsnips.

Fair words feed neither cat nor kitten.

Fair words fry no fritters.

In all these cases the fawner, and the flatterer, and the fine promiser are truly estimated. Beware of Mr. Plausible Prate.

Fair words make me count my money.

Who uses fawning words, of him beware thee straight :
Be sure he would entrap , or why such dainty bait ?

Faith in God is reason acting reasonably.

Although faith in God is the gift of God, it can be justified by the clearest logic. There is every reason why we should believe the God of truth, and no reason whatever for doubting him. True religion is common sense enlightened by uncommon grace. Faith is not reason in labour, but reason at rest.

Falling leaves are nature's sermons.

"We all do fade as a leaf." "In the amber autumn the leaves drop with an 'Amen.'"

Falsehood follows at the heels of debt.

The man fails to be upright, and lies.

Fame is not found on feather beds.

We may expect conflict if we are to win glory. *Dr. Watts* says :

"Must I be carried to the skies
On flowery beds of ease,
While others fought to win the prize
And sailed through bloody seas ? "

Familiarity breeds contempt.

Men are seldom heroes to their valets, or honoured prophets in their own country. Yet familiarity with the Lord Jesus breeds a deeper reverence ; for the more we know him, the more we adore his infinite perfections.

Fancy is a pretty dog, but needs a deal of feeding.

Doubtless whims are more expensive than necessities.

Fancy you are miserable, and you are so.

Some of the worst griefs are those of a sentimental kind. They have been called "the vapours," and they are as vapoury and as hard to deal with as malarious gases. It is the same with the body as with the mind , you can make yourself ill by fancy, hence *Churchill* says :—

Most of the evils we poor mortals know,
From doctors and imagination flow.

Far-off water won't quench near fire.

> When you are in immediate want, money to come to you in a year, or a legacy at the death of an aged but immortal uncle, or castles in Spain are a very poor help. "Better is a neighbour that is near than a brother far off."—Prov. xxvii. 10.

Farmer! Don't rake your fields with a small-tooth comb.

> Some would do so, if they could, to get up the last ear of corn from the gleaner. This is a wretched form of economy.

Far sought and dear bought,
May be good for nought.

> Yet many think things fine because they are foreign. Britons ever will be slaves when fashion is in the case.

Fast bind, fast find.

> Make a business clear and sure from the beginning, that it may remain so in days to come.

Fat kitchens make lean wills.

> You cannot both eat an estate and leave it to your heir.

Fat or lean, always see the cloth is clean.

> Housewives of working-men will find this trifle to be no trifle.

Father's a father till he gets a new wife,
But mother's a mother all her life.

> A tender mother's love keeps to her children under all circumstances, when even the father's affection may grow cold, because the second wife weans him from the offspring of his first love. A step-mother may turn her husband into a step-father.

Fatten the pig, or you'll have no fat bacon.

> Put money into the business or you will get none out.

Faults are thick where love is thin.

> Love, when fervent, admires the very thing which is greatly denounced when love has grown cold. Of course I·have many faults when you have little love.

Faults we own ever, but false we are never.

> May God grant that we may never become untrue, for that is a fatal fault, and one which, speaking after the manner of men, cannot be cured. As a rule, a liar is a leper, and no waters of Jordan will wash him clean.

Favour those whom God favours.

> These should be our companions, and it should be a luxury to do them good for the Lord's sake.

Fear gives more pain than the pain it fears.

> Certainly men "feel a thousand deaths in fearing one."

Fear God, and you will have nothing else to fear.

> He will preserve you from all evil, and keep you in perfect peace.
>
> > True virtue, whatsoe'er betides,
> > In all extremes unmoved abides.

Fear hath many eyes, and yet trembles at what it does not see.

> The unseen is indeed the most terrible to our feeble minds. "There were they in great fear, where no fear was." We look through the telescope of apprehension, breathe on the glass, and then think we see clouds, when indeed it is only our anxious breath.

Fear kills more than the physician.

> No doubt illness is often a matter of nervousness and dread; as says the old rhyme—
>
> > "Here lies a man who lived to age,
> > Yet still from death was flying;
> > Who, though not sick, was never well,
> > And died for fear of dying."

Feather by feather the goose is plucked.

> Small expenses are overlooked, and at last the man finds himself without a feather to fly with. Economy must preserve what industry gains.

Feed a bear, and his claws will grow.

> Feed a quarrel by saying fresh words of strife, and the result will be more anger and malice than at the first.

Feed a pig, and you'll have a hog.

Those who are of a swinish nature only grow worse when they receive either kindness or consideration.

Feed your farm before it is hungry, and weed your garden before it is foul.

In this and all other cases prevention is better than cure. It is better to keep things right than to get them right after they have run down.

Feel for others—in your pocket.

Practical, pecuniary sympathy is more useful than mere talk. "I feel for the poor man," said one. "Friend, how much dost thou feel?" said the Quaker: "Dost thou feel five shillings for him? If so, I will put my feelings and shillings along with thine."

Few are fit to be trusted with themselves.

And if they cannot keep themselves right, how shall they be trusted by others?

Few men ever repent of being silent.

Few people get fat on wind-falls or wind-bags.

Hard work pays better than looking for legacies or dreaming of fortunes. Great expectations are a breakfast for fools.

Few words, and kindly meant,
Are a woman's ornament.

Fierce fires soon burn themselves out.

The excitements of zeal are not to be much reckoned on.

Fiery men are easily put out.

The least little thing provokes them, and they often blaze up without any apparent cause. Such men are like John Lilburne, of whom it was said that he must quarrel; and if there had been no one else in the world, John would have quarrelled with Lilburne and Lilburne with John.

Fight, but fight only with yourself.

Self-conquest is the greatest of victories. Many have vanquished all others, and yet have been slaves to their own passions.

Fighting dogs get bleeding ears.

Find contentment in God's appointment.

Find you out your sins, or your sins will find out you.

Fine birds are all the more likely to be plucked.

> Pretty people are tempted, and great men are assailed.

Fine clothes cannot hide the clown.

> They far oftener betray him : he does not feel at home in them any more than a dog in a blanket, or a hog in armour.

Fine feathers make fine birds.

> Yet garments can only make a vain person what *Masson* calls "a decorated fool." A puritanic student once called certain fine ladies "ambulating blocks for millinery." Well, dress as they may, it is, at least, a pity that they do not leave feathers to birds, and not murder our songsters to bedeck their own heads.

Fine promises are frail securities.

> That is to say, when they come from our fellow mortals. Many have been ruined by the rascality which promised, but never intended to perform. Such promises are solid lies : not so much falsehood in word as falsehood in fact.

Fine stables do not make good horses.

> A man may live in a college and be a dunce, or dwell under the eaves of the house of God and be an infidel. A villa may have a villain for its tenant, and a mansion may hold a lord without either manor or manners. Ecclesiastical architecture does not secure piety. Many a poor drone of a preacher has had the emptying of a fine Gothic edifice.

Fine words have great weight with feeble minds.

> The authors of proverbs to this effect, of which there are very many, had evidently been misled by fine oratory, and at last arrived at the conclusion that words are but air, and that there is no building upon them.

Finery is foolery.

> A lady asked the Rev. John Newton what was the best rule for female dress and behaviour. "Madam," said he, "so dress and so conduct yourself that persons who have been in your company shall not recollect what you had on." When so much is spent on dress, that the house is impoverished, the folly is extreme. It suggested the epigram—
>
> > "What is the reason, can you guess?
> > Why men are poor and women thinner?
> > So much do they for dinner dress ;
> > There's nothing left to dress for dinner."

Fire begins with little sparks: crime begins with evil thoughts.

First come, first served.

> A fair rule. No one ought to wish to go out of his turn at the expense of others, even though he may think himself a person of importance.

First comes owing, and then comes lying.

> For the debtor invents false excuses, and makes untruthful promises, so as to stave off the day of payment.

First look up, and then look out.

> Look to God first, and then watch for every honourable opportunity of getting on in business.

First practise at home, then preach abroad.

> It is not every man that would like to preach to his neighbours from his own door-step.

First the distiller, then the doctor, then the undertaker.

First thrive, then wive, then strive.

First understand, and then undertake.

> It is the height of folly to undertake a matter of which you do not know the ins and outs. Many have burnt their fingers with such blind agreements. Never sign what you have not seen.

Fish bred in dirty pools will surely taste of mud.

> I remember having received, as a present, some fine carp taken from the village pond. To put the knife into them was quite enough for me: a friend who ate of them was seriously ill. The fish had lived upon the filth of the parish, and could not be clean eating. Those who are bred in vice are sure to show it in their character.

Fit words are fine; but often fine words are not fit.

> If the language is suitable to express the truth, it is everything. Sometimes grand oratory is great absurdity.

Flattery is pap for fools.

> 'Tis an old maxim of the schools
> That flattery's the food of fools;
> And whoso likes such airy meat,
> Will soon have nothing else to eat.

Flattery fouls the flatterer and the flattered.

Mr. Simeon said : " We ought to feel as if our ears were stung with blasphemy, when we discover any attempt to transfer the crown of glory from the head of the Redeemer to that of any of his servants." *Flavel* also exclaimed : " Christian, thou carriest the gunpowder of pride about thee. Desire those who carry the fire of flattery to keep their distance. It is a dangerous crisis when a proud heart meets with flattering lips."

Flowers are sweet, but men need meat.

This is in allusion to florid sermons in which there is an absence of sound instruction.

Flowers smell sweetly, whether men are near or not.

They do not " waste their sweetness." He who made them enjoys them, and that is enough for them. We must do good, however unnoticed our work may be.

Flowery meadows have none the better grass.

Poetical preachments are by no means promotive of edification. The soul feeds on truth, not on pretty periods.

Foes may rise, and thrones may fall;
God is mightier far than all.

Follow the river, and you'll come to the sea.

Trace a stream of mercy, and you come to the infinite God.

Follow the wise few, and not the learned many.

Some read the *vulgar* many : but it little matters, the learned are often vulgar also. To follow any multitude to do evil is a thing to be avoided.

Folly and learning may live under one hat.

Book learning may carry a man far from truth and common sense : experience is needed, and grace from God, to make true wisdom.

Folly is wise in her own eyes.

And this prevents her ever attaining to wisdom. Men can only be wise by finding out their own folly.

Folly taxes us four times as much as Parliament.

Calculate the expenditure under the heads of Drink, Dress, Show, Idle Amusement, and Fads, and you will be astonished.

Fond of doctors, little health ;
Fond of lawyers, little wealth.

> These learned practitioners are excellent in their way, but they are not intended to be called in every day.   When we are well, or none dispute with us, we are apt to make fun of them.   Here is one of the witty things of a man who was well : —
>
> " The homœopathic system, sir, just suits me to a tittle,
>   It clearly proves of physic you cannot take too little :
>   If it be good, in all complaints, to take a dose so small,
>   It surely must be better still, to take no dose at all."

Fond pride of dress is sure a dreadful curse :
It shows an empty head, and makes an empty purse.

Foolish fear doubles danger.

> For it unfits you for acting so as to avoid danger, and even drives you further into it.   Most of the accidents which occur in the street happen to nervous people.

Foolish tongues talk nineteen to the dozen.

> The less they have to carry, the faster they go.

Fools and children should never see unfinished work.

> Because they form a judgment without having the whole matter before them, and that imperfect opinion they are apt to retain.

Fools and churls make lawyers rich :
Concessions fair jump o'er the ditch.

> This is one among many wise sayings which would keep us from law, its uncertainty, its cost, and its worry.   The proper use of a lawyer is that he may keep you out of law.

Fools are not great fools unless they know Latin.

> The affectation of scholarship enables a man to be more egregiously foolish than the utterly ignorant.

Fools are pleased with their own blunders.

Fools build, and wise men buy.

> Thus they get a house more cheaply as a general rule.   According to the rhyme,
>
> " He that buys a house ready wrought,
>   Hath many a tile and pin for nought."
>
> But nowadays full often knaves build, and fools buy.

Fools feast forgetful of the reckoning.

And this they will do through life till at last they have to say with the epicure :—

> " At length, my friends, the feast of life is o'er ;
> I've ate sufficient, and I'll drink no more ;
> My night is come ; I've spent a jovial day ;
> 'Tis time to part ; but oh ! what is to pay ? "

Fools grow without watering.

A wise man says that a fool may be known by six qualities : anger without cause, speech without profit, change without motive, enquiry without object, putting trust in a stranger, and want of capacity to discriminate between a friend and a foe. We could mention other equally clear characteristics, but there is no need. Fools are common objects by the seaside, and everywhere else.

Fools have made wise speeches, and wise men have made foolish speeches.

Of course the foolish must now and then be right by mere chance, and the wise are wrong through natural imperfection.

Fools live, but do not learn.

Like a spoon in the gravy, they imbibe no flavour of that which surrounds them, even though they live with the wise and gracious. So say the Burmese sages :

> But fools are fools where'er you go !
> Experience cannot reach them ;
> The only thing they'll ever learn
> Sure death itself must teach them !

Fools make feasts, and wise men eat them.

When a king of Scotland heard this speech at one of his banquets he pulverized it with another, " Wise men make proverbs and fools repeat them."

Fools make those enquiries afterwards which wise men make before.

Fools may make money, but only wise men can keep it, or spend it properly

Fools run in packs ; the wise oft walk alone.

Fools set stools for wise men to stumble over.

They raise puzzling questions, and in the answering of them men of knowledge are confounded. The Spaniards say, "A fool can cast a stone into a well, which many wise men cannot get out." The Italians say, "A fool can ask more questions in an hour than seven wise men can answer in seven years."

Fools should never be set on eggs.

They will addle them or break them, but never hatch them. This saying means that designs which need patient attention must never be left to unwise people.

Fools think nothing right but what they do themselves.

Fools think that others do not think.

But others do think, and thus the fool is greatly mistaken.

Fools worship mules that carry gold.

Alas! many do this who would not like to be called fools. "Having men's persons in admiration because of advantage."—Jude 16.

Fools' names you see on seat and tree.

Go where you will, you will see these disfigurements. In every instance initials cut in public places are those of fools.

Foot firm, and faith fast,
Stand still till storm past.

"Having done all, still stand."—Ephesians vi. 13.

Foppish finery suits puppies and puppets.

For a dead opportunity there is no resurrection.

Sir Richard Baker saith :—

"To let time slip is a reverseless crime :
You may have time again, but not *the* time."

For better for worse, some follow the purse.

Worshippers of the golden calf, they are always of the opinion of the squire, or some other man made of money.

For every ill beneath the sun, there is some remedy or none :
If there be one, resolve to find it ; if not, submit, and never
mind it.

For God expend, and he will send.

Many happy years I have found it so at the Stockwell Orphanage. Our five hundred mouths never lack a meal, for our Father feeds us.

For little birds there are little traps.

Children and youths are preyed upon by the wicked; and even the poor are entrapped by rogues, who are content with little fishes if they can get many of them.

For love of the nurse they kiss the child.

Many pretend affection for one to gain the affection of another. Love me, love my darling.

For rainy day lay store away.

This was the young gentleman's reason for keeping the umbrella which had been lent him. It is good in the day of abundance to prepare for days of need. When our strength declines it will be pleasant to eat the honey laid up in the early summer of our youth.

For the light of day we have nothing to pay.

God has made this choice blessing common. It is the true emblem of his enlightening grace, which is free as the day

Forbid a fool, and he'll do it directly.

This folly seems to be universal in the race. At the beginning, the fruit was desired because it was forbidden; and Paul said that "when the commandment came, sin revived."

Forget the corn on Sabbath morn.

It will grow just as well without your thinking upon it, and on the Lord's-day you have other subjects to consider.

Forgive and forget : when you bury a mad dog don't leave his tail above ground.

Here is the difficulty with some, they harbour the memory of wrong, and so the snake of anger is scotched and not killed, and it wriggles itself to life again. Have done with it, and let the remembrance of it die altogether.

Forgive every man's faults except your own.

Be much harder with yourself than with others. Say as one did, "God may forgive me, but I shall never forgive myself."

Forehand payments make hind-hand work.

Fellows don't care to work for a dead horse; they have had their money, and spent it, and now they have no heart to work.

Fore-think, though you cannot foretell.

We cannot foresee, but we can forecast and prepare for what is likely to happen.

Forethought will spare afterthought.

Consideration may prevent regret.

Before thou bring thy works to light,
Consider on them in the night.

Foul breath is a calamity; but foul speech is criminality.

Foul deeds will rise before men's eyes.

However carefully concealed, they have the knack of making themselves known. Sin has a resurrection. Many other sins besides murder "will out." A bird of the air shall tell the matter.

Fowls should roost where foxes cannot reach.

It is wise to rise above the tempter's grip by living on high with God. Also let the young be lodged out of harm's way.

Fox sly-boots is quiet, but waiteth his day;
While you make a riot, he seizeth his prey.

Sin is a crafty enemy. Beware of that fox. While you are enjoying your pleasure sin will destroy your soul.

Fraud and frost both end in foul.

When they break up, the discovery and the thaw are by no means pleasant or clean.

Frenzy, heresy, and jealousy, these three
Seldom or never curèd be.

They feed upon themselves, and grow most rapidly without other food, and hence there is little hope of their abatement.

Fretting cares make grey hairs.

And this is all they make. What is the use of them?

Fretting mends no broken dishes;
Brings us none of all our wishes.

Why, then, do we fret? Better far to trust in God, and be at peace.

Friends are like fiddle-strings, they must not be screwed too tight.

We must not expect unreasonable things of them, nor provoke them, even in jest, nor exact excessive esteem from them.

Friendship cemented by Christian brotherhood has a firm foundation.

That friendship firm will ever bide
Whose hands unto the cross are tied.

Friendship, like a bird, has two wings.

Something should be rendered on each side. "He that hath friends must show himself friendly." I must be a friend to him, who is a friend to me. One good turn deserves another.

Friendship made in a moment is of no moment.

Douglas Jerrold said of one, "His friendships are so warm that he no sooner takes them up than he puts them down again."

Frogs betray themselves by their own croaking.

Many bring sorrow on themselves by their own lamentations.

Frogs in a well know nothing of the high seas.

Men with narrow range of knowledge and experience cannot calculate the greatness of the divine designs, nor even understand the larger ideas of more instructed men.

From an empty pot,
Pudding cometh not.

No, not even if you set that pot simmering in a pulpit.

From nothing comes nothing.

What gracious or holy thing can come out of our vain and worthless nature? We are less than nothing, and something far worse than nothing is all that can come of us.

From one who always calls thee " dear "
Preserve thyself and pocket clear.

> This comes of my own observation. Cant phrases should excite
> suspicion. They are the chosen trade-marks of certain parties,
> religious or otherwise, who believe that all men can be fooled if
> you will only use enough treacle.

From saving comes having.

> Of little gains let care be had,
> For of small ears great mows are made.

From saying to doing is a long stretch.

> Especially with some who are very lavish with their promises.
> Trust in that man's promise who dares to refuse that which he fears
> he cannot perform. A promise and its performance should balance
> like a pair of scales ; but too often they do not.

From thence where nets and snares are laid,
Make haste, lest else thou be betrayed.

> Go not down to the plain of Sodom, which is full of slime pits.
> Fly : there is no safety but in flight.

Fuddle makes muddle.

> Those who are given to drink do not clearly think, and so stagger
> into messes.

Full ears of wheat bend low with weight.

> The more there is in a man the more lowly is his behaviour.

Full many a pleasing, praising speech,
Prepares the way to over-reach.

> Fulsome flattery is fodder for fools, and is used as bait by knaves.

Full many a shaft at random sent
Finds mark the archer little meant.

Sayings of a more Spiritual Sort.

Faint, yet pursuing ;
Weak, yet subduing ;
Spent, yet renewing ;
Christ ever viewing.

> This is much as our life has been. May God be glorified both by its weakness and its strength, its change and its constancy !

Faith builds a bridge from this world to the next.

Faith cannot die, nor can he die who hath faith.

Faith fears no famine.

> How can she, when she can sing, " Jehovah-jireh " : the Lord will provide ? Sooner will the clouds rain bread than the people of God be left to die.

Faith *gets* most, humility *keeps* most, love *works* most.

Faith honours Christ, and Christ honours faith.

> He said to the blind man, " Thy faith hath saved thee." He puts the crown on the head of faith because faith always puts the crown upon the head of her Lord.

Faith in God is never out of season.

Faith looks to precepts as well as to promises.

> It takes the whole Word of God, and obeys commands as well as trusts promises.

Faith makes all things possible, and love makes them easy.

Faith makes the Christian, but love proves him.

> Faith justifies the believer, but love justifies his faith by the works which it produces. Faith believes God to be true ; love proves faith to be true.

Faith sees God, and God sees faith.

> Faith sees God, who is invisible, and God sees even that little faith, which would be invisible to others.

Faith unfeigned breeds hope unfailing.

Faith which never wept was never true.

> Repentance is the inseparable companion of a true trust in Christ. It is the tear which falls from the eye of faith at the remembrance of pardoned sin.

Faith works love, works by love, and loves to work.

Faith's barque is often tost, but never lost.

> An untried faith will turn out to be an untrue faith ; but, however much tried, true faith will bear the strain.

Faith's eye sees in the dark.

> It is a God-given eye, and it is like the eye of God.

Faith's hand never knocks in vain at mercy's door.

Feeble-mind is a true pilgrim, and the Lord will be mindful of his feebleness.

Fiery trials make golden Christians.

Filial fear is the safeguard of sanctity.

Follow the Master more than the pastor.

> The pastor must only be followed while he follows *his* Pastor. Happy is it for a people when their minister walks with God, for then they may follow him everywhere.

Forget a frowning world, and serve a smiling God.

Forget not him who forgets not thee.

Free grace and dying love
Lift believing souls above.

> Sweetest of all comforts here, and sweetest of all hopes hereafter, are these two things.

AIN when badly gotten
Is sure to turn rotten.

This has been seen to be so in a thousand instances.
It is no pious dream, or religious superstition, but a
matter of common observation. I have noted it often.

Galled horses can't endure the comb.

Plain truth suits not the man whose conscience it annoys. Those
who live upon abuses are very savage against reformers.

Gamblers and swindlers are first cousins.

Gambling is an express train to ruin.

Nothing corrupts the entire nature and character of a man more
fully than gambling. Who but gamblers would have rattled dice
at the foot of the cross? Thousands of young men are led to
embezzlement through betting, and from fear of discovery they
plunge on from one crime to another.

Gambling is play in name, but crime in reality.

So common is this vice, in one form or another, that it would seem
as if the devil were firing dice out of a mitrailleuse, and slaying his
tens of thousands. This vice brings every other in its train, in-
cluding suicide and murder. Great families have been dragged
down to degradation by this infatuation. That old prophecy has
been fulfilled many a time :—

" An ancient house and a noble name,
An honest heart and a spotless fame,
By the viper's sting and the demon of play,
Shall be blighted and lost for ever and aye."

Games of chance are best avoided altogether.

" Some play for gain : to pass time others play
For nothing. Both do play the fool I say :
Not time nor coin I'd lose, or idly spend.
Who gets by play proves loser in the end."

Garments should never be made too tight :
Homes should be healthy with air and with light.

Gather of patience enow; it's in season, I trow.

For certain it is greatly needed in these trying times; but it does not grow in all gardens. Go with the Man of Sorrows, and learn of him, and you will be made patient under all trials.

Geese can hiss, but who minds them?

The same is true of foolish persons and their censures, they hiss but cannot bite. Why should their opinions influence us?

Geese with geese; sots with sots.

Every man by the choice of his society confesses what he is.

Gentle answers kill growling speeches.

Gentle manners make the gentleman.

Gentle words are hard to answer.

A company of drinking men in Boston, New England, saw Mr. Cotton, the venerable pastor, coming along the street. "I will go," said one of them, "and put a trick upon old Cotton." Crossing over the road the rude fellow whispers into the minister's ear: "Cotton, thou art an old fool." Mr. Cotton replied, "I am afraid I am so. The Lord make both thee and me wiser than we are, even wise to salvation." The fellow returned to his companions thoroughly ashamed; and, when they had forced him to repeat good Mr. Cotton's words, their frolic came to an end. Hard language would have set them on reply, but the soft word silenced them.

Gentle words fall lightly, but they have great weight.

Get clean money, or none:
Mark this, my son!

The reverse of the old advice—"Get money: get it honestly, if you can; but if not, get it—anyhow." Some money ought to smell badly. If the conscience had a nose, and the man had a conscience, he would not be able to live within ten miles of his money.

Get light from smoke, not smoke from light.

Learn from obscure sayings, but do not make plain doctrines obscure. German smoke has had a good deal to do with "modern theology." Many follow the negro's advice when he said "Bredren, let us proceed to confound this text."

Get rid of slugs and sluggards.

Neither of them are good in gardens, or anywhere else.

Get the coffin ready, and the man won't die.

Often it happens that the expected comes not, but the un-expected happens. Some men find all things go wrong with them. If they went to the sea it would be dry. One of them wrote : —

> 'Twas ever thus from childhood's hour,
> That chilling fate has on me fell,
> There always comes a soaking shower,
> When I hain't got no umberell !

Others are so fortunate that if they fell overboard they would come out of water with their pockets full of fish. Thus is a manifest sovereignty seen in providence in more ways than some men care to own.

Gifts are not grace, yet grace is the gift of gifts.

"He that hath the least grace is a Christian; he that hath the greatest gifts may be no more than almost a Christian."— *Mead.*

Give a dog an ill name, and hang him.

The Quaker is reputed to have said to the cur, "I'll not beat thee, nor hang thee, but I'll give thee an ill name."

Give a Yorkshireman a halter, and he'll find a horse.

Both because he is a shrewd man, and also because he is fond of horses. No doubt there is a hint here of something worse ; but we do not suppose that there is any ground for the charge. Yorkshire-men, like all other men, look well to their own interests.

Give alms to the lazy, and you license their laziness.

Giving should be performed with discretion, or we may do harms with our alms. Some give only to indulge their kindly feeling, like one of whom it was said, "He would have held an umbrella over a duck in a shower of rain."

Give an inch, and he'll take an ell.

This is called "cheek"; and cheek is commonly indulged at the expense of those whose generosity verges upon greenness.

Give no man counsel or physic till he asks it.

He will not value it even if it should prove to be wise, and you will have the blame if it turns out to be unsuitable.

> Advice gratis
> Seldom great is.

Give rocks and rascals a wide berth.

Either of them may wreck you; they cannot do your ship or yourself any good.   Distance lends enchantment to the view.

Give the benefit of doubt
Till the truth is fully out.

This is what you would claim if it were your own case, and therefore act thus towards others.

Give the birds crumbs; God gives you loaves.

In the winter pay the birds for the songs of spring by feeding them.   In Sweden a sheaf is always left for the birds.

Give the devil your eye, and he'll win your whole body.

It was so with mother Eve.   "And when she saw."—Gen. iii. 6. *Trapp* says, that " thousands thus die of a wound in the eye."

Give the man his bread and cheese,
Then applaud him if you please.

But many give a man praise, but no pudding; and this is poor pay.   *Luis Camoëns*, author of the "Lusiad," was god of poetry in Portugal, but was allowed to die in the streets of Lisbon like a dog, literally of starvation.   Poor fellow, he would gladly have exchanged for solid pudding some of his empty praise !

Give the mouse a hole, and wonder not that the cheese is
**   taken.**

Let in an ill habit, and it will soon work mischief.   Other interpretations readily suggest themselves.

Give thy purse rather than thy time.

You may earn more in the time than the money would come to. Time, though little thought of, is worth more than gold.

Give to Peter; but save a penny for Paul.

Why should one good person, or work, absorb all that you have?

Give to some people once, and they will expect for ever.

The Kashmirs say : " An old woman found an apple under a tree, and afterwards she went to that tree every day with a basket."

Give to the poor, and you shall have more.

Generosity is not a waster of men's substance, but an improver of it.

> "We all can do better than yet we have done,
>   And not be a whit the worse ;
> It never was loving that emptied the heart,
>   Nor giving that emptied the purse."

Give us the meat, and the bones won't choke us.

Rowland Hill, combating the doctrine of priestcraft, that the common people should not be trusted with the Bible, because there are in it things hard to be understood, said : "A boy came running to his father, crying, 'I am very hungry; do please give me some meat.' 'No, my dear son, for there are hard bones in it, and you cannot eat the bones.' "

Give your horse more corn than cord.

Give your order, and then do it yourself.

Thus only can you be sure that it will be done. There is an old saying. "If you send your man, your man will send his dog, and the dog will send his tail, and the tail will be busy wagging, and so nothing will go."

Give your tongue more holidays than your head.

Old *Sir Richard Baker* says—

> " The tongue hath this most rare but certain notion,
>   Its virtue shows as much in rest as motion."

And indeed, O rare Sir Richard, in rest it shows more excellence than in any other state ! How musical is its silence ! Woman, with all thy faults I love thee *still!* Thy stillness is no mean part of thy loveliness. " The ornament of a quiet spirit " is an ornament indeed.

Giving feeds love, and lending loses it.

Because the borrower is shy of you ; and, as he does not repay you, you soon grow shy of him.

Giving is generally a kind of fishing.

They give a sprat to catch a salmon. Orientals are great at this art, and some in these western parts are becoming proficient.

Giving is living.

> Give strength, give thought, give deeds, give pelf,
> Give love, give tears, and give thyself.
> Give, give, be always giving :
> Who gives not, is not living.

Giving is sowing; the larger the sowing, the larger the reaping.

> For this we have inspired assurance, "He which soweth bountifully shall reap also bountifully."—2 Cor. ix. 6.

Glowing coals will sparkle.

> Where there's passion there will be burning words : where there's great talent there will be indications of it, &c.

Gluttons dig their graves with their teeth.

> Very curious are the instances of this. Here is one, which is reported as an epitaph ; but we take leave to doubt if it ever was carved on a stone :—

> > "This disease you ne'er heard tell on,
> > I died from eating too much melon,
> > Be careful, then, all you that feed, I
> > Died because I was too greedy."

Gnaw your own bone, and let others alone.

> Many need this advice, for they are always prying and interfering. It is wonderful how few people mind their own business.

Go after wisdom, or it will never come to you.

> A suggestive preacher once said, "Do not suppose that wisdom is so much flattered at having you for a pupil that she will set you easy lessons, and yet give you the gold medal."

Go down for a wife, and up for a friend.

> We are not sure of the wisdom of this proverb. Still a very superior wife may look down on her husband, if the superiority lies only in rank ; but this a true friend will not do.

Go into the country to hear town news.

> It is often so : that which is done in our own street may be first made known to us when we are far from home.

Go not astray from the King's highway.

It is the best and safest road, and in it you are under royal pro-ection. "It shall be called the way of holiness."—Isa. xxxv. 8.

Go not every day to your neighbour's house.

So Solomon saith :—"Withdraw thy foot from thy neighbour's house ; lest he be weary of thee, and so hate thee."—Prov. xxv. 17.

Go through your closet to your shop or your field.

Let prayer be the preface to all your business.

"Go to Bath !"

This is good advice if taken literally : the oftener the better. The saying is, however, varied, and takes the form of "Go to Halifax !" "Go to Jericho !" and "Go to Hanover !" In the last shape it may have been a Jacobite wish for the reigning house.

Go to bed with the lamb, and rise with the lark.

Go to strangers for charity, to acquaintances for advice, and to relations for nothing—and you will generally get a fair supply.

Go to the ant—but don't go to your uncle's.

The pawnbroker's shop is not for the industrious and thrifty.

God and the doctor we alike adore,
But only when in danger, not before.
The danger o'er, both are alike requited :
God is forgotten, and the doctor slighted.

God can send meat by ravens as well as by angels.

He can make bad men the servants of providence for his people.

God defends the right.

God gives sleep to the bad that the good may be un-disturbed.

If lions and wolves never slept, it would be all the harder for the sheep : if knaves were always awake, where were honest men ? No doubt wicked men are allowed prosperity, that they may be good-tempered, and the righteous may have rest.

God gives thee six days ; steal not the seventh.

God helps those who help themselves.

God helps those who cannot help themselves.

> These two proverbs are equally true; but the last is very sweet to the hopeless and helpless.   Our extremity is God's opportunity, and he is never slow to begin when we have reached the end of our own power and wisdom.

God is no man's debtor, but every man's creditor.

God knows best how the weather should be,
It is better with him than if left to thee.

God pities weakness, but punishes wickedness.

God sends clothes when he sends cold.

> This is a matter of experience.   God's own children affirm it to be so.   Though, sometimes, the clothes are not quite what we would prefer, they are better than we deserve.   We are "gentlemen commoners upon the bounty of Providence"; or, as another puts it, "Our Lord finds us our livery."

God sends meat and the devil sends cooks.

> The gift of his providence is often spoiled by those who have the management of it.   Cooks, however, to turn to the letter of the proverb, would appear to come from a better quarter than that which is mentioned, for the rhyme has it:—
>
> > We may live without learning, may live without books;
> > But civilized men cannot live without cooks.

God tempers the wind to the shorn lamb.

> Does he?   Should lambs be shorn?   Is this an excuse for cruelty?
> Some have even quoted this saying as a Scriptural text!   Find it!

God, who thinks of sparrows, cares for souls.

God will grind to powder those who grind the poor.

Godliness is gain; but gain is not godliness.

God's mills grind slowly, but they grind small.

> *Longfellow* puts it:—
>
> > "The mills of God grind slowly,
> > Yet they grind exceeding small.
> > Though with patience he stands waiting,
> > With exactness grinds he all."

God's providence is mine inheritance.

> The motto on the old house in Chester. A glorious one.

God's wrath comes by measure; his mercy without measure.

Gold is a base metal in base hands.

> " Gold begets in brethren hate ;
> Gold in families debate ;
> Gold does friendship separate ;
> Gold does civil wars create.
> A curse, all curses else above,
> On him who used it first in love."

Golden cups may carry deadly draughts.

> Riches, fame, honour, may be ruinous temptations. Eloquence, architecture, pomp, music, and so forth, are the golden cup in which false doctrine is proffered to the unwary.—Rev. xvii. 4.

Golden dreams cannot fill an empty purse.

Gone is gone, for ever gone,
No Jew will lend a groat thereon.

> Once spent there is no calling money back into the purse, and there is no use in saying, " I used to be worth my hundreds."

Good articles sell themselves.

> " Good wine needs no bush " ; and yet who is to know where they sell wine, if there is no sign over the door? Suppose it is true that " the sign is in the cellar," who is to see it when walking the street ? And who is to know where goods can be bought, if there is no advertisement? Yet it is true that " Good stuffs need no puffs " ; and " the best advertisement for the shop must be kept inside "—the quality of the merchandise must attract purchasers.

Good bees never turn into drones.

> Such a miracle of natural history has never been reported ; there is a final perseverance of workers and of saints.

Good books enrich; bad books bewitch.

> Yet there is a third class which simply weary the reader. Of such books one wrote :—
>
> > If there should be another flood,
> > For refuge hither fly ;
> > Though all the world should be submerged,
> > This book will still be dry.

Good cakes and bad customs ought to be broken.

The older the cakes or the customs, the more need that they be at once broken. A courageous man will never sin because others do, but will instantly bear his practical protest.

Good comes to better, and bad to worse.

There is a law of development in character which runs on this wise: but bad does not come to good except by conversion.

Good fences make good neighbours.

Experience has proved that all rights must be respected between friends as well as foes. *Meum* and *tuum* must be rigidly distinguished among the dearest relatives. A clear separation of properties, and a keeping out of strays, are both very needful for harmony. Even a wandering hen may scratch up a quarrel, and a hog may uproot an old friendship.

Good health is above wealth.

Sir Richard Baker says :
To gather riches do not hazard health ;
For, truth to say, health is the wealth of wealth.

Good husbands like the Fireside Club best.

Some philanthropists advocate clubs for working-men ; but it is to be feared that they disturb the home, and keep away the husband who should be the band of the house.

Good is good, but better beats it.

It is for us to endeavour to reach the highest degree of comparison. "Not as though I had already attained."—Phil. iii. 12.

Good leading deserves good following.

With such a Leader as Christians have, what manner of people ought they to be?

Good men take good advice.

Good milk, good water; but the mixture is not good milk.

Londoners have abundant opportunity of proving the truth of this sentence. Our skies are not often blue; but we too often see "sky blue."

Good nature and good sense must ever join:
To err is human, to forgive divine.

Good pastures make fat sheep.

A ministry rich in gracious doctrine will produce useful and holy Christians.

Good people live wide apart.

Yet not so wide apart as they think. There are thousands of reserved ones who have not bowed the knee to Baal.

Good professors can make good scholars,
Good mothers only can make good men.

Sydney Smith said, "An ounce of mother is worth a pound of clergy." The future of society is in the hands of mothers.

Good sees good, and foul sees foul.

This accounts for the various reports which men give concerning the moral condition of a neighbourhood. Each man notices that which is after his own mind. If a vulture should fly over a region it would spy out carcases, where a dove would note clean corn.

Good sermons need not be long, and bad ones ought not to be.

Yet, when sermons are very good, the length is not noticed; and bad sermons are always too long, however short they may be.

Good stuff is often twisted into queer shapes.

The truth can be distorted. Excellent people are sometimes ugly.

Good tales marred in the telling,
Like peas lost in the shelling.

Good temper oils the wheels of life,

But bad temper puts grit into them. Some men are like pickles, a little of them at a time is quite enough ; others are like saccharin, a dust of them sweetens the cup of life.

Good things are often hard.

Of course. A thing that can be produced without labour must necessarily be of small value. In this evil world virtue and holiness can never be easy things.

Good ware makes a good market.

Few seem to believe this, for they palm off all manner of trumpery ; but, in the end, when it is well known, the really good article will win its place.

Good wine ruins the purse, and bad wine ruins the
stomach.

> It is marvellous what connoisseurs spend on choice wines. It is
> still more marvellous that men suck in, as wine, the vilest mixtures
> that can be concocted.

Good wives if they were sold,
Were well worth crowns of gold.

> But nobody wishes to sell them ; and nobody could buy them if
> he wished to do so.

Good wives, like echo, should be true,
And speak but when they're spoken to ;
Yet *not* like echo, so absurd,
To have for ever the last word !

> This "last word" business is a miserable one. It would seem
> the best for both husband and wife to leave off angry words at once,
> and so both hasten to have the last word. As for the wife's being
> quite so humble as to speak only when she is spoken to, the notion is
> a relic of savage life, and finds no echo in a Christian man's head.
> Among true Christians the wife is the equal of her husband, and is
> had in honour by him. The wife is not the head, but she is the
> crown, and that is higher still.

Good words cost little, but are worth much.

Good words without deeds are rushes and reeds.

Good work ought to get good wages :
Good wages ought to get good work.

> If masters would accept the first line, and workmen the second
> line, we should be all upon a good line of things. Too often the
> master cuts down the wage, and the man cuts down his work, and
> not only do both sides suffer, but the public suffer also.

" Good-fellow " is a costly name.

> To keep up its repute many a foolish person has made of himself
> a poor fellow, and at last a sad fellow, and a bad fellow.

Goods are not good unless we do good with them.

> " To have, and not to use the same,
> Is not our glory, but our shame."

Goose and gander are very much alike.

> What is true of woman is true of man, for bad or good.

Gospel truth must *re*form us, as well as *in*form us.

> Religion is practical, if true: it is a light which removes the darkness of sin, as well as the darkness of ignorance.

Gossiping and lying are brother and sister.

> Alas, for the misery which is caused by a long tongue! The quantity of the gossip could not be kept up if it were restricted to truth, and so evil inventions are added thereto. These at first are a sort of spice and flavouring, but in time they become the principal ingredient. A modern essayist defines gossip as "the putting of two and two together, and making five of them." Say *fifty*, and you are nearer the mark.

Gossips and frogs drink and croak.

> Certainly it is so with the gossips. Is it tea they drink? Their gossip is tedious. Do they take spirits? There is an evil spirit in them.

Gossips speak ill of all till all speak ill of them.

Grace will last when gold is past.

Graciousness is better than greatness.

Grantham gruel: nine grits in a gallon of water.

> Why Grantham is mentioned we know not, except it be that it begins with the letter G. The gruel is nearly as poor as a modern sermon, one globule of gospel in an ocean of words.

Grape-juice kills more than grape-shot.

> Is it grape-juice? Perhaps Cette and Hamburg can tell us. Much wine comes from places where grapes do not grow. Whether or no, we feel sure that the bottle kills more than the battle.

Grass, grow while you may!
Alas! how soon you'll turn to hay.

> Life is short, death is sure. Let us live while we live.

Graves are the same, bedeck them how you may.

The grave is the common bed of rich and poor; and so long as we moulder back to dust, it matters little how we are buried. Yet some distinction is aimed at even among ashes and worms. Hence the complaint upon the tomb at the church door :—

> " Here I lie beside the door,
> Here I lie because I'm poor,
> Further in the more they pay,
> Here I lie as warm as they."

Great bargains are great thieves.

It usually turns out so. The cheap thing is soon worn out, or there is some concealed flaw which makes it practically useless.

Great boast, little roast.

> The more of the mouth, the less of the meat
> The bigger the brag, the poorer the feat.

It is so almost always; the smallest boy beats the biggest drum.

Great bodies move slowly.

It must be so. Hence the difficulty of moving a corporation, a parliament, or a committee.

Great cry and little wool, as the man said when he sheared the hog.

Where there is wool there is no cry, for " the sheep before her shearers is dumb." Where there's nothing but bristles, the cry is enough to wake the whole parish, and the church too.

Great greediness to reap, helps not the money heap.

In his haste the covetous man makes ducks and drakes of his money. He is apt to try some shady scheme, and his investment shades off into nothing.

Great oaks were once little acorns.

Despise not the day of small things. Despair not because your strength is little. Who knows what you may be or do?

Great peace is better than a great purse.

Those who have had experience of both of these can certify to the truth of the proverb. Money breeds care, but peace is a jewel.

Great promisers are bad paymasters.

> This is frequently and notably the case.

Great quarrels have small beginnings.

> Oh, that they could be crushed in the egg ! By a little word, and a slight concession, years of hate would be avoided.

Great scholars are not always wise men.

> They are sometimes very foolish. Indeed, to make a very special fool the best raw material is a man of unusual education.

Great scholars may be great sinners.

> Learning does not necessarily better men morally. Satan knows more than any of us, and yet he is not improved by all he knows. An educated villain has all the more tools at command with which to do evil.

Great show and spread, no beef, and little bread.

> Like the Ḥidalgo's dinner : very little meat, and a great deal of table-cloth. How often is this the case with mental and spiritual feasts !

Great thieves wear gold chains, while little thieves have iron ones.

> It would be very shocking to steal a loaf, but to set up a sham company, and net ten thousand pounds by other peoples' folly, is quite respectable.
>
> > " A little stealing is a dangerous part,
> > But stealing largely is a noble art :
> > 'Tis mean to rob a hen-roost or a hen,
> > But stealing thousands makes us gentlemen."

Great weights may hang on small wires.

> On a word or even a look the history of a nation has depended. On a single act a man's whole life may turn.

Greed gathers itself poor, and generosity gives itself rich.

> Those who watch men must have seen that this is frequently true. I have noticed remarkable instances of it.—C. H. S.

Greed wants the first cut, and all the rest of the joint.

In the Hindoo story a guest is asked whether he would take biscuits, or a cold breakfast; he replied that he would take biscuits, and a cold breakfast first, and a hot breakfast afterwards. Thus would some men have all they can get, and a great deal they will never get.

Greedy carvers lay all the meat on their own plates.

Have you noticed how they save up the green fat of the turtle, and carve the breast of the fowl for themselves?

Greedy grabbers grudge gleaners.

It is a miserable policy which shuts out the poor from the stubbles, and sends the horse-rake again and again to get in every single ear. Let the poor have their portion; they get little enough. A correspondent of *The Guardian* writes :—"The remarkable progress of engineering skill in agriculture has well-nigh abolished sweet Ruth and her friends. The modern reaping-machine and self-raking reaper leave behind them no ears of corn of appreciable value to be picked up by industrious mothers and their children."

Green are the hills that are far away,
But greener the garden where I stay.

There's no place like home.

Grey and green make a bad marriage mixture.

If the husband is greatly older than the wife he cannot live to bring up the children, and he will probably leave his wife a widow. It is not seemly, and hardly natural, to see sixty wedding twenty.

Grey hairs are death's heralds.

Are they not also the snows of past winters, and the silver of crowns of glory?

Grief grows by repression; joy by expression.

Silence causes pent-up griefs to swell; it is a great solace to tell your sorrow.

> Sorrow shared is half a trouble,
> Joy that's shared is joy made double.

Grind no man's name; seek other grist.

Yet some are never so pleased as when they have a gracious man between their millstones, and are reducing his character to dust.

Grow angry slowly; there's plenty of time.

If you must let anger rise sooner or later, prefer later, and the later the better. In this matter better never than late.

Growling will not make the kettle boil.

Grumbling makes the loaf no larger.

Grunting won't buy me new shoes.

These three sayings, and many more, show the uselessness of murmuring; yet we go on with this worthless business, and almost regard it as an Englishman's privilege to complain. Well may we call the world "a howling wilderness," if we will persist in howling!

Guilt on the conscience puts grief on the countenance.

Where it is real and deep, it is a hard matter to conceal conviction of sin. This heaviness of the heart makes a man stoop.

Guilty persons are always suspicious.

They measure others by themselves, and expect others to treat them as they have treated their fellows. One reason for "setting a thief to catch a thief" is because the thief is quick to suspect.

Gut no fish till you get them.

A rough form of the same advice contained in the warning, "Do not count your chickens before they are hatched."

Sayings of a more Spiritual Sort.

Give me the Christian that is better seen than heard.

God breaks the cistern to bring us to the fountain.

> Our creature comforts fail us, and then we go to the Creator himself. Gainful are the losses which bring us nearer to God.

God can strike straight strokes with crooked sticks.

> He can work out a holy purpose by overruling the actions of the vilest of men.

God chose his people for his love, and he loves them for his choice.

God conceals his purposes, that we may live on his promises.

> It is not for us to pry into his decrees, or seek to know the future; the promise should be sufficient to stay the heart as to the Lord's ways.

God fills the empty, and empties the full.

> See the Virgin's Song.—Luke i. 53.

God furrows the heart, and then sows it with grace.

> Conviction prepares the soul to receive gospel truth.

God gives much grace, that he may give more grace.

God gives to thee his firm decree,
That as thy days, thy strength shall be.

God grants grace, and we should give gratitude.

> "Many favours which God giveth us ravel out for want of hemming, through our unthankfulness."—*Fuller.*

God hath promised to keep his people, and he will keep his promise.

God is a sun that never sets.

God is both the rewarder and the reward of his people.

God is where he was.

> He has not changed in place or power. Go to him by prayer and he will hear your requests.

God looks most, where man looks least—at the heart.

God loves his people when he strikes them as well as when he strokes them.

God loves us, not for what we are, but for what he can make us.

God never yet forsook in need
The soul that trusted him indeed.

God not only gives his people promises to believe, but gives them to believe his promises.

God may as soon cease to be God as cease to be good.

> Let this be a settled matter of faith with us, for it is even so.

God may cast thee down, but he will not cast thee off.

God provides a full Christ for empty sinners.

God sees Christ in his people, and his people in Christ.

God sees grace where we see none.

> We judge hastily, but He knows the circumstances, and the inward thoughts of the feeble in grace.

God sends us food by our own hands.

> It is God's plan to employ us to provide food for his children, and for ourselves among the rest.

God waits to be gracious, and the gracious wait on God.

God, who feeds his ravens, will feed his doves.

> Or, as *Matthew Henry* puts it, "He that feeds his birds will not starve his babes."

God will be only theirs who are truly his.

God wills changes, but changes not his will.

God works *with* and *without* means. *With*, that man should not be *indolent;* and *without*, that he should not be *self-confident.*

God's best comforts are reserved for our worst times.

One who was greatly afflicted, but graciously comforted, bore this testimony :—

> "The love of Jesus, what it is,
> None but his *sufferers* know."

God's chariots of fire conquer men's chariots of iron.

He has forces of a spiritual order which prevail over the most stubborn wills and the strongest arms

God's children are made to smart when they yield to sin.

> "But woe to the man that sins without pain ;
> He feels no correction, and sinneth again."

God's crumbs are better than the world's loaves.

God's ear lies close to the believer's lip.

God's friends should be one another's friends.

Christians should know, love, and help one another.

God's gentleness makes his saints great and grateful.

David said, "Thy gentleness hath made me great."—Ps. xviii. 35.

God's giving deserves our thanksgiving.

God's patience is lasting, but not everlasting.

God's rest-day is our best day.

God's thoughts of love should move us to deeds of love.

God's Word is the soul's medicine.

God's worst is better than the devil's best.

The reproach of Christ is greater riches than all the treasures of Egypt.—Heb. xi. 26.

Gospel commandings are gracious enablings.

John Berridge wrote :—

> Run, John, and work, the law commands,
> Yet finds me neither feet nor hands:
> But sweeter news the gospel brings,
> It bids me fly, and lends me wings.

Grace makes no man proud.

> He that is proud of the grace he thinks he possesses must therefore be a mere pretender.

Grace not only makes a man more a man, but it also makes him more than a man.

Great sorrows are nothing compared with great sins.

> Holy men would prefer life-long sickness to wilful sin. He was a wise man who prayed that he might sooner die than deny his Lord.

Greatest evils oft begin
In some unsuspected sin.

Greatness is the fairest object to the eye of the world; goodness, to the eye of heaven.

Groanings unutterable lead to joys unspeakable.

> "These are they that came out of great tribulation."— Rev. vii. 14.

Guard well thy thoughts; for thoughts are heard in heaven.

ABIT with him has all the test of truth ;
"It must be right—I've done it from my youth."

This stands for argument with many. What they
have done they will do ; as if continuance in evil
produced an excuse for it, whereas it aggravates the
wrong exceedingly. Is a Thug justified in murder because he
has always done so ?

Habits are soon assumed ; but when we strive
To strip them off, 'tis being flayed alive.

At first, a bad habit is a spider's web, then a net of thread, next
a bond of rope, and soon a fetter of steel. Cease from an evil habit
before it holds you like an octopus.

Hair by hair old heads grow bare.

Decline is gradual, and therefore sometimes it is unnoticed. It
may be thus with us spiritually : "Grey hairs are here and there
upon him, yet he knoweth not."—Hosea vii. 9.

Half an acre is better than no land.

Especially half an acre in the City of London.

Half an hour's hanging is quite long enough.

One could be content with much less than that.

Half doing is many a man's undoing.

Those fellows who never really finish anything are regarded as
being only half-baked themselves, and no man cares to hire them.

Half-heart is no heart.

To be half inclined is to be disinclined ; to be half persuaded is to
be unpersuaded ; to be half-hearted in a matter is to have no heart
at all for it.

Half the world's mischief, folly, and woe,
Comes from a " Yes," which ought to be " No."

One of the first words a young man should learn to say is "No."
It ought to be as easy to say "No" to a man as to say "Boo" to a
goose, but it is not ; and so the young fellow is led by the nose,
and to ruin he goes.

Handle your tools without mittens.

Dainty gentility spoils people for labour. Preachers in gloves remind us of the saying, " Cats in gloves catch no mice."

Hands are many, but heads are few.

The thinkers are still in the minority. Plenty of bellows, but where are the brains? Pimples everywhere, but few capacious sense-boxes.

Handsome apples are sometimes sour.

Pretty women may have very bad tempers.

Handsome is that handsome does.

"Now, my pretty gentleman!" as the gipsy says, mind you behave handsomely.

Happy is he that is happy in his children.

John wrote, " I have no greater joy than to hear that my children walk in truth." It is a choice mercy, a crowning mercy.

Hard of feeling is worse than hard of hearing.

We can buy the deaf man a horn, but the unfeeling man has a horny heart already. None are so deaf as those who refuse to hear in the heart. Hard rocks need hard hammers. Hence the heavy blows which God deals with his law and with afflictions, so as to break stubborn hearts.

Hard with hard builds no houses; soft binds hard.

Mortar is wanted as well as stone, and love must be mixed with our firmness. Two strong-minded persons will have need of a great deal of love to keep them together.

Hard words often come from soft heads.

Very generally this is true; and yet certain very hard-headed men can speak bullets.

Hard work wins soft rest: sweat earns sweet.

He that has earned rest shall have it: but he who never works does not know what rest means.

No restful age shall come to me
Unless in youth I've industry.

Hares and cares start up unawares.

But if the cares run away as fast as the hares we need not mind them.

Hares are not caught with drums.

It remains to be seen whether men will be won to religion by brass bands. In other matters, timid people are rather repelled than won over by loud argument.

Harm watch, harm catch.

Look for evil, and it comes; and the same with good.

Harry Heartless will make a bad husband.

Better let him remain a bachelor.

Hast thou a soft heart? It is of God's breaking.
Hast thou a sweet wife? She is of God's making.

Haste trips up its own heels.

Hasty climbers have sudden falls.

"Up like a rocket, and down like a stick," is often verified. It is a good thing for a man to endure difficulty and opposition when rising in life, for such an experience gives permanence to character.

Hasty questions should have slow answers.

Perhaps no reply at all would be better. Two hasty persons going at it, hammer and tongs, make great mirth for the devil.

Hat in hand goes through the land.

Politeness, courtesy, obligingness clear many a man's path.

Haughty looks are naughty looks.

Have a deaf ear for hasty words.

It will serve your turn better than quick hearing, for that might provoke you. Let rash and foolish language go in at one ear and out at the other, and let nothing wrong remain on the memory.

Have a hand to give, and a heart to forgive.

Have a mind before you speak your mind.

Some blunder out whatever comes first, and then they feel bound to stick to it through thick and thin. If they only thought wisely at the first, they might save themselves and others a world of trouble.

Have an open ear and a closed mouth.

> Hear, see, and say nothing, and live in peace.

Have four and spend five ;
Be poor and never thrive.

Have more than thou showest,
Speak less than thou knowest,
Spend less than thou owest.

Have no faith in a man who has no faith.

> If he does not believe in God, do not believe in *him*.

Have not a mouth for every matter.

> Leave things alone which are no business of yours, and which you do not understand.

Have not thou such friends abroad
Thou couldst not welcome to thy board.

> If a man ought not to be introduced to your wife and daughters, he is not likely to be of much benefit to you or your reputation.

Have not thy cloak to make when it begins to rain.

Have peace with men, but war with sin.

> A good distinction ; hate the sin, but love the sinner.

Have the potatoes and bacon done,
And nice white cloth as the clock strikes one.

> The meals nicely cooked keep the husband in humour, and prevent his seeking the public-house and its temptations.

Have thy distaff ready, and God will send thee flax.

> Be prepared to do your work, and work will come sooner or later. Don't so much look for a position as for fitness to fill it.

Have you a good master ?
Stick to him the faster.

> Don't impose on his good nature ; but the more kind he is, the more be you worthy of such kindness. Alas ! the British workman is too much like the man in the story, who said, " My master is so good, that I cannot do too much for him ; and I don't mean to try."

He begins to grow bad who thinks himself good.

> Pride is growing up in his heart; and what is worse than that?

He boiled four eggs for himself, and gave the poor the broth.

> It is wonderful what worthless rubbish some people will give away. The man in our proverb is like that other benefactor in the epigram—
>
> > "Ancho is charitable, all must own,
> > He steals a ham, and gives the poor the bone."

He cannot speak well who cannot hold his tongue.

> He lacks power over himself; and this is fatal to the success of an orator. No man can be called a good driver, who cannot hold his horse in when the time comes.

He deserves no sweets who will taste no sours.

> We must take things as they come. He ought not to eat who must needs have all the fat, or all the lean. In no country can a man have all fine weather. In no form of life will all things happen to our mind.

He does much who does a little well.

He doeth much who loveth much.

> Love to God is the mainspring of activity, and sets a man doing much. Even when the good work is apparently little, the abundance of love which is in it makes it much in the sight of God.

" He doeth well who doeth good
To those of his own brotherhood;
He doeth better who doth bless
The stranger in his wretchedness:
Yet best, yea, best of all, doth he
Who helps a fallen enemy ! "

He drinketh wine; his nose will shine.

He enjoys much who is thankful for a little.

He fawned on me, and then bit my heel.

> It is the nature of curs to curry favour with you, and then curse you. Curs occur to most men.

He fishes on who catches one.

The smallest success keeps him at his sport. We have seen anglers who have gone on day after day, though they caught nothing. One of them said he had been by the water three days, and had only one bite. To the remark, "How can you keep on?" he answered, "You get to like it, and feel as if you must keep on even when you get nothing." It would be well if fishers of men had always the same constraining love for their work.

He has a nose of noses,
And sniffs more things than roses.

Some are great discerners of spirits, and live by finding out what nobody else suspected. They have no nose for virtue, lavender, and other sweet things; but at Stinker's Reach they feel at home, for there they are able to enjoy the sensation of shouting—"Horrible! Abominable! Enough to poison a fox!" Never at ease till they cannot bear it any longer; their superior nose of discernment is the organ of misery to them.

He has bad food who feeds on others' faults.

Yet to some the faults of others are a sweetmeat. A dish of scandal is very savoury to gossips. Only a foul bird will feast on carrion; but such foul birds go in flocks.

He has found a mare's nest, and is laughing at the eggs.

Spoken of one who has found something very ludicrous where he expected a great discovery. The case often occurs.

He has most who wants least.

He has much to do who would please everybody.

Yes: he has more to do than he will ever accomplish. Who can serve a hundred masters?

"Suit every one? You never will!
    That's settled any minute;
The task is far beyond your skill,
    So never you begin it.

Whate'er the world says, *Never mind!*
    Go on, your duty doing;
On every side there's some fresh kind
    Of gossip ever brewing."

He has not a penny, but yet he boasts his pedigree.

He talks about Lord Donomore and Lady All-spent. If his gentility were put up to auction, it would not bring him in a pennyworth of cabbages. Yet see how high he holds his head. He is a horse of pedigree with three game legs, and broken wind.

He has not five farthings, but he gives himself fifty airs.

The poorer the prouder. There is no repressing "His Emptiness."
He spreads himself over all things and questions; and yet he
cannot manage a shop where the stock-in trade is a herring and
a half.

He hath little joy of life
Who hath found a scolding wife.

He hath peace who holds his peace.

He is a bad gardener who roots up the plants.

He is a bad minister who drives away the congregation, scatters
his church, alienates his friends, and destroys all the useful societies.

He is a fool who fools other people.

Nothing is more ridiculous than the hoax or practical joke; and
yet it passes for wit among those who are short of wit.

He is a good speaker who makes his hearers good.

Whatever his style may be, he has spoken well if he has led his
hearers to the Lord Jesus, who makes all good who come to him.

He is a good waggoner who can turn in a little space

To manage comfortably and economically with a very small
income is the height of wisdom. We know women who can do
more on £100 a year, than others will with three times the amount.

He is a great coward who is afraid to do good.

He is a great thief who would steal the ten commandments.

Much more he that would steal from us the whole Bible!

He is a man who acts like a man.

He is a poor fiddler who has only one tune.

Monotony is wearisome: but some speakers, preachers, and talkers
harp for ever on one string. There are more subjects in the world
than one. "Always partridge," as the French say, is very wearisome: what would "always *frog*" be? Ding, dong; ding, dong,
and that without end, is a thing of horror, and a woe for ever.

He is a poor smith who cannot bear smoke.

In all pursuits there are inconveniences which we must put up
with; and it is so in every form of holy service.

He is a stupid who loses patience with a stupid.

"Ye suffer fools gladly, seeing ye yourselves are wise."—2 Cor. xi. 12. We find out how foolish we are when a great stupid brushes our fur the wrong way, and raises our dander.

He is a weak friend who cannot bear with his friend's weakness.

He is best who has done best.

With few exceptions this is the rule. "By their fruits shall ye know them."—Matt. vii. 20.

He is blind who thinks he sees everything.

The observant man recognizes many mysteries into which he cannot pretend to see, and he remembers that the world is too wide for the eye of any one man. But modern sophists are cock-sure of everything, especially if it contradicts the Bible.

He is free who dares to be
In the right with two or three.

This liberty has to be paid for; but there is a sweetness in it which those only know who have tasted it.

He is kind to himself who is kind to his wife.

Is she not bone of your bone? Does not your happiness inter-weave itself with hers?

He is no one's friend who is his own enemy

He is not the best carpenter who makes the most chips.

But the reverse. He who does his work in a masterly manner is usually very neat and clean in it. The proverb, however, means that the best workers make no fuss, and create no disorder.

He is right sure who is surely right.

He is very absent-minded who searches for the ass on which he is riding.

He must be brother to that other Celestial, who cried out, "Here's my bundle, here's my umbrella; but where am I?"

He is very blind who cannot see the sun.

How blind must he be who cannot see the God who made the sun!
He that is blind will nothing see,
What light soe'er about him be.

He is wise who follows the wise.

He is wise who knows his own business.

He may not be a university man, but he knows enough to get through the universe.

He knows the water best who has waded through

There is nothing like personal experience.

He laughs at scars who never felt a wound.

The power to sympathize can only come by personal suffering.

He laughs best who laughs last.

Because he will be surest of his laugh, and will probably laugh at those who laughed at him. If he can laugh when the whole thing is ended, he has the best cause for his merriment.

He likes mutton too well who eats the wool.

We are not bound to follow a man, faults and all.

He lives longest who is awake most hours.

That is to say, if he is not kept awake by sickness, or care, or excessive labour ; for these may shorten life though they add to the waking hours. Doubtless early rising is a great addition to our opportunities for work.

He liveth long who liveth well.

Indeed the way to measure life is not by its years, but by its deeds.

He looks as if butter would not melt in his mouth.

This is the sort of man whom you must never trust.

He loses indeed who loses at last.

He loses least in a quarrel who has had least to say in it.

He may well swim who has his head held up.

Just so ! We are able to swim the seas of temptation only because grace keeps us from sinking.

He may wisely run who finds he cannot stand his ground.

He means to buy, for he finds fault with the goods.

"It is naught, it is naught, saith the buyer." Just because he means to be a buyer.

He must be a wise man himself who can distinguish one.

So said *Diogenes*, and we will not contradict him.

He pares his apple that would cleanly feed.

Well said, *Mr. Herbert.* Tell the story, if worth telling, but not with the oath or the smut: that can be left out with great advantage.

He preaches well who lives well.

Even if he does not open his mouth his example is a sermon.

He promiseth to turn your iron into gold, but he will turn your gold into iron.

True of the gentleman who presents you with a prospectus of a Company which is to pay a quite impossible dividend. No doubt the concern will pay those who get it up.

He put his finger in the pie, and burned his nail off.

He rides well who never stumbles.

Where is that man? Where is his horse?

He runs far who never turns.

Unless he breaks his neck. He will run too far, if his way be not the right one.

He shuts his eyes, and thinks none see.

He talks much who has least to say.

"How would you wish your hair to be cut?" asked the barber one day of Archelaus, King of Macedon, and the King made answer, "Silently." Alas! this is too rare a method anywhere, in anything.

It was said of one man,

> He argued with the greatest zest,
>   'Twas very hard to put him out;
> And strange to say, he talked the best
>   Of what he knew the least about.

He that a watch would wear, just this must do,
Pocket his watch, and watch his pocket too.

> We have heard of one who covered his watch with fish-hooks; but the worst of it was that he only remembered what he had done when he put his own fingers into his watch-pocket.

He that asks too much is likely to get nothing.

He that burns most, shines most.

> There must be a self-consumption to produce light. John was a burning and a shining light, and the burning is not to be separated from the shining.

He that by the plough would thrive,
Himself must either hold or drive.

> A living can be made by one who works himself, even where a gentleman farmer is a heavy loser. So we have heard. At any rate, if the farmer cannot live who drives the plough, how can he live who drives a fast-trotting mare?

He that can be won with a feather will be lost with a
straw.

> Easily persuaded persons are no great catch, for no reliance can be placed upon them: they are soon led to the opposite side.

He that cuts himself wilfully deserves no salve.

He that deals in dirt will not keep clean hands.

He that delights to plant and set
Puts coming ages in his debt.

> This, after all, is only justice; for we also eat of many trees which our fathers planted.

He that deserves nothing should be content with anything.

He that doth jest must take a jest;
Or else to let alone were best.

He that dwells in a city where there is a synagogue, and
comes not to prayer there, is the person that
deserves the name of a bad neighbour.

> This is a saying of the Jews. But how many bad neighbours do we live among, who are seldom seen in the public assemblies of the saints from year to year!

He that eats least will live to eat most.

Reform is as much needed in eating as in drinking. We want a Moderate Eating Society. *Basil Montague* tells us :—" In one of the annuals there is the following anecdote : A traveller, who had been much distressed by a terrible nightmare, thus accounted for it : 'If you will believe me, sir, my supper had been nothing particular ; it was but one blood-pudding, a trifle of pickled salmon, a beefsteak and onions, and some Derbyshire toasted cheese, which I relished exceedingly ; and not one drop did I drink but a jug of egg-flip. It must have been all owing to the bread ! ' "

He that fears pricking must not be picking roses.

Squeamishness and extreme delicacy unfit people for ordinary life. Roses will have thorns, and fingers will get pricked, unless we all go to the Fool's Paradise, where all is pap and sugar.

He that gets money before he gets wit
Will be but a short time master of it.

Certain unscrupulous folks who have no cash, but plenty of spare brains, will devise a pretty scheme for relieving simpletons of their surplus, and before they are aware of it they will be plundered. These clever people are not called thieves, but they are conveyancers, and they execute a transfer of property in an ingenious manner. Mr. Shortwit takes shares in their company *limited*, and his gains are more limited still.

He that gives his heart will give his money.

Yet some who profess great love to the cause are very slow in their gifts. One said, "If you want to reach my purse, you must touch my heart." "That's true," said a discerning friend, "for that is where his purse lies."

He that has nothing is frightened at nothing.

> The man that is poor may be void of all care,
> If there's nothing to hope, there's nothing to fear :
> Whether stocks rise or fall, or whate'er be the news,
> He is sure not to win, and has nothing to lose.

He that has the worst cause makes the most noise.

He that hath a big nose thinks that all are looking at it.

He that hath a trade hath an estate.

He that hath but one eye should take great care of it.

He that hath guineas shall soon have cousins.

There is a great disposition to claim relationship with a wealthy man, for the honour and glory of it, if not with an indistinct hope that a trifle may in some way trickle down to the distant relative.

He that hath it, and will not keep it,
He that wants it, and will not seek it,
He that drinks, and is not dry,
Shall want money as well as I.

He that hath love in his heart hath spurs on his heels.

" 'Tis love that makes our willing feet
In swift obedience move."

He that hath much corn may bear with a few thistles.

We may put up with trifling trials considering our many mercies.

He that hath rent his trousers had better sit still.

A person whose character will not bear examination should be quiet, and not put himself forward.

He that hath tin shall soon have kin.

Unless he is very distant to them he will be eaten up by the crowds who are distantly related.

He that hunts another has no rest himself.

Thus malice and revenge are a man's own loss. Ill-will chews its own heart, and heats its own blood.

He that is bored of works will soon try thefts.

He must have a living, and if he does not care to work for it, he will get it by some other means, specially by ill means

He that is down needs fear no fall,
He that is low no pride ;
He that is humble, ever shall
Have God to be his guide.

This is a verse by Honest John ; and if the poetry be not brilliant, the expression is pastoral and the sense most truthful. The valley of Humiliation is a lovely place.

He that is down, the world cries, "Down with him!"

It is a cruel world, and treats men as beasts are said to treat each other, namely kill the weaker sort.

He that is full of himself is very empty.

He that is in love with himself needs fear no rival.

He may have himself all to himself : no one will ever think more of Number One than he does.

He that is not humble shall be humbled.

Thomas Adams, speaking of pride, says, "It thrust proud Nebuchadnezzar out of men's society, proud Saul out of his kingdom, proud Haman out of Court, proud Adam out of Paradise, proud Lucifer out of heaven."

He that is out at sea must either sail or sink.

Now that you are in this world, and in the midst of its cares, you must either do your best, and struggle manfully, or you will sink for certain.   Oh for a good pilot on board !

He that is out of will, will soon be out of work.

He will find nothing to do, because he has no will to do it. The Creoles say, "Lazy folks ask for work with their lips, but their hearts pray God that they may not find it."

He that is religious by proxy will be lost in person.

There is no truth in religious sponsorship : there can be none.   All forms of representative piety are empty, and vain, and void.

"By proxy I pray, and by proxy I vote,"
Said a graceless peer to a churchman of note,
Who answered, " My lord, then I'll venture to say,
You'll to heaven ascend in a similar way."

He that is slow in seeking is afraid of finding.

He that is thy friend indeed,
He will help thee in thy need.

He that is not thy friend will help himself when he sees thee in difficulties.   When thine estate is breaking he will pick up the pieces.   The crow is a great friend to the sheep, and picks out his eyes when he finds him dead.

He that knows not, and knows not that he knows not, is stupid.   Shun him.

He that knows not, and knows that he knows not, is good.   Teach him.

He that knows, and knows not that he knows, is asleep. Arouse him.

He that knows, and knows that he knows, is wise.   Follow him.

> These are four Arabian proverbs worth preserving, and practising.

He that leaves certainty for chance,
When fools pipe, he may dance.

He that lives with cripples learns to limp.

> Such is the force of example.

He that marries for money sells himself.

> Put into rhyme we have the same sense—
>
> > He who for money takes a wife
> > Has made himself a slave for life.

He that meddles with all things may go and shoe the goslings.

> He may do any silly thing he likes.

He that on earthly things doth trust,
Dependeth upon smoke and dust.

He that spendeth much,
  And getteth nought;
He that oweth much,
  And hath nought;
He that looketh in his purse
  And findeth nought,
He may be sorry,
  And say nought.

> He has come in his estate very near to nothing, which Patrick describes as " a footless stocking without a leg," and Jonathan calls "the ashes of gunpowder." Some people rise from nothing, but this gentleman has gone down to nothing, and does not like the situation.   The more quiet he is, the better.

He that pours water hastily into a bottle spills more than goes in.

> So he who tries to teach a child too much at once loses most of his pains. You cannot put a quartern loaf into a child's head; you must break it up, and give him the crumb in warm milk.

He that sponges upon a friend wipes out his love.

> Friendship stands a good deal, but when at last it discovers that it is made a beast of burden to carry a lazy lubber it throws off the office in disgust.

He that stumbles, but does not fall,
He mends his pace, and that is all.

> Many a traveller to heaven has grown more cautious and earnest by observing that his steps had well-nigh slipped.

He that sweareth
   Till no man trust him;
He that lieth
   Till no man believe him;
He that borroweth
   Till no man will lend him,
Let him go where
   No man knoweth him.

> But Dr. Johnson says wisely, "Let him not go to the devil, for there he is known." It were better far that he should repent, and be made a new creature, and see what he can do in a new world.

He that takes the raven for a guide shall light upon carrion.

> If we surrender our minds to dirty men we shall soon be amid rottenness ourselves.

He that talketh much sinneth much.

He that thinks time long enough will find it short enough.

He that wants looking after is not worth looking after.

> We ought to be able to trust a servant who has come to years of discretion, and if we cannot, we have not yet been happy in our selection.

He that will not when he may,
When he will he shall have nay.

He that will not be ruled by the rudder will be wrecked on the rock.

Thousands are unhappy witnesses to this solemn truth. Without prudence and godliness to conduct them they have come to ruin.

He that will not work shall want.

He that works on wins honour, if he keeps honest.

It is said of a lawyer that he began his practice to get on, continued at it to get honour, and then left it to become honest. Rather hard! It reminds us of one who gave up the law, and built himself a villa, which he called "Dunrobin."

He that would be sure must never be surety.

He that would catch birds must not throw stones at them.

No unkindness or anger must be shown by those who would win their fellow-men to better things.

He that would have a loaf from his wheat must wait the grinding.

They say, "The king himself must wait while his beer is being drawn, and the queen cannot eat honey till the bees have made it." Reasonable patience must be exercised by all.

He that would have his secrets kept must keep his secrets.

When Charles II. was entreated to communicate something of a private nature, the subtle monarch said, "Can you keep a secret?" "Most faithfully," returned the nobleman. "So can I," was the laconic and severe answer of the king.

He that would thrive must rise at five.

No doubt this is quite correct; but some wag has improved upon it thus :—

"He who would thrive must rise at five;
Who would thrive more must rise at four;
He who would still more thriving be
Must leave his bed at turn of three;
And who the latter would outdo,
Will rouse him at the stroke of two;
And he who would not be outdone
Should always rise as soon as one;
But he who'd flourish best of all
Should never go to bed at all."

He that would keep a clean face should often look in the glass.

> He who would be holy should examine himself by the word of God, that he may know wherein he transgresses. "Commune with your own heart, and be still."—Ps. iv. 4.

He uses different levers, but he is always rolling his own log

> Always bent on his personal ends, he makes all things contribute towards that which he has in hand. This is laudable persistence, or sheer selfishness, as the case may be.

He who basely runs away
Will not fight another day.

> Of course he will not. There is no fight in him. In him prudence is the only form of valour ; and it runs into his feet.

He who beats a donkey is worse than a donkey.

> Cruelty to animals is utterly senseless.

He who begins many things finishes few.

He who blabs about others will blab about me.

> Those who fetch will carry. He who finds fault with my neighbours to me will in turn find fault with me to my neighbours.

He who blows in the dust will hurt his own eyes.

> Get prying into dirty matters, and you will cause yourself trouble. Meddle with deep mysteries, and you will hurt the eye of your understanding.

He who boils his pot at the fire should bring a stick to it.

> If we share the benefit we should contribute to the expense.

He who builds by the roadside will have many surveyors.

> Everyone will favour him with an opinion ; and if he be so unwise as to take note of all that he hears, he will build a fool's castle, or nothing at all. Some of us have had quite enough advice to have ruined us ten times over if we had hearkened to it.

He who buys by pennyworths pays double price.

> Our poor thus put themselves to a great disadvantage. If they could but save a little and take a quantity, they could buy better.

He who buys bargains is often sold.

> Remember Hodge with the razors made to sell, and Moses with the green spectacles. Eagerness to get too much for little money is a sort of greed which deserves to be punished. People who are too sharp cut their own fingers.

He who buys fancies may have to sell necessaries.

He who buys hath need of four eyes.

> Unless he goes to a good shop, and pays a fair price. Bargaining certainly does need a man's eyes to be sharp as needles.

He who buys what he don't want will soon sell what he does want.

He who can conceal his poverty is almost rich.

> When its only the shoes that know of the stockings having holes in them, half of the worry caused by the dilapidated garments is gone. What some people suffer to hide their need! These are often the worthiest of people.

He who can dig ought not to beg.

> And if he will not dig for a living he ought to be allowed to try the medical virtues of a protracted fast. Able-bodied idlers are the pest of society.

> > "The wretch who works not for his daily bread
> > Sighs and complains, but ought not to be fed.
> > Think, when you see stout beggars on the stand,
> > 'The lazy are the locusts of the land.'"

He who cannot mind his own business is not to be trusted with mine.

He who cannot obey is not fit to command.

> The spirit of discipline is not in him.

He who cannot say "No"
Will soon be in woe.

> Above all things we advise young people to learn to say "No." It will save them from a thousand ills if they can clearly and distinctly pronounce that monosyllable.

He who cannot stand should not boast of his running.

> He who cannot do the less should not brag of doing the greater; for it is self-evident that he is not speaking the truth.

He who cannot swim should never dive.

Keep out of matters with which you are not practically acquainted. In business do not run risks to which you are not equal. In theology do not get into speculations which carry you away.

He who ceases to pray ceases to prosper.

That is to say, in the truest and highest sense.

He who considers all lets the wine-cup fall.

It is expensive, it is perilous, it sets a bad example; to take it is a mere self-indulgence, to abjure it may help a brother. It may let me fall if I do not let it fall.

He who courts in sport may be caught in earnest.

First he courts, and then he gets into court through an action for breach of promise. Or else he is caught in a marriage which he never intended, which turns out a life-long bondage.

He who dances on the brink may soon be dashed on the bottom.

Keep as far from danger as you can. The verge of temptation is perilous ground.

He who deals with the devil will make small profits.

He may be infinitely and eternally a loser: and even if he can escape this greatest ill, he will be robbed of his comfort, and his purity. Never sup with Satan, even if he says grace, or asks you to do it. Do not even exchange the time of day with this arch-enemy of souls.

He who depends on another dines ill and sups worse.

His patron's gifts decline as time passes, although he is never too well provided for.

He who does nothing is the man to find fault.

Out of imbeciles men make critics. They can only do the magpie's part, and pull things to pieces. For every other art men are prepared by education, but fault-finders are born fully equipped.

He who does me good teaches me to be good.

He who falls in the dirt, the longer he lies the dirtier he is.

Quick repentance comes none too soon. This is the mark of a child of God, that he may fall into the mire, but he will not lie there. The sheep slips, and is up again; the sow lies down and wallows.

He who fears to suffer suffers from fear.

Usually suffering more from the fear, than the evil itself would have brought upon him. *Emerson* gives a translation of an old French verse, which is much to the point :—

"Some of your griefs you have cured,
And the sharpest you still have survived;
But what torments of pain you endured
From evils that never arrived!"

He who feeds on charity eats cold victuals.

People get weary of him, and, after being known as a regular cadger, he is by no means sure of a warm welcome. Cold is the hand of charity, and this chills the victuals it hands out. Often that hand has been made cold by the frost of ingratitude.

He who fights and runs away,
May live to *run* another day.

We have had this before in rather a different shape. Certainly, running has this advantage over being killed, that there can be a repetition of it. But when one is killed, it is like the dog, who, when a brutal wretch cut off his tail, barked at him this challenge, "You can't do *that* again."

He who flattereth bespattereth.

Instead of being honoured by false praise we are likely to be disgraced by it. Judicious persons will think all the less of us because of the ill-judged praises of our silly friends. The world always takes a discount from friendly opinions, and sometimes this reduces a man below his fair value.

He who follows Christ for his bag is a Judas.

And of these creatures the apostolical succession has never failed. To make religion a stalking-horse for personal ambitions is to act like a true son of perdition.

He who gambles picks his own pocket.

And he is virtually guilty of picking other people's pockets, for he would do so if he could, and does do so when he can. Crime, suicide, murder, track the footsteps of gaming. Here indeed we have *rouge et noir*, red murder and black villainy.

He who goes a-borrowing goes a-sorrowing.

Except some brazen-faced creatures who borrow with great delight, because they never mean to pay.

He who goes to bed mellow, gets up a rotten fellow.

Oh those night-caps!

He who governs himself can govern others.

He who greases the wheels helps the horses.

Some little word of encouragement may help a work as much as a great effort.

He who has a goose can get a goose.

He has capital to work with, to sustain his credit. Moreover, geese and guineas like to go where there are some already.

He who has high spirits wears himself, and he who has low spirits wears others.

He who has least sense is least sensible of it.

He who has most pride has least sense.

He who has no appetite has no appreciation.

He quarrels with every diet, and is pleased with nothing. What a blessing it is to have food, and to be able to enjoy it! Here is a grace which may suit those who are in that happy case :—

> Some have meat and cannot eat,
> Some can eat and have no meat ;
> We have appetite and food,
> Bless the Giver of all good.

He who has no wife is only half a man.

Let him look out for his other half, and mind that she proves his better half.

He who hath no wife hath no house.

He is a sort of lodger in the universe till some one has pity upon him. "Housekeeping without a wife is a lantern without a light."

He who hath scalded himself once blows the next time.

He who hides truth is as bad as another who spreads falsehood.

Augustine has a sentence to that effect, and there is truth in it; but we doubt the equality of the guilt. Concealment of truth is a sort of negative lying, and tends to the same result as telling a falsehood.

He who holds the sack is as bad as he who fills it.

The receiver is always reckoned to be as bad as the thief.

He who hunts with cats will catch mice.

He will take nothing better than such small deer. When we work with mean men of small ability, what can we accomplish?

He who is above his business is beneath contempt.

Young lads are apt to look down on their trade as unfit for young gentlemen. This is despicable vanity, such as only fools would indulge in.

He who is always full does not feel for the hungry.

He who is always resting will soon be rusting.

He who is at the bottom will fall no lower.

There is some sort of comfort in this. When it is pitch dark, and you cannot see your hand, it can't be darker. Things must turn when they can go no further.

He who is doing nothing is seldom without helpers.

" What are you doing, Joe ? " said I.
" Nothing, sir," was his reply.
" And you there, Tom, pray let me know ? "
" I'm busy, sir—I'm helping Joe."
" Is nothing, then, so hard to do,
That thus it takes the time of two ? "
" No," said the other with a smile.
And grinned and chuckled all the while ;
" But we're such clever folks, d'ye see,
That nothing's hard to Joe and me."

He who is fit to die is fit to live.

The converse is true :—He who is fit to live is fit to die.

He who is full of care is like a hare.

He rests not anywhere, but starts at every footstep.

He who is giddy thinks the world turns round.

Every drunken man agrees with astronomers as to the rotation of the globe.

He who is his own tutor has a fool for a scholar.

If he knows nothing, why does he go to school to himself?

He who is ill to his own is ill to himself.

He is depriving himself of domestic comfort, and preparing a rod which will sooner or later make his own back sore.

He who is least excited is least exhausted.

He who is not happy at home is not safe abroad.

He who is not his own friend is nobody's friend.

"Be friend to others ; but thine own friend first ;
The kind fool of all kinds of fools is worst."
Sir Richard Baker.

He who is rusty is sure to be crusty.

He has no fitness for anything else but growling at other people.

He who is short of grace thinks sermons long.

He takes no interest in the subject, and therefore, the less said the more to his taste. The proverb reminds us of the story that a German gentleman was in the habit of attending a Unitarian chapel at Manchester, for this reason : "The people do go in late, and do come out early, and there is no devil."

He who is sick of the lazies cannot work.

A divine was once asked by a man to help him, because he was suffering from a disease too terrible to be mentioned. The good man promised him relief if he would tell him what his malady was, which the beggar promised to do, as soon as he had the money. Then he replied, "Sir, I am incurably lazy." I heard of a boy in Wiltshire, who was afflicted with a strange disease. Describing his symptoms, he said that he could eat well, and sleep well, and had no particular pain, but when they told him to go to work, he began to tremble all over.

He who is too wise becomes a fool.

Here again that quaint old knight, *Sir Richard Baker*, comes in with his couplet—

"In stinting wisdom, greatest wisdom lies ;
No man is ever wise that's over wise."

He who is weighty is willing to be weighed.

The base pretender, being short in weight, dreads the scales. Testing is what he abhors. He cannot endure a creed for his faith, nor a law for his practice. But the man who is sound at heart comes to the light and to the scale.

He who is well lathered is half shaved.

When well flattered, he is ready to be robbed.

He who is willing to work finds it hard to wait.

> Oh, while ye feel 'tis hard to toil,
> And sweat the long day through,
> Remember it is harder still
> To have no work to do.

He who is wise is strong.

Knowledge is power, but wisdom is far more truly so.

He who is wrong in the tens will be wrong in the hundreds.

Evidently he cannot be trusted, for honesty is seen in little things.

He who is your flatterer cannot be your friend.

He who keeps off the ice will not slip through.

If we avoid the temptation we shall not fall into the sin. It is good never to go into the company which leads into evil.

He who knows everything knows nothing well.

His knowledge is spread over too wide a surface to be deep. There is some truth in the couplet :—

> " A little knowledge is a dangerous thing,
> Drink deep, or taste not the Pierian spring ;
> For shallow draughts intoxicate the brain,
> But drinking largely sobers us again."

He who knows himself best esteems himself least.

He who knows least is generally most positive.

He who knows little soon tells it.

He who lays out for God lays up for himself.

" He that hath pity upon the poor lendeth unto the Lord; and that which he hath given will he pay him again."—Pro. xix. 17. *Dean Swift* said, " If you like the security, down with the dust."

He who lied before will lie again.

Usually he is forced to do so to keep his former lies in countenance. Moreover, the force of habit is upon him, and he cannot put on the brakes exactly when he pleases. He can leave off lying when he pleases, but he cannot please to leave off lying.

He who lies with dogs will rise with fleas.

And fleas which take very kindly to human flesh. Go into bad society, and you will bring a good deal away which you will wish away.

He who likes borrowing dislikes paying.

Honest men cannot bear loans, and it is great relief to them to clear them off : but those who borrow with a light heart are not the men to pay. One even spoke of the folly of frittering away money in paying debts. The rascal !

He who little sweats but little gets.

Unless he gets up a company, or marries a rich wife.

He who lives by his wit needs a good stock of it.

And as he usually runs short, he is very apt to take what is not his own, and then the convicts' distich comes true :—
" He that takes what isn't his'n,
When he's cotched will go to prison."

He who lives fast cannot live long.

Life has only a certain quantity of fuel ; and if we burn it away in a roaring blaze, we shall soon have nothing left with which to feed the flame.

He who lives idly does not live honestly.

A lazy man does not live by his own exertions, and therefore he must be taking from others what he has no right to.

He who lives longest will see most.

Spoken of things which we feel sure will happen in due time, and will clear up much that is now a mystery.

He who lives not wise and sober
Falls with the leaf in dull October.

> The fall of the year is reputed to be an unhealthy season, and peculiarly trying to those who have injured their constitutions with drunken follies.

He who lives on his beer will soon lie on his bier.

> Men of great bulk and vast strength are seen in breweries; but it is said that if they scratch their legs it is very hard to cure them, and they are soon gone. Life based on malt and hops has a poor foundation.

He who lives too fast may live to fast.

> How he will remember his lavish luxuries, and wish for the portions which he threw away in waste!

He who lives without fear shall die without hope.

He who lives without prayer dies without hope.

He who looks not before will soon be behind.

> If he makes no provision for old age, he will come to poverty. A little foresight will prevent a world of trouble.

He who loves nobody is nobody.

> For a man is as he loves.

He who loves right hates wrong.

> His integrity moves him to indignation when he sees injustice. He is "a good hater." A man who has convictions is never looked upon as "a moderate man"; nor need he desire the doubtful compliment.

He who makes a fool of himself has many to help him.

> Persons who would not or could not help you to grow wise will be indefatigable in developing your folly.

He who makes constant complaint gets little compassion.

> People know him as Mr. Petty-Grievous, and listen to his murmurs as they would to the hum of a water-wheel; but it is so much a matter of course that nobody thinks it matters.

He who marries a fool is a fool.

> He did not use sufficient discretion and discernment. However, fool or not fool, he is in for it, and must bear the consequences.

He who marries a good wife has prospered in life.

> Even if he be poor as a church-mouse he has found a great treasure. So says the old-fashioned love-song—

> > " Richer than rubies,
> > Dearer than gold,
> > Woman, true woman,
> > Glad we behold !
> > Thus said the wise King,
> > In the old times,
> > And thus re-echo
> > These idle rhymes."

He who masters himself can rule others.

> All his passions being under due control, he will be of equable temper and impartial judgment, and so will win the esteem and confidence of those under him : thus his rule will be easy.

> > " We best shall quiet clamorous throngs
> > When we ourselves can rule our tongues."

He who minds need never mind.

> As he is careful, he will be saved from many a care.

He who mounts before he has put on the saddle loses his time.

> Time is well spent in preparing for action. Hasten slowly, that you may hasten surely.

He who never begins will never finish.

He who never rides never falls off the horse.

> If therefore we are not expert riders our safety lies in keeping off the horse. The same is true of every questionable practice. He who does not bet will not lose. He who does not brag will not make himself ridiculous. He who does not frequent debatable amusements will not be defiled by the evils which come of them.

He who never turns will one day wish he had.

> He will sorrow to think that he obstinately persevered when wisdom would have suggested retracing his steps,—

> > Of all sad words of tongue and pen,
> > The saddest are these, " *It might have been.*"

He who never was ill is the first to die.

> How often do we notice that strong men yield to their first illness, while the sick live on !

He who often hugs the pewter,
Sure his thirst becomes acuter.

He who once hits the mark keeps on shooting.

> Many, having enjoyed one success in a certain pursuit, are induced to persevere in it, in hope of a continuance of prosperity. When we are once heard in prayer, should we not pray on ?

He who owns the cow may milk her.

> If a privilege is really ours let us avail ourselves of it. This applies both to temporals and spirituals.

He who peeps through the keyhole may lose his eye.

> This proverb dissuades from eaves-dropping and prying.

He who pelts every barking cur must pick up many stones.

> He who answers every slander will have work cut out for him which will leave little time for anything else.

He who plants a walnut tree expects not to eat the fruit.

> It is usually so ; yet it fell to my lot to plant two or three and eat of their produce. Our fathers planted many trees for their posterity, and we may be well content to do the same. Our institutions should be carefully considered in the light of their influence upon future generations. One of our senators of a former period is reported to have said that posterity had never done anything for him. Posterity has made up for its fault, for it has laughed at him.

He who pleased everybody died before he was born.

> That is to say, there never was any such person, and never will be.

He who praises himself bespatters himself.

> People consider that he must be very short of repute to be obliged to extol himself, and they take his self-praise to be the reverse of a recommendation. They say that his trumpeter is dead, or has resigned the office in disgust.

He who pries will vex his eyes

> He will see what he had better not have seen if he had consulted his own comfort.

He who promises too much means nothing.

He who receives a good turn should never forget it; he who does one should never mention it.

He who resolves suddenly will repent sorrowfully.

He who rides between two camels is kicked by both.

Jack-o'-both-sides is, before long, trusted by nobody, and abused by both parties.

He who says nothing tells no lie.

He who says what he likes will hear what he don't like.

Of course others will take the same liberty with him which he takes with them, and then he will hear truth more plain than pleasant. *Boswell* said to *Dr. Johnson,* "Every man has a right to say what he likes." "Yes, sir," said the *Doctor,* "and everybody has a right to knock him down for saying it."

He who scrubs every pig he sees will not long be clean himself.

Entering into every squabble, and trying to set everybody right, a man usually ends in implicating himself in some way or other. If he would scrub his own pig, and have done, it would be all very well.

He who seeks trouble will have no trouble in finding it.

There's plenty of it, and it comes readily to the ill-humoured.

He who sells truth buys sorrow.

Yet for the time being he may save his skin and win popularity. It is a very risky business.

He who sends mouths will send meat.

The God of providence will provide for those who trust in him. But we all remember the story of the poor man with ten children who thought that the Lord had sent all the mouths to him and all the meat to the parson, and so applied for a little of that which had been delivered at the wrong house.

He who sharpens a knife may cut his own fingers with it.

Haman's gallows were used for his hanging. Many are lifted by their own crane, or blown up with their own dynamite.

He who shoots often hits the mark at last.

> " If at first you don't succeed,
>   Try, try, try again."

He who sows brambles will reap thorn

He who sows thorns should not go barefoot.

> Those who do mischief should look out and be abundantly careful
> that it does not wound themselves.

He who speaks ill of others is none too good himself.

He who stands may fall.

> Therefore let none presume or become censorious.

He who stays in the valley will never cross the mountain.

> Like the old man who lived at the foot of Snowdon.   " Have you
> ever been up the mountain?" asked a visitor.   "No, but I have
> intended going up all my life."

He who steals eggs would steal hens if he could.

He who steers our vessel sends the storm.

> The Great Pilot of the universe, even the Lord of all, is with us ;
> and, as *Herbert* says :—
>
> > " Though winds and waves assault my keel,
> >   He doth preserve it, he doth steer,
> >   Even when the barque seems most to reel."

He who sups with the devil will need a long spoon.

> And even then the steam of the broth will injure him.

He who swells in prosperity will shrink in adversity.

> The wood he is made of is green, and yields to the weather.
> His conduct in the first case proved the weakness which is seen
> more clearly under the opposite circumstances.   If we are lifted up
> by praise, we are cast down by censure.

He who swims in sin will sink in sorrow.

He who takes a partner takes a master.

> Of course he yields a part of the control of his business.   The
> proverb, we fear, alludes to a certain sleeping partner, who too
> often aims at mastery.

He who the squalling cannot bear
Should take no piggy by the ear.

In attacking abuses we must look for abuse, and stand prepared for it. Interested persons will be sure to defend the source of their gains. Pigs will squeal if you pull their ears.

He who thinks he was always good was never good.

He was all along a proud man, and a proud man is not good.

He who thinks himself cunning is sure to be deceived.

They that know most are the most often cheated. This is a very curious and edifying fact.

He who thinks himself nothing is something.

Humility is evidence of virtue; it is the hall-mark of excellence. *John Newton* says: "Young Christians think themselves little; growing Christians think themselves nothing; full-grown Christians think themselves less than nothing."

He who thinks it's too soon may find it's too late.

Luther said: "How soon *not now* becomes *never !* "

He who throws fire-brands will burn his fingers.

He who tries to stand in two boats at once runs great risk of drowning.

To have two grounds of dependence will lead to disappointment. A man of two trades stands two chances of liquidation.

He who waits to do a great deal at once will do nothing.

Ladders must be climbed by taking one step at a time, and he who would put his foot upon the highest round at first will wait at the bottom all his life.

He who walks too fast is likely to stumble.

He who wants to dig will find a spade somewhere.

Where there's a will there's a tool.

He who wastes pence may one day want them.

And then, what regretful remembrance of the former waste !

He who will have his will, will have plenty of ill.

Obstinacy leads to folly, and folly has to be paid for; sometimes the price is minted from the eyes.

He who will not hear must feel.

Afflictions, if not the pains of hell, will come to him who refuses to take warning.

He who will not live in love will never live in heaven.

The very element of heaven is love; for God is love. The best preparation for life in heaven is to be filled with the heavenly life on earth, and this will cause us to live in love to God and man.

He who will not mend shall have an evil end.

He who will not save in youth will have his nose to the grindstone all his life.

If he eats all at breakfast he will be hard-up for dinner, and in worse case for supper. For lack of the capital, which in youth he might have saved, he must be a workman for another all his days.

He who will not save pence shall never save pounds.

Thrift must begin with little savings. The Post Office does good service in allowing children to put in their stamps. The reckless expenditure of many is a sad cause of national poverty. If people will not keep an old stocking they will have to go barefoot.

He who works best must sometimes rest.

He who would be rich in a year, begs in six months.

Because he makes a desperate plunge, sustains a great loss, and gets his name into the *Gazette*.

He who would be young in age,
Let him in his youth be sage.

He who would carry the cow must every day shoulder the calf.

Then he will grow used to the load, which will increase so insensibly that he will hardly perceive it.

He who would catch fish must not mind a wetting.

He who would catch fish should mend his nets.

Those fishermen whom Jesus called were either fishing or mending their nets. Ministers should be either preaching or studying.

He who would eat long, let him eat little.

This will prolong his life; for he will digest what he eats, and will not clog the organs of the body by excess.

He who would eat the kernel must crack the nut.

Study a truth till you get to the essence of it, or you will not enjoy it. We must overcome difficulties to get at the prize.

He who would escape the punishment must leave the sin.

He who would die single must beware of widows.

There is a general belief that widows are very insinuating. Perhaps they know the helplessness of men without wives, and are moved with compassion for them. Still, "Beware of the widows Sammy," has passed into a proverb.

He who would go to sea should learn to pray.

He who would learn to pray should go to sea.

Both proverbs are true. The dangers of the sea call for prayer, and the wonders of the sea lead to prayer, if there be any religion in the sea-goer. Storms bring many to their knees, and make atheism a hard matter. When certain sailors heard that a passenger was an "atheist" they wondered what queer fish he might be; and when a storm came on, and they heard him cry to God, they wanted to put him overboard while he was in a good frame of mind.

He who would please all, and please himself too,
Has taken more in hand than he can do.

He who would reap must sow.

He who would rest must work.

He cannot enjoy rest if he does not work, neither is he likely to get much chance of resting. And, on the other hand, he who would work long and well must take a fair measure of rest, or he will run down.

He who would rise in life must rise in the morning.

The morning hour has gold in its mouth. Early rising, in many cases, shows an energy which will enable a man to fight his way up.

He who would save should begin at his mouth.

It is wonderful what a saving it is when the beer jug no longer goes to and fro. The mouth makes all the difference between poverty and plenty in a working man's house.

He who would sleep soundly, let him borrow the bed of a bankrupt.

It is said that a Roman emperor who could not sleep desired the couch of a debtor, for he thought it wonderful that a man should sleep while in debt.

He who would speed must take good heed.

He who would stop everybody's mouth needs plenty of cakes.

Indeed, if he gave away cakes, mouths would open to receive them, if for nothing else.

He who would thrive must look alive.

In these times, especially, one must not be asleep, or we shall have our teeth drawn while we are dreaming.

He who wronged you will hate you.

It is so, that, when a man has done you an ill turn, he takes a dislike to you.

He whom God steers sails safely.

But keep your own hand off the tiller, saying "Not as I will, but as thou wilt."

He whose worth speaks will not speak his own worth.

Chinese shop-keepers write on their doors, " *No cheating here.*" This suggests that there is need for such an assertion. "You can trust me," said one, "I am beyond temptation." He who heard this boast suspected him at once, and not without justification.

He will not drink too much who never drinks at all.

This is the simple fact which justifies total abstinence from all intoxicating liquors. Is it not a sure cure if followed out? A little drinking is a dangerous thing.

He winneth that waiteth.

He wins all things who waits upon the Lord of all.

He works hard who has nothing to do.

There is no fatigue so wearisome as that which comes from want of work.

He's a man who dares to be
Firm for truth when others flee.

Where are such men? Nowadays compromise and indifference
rule supreme, and instead of solid grit we have putty or wax.

He's a mouse who feeds on other people's cheese.

Shame on able-bodied men, who live upon their wives, or pick up
the doles of charity! We libel a mouse in likening such a wretch to
it. Such fellows want the old Dutch system tried on them:—to be
put in a cell, into which the water comes so fast that they can only
save their lives by pumping as hard as they can. What a picture
it would be to see them taking to the pump when the water was
nearly up to their necks!

He's a whole team, a horse extra, and a dog under the
waggon.

That is to say, he is fully efficient; nay more, he could accomplish
a far more difficult work. He fulfils the saying, "He is all there
when the bell rings."

Health is not valued till sickness comes.

Hear both sides or none.

Hear first, speak afterwards.

Trapp says, "We read oft, 'He that hath an ear to hear, let
him hear;' but never, he that hath a tongue to speak, let him
speak; for this we can do fast enough, without bidding."

Hear for yourself, and hear for eternity.

Mr. Philip Henry notes in his diary the saying of a pious hearer
of his own that much affected him:—"I find it is easier," said the
good man, "to go six miles to hear a sermon than to spend one
quarter of an hour in meditating and praying over it in secret, as
I should when I come home."

Hear God, and God will hear you.

Hear the other side before you quite decide.

Aristides, they tell us, would lend but one ear to any one who
accused an absent party, and used to hold his hand on the other;
intimating, that he reserved an ear for the absentee accused.

Hear with patience, that you may answer with prudence.

The Danes say, "Hear one man before you answer, several
before you decide."

Hearsay is more than half false.

Heart of gunpowder, shun the candle of temptation.

> *Whitefield* used to say when any one praised him, "Take care of fire; I carry powder about with me."

Hearts may agree though heads differ.

> But it is a sounder agreement when heads and hearts go together, so that we are one in belief as well as in feeling.

Heartsease bloweth for the true;
For the false there groweth rue.

Heartsease is a flower that groweth only in the garden of grace.

> "There is a little flower that's found
> In almost every garden ground;
> 'Tis lowly, but 'tis sweet;
> And if its name express its power,
> A more invaluable flower
> You'll never, never meet."

Heaven is as near by sea as by land.

> What multitudes will find it so when the sea gives up her dead! The ocean is even now a cemetery where bodies of saints are awaiting the sound of the trumpet: —
>
> "The sea's abyss is one large grave,
> A churchyard is its face,
> A tombstone is each rising wave,
> To mark the burial place."

Hedges between keep friendship green.

> By a proper separation persons do not grow weary of each other, quarrels do not arise, and rights are secured. This is wise.

Hedges have eyes, and walls have ears.

> As you walk along roads and garden paths be cautious what you say; for you can never tell who is listening.

Help, hands! for I have no lands.

Help those who help themselves, and those who cannot help themselves.

> These two classes of persons are evidently most fit objects for charity.

Help which is long on the road is no help.

> The man is drowned while his friend is pulling off his coat to rescue him.

Help yourself, and God will help you.

Help yourself, and your friends will love you.

> But not if you help yourself to the wine and to the meat, as some do. Every man admires a relative who pays his own charges by his own honest endeavours.

Hens that lay should not be put in the pot.

> Don't spend the capital which brings in your living.

Here my master bids me stand,
And mark the time with faithful hand;
What is his will is my delight,
To tell the hours by day, by night.
Master, be wise, and learn of me
To serve thy God as I serve thee.

> This was the verse which John Berridge placed on his Clock.
> A Hindoo who had become a Christian, first had a Bible given him, and afterwards a clock. "The clock will tell me how time goes, and the Bible will teach me how to spend it," said the old man.

High birth is a cold dish for a poor man.

> Many a poor man tries to get a taste of it. The Creoles say, "When a mulatto gets a mule, he will not own his mother was a negress." Pride of birth is ridiculous anywhere, but most in the man whose only coat of arms is out at the elbows.

High learnt niggers ain't much at rolling logs.

> No doubt some people are spoiled for hard work by their superfine education.

High looks are not good looks.

> Pride is uncomely

His mother's duck turns out to be his father's goose.

> He gets so spoiled when young, that he grows up a simpleton.

His mouth never keeps Sunday.

> Said of a man who is always talking or eating.

Hit the nail on the head.

When you aim at a thing, don't miss it. In dealing with an evil be plain, pointed and direct. Fail not to make your words tell upon the evil you aim at.

Hobby-horses are as dear as race-horses.

Men will spend anything on their fancies. Often they are boobies with their hobbies.

Hoe your own garden, but owe not a farthing.

Cut up your debts, for they are a nasty kind of weed.

Hoist your sail when the wind is fair.

" Hoist up the sail while gale doth last—
    Tide and wind stay no man's pleasure !
Seek not time, when time is past—
    Sober speed is wisdom's leisure !
After-wits are dearly bought :
    Let thy fore-wit guide thy thought."—*Southwell.*

Hold the ear, and the head will follow.

Constantly teach the truth, and we may hope to win the mind to it.

Hold your tongue, and hold your friend.

There are times when a few words will part you. Bite your tongue rather than let it bite your friendship in pieces.

Holy things are for holy men.

The promises, the doctrines, and the ordinances would be polluted if grasped by wicked hands.

Home is home, be it ever so homely.

Is there any word concerning things human which has more sweetness in it than the word " home " ? Is not the Christian home one of the fruits of Christianity, which prove the goodness of the tree ?

A man can build a mansion,
    And furnish it throughout ;
A man can build a palace,
    With lofty walls and stout ;
A man can build a temple,
    With high and spacious dome :
But no man in the world can build
    That precious thing called Home.

Honest toil is no disgrace ;
Pride is always out of place.

Honesty in little things is not a little thing.
> On the contrary, it is the great point in life.

Honesty is exact to a penny.
> It is in such little matters that genuine integrity is seen.

Honesty is the best policy.
> But he who is honest out of policy is not an honest man.

Honey is sweet, but bees sting.

Honour and fame from no condition rise :
Act well your part—there all the honour lies.

Honour your parents, and your children will honour you.

Hope and strive is the way to thrive.

Hope is sweet music.
> It is the music of the future, with an undertone of heavenly song.

Hope may be drenched, but it cannot be drowned.

Hope well, and have well.

Horse-racing is a galloping consumption.
> That is to say, for the pocket, the reputation, the morals, and the soul. Racing is supposed to improve the breed of horses, but it sadly deteriorates the breed of men.

Horses will do more for a whistle than for a whip.
> That is to say, as a regular thing. Of course the whip may do wonders for a moment, but the constant use of it is infamous. When kindly used the horse becomes intelligent, and performs marvels without requiring so much as a harsh word.

Hot heads make their brains bubble over.
> They take up with wild notions, and then nothing will do but they must run after them like wild horses. They are so hot that they scald other people, and at length they themselves evaporate in steam. It is a good rule to keep the head cool and the heart warm.

How can a slut be a saint?

This is a hard question; and while it is being answered, the slut had better wash, and be clean. Godliness ought not to be lodged in a pig-sty.

How can he be godly who is not cleanly?

Time was when filth produced "the odour of sanctity"; but nasty saints are now held very cheap.

How easily a hair gets into the butter!

How readily do we err even in our best things!

"How not to do it" you shall see,
Just leave it to a committeè.

Resolutions will be passed, and the business will be past too; or else the committee as a whole will do what no man among them would be bad enough to do by himself.

How oft the fear of ill to ill betrays!

The fear is father to the fact: the dread brings on the calamity. Or, men do evil from fear of evil, and so ensure evil.

How will it look by daylight?

A very proper question to ask. Every secret thing must be revealed in the light of the day of judgment, if not before. Act as if all men saw you.

Live as in the light of day:
Nothing have to hide away.

However blind a man may be,
Another's faults he's sure to see.

However small a bush, it casts its shadow.

Everybody has some influence. Everyone can render a little help in the hour of need.

Humility is better than gentility.

A lowly deportment is the backbone of gentlemanly behaviour.

Hunger is fine sauce for plain dishes.

Hungry dogs will eat dirty puddings.

So, we suppose, will hungry men; but that is no reason for making them dirty. It is said that "we must all eat a peck of dirt before we die"; but we don't want it all at once. The proverb also means that men who are hungry for place and office will do very dirty things. Notice members of Parliament, and you will soon have proofs enough.

Hungry horses make clean mangers.

None are more ready to receive all the truth of God than those who feel and know their own spiritual need. There would not be so much picking and choosing of Scripture if the Lord had wrought a holy hunger in the soul.

Husbands can earn money, but only wives can save it.

Hypocrites will serve God while God serves them.

Yes, and they will just as soon serve the devil if it answers their purpose better. They are mere traders in the market, and they will buy or sell as the price may happen to go.

Sayings of a more Spiritual Sort.

Halfway to Christ is a dreadful place.

A dreadful place to stop in ; for it tempts to presumption, and yet it is no better than being far off.

Have a good memory.   Remember the Sabbath-day to keep it holy.

A minister, one Sunday, was accosted by a man, who said, "Sir, have you seen a family going along here travelling?" "What sort of family were they?" said the good man. "Oh, they had a cart." "Yes," said the minister. "Were they a family with short memories?" "I don't know much about that," said the young man. "What do you mean?" "Why," replied the divine, "I thought they must be, for it is written, 'Remember the Sabbath-day, to keep it holy,' and they seem to have forgotten it." There are many families with short memories nowadays.

He alone lives who lives to God alone.

The rest is death.   Paul saith, "She that liveth in pleasure is dead while she liveth."—1 Timothy v. 6.

He gains a loss who shuns the cross.

He is no man who needs no mending.

He is safe who is where God puts him,
He is right who is what God makes him.

He knows God who imitates him.

Certainly imitation is the truest form of praise.   It can only be carried out so far as the great Original is known to us.

He loseth nothing that keepeth God for his friend.

He only is a Christian indeed who is a Christian in deeds.

He pleases God best who trusts him most.

"Without faith it is impossible to please God"; but with much of it we can delight him.

He prizes grace too little who prizes gifts too much.

He shall have hell as a debt who will not have heaven as a gift.

He shall never want mercy that does not wanton with mercy.

And even he that has so wantoned with mercy shall obtain it if he turn and repent ; for the Lord is not only merciful, but he is mercy full.

He that believes God for the event must believe him for the means also.

If the harvest is sure you must be sure to make sure the sowing.

He that can repel a temptation to gain, gains by the temptation.

He that contemns a small sin commits a great one.

He that doth not fear God continually has cause for continual fear.

He that doth not hear the Word of God to his renovation, shall hear it to his condemnation.

He that falls into sin is a man ,
He that boasts of sin is a devil ;
He that grieves over sin is a Christian ;
He that forgives sin is God.

He that forsakes the truth of God, forsakes the God of truth.

He that good thinketh good may do,
And God will bless him thereunto :
For no good work was ever wrought
Without beginning in good thought.

Want of thought is a far more pernicious want than it may seem to be. " I thought upon my ways," said the Psalmist, " and turned unto thy statutes."

He that hath Jesus Christ for his daily bread, may (*without sin*) fare sumptuously every day.

He that is graceless in the day of grace will be speechless in the day of judgment.

He that is rotten within will soon be specked without.

> Before long evil principles display themselves in unhallowed actions.

He that is most full of God is most empty of himself ; and he that is most full of himself is most empty of God.

He that makes earth his heaven shall have no other heaven.

He that will make God's will his will, will have his will.

He that will not be saved needs no sermon.

He that wills to serve God for nought, will find that he does not serve God for nought.

> Our motive must be free from selfishness, but in the end the Lord will reward all the faithful. Satan asked, "Doth Job serve God for nought?" But we might answer, "Dost thou think that God is such a Master that he would let a man serve him for nought?"

He that would find Christ must seek him.

He that would have his sins covered by God must uncover them before God.

He that would never die must die daily.

He walks uprightly who leans on God.

> None else will long do so. The leaning of faith balances the natural leaning to our own understanding.

He who brings good tidings may knock boldly.

> How bold may he be who brings the gospel—"glad tidings of great joy"!

He who can wrestle with God can conquer man.

> Or put it in these words, "He that overcomes heaven can overcome earth." We shall have power with men for God in proportion as we have power with God for men.

He who closely clings to God
Oft escapes the chastening rod.

> The further off the heavier the blow when a man is striking. By running into God's arms we escape the full force of the stroke. Complete submission renders affliction light.

He who covers his sin, discovers himself to be a sinner.

He who creates his image in us, will love his image in us.

He who dwells in high heaven never dwells in a haughty heart.

He who gives before we ask will give when we ask.

The spontaneous bounty of God should be a great incentive to believing prayer.

He who gives thee Christ will not deny thee a crust.

" He that spared not his own Son, but delivered him up for us all, how shall he not with him also freely give us all things ? "

He who grieves for his sin may be glad of his grief.

Indeed, it is such blessed sorrow that one holy man was wont to regret that the tear of repentance would not wet his eye in heaven.

He who has God has all.

Therefore, let him not fret though he should seem to lose all.

He who is angry with sin does not sin in his anger.

He who is good to the saints for God's sake, shall find God good to him for the saints' sake.

He who is heaven-bound must first be heaven-born.

He who is of the religion of the time, will in time have no religion.

He who is only half God's is wholly the devil's.

The more surely so because of his half-hearted religion.

He who is the friend of God is the enemy of priests.

For they are the enemies of the one Great High Priest. Their pretentions are in direct opposition to the way of salvation by faith.

He who learns Christ unlearns sin.

He who leaves the saints of God will not cleave to the God of saints.

He who lifts clean hands in prayer,
God will have him in his care.

He who lives in God will never be weary of living.

He who lives most in sin, and in most sin, is most dead in sin.

He who loses Christ is lost himself.

He who loves Christ sincerely, loves him superlatively.

> A second place in the heart our Lord will never occupy; the very idea is a dishonour to him.

He who made man was made man.

He who made the smallest flower
Regulates the tempest's power.

He who makes the world his god, worships the god of this world.

He who serves God serves a good Master.

He who sins for profit, will not profit by his sins.

He who would find Christ must lose self.

> For self-confidence and confidence in Christ will no more agree than Dagon and Jehovah.

He who would have a clean life must have a clean heart.

> Only from a pure fountain can there flow pure streams, and the heart is to be kept with all diligence; for out of it are the issues of life.

He will never go to heaven who is content to go alone.

Hear to believe, and believe to do.

> This is the hearing which is saving; faith comes by it, and works meet for repentance come of the faith.

Heaven alone has all roses, and no thorns.

> No traveller ever reached that blest abode,
> Who found not thorns and briars on the road.

Heaven is a prepared place for a prepared people.

> Our Lord came to earth to prepare the people, and he is gone to glory to prepare the place.

Heaven is never deaf but when our hearts are dumb.

Heaven must be in thee ere thou canst be in heaven.

> At the bottom of a portrait of *Sibbes* we find this couplet:—
> Of this blest man let this just praise be given:
> Heaven was in him, before he was in heaven.

Heirs of blessing should also bless their heirs.

> Holy training should be given to all the sons of the sons of God, that then the grace of God may abide upon the family from generation to generation.

Hell is truth seen too late.

> Note this definition. May none of us learn its truth by practical experience!

Hem your blessings with praise, lest they unravel.

> A notable piece of advice. Doubtless our enjoyments become a danger unless we humbly trace them to the hand of God, and gratefully praise his name for them.

Here we are to labour for rest; hereafter we shall rest from our labours.

> We are to "labour to enter into that rest" (Heb. iv. 11). This is a singular expression, and reminds us of our Saviour's words: "Labour not for the meat which perisheth, but for that meat which endureth unto everlasting life" (John vi. 27). Here he utters a paradox. He bids us not to labour for that which we cannot get without labour, and commands us to labour for that which we cannot earn by labour. Blessed is he that understandeth!

His heart cannot be pure whose tongue is not clean.

His voice is most eloquent whose life is most innocent.

Hold forth the truth, and hold fast the truth.

Hold on, hold fast, hold out.

> Three things which must be attended to by all who would reach the eternal rest.

Hold the truth, because it holds you.

> No one else will continue to hold the gospel in times when it is unpopular; but if it has full possession of the soul, there is no fear of its being given up. A cross with the motto ET TENEO, ET TENEOR— *I hold, and am held*—is a fine coat-of-arms for a Christian.

Holiness is not the way to Christ; but Christ is the way to holiness.

Holiness is the best Sabbath dress.

>   But it is equally suitable for every-day wear.

Holiness is the wholeness of the soul.

>   It is our spiritual health, even as sin is the soul's disease.

Holy hearts make holy tongues.

>   The Holy Spirit, both in his miraculous and in his common gifts delights to work upon tongues. The tongue is the glory of the man, and when grace purifies it, it sets forth the glory of God.

Honour the Lord with thy substance, and there will be substance in it.

>   God's blessing makes consecrated possessions to be real goods, whereas, without his blessing, they are a vain show.

Hope is a good anchor, but it needs something to grip.

Hope is never ill when faith is well.

>   That hope flourishes
>   Which true faith nourishes.

Hope on, hope ever.

How shall the blind see when the *seers* are blind?

>   When the pastors err, where will the sheep go?

Hunger breaks through stone walls.

>   Nothing can keep back the man who hungers after Christ: he will force his way to the bread of heaven.

Humble we must be if to heaven we go:
High is its roof of light, but yet its gate is low.

Humility is to have a just idea of yourself.

>   To sham humility by a fictitious depreciation of one's self is sickening hypocrisy. We are not without ability, nor without some measure of moral virtue: and we should not profess that we think we are. It cannot be necessary to modesty that we should deny the truth; still, if any man's opinion of himself is very high, he may depend upon it that he has made a mistake in the adding up.

Hypocrites love the gold of the altar better than the God of the altar.

CANNOT swallow the sea for the sake of the fish.

To subscribe to a long creed for the sake of one article in it, or to put up with a heap of ill-conduct for a little benefit, or to go into an evil trade for temporary gain, will all come under this sentence.

I can't work for nothing, and find thread.

He did so who gave a lecture with free admission, and paid the hire of the hall and his own expenses.

" I do not like you, Dr. Fell ;
The reason why I cannot tell ;
But this I know, and know full well—
I do not like you, Dr. Fell."

Prejudice cannot give a reason for its own existence; but there it is.

" I don't care " is a deadly snare.

When youth grows reckless shipwreck is near.

" I feel as queer as Dick's hat-band."

This was too long to go round his hat once, and not long enough to go round twice; and so, according to his own description, it was neither one thing nor the other. Has not the reader some-times felt somehow, nohow, all sorts, and out of sorts ?

I have a fine cloak, but I left it in France.

The man has everything somewhere else, but nothing for immediate use. This sort of talk is common, but silly.

I have other fish to fry.

A good reason for leaving second-rate things alone. Fry your own fish, and don't be in a hurry to lend your frying-pan.

I much commend to make a foe into a friend.

This is the Christian way of conquering enemies. May we understand the divine art of which our Lord Jesus was the great example !

I saw an honest lawyer and a white crow.

> Are they equally rare? So one would gather from an epitaph which comes to our mind :—
>
>> "God works wonders now and then.
>> Here lies a lawyer, an honest man."
>
> Even he is dead, or rather, even "here he lies." Let us hope that all this is mere fun. No doubt the good people who are called lawyers are as honest as others; though I once knew a gentleman who used to sigh for a day's shooting in Lincoln's Inn Fields. He had doubtless been unfortunate in his transactions with gentlemen of the long robe.

"I saw" is ten times better than "I heard."

> Because the eyes are not so likely to be deceived. "Seeing is believing"; but hearing is deceiving, when we only hear.

"I was taken by a morsel," says the fish.

> How small a crumb has served to bait the hook of the great destroyer of souls! May we never have to lament as the fish did!

I wot well how the world wags.
He is most loved that hath most bags.

"I'll try, I'll try."
He'll rise by-and-by.

> Perseverance is the pledge of success.

I've lived too near a wood all my life to be afraid of an owl.

> Spoken to one who is threatening you, and yet is a nobody. It is not a speech that we should recommend.

Idle bodies are generally busybodies.

> And busybodies are nobodies, except that they are nuisances to everybody.

Idle brains are addled brains.

> Out of them comes nothing but folly, or worse. "Of idleness comes no goodness." The thoughts of an idler are barren.

Idle men are the devil's playmates,

> And he is so ashamed of their idleness that he sets them to work.

Idle people are dead people that you can't bury.

The more's the pity. We have to endure their carcases above ground. An idler is the sepulchre of all that is good.

Idle people take the most pains.

They cause themselves double work by trying to do the thing easily.

Idle young, needy old.

The Germans say, "Idleness has poverty for wages," and the Dutch, "Idleness is hunger's mother." Noteworthy is the other old saying, "Idleness is the key of beggary."

Idleness and vice are twin brothers.

They are the Siamese twins of immorality.

Idleness breeds sleep, and sleep breeds idleness.

This, of course, is to be taken *cum grano salis.* To sleep as much as nature requires is not idleness.

Idleness is hard work to those who are not used to it, and dull work to those who are.

Idleness is the devil's bolster.

When we lay our heads on it, we are very near to the evil one. It is not the devil's couch of ease as some say, for it is a disease, and brings a world of uneasiness with it.

Idleness is the mother of all vices.

It produces a state of mind which is favourable to every form of evil. Say a fellow is lazy, and nothing worse remains to be said of him. Idleness is the shipwreck of chastity, and the root of all evil.

If a cow gives milk, it need not play the piano.

Persons who can do their proper work are not to be censured because they cannot display accomplishments, or do other things which are not in their line.

If a dog is vicious, tie him up short.

That he may have small space in which to do mischief. Some men must be dealt with very carefully, and we must see that they have not the opportunity of doing us wrong.

If a donkey brays at you, don't bray at him.

Which you will do if you answer railing by railing. Take as a specimen and a warning the following : An American editor speaks of his rival as " mean enough to steal the swill from a blind hog ! " That rival retorts by saying, " He knows he lies : I never stole his swill." Do not fall into the style (we had almost said sty) of these editors.

If a fool has success it ruins him.

His head is turned, and he becomes more of a fool than before. Want of ballast renders even a fair wind a great danger.

If a mouse lives in a cat's ear, the mouse is very daring, or the cat is very dull.

When fellows thieve under the eye of the police, or other watchers, there is something strange about it.

If a nag is meant to go,
Do not keep his feed too low.

And when a servant is worked hard, don't stint him in wages. A miserly farmer once said to his man, " A fat horse can't work, you know, John." " Neither can't a lean 'un, Maister," said poor John, who had reason for knowing, for he had never a chance of being anything else but lean as a strap.

If a thing be easy, do it as well as if it were hard.

This would prevent slovenly work. Let the hare keep to the course as steadily as the tortoise, and she will win grandly.

If a woman were as swift of foot as of tongue, she would catch enough lightning to kindle the fire in the morning.

These wicked observations are shamefully plentiful. Do women really talk more than men ? If they do, is it because they have more to tell ? Or are men so stupid as to need often telling ?

If a word is worth a shilling, silence is worth two.

If all men lie, speak you the truth.

There is the more reason that you should do so. Surely truth should have one advocate !

If an ass goes a-travelling, he won't come home a horse.

> Persons who go abroad may come home as ignorant as they went out. Unless we carry brains with us, we shall bring none home.
>
> > A dunce that hath been sent to roam
> > Is still a dunce when he comes home.

If better were in, better would come out.

> The man would talk more sense if he had more sense.

If cold, don't scold; if warm, don't storm.

> The weather should not have such an effect upon us as to make us ill-tempered. We must not be so mercurial as to go up and down with the temperature.

If England sink, 'twill be by drink.

> This is the sin which swells the revenue, but also brings un-numbered ills upon us. The heathen might picture an English-man with a bottle in one hand, and a Bible in the other. Such inconsistency is inconsistent with God's blessing.

If envy were a fever, half the world would be ill.

> Let us hope that this is too sweeping; but certainly our fever hospitals would never hold all the patients.

If every fool were crowned, we should all be kings.

If every unwise man died, no one would be buried; for there would be no one to dig a grave.

If everyone would mend one, all would be mended.

If flies will dip into people's cream jugs, they will get drowned.

> Meddling and pilfering will have evil consequences to men as well as flies. Those who taste every man's broth will burn their mouths.

If folly were grief, every house would weep.

If fools ate no bread, corn would be cheap.

If fools went not to market, who would buy the bad goods?

> Many of the preceding proverbs were evidently written by an ancient Thomas Carlyle. When a man knows exactly how many fools there are, may he not be one of the confraternity? How else could he be so well acquainted with the statistics of the community?

If God bolts the door, do not get through the window.

> Don't go where it is evident that you cannot go without doing wrong. Take to heart the warnings of providence, which are often as plain as if we heard voices from heaven.

If God did not mean to hear us, he would not bid us pray.

If God has helped thee, help thy neighbour.

If husband and wife fall out, they had better fall in again.

> For they must go on together, and they may as well make matters as agreeable as possible. The French say that "No one marries without repenting it"; but this, we trust, is not true. It is far better, and far easier, to repent of the quarrel than of the marriage.

" If I drink beer, it makes me queer."
> > And so it ought'er,—
> > Try pure water.

If I e'er shall married be,
Somewhere in the world is she,
Whom the Lord ordains for me;
So for her I now will pray,
And continue every day.
"Bless her, Lord!" my heart shall say.

> The idea of this rhyme is borrowed from "Proverbial Philosophy."

If I have not done well, will you do better?

> A question which should not be used in self-defence; but should suggest itself to anyone who censures the conduct of another.

"If I rest I rust," says the key.

> We find it so: even industrious people grow a bit rusty when out of work. As for idlers, they are nothing but rust.

If I think my wife is fair,
What need other people care

"If, If, If,"
Very small, very stiff.

> Only one syllable, and yet "if" stubbornly stops many things.

If it were not for "if" I should be rich as Rothschild.

If it cannot be better, be glad it's no worse.

Thus will there always be room for gratitude.

If it must be done, do it, and have done.

A rebuke for shilly-shallying, such as you see in some people who never come to the point.

If it rained porridge, the lazy man would have no basin.

If it rains to-day, it will keep on till it leaves off.

A safe prophecy. Given as a specimen of the only kind of uninspired prophecy which has anything in it worth a moment's attention. Neither Mother Shipton, nor Dr. Dee, nor the astrologers, nor the soothsayers, nor the spiritualists, can see any further into a millstone than other blind people.

If it rains—well! If it shines—well!

This is the contented man's feeling. He leaves the skies and clouds with him who manages them far better than short-sighted mortals could. "I wish you a good day," said the divine to the peasant. The answer was, "Sir, every day is a good day to me, for God sends it."

If it's dirt to me, it's not clean to my neighbour.

I ought not, therefore, to ask him to do what I would not do myself. Wrong for me is wrong for my servant.

If it's nothing to you, say nothing about it.

You are poking your nose into other people's business, and you may get an uncomfortable punch.

If Jack drinks the wages, Jill cannot save them.

Economy must begin with the beer-money. The money spent in drink just makes the difference between comfort and want.

If Jack were better, Jill would not be so bad.

Often the husband creates the wife's faults, and *vice versâ*.

If Johnny does not learn it, John will not know it.

Education is best received in early days, and especially the moral part of it. Teach Polly, and Mary will know.

If lies were Latin, learned men would be common.

> Perhaps this saying was suggested by the other, "Lies and Latin go round the world." Many who know no Latin are proficients in the other universal tongue, which is not one of the dead languages.

If love finds fault, it is that fault may not be found by others.

> The most amiable reason for criticizing a husband or a friend.

If men had not slept, the tares would not have been sown among the wheat.

If men would think,
They'd give up drink.

> On the other hand, while drink sways them they will not think.

If money be not thy servant it will be thy master.

If my aunt had been a man she would have been my uncle.

> Wonderful news! Almost as striking as the information that the Dutch have taken Holland. Sometimes we are obliged to rebuke great wonder-makers with some such sentence.

If on your journey you want speed
Give the mare an extra feed.

If one door shuts, another will open.

> Often have I heard good men declare that this is true, and I have rejoiced with them in hearing of the goodness of God in providing for his servants new openings when others have closed.

If one sheep break the hedge, a dozen will follow.

> True of men also. One who was forty years a shepherd of sheep, and then forty years a shepherd of men, was wont to say that his second flock was the more sheepish and more apt to wander of the two.

If others say how good are you,
Ask yourself if it is true.

> Modestly suspect yourself. Also suspect others of having some object in flattering you.

If others' purses be more fat,
Why should we groan and grieve at that?

If prayers were puddings, many men would starve.

And others would be reduced to skin and bone.

If sin be in fashion, let us be out of fashion.

If slighted, slight the slight, and love the slighter.

This is conduct worthy of a noble mind.

If the beans are blighted, the peas must pay for it.

One crop makes up for another. All parts of our business do not fail at the same time. Therefore, let us cheer up.

If the best man's faults were written on his brow, he would wear a broad-brimmed hat.

And feel as great an objection to taking it off as the Quaker did when he met Charles II.

If the camel once gets his nose into the tent his whole body will enter.

Allow the beginnings of evil, and the rest will follow as a matter of course. Give intrusive people a chance, and they will take a world of liberties.

If the cap fit wear it.

Whenever a rebuke comes home to the conscience, profit by it.

If the devil be the vicar, don't be his clerk.

If the devil catch men idle, he sets them to work.

" He will find them work to do,
He will pay them wages too."

If the eye do not admire, the heart will not desire.

If the man is ugly, he blames the looking-glass.

It does not reflect him fairly, so he says; the fact being that it is too accurate. When a sermon is too true it is too personal.

If the mountain will not come to Mahomet, Mahomet must go to the mountain.

If circumstances will not yield to you, you must yield to the circumstances, or let the matter alone.

If the sun shines on me, what matters the moon ?

If God's blessing be ours, we can afford to do without the smiles of men.

If there were no fools, there would be no wars.

It may be no wonder that foolish monarchs should go to war, but the marvel is that their subjects should be so eager to spill their blood in quarrels which very little concern them.

If they call thee reaper, whet thy scythe.

Try to deserve the credit which is given you.   What's in a name? Make it a reality.

If things were to be done twice, all would be wise.

True in many instances ; but some persons are more foolish the second time than at the first.

If thou wilt love, thou shalt be loved.

It is so in the domestic circle generally ; but out in the wide wide world the most loving have oftentimes been the most hated.

If thou wilt not learn, nobody can teach thee.

If thou wouldst reap money sow money.

To hope to conduct trade without outgoings is absurd ; and yet some are so stingy that they starve their business, and it dies under their hand.   You can't make the pot boil and yet save your sticks.

If to do were as easy as to know, how good men would be !

If two men ride a horse, one must ride behind.

The question of position should be settled before starting, for it will be awkward to arrange it afterwards.   In partnerships of all sorts this is to be thought of.

If we cannot all gather a sheaf, let us each glean an ear.

If we did not flatter ourselves, nobody else could.

Flatteries from others would be nauseous to us, and would not be offered.

If wet, don't fret ; if dry, don't cry.

In any case be not unduly troubled, especially by matters of weather which you cannot alter.

If wisdom's ways you wisely seek,
  Five things observe with care:
Of whom you speak, to whom you speak,
  And how, and when, and where

>Here we have the five points of courtesy and caution in conversation. To observe them would save a world of trouble.

If wishes were dishes, beggars would dine.

If wishes would bide, beggars would ride.

>"How many sick ones wish they were healthy!
>How many poor men wish they were wealthy!
>How many ugly ones wish they were pretty!
>How many stupid ones wish they were witty!
>How many bachelors wish they were married!
>How may Benedicts wish they had tarried!
>Single or double, life's full of trouble;
>Riches are stubble, pleasure's a bubble!"

If with the law you once begin,
Twill strip you to the very skin.

>Burton says, "He that goes to law does as the sheep does that in a storm runs to a briar." He loses his wool while seeking his shelter. Our weekly satirist once said, "He who is fond of maintaining an action will soon be without the means of maintaining himself."

If you agree to carry the calf, they'll make you carry the cow.

>A yielding spirit is apt to be imposed upon.

If you always say " No," you'll never be wed;
If you always say " Yes," you'll be horribly bled.

>The right use of these monosyllables is a main point of practical wisdom.

If you are a beauty, do without paint.

If you are deaf to God's voice, he'll be deaf to yours.

If you are in great haste, wait a bit.

>Sound advice! You may blunder into great evils, if you do not take time to consider. The Kashmiri saying is, "If he delays he will come quickly: but if he hastens he will come slowly." The more haste the less speed.

If you are kind to the creature, be not unkind to the Creator.

Alas! few think of Him, of whom they should think most.

If you are losing money, save some by giving it away.

The following story will explain the proverb :—*Mr. Thornton*, of Clapham, was waited upon by a minister, to whom he gave the liberal subscription of £15. Before the grateful clergyman left the house the mail came in, and brought information that *Mr. Thornton*, through a storm at sea, had lost more than £20,000. He remarked to the minister that after so heavy a loss he must ask for his cheque to be returned to him. The minister handed it back with a heavy heart; for his case was one of great need. *Mr. Thornton*, to his astonishment, gave him a cheque for £50, and added, "The Lord seems resolved to deprive me of much of my wealth, and therefore I must make haste to use what remains to me. Before I lose all, I must save some."

If you are weak, you need not be wilful.

But usually these two things go together, and fools are generally obstinate. He that is weak in the head is often headstrong.

If you argue, pray that it may be with those who can understand you.

Otherwise it will not be a fair debate, but a mere jangle, very trying to the temper.

If you blacken others, it does not whiten yourself.

If you blow out another man's candle, it will not light your own.

If you box a boy's ears, you'll addle his brains.

This common form of chastisement should for ever be abandoned.

If you cannot drive the engine, you can clear the road.

Every man may contribute something to the common-weal.

If you cannot find water in the sea, where will you look?

If God does not help you, who can? Why go to the streams when the ocean of mercy is before you?

If you cannot have the best, make the best of what you have.

If you cannot paint, grind the colours.

Do something towards that grand work of art—a renovated world.

If you can't be clever, you may be clean.

If you can't bite, don't show your teeth.

Don't threaten beyond your power. The Hindoos tell of a certain custom-house official who had no legs, but he used to threaten travellers who tried to evade the duties by saying what he would do when he got up. At length his secret was found out, and he became the butt of ridicule.

If you can't get a loaf, don't throw away a cake.

If you can't get crumb, you must fain eat crust.

If you can't help, don't hinder.

If you can't take things easy, take them as easy as you can.

Some are naturally so nervous that this is all we can say to them with any hope of their following out our advice. Don't let nervousness be more than need be.

> If you must fidget,
> Please to abridge it.

If you come uncalled, you may sit unserved.

Those who intrude cannot expect to be welcomed. There are no such guests at the banquet of divine love.

If you command, and hope to be obeyed,
Observe yourself the laws yourself has made.

Obviously wise advice: yet we know law-makers who are the first to break their own rules, and seem to think that having been so good as to draw up the regulations they had done their part, and could not be expected to pay any further attention to them.

If you could run as you drink, you would catch a hare.

True of many who support the brewers and wine dealers.

If you deal with a fox, look out for tricks.

Make your dealings few and brief, or you may learn to be tricky while watching against tricks.

If you don't like crab-apples, don't plant crab-trees.

If you prefer peace and quietness, be peaceful and quiet. A member of the Peace Society must not break the peace himself. Married people should not create causes for contention, lest contention should spoil their union.

If you don't open the door to the devil he goes away.

If you don't say it you'll not have to unsay it.

A capital reason for silence where the prudence of speech is doubtful.

> You can't make me unsay what I never have said,
> Nor make me get up if I've not gone to bed.

If you don't touch the rope you won't ring the bell.

Do not place in his way the temptation which leads a man to sin, nor name the topic which makes your companion angry, nor play with causes whose results are mischievous.

If you eat all for breakfast, what will you do for dinner?

Thrift should begin with youth, that there may be some little provision for old age.

If you fall out with the only road, which way will you go?

There is one way to heaven; and if you refuse it, what will you do?

If you get the best of whisky, it will get the best of you.

A clever American saying. Very true.

If you have a diamond necklace, don't hang it on a sow's neck.

Give your love and your approbation to worthy objects. Do not devote your life's powers to a mean object.

If you have a good seat, keep it.

In running about for change sake, or pressing up for ambition's sake, you are apt to have your seat withdrawn, and yourself on the ground.

If you have an iron hand, wear a velvet glove.

Let strength be veiled with courtesy.

If you have no beef, thank God for beans.

Another proverb of the same sort says, "If you can't get chicken, enjoy your onion."

If you have no money, you must have manners.

It will be all the more incumbent upon you to behave courteously if you are needing help.

If you have no son, don't give him a name.

Don't act a boastful part. It's ill for either a king or a cobbler to talk of things he has not.

If you have two hands, beware of having a third.

That third is a little behind-hand, which has ruined, in many cases, the work of the other two hands.

If you hold the stirrup, Satan will mount the saddle.

If you jump into a well, don't blame providence if it leaves you there.

He who is lazy, and comes to the workhouse, should not lay his poverty at the door of Providence.

If you let a dog kiss you, it will lick you all over the face.

Some people know no medium, but carry affection and everything else to an intolerable excess. You cannot make people what an old farmer used to call "judgmatical."

If you let the devil into the cart, you'll have to drive him home.

Begin with a sinful action, and the force of circumstances will urge you onward. Better not commence a drive to hell. It is easy to let the devil in, but hard to turn him out.

If you live with dogs, you will learn to howl.

And so if you live with the quarrelsome you will be apt to grow cantankerous ; and with the mean you will get to be mean before you know it. Don't take lodgings in such kennels.

If you love independence, do not live in dependence.

Some would like to have all they can get from others, and yet enjoy the freedom of men who support themselves. This is unreasonable. At the same time there are persons who err in the other direction, and are so independent that you cannot depend upon them.

If you lose your temper don't look for it.

It is not worth finding; do without such a temper. Remember the story of the man who gave his master notice because he could not stand his temper. "But," said the master, "you had better stay, James; for you know I am no sooner out of temper than I'm in again." "No, sir," said the servant, "I cannot stay; for the trouble is, that no sooner are you in a good temper than you're out again." A boiling temper may soon cool down; but, in the meanwhile, those who have been scalded do not forget it quite so easily.

If you love liberty, don't keep it all for yourself.

Allow other people to be as free as you are. In the name of liberty of conscience much illiberality is displayed. We have quite enough to do if we use our own liberty well.

If you love me show it.

This is but a reasonable demand, whether it comes from our fellow-servant or from our great Master.

If you make a good profession, make good your profession.

This proverb should be appointed to be read in churches.

If you meddle with dirt, some of it will stick.

Stick to your own hands, remember. Few touch a foul business without being fouled.

If you meddle with many things, you will muddle them all.

Some few seem to be able to manage many things; but, as a rule, if we have too many irons in the fire, some of them burn. Concentration of energy is needful to any great success.

If you miss one post, don't run your head against another.

A certain doctrine you may not receive, but don't rush to the opposite extreme.

If you mock the lame, you may limp the same.

Nothing can be more cruel and mean than to ridicule the afflicted; and it seems a very natural judgment that those who do so should suffer a similar calamity.

If you must fly, fly well.

There is no need for you to attempt the unusual; but, if you do venture upon such things, mind that you justify the attempt.

If you pay nothing, don't grumble about the score.

When a thing is absolutely gratis, one is hardly at liberty to criticize; and yet some men *will* murmur anyhow. Even if hanged at the country's expense they would not like it.

If you pay your servant badly, he will pay himself.

How often are pilferings the result of paltry wages!

If you play with cats, expect to be scratched.

Among rough or wicked companions we may look for harm; and we shall get it, whether we look for it or not.

If you play with dirt, you will foul your fingers.

If you play with the bull, you will feel his horns.

If you put butter by the fire, expect it to melt.

Expose youths to temptation, and wonder not if they yield.

If you put more water in the pot, put in more tea.

More work will require more grace; more speech more thought; more care more prayer.

If you raise one ghost you will have the churchyard in motion.

One cannot do a certain measure of evil and stop there; the ball once set a-rolling goes further than we thought.

If you rake a dunghill, you will raise no lavender.

Offensive subjects are better let alone.

If you ride the horse, you ought to pay for his shoeing.

Certainly. If you hear a man preach, you ought to support him; if you have a wife, you should maintain her; if you have a government, you should pay for its expenses; if you use a man's time, you should pay him for it.

If you say A, you'll have to say B.

Yielding to one evil demand will only bring another upon you. Go not one step in a way in which it would be wrong to go two.

If you say nothing, nobody will repeat it.

If you seek flowers, you must sow seeds.

If you sell the cow, you sell her milk too.

> If you renounce a truth you will lose all the comfort of it.

If you shut out love, love will shut out you.

> When it comes to that, a man is in a poor case. He generally becomes a snarling misanthrope, whom it is wise to let alone. He sings, " I care for nobody, and nobody cares for me."

If you sow thorns, you will not reap roses.

If you squeeze a flint, you will get no juice.

> Press some as much as you like, and they will give you nothing.

If you swallow the church, swallow the steeple.

> It is a rebuke for those who do the major part of a wrong thing, and then stickle at some small point.

If you tell everybody your business, the devil will do it for you.

> Thus say the Italians; and they do but express what experience proves true. The Creoles say, " Eat everything, drink everything, but don't tell everything."

If you touch pitch you'll blacken yourself.

> See Ecclesiasticus xiii. 1. This is not Scripture, as some suppose, but it is sound sense notwithstanding.

If you trust before you try,
You'll repent before you die.

If you turn sweep you must wear black.

If you walk on a tight-rope, you will need a balancing-pole.

> Great prudence is needed when the path is perilous. A man may safely be rich or great if grace gives prudence ; but not else.

If you want a boy to move fast, say: " Now, my man!"

> When, on the other hand, you would stir an aged person, you may shout: " Now, young man ! " In either case the person puts his best foot foremost to seem to be what you call him.

If you want a good servant, wait on yourself.

There will be no wages to pay, and you will receive neither warning nor sauce. In this respect "self is the man."

If you want a pretence to whip a dog, say that he ate the frying-pan.

When a malicious desire to rail at a person has taken possession of a man, it matters not how gross the falsehood; it will be used without remorse. Remember the story of the wolf and the lamb at the stream.

If you want easier travelling, mend your ways.

A right life is the happiest after all.

If you want the cart to go, you must grease the wheels.

Give workmen encouragement. Practically aid desirable objects. Golden oil will help the cart-wheel wonderfully.

If you want to die, take a quack's medicine.

Especially take those remedies which are said to cure everything, from corns to consumption. What cures Mary may kill Martha; and when a medicine is said to be equally good for everything, be sure that it is good for nothing.

If you want to know what a pound is worth, try to borrow one.

He said "a trifle" when he borrowed it of me;
A pound's no trifle now when I'd a borrower be.

**If you wear the ribbon blue,
Mind you're to your purpose true.**

If you were a cat, you would hunt for mice.

People say: "If I were he, I should do so and so." Nonsense. If you were he, you would do as he does.

**If you wish to be well—as you do, I've no doubt—
Just open the windows before you go out.**

Some people are as afraid of the fresh air as if it were poison. If the air could come into our rooms both by day and night, it would bring health with it.

If you won't do better to-day, you'll do worse to-morrow.

We shall either grow ripe or rotten. In the road of morals, we are always going forward or backward.

If you would be a smith, begin with blowing the fire.

> He is the best workman who has gone through all the grades, and worked at every part of the trade. So in holy service, our young people should begin with easy and lowly work, and then advance to more difficult labours.

If you would be graceful, be full of grace.

If you would be obeyed willingly, command kindly.

If you would drink pure water, go to the fountain-head.

> Read the Scriptures. Both preachers and books may err, but not the inspired Book. This is the well of doctrine undefiled. The old Bibles have in them this rhyme :—
>
> > "Here is the Judge that stintes the strife,
> > When men's devices faile ;
> > Here is the bread that feedes the life,
> > That death cannot assaile."

If you would have a friend, be a friend.

> For friendship feeds on friendship, and starves if it finds itself alone.

If you would keep right, mind what you write.

> *Verba scripta manent.* Words written remain, and can be produced in evidence.
>
> > Put not things in black and white
> > If they will not bear the light.

If you would know, and not be known, live in a city.

If you would shun the sin, shun the temptation.

> "They that fear the adder's sting will not come near his hissing." If you don't want to fall into the river, keep off the bank.

If you'd learn patience superfine,
Go you to fish with rod and line.

> Yes, *Isaac Walton* must have been the happiest of martyrs, the gentlest of killers. But what perseverance his followers exhibit ! Oh, the joys of angling !
>
> > "Still with patience on the shore,
> > They clear the line, and try once more ;
> > And thus they toil from morn to night :
> > But then they get—Get what ? A BITE.
> > 'Ere they get their fish to shore,
> > He snaps the line, they're balked once more.
> > Then home they go : their tale is told,
> > That they have caught—Caught what ? A COLD."

If you've breath to spare, cool your pudding.

> Don't spend breath in talking, but turn it to some useful account. Oh that some would be sensible enough to do this!

If you've no good reason for doing it, you've one good reason for letting it alone.

If your brother is a donkey, what are you?

If your children you will pet,
They will surely make you fret.

> Some children have had reason to think, in after-life, that if their parents had loved them wisely, they would also have whipped them well. Yet, too much Cain is apt to kill Abel.

If your head is in the lion's mouth, get it out as quick as you can.

> Such a risk ought not to be prolonged. By all means make matters right when you see that you are altogether in the power of a great adversary, be he human or diabolical.

If your husband is a dog, don't be a cat.

> If you are, you will lead a cat-and-dog life.

If your wife is crust, mind that you are crumb.

> Be resolved to be specially patient and gentle when you see that there is irritation in your partner. *Mr. Shelly*, a clergyman at Cambridge in the seventeenth century, is described as "an old-fashioned, good man." He made the following rhymes on a sudden, as he was going to preach in his parish church, in answer to one of his parishioners, who asked, "How long, sir, have you and *Mrs. Shelly* been married?"
>
>> "Fifty years and three,
>> Together in love, lived we:
>> Angry both at once none ever did us see.
>> This was the fashion
>> God taught us, and not fear:
>> When one was in a passion,
>> The other could forbear."

If your wife is flint, don't be steel.

> Or, if you are so, don't try the effect of striking.

If your wife is short stoop to her.

If youth be sick of the will-nots, old age is in danger of
    dying of the shall-nots.

If youth but knew what age would crave.
Most surely it would try to save.

" Ifs " and " buts " spoil many a good character.

Ignorance confessed sets all dispute at rest.

> This is a fine conclusion of controversy; and if we were not too
> proud we might end many a debate in this manner.

Ignorance is the mother of impudence.

> The father is pride.

Ignorance is the mother of superstition.

> Not of *devotion*, as has been ignorantly asserted.

Ignorance shuts its eyes, and swears that it sees.

> None are more positive than those who know nothing.

Ill doers are ill deemers.

> They measure other men's corn with their bushel ; and, as they
> know their own baseness, they reckon that all others are like them-
> selves.

Ill-gotten gain is no gain.

> It brings a curse with it, and seldom lasts to the third generation.

Ill habits gather by unseen degrees,
As brooks make rivers, rivers run to seas.

Ill husbandry trusteth to him and to her ;
Good husbandry putteth itself all astir.

> Those who leave their business to others very soon find that it is
> gone from themselves altogether. Do not say " Go," but " Come
> along." This will make all the difference between a clean farm
> and a slovenly one.

Ill huswifery lieth
    Till nine of the clock ;
Good huswifery trieth
    To rise with the cock.

Ill in kits is worse in cats.

For old people to do wrong is inexcusable, but youth may be pleaded as some little apology.

Ill-matched horses draw badly.

If one pulls and the other jibs, it is a bad thing for the family coach. Husband and wife should be of one mind, and specially in religion. "Be ye not unequally yoked."

Ill news flies fast enough.

Hence, "no news is good news"; for, if there had been bad to hear, we should have heard it. People seem more eager to publish the evil than the good; probably because they are evil.

Ill weeds always grow apace;
Folly runs a rapid race.

Ill won is generally ill worn.

A righteous fatality seems to prevent the dishonest from enjoying their plunder. He who steals eels finds them turn to snakes. Ill-gotten goes rotten. What the devil brings the devil takes away.

Ill words are bellows to the fire of anger.

He that is quiet causeth no riot.

Ills that God blesses are my good;
All unblest good is ill;
And all is right that seems most wrong
If it be God's dear will.

A fine distich, which deserves to be made proverbial, seeing it is a conglomerate of proverbs, and full of grace. It has been wisely said that "ills are wells when God blesses them."

Imitate the best, not the worst

Our propensity to imitate is very strong, hence the importance of selecting a good model. Johnson says that no man becomes great by imitation, but we doubt it: in the beginning of life the imitation of a good model leads on to originality.

Improve time in time while time doth last;
For all time is no time when time is past.

Impatience is the sting of affliction.

And this we put into it ourselves. What folly!

In a calm sea we are all good sailors.

> We suppose that we can endure trouble with great equanimity; but when it really comes, we are as much vexed by it as others are.

In a fiddler's house one learns to dance.

> The motion of the music makes the feet move almost involuntarily. When one gets into a family one is apt to fall into the ways of the house.

In a large flock there will be one lame sheep.

> Large families are seldom without one weak child. In religious communities we may look for a proportion of feeble souls.

In a leopard we expect spots.

> In irreligious men we look for ill habits, which could not be tolerated in members of churches.

In strangers' company beware;
Of both thy tongue and purse take care.

In a walking newspaper the leading article is scandal.

> Our advice is—do not take it in, nor do anything else to increase the circulation of the red rag.

In buying a horse expect to be sold.

In choice of bride let grace preside.

> We fear that as a rule nature has far more to do with it than grace.

In company guard your tongue, in solitude your heart.

> Our words need watching; but so also do our thoughts and imaginations, which grow most active when we are alone.

In conduct don't make trifles of trifles.

> Regard the smallest action as being either right or wrong, and make a conscience of little things.

In deep waters men find great pearls.

> Our worst troubles are often our greatest enrichments.

In every beginning think of the end.

> In that case many things would be quitted in their beginnings, for no one would wish to encounter the end.

In every fault there is folly.

It is always unwise to sin.

In fair weather prepare for foul.

The beauty of our English weather is, that when it is bad, we may hope that it will soon change. Its fault is, that when it is good, we may be pretty sure it will soon alter.

In for a penny, in for a pound.

It is so with a certain order of expenses : once begin and you must go on, and cannot pull up when you would.

In giving and taking,
It's easy mistaking.

Therefore allowances should be made for error. Say not: "It is a fraud," but judge it to be a mistake. Count money twice, even after your own kin. Keep correct books. When you err yourself, let it be against yourself.

In half the affairs of this busy life
(As that same day I said to my wife),
Our troubles come from trying to put
The left-hand shoe on the right-hand foot.

A little adjustment would save a world of trouble ; but common sense is very uncommon sense. We put salt upon the plum-pudding and grumble at its taste ; we mix the unsuitable, and the result is uncomfortable.

In judging what a boy will be,
Mark what he is in infancy.

For the child is the father of the man. Quick eyes may see the future life of the man in the little ways of the child.

In law there's many a loss without a gain, but never a gain without a loss.

In Orange everything grows except oranges.

A name is frequently a mere name. Orange is too cold a region for the orange tree : the province bears the name of the fruit it cannot grow. Some Christians have little that is Christian about them. Some "Brethren" are sadly unbrotherly. Surnames are said to go by contraries : "Mr. Makepeace was bred an attorney."

In showers, the umbrella at home is of no use.

It is like the Dutchman's anchor. When the storm came on he said that he had a first-rate anchor at home.

In spending spare,
Of debts beware.

In talks prefer quality to quantity.

Don't utter sheer nonsense, such as *Dr. Darwin* alludes to in his lines :—

> " Hear the pretty ladies talk,
>   Tittle tattle, tittle tattle !
> Like their pattens when they walk,
>   Pittle pattle, pittle pattle."

In the coldest flint there is hot fire.

Persons who seem slow and patient have still a temper, and will fire up if too much provoked. Let us be careful not to arouse dormant passion. It's ill waking sleeping tigers.

In the end things will mend.

Time sides with patience, heals sorrows, and moves difficulties ; therefore let us " learn to labour and to wait."

In the evening one may praise the day.

But it is well to see how things look as the hours pass away. Some acts which seemed to promise well at first may not in the long run turn out to be quite so wise as they looked.

In the front they bear the brunt.

No one who considers his own ease or pleasure should desire to be a leading man : he is little more than the chief drudge, while he is supposed to be a king.

In the wedding cake hope is the sweetest of the plums.

In this life repentance is never too late.

On the other hand, it is never too soon. It is also to be remembered that God, who will accept late repentance, may never give it.

In trade, competition prevents imposition.

No doubt the public are gainers, though tradesmen grumble.

Industry is a fine fire for frozen fingers.

Flowing rivers seldom freeze, and men and boys who keep diligently at work keep themselves warm.

Industry is the parent of independence.

Ingratitude is the basest of vices.

No one ever owns to it : even the devil would not defend it.

Ingratitude wearies benevolence.

Yet let it not succeed with us. This is its natural tendency, but we must take an antidote, and "do good to the unthankful."

Injure not another whilst help thou dost borrow.

This reminds us of *Herbert's* verse :—

" Bees work for man, and yet they never bruise
    Their master's flower, but leave it, having done,
As fair as ever and as fit for use :
    So both the flower doth stay and honey run."

Injuries slighted are very soon righted.

But when they are laid to heart they become of exaggerated importance, and it is difficult to deal with them.

Innocence needs no eloquence.

It pleads its own cause ; and yet in too many cases, in this rough world, "innocence is no protection."

Inquire and inquire ; for report is a liar.

Instruction in truth is destruction of error.

Insults are very much what we make them.

They are like bad coins : we cannot help their being offered to us, but we need not take them.

Intentions which die are pretensions which lie.

Intending, intending, but never amending,
Pretending, pretending ; lies not worth defending.
The wheel is turned round, but no progress is found.

Into courts of law and courtings of love go cautiously.

Well may you go cautiously, for you cannot return easily. These things are like mouse-traps—easy to enter, but hard to leave.

It cannot always be honeymoon.

Therefore eat up the moon and keep the honey : some eat all the honey, and have nothing left but the moon.

It can't come out of the sack, if it's not in it.

If not in the brain, you cannot produce it.   *Pope* says :—

" You beat your pate, and fancy wit will come :
Knock as you please ; there's nobody at home."

It grieves one dog that another goes into the kitchen.

He would like to go there on his own account, and he envies one who is more favoured than himself.   Or if he himself has a free pass to the kitchen he wants no one else to share with him.

It is a bad coat that will not bear brushing.

Yet some people will not bear with half a word of correcting.

It is a fortunate head that never ached.

Where is such a head?   It is to be feared that it has a deal of aching to come

**It is a good horse that never stumbles,
And a good wife that never grumbles.**

If a man has such treasures, let him treat them well, and wish that they may live for ever.

It is a great blessing to know your blessings.

We are apt to be like swine under an oak, eating the acorns, but never praising the tree ; better to be like the little chick, which, when it drinks, lifts its head towards heaven.

It is a long lane that has no turning.

It is a mad hare that will be caught with a drum.

He must be of the same sort who is made religious by a band of music.   If such there be let the drum be beaten still.

It is a poor bee that makes no more honey than it eats.

This, of course, depends, in a measure, upon the season and the position of the hive.   A little honey costs more labour when flowers are few, than a great deal in good weather among the heather.

It is a sin to steal a pin.

> So said Chubbins; and then Padley topped it by adding—" It is a greater to steal a 'tater."

It is a very easy thing
To make a man into a king ;
But ever since the world began,
'Tis hard to make a king a man.

It is always dark just under a lamp.

> Thus Orientals declare the injustice of their rulers.   Is it not also true, that, near a great truth, there is a mystery ?

It is an ill house where the hen crows.

> It is unnatural and uncomfortable to see the wife domineering over the husband.   *Hood* makes a poor little man say :—
>
> > " And when I speak, my voice is weak ;
> > But hers, she makes a gong of it :
> > For I am short, and she is tall,
> > And that's the short and long of it."

It is an ill wool that will not take a dye.

> Most men are too ready to be influenced ; but, if we find one who is impervious to all teaching, what is to be done with him ?

It is bad combing where there is no hair.

> Trading in a district where there are no customers, preaching where there are few people, or teaching where there seems to be no understanding—any one of these is hard.

It is bad mustard that never bites the tongue.

> If a preacher never touches the conscience, what is the good of him ?

It is barely possible to bear with a bear.

> Yet you may as well bear with the creature, for, in resisting him, it is more than barely possible that you may lay bare your temper, and become a bear yourself.

It is best to make the best of the worst.

> If fortune give thee less than she has done,
> Then make less fire, and walk more in the sun.—*Sir R. Baker.*

It is better to be puffed *at* than to be puffed *up*.

It is better to deserve praise than to receive it.

> The noblest characters can be formed by missing deserved honour: but to receive praise is perilous even when it is our due.

It is better to feed five drones than starve one bee.

> Therefore in distributing alms, it is better to be deceived by the bad than to neglect the deserving.

It is better to wear a shabby coat than lose a good conscience.

> *Havelock* said : " I humbly trust I should not change my opinions and practice, though it rained garters and coronets as the reward of apostasy." Bravely spoken !

It is better to whistle than whine ;
It is better to laugh than to cry ;
For though it be cloudy, the sun will soon shine
In the blue, and the beautiful sky.

It is bitter fare to eat one's own words.

It is cheaper to *give* one shilling than to *lend* five.

It is cheaper to *lend* one shilling than to *give* five.

> Lending and giving come to much the same thing, and thus the smaller the investment the better.

It is cruel to smite those with our *tongues* whom God has smitten with his *hand*.

> Hence no unkind word should be said of the deformed, or the unfortunate, or those whose gifts are small.

It is easier to build two chimneys than to keep one going.

> Setting up an establishment is simple enough, but to keep the affair going costs far more money than we could have thought.

It is easier to find a wife than to feed a wife.

> They are very dear to their husbands. You have no right to drag a loving woman into poverty. Do not seek a housekeeper till you can see the means of keeping the house.

It is easier to go up hill rapidly, than to go down hill gracefully.

> In the heyday of success prosperity may be admirably borne ; and yet in times of loss and decline the man may fail to display a noble and patient spirit.

It is easier to hurt than to heal.

It is easier to leave home than to come back again.

> True. To his cost, many a wanderer has found it so.

It is easier to make money than to keep it.

> Money is like an icicle, soon found at certain seasons, and soon melted under other circumstances. How often we see a man wise enough to grow rich, but very foolish with his riches!

It is easier to pull down than to build.

> The reformer's work is easy so long as he destroys, but to reconstruct is difficult.

It is easy to fetch water when a river is near.

> Ought we not then to find all the grace we need? Prayer is the bucket, and the river of life is close at hand.

It is eight ounces of the one, and half a pound of the other.

> They are alike guilty. They are both in the same boat. They are much of a muchness.

It is good fish enough if we could but catch it.

It is good to be deaf of one ear.

> It is wise not to hear some things, or to act as if we did not hear them. A man who could not explain himself at last lost his temper, and said to his fellow-traveller, "How dull you are! Why the matter is as simple as A B C." "It may be so," said the other, "but suppose I am D E F?" It is well sometimes to be in that condition.

It is good to get out of the net, but better not to get into it,

> Watchfulness against sin is better than repentance after sin.

It is hard to be high and humble.

> To be eminent for riches or rank, and yet to be lowly, is what only grace can teach us to be.

It is hard to be idle and innocent.

> "Satan finds some mischief still
> For idle hands to do."

It is hard to get two heads under one hat.

> Two men will seldom think alike. Two sets of opinions cannot meet in one man.

It is hard to talk sense, but harder to find listeners if you do.

> Nonsense charms the multitude ; plain truth is despised.

It is idle to spread a plaster where there is no sore.

> Vain is it to administer religious consolation where the conscience never smarted under a sense of sin.

It is more easy to be wise for others than for yourself.

> We come across persons noted for giving judicious advice to others whose lives are failures as to themselves. We remember one such who was a sort of Solomon, and yet made a hash of the home department in a way which was a warning to all who knew him.

It is never too late to learn ;
It is never too late to turn.

It is never too late to mend ;
It is always too soon to rend.

It is no joke to bear with a man who is all jokes.

It is not enough to run, you must start in time.

> Neither is this enough; you must run the right way, and keep on in it.

It is not every couple that is a pair.

> Alas ! many are coupled together who will no more unite than oil and water. Of many a wife it may be said : " She is his fate, but not his mate."

It is not everyone that is lying in lavender like Paddy's pig,

> Or feeding in clover like the British lion

It is not the load, but the overload, which kills the horse.

> The little too much is the last straw which breaks the camel's back. Very few think of this in reference either to men or horses.

It is poor work fishing without bait,

> Or trying to convert people when there is nothing in your gospel that is worth having.

It is sometimes harder to get a penny out of a full purse than ten shillings out of a purse that is half empty.

Benevolence does not increase with wealth. We have known it to go the other way. The guinea heart has the shilling purse , and the shilling heart the guinea pocket.

It is sure to be dark if you shut your eyes.

When men don't want to understand, the subject is sure to be beset with difficulties.

It is the bright day that brings out the adder.

Prosperity develops pride and other vices, and men are then seen who else would hide away.

It is the frog's own croak that betrays him.

If foolish people would not talk, their folly would not be known.

It is the master-wheel which makes the mill go round.

The master force in our nature will set in motion all the rest, whether for good or for evil.

It is the truth that makes a man angry.

One came to me in a high passion because of what another had said of him; for, said he, "I should not have minded if it had been true." "Nay," said I, "then you should have minded" I have heard of another that when one said, "You need not be angry, for it is not true," "Ah !" said he, "there's the rub of it, it *is* true" If the charge is true, we ought not to be angry, but ashamed.

It is the truth that blocks the way of bad men, and balks their designs. They can't get over it. It would be fine for them if the Bible could be proved to be false ; but its solemn teachings are their stumbling, and hence their hatred of sound doctrine.

It is too late to cover the well when the child is drowned.

It is well to spend a penny to save a pound.

There is great economy in a wise expenditure. Don't spoil the house for a tenpenny nail.

It may be hard to work, but it must be harder to want.

It is harder to need bread than to knead it, and better to grind hard at the mill than to have no meal to grind, and more pleasant to carry a load of wood than to have no wood for the hearth.

It may be little, and yet every bit of the little may be bad.

> The same may possibly be true of a little wife, a little strife, a little clique, and a little sneak, &c., &c.

It may be true, it may be true;
But has it aught to do with you?

> If not, do not rush in where the peaceful fear to tread.

It must be a very bad cause if the lawyer is ashamed of it.

> How well it would be if they all acted like one of whom I have read :—" A pious attorney, being asked how he could conscientiously plead for some of his clients, replied, ' Sir, I have not for many years undertaken a cause which I could not pray for ; and I never lost a case for which I could pray.' " This attorney is deceased, and we are not able to mention the place of his burial.

It needs great wisdom to play the fool.

It needs greater wisdom not to play the fool.

> Both proverbs are true. The court fools of the olden times were not fools, or they would soon have lost their heads as well as their caps and bells. He who never commits a folly has great wisdom indeed.

It needs more skill than I can tell,
To play the second fiddle well.

> Any one can take the lead, or at least everybody thinks he can; but he who will gracefully remain second to another exhibits rare virtues, and deserves far more honour than he usually gets.

It needs much skill to wield the quill.

> Those who think of writing for the press had better think again.

It never rains but it pours.

> When things do come they frequently come in plenty ; especially when trials come, the downpour is generally very heavy.

It requires many brains to deal with a blockhead.

> Because you have to find judgment both for him and for yourself, and you are never sure that he understands an agreement when it is made.

It takes a good many mice to frighten a cat.

> Addressed to little men when they set themselves against one who knows his power.

It takes a long time to say nothing.

> He who has really nothing to say will speak on and on as if he were wound up like a clock, and must keep on till he had run down.

It takes all sorts of people to make up a world.

> We must, therefore, bear with the eccentric; and in general, make use of such people as come in our way. But really some odd folks are odd indeed, and we wonder what next we shall see.

It takes four living men to carry a dead man out of the house.

> Yes, and to get rid of worldlings and hypocrites out of the Lord's house is a great tax on the energies of living Christians. Four living men were better employed in bringing a sick soul before the Lord Jesus than in bearing out an Ananias or a Sapphira.

It takes many a load of earth to bury the truth.

> And then it will rise again.

It takes many feathers and more big words to make a pound.

It takes many gallons of water to fill a sieve.

> Instruction may be poured into the mind of a forgetful person, and yet he is never the wiser.

It takes two to make a quarrel.

> The *Rev. John Clark*, of Frome, was a man of peace. He was asked one day, by a friend, how he kept himself from being involved in quarrels. He answered, " By letting the angry person always have the quarrel to himself." This saying seems to have had some influence on some of the inhabitants of that town ; for, when a quarrel has been likely to ensue, they have said, " Come, let us remember old Mr. Clark, and leave the angry man to quarrel by himself."
> This is an old story. Is it true of Frome now ?

It's a bad bargain when both sides lose.

> Yet it happens so occasionally—in marriage, to wit, and in war.

It's a great thing to do a little thing well.

> A man's entire character and capacity may be seen in a small matter quite as well as in a greater affair. We ought to do our best in all that we do.

It's a great weariness to do nothing.

There is no fatigue like that of one who is tired of having nothing to do. When Napoleon was slowly withering away, from disease and *ennui* together, on the rock of St. Helena, it was told him that one of his old friends, an ex-colonel in his Italian army, was dead. "What disease killed him?" asked Napoleon. "That of having nothing to do," it was answered. "Enough," sighed Napoleon, "even had he been an emperor."

It's a pity to be grey before you're good.

It's a silly mouse that falls in love with a cat.

Yet it happens. Infatuated women marry villains, who devour all their estate and then forsake them.

It's a silly pig that's proud of its ring.

That ring in the nose, which proves him to be a doer of mischief, the foolish pig is supposed to prize as an ornament. There are men who glory in their shame.

It's all very fine,
To give what's not thine.

Servants and others need warning against that kind of generosity which amounts to thieving. Persons who flourish with large donations and are deep in debt, are worse.

It's an ill bird that fouls its own nest.

To revile your family, your church, your trade, your country, is a very unsavoury thing

It's an ill wind that blows nobody good.

The worst calamities to the many, bring benefit to the few.

It's bad for a rat when he's too big for his hole.

There are such people, much too great for their position, and therefore quite unable to enjoy the comforts which might be theirs. Poor rats, they can't get into their holes!

It's bad going to market with an empty purse.

It's bad when the tail wags the dog.

When the least and lowest control affairs, it is unnatural and unprofitable.

It's easier to deal with a whole fool than with half a fool.

In the first instance you set the man aside; but, in the second, the case is not bad enough for that. When a man gets into an asylum, the matter is easy; but what of those who are mad, but not quite mad enough to be confined? They are plentiful as blackberries.

It's easy to put the pot on, but is there anything in it?

To act the big man is easy, but to be really great is another matter.

It's good sailing with wind and tide.

It's hard blowing at cold coals.

And harder warming frozen souls.

It's hard keeping shop where there are no customers.

One grows weary with waiting, when, as the Chinese say, "You have only sold a couple of cucumbers in three days."

It's hard to be bitten by your own dog.

You have fed him, and he owns you as master, and yet he bites you. Some of us know all about this, and cannot soon forget the pain; yet we are not mad.

It's hard to get a pound of butter out of a dog's mouth.

Or to obtain your money when certain persons have once managed to grasp it. A friend assured me that he was acquainted with many funds, but that in all his life he had never received a penny from the fund called REFUND.

It's hard to get the leaven out of the dough.

Indeed, it is impossible. How is sin to be gotten out of the nature of man, except by a miracle of grace?

It's hard to make a good thing of a bad marriage.

So hard that he who is happily mated may rejoice that he has not so hard a problem to work out.

> If tied thou be
> To a sour apple tree,
> I pity thee and I pity she;
> But right glad I be
> That it is not me.

It's hard to pluck a magpie, and not make her scream.

When you are exposing faults, those who are personally touched are sure to cry out, and to express great indignation at your personalities, your uncharitableness, your inaccuracy, or something.

It's hard to turn in a narrow road.

But if you are truly in the straight and narrow way which leadeth unto life, you have no need to turn, and, indeed, you must not.

It's " Hobson's choice "—the next or none.

Hobson, the carrier of Cambridge, let out horses to the young collegians, and he would have the horses go out in turns. When a young gentleman wanted to take another horse than the one whose turn it was, the old carrier would answer, " This, or none." For many people, it would be a great blessing if they had a *Hobson* to choose for them, for they do not know their own minds.

It's hope that cheers us, but it's soap that cleans us.

Both articles are cheap, and may be used to advantage.

It's ill jesting with God's judgments.

Anything which has to do with divine things should be regarded as beyond the range of jesting. He must be hard pressed for mirth who can make merry with sacred things. Remember Belshazzar.

It's ill living where everybody knows everybody.

> A village is a hive of glass,
> There nothing unobserved can pass

It's ill putting fair glove on foul hand.

Pretending to purity while covered with sin is sheer hypocrisy.

It's ill when the physician had need be the patient.

Note what *Selden* says upon such a case. " Preachers say, ' Do as I say, not as I do.' But if a physician had the same disease upon him that I have, and he should bid me do one thing, and he do quite another, could I believe him ? "

It's mean to say what you don't mean.

It's no use diving deep to bring up a broken pot.

Making a great search after something not worth knowing.

It's no use killing nettles to grow docks.

If we only supplant one evil by another the gain is small.

It's no use mending the tank when the water's gone.

An Eastern way of describing the common fault of being wise too late. "I know how he could have been saved," cried a slow-minded creature, after his friend had been drowned.

It's no use playing the cornet to a cow.

She has no ear for such music. There are plenty of instances in which want of taste on the part of the person will render all the instructor's efforts vain.

It's no use pumping a dry well.

It's much the same if you ask Mr. Screwmaker for a donation.

It's no use sparing at the spigot, and letting it run at the bunghole.

Some are mightily economical in trifles, and yet indulge in expensive vices.

It's no use running from the bear to the wolves.

A change of loan-offices is no great gain ; neither is a change of vices, or prodigalities, or ill companions.

It's not always the worst fish that bites first.

No : a very excellent convert may come forward at the very first time of asking. There are first that shall be first.

It's not always the worst fish that bites last.

Therefore persevere, for there are good converts yet to come. and "there are last that shall be first."

It's not the bonnet, but the head that's in it.

Yet you may depend upon it,
Heads are judged of by the bonnet.

It's not "What has she?" but "What is she?"

Seek a fortune *in* a wife rather than *with* a wife.

It's pleasant to see it rain when you're in the dry.

A cruel and selfish observation; but there is truth in it. We are interested by the account of wars which should make us weep, and we read with avidity stories which ought to excite our horror. We are pleased to hear of others sailing on the sea, even though we should be sick if we were there ourselves. A writer speaks of the peculiar pleasure of seeing two strong men pulling the oars at a splendid rate on a hot day, while you coolly survey them from the cushioned seats of your boat.

It's the old pot that makes the good soup.

A Conservative sentiment this, but we fully agree with it as regards the old gospel.

It's too late to cast anchor when the ship is on the rocks.

When at last the soul is ruined by sin, and the mind is losing consciousness, the time for faith is over.

It's too late to cry when your head's off.

When the catastrophe has come, and the trader is a bankrupt, it will be of no use for him to cry out. Better see to the matter at once, while you are yet able to pay your way, and your head is still on your shoulders; unless, indeed, it is so poor a head that the old saw applies: "You have a head, *and so has a pin.*"

Sayings of a more Spiritual Sort.

I have a great need of Christ ; but I have a great Christ
for my need.

If Christ and thy heart are one, sin and thy heart are two.

We cannot hold to our Lord, and yet love that which he hates.

If Christ be sweet to thee, sin will be bitter to thee.

If Christ hath made us kings, why do we live as beggars ?

Which we do, if, through unbelief, we miss the comforts which
are stored up in his Word.

If God be our guide, he'll be our guard.

If God bids thee ride, he'll find thee a horse.

We are not called to a work for which we have no capacity. If
God means a man to preach, he gives him thought, voice and
common sense. Alas ! men attempt what they were not meant for ;
and then we see in the pulpit—

" The intent of kindly nature foiled,
A tailor or a butcher spoiled."

If God lights the candle, Satan cannot blow it out.

This reminds us of the old Reformation picture of a candle with
the Pope, Monks, and the Devil all puffing at it.

If God's mercies are not loadstones, they will be millstones.

If they do not draw us to God and his salvation, they will sink
us under a load of condemnation.

If God's to-day be too soon for thy repentance, thy to-morrow
may be too late for his acceptance.

If God's work, 'twill aye endure ;
If man's, 'tis not a moment sure.

This is the famous saying of Gamaliel.—Acts v. 39.

If in God you delight,
You'll have songs in the night.

If Jesus help thee, none can hinder thee.

If our best is bad, what must our worst be?

A humbling consideration for every soul that would know its true condition before God.

If sin were not deceitful, it would never be delightful.

If it could be seen in all its native deformity, men would loathe it.

If study makes men of us, prayer will make saints of us.

If the love of God sets us to work, the God of love will find us wages.

God is a sure paymaster, though he does not always pay at the end of every week.

If thou wilt not pray for thyself, who can pray for thee?

If thou wilt spin, God will find thee yarn.

Holy work is God's work, and he will provide for it. So have I found it.—*C. H. S.*

If thou wouldst preserve thy faith, labour to increase thy faith.

If we did what we should, God would do what we would.

Prayer would be heard if we'd hearken to the Word.

If you are God's child, behave yourself accordingly.

If you are not a sinner, Christ is not your Saviour.

If you cannot go to the house of the Lord, go to the Lord of the house.

If you have chosen God, God has chosen you.

For your choice of God is the result of his grace, which flows to you because of his choice of you.

If you have found Christ, he has found you.

Of that you may be quite sure, for we may truly say to our Lord:

No sinner can be
Beforehand with thee;
Thy grace is most sovereign,
Most rich, and most free.

If you have grace, you have none to boast of.

> That which we receive as a free favour, how can we boast of it, as though we had not so received it?

If you have to swim, the depth is of no consequence.

> Since the godly man must swim the sea of life by faith, the depth of his necessity is a very small item.

> > If we trust at all,
> > Let us trust for all.

If you lose a penny for Christ he will give you a pound.

> But do not seek to have it so, lest it should prove that he returned your offering because he would not accept it at your hands.

If you starve the preacher, how can he feed *you* ?

If you were not strangers here, the dogs of the world would not bark at you.

If you would know the heart of your sin, you must know the sin of your heart.

> An old divine says, "You say, 'I have my faults, but at bottom I have a good heart.' Alas! it is this that deceives you, for your heart is the worst part of you."

In Adam's fall
We sinnèd all.

> This is unfashionable doctrine, but none the less true. Some call the fall a fable, but of such we shrewdly suspect that all their religion is fabulous.

In God's works we see his hand, but in his Word his face.

In one sin there are many sins.

> The first sin is a specimen of this. It would be hard to say which was the chief point in Adam's transgression—unbelief, pride, presumption, self-will, selfishness, irreverence, or dishonesty.

In sermons, the less of man the more of God.

In weighty matters wait on God.

> And count nothing too light to be brought to the mercy-seat. "Bring hither the ephod" was David's cry, and true believers should imitate his wise example.

Inordinate affection brings extraordinary affliction.

> We are punished for idolatry through our idols.

Invited guests bring no provisions with them.

> Why, then, should sinners hesitate to come to Christ, because they are empty-handed. One who was invited to tea by a poor woman carried two cakes with him, but the good creature was so wounded thereby that he deeply regretted it. Will we insult our Saviour by such an act as even a poor woman might resent?

Inward guilt makes outward fear.

It is a great sin to love a small sin.

It is better to obey God than to work miracles.

> Obedience is the hall-mark of faith, and the proof of grace; but Judas and others worked miracles, and were lost.

It is easier to *build* temples than to *be* temples.

It is God's will that I should not do mine own will.

> If I will make God's will my will, my will will be God's will.

It is not every one who *looks* like a Christian that *lives* like a Christian.

It is terrible to be born if not born again.

It is the Christians' joy to give Christ joy.

It is the devil's masterpiece to make us think well of ourselves.

> Yet we do this so naturally that we hardly need his help in the business.

It were better for us to have *no* being than not to have a *new* being.

It's all in vain to paint the dead.

> To colour a dead profession of religion with appearances of piety is terrible folly.

It's hard sailing when there is no wind.

> It is very hard preaching when we have no help from God,

ABBER, jabber, I won't have her.

A woman who has a long tongue is not a wife for a sensible man. And yet, it may be, she is one who might fairly say, "Hold your tongue, husband, and let me talk; for I have all the wit." Those of whom this would be true never say it.

Jack has been to school
To learn to be a fool.

What a pity that this was the net result of his learning! We fear we have met with many young gents who have given themselves mighty airs because they once 'learned "Hic, hæc, hoc." They thought they knew a great deal, but they did not.

Jack gets on by his stupidity.

This might be so once; but, now that the schoolmaster is abroad, such a Jack will have little meat to roast, and no boots to pull off unless he brightens up.

Jack-in-office is a great man.

Generally much too large for his waistcoat. He cannot contain himself, and the world is hardly large enough to accommodate him.

Jack is as good as his master.

They are very much alike in their greatness, especially Jack. In many instances the fine livery makes the servant appear the greater man of the two in the eyes of the vulgar.

Jack is great because of his master.

But he is apt to forget that his plumes are borrowed. Even servants of God can be so foolish as to forget that they are nothing without their Lord.

" Jack-of-all-trades is master of none."

He who brags of doing everything, does nothing.

> "Jack his own merit sees—
>   This gives him pride;
> And he sees more than all
>   The world beside."

Jack-of-all-trades, show and sound,
Good for nothing, I'll be bound.

Jack-of-both-sides is kicked by both sides.

When his double-dealing is found out, he becomes the foot-ball of contempt.

Jackets sometimes need a little dusting.

Boys are none the worse for tasting the results of disobedience, and making the acquaintance of a cane which does not yield sugar.

Jacob's voice should not go with Esau's hands.

This almost led to Jacob's being found out by his father; and when men are not dealing with a blind Isaac, they will soon be seen to be deceivers if they talk one way and act another.

Jaundiced eyes see all things yellow.

Prejudiced persons view everything in an untruthful light. They see what is in their own minds rather than that which really exists. One who returned to a minister whom he had formerly left, apologized and said, "Sir, I used to find fault, but then *I heard you with a jaundiced eye.*" He was not an Irishman.

Jeering and sneering
Are not worth fearing.

They will have no power to harm if we refuse to be harmed. It is only the thinness of our skin which can give them power to wound.

Jest only with your equals,
And with them leave no sequels.

Older and wiser men than ourselves may not care for our nonsense, and they ought not to be tried with it. Those with whom we may make merry should never have anything bitter to remember. Let us use friendly pleasantry, if any.

Jesting falsehoods are serious sins.

God has given us no license to lie, even though we only do it in sport. He that will lie in jest will be lost in earnest.

Jesting is unwise if it be not very wise.

It is difficult to keep within fitting bounds, so that no rule of truth, kindness, or religion be broken. As a rule, jesting is "not convenient." With some men, an approach to a certain subject must be carefully avoided, or they will be aggrieved. The Creoles say, "Jest with a monkey as much as you please, but take good care not to handle his tail." So should we be careful not to touch a man's sore places, even with the lightest finger.

Jesting may end in sorrowing.

If it be unkindly done it will vex the object of it, and then bring harm to the utterer of it. Some must have their joke; but the game is not worth the candle when the mirth gives pain.

Jests are not arguments, and laughter is not demonstration.

Yet many look round very knowingly, as if the roars of laughter they have called forth settled the matter; but it is not so.

Jests which go too far bring home hate.

Some men's backs are not broad enough to bear a joke, and they are provoked to anger by that which ought only to have tickled them. If you must joke, neither do it with stupid people, nor sensitive people. In their case, what you think sweetmeats will be followed with sour sauce.

Jill is what Jack makes her;
But for better for worse he takes her.

It is said that some are "all worse and no better"; but, still, the deed is done, be it kill or cure, and both parties must make the best of it. How much bliss or blister may lie within the small circle of a wedding-ring! But once on the finger it comes not off with honour till death doth us part.

Joe hates a hypocrite, and this doth show
Self-love is not a glaring fault with Joe.

John Blunt may often cause affront,
But bravely he will bear the brunt.

The man who is so honest as to speak his mind is, or should be, ready to bear all consequences without losing his temper.

John Ploughman says, Of two evils choose neither.

Don't choose the least, but let all evils alone. There is a wicked way of using this saying, "Of all evils choose the least," by applying it to an undersized wife. When the Lacedæmonians fined their king for marrying a little woman, he excused himself by saying that of two evils he had chosen the less. The old rhymster said:—

> "If wives are evils, as 'tis known,
>   And wofully confessed,
> The man who's wise will surely own,
>   A little one is best."

John the Ploughman often said,
Never carry care to bed.

> Leave it at the place where you kneel in prayer. "Casting all your care upon him; for he careth for you."

Join not in hand where thou canst not join in heart.

Joke with an ass, and he will kick you in play.

> Rough people take undue advantage of familiarities tolerated in sport. It is better to know your company before you joke, or a rude fellow may wound you sorely.

Jokes never gain over an enemy, but they sometimes lose a friend.

> Therefore, like edged tools, they should be handled carefully. Never drive a jest so far as to create anger.

Joseph is not known when a new king arises.

> Past services are not often recognized by new masters.

Joy and sorrow are next door neighbours.

> Some say that life is like the ague—one good day between two bad ones. We suppose *they* find it so; but *we* joy in God. In an earthly sense, however, it is still true,
>
> > "Joy and sorrow
> > Make to-day and to-morrow."

Joy, and temperance, and repose,
Slam the door on doctor's nose.

> The Latin has it: "Be these three thy doctors: rest, cheerfulness, and moderate diet."

Joy pours oil into the lamp;
Sorrow is a grievous damp.

Judge a man by his questions, as well as by his answers.

> This is a bit of French wisdom; and there is much in it.

Judge by your own pot how the others are boiling.

> If this were done, many would abstain from provocation.

Judge not a tree by its bark.

> Nor a man by his clothes, or other outward appearance.

Judge not a woman by her dress, nor a book by its binding.

> The best books are generally bound very soberly ; while novels, and such like trash, are in flashy coloured wrappers. As for the grand old Puritans, "They wander in sheep-skins, and goats' skins"; yet we say of them, "of whom the world was not worthy."

Judge not by appearances.

> If you do, you are no judge. Look a little closer than a passing glance will enable you.
>> Take not dislike to a man in the street ;
>> Yet be not "hail fellow" with all that you meet.

Judge not of a ship as she lies on the stocks.

> Wait till she has accomplished a voyage. Test everything by experience. Human beings cannot be added up like a column of figures : you can only know men by living with them. The Chinese say, "Every character must be chewed to get its juice."

Justice is one thing, law is another.

> Justice would act with mathematical certainty, but the result of an appeal to law is a lottery ; and this, not because the law is unjust, but because the procedures and judgments of courts are fallible.
>> The law's a shuttle-cock, you'll none deny,
>> Which parchment battledores compel to fly.

Sayings of a more Spiritual Sort.

Jacob saw angels ascending and descending, but none standing still.

> Activity is the mark of holy spirits, and should be the mark of holy men.

Jesus Christ is light to the eye, honey to the taste, music to the ear, joy to the heart.

Jesus Christ to a believer is fairer than the fairest, sweeter than the sweetest, nearer than the nearest, dearer than the dearest, richer than the richest, and better than the best

Jesus has many lovers of his crown, but few bearers of his cross.

Jesus is our sole hope as well as our soul's hope.

I saw on a cross in Italy the words "*Spes unica.*"

Jesus lived that he might die, and died that we might live.

Jesus saves *from* sin, not *in* sin.

Jesus will be all or nothing.

Joys are our wings; sorrows are our spurs.

Joy in the Lord always, and you will always have cause for joy.

Joy suits no man so much as a saint, and no day so much as a Sabbath.

"Religion never was designed to make our pleasure less."

Don't make the Lord's day dreary. Enjoy the most sun on Sunday. "Call the Sabbath a delight."

Judge not God by his providences, but by his promises.

His love hides itself in afflictions, but shines forth with unchanging glory in his promises.

Judge not the Word, but let the Word judge thee.

Alas! that so many are proud enough to call the Holy Spirit to their bar, and have never received grace to bow to the infallible Teacher.

Justice is the activity of God's holiness.

EEP a cool head in hot weather.

> And in any other weather : a hot head is always a danger.

Keep a nest-egg ; money lays to money.

With many people the saving of the first five pounds is *the* struggle. Let them resolve, before the cares of a family pour upon them, to learn the art of proper economy.

Keep a thing seven years, and you'll find a use for it.

Even a tea-pot without a spout, and a saucepan without a bottom have been found at last to have a use.

Keep as far as can be
From the "Marquis of Granby.'

And from all other drink-shops. The best side of a public-house is the outside. There's nothing within which a sober man wants.

Keep cats out of pantries, and children out of temptation.

Put not a temptation in the way of the young, or you will be a partaker in their sin, if they fall into it.

Keep clear of Red Lions and Blue Boars.

These are such strange animals, that he who haunts their dens will by degrees become a strange animal himself.

Keep clear of the rout who would clear thee out.

There are certain people who would gladly egg on a man to spend all that he has, and the only safety from them is to put a good mile between yourself and them.

Keep cool, and the hot-tempered cannot harm you.

You will be more than a match for the most furious, if you are quite calm yourself.

Keep far from the bar and the barrel.

From the bar of drinking to the bar of justice is a short cut; bar the road by abstinence.

Keep good company, and may the company keep you good.

It will be a great help in that direction, for we are all greatly influenced by our associations.

> As cloth is tinged by any dye
> In which it long time plunged may lie ;
> So those with whom he loves to live
> To every man his colour give.

Keep good company, and you will be of the number.

But if you keep company with bad men, their number will soon be increased by one.

Keep no more helps than thou canst help.

For there is truth in the saying, "The more servants, the more plagues." When too numerous servants tumble over one another, and make work instead of doing it.

Keep not from sowing for fear of the birds.

True, something of your work will be lost, but the major part will bring forth a harvest ; therefore, sow on.

Keep not two tongues in one mouth.

To say one thing to one, and another to another, is unwise and wicked. The double-tongued will receive double condemnation.

Keep road-dust out of your eyes, and gold-dust out of your hearts.

This last is terribly blinding, hardening, and even killing. More are ruined by riches than by poverty.

> Who live for getting
> The wealth men covet,
> Live, too, forgetting
> Wealth far above it.

Keep the head cool, and the feet warm.

Some say, "Keep your feet dry, and your head hot"; but the former proverb is preferable. At least, it cannot be wise to be hot-headed in a mental sense.

Keep the highroad, and none may challenge thy right.

Do what is clearly just, and follow no doubtful policy, and then you are safe from any righteous censure.

Keep the ferret of suspicion out of the hen-house of your friendship.

If you don't, you will not have a friend left; for when a man is given to suspect, everything that happens suggests a reason for doubt. The following verse by *Alice Cary* is worthy to be quoted continually :—

> Do not look for wrong and evil—
> You will find them if you do ;
> As you measure for your neighbour,
> He will measure back to you.
> Look for goodness, look for gladness,
> You will meet them all the while ;
> If you bring a smiling visage
> To the glass, you meet a smile.

Keep the powder far from the fire.

The powder of depravity is in the heart, therefore avoid the fire of temptation. "Lead us not into temptation."

Keep thine own counsel, so I counsel thee.

Bailey advises : —

> "Let no man know thy business, save some friend,
> A man of mind."

Keep thou some, and more will come.

Get people to begin saving, and half the battle of thrift is won.

Keep to the bridge which has carried you over.

Don't forsake the old gospel and the truths which feed your soul. Leave not the old business. Quit not an old friend. Alonso, King of Aragon, used to say, in commendation of old age, "Old wood is best to burn ; old wine to drink ; old friends to trust ; and old authors to read." We may add, "Old shoes to wear."

Keep truth, and truth will keep thee.

Whatever truth costs thee, even if she put thee to heavy charges, she will repay thee with the largest interest.

Keep your finger out of your neighbour's pie ;

Or you will burn your finger, or get it cut. Let not that concern thee which does not concern thee. Remember that sarcastic verse :—

> "I know your assistance you'll lend ;
> When I want it I'll speedily send ;
> You need not be making such stir ;
> But mind your own business, good sir ! "

Keep your grease for your own cart-wheels.

Spoken to those who are full of palaver, and are worrying you with those soft nothings which disgust honest people.

Keep your hand out of the fire, and yourself out of quarrels.

Keep your hook always baited.

Who can tell when a fish may come? Be ready for a customer in the shop. Be ready to say a good word for true religion when an opportunity occurs. "Keep your powder dry."

Keep your lip from sip and sip.

For by constant drops the habit of drinking is acquired more surely than even by occasional excesses. Young men begin to take nips in business, and this becomes their sure ruin.

Keep your mouth shut, and no flies will get in.

And no lies will come out. Wisdom is not garrulous, but folly stands with gaping mouth :—

"The prophet Balaam was in wonder lost
To hear his ass speak :—asses now talk most."

Keep your mouth shut and your eyes open.

See and say nothing. This is wise for eyes and mouth too.

"Think *all* you speak, but speak not all you think.
Thoughts are your own ; your words are so no more.
Where Wisdom steers, wind cannot make you sink.
Lips never err when wisdom keeps the door."—*Delaune.*

Keep your old shoes till you get new ones.

Excellent advice. Never leave a place of business or a situation till you see something else. He who gave away his clothes before he had a new suit, found himself as much a prisoner as if he had been in Newgate.

Keep your room always tidy and clean;
Let dust on the furniture never be seen.

Mind this, young housewife !

Keep your shop, and your shop will keep you.

So said *Benjamin Franklin;* and Poor Richard was wise in his generation. The precept is more necessary now than ever.

Keep your sickle out of your neighbour's harvest.

Let him have the full reward of his toil. Don't fish in his waters, nor poach on his manors. Do not run off with what should be his own proper gains. Don't even meddle with his business, nor seem to do so, if you can avoid it.

Keep your spoon out of my porridge.

Don't meddle with my matters, for they matter not to you.

Keep your tongue, and keep your friend.

It will often happen that talk will cause disagreement, while prudent silence will cement fellowship.

Keep your weather-eye open.

You may have your eye-tooth drawn if you don't watch. People must wear wide-awakes nowadays: these are so called because they are hats which have no nap.

Keep your wife's husband out of the public-house.

> Get him quick to sign the pledge;
> Keep him thus from danger's edge.

**Keep within compass, and then you'll be sure
To avoid many troubles which others endure.**

Kick not against the pricks.

This is hard work for a naked foot; yet many are doing it, as Saul did of old.

Kill the cat, and what will you do with the mice?

One has to look at the result of parting with a useful servant. The police may be expensive, but what would thieves cost?

Kill the weeds, or they'll kill the seeds.

Errors and vices are the enemies of truth and virtue.

Kill your enemies with kindness.

They will be slow in dying; but the method makes a sure and happy end of them.

Kind words are never wasted.

Like scattered seeds they spring up in unexpected places.

Kind words bring no blisters on the tongue that speaks them, nor on the ear which hears them.

Kindle not a fire which you cannot put out.

> To commence a family quarrel is one of the things condemned by this sage sentence.

Kindness is a conquering weapon.

Kindness should not be all on one side.

> One good turn must have another as its return, or it will not be fair. He who expects kindness should show kindness.

Kings, bears, and wealthy old folk, are apt to worry their keepers.

> Who aspires to the office of bear-ward? Yet it is the easiest post of the three which are mentioned in this sentence. Those who have tried the other two will fully confirm the assertion.

Kings should have heads, as well as crowns.

> It is sad for them, and bad for their people, where this is not the case. Some men would like to be the head of everything, but they are not ; and nobody regrets it.

Knack can carry, in a crack,
Pack which breaks poor labour's back.

> Get into the way of the thing, and you can do it. But it is only by hard labour that men learn to do their work easily. Tact is a great thing ; it does not remove difficulties, but difficulties disappear before it.

Knaves often cheat themselves.

Kneeling never spoiled silk stocking.

> It is to be feared that few silk stockings try it long enough. Prayer brings no hurt to any man.

Knock at no door which thou wouldst not have opened.

> Or it may open on a sudden, and thou wilt stand confounded. When persons speak for a cause which they do not really believe in, they may have to pay dearly for their words. Some who defend Socialism may soon have too much of it.

Knotty timber needs sharp wedges.

> Hard hearts must be broken, and God will use stern truth and severe affliction, that it may be done.

Know chalk from cheese, and talk from deeds.

Especially when it is your own chalk and your own talk.

Know the secrets of thine own house, but not those of another.

Avoid being made the keeper of a secret. It is a difficult task, and if you fail in it you may cause great mischief, and embroil yourself. When any ask, "Can you keep a secret?" Answer, "It is no secret that I cannot keep a secret."

Know when you are well off.

One would think that this was very elementary knowledge, and yet many are so given to change that they are never satisfied. They run under the spout to get out of the rain, and leave home to wander in the bush.

Know your opportunity.

Many have missed the tide, and their barge has laid high and dry without a chance of floating.

Knowledge is no burden.

We are not quite so sure of this. Some knowledge terribly burdens the heart. The tree of knowledge of good and evil yields fruit which is hard to carry. Yet in practical business it is well to know all the ins and outs of your trade.

Knowledge is power.

But wisdom is needed to use it properly; for
Knowledge, when wisdom is too weak to guide her,
Is like a headstrong horse, which throws its rider.

Sayings of a more Spiritual Sort.

Keep out of sight and scent of old sins.

Thus shall we be preserved from looking, longing, and lingering, which were the ruin of Lot's wife.

Keep such company as God keeps.

Holy men will be our safest companions, and they will be such society as we may enjoy for ever with God.

Keep the whole Sabbath holy.

It is none too long for those who delight in its heavenly service.

Keep up grace to keep down sin.

Kill sin, that it kill not thee.

Knock at mercy's gate, but wait till it opens to you.

Too many prayers are a sort of runaway knock, for they are not attended with expectant waiting upon God.

Know the love which passes knowledge.

For according to our apostle it is to be known, and it should be our ambition to know it.

Know thyself; but, better, know thy Lord.

Else self-knowledge may lead to despair.

ABOUR past is pleasant.

We reflect upon it with satisfaction, we rest after it with delight. He who never labours heartily can never know what true "rest" means. We must labour to enter into rest. To the industrious, labour is in itself a pleasure. "Labour conquers all things," and to conquer is always a joy.

Lambs die as well as wethers.

Or, "As soon dies the calf as the cow." None are too young for the grave. The sun of life often goes down ere it is yet noon.

Language was given us that we might say kind things to one another.

Large interest means small security.

When will persons with small savings learn this? To get ten per cent. they lose every cent they possess.

Last not least.

Indeed, in some respects the last are the greatest. The four last things are the four important things: death, judgment, heaven, and hell.

Laugh and grow fat;
Care killed a cat.

"Which, being interpreted in a philosophical spirit, means nothing more nor less than this, that the obese are jolly and genial, whereas the thin are acid of temper, and consumed with solicitude. A cat who, instead of making the best of it, takes things to heart, grizzling wofully over the scarcity of mice, or any kindred calamity, grows thin and haggard, till at last her nine lives vanish one after another, and she herself altogether disappears. So it is with human bodies. Men and women who 'grill' over the petty annoyances incident to existence, and inseparable from it, go to ruin like a careworn cat." —*Charles J. Dunphie, in "Sweet Sleep."*

Law hath a sharp claw and a hungry maw.

One writer calls it a cormorant, another likens it to the horse-leech. A suitor cries out bitterly:

"I am without a sou,
Thanks to the law and you;
For, oh! I feel the law
Has clapped on me its paw."

Law is a bottomless pit; keep far from it.

Therefore " agree with thine adversary quickly," or thou and he may both be in the abyss. "The suit is ended," said the lawyer ; "both parties are cleaned out."

Law is a lottery.

Who has not heard of the glorious uncertainty of the law ?

Law-makers must not be law-breakers.

In the family, parents should be sure to keep their own rules ; and the same should be observed in every business establishment, and in the law-making houses of Parliament.

> The laws you make
> You must not break.

Lawyers and painters can soon make black white.

They have only to lay it on thick, and produce the desired effect by colouring. It was said of an eminent lawyer now dead —

> "When facts were weak, his native cheek
> Brought him serenely through."

Yet *Charles Lamb* says, "Lawyers were children once, I suppose."

Lawyers and woodpeckers have long bills.

This is natural. Therefore let the man and the bird alone. But it seems as if in the olden times lawyers' bills were not just. Of course all that is altered now ; but think of this as a sarcastic epitaph :—

> " Here lieth one, believe it if you can,
> Who, though an attorney, was an honest man !
> The gates of heaven for him shall open wide,
> But will be shut 'gainst all the tribe beside."

Lawyers are needful to keep us out of law.

Brougham, however, said, " A lawyer is a gentleman who rescues your estate from your enemies, and keeps it to himself."

Lawyers' houses are built on fools' heads.

If men are obstinate and litigious they make work for lawyers, and thus supply them with an income.

> When fools fall out for every flaw,
> They run horn mad to go to law ;
> A hedge awry, a wrong plac'd gate,
> Will serve to spend a whole estate.

Lay by, like ants, a little store,
For summer lasts not evermore.

"Save for the man on the white horse," namely, old age.

Lay by your pence for a rainy day,
If you don't need you can give them away.

The Chinese say :—"Don't keep your coals in a volcano." Don't
be extravagant with your possessions. Prodigality is as much a
vice as hoarding.

Lay not all the load on the lame horse.

People are apt to pack all the blame on the man least able to
defend himself ; this is not fair. "Lay the blame at the right
door." Put the saddle on the right mule.

Lay up and lay out should go together.

Their separation will make a man either a miser or a bankrupt.

Lay up that you may lay out.

Spend not nor spare too much : be this thy care,
Spare but to spend, and only spend to spare :
He that spends more may want, and so complain :
But he spends best that spares to spend again.

Laziness begins with cobwebs, and ends with iron chains.

Habits which are easy to shake off at first become unconquerable
in after years.

Laziness is nothing unless you carry it out.

And if you do, it is monstrous, the theme of all men's ridicule.
One said :—

" Your lazy loon, if dainty pigeons
Up to his mouth well roasted flew,
He would not taste them, no, not he,
Unless all cut in morsels too."

Laziness travels so slowly that poverty soon overtakes him.

Most true, "As poor Richard says." "The lazy man goes to
his work like a thief to the gallows," and therefore no wonder that
want soon has him by the heel.

Lazy folks' stomachs don't get tired.

So says *Uncle Remus ;* and we also notice that this organ is
usually very active in persons who have no passion for hard work.

Lean liberty is better than fat slavery.

> Thus *Horace* sang :
>
>> "Give me again my hollow tree,
>> A crust of bread and liberty."

Learn a craft while you are young, that you may not have to live by craft when you are old.

> It is a pity when we see an old man cadging and scheming when he ought to be living upon the fruits of former industry.

Learn the noble art of self-restraint.

> This will serve you in better stead than " the noble art of self-defence."

Learn to be little if thou wouldst be great.

Learn to creep before you leap.

>> " The wee birdie falls when it tries over-soon to fly :
>> Folks are sure to stumble when they climb over-high."
>
> Prudence in our attempts is to be commended. We shall do more by attempting less.

Learn to hear, and hear to learn.

> Hear so as to heed.   Learn so as to live.

Learn to hold your tongue.

> Five words cost Zacharias forty weeks' silence.

**Learn to live well, and thou mayst die so too :
To live and die is all we have to do.**

Learn wisdom from the follies of others.

**Learn young learn fair
Learn old learn sair.**

> We teach the young, but we have no schools for the old : it would seem out of order, if not useless. The young should learn ; the old should teach.

Learning makes a wise man wise, but a fool is made all the more of a fool by it.

> It is said : —
>
>> You can't make a fool of biggest pattern,
>> Unless you teach him both Greek and Latin.

Learning without thought is labour lost.

Thought without learning is perilous, but learning without thought is useless.

> " My garden neat
> Has got a seat,
> That's hid from every eye, sir ;
> There, day and night,
> I read and write,
> And nobody's the wiser."

Least said soonest mended.

But it is best to say nothing that needs mending.

Leave a welcome behind you.

Go before you have a hint to begone.   So go that folks may be glad to see you when you call again.

Leave Ben Lomond where it stands.

Don't attempt impossibilities ; and when you are shifting everything, do let some of the grand old doctrines and institutions remain where they are.   Sometimes the proverb is, " Leave the minster where it was built."   Do not accept of the radical motto, " Down with everything that is up."

Leave grunting to hogs, and snarling to dogs.

You have quite enough to do to praise God with the birds of heaven.   Hogs and dogs are by no means examples for saints.

Leave it if you cannot mend it.

What's the use of idly finding fault ?   Shun such fruitless labour.

> Any little silly soul
> Easily can pick a hole.

Leave not the meat to gnaw the bones,
Nor break your teeth on worthless stones.

Don't forsake the gospel for the emptinesses of philosophy.

Leave off no clothes,
Till you see a June rose.

Our climate is so uncertain, that cold weather may return at any time through May ; therefore keep on your winter flannels.

Leave the brown October, and keep yourself sober.

Leave the Magpie and Stump, and stump home.

> Better still, let the magpie have its stump to itself altogether.

Leave to-morrow till to-morrow.

> "Sufficient unto the day is the evil thereof."—Matt. vi. 34.

Leaving for gleaner makes farmer no leaner.

Lend only what you can afford to lose.

> Lending is like pelting dogs with bits of meat : all is lost which goes in that way. Pour water into a hole in the ground, and when it bubbles up again expect to get back the money you have lent. Yet "Lend, hoping for nothing again."—Luke vi. 35. Only mind that what you lend is your own, and not your creditors'.

Less in the pewter pot, more in the iron pot.

> Wives and children would have more to eat if husbands and fathers spent less on drink. Going to the pot as a sot causes many to "go to pot" in the worst sense of that vulgarism.

Less of your honey, and more of your honesty.

> Spoken to one who did not pay his debts, but was very complimentary. He that hath no money in his hand need have honey in his mouth ; but even then he will not please his creditors.

Lessons hard to learn are sweet to know.

> Affliction is a stern schoolmaster, but a good instructor.

Let a good pot have a good lid.

> A good woman should have a good husband, a good church a good minister, and so forth.

Let a man be a man, and a woman a woman.

> No good can come of their entering upon each other's sphere, or copying the points peculiarly fit for the opposite sex. A womanish man is about as objectionable as a masculine woman. With regard to women appearing in Parliament, there is truth in the witty verse :—
>
> > "Should women sit in Parliament,
> >   A thing unprecedented—
> > A great part of the nation then
> >   Would be *Mis*-represented."

Let anger's fire be slow to burn,
And from thy wrath right quickly turn.

> Anger should be like damp wood, slow in lighting and quick in going out.
>
> > Be not quick to take offence,
> > Anger is a foe to sense.

Let another do what thou wouldst do.

> Liberty is not for ourselves only, but for all. Especially must we concede the religious liberty which we so earnestly claim for ourselves. "Think and let think;" and this you may do without being compromised in your fidelity to truth, if you keep from all personal connection with the error.

Let another's shipwreck be your beacon.

> Take warning by the ills of others. There can be no need for your vessel to feel the rock'for itself when you see that another ship has struck upon it.

Let by-gones be by-gones.

> A very good agreement to make after disagreement. Clean the slate and begin as if misunderstandings had never occurred.

Let charity be warm, if the weather be cold.

> And all the warmer because the poor are suffering from the inclemency of the season. Send your charity abroad wrapt in blankets.

Let each tailor mend his own coat.

> Or his customers will judge that he cannot mend theirs. He who does not amend his own faults will make a poor reformer.
>
> > Let reforms begin at home,
> > Then the nation they may roam.

Let every bird whistle its own tune.

> Be sure it will not whistle another tune half so well.

Let every dog scratch his own ear.

> He will be a lazy dog if he asks another dog to do it for him. Some people will do nothing for themselves: they almost require a deputy to chew their victuals for them.

Let every fox take care of his own brush.

> A selfish proverb; and yet there is sense in it.

Let every husband stay a lover true,
And every wife remain a sweetheart too.

Let every man do what he was made for.

"What! you a hare, and out hunting?" was a good question of the ancients. In too many cases men mistake their calling, and frogs try to be as big as bullocks.

Let gleaners glean, though crops be lean.

We repeat this sentiment, because the good old practice seems dying out, and we love to see Ruth carrying home her gleanings.

Let him hang by the heels.

A good prescription for a miser. Let him hang till his money drops out of his pocket, and the poor catch the dripping.

Let him never have a wife
Who will not love her as his life.

Let him that does not know you, buy you.

As much as to say, "I would not give a penny for you, if you were put up for sale."

Let him that earns, eat.

Good rule. He that will not work, ought to want.

Let him who is well off stay where he is.

For he that changes without need
Is not a likely man to speed.

Let John Bull beware of John Barleycorn.

Generally they say *Sir* John Barleycorn; but he is not knighted, it is his admirers who are benighted.

Let no man ever see
A green gosling in thee.

Act prudently. When any man would take thee in, let him find thee "all there when the bell rings," and quite prepared for him.

Let not fifer play the fiddle, nor fiddler play the fife,
But each man fully follow his own fitting course of life.

Let not mirth turn to mischief.

It is too apt to do so. When sport turns to sin, it is time to turn from it. When a jest becomes earnest, it should be dropped.

Let not my anger with men make God angry with me.

This will happen if my anger sees the sun rise and set, or if it leads to malevolence and desire of revenge. *Franklin* said :—

" Take this remark from Richard, poor and lame,
Whate'er's begun in anger, ends in shame."

Let not plenty make you dainty.

A little workhouse fare would greatly improve some people's appetites ; for now they turn up their noses at the best of food.

Let not poverty part good company.

Rather let us cling to our friend in his distress, and give him practical proof of our sincere esteem.

Let not property bring thee pride ;
Let not poverty turn thee aside.

Let not the devil dance on your lips.

If he does he will prove himself to be reigning in your heart. If the tongue is kept free from Satan's power, the whole body will be governed aright. We are able by divine grace to resist his temptations ; for though he may strike a thousand sparks he can never get a light unless we lend him our tinder.

Let not your money become your master.

You could not have a worse. The name of the servant of Mammon is *miser*, that is, miserable.

Let not your mouth swallow you.

Neither by expensive feeding, drunkenness, or ill language.

Let not your sail be bigger than your ship.

Or you will be upset. He that makes a great show, and goes on at a faster rate than is safe will soon be a wreck.

Let the church stand in the churchyard.

Everything should be in its own place : there it has a right to be, and no one can remove it.

Let the young people mind what the old people say,
And where there is danger keep out of the way.

Their temptation is to get into the way of danger just to see
what it is like.   If people were content to believe the statements of
experienced persons, they might be saved much sorrow; but it
seems that everybody must himself tumble into the ditch before
he will believe that there is mud in it.

Let thy words be true, few, and due.

Let us have crowns, and we shall have cousins.

These are sure to turn up.   No man has any idea of the extent
of his clan till he has something to give away; then he may
reckon that every third man in the street is his second cousin.

Let well alone : if you've little meat, pick the bone.

"Fools are aye fond of flitting," and are hot for change; but
wise men will be content with what they have.

Let your body be busy; but be not a busy-body.

Let your eye be quick, and your tongue be quiet

Let your hand be longer than your tongue.

Don't brag.   Do more than you say.

Let your neighbour wash his dirty linen in peace.

He has quite enough trouble without your interference.

Let your nose go in front; but don't always follow it.

We need a far better guide than our own fancy, or we shall be
like Mr. Knight, of whom the ditty says,—
> "Old Mr. Knight never goes right,
> And what's the reason why ?
> He follows his nose wherever he goes,
> And that's the reason why."

Liabilities often create abilities to lie.

Being hard up for money, and pressed by creditors, the man
becomes inventive, and develops a faculty for sailing very near the
wind.   Empty sacks, since they cannot stand, are apt to lie.

Liars should have good memories.

If not, they will soon contradict themselves.   It must be hard to
remember how you have stated your invention, so as to keep the
rest of your lying consistent with the commencement.

Lies are very nimble, but they soon trip themselves up.

They usually tread on their own garments. One part of the tale is inconsistent with the other, and thus its falsehood is betrayed.

Lies hunt in packs.

One lie needs ten to wait upon it, and these need ten each to keep them company. A lie will multiply like the aphis, from generation to generation. The old tale is, "A crow; two crows; three crows; a hundred crows: thus one to a hundred grows."

Lies may be acted as well as spoken.

This makes many men to be really liars who would scorn the appellation. In this sense David was right, and the commentator upon him is also right, who wrote—

"'All men are liars in my haste, I said,'
Quoth David to quick wrath by falsehood led.
Those in this place, could holy David view,
He'd say the same, and at his leisure, too."

Lies need a great deal of killing.

A lie has as many lives as a cat. "At the scent of water it will bud." After a falsehood has been answered a hundred times it will be repeated. "A lie never grows old," says one; and yet another declares that "Lies melt like snow."

Lies that are half true are the worst of lies.

When altogether false their smell betrays them, but a little truth conceals their character.

And the parson made it his text
That week, and said likewise,
That a lie which is half the truth
Is ever the blackest of lies.

**Life is a bubble,
And full of trouble.**

Yet, on the other hand, when we walk with God,—

While onward we go
We find heaven below.

Life is half spent before we begin to live.

With too many it is gone before they even think about it. Their whole experience will be summed up in the miserable exclamation, "What a fool I've been!"

Life is made up of little things.

Attention to these littles is by no means a little thing.

Life is made up of the rose and the thorn :
What can't be enjoyed must be patiently borne.

Life isn't all sunshine, nor is it all shade ;
There are profits and losses in every trade.

Life is short, but death is sure.

> Life's like a cobweb ;
> Be we e'er so gay,
> Death with his besom
> Sweeps us all away.

Life would be too smooth if it had no rubs.

If too smooth, it would be slippery and unsafe.

Light another's candle, but don't put out your own.

Nor need you. Indeed, by holy prudence you may help to keep your own flame burning by lending light to others.

Light come ; light go.

It is generally true that those who get money easily are apt to waste it, or otherwise to get rid of it speedily. He who earns his fortune with difficulty takes care of the fruit of his labour.

Light is good, but sore eyes don't like it.

"Everyone that doeth evil hateth the light."—John iii. 20.

Light is light, though blind eyes cannot see it.

Light not your candle at both ends.

This is the spendthrift's economy. He says :—

> "With cards, and dice, and dress, and friends,
> My savings are complete :
> I light the candle at both ends,
> And thus make both ends meet."

Like a tailor's needle, say, "I go through."

Persevere. Don't be beaten. Mean success.

If bad be your prospects, don't sit down and cry,
But jump up and say to yourself, "I WILL TRY."

Like blood, like goods, and like age,
Make the happiest marriage.

> God's blessing resting upon the union, these are likely elements of a happy marriage. Oil and water will not mix, neither can men and women of opposite temperaments make happy unions.

Like cures like.

> This is the Homœopathic dogma, and who can disprove it?

Like draws to like the world over.

> "Like to like, and Nan to Nicholas"; people generally find partners of their own sort. This is true, even for the next world, as the rough proverb hath it: "Like will to like, as the devil said to the charcoal-burner."

Like likes like: at least, its likely.

> In all probability, those who are fond of each other's company are much of the same kidney. Its "owl to owl, and crow to crow." The old adage is, "Like to like, Jack to Jill, a penny a pair."

Like master, like man.

> Apt enough are we to copy the manners of our superiors, especially if they do wrong. We imitate our associates. "Like priest, like people," and "Like mistress, like maid," "Like well, like bucket," are all forms of the same observation.

Likely tumbles in the fire,
When unlikely rises higher.

> Those whom we think sure to succeed, often fail; while others, of whom we hoped little, succeed.

Limit your wants to your wealth.

> "This is the maxim I'll hold to the end,
> Whilst Providence gives me my health.
> If little I have, then little I'll spend,
> And measure my wants by my wealth."

Linseys are warmer than silks.

> Linseys paid for keep out cold;
> Silks on credit soon grow old.

Lions are not frightened by cats.

> Men of strength of mind are not turned aside by the sputterings of nobodies.

Lions' skins are not to be had cheap.

If you mean to overcome a really brave man, you have your work cut out, for he will not tamely yield.

Liquor very loudly talks,
When the screw has drawn the corks.

What a noise and hubbub the stuff will cause when a company of men are discussing politics and spirits !

Listen to others, if you would have them listen to you.

It is only fair.   " Turn and turn about " is justice.

Listeners hear no good of themselves

It is meanness itself to hear what is not intended for you.   A gentleman will carefully abstain from over-hearing.   Inquisitive people stick their heads into a beehive, but they should not complain if they receive more instruction than they like.

Little and often is good for little ones.

" Children and chicken will be picking."   They do not thrive on great feasts and long fasts.   In teaching children, precept should be upon precept, line upon line, here a little and there a little.

Little and often fills the purse;
But haste for riches brings a curse.

Little bantams are great at crowing.

Wonderful, indeed, it is how loudly little people can boast.   It seems as if the less people can do, the more they can brag.

Little boats must keep near shore;
Larger ships may venture more.

Caution is wise.   When our estates do not permit of large expenses, or great ventures, let us be content with smaller things

Little bodies have great souls.

This is often the case.   Dr. Watts was a little man, but a great poet, and when he was despised for his low stature, he wrote :—

> " Were I so tall to reach the pole,
> Or grasp the ocean in my span,
> I must be measured by my soul :
> The mind's the standard of the man."

Little by little, the little bird builds its nest.

Thus, by diligence and economy, the man of moderate abilities succeeds in gaining a comfortable living.

Little chips light great fires.

Thus, the worst of quarrels have arisen from a few angry words.

Little enemies and little wounds must not be despised.

To despise an enemy is to give him a great advantage. This proverb is specially true of spiritual and moral mischiefs.

Little fishes are sweet, and little rooms are warm.

A small estate has its peculiar comfort.

Little fishes should not spout like whales.

This they are very apt to attempt, but they make themselves ridiculous.

Little folks like to talk about great folks.

Some are as proud as peacocks if they once rode in the same train with Sir John, or my Lord Harry.

Little griefs are loud, great sorrows are silent.

Hence, when a man sits alone and shuns all mention of his woe, we ought to give him all the greater sympathy.

Little is done when every man is master.

But a good deal is likely to be undone, and great uproar created. The worst despot is better than no head at all.

Little pigeons can carry great messages.

And they will do so. Therefore, mind what message you give them. Say not that which thou wouldst not hear again.

Little pigs eat great potatoes.

If they can get them. Children are great feeders. Very small men concoct great political schemes.

Little pitchers have great ears.

Children hear very quickly. Say nothing which you would not wish them to repeat, for they will repeat all they hear, even as parrots do. The proverb is sometimes varied by the word "pigs" being inserted instead of "pitchers."

Little pot,
Don't get hot
On the spot.

An angry person is a ridiculous person; and if he is very little, he makes all the greater stupid of himself.

Little strokes fell great oaks.

Little things please little minds.

Which may be spoken to disparage those who are delighted with trifles; but may also be to their credit, since it is most commendable to be easily contented and pleased.

Little troubles are great to little people.

It is therefore cruel to laugh at the griefs of children, which may be as great to them as some huge calamity would be to us. The sorrows of the little are not little sorrows to them. This may teach humanity to animals and insects. May it not be true also that a beetle suffers as much in death as an elephant?

Little wit in the head makes much work for the feet.

Little wrongs done to others are great wrongs done to ourselves.

The moral sense is blunted, and this is a serious injury.

Live and let live.

Capital motto. Many people think they can only live themselves by grasping the living of everybody else.

Live as if each day were thy first day and thy last day.

With the freshness of a beginner and the earnestness of one who is nearing his end.

Live *in* to-day, but not *for* to-day.

The cattle see no further than their eye can reach, but we look into a vast eternity, and endeavour to prepare for it.

Live not for yourself alone.

For that will be to make a sepulchre of your own personality. Self is a grave.

Live only a moment at a time.

> Trusting for constant help from heaven. Our long ranges are difficult firing, we do best when we "do the next thing."

Live to die that thou mayest die to live.

Live to learn, and learn to live.

> Do not think that you know everything, but ever be learning more, and let that learning touch most on the practical concerns of every-day life.

Live upon trust,
And pay double you must.

> Of course, the seller has to charge us for interest, and for the risk he runs of our never paying. "The Hire System" is also a higher system of charging and paying. Pay down on the nail.

Live we may : die we must.

> A few days may, a few years must,
> Repose us in the silent dust.

Live with a singer if you would learn to sing.

> Association is an insensible instruction. We do, as it were, imbibe habits as Gideon's fleece drank in the dew.

Live within your means, but never be mean within.

Live while you live.

> Doddridge has set this in the right light :—

> " ' Live while you live,' the epicure would say,
> ' And seize the pleasures of the passing day ' ;
> ' Live while you live,' the sacred preacher cries,
> ' And give to God each moment as it flies.'
> Lord, in my view, let these united be ;
> I live in pleasure when I live to thee."

Loans and debts make worries and frets.

Loans should come laughing home.

> One who lends likes to have his money back at the promised time, and he ought to have it. Many could truly say, " We would lend willingly : but when shall we get it again?" There should be a prompt and cheerful return of anything borrowed : but some keep an article till it is half worn out before they send it home.

Loaves put awry in the oven, come out awry.

The commencement of a work must be looked to. If we are wrong in the first stage it will affect the result.

Lock the stable before you lose the steed.

Generally, this is done just after the horse is stolen.

Long is a day without bread.

Let those who fare sumptuously think how long four-and-twenty hours must be to one who is starving.

Long lent is not given.

Yet after keeping a borrowed article much longer than they should, some treat it as if it belonged to them. Shame!

Long looked-for comes at last.

"The expectation of the poor shall not perish for ever."—Ps. ix. 18.

Long talk makes short work.

Gossiping over the pales stops the mops and brooms. Endless speeches in Parliament cause barren sessions.

Long-tongued people are generally short-handed.

The Orientals say, "He has only one cowry to spend, but he rushes all over the bazaar and makes a great stir everywhere."

Look above you, and then look about you.

First seek the blessing of God, and then watch your opportunities.

Look at paintings and fightings from a distance.

They do not improve upon near inspection.

**Look at your corn in May,
And you'll come weeping away;
Look at the same in June,
And you'll sing another tune.**

Fret not in a hurry. Tarry a bit and see what time will do. "The husbandman waiteth for the precious fruit of the earth, and hath long patience for it."—James v. 7. In spiritual things we must learn to wait patiently.

"Our husbandmen for harvest wait and stay;
Oh, let not any saint do less than they!"

Look before you leap ;
The ditch may be deep.

> Do not be in a desperate hurry, or you will get into **trouble, or at** the least fail in your endeavours. The Chinese say that " **a hasty** man drinks his tea with a fork."

Look before you, or you'll have to look behind **you.**

> Foresight may save regret. If men used their eyes before **acting,** they might not have to wipe them afterwards. In every case there is need to be on our guard. The Siamese say, " Go up by land you meet a tiger ; go down by water you meet a crocodile." Always keep a good look-out, for you are in an enemy's country.

Look for hogs in the sty.

> Bad men have their haunts, and there you may expect to find them. Another proverb is, " Look for the hog at the oak." Look for a tippler in the public-house.

Look for squalls, but don't make them.

> " Accidents will occur in the best regulated families " ; but we must, if it be possible, as much as lieth in us, live peaceably with all.
>
> > Earn the laurels of peace,
> > And make quarrels to cease.

Look not a gift horse in the mouth.

> Gratitude should prevent a churlish criticism of a gift. Whatever the nag's age may be, it costs you nothing.

Look not for musk in a dog-kennel.

> Do not expect virtue where wantonness and sin hold their reign.

Look to your own failings before you look at **my faults.**

> > " In other men we faults can spy,
> > And blame the mote that dims the eye :
> > Each little speck and error find ;
> > To our own strongest errors blind."

Look through a keyhole, and your eye will be sore.

> Paul Pry with his " hope I don't intrude " is sure to meet with unpleasant discoveries.

Lookers on see more than players.

> Or think they do. Every man could do my business better than I can. Can he ?

Lose thy fun rather than thy friend.

"He that will lose his friend for a jest deserves to die a beggar by the bargain. Yet some think their conceits, like mustard, not good except they bite. Such let my jests be, that they grind not the credit of my friend."—*Thomas Fuller.*

Lost time is never found again.

Love all ; trust few ;
To each be true.

Love and lordship like not fellowship.

So far as the sexes are concerned, there is only room in love's kingdom for itself : jealousy, like the cherub with drawn sword, keeps others from intrusion.

Love and poverty are hard to hide.

Some put with these "fire and a cough." and others "smoke and money." Those lovers who try to act as if they were perfect strangers to each other, so much overdo the part that everyone sees how love is struggling for fresh air. Newly-married people need not try to conceal the fact : it is visible to the naked eye.

Love hath a large mantle.

"Love covereth a multitude of sins."—1 Peter iv. 8 (R.V.). It forgives and forgets, and therein it proves itself to be of God.

Love in married life
Makes husband and wife
Each rule without strife.

They were a happy pair of whom it was said :—
    " They were so one that none could ever say
        Which of them ruled, and whether did obey ;
        He ruled, because she would obey, and she,
        In the obeying, ruled as well as he."

Love in the heart is better than honey in the mouth.

Love is a secret no man knows,
Till it within his bosom glows.

Only those despise the emotion who have never come under its sway. It is a weakness in which lies our strength : a mystery which is simplicity itself.

Love is as warm in fustian as in velvet.

            " Love's voice doth sing
        As sweetly in a beggar as a king."

Love is blind.

It is often born so, but, like the puppies, its eyes open in due time. "Though blind it yet sees far," as the old saying tells us. "A lover's eyes will gaze an eagle blind." Paradoxes often convey much truth in a pithy form. Love is all eye for beauties, and has no eye for blames.

Love is neither bought nor sold.

Love is the only price of love. It is said by the old proverb, "Love works wonders, but money makes marriage"; but money cannot bring love, and without love marriage is penal servitude for life. Where love comes for the sake of gain, it is generally false, and the old rhyme stands true:

> Thy seeming lover false will be,
> And love thy money more than thee.

Love is the mother of love.

It is born of love and nurtured by it. "Loving and singing cannot be forced." The parentage of love is free; its parents are as itself. Love if thou wouldst be loved. Even of God we know from Scripture and from experience that, "We love him because he first loved us."

Love laughs at locksmiths.

When set upon its object, the loving heart will find its beloved; as the old ballad puts it:—

> "If the earth should part them,
> He would gallop it o'er;
> If the seas should o'erthwart him,
> He would swim to the shore.
>
> Should his love become a swallow,
> Thro' the earth to stray,
> Love will lend wings to follow,
> And will find out the way."

Love lightens labour, and sweetens sorrow.

"Instead of love being the occasion of all the misery of this world (as is sung by fantastic bards), the misery of this world is occasioned by there not being love enough."—*Disraeli*.

Love lives in cottages oftener than in courts.

> Love may be found in huts where poor men lie,
> But pride which shuts the heart makes love to die.

Love makes labour light.

Love makes marriage merry age.

> Without love it is mar age. Too often after marriage people grow cold, and then their union is mere bondage. The following paragraph is sometimes true :—
>
> It appears that in New Zealand, when the marriage ceremony takes place, it is a very old custom to knock the heads of the bride and bridegroom together previous to their union. But,
>
> > In Christian lands it isn't so :
> > The bridegroom and the bride
> > To loggerheads but seldom go
> > Until the knot is tied.

Love maketh time to pass away,
Time cannot make true love decay.

Love me, and then say what you please about me.

> For if love thinketh no evil, we may be sure that it speaketh none. " Charity is no churl."

Love me, love my dog.

> When the cup of love is full, it flows over to those who are dear to its object. It's hard, however, to love a man's dog if it's a French poodle, clipped in the fashion.

Love rules without a sword,
And binds without a cord.

Love should not be all on one side.

> It must be mutual to be abiding, according to the legend:
>
> > " Two souls with but a single thought,
> > Two hearts that beat as one."

Love sought is good, but love unsought is best.

> Surely this is the kind of love which God hath bestowed on sinful men.

Love your house, but don't ride on the ridge.

> Don't be silly and over-fond. Better "love me little and love me long " than act like an idiot. " Love teaches asses to dance," but they are all the more asses for it. Be sober in love, as in all else.

Love your mother ; you'll never have another.

> A distinguished author, Jean Paul Richter, used to say, " Unhappy is the man for whom his own mother has not made all other mothers venerable."

Love your neighbour, but mend the hedge.

If not you will in due time wish you had. You cannot mix *meum* and *tuum*, and separate them again at pleasure.

Love your " uncle," but don't pledge the flat-iron.

Nor anything else if you can help it. Remember the balls outside the Pawn-shop. Two and one, to warn you that it is two to one that what goes in will ever come out again.

Lovers' purses are tied with cobwebs.

They are always ready to spend their money on those they love.

Lovers' time runs faster than the clock.

They are sure to meet before the time appointed; and when they get together, the moments fly at a double rate. One of them read on a clock *Tempus jugit*, and said, " Yes, *Time fidgets*"; and so it does when we want yet a few more last words.

Love's fire, if it once goes out, is hard to kindle.

Old flames are extinguished, and it is idle to ask what becomes of quenched fire.

> Violets plucked, the sweetest rain
> Makes not fresh to grow again.

Luck is the idol of the idle.

They are looking for something to turn up, and staring to see their ship come home. Turn from such a dumb idol as luck.

Lying and gossiping are as like as soup and broth.

They are very much alike, especially gossiping.

Lying and stealing live next door to each other.

Lying pays no tax.

The more's the pity. It might bring in enough to pay the National Debt.

Lying rides on debt's back.

The debtor promises and promises, and then makes false excuses. Debt soon destroys a reputation for truthfulness.

Sayings of a more Spiritual Sort.

Lay self aside, or God will lay you aside.

> For he will not endure a rival.   If we trust self we cannot truly trust the Lord.

Lay your head to rest on the bosom of omnipotence.

> Leave your cares and needs with almighty love.

Late repentance is seldom true; true repentance is never too late.

> The first sentence is most sadly true, as many a minister can testify, for when men recover they are all too apt to forget the vows they made in sickness.

Learn the wretchedness of self and the riches of Christ.

Leave thy salvation in thy Saviour's hands.

> If he cannot save thee, be sure thou canst not save thyself.

Let faith shut the door at night, and mercy will open it in the morning.

Let God's ways be in your heart, and your heart in God's ways.

Let not our prayers die while our Intercessor lives.

> Because he prays we should pray also.
> > And wilt thou in dead silence lie,
> > While Christ stands waiting for thy prayer?
> > My soul, thou hast a Friend on high;
> > Arise, and try thy interest there.

Let me be a sorrowing saint, rather than a merry sinner.

> Let me rather sigh for sin, than sing in sin.
> > The sacrifices God loves best
> > Are broken hearts for sin oppressed.

Life in prayer
Brings death to care.

Lightness of spirit may bring darkness of soul.

Too often has it been so ! Tender consciences soon discover that something is wrong between God and their souls, and then their sinful levity is followed by heaviness of heart. Thus *Berridge* complained of himself :

> Brisk and dull in half an hour,
> Hot and cold, and sweet and sour ;
> Sometimes grave at Jesus' school,
> Sometimes light, and play the fool!

> What a motley wretch am I,
> Full of inconsistency !
> Sure the plague is in my heart,
> Else I could not act this part.

Lip prayers are lost prayers.

> " In prayer the lips ne'er act the winning part,
> Without the sweet concurrence of the heart."—*Herrick.*

Little-faith is heir to great promises.

The title to an estate does not depend upon the health, strength, or wealth of the heir ; but upon his being of true birth.

Live for HIM in whom you live.

Live here as those who have to live hereafter.

Live *to* God's glory and you shall live *in* God's glory.

Living, loving, lasting union exists between Christ and believers.

Living without God means dying without hope.

Look not for a golden life in an iron world.

Where Jesus wore a crown of thorns we cannot expect coronets of honour. Should the servant be above his Lord ?

Look to the Lord even when the wind blows sand in your eyes.

If you cannot see as you would, yet look that way. The Lord knows what blinds you, and will see you when you cannot see him.

Look up, for God looks down.

Happy are our eyes when they meet his eyes : then is our whole nature transformed.

Lord, accept our willingness, and forgive our weakness.

Lord, hold me up : yet keep me down.

> Upright in conduct, and lowly in spirit.

Lord, keep me, that I may keep thy commandments.

Lord, keep us from evil, and evil from us.

> " Lead us not into temptation, but deliver us from evil."

Lord, teach my teacher, that he may teach me.

> Recommended as a Sabbath prayer.

Lord, touch my ear, that I may hear.

> And if it has been wounded by sin, or stopped up by error, Lord
> heal it, and open it to hear thy word.

Love all for Christ; but love Christ for himself.

Love is the livery of Christ.

> Make sure that you wear it in every place.
>
> > " No outward mark we have to know,
> >   Who thine, O Christ, may be,
> > Until his Christian love doth show
> >   Who appertains to thee :
> > For knowledge may be reached unto,
> >   And formal justice gained,
> > But till each other love we do,
> >   Both faith and works are feigned."— *Wither.*

Love is the perfect of the verb " live."

> Oh, to be intense in that perfect tense !

Love those who love God.

> For such love may continue throughout eternity.

Love we to drink the sweet, and shall we lower
If God be pleased to send a little sour?

SPURGEON'S
PROVERBS and SAYINGS
WITH NOTES

SPURGEON'S
PROVERBS and SAYINGS
WITH NOTES

VOL. II — M TO Z

C. H. SPURGEON

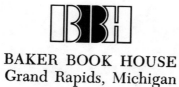

BAKER BOOK HOUSE
Grand Rapids, Michigan

Proverbs and Quaint Sayings.

AD bulls cannot be tied up with a pack-thread.

> Far greater restraints are needed. Obstinate people must be held in with strong measures. Our corrupt human nature in its madness is not to be ruled by mere resolves, nor by any power less than divine.

> " Some men demand rough treatment everywhere :
> Will apples tempt a wild bear to a sty ?
> You cannot with a whistle tame a bear :
> You cannot with a beckon lure a fly."—*S. C. Hall.*

Mad dogs cannot live long.

The furiously wicked have but a short career. Bad for them, but good for the universe.

Mad folk are not to be argued with.

Any more than mad bulls. They are not in a condition of mind to appreciate argument, and should be let alone. To stand reasoning with a wild bull would be very absurd, and it is equally so to debate with a hot-headed partisan.

Mad people think others mad.

The judgments of men are warped by their own follies, and we should not pay too much heed to them. When a man is "mad as a hatter," or "mad as a March hare," his opinion of others is of small consequence.

Maidens should be mild and meek,
Swift to hear and slow to speak.

The same advice will apply to men also ; but the men like advising the women, better than doing right themselves.

Make all sure, and keep all pure.

Make every bargain clear and plain,
That none may afterwards complain.

> This would save a world of heart-burning, and greatly tend to peace and quietness. If possible, put it down in black and white that there may be no after quibbling.

Make good cheese, if you make little.

> Keep up the quality of your work, even if you cannot excel in the quantity of it.

Make great excuses for people in love.

> They have not all their wits about them. A temporary insanity possesses them.
>
> > " Love is a dizziness :
> > It winna let a poor body
> > Gang about his business."

Make haste slowly.

> A wise Eastern proverb says, "Hurry is of the devil, but slow advancing comes from God." What is done hastily is seldom done well ; and being ill done, it has to be undone, and this wastes time. "With eager feeding food will choke the eater."

Make hay while the sun shines.

> You cannot make it when it is pouring with rain, therefore seize on the season, and, like the busy bee, improve each shining hour.
>
> > " Make your hay fine
> > While sun doth shine."

Make home happy, and you will be happy at home.

> A golden sentence. When any one ceases to care for his home, it is one of the worst possible signs of moral sickness.

Make matters of care matters of prayer.

> This is the wisdom of the anxious. To lay the matter before the Lord is to take the sting out of trial.

Make much of little.

> By economy use a small income well ; by grateful praise express your value of the least of God's mercies ; and by charitable judgment come to a favourable conclusion concerning those in whom you see even a little grace. One can see the sky in a single drop of rain, and a work of grace in a tear of repentance.

Make no debts, and lay no bets.

A debtor is a slave, and a bettor is no better; for before long his losses will bring him into the same condition of bondage. *Rowland Hill* said, "I never pay my debts, and for the best of reasons—*I never have any debts to pay.*"

Make not another's shoes by your own foot.

For that which suits you very well may be quite unsuitable for another person. Every foot needs a last of its own. Allow latitude of thought and manner within the bounds of truth and holiness. Avoid Chinese shoes both for yourself and others.

Make not fish of one and flesh of another.

Unless they are really distinct. Give equal justice to all; but yet discriminate, and judge none sweepingly.

Make not friends with an angry man or a drinking man.

The first is Solomon's advice; the second does not need a Solomon to see its common sense. We grow like our friends; therefore let us choose them with care.

Make not much of little.

That is to say, when finding fault, don't make mountains of molehills, nor crimes out of blunders. This is the apparent reverse of a proverb a little back; but then it applies to another set of things.

Make not thy tail broader than thy wings.

Have not more show than substance, more outgoings than incomings, more promise than ability to perform.

Make not two sorrows of one.

Do not so worry as to create a second sorrow, nor so sin as to involve a repetition, and perhaps an aggravation, of your grief.

Make not your holiday an unholy day.

Make one wrong step, and down you go.

This may be the case at any time; therefore cry unto "him who is able to keep you from stumbling." With certain uncharitable people this proverb is bitterly true; for all your years of acceptable service will be forgotten if, for once in your life, you give them the least cause for complaint.

Make others happy, and you will be happy yourself.

When out for a holiday, a sour-visaged lady said to another, "Are you enjoying yourself? I am sure I am not." "No," said her friend, "I did not come out to enjoy myself, but to enjoy other people, and I am doing it heartily." This is a surer way to pleasure than self-consideration.

"For the sake of those who love us,
For the sake of God above us,
Each and all should do their best
To make music for the rest."

Make short the miles with talk and smiles.

Cheerful conversation causes time to fly by unnoticed.

Make speed to-day, you may be stopped to-morrow.

Whenever we have a chance for undisturbed work, let us use it, for there are many hinderers. If the train does not get over the ground where there are few stations to stop at, it will certainly make small speed upon other parts of the road.

Make sure of nothing, but that God is true.

Make the best of a bad bargain.

Say as little as you can about it, or you will be injuring your own reputation for good judgment. If you have entered upon marriage, and find yourself mistaken, "bear and forbear." In all trying cases, among a trying people, say—

"I'll not willingly offend,
Nor be easily offended;
What's amiss I'll strive to mend,
And endure what can't be mended."

Make the plaster as large as the sore.

If you have given offence, let the apology and, if need be, the reparation, be ample. Make it up; leave no back reckonings.

Make your hay as best you may.

If the season is wet, watch the intervals between the showers, and use them with diligence. If we cannot alter our circumstances, we must do the best under them.

Make your mark, but mind what the mark is.

Too many seem eager for mere notoriety, but if we are not famous for goodness we are practically infamous.

Make your pudding according to your plums.

> Arrange your whole plan of life so as to suit your means, and thus avoid debt, and other forms of failure. Some men try to do too much, and do it to their ruin.

Make your will without delay,
For death may come on any day.

> Great sorrow has been brought on families by neglect in the making of wills. It is cruelty to one's own flesh and blood to leave one's affairs unsettled. Yet some persons have a strange aversion to do what ought to be done by every sane man. Do they think that it will be signing their death-warrant, to sign their will? Reader, are you one of these wilful waiters?

> > Come, swallow the pill,
> > And draw up your will.

Make yourself an ass, and everyone will lay his sack on you.

> Too great softness is a rare fault, but a fault it is. We need not invite all the world to impose upon us. They will burden us if they can, and it is as well to let them see that we are not quite so stupid as they suppose. When the sheep is too meek, all the lambs suck it.

Malice is mental murder.

Man by nature is poor, proud, peevish and pig-headed.

> You cannot slander human nature; it is worse than words can paint it. Man is an animal that sins. He is often a wolf to man, a serpent to God, and a scorpion to himself.

Man does not grow perfect in a hundred years; but in one day he becomes corrupt.

Man is a puff of wind and a pile of dust.

> Yet "all men think all men mortal but themselves." In truth, "Life's but a walking shadow." We rather seem to be than really exist. Our life's a shade.

Man proposes, but God disposes.

> Napoleon boasted that he proposed and disposed too, but God's answer was given when Napoleon was deposed.

Man's saying is only saying; but God's saying is doing.

> With men, "between saying and doing many a pair of shoes is worn out"; but God speaks and it is done. *Dictum, factum.*

Man's security is Satan's opportunity.

When we think ourselves wise and strong, our enemy soon trips us up, and proves us silly and weak. Carnal security is a strange fatuity. He is not safe who thinks himself so.

Man's twelve is not so good as the devil's dozen.

He is older and craftier than we are. How can we hope to cope with one whose experience is so wide, and of so long a duration?

Man's work lasts till set of sun;
Woman's work is never done.

She has to prepare the meal before the man goes out, and also to have another ready when he comes home, and even through the night the children demand her care. It is as *Tusser* wrote :—

" Some respite to husband the seasons may send ;
But housewife's affairs have never an end."

Manners maketh man.

Not money, nor birth, nor office, but behaviour makes the man among his fellows. To the proverb above is generally added the words, " Quoth William of Wickham."

Manners you may have though you have no manors.

The man who has not a foot of land, nor a pound in money, may yet be a perfect gentleman. In certain cases we might justly say, " He hath of manors and manners, none at all."

Many a child is hungry because the brewer is rich.

What should have been spent in bread and butter has gone in malt and hops. A little fellow was asked by a lady, " Why do you not come for cold victuals any more ? " and replied, " Because father's signed the pledge, and we get hot victuals at home." This story was told by *J. B. Gough.*

Many a cloudy morning leads on to a fine day.

So that we may live in hopes of its clearing up. Carry your umbrella, but don't always put it up. Be careful, but not fearful.

Many a cow stands in the meadow and looks wistfully at the common.

Anxious to go from better to worse ! Men often envy those whom they should pity. Mice outside envy those in the trap.

Many a dog is dead since you were a whelp.

You are not so young as you would wish me to think you.

Many a fine dish has nothing on it.

Many a person who is comely is also a dummy. An open countenance and a noble head may only be an apology for absent intelligence. We must not judge of men by their elegant appearance. A dish of finest ware only mocks a hungry man, if it brings him no food ; and many a learned discourse is of this nature.

Many a good drop of broth may come out of an old pot.

An old text, an old minister, an old book, an old friend, an old experience, may yet yield us consolation.

Many a good tale is spoilt in the telling.

Let the speaker be too long, too loud, too low, or too lofty, and the best story will be sadly marred in the telling. It is a pity when it is so with the gospel.

Many a man cuts a stick to break his own head.

He, unknowingly, does that which will be to his own serious injury. A man's folly is his worst foe.

**Many a one for land,
Takes a fool by the hand.**

Marrying property instead of wedding a sensible wife is a great absurdity. Surely, if the woman who is chosen for her land turns out a fool, there is a pair of them !

Many a one is good because he can do no mischief.

Involuntary virtue wins no commendation. He who would do mischief if he could, should remember that in a bad as well as in a good sense, the will is often taken for the deed.

**Many a pang has been incurred
Through a single hasty word.**

Many a pearl is still hidden in its oyster.

No doubt there are as good pearls in the sea as ever came out of it. Let us not despair for the times. God has jewels in hiding.

Many a stroke must fell an oak.

Many a true word is spoken in jest.

That which was the subject of mirth turns out to be a real cause for sorrow. We are all, at times, unconscious prophets.

Many acres will not make a wiseacre.

Broad lands and breadth of wisdom do not necessarily go together, and yet many seem to think that everything a rich man says is eminently important. Yet in the parable the rich man was a fool. Riches cannot really cover folly, neither can they make an empty mouth speak golden words.

Many are betrayed with a kiss.

Judas did this with our Lord, and we need not wonder if others do so with us. Yet let us not be betrayed by the kiss of Delilah: that form of kiss we *can* refuse.

Many are brave when the enemy flies.

They pursue to share the spoil. Win you the victory alone, and thousands will then fight the battle o'er again.

Many are lighter in the heels than in the heart.

They dance with their feet, but they limp in spirit. They have a fantastic toe, but a fainting heart. Grief is all the more oppressive when it is forced to wear the mask of cheerfulness. ,

Many are wise in jest, but fools in earnest.

It is a small attainment to be great in foolery, and to be useless for all practical purposes; yet many are in that condition.

Many beat the sack and mean the miller.

They find fault with the sermon, but really dislike the preacher. They have a personal animosity which prevents their speaking well of what the good man does or says.

Many can get money; few can use it well.

Even to keep it is not easy. Many of the silliest investments have been made by men who, in their own business, were shrewd to the highest degree. It is harder to weave than to gather wool.

Many can help one.

Without hurting themselves they can put their littles together, and aid a friend in the day of his need.

Many can make bricks, but cannot build.

They lack the organizing faculty, though otherwise good workers.

Many captains, and the ship goes on the rocks.

Divided authority is as bad as none at all. What would a man do with two heads differing in thought? " There can only be one captain to a ship," one central source of rule.

Masters two,
Will not do.

Many commit sin, and blame Satan.

Just as Eve said, "The serpent beguiled me, and I did eat." Satan has quite enough sin of his own, without having our iniquities fathered upon him. Even the evil one can be libelled.

Many cut broad thongs out of other people's leather.

Preachers and authors make bountiful extracts. Servants help themselves lavishly to sugar and butter at their master's expense; and, in general, men are very generous with that which costs them nothing. Find a man in coals, and he will keep up a great fire at midsummer: pay his travelling expenses, and he will become a globe-trotter, and go nine times round the world.

Many dogs soon eat up a horse.

A number of fellows drinking and feasting at the expense of a man of means, will soon devour his fortune, as hounds will swallow a dead horse. These dogs are always prowling about.

Many drops make a shower.

Combinations of littles may accomplish great results.

**Many find fault without any end,
And yet do nothing at all to mend.**

Many give an egg to get an ox.

Or a sprat to catch a mackerel. This is the Oriental manner of giving presents to great men, to get a large return.

Many go out for clothes and come home stript.

Especially when they invest in a Limited Company, and the concern gets into liquidation.

Many good purposes lie in the churchyard.

Dead and buried, like those who brought them forth. What we should be if we did but carry out our good resolves !

Many hands make light work : this is clear.
Many hands make slight work : this I fear.

Many have come to port after a great storm.

Especially if they have taken on board the pilot of the Galilean lake. Courage, ye who are tost with tempest, and not comforted !

Many hostlers starve the mare.

"What!" say the Kashmiri, "eleven grooms for a one-eyed mare!" Alas, for the creature whose welfare depends on many ! The business of many is the concern of none.

Unless you leave the work to one,
I'm pretty sure it won't be done.

Many hounds are the death of the hare.

She might baffle the pursuit of one dog; but when another and another join in the hunt, what can she do ? Many cares, pains, and losses, coming close upon one another, prove too much for weak minds. If God help not, the many hounds will kill the hare.

Many leaves fade in summer, and many men die soon.

Many lick before they bite.

This I know by experience : and the worst lick-spittles bite the most venomously.

Many littles make a mickle.

Drop by drop the sea is filled. Add small to small, and it comes to great. Little grains make up the terrible quicksand.

Many love our persons for our purses.

Hear what the man said : "Leave you, dear girl ! No, never; so long as you have a shilling."

" Sage Plutarch said in ancient days :
'When the strong box contains no more,
And when the kitchen fire is out,
Both friends and flatterers shun the door.' "

Many make straight things crooked, but few make crooked
things straight.

> Most true. But the former is a far easier task than the latter.
> To make crooked things straight is the peculiar work of God's
> grace and providence. This he has promised to do.

Many men, many minds.

Many men mean mending, but more need it.

Many patients die of the doctor.

> This is what people say when they are well. Then they talk of
> having no doctor, but "dying a natural death"; but, after a little
> pain, they pitifully cry out, "Send for the doctor."

Many persons think they are wise, when they are only
windy.

> During a stormy discussion, a gentleman rose to settle the matter
> in dispute. Waving his hands majestically over the excited dis-
> putants, he began: "Gentlemen, all I want is common-sense——"
> "Exactly," Douglas Jerrold interrupted; "that is precisely what
> you do want." The discussion was finished in a burst of laughter.

Many rendings need many mendings.

> Applicable, not only to garments, but to communities, to churches,
> and to the lives of men.

Many save their silver, but lose their souls.

> Many a man's soul has been ruined by his great love of money,
> although he had but little money to love.

Many sin like David, but do not repent like David.

> Yet they readily quote David's faults as their excuse. If, like
> David, I am defiled, let me, like David, be washed.

Many speak much, but few speak well.

> And those who speak well are not eager to speak much. From
> mountains of labouring words there may only come a mouse of sense.

Many suffer long, but are not longsuffering.

> Because they suffer unwillingly, and are angry and impatient.

Many talk like philosophers, and live like fools.

Many talk of *Robin Hood*, that never shot with his bow,
And many talk of *Little John*, that never did him know.

> Of course, talk goes ahead mightily. If you cannot do any-
> thing great yourself, it is something to say that you know those
> who are famous, or, at least, that you know their cousin's grand-
> mother's housemaid.

Many tickle with one hand, to strike with the other.

> Pleasing in order to betray. The flatterer is a vile reptile; like
> a boa-constrictor, he covers his victim with saliva, and then pro-
> ceeds to swallow him.

Many words will not fill a bushel.

> They are but wind at the best. The Scotch say, " Meikle crack
> fills nae sack."

Many would run away if they had courage enough.

> Strange to say, fear has kept many men from playing the coward.

Mar not what marred cannot be mended.

> If the mischief cannot be undone, we must avoid it with tenfold
> care. Do not break the shell if you wish to save the egg, for there
> is no repairing the damage.

March comes in like a lamb, and goes out like a lion; or it
    comes in like a lion, and goes out like a lamb.

> It seems ordained at one part or the other to rage and roar with
> tremendous wind. In this it resembles the lives of different men:
> some begin with peace and end with trial, and others commence
> roughly, but end in tranquillity.

March has many weathers, and life has many changes.

March is a lion or a lamb;
Which it will be uncertain I am.

> If this month comes in with raging winds, it often finishes
> delightfully; and, on the other hand, if it opens gently, it will
> rave before it is over. The month is near the vernal equinox,
> when wind is to be expected. We leave prophecies about the
> weather to Old Moore and Zadkiel, who know as much about it as
> the dead crow knows about the sea-serpent.

March winds and April showers,
Bring forth May flowers.

> Sorrows and troubles produce lovely graces when God sanctifies
> them to that end.

Mark this, one and all :
Pride will surely have a fall.

A striking instance was given in the life of Elizabeth Stuart, sister of Charles I. When her husband, the Elector Palatine, hesitated to accept the Bohemian crown, she exclaimed, "Let me rather eat dry bread at a king's table, than feast at the board of an Elector"; and, as *Mrs. Jameson* says, "it seems as if some avenging demon hovered in the air, to take her literally at her word; for she and her family lived to eat dry bread—ay, and to beg it before they ate it—but she would be a queen."

Marriage for love is risky, but it's right.

Without love marriage is wicked. But love must not be blind or mad. True love will not drag its object into hopeless poverty. Where love reigns supreme, the married life will be joyful, whether in wealth or in poverty : yet love is apt to fly out of the window when the wolf of want comes in at the door.

Marriage is either kill or cure.

It is either mar age or merry age, as the case may be.

> " O matrimony ! thou art like
>   To Jeremiah's figs—
> The good are very good indeed ;
>   The bad too sour for pigs ! "

Yet people will venture upon it still, so long as the world standeth. Aunt Rachel said it was a solemn thing to be married; but her niece replied that it was a great deal more solemn not to be.

Marry a man, not a clothes-horse.

Fops, who give their whole mind to a hat or a waistcoat, are not worth looking after. As well marry one of the dummies in a tailor's window. It is a great pity when the man who should be the head figure is a mere figure-head. In such a case it is a mercy if the grey mare is much the better horse.

> Says Giles, "My wife and I are one,
>   Yet, truth, I know not why, sir."
> Quoth Jack, "If I think right, you're ten :
>   She's one, and you're a cipher."

Marry for love, and work for the lucre.

The prudent father said : "Do not marry for money, but only for love; yet let not your love go where there is no money." Our proverb is better advice by far. When a couple are united in love, then their joint exertions can be given to obtain the supply of their necessities, and in general they will succeed.

Marry for love, but only love that which is lovely.

Marry in a hurry, and live in a worry.

Marriage is harness for a pair, and it should be adjusted with care, blinkers and kicking-straps included, wherever they are required. This harness should be put on with due deliberation. Take time to do that which time cannot undo.

Marry in haste, and repent at leisure.

Marriage is a desperate thing. "The frogs in Æsop were extremely wise : they had a great mind to some water, but they would not leap into the well because they could not get out again." Blessed is the man who can say, after twenty years :

"I did commit no act of folly,
When I married my sweet Molly."

Marry not without love, but love not without reason.

Marry your first love if you can,
And hope to be a happy man.

Marrying is easy, but housekeeping is hard.

Thoughtless young people need to be reminded that they cannot live upon love, nor keep house upon none-pence a day.

Masters and mistresses are the greatest servants in the house.

On them lies the care of providing and directing, and they often lie awake when Sarah and Ann are sound asleep.

Matches may be made in heaven, but they are *sold* on earth.

That is to say, they are too often a matter of bargain, and the lowest motives are brought into play.

Many a match is made for gold :
The bride is bought—the bridegroom sold.

Match-making is a dangerous business.

Literally it is so ; for these little light-makers are apt to burn. The allusion is, however, to marriage. Match-makers often burn their fingers. If a mistake is made, the couple are apt to blame the persons who brought them together, and led them into matrimony. To recommend anyone for a husband or a wife is a very responsible business, and it is, as a rule, best let alone.

Matrimony should not be a matter of money.

He that marries for gold is bought and sold. Yet, even in the old times, men did such mercenary things ; for the rhyme ran :—
> "Bring something, lass, along with thee,
> If thou intend my wife to be."

This also is a curious memorandum :

	£	s.	d.
The girl was worth	1,000		
The man wasn't worth		1	
And when she found that he had			0
To wed she was unwilling.			

" May-be " is very well, but " must " is the master.

May good digestion wait on appetite, and health on both !

A good wish, having far more in it than at first appears. The joy of life depends more on digestion than on any other earthly thing. He that would have a good life must have a good liver. A great deal of misery is born of the stomach.

May that flirt soon light on a limed twig.

May he or she be caught, and held fast, so that the indecency of flippant flirting may be finally finished, in that case at least.

Measure men around the heart.

A man of great soul and large heart is a man worth knowing.

Measure three times before you cut once.

For you cannot uncut it, and you may waste the material.

Medicines are not meant to feed on.

"Mirth," according to Solomon, "doeth good like a medicine." It should not be our daily bread, but it should be measured out in proper quantities as a tonic, and not as a constant food.

Meekness is not weakness.

On the contrary, it is a sign of strength, and a cause of it. The ox lies still while the geese are hissing. The mastiff is quiet while curs are yelping. As an instance among men : Moses was king in Israel because of his great meekness among a provoking people.

Men are strong and hale without strong ale.

Lions and horses drink water, and so did Samson. It is a popular fallacy that there is strength in strong drink.

Men are seldom rashly bold
When they save a little gold.

A conservative tendency takes the desire for risk out of them, and they had rather let things be as they are. A Socialist was advocating an equal division of property. "And how much," asked a Scotchman, "wad there be for ilka ane?" "Oh, maybe near a hundred pounds!" "Then I'll na gang alang wi' ye, for I've saved a matter o' a hundred and twenty mysel'."

Men hate where they hurt.

Men love best those whom they have benefited, and hate those whom they have injured.

Men, like puppies, are born blind, but they do not so soon have their eyes opened.

"Man, a poor deluded bubble,
    Wanders in a mist of lies;
Seeing false, or seeing double,
    Who would trust to such weak eyes?

"Yet, presuming on his senses,
    On he goes, most wondrous wise;
Doubts the truth, believes pretences,
    Lost in error, lives and dies."

Men make houses, but women make homes.

Ruskin says: "Wherever a true woman comes, home is always around her. The stars may be over her head, the glow-worms in the night-cold grass may be the fire at her foot; but home is where she is; and for a noble woman it stretches far around her, better than houses ceiled with cedar, or painted with vermilion, shedding its quiet light far for those who else are homeless."

Men may bear till their backs break.

But they very seldom do. They are generally more ready to put their backs up if you would lay a single ounce upon them.

Men may die of the plague, though the spots never appear.

Alas! sin may reign in the heart unto eternal death, and yet the life may appear free from grave moral fault. This leprosy lies deep within, and is fatal even when unseen.

Men muse as they use.

They think of others as they are and do themselves. They weigh other folk's meat with their own steel-yard.

Men praise themselves, to save praising others.

None are more unjust in their judgments of others than those who have a high opinion of themselves. He who is greedy of applause never gives a cheer for a rival.

Men rattle their chains to show that they are free.

The wicked, who are slaves to sin, make much noise and shouting, that they may appear to be happy and at ease.

Men readily believe what they wish to be true.

The wish is father to the thought, and the thought is father to the belief. Hence we should be jealous of our beliefs when they coincide with our personal interests.

Men who carry honesty in their faces are often rogues.

I remember a very eminent bubble-blower, whom I mistook for an Essex farmer of the most plain and outspoken sort; and after looking at his honest face, and hearing his bluff speech and jolly laugh, I never wondered that people believed in him. An honest manner is essential to the success of a great rascal.

Men who have weak heads are generally headstrong.

So that if you forbid them a thing they will be sure to do it. Of such we have to say, "He that will to Cupar maun to Cupar." There's no keeping fools from hurting themselves.

Men will blame themselves for the purpose of being praised.

This is called "fishing for compliments," and it is not even so profitable a business as fishing for sticklebacks.

Men with nought in purse to spare
Go most quickly through the fair.

So do some pass through life with less of hankering for the world by reason of their poverty.

Mendings are honourable; rags are abominable.

Women who are worth their salt will use their needle to darn and patch. *Tom Fuller* says: "Needle means ne idle, or not idle"; but surely rags mean rogues.

Mercies and miseries seldom come alone.

These fly in flocks. It never rains but it pours.

Mercy to the criminal may be cruelty to the innocent.

Gentleness to those who commit burglary with violence is certainly cruelty to their victims; and there are many other cases equally to the point. We shall be glad to do away with the infliction of death when murderers set the example.

Mere wishes are bony fishes.

There is nothing solid and sustaining about mere dreams and schemes. The wishing-gate opens into nothing.

Merit only can measure merit.

A Sanscrit writer says:

"No man can others' virtues know,
While he himself has none to show."

Mice have tails.

Meaning that something may follow by way of consequence, even out of a trifling action. We should consider the results of little acts, for these may be greater than at first appears.

Mice must not play with kittens.

Nor must men toy with temptations, for they are not able to resist them.

Miles test the horse, and years prove the man.

They say, "It is the pace which kills," and it may be so; but it is far easier to make a great rush than to plod steadily on through a long life. Roasting before a slow fire is worse than burning.

Mind how you feed, especially when you feed your mind.

For as the silkworm is coloured by the leaf it feeds on, so do men take the hue of their reading. As we would not eat carrion, let us not read garbage. *Thackeray* once said to a visitor: "I read very few novels. I am a pastry-cook. I bake tarts and sell them. I do not eat them myself: I eat bread and butter."

Mind your " p's " and "q's."

These letters are exactly alike, save that one is turned one way, and the other the other. If mistakes are made in them even a peer is queer. Great errors may arise from carelessness in little things. Mind etiquette, or you will have the wrong ticket.

Mind that no doubting mind undermines your mind.

A danger very pressing just now. For many are the deceivers
"Who, wheedling round, with metaphysic art,
Steal true religion from the unguarded heart."

Mind that *porter* does not carry you off.

Double stout, though said to be nourishing, may readily carry a
man half seas over. "*Porter* was a name given in the last century
to a new mixture of malt liquors, which was at first chiefly drunk
by porters; but it has twice earned its name by the tendency it
displays of carrying heavy burdens and placing them upon men's
hearts, and by the success it has attained in carrying men from
their homes, reason from the brains, money from the pocket, love
from the bosom, peace from the conscience, reputation from the
character, and too often life from its victim."

Mind the corner where life's road turns.

For as you turn that point, so will you be likely to continue. If
one foot should there be placed awry, many a day may have to rue it.

Mind the main chance.

But what is it? Take care to answer this question wisely, and
then obey the proverb.

Mind the paint! Keep clear of the face that wears it.

What good can you get from a picture painted on flesh? Paint
is the outward and visible sign of inward and spiritual deceit.

When a woman is painted up to the eyes,
She's a Jezebel even the dogs will despise.

Mind *what* is preached, more than *how* it is preached.

Meat is more than its carving, and truth is more than oratory.

Mind *what* you do, and *how* you do it.

Let the matter be good, and let the manner befit it.

Mind you get the right sow by the ear.

Don't blame the innocent, nor pounce upon a person whom you
ought not to assail. Leave all piggies' ears alone, rather than seize
upon the wrong one.

Mind your courting does not end in court.

Breach of promise has overthrown many a promising young man.

Mind your own business, and you will be sure
To avoid many troubles which others endure.

> Men who mind their own business will be very likely to succeed; for there is very little competition in that line. You will do better at your own business than at anything else: " Every man can blow best on his own horn." Let every tailor keep to his goose.

Mind your till, and till your mind.

> Look to your business, its takings and makings; but do not forget the nobler part of your being. Don't put your soul along with the coppers; keep it cultivated with reading and thought.

Mind your work, and God will find your wages.

> If not to-day, nor to-morrow, yet very certainly and abundantly, according to his grace, he will reward every good work.

Mirth should never run into mischief.

> Boisterous boys should take heed to this. Mirth has its bounds. When we meet merrily, let us so act that we may part merrily too. There is an old saying not often quoted, but very true: " No mirth is good without God."

Misers' hearts are as hard as their hard cash.

> Of such a man it could be said:
>
> " Iron was his safe,
> Iron was its door;
> His hand was iron,
> His heart was more."

Misery hath strange bed-fellows.

> In a common calamity men of different classes are thrown together without question of rank or character.

Misfortune comes on horseback, and goes away on foot.

> Adversity pounces upon us like an eagle; but to retrieve a disaster is slow work. Sorrow seems to linger long.

Misreckoning is no payment.

> This is clear enough in trade, and it is equally so in morals. Because a man thinks well of himself, is it therefore well with him? If a man's conscience reckons amiss, this does not make a breach of the law an innocent thing.

Mistress Margery, do not scold,
It makes you look so very old.

> *Ovid* wrote :
> " Look in the glass when you with anger glow,
> And you'll confess you scarce yourself would know."

Misunderstanding brings lies to town.

People are apt to misinterpret those whom they dislike, and then the misrepresentation leads on to libel and slander.

Mock not a cobbler for his black thumbs.

His disfigurement comes of honest labour, and, therefore, it is no theme for jest. Napoleon said, " Respect the burden," and truly all labour, and all that necessarily comes of labour, deserves to be had in honour. In the cobbler's case be very generous; for you ought to remember that while other trades take an earlier turn, he has to wait for his *last*.

Modest dogs miss much meat.

No doubt one can stand in his own light by extreme bashfulness. Some puppies we know of never lose a mouthful from this cause.

Moles and misers live in their graves.

Scarcely can we say this of moles; but they are of the earth earthy, and so is the man whose heap of yellow dust is all he cares for : he is buried in the earth he has scraped together.

Moles don't see what their neighbours are doing.

Some persons are so absorbed in their own earth-grubbing, that they know nothing of anybody else. This selfish isolation is, on the whole, not so mischievous as perpetual interfering.

Monday religion is better than Sunday profession.

Money answers everything,
Save a guilty conscience sting.

Golden ointment is no cure for a wound of the heart. Ready money is ready medicine, but not for the sting of remorse. Some call it " the one thing needful," but they know not what they say.

Money borrowed is soon sorrowed.

He that lends it begins to sorrow, even if the borrower does not; for, in general, he may mourn that he has parted from it to meet no more.

Money burns many.

They are injured by their wealth. Some by bribes are burned; for

> When money's taken,
> Freedom's forsaken.

Money calls, but does not stay; It is round and rolls away.

It makes the mill to go, but it goes faster than the mill-wheel. It is no more to be kept in the purse than snow in an oven; at least, so I find it. But why should we wish it to stay? It is the circulating medium! why should we detain it? If it rests it rusts. Let it go about doing good.

Money gained on Sabbath-day Is a loss, I dare to say.

No blessing can come with that which comes to us, on the devil's back, by our wilful disobedience of God's law. The loss of health by neglect of rest, and the loss of soul by neglect of hearing the gospel, soon turn all seeming profit into real loss.

Money gilds over guilt.

Money is said to be a composition for taking out stains in character; but, in that capacity, it is a failure. Those characters which can be thus gilded must surely be of the gingerbread order.

Money has no blood relations.

There is no friendship in business. Sad that this should be a proverb in any land, but so it is. The Chinese say: "Though brothers are closely akin, it is each for himself in money matters." They also say: "Top and bottom teeth sometimes come into awkward collision." So little power has relationship in the savage customs of business that, in some instances, one hand would skin the other, if it could make a profit by it.

Money is a good servant, but a bad master.

Even as a servant it is not easy to keep it in due subordination. If "money makes dogs dance," it makes men proud. If we make money our god, it will rule us like the devil.

Money is often lost for want of money.

It is so when men cannot get their rights, from inability to pay legal charges. Yet if one had plenty of cash, it would not be wise to throw away good money after bad.

Money is the best bait to fish for man with.

He bites greedily at a gold or silver bait : but is the creature which is thus taken worth the catching?

> He who can be bought,
> I think is worth nought.

Money is the servant of the wise, and the master of fools.

Money makes money.

The goose that lays the golden eggs likes to lay where there are eggs already ; perhaps because it is a goose. The lard comes to the fat hog. Capital grows by interest, or by wise use it brings in profit, and thus increases. Money is money's brother. " If riches increase, set not your heart upon them."—Ps. lxii. 10.

Money makes the mare to go and the dog to dance.

Pecuniæ obediunt omnia. " All things obey money." This saying comes from the Latin, but it is true in English. A little palm oil will gain entrance where nothing else will do it. Officials are greatly mollified when their hands are crossed with silver. In a more allowable sense, a good wife would be happier and more active if her allowance could be increased. If she has too little money to keep house upon, it takes the "go" out of her.

Money often unmakes the men who make it.

It has a defiling and degrading power over the mind which thinks too much of it.

> "Money and men a mutual falsehood show ;
> Men make false money ; money makes men so."

Money speaks more powerfully than eloquence.

Too often, because the speaker is a rich man he commands attention, and secures the approbation of persons who see no sound sense spoken by one who has no money bags. This is very well put in the following verse :—

> The man of means is eloquent :
> Brave, handsome, noble, wise ;
> All qualities with gold are sent,
> And vanish where it flies.

Money spent on the brain
Is never spent in vain.

Pour your money into your brain, and you will never lose it all. Education is such a gain, that it is worth all that it costs, and more. Yet some fellows learn nothing in the schools. Many a father, when his son returns from the University, might say, " I put in gold into the furnace, and there came out this calf."

Money will make the pot boil, though the devil should pour water on the fire.

But such fuel is not to be depended on. We need something better than mere money to keep our pot a-boiling. Such boiling is apt to scald a man sooner or later.

Money wins where merit fails.

It is a pity it should be so; but, with worldly minds, to be rich is to be good. This vulgar error is long in dying. "The boy in yellow wins the day." Canaries are still the favourite birds.

"This is the golden age: all worship gold:
Honours are purchased; love and beauty sold."

Monk's-hood is very poisonous. Beware!

Whenever a smell of Romanism is discernible, be on the watch.

More belongs to riding than a pair of boots.

So in most things there is much to be learned, and the thing is not so easy as it looks. Even in pastimes this is true, as the proverb saith, "More belongs to dancing than a pair of pumps."

More die of idleness than of hard work.

A very small burial-ground will hold those who kill themselves with excessive industry; but the cemetery at Idler's End covers many acres, and the ground is rapidly filling up.

More die of overfeeding than of underfeeding.

Death feeds himself at banquets, but fares ill where there are short-commons. Lean ribs last longer than fat collops. More die of suppers than of the sword.

When other forms of physic fail,
Try if fasting will avail.

More flies are caught with honey than with vinegar.

Gentleness and cheerfulness attract more to religion and virtue than severe solemnity, or stern manners.

There's but little power,
In religion sour.

More have repented of speech than of silence.

How seldom are men sorry for holding their tongues! How often have they had to bite their tongues with anguish at the memory of unguarded speech! Say nothing, and none can criticize thee.

More know Tom Fool than Tom Fool knows.

Public characters are known by thousands, but they cannot know thousands themselves. "Don't you know me? I heard you speak at Exeter Hall." Wonderful argument!

More light, more life, more love.

Worthy to be a common wish, and to grow into a holy proverb.

Light without life is a candle in a tomb;
Life without love is a garden without bloom.

More meat, and less mustard.

Often we would like more solid argument and fewer angry words; more gospel and less controversy; more wages and less scolding; more gifts of charity and less lecturing upon thrift.

More pith and less pride.

Generally your boaster has nothing in him of true grit. The more of the solid there is in a man, the less does he act the balloon.

More potatoes and fewer potations.

A capital motto for a labouring man. *Father Matthew* and plenty of *murphies* will be of more use to the Irish than all the whisky of all the stills in the Emerald Isle.

More than we use, is more than we want.

Except so far as we make reasonable store, like Solomon's ant, whose ways he bids us consider and be wise.

More words than one go to a bargain.

Because one man says he would like it to be so, it does not follow that the matter is settled for both sides. It takes two to make a binding agreement; and that agreement should be well talked over by both parties before it is finally decided.

Morning dew is good for the eyes.

Our forefathers thought much of dew in May; hence the rhyme:

"The fair maid who, the first of May,
Goes to the fields at break of day,
And washes in dew from the hawthorn tree,
Will ever after handsome be."

But early rising at any time is beneficial to body and soul. "The muses love the morning," and so do the graces.

Most felt, least said.

Deep and true feeling often causes an eloquent silence.   The frost of the mouth goes with the thaw of the soul.   Waters that are deep do not babble as they flow.

Most horses that are very fat have fed by night as well as by day.

This is an insinuation that those persons who have amassed great riches have done things which would not bear the light.   Let it be hoped that this is not largely true.   It is true in a measure.

Most men get as good a wife as they deserve.

And some get a great deal better.

Most things are difficult before they are easy.

Most trees have enough rotten wood about them to burn them.

We have enough of evil tendency in our nature to ruin us.

Motherless husband makes happy wife.

We don't believe it.   This is a shot at mothers-in-law, who are constantly made a butt of.   Some of them deserve it, but many do not.   Why not abuse fathers-in-law ?

Mothers make men.

They have the formation of their boys' characters.

Mother's love is the cream of love.

It is most pure, holy, and unselfish.   "A mother's heart is always with her children."   Hence the return on the part of her sons of the sweet proverb, "The mother's breath is aye sweet," and that other : "There is no mother like the mother that bore us."

Mother's truth makes constant youth.

Doubtless a good man generally comes of a good mother.   It was usually so in Scriptural times, and it is so still.

Mourning tendeth to mending.

Sorrow is salutary, and when blest to us by God's Spirit it leads to thought, and to our seeking for salvation.

Mouth and heart should never part.

True men speak only what they believe and feel. When the mouth is white and the heart black, the man has a plague upon him.

When tongue and heart go different ways,
The very soul of man decays.

Mr. Facing-both-ways is not to be trusted.

If we can scarcely trust an honest man, we ought by no means to put confidence in the double-faced.

Mr. Too-good is not Mr. Good-enough.

Those that think that they are a little better than there is need to be, may be sure that they are far below what they ought to be.

Mrs. Chatterbox is the mother of mischief.

They say that when ten portions of speech were given out, the women seized on nine of them; and, really, it would seem to be true of certain of them, though not more so than of the same order of men. Mr. Chatterbox is a worse mischief maker than his wife.

Much ado and little done.

Often the case; great horn-blowing, and yet no hunting. All sound and fury, and there's an end of it.

The King of France with might and main,
Marched up a hill and down again.

Much banqueting, quick bankruptcy.

No doubt the kitchen fire has often burned up the house, and the table has devoured the estate.

Much broth is often made with little meat.

Long talk and short sense often meet in one. A very long story is often concocted out of a very tender supply of fact. Lengthy discourses are also manufactured out of the tiniest measure of thought and doctrine.

Much chatter, little wit; much talk, little work.

Pope says:
"Words are like leaves, and where they most abound
Much fruit of sense beneath is rarely found."

Much din and little done.

Often the case in religious movements, and political contests.

Much haste, much waste; much drink, little chink.

Much illness is caused by the want of pure air:
To open your windows be ever your care.

> The fear of draughts leads many foolish people to live like rats in a drain. They dread fresh air, which is one of God's best gifts. Would they not have been happy in the Black Hole of Calcutta?

Much in bed, dull in head.

> Unnecessary sleep prevents men from fully waking up at any time. Many walk in their sleep all day long.

Much is expected where much is entrusted.

> Most justly and rightly so. "Unto whomsoever much is given, of him shall be much required."—Luke xii. 48.

Much kindred, much hindered.

> Demands from a large family and numerous poor relations, tend to keep a man poor. Still, there is a blessing in helping one's kin.

Much laughter, little wit.

> The flame is fast and furious when the fuel is light and unsubstantial. A bush blazes greatly, but the flame is soon over, and nothing remains. When people laugh at their own jokes their wit is very small beer, and is lost in its own froth.

Much rust needs a rough file.

> Hence the sharp afflictions which some of us require to put us in a right condition.

Much to read, and nought to understand,
Is to hunt much and nothing take by hand.

> It is possible for a great reader to become a donkey loaded with paper. Brains can be buried under a pile of books.

Much water runs by while the miller sleeps.

> Many opportunities are lost by neglect, and others by necessity; for there is a sleep which is needful as well as a slumber which is slothful. Be it how it may, the past is passed, and we can do nothing with it. The Poet was right when, listening to the clicking of the mill-wheel, he wrote—
>
> > "And a proverb haunts my mind,
> >   And as a spell is cast;
> > The mill will never grind
> >   With the water that is past."

Much would have more, and lost all.

Mud chokes no eels.

They have lived in it too long to feel its foulness. Use is second nature. People who dwell in filth lose sensitiveness, and grow used to abominations. No doubt, to a fox his hole is sweet, and pigs think they are cleaning themselves in the mud. People should be clean now that soap is so advertised. Let us hope so.

Muddle at home
Makes husbands roam.

Slatternly wives drive their husbands from the fireside; and if they go where they waste the money in drink, their wives may thank themselves for it.

Muddy spring, muddy stream.

"Who can bring a clean thing out of an unclean?" A depraved parentage cannot bring forth perfect children. Impure motives produce unholy actions. Impure amusements create vice.

Music will not cure the toothache.

Much less the headache. "Music has charms to soothe a savage breast;" but in great grief it becomes a trial rather than a solace, and we think the man who offers it "more fool than fiddler."

Must is a hard nut.

There's no cracking it. We must even let it alone.

Must is for THE KING.

He alone can say that so a thing must be: yet even he for our sakes came under a necessity of love. "He must needs go through Samaria."—John iv. 4. "I must work the works of him that sent me, while it is day."—John ix. 4.

Muzzle not the ox which treadeth out the corn.

Don't starve the man who works hard to find you spiritual food.

Muzzled dogs bite no burglars.

If we are not allowed to speak truth boldly, we cannot save the church from teachers of error. Dumb dogs are not worth their bones. If they will not bite burglars, what is the good of them?

My dame fed her hens on thanks, but they laid no eggs.

And men who earn nothing but compliments are not likely to be very diligent in so unprofitable a service. "Pretty Pussy" and "Pretty Pussy" will not feed a cat. Fine speeches make poor suppers, and votes of thanks are notes of nothing.

My daughter-in-law tucked up her sleeves and upset the kettle into the fire.

She went at it with desperate zeal, as most newly-aroused people do, and, therefore, in her hurry she did more harm than good. Some stir the fire and poke it out ; others make up such a fire that they set the chimney alight, and burn the house down. Too much zeal may be as harmful as too little.

My house is my castle, but "The Castle" is not my house.

My kingdom is what I do, not what I have.

A clear conscience is better than a golden crown.

My mind to me a kingdom is.

The man is more to himself than an empire could be. Mind that your mind is worth the having, for it is your only kingdom.

My son's mother—where's such another ?

There is one good wife in the country, and many a man *thinks* that he hath her ; but I know a man who *knows* that he is the man who hath the best wife in all the world.

My own dear wife,
Joy of my life.

My ugly dog is a beauty.

To me he is by no means a horribly ugly pug, but his black muzzle and red tongue are charming ; for he loves his master, and rejoices at the sound of his coming home.

Sayings of a more Spiritual Sort.

Make a crutch of your cross.

> Use it as a help on the road to heaven.

Make a saviour of nothing but the Saviour.

Make God your end, and your joy shall have no end.

> "Man's chief end is to glorify God, and to enjoy him for ever."
>> "What is my being but for thee,
>> Its sure support, its noblest end?
>> Thy ever smiling face to see,
>> And serve the cause of such a friend?"

Make the Sabbath a delight from morning to night.

> The poet *Coleridge* said to a friend, one Sunday morning, "I feel as if God had, by giving the Sabbath, given fifty-two Springs in every year."

Make Thou my spirit white and clear
As the first snowdrop of the year.

Man's extremity is God's opportunity.

> Let the believer who is sorely tried remember this. The darkest part of the night is that which precedes the dawning of the day. When we are quite empty, the Lord will fill us.

Man's holiness is "Much-ado-about-nothing."

Man's life's a book of history,
  The leaves thereof are days;
The letters, mercies closely joined;
  The title is God's praise.

Man's merit is a madman's dream.

>> The legal path proud nature loves right well,
>> Though yet 'tis but the cleanest road to hell.

Many have gifts from God, but not "the gift of God."

> They have the comforts of life, but not eternal life.

Many things may dim a Christian's view of Christ, but nothing can separate him from Christ.

Many wear God's livery, but are not his servants.

Many worlds would not be enough for *one carnal* man; but one heaven shall be enough for *all Christian* men.

Mary was not praised for sitting still, but for sitting at the feet of Jesus.

Meditation fits a man for supplication.

It provides thought-fuel for the flame of prayer.

Meekness is the bridle of anger.

It is love put to school to the Man of Sorrows.

Men cannot practise unless they know, but they know in vain if they practise not.

Men lose their lives by accident, but not their souls.

No. It is their wilful fault, and not their misfortune, which ruins the souls of men.

Men may live fools, but fools they cannot die.

If they die in their senses, conscience usually drives out their foolish indifference.

Men may live in crowds, but they die one by one.

A saying which recalls *Faber's* pathetic lines:

" Alone to land upon that shore,
To begin alone, to live for evermore;
To have no one to teach
The manners or the speech
Of that new life, or put us at our ease;
Oh, that we might die in pairs or companies!

" Alone? The God we know is on that shore;
The God of whose attractions we know more
Than of those who may appear
Nearest and dearest here.
Oh, is he not the life-long Friend we know
More privately than any friend below?"

Men who love much, will work much.

"The love of Christ constraineth us." It is the most powerful of the forces which work for good.

Mercy despised brings misery deserved.

Mercy is "*from* everlasting" to contrive thy salvation, and "*to* everlasting" to perfect it.

Mercy is without price, and beyond all price.

> 'Tis heaven, and yet it is given away :
> 'Tis all in all, and yet " nothing to pay."

Mercy's gate opens to those who knock.

Ministers can persuade, but God alone can prevail.

> We can explain truth, but God must apply it.

Ministers should be stars to give light, not clouds to obscure.

> In some cases the text is as clear as a mirror, till the preacher's breath bedims it. We ought to pick out all hard words from our speech : good cooks stone the plums.

Ministers should study as if all depended on study, and preach knowing that all depends on the Holy Spirit.

Miseries often drive men to their mercies.

> Even as the black dog drives the stray sheep to the shepherd.

Most men forget God all day, and ask him to remember them at night.

Most people would sooner be told their fortunes than their faults.

> Yet the first would be an idle lie, and the other a practical truth.

Mourners in Zion are more blessed than merry-makers in the world.

> "Blessed are they that mourn : for they shall be comforted." Matt. v. 4.

Mourning only lasts till morning with the children of the morning.

My only plea—
Christ died for me.

AG, nag, nagging,
  Is very, very fagging.

This may come from either side of the house, and it is equally bad whoever is the first hand at it. It is a weariness to hear it as a visitor; but it must be horrible to bear it as a partaker in it. We know instances in which the husband is the more guilty of the two; but that makes it none the better.

> What *she* proposes,
>   Be it good or bad,
> *He* still opposes,
>   Till he drives her mad.

As married people grow old, the tendency to correct each other in every trifling mistake is often developed; and it is so trying that they will be wise to watch against it with the utmost care.

Nail your colours to the mast.

If you carry the flag of truth, never strike your colours, nor sail under false ones. Never be a turncoat or a traitor.

> Be ready to die,
> But never deny.

Nails unclinched are unsafe.

Make assurance doubly sure. Do not hang much on a nail which is not surely fastened. We are not saved by faith when dealing with our fellow-men.

Narrowness of waist shows narrowness of mind.

Nobody with a large mind would think of injuring all the delicate organs within the body by wickedly compressing them within unnatural limits. There is neither sense nor beauty in a figure shaped like a wasp or a half-quartern loaf.

Nature abhors a vacuum.

When a man's head is empty some nonsense or other is sure to get in, and when his stomach is empty it will not be comfortable till it is filled. Empty purses also are very restless things.

Nature needeth nurture, minds want minding.

> Even as the vine needeth pruning,
> And the harp still needeth tuning.

Nature, though driven out with a fork, will return.

So said the Latins : nature will assert itself, and have its way.

Near to church should not be late to service.

Yet is it often so. People who can run in so quickly wait till the last moment; till we half think that "the nearer the church the further from God."

Necessity cannot stand upon nicety.

It dispenses with decorum, and knows no law.

Necessity is a hard nurse, but she raises strong children.

Captain Butler, recounting his hardships in the Great Lone Land, says, "And yet how easy it all was, and how soundly one slept! *simply because one had to do it.* That one consideration is the greatest expounder of the possible." The sons of need are driven to exertion : their muscle is tried and strengthened, and we get a race of sturdy, independent men.

> Hard work and harder fare
> Breed men of vigour rare.

Necessity is the mother of invention.

When a want becomes pressing and common, somebody's mind is exercised to supply it, and a new discovery is the result. The necessity of the masses is great; how can we reach them? Now for a holy invention!

Necessity makes lame men run.

It would cure many a nervous lady if she had to work for her living, and many a dyspeptic man would be well if he lived upon sixpence a day, and earned it. We know not our force till we are forced to know it.

Necessity never made a good bargain.

Because the man wants money so badly that he cannot wait, but must take whatever he can get. This is the reason why poor manufacturers have so bad a market : they must sell, or be sold up.

Necessity sharpens industry.

The call for daily bread sets all the world to work, and rigorous climates tutor men to hardihood of labour. A man driven by distress will do as much as thirty, at least the Spaniards say so.

> Adam delved and Eve span;
> Need allowed no gentleman.

Necessity's budget is full of schemes.

> Kite-flying, speculation, day-dreaming, &c., make up the stock-in-trade of men who are hard up for hard cash.

Necks may be bent by the sword, but hearts will only bend to hearts.

> So say the Arabs; and they ought to know, for they once set up an empire by force, and they have seen it melt away.

Need is the frying-pan, but debt is the fire.

> Whatever trouble it may cause us to bear the want of comforts, we shall gain no comfort by running into debt.

Needles and pins, needles and pins;
When a man marries his trouble begins.

> A Quaker who married a couple said, "Now you are at the end of your troubles." Some time after, the afflicted husband reminded him of the saying, and charged him with misleading him. "Nay," said the friend, "I said ye were at the end of your troubles, but I did not say at which end."

Needles are not sharp at both ends.

> We ought not to be all sharpness; we must have an eye as well as a point—judgment as well as courage.

Ne'er let your tongue outrun your wit:
Wise men full oft in silence sit.

Neighbours are good when they are neighbourly.

> Some say, "No neighbour is best"; but another says, "No one is rich enough to do without his neighbour." Good neighbours make good neighbours. He that would have good neighbours must show himself neighbourly.

Neither break law nor go to law.

> Keep law, and keep from law.

Neither colour the truth nor the face.

> "When fair, no colour is required:
> When true, no colour is desired."

Neither crow nor croak.

Neither of these sounds is becoming in men; leave them to fowls and frogs.

Neither give nor take offence.

The world would be happy and peaceful indeed,
If all men on this point were always agreed.

Neither seek a secret nor speak a secret.

Don't want to be told it, and if told it, never tell it again. When any would tell thee a secret, be deaf; but once having heard it, be dumb. Secrets are useless and dangerous curiosities.

Neither shoot without aim, nor speak without thought.

Or you may do as much mischief by a hasty speech as by a random shot.

Sometimes our words
Hurt more than swords.

Neither trust nor contend,
Nor lay wagers nor lend,
And you may depend,
You'll have peace to your end.

That is to say, as much peace as this troublesome world allows of. Great worries arise out of the four things mentioned; but the old rhyme can only be accepted with a grain of salt.

Nettles are to be boldly dealt with.

Tender-handed stroke a nettle,
And it stings you for your pains;
Grasp it like a man of mettle,
And it soft as silk remains.

'Tis the same with vulgar natures,
Use them kindly, they rebel;
But be rough as nutmeg graters,
And the rogues obey you well.

Never argue for victory, but for verity.

Controversy would wear a very different complexion if this were observed. We ought to fight for truth, not for party.

Never ask pardon before you're accused.

For those who excuse themselves accuse themselves.   To answer an idle rumour is to confirm it in the minds of many.   Why go into the dock when you have never been summoned ?

Never bark up the wrong tree.

Don't accuse the wrong man, nor denounce a procedure mistakenly.   Be quite sure before you open your mouth.

Never barter a pearl for a pippin.

You will do this if you lose modesty for pleasure, and still more if you lose your soul to gain the world's applause.

Never be a dog in a manger to friend or stranger.

Nor to anyone else.   Surely, what you do not require should be cheerfully given up to others who can use it.

> The cur could never eat the hay,
> And yet he drove the ox away :
> So some who ne'er a penny made
> Yet do their best to spoil the trade.

Never bet even a gooseberry.

A friend of mine, who was a great enemy to gambling, once felt so sure of a matter that he incautiously said, "I'll bet a thousand pounds to a gooseberry that it is so."   His companion cried, "I'll take you," and entered the bet in a book.   The good man was in some trouble because of the bet, and would have given the thousand pounds to be out of it.   As it happened he was right, and his friend in mirthfulness sent him a silver gooseberry as his winnings; but he never used the phrase again, nor ventured on such treacherous ground.   In this matter excessive caution is justifiable excess.

Never bite a farthing in two.

Nor split a plum, nor dispute about a casual expression, nor make miserable debates over mere trifles.

Never bite back at back-biters.

If you do so, they have caused you a serious injury of soul by bringing you down to their level.   Leave them their miserable trade to themselves.   " Bless them that curse you."

Never boil your rabbit till you've got him.

There are many such proverbs, and hence we gather that people are very prone to deal with mere hopes as if they were realities; like the milkmaid with her eggs.

Never bray at an ass.

Let a foolish person have the talk to himself. Do not imitate his folly. Your silence will be quite as melodious as his voice.

Never buy a pig in a poke.

Examine the article before you part with your money. If you do not so, and are taken in, you will have yourself to blame. If the pig in the poke should turn out to be very lean, it will be no wonder. If it had been fat, the seller would have allowed you to see it.

Never cackle till your egg is laid.

And you need not do much of it when the brave deed is done; leave cackling and crowing to feathered fowl.

Never challenge another to do wrong, lest he sin at thy bidding.

And in that case thou wilt have to share the sin; for thou wilt have acted the part of the tempter.

Never comb a bald head.

Don't criticize where there is nothing to work upon. Treat a poor helpless man with tenderness. If a man has no religion, don't dispute with him about its doctrines. When you meet with a person who has no money, don't ask him for a contribution.

Never commit what you would wish to conceal.

Do only that which will bear the light of day.

Never despise the day of small things.

Whether good or bad, things must begin as littles.

Out of small,
Cometh all.

Even the great eagle was once in an egg, and the terrible lion was a playful cub. The mother of mischief is a midge's egg.

Never dispute about the wool of a cat.

See if there is anything in a question before you discuss it, or you may make much ado about nothing.

Never fall out with your bread and butter.

To find fault with the way in which you earn your living is very absurd. Speak well of the ravens which bring you your bread and flesh, and don't find fault with the brook of which you drink.

Never find fault with the absent.

It is cowardly. Accuse a man when he can defend himself.

Never fish in troubled waters.

Or you may draw forth trouble for yourself. Yet some read the proverb the other way, and delight in a stir, because troubled waters are best for their sort of fishing.

Never flog the dead.

They cannot be improved by your remarks, neither can they meet your charges. Let them sleep on. When an error is clean dead, do not go on disproving it, lest, like the boy with his top, you set it going again by whipping it.

Never fry a fish till it's caught.

It will be a waste of fire and butter to attempt it. Yet angry folks threaten loudly what they will do when they get us in their power. *When?*

Never give up the ship.

Stand to your trust. As long as she is above water, never desert the ship; as long as hope remains, do not give up a good undertaking. Above all, never quit the glorious ship of the church, in which our Lord is captain : she will never go down.

Never grudge a penny for a pennyworth.

Pay a fair price cheerfully, and do not beat down the seller; for he in his turn will have to sweat the workman.

Never grumble nor mumble.

Take things as they come,
Eat crust as well as crumb.

As for mumbling, when men are making a complaining speech, they generally talk so fast that they eat one-half of their words, and whistle the rest. It would not matter much if they whistled all of them, for they are not worth much.

Never hang a man twice for one offence.

If he has borne his punishment, cease to persecute him. Some accusers can never have done; they would hang a man every morning for the offence of years ago.

Never have an idle hour, or an idle pound.

For these are buried talents, the Lord's goods wasted.

Never hold a candle to the devil.

Do not aid him in his work, nor pay deference to the powers of evil. "To hold a candle to the devil" is to abet an evil-doer out of fawning fear. The allusion is to the story of an old woman, who set one wax taper before the image of St. Michael, and another before the devil whom he was trampling under foot. Being reproved for paying such honour to Satan, she naïvely replied, "Ye see, your honour, it's quite uncertain which place I shall go to at last, and sure you'll not blame a poor woman for securing a friend in each." This policy is the sure way to ruin.

Never is a long day.

Therefore it is well not to vow so indefinitely, for we may change our mind. Moreover, it is wise never to despair, or say that we shall never be happy again; for after a while things will look brighter.

Never judge a horse by its harness, nor a man or a woman by outward appearances.

Very poor horses may be finely caparisoned, or decked with ribbons at a fair; and the same is true of two-legged creatures.

Never lean on a broken staff.

This you do whenever you trust in man; especially in yourself.

Never leave a certainty for an uncertainty.

Multitudes have quitted a small assured income for "the larger hope" of speculation. They have left rock for sand, and have been swallowed up. The same is specially true in religious matters.

Never leave till afternoon what can be done in the morning.

This the boy quoted as a reason for eating all the cheese for breakfast. In other directions it is a good rule of promptitude. We are informed that this proverb does not apply to lawyers, with whom "Procrastination is the hinge of business."

Never let plain-dealing die.

If all the world should twist and twine,
Still be thou straight as plummet line.

Never look for a knot in a bulrush.

Don't look for difficulties where there are none.

Never look for a ram with five feet.

Expect not the abnormal, the monstrous, the singular. Leave "the Derby ram" to those who are in love with penny shows.

Never look for pippins on a crab-tree.

Everything yields according to its nature. Sour yields sour, and it would be folly to look for sweet from it.

Never meet trouble half-way.

It will come soon enough, and then you will meet it where God meant you should meet it, and where he will help you to bear it.

Never mind who was your grandfather: what are you?

The man who has nothing to boast of but his good ancestors, is like a potato : all that is good of him is under ground. So said an author long since under ground himself.

Never mix mirth and malice.

It is a sort of treachery to do so : like Absalom inviting Amnon to a feast to kill him.

Never offer to teach fish to swim.

They know better than you do. It is absurd for young greenhorns to set up to instruct experienced persons.

Never overdrive
The best horse alive.

He is just the horse you ought to take care of. If he be a weak horse it is cruel to overdrive him, and if he is a willing horse it is unfair to take advantage of him.

Never play with a mad dog.

Or you will soon have cause to repent of your play. Do not sport with sin, or speculate in false doctrine. Keep out of the way when a man is in a savage temper.

Never prophesy till you know.

And then it is too late to foretell. We had better not so despise prophesyings as to think ourselves capable of manufacturing them.

Never put your finger between the anvil and the hammer.

Keep clear of violent opponents when they are in full action, or you may receive upon yourself the force of their blows.

Who interferes gets double blow :
It's not my business, off I go.

Never put your hand into a wasp's nest.

It will be prudent to respect the quiet of that domestic circle. *Josh Billings* says, "When I see the tail of a rattlesnake sticking out of a hole, I say to myself, 'That hole belongs to that snake, and I am not going to try to take it from him. I believe in respecting the rights of property.'" Even if a man does not regard the rights of others, it may often be wise for him to consider his own peace before he commences to meddle.

Never raise
Your own praise.

"Let another man praise thee, and not thine own mouth."— Prov. xxvii. 2.

Never ride a broken-kneed horse.

Trust not the man who has failed you. Moreover, he who has been a bankrupt once is very apt to fail a second time : be cautious.

Thou didst deceive : the fault was thine.
A second time it will be mine.

Never roast so as to burn, nor sport so as to sin.

Observe the bounds of righteousness, kindness, and truth.

Never say die !
Up, man, and try !

Despondency does nothing ; perseverance works wonders.

Never say die till you're dead, and then it's no use.

Bravely hold on, and do not give way to despondency under any circumstances whatever. (Easier said than done.)

Never say of another what you would not have him hear.

This precept would put the extinguisher on many a tattler.

Never sell your customers by selling bad goods.

It will be a rogue's action, and in the long run you will sell yourself, and be obliged to shut up shop.

Never shirk the hardest work.

Some do so habitually. If they can live on others they will not do a hand's turn. The age of chivalry is over, but the age of loafers lasts for ever. Let us be of another clan. Two negroes were loading goods into a cart. One of them was disposed to shirk; the other stopped, and looking sharply at the lazy one, said, *"Sam, do you expect to go to heaven?"* *"Yes."* *"Then take hold and lift."*

Never sigh, but send.

Do not long for a thing despondingly, but do your best to get it, if it is to be had, and is really desirable.

Never speak ill of those whose bread you eat.

Even a dog knows who feeds him. If he bites his keeper, he is likely to be hanged, and nobody will pity him.

Never stint soap and water.

The soap-makers seem, to judge by their advertisements, to be doing a thriving business; but we still know a few people who need to patronize them. We do not admire Pharisees, but we should like to see some persons become Pharisaical in one respect, namely, in their objection to eat with unwashen hands.

Never stint the cause of God.

Cut down expenses for self before you diminish offerings to God.

Never swap horses while crossing a stream.

While a difficult business is going on, make as few changes as possible. *Abraham Lincoln* quoted this with much effect.

Never tell in the parlour what you heard in the kitchen.

Servants' gossip, if repeated, may make mischief, and it cannot possibly do any good. Carry no slops into the parlour.

He that heareth much, and speaks not at all,
Shall be welcome both in kitchen and hall.

Never throw a hen's egg at a sparrow.

That will be an expensive throw. Do not spend a pound in the hope of getting a groat, nor waste great effort on an insignificant object.

Never too old to turn; never too late to learn.

If not too old to sin, we are not too old to repent.

Never trouble yourself with trouble till trouble troubles you.

Forestalling trouble is like burning yourself at a fire before it is lit. *Mr. S. C. Hall* tells of an underwriter at Lloyd's, an excellent and estimable gentleman, who had all his wealth in ventures on the sea, or thought he had. One night a terrific storm shook the house in which he lived. He awoke frightened, was haunted by a terror that all his ships were wrecked, and that he was ruined; and he was found in the morning under his garden hedge dead, having taken laudanum. It was afterwards ascertained that his losses were trifling.

Never trust a man who speaks ill of his mother.

He must be base at heart. If he turns on her that bore him, he will turn on you sooner or later.

Never trust a swearer, nor believe a boaster.

A friend once drove me out to a village to preach, and he put up his horse at an inn. When we stopped, the ostler used profane language at some one in the yard. I noticed that my friend did not come in to the service, and on asking him why, he replied: "I stopped in the stable to see my horse eat his feed of corn; for I felt sure that the ostler would steal it. He that will swear will steal." I admired his wisdom, and I doubt not that his horse profited thereby; for a swearing ostler is likely to be an oat-stealer.

Never trust a wolf with the care of lambs.

And least of all if he offers to do it for nothing. He will take it out in lamb.

Never try to prove what nobody doubts.

This is often done by preachers, and the result is that ever so many are made to doubt who never doubted before. It is like the minister who spent his time in harmonizing the four evangelists, and the old woman said, "Our minister is well set to work to try and make four men agree who never fell out." There is so much of this useless labour done, that the necessary work of preaching the gospel gets neglected. In *Carlyle's Reminiscences* we find an appropriate illustration: "Accidentally, one Sunday evening, I heard the famous Dr. Hall (of Leicester) preach; a flabby, puffy, but massy, earnest, forcible looking man, *homme alors célèbre!* Sermon extempore; text, 'God, who cannot lie.' He proved beyond shadow of doubt, in a really forcible but most superfluous way, that God never lied (had no need to do it, &c). 'As good prove that God never fought a duel,' sniffed Badams on my reporting at home."

Never use religion as a stalking-horse.

When a man endeavours to take you in by religious talk, he imitates the devil, of whom the French negroes say, that when he wants to get a man into his clutches he talks to him about God. Very hateful is this trying to make gain by the false pretence of superior godliness.

Never wake a sleeping lion.

Rouse not angry man or woman. Don't stir the fire of strife when it is dying out.

Never wash sheep in scalding water.

This is done when the faults of good men are rebuked in anger. They are Christ's sheep, and must be tended with gentleness akin to that of the Great Shepherd of souls. We have heard it said of certain hot-tempered church members, that they must have been baptized in boiling water. The fewer of such the better.

Never wear mourning before the dead man is in his coffin.

This is a Creole warning against anticipating evil for others. It may not come, and then malicious forecasts will prove wicked folly.

Never write what you dare not sign.

An anonymous letter-writer is a sort of assassin, who wears a mask, and stabs in the dark. Such a man is a fiend with a pen. If discovered, the wretch will be steeped in the blackest infamy.

New bread is a waster, but mouldy is worse; Day old suits the stomach, and also the purse.

Housekeepers will endorse this, and perhaps be glad to quote it to those who grumble for new bread.

New breeches shame an old coat.

Partial reformations only make old faults the more glaring. When we morally improve, we need a new suit from top to toe.

New churches and new taverns are seldom empty.

People rush to see the new place; like children who are eager to play with a new toy.

New corn grows in old fields.

There can be no need to run off to the fresh fields of new theology : the old land of promise bears food ever new.

New hearts are more needful than new hats.

Those who are so particular about their go-to-meeting clothes should take good note of this.

New things are fine to look at.

But whether they will be as fine in the using remains to be seen, or, quite as likely, not to be seen. Fine new rubbish is common.

Newspapers are the Bibles of worldlings.

How diligently they read them ! Here they find their law and profits, their judges and chronicles, their epistles and revelations.

Next to no wife a good wife is best.

This must have been the grunt of some spiteful old bachelor, or of a bad husband who never deserved a wife. Solomon says, " He that findeth a wife findeth a good thing."

Nick-names are stick-names.

There is no shaking them off. Therefore let us not be guilty of affixing them to anyone. Call every man by his proper name.

Nightingales will not sing in a cage.

Liberty is essential to the full development of talent.

Nine tailors cannot make a man.

Nor ninety of them. Yet some think so, and dote upon the fashions. One tailor can make a masher, but that is not a man.

No answer is also an answer.

And it will be wise in many cases to accept it as such.

No Autumn fruit without Spring blossoms.

There must be the hopeful beginning of repentance and faith, or there will be no enduring piety.

No bees, no honey ;
No work, no money.

No carrion will poison a crow.

It is used to the filthiness. So, no immorality disgusts a man of debauched habits, and no error will be too flagrant for one who hates truth.

No cloth is too fine for moth to devour.

No estate is too honourable to be touched by decay; no man too great to die; no character too established to be injured.

No cross, no crown.

No conflict, no conquest.

No cure, no pay.

A fair principle, but it might be carried still further with advantage. Kien Long, Emperor of China, enquired of Sir G. Staunton the manner in which physicians were paid in England. When, with some difficulty, his majesty was made to comprehend the manner of paying physicians in England for the time that the patients were sick, he exclaimed: "Is any man well in England who can afford to be ill? Now I will inform you how I manage my physicians! I have four, to whom the care of my health is committed; a certain weekly salary is allowed them; but the moment I am ill, the salary stops till I am well again. I need not inform you that my illnesses are very short."

No fishing like fishing in the sea.

There you have plenty of room, and the largest sort of fish. A man naturally desires scope for his endeavours, whether he is engaged in business, in literary pursuits, or in religious work.

No fool was ever so foolish but some one thought him clever.

Let us hope that his wife and children think him a fine fellow: they will, if they love him; for love is blind.

No frost can freeze providence.

Despite all weathers, the river of God flows on. In the very worst of times God's providence is to the believer an ample heritage.

No gains without pains.

At least, none to be relied upon: windfalls are generally rotten apples; the sea of chance mostly washes up empty shells. In all labour there is profit; but labour withheld withholds the gains on which men live.

> " No gold is found beneath the ground
> 　　By idleness or shirking;
> 　The noblest brains have labour pains,
> 　　And live by honest working."

No gift on earth pure water can excel;
Nature's the brewer, and she brews it well.

"Not in the simmering still, over smoking fires, choked with poisonous gases, and surrounded with the stench of sickening odours and rank corruption, doth your Father in heaven prepare the precious essence of life, pure, cold water; but in the green glade and grassy dell, where the red deer wanders, and the child loves to play. There God himself brews it, and down, low down in the deepest valleys, where the fountains murmur and the rills sing; and high upon the mountain-tops, where the naked granite glitters like gold in the sun; where the hurricane howls music; where big waves roar the chorus, 'sweeping the march of God'—there he brews it, that beverage of life, health-giving water!"

No grave-digger can bury the truth.

Or if he did, it would have a resurrection.

No greater promisers than those who have nothing to give.

They are lavish with a generosity which cannot cost them anything; but it is all wind. Here is another application of the proverb: "All this will I give thee," said Satan; but out of all the kingdoms of the world not one of them was really his to give. Satan owns nothing but sin; and he is so great a liar that he will not own to that.

No horse so bold as the blind mare.

She sees no danger, and therefore knows no fear. No men are more reckless than the utterly stupid, who have not sense enough to know the perils which surround them.

No house without mouse; no throne without thorn.

Both great and little people have their troubles. Thorns grow at Windsor as well as at Whitechapel.

No joy without alloy.

No gain on earth without its loss;
No back of man without its cross;
No pleasure here without its pain:
This earth and earthly things are vain.

No land without stones,
No meat without bones.

Some measure of loss and discomfort attends all earthly affairs, and there is no use hoping to find perfection in an imperfect world.

No man can call again yesterday.

He may call, but it will not come. It is "with the years beyond the flood." Take time in time.

No man can make a good coat with bad cloth;

Nor fashion a pure life on bad principles, nor form a good government with bad men, nor a holy church with unregenerate persons.

No man hath a velvet cross.

Neither hath he an iron one, though it may be painted with iron colours. Each man has a real burden to bear.

No man is always wise except a fool.

The man who makes no mistakes usually makes nothing. The fool's abiding wisdom is the invention of his own folly. We have all blundered.

> "If every one who's played the fool
> Had died and turned to clay,
> How many people would be left
> Alive and well to-day?"

No man is bound to snuff the moon.

We cannot alter the laws of nature, nor mend that which is of necessity beyond our reach.

No man is made top-heavy by a pull at the pump.

He may empty the bucket, but he will not take a drop too much, so as to make him half-seas over.

No man is the worse for knowing the worst of himself.

He will be the more humble and cautious. So far to know the worst helps towards the best. The celebrated Abernethy often gave this advice to the students of his hospital class: "Gentlemen, probe always to the bottom; find out the worst; and then act."

No man should live in this world who has nothing to do in it.

> He who will not live by toil
> Has no right on English soil.

No mill, no meal; no sweat, no sweet.

No need to be a cripple because crutches are cheap.

> We must not be feeble in grace because help will come, nor fall into sin because repentance is accepted, nor limp with despondency because there are gracious consolations.

No news is good news;

> For if there were an evil to tell, it would have been told you. It is the wisest course to hope that when no complaint reaches you, all is going well: it is generally so.

No one eats gold fish : riches yield small comfort.

> In the life of the Rev. W. Harness it is said, "that when at Deepdene the tone of conversation amused him much, as when Rothschild observed to Hope that a man must be a poor scoundrel who could not afford to lose two millions, or replied to a nobleman who said he must be a supremely happy man : 'I happy ! when only this morning I received a letter from a man to say, that if I did not send him £500, he would blow out my brains.'"

THE SENTENCES WHICH FOLLOW ARE THE SAYINGS OF CATWG THE WISE :—

No one is discreet but he that perceives himself to be simple :
No one is knowing but he that knows himself :
No one is mighty but he that conquers himself :
No one is sensible but he that is aware of his misconception :
No one is wise but he that understands his ignorance :
No one is watchful but he that watches over himself :
No one is wary but he that avoids what his desire craves for :
No one is blind but he that sees not his own fault :
No one is discerning but he that discerns his own failing :
No one is strong but he that overcomes his weakness.

No one is so poor as he was when he came into the world.

> We brought nothing with us when we came hither. "Look," said one, "at that man : he is rich, and yet he is a nobody ; for he came into this parish without a second shirt." "Well, well," said one who stood by, "you were born here, and so you came into the parish without even one shirt."

No one knows the weight of another's burden.

Hence the lack of sympathy. It is said that "other people's trials are easy to bear." Nay, some go the length of saying that "the misfortunes of our friends are not altogether painful to us." This last, it is to be hoped, is a calumny.

No one likes to bell the cat.

The mice all say, "Let a bell be fastened to the cat's neck," but no one mouse will accept the task himself. Here and there a brave soul cries, "I'll bell the cat." Bravo!

> In words to draw a pretty plan
> Is easy work for any man ;
> To execute the scheme designed,
> The proper man is hard to find.

No one man
All things can.

It would be a pity he should, for then there would be nothing for the rest of us to work at.

No one pays God, but all should praise God.

Praise is our peppercorn of rent to the great Owner of all things ; and it is such a joy to pay it, that he who robs God of praise robs himself of pleasure.

No pain, no palm.

We must endure the toil and the suffering, or we may not expect the reward. The winner must first be a runner.

No piper can please all ears.

Nor can any preacher do so. Two aged women of a village where John Foster preached gratuitously, were greatly divided in opinion respecting him—one setting him down for "a perfect fool," the other "longing to hear that good man all the winter."

No road is good if it leads to a bad end.

Pleasant it may seem, but not to those who see the dreadful end.

No Rome Rule for England or Ireland.
No sauce like appetite.

This is the "Chef Sauce." This puts a flavour into dry bread.

No sense so uncommon as common sense.

Old John Brown, of Haddington, used to address his students of the first year to this effect:—"Gentlemen, ye need three things to make ye good ministers; ye need learning, and grace, and common sense. As for the learning, I'll try to set ye in the way of it; as for the grace, ye must always pray for it; but if ye havena brought the common sense with ye, ye may go about your business."

No shine but hath its shade.

"All sun," say the Arabs, "makes the desert."

No showers, no flowers, nor summer bowers.

"God sendeth sun, He sendeth shower;
Alike they're needful for the flower;
And joys and tears alike are sent
To give the soul fit nourishment:
As comes to me or cloud or sun,
Father, Thy will, not mine, be done."

No two things can agree much worse
Than notions high and beggar's purse.

They irritate their owner. His tastes call for a large expenditure, but his purse forbids it, and so he is dragged to and fro by opposing forces. He must lower his notions, or he will be an unhappy man.

No whip cuts so sharply as the lash of conscience.

Those under conviction of sin are in more pain than a felon at the whipping-post. Flesh-pain is terrible, but soul-pain drives the man to madness.

No wonder if he breaks his shins that walks in the dark.

Of course he stumbles, for he cannot see his way. When we quit the light of God's Word we are on the way to many a blunder, stumble and fall.

No wool is so white that the dye cannot make it black.

The best character will be injured by society. The cleanest reputation can be darkened by slander.

No word is ill spoken if it be not ill taken.

Really unkind words have been made to lose their sting by being left unnoticed. If we won't be offended, nobody can offend us.

No work is worse than overwork.

Nobility without ability, is like a pudding without suet.

> A noble nobody is a poor peer, a barren baron, a benighted knight, a count of no account.

Nobody calls himself rogue.

> 'Tis not likely he would ; and yet when he calls himself he calls a rogue.

Nobody can live longer in peace than his neighbour pleases.

> That neighbour can pick a quarrel if he pleases ; and the less cause he has for it, the more fiercely will he contend.

Nobody can repeat it if it is not said.

Nobody may quarrel in my house except the cat and dog.

> And they are so friendly that to me a cat-and-dog life seems a most desirable one.

None are so credulous as the incredulous.

> No one is so readily duped as the sceptic.   Nobody thinks he knows so much as the man who calls himself an agnostic, or knows nothing.

None are so well shod but they may slip.

> Therefore let no man presume that he can never fall.

None but fools and knaves lay wagers.

> When thou art sager,
> Thou'lt lay no wager.

None can tell what's in the husk until it's shelled.

> Many matters must be left for time to reveal.

None so blind as those who will not see.

> Prejudice makes a man resolve that he will not see, and he becomes blind indeed.   No blinkers are like those of conceit.   If a man will shut his eyes because he knows enough already, how can we make him see ?

None so busy as those who do nothing.

None think the great unhappy but the great.

Nonsense is not sense.

Not a long day, but a good heart, gets through work.

> The longest day is not long enough for some to do their work in, for they are not in love with it. Of the slothful man Solomon says: "His hands refuse to work." We know the breed. An officer, seeing a man professedly employed in breaking stones for the road, doing his work as if he were half asleep, said, "Take care, my man, you will break that stone." "Oh, no, your honour," was the reply, "I knows too well for that."

Not all the strongest live the longest.

> It was said of Henry Jenkins, who was older than Old Parr:
>
> > He lived longer than men who were stronger,
> > And was too old to live any longer.

Not every light is the sun.

> Why praise up a farthing candle as if it were the orb of day? Some are greatly given to such laudations.

Not every parish priest can wear Martin Luther's shoes.

> Yet he probably thinks he can. If some men could but see themselves once they would never look again. Possibly a little conceit may help some poor souls to do more than they otherwise would have the courage to attempt.

Not everything which fair doth show,
When proof is made will turn out so.

Not race, nor place, but grace makes a man.

> Such was the argument of the young lady whom Philip Henry desired to marry. She belonged to an old and wealthy family, and her father opposed the match. Mr. Henry, he admitted, was a scholar and gentleman of no ordinary type, but, "we do not know where he comes from." "Perhaps so," replied his daughter; "but we know where he is going, and I should like to go with him."

Not that which is much is well, but that which is well is much.

> The apparent quantity vanishes when the quality is found to be inferior. There is not so much in a pound of copper as in an ounce of gold. Truth is the test. Nothing can be great which is not right. A little which is consistent with righteousness has more in it than the great thing which is questionable.

Not to break is better than to mend.

Prevention is better than cure. A dish well rivetted is not so good as one which was never cracked.

Not to wish to recover is a mortal symptom.

He who does not desire to reform gives evidence of desperate sinfulness.

Nothing comes amiss to a hungry man.

To him, even bitter things are sweet.

Be it cold, or be it hot,
Hungry man refuses not.

Nothing endeavoured, nothing discovered.

If we do not try we shall never find out the way. Without effort we shall stick in the mud, and never get further.

**Nothing is a man's truly,
But what he came by duly.**

That which we gain wrongfully can never be rightfully ours. Be ashamed to harbour stolen goods.

Nothing is cheap if you don't want it.

A great bargain is a pick-purse. If merely bought because the price was low, and not because we needed it, it is dear.

Nothing is clean to a carrion crow.

Its eye searches out rottenness, and sees nothing else; and thus men of vile character believe others to be vile, spy out all their faults, and shut their eyes to their virtues, and speak evil of the good.

Nothing is safe from fault-finders.

Even *Milton's* "Paradise Lost" was censured by a hard-headed Scotchman because, said he, "It proves nothing." Even proverbs come under the lash of *Chesterfield's* elegance. He says, "A man of fashion never has recourse to proverbs and vulgar aphorisms."

Nothing is so graceful in a woman as grace.

When she is full of grace she is graceful indeed, and all are compelled to see the beauty of her character, whether she has beauty of person or not. Moreover,

Grace will last
When beauty is past.

Nothing is so strong as gentleness; nothing so gentle as strength.

Nothing sharpens sight like envy.

It spies out the smallest fault, but at the same time refuses to see anything which might excuse it. Was there ever one so holy that envy would not see evil in him?

Nothing should be done in haste except catching fleas.

Nothing stands in need of lying but a lie.

Truth is always consistent with itself, and needs nothing to help it out; it is always near at hand, sits upon our lips, and is ready to drop out before we are aware; a lie is troublesome, and sets a man's invention upon the rack, and one trick needs a great many more to make it good. It is like building upon a false foundation, which continually stands in need of props to shore it up, and proves at last more chargeable than to have raised a substantial building at first upon a true and solid foundation.—*Addison.*

Nothing succeeds like success.

Men are apt to aid that which is getting on; the very report of success helps to make itself true. Hence a crafty man recommends another to look like getting on, or he never will get on.

Nothing that is violent is permanent.

The rushing torrent is soon over, and so is it with other things of the same impetuous character. Gently goes far.

Nothing venture, nothing win.

Some measure of risk must attend all trading. We must also venture all, even to life itself for Christ's cause.

Novels contain little that is novel.

But, alas! much that is unnatural, and many a time that which is polluting. The lives of many are rendered false by reading false lives. Truth is made sick by fiction.

Now that I have a hat, others take off theirs to me.

The man has come to be what the world calls "respectable," and he is respected accordingly; but he ought not to be proud, for the respect is evidently paid to the hat rather than its wearer.

Now that I have got no gun,
Rabbits run about like fun.

But why not have had a gun? Opportunities often come to men who are not ready for them. Why are they not ready?

Now the poet's starved and dead,
Raise a stone above his head.

’Tis the old story of *Homer*, begging in life, and honoured in death.
The man needs bread, and they give him a stone; but not even that
till he is gone.   Alas, poor world! thy gratitude is as late as it is
worthless: after death a stone!

Now the thief is out of sight,
The police have come to light.

Hardly fair! In many cases the police have been singularly
prompt and courageous.

Now that I have a sheep and a cow everyone bids me
good morrow.

So much does even the courtesy of our fellow-men depend upon
our possessions. A court of law decided that a man who keeps a
gig is respectable, and three acres and a cow are the recognized
limit of competence. What is that respect worth which depends
on our owning cows and sheep?

Now that I no longer need
I can get full many a feed.

People run to grease the fat sow. Who will not give to a prince?
Poverty craves in vain, where wealth asks and receives.

Now is now here, but to-morrow's nowhere.

Now is the only time we have; even when to-morrow comes, if it
ever comes, it will also be "now." So *Doddridge* put it :—

" Strength for to-day is all we need,
For there never will be a to-morrow ;
For to-morrow will prove but another to-day,
With its measure of joy and of sorrow."

‘Now" is the watchword of the wise.

"To-morrow " is the devil's great ally—the very Goliath in
whom he trusts for victory : "Now" is the stripling sent forth
against him. A great significance lies in that little word ; it marks
the point on which life's battle turns. That spot is the Hougomont
of life's Waterloo ; there the victory is lost or won.—*Arnot.*

Nuts are given us, but we must crack them ourselves.

Providence does not spare us the necessity for exertion, even
when it is most favourable. Herein is wisdom.

Sayings of a more Spiritual Sort.

Natural men are spiritual monsters.

The natural man's heart is where his feet should be, fixed upon earth; his heels are lifted up against heaven, which his heart should be set on. His face is towards hell; his back towards heaven. He loves what he should hate, and hates what he should love; joys in what he ought to mourn for, and mourns for what he ought to rejoice in; glories in his shame, and is ashamed of his glory; abhors what he should desire, and desires what he should abhor.—*Boston.*

Neither neglect the means nor rest in the means.

Services and Sacraments are to be humbly used as channels for the water of life, but they are not that life in themselves.

Never dare to despair
While God answers prayer.

There is a strange presumption in the wicked act of doubting the goodness of the Lord.

New sinnings call for new repentings.

" No answer required."

This note often accompanies messages sent to man, but oftener those sent up in prayer to God.

No grace, no glory.

No happiness without holiness.

There is no felicity in what the world adores. That wherein God himself is happy, the holy angels are happy, and in whose defect the devils are unhappy—that dare I call happiness.—*Sir Thomas Browne.*

No man is necessary.

With this saying of Napoleon, we may compare the sentence on the monument to the two Wesleys, in Westminster Abbey—" God buries his workmen, but carries on his work."

No pillow so soft as God's promise.

No skin, no hair;
No grace, no prayer.

There can be no hair where there is no skin, and no true prayer where there is no grace. A prayerless soul is a graceless soul.

None can pray well but he who lives well.

> Prayer will make us leave off sinning, or sinning will make us leave off praying.—*Fuller.*

None should wear the name of saints but those who have the nature of saints.

> The Seventh General Council which met at Constantinople in 754 under the Iconoclast Emperor Constantine V., decreed, "If any one spend his labour in setting up figures of saints, or lifeless and deaf images, which cannot do any good; and has no care to represent in himself their virtues as he finds them on record in the Scriptures, let him be Anathema." Equally worthy of condemnation are they who profess to be saints, but have nothing saintly about their character and life.

Not a leaf moves on the trees,
Unless the Lord himself doth please.

> The wind shall not blow on the earth, nor on the sea, nor on any tree, till the permission of God be given.—Rev. vii. 1.

Not more *than* Christ, but more *of* Christ.

Not to love God is madness.

> It shows a mind disordered by the madness of sin.

Nothing is simpler than faith, and nothing more sublime.

> Faith is simple from the human side: it is a childlike trust. But it is sublime from the divine side, since it grasps the Invisible, and has power with the Omnipotent.

Nought can be gained
By a Sabbath profaned.

THOU Nazarite, go about, go about, and do not come near the vineyard!

The meaning is, that we should avoid the occasions of sin. The Nazarite was forbidden the use of wine; and it was therefore his wisest course to avoid all occasions of trespassing, by even keeping out of the vineyard. In matters of evil it is well to avoid the appearance of it, and the suggestion of it. He who dreads a spark will not play with fire.

Oaks fall when reeds stand.

To yield may sometimes be greater wisdom than to defy the storm; and it is always so when the hand of God goes out against us. Then we must either bow or break.

Obedience should be a child's first lesson.

And it will need to be repeated. If he learns it well as a child, it will be the foundation of his character as a man. Colts must be broken in, or they will be useless horses. All human beings need to be taught obedience; for as *Judge Halyburton* says—"Wherever there is authority there is a natural inclination to disobedience."

Obedience to his master is the wisdom of the disciple.

Thus he learns practically, and if he does not learn practically, he does not learn truly. The apprentice learns his trade by working at it; and even so we must learn Christianity by living like the Lord Jesus Christ. He who will *do* shall *know*.

Obedient wives lead their husbands.

Sensible men know when they have good wives, and they are glad to let them manage the house, and lead them on to prosperity. The author of the "Five Talents of Woman" tells the following story:— "As a clergyman was riding through a village in Fifeshire one day, a man came out and stopped him, addressing him in the following remarkable words: 'D'ye mind, sir, yon day, when ye married me, and when I wad insist upon vowing to obey my wife? Weel, ye may now see that I was in the richt. Whether ye wad or no, I hae obeyed my wife; and behold, I am now the only man that has a twa-storey house in the hale town!'"

Obey orders if you break owners.

Meaning that the result of obeying orders is not for the mariner's consideration. He is a man under authority: his not to reason why.

Obstinacy is absurdity.

There are people who, like pigs, always go the reverse way to that in which they are driven. One pig went all the way upstairs by having his tail pulled downwards. So *Swift* wrote of a woman :—

> " Lose no time to contradict her,
> Nor endeavour to convict her,
> Only take this rule along,
> Always to advise her wrong,
> And reprove her when she's right,
> She will then grow wise for spite."

We recommend no such method ; but with some it might be more successful than good advice. There are men also of this breed ; and indeed the English stock has a full share of obstinacy in it ; so that one said, "The crest of the southern English is a hog, and their motto is, ' We wun't be druv'."

Of a little spend a little and save a little.

Give a little, too, to consecrate the whole. What we give in alms will prevent covetousness.

> What is given
> Stops the leaven.

Of all cocks the worst is a weathercock.

From its turning with every wind. Men who are twisted about by every breeze, and are not to be depended upon, become the objects of supreme contempt.

Of all crafts honesty is the master craft.

He who is not crafty, but candid and open, will carry the day in the long run against all the cunning in the world. Cunning is folly wearing the mask of prudence, wisdom soured with falsehood. But plain honesty so puzzles the men of policy that they suspect it is working a scheme of more than ordinary depth, and so it baffles them.

Of all tame beasts I like sluts least.

Nobody can endure them : they make you feel sick. Dirty dishes, foul linen, filthy rooms, and so forth, cause nausea to clean people.

Of all things, men are most fond of their wrong notions.

Even as mothers love most their weakest children.

Of bowers and scrapers beware.

Too much politeness is suspicious. When men bow very often, they may be suspected of stooping because they think there is something to pick up.

Of dead and gone speak good or none.

De mortuis nil nisi bonum. Which one translates, " Concerning the dead nothing but *bones* " ; another says, " Nothing but a *bonus*."

Of hard striving comes sure thriving.

He that would thrive,
His work must drive.
If work drives thee,
Right poor thou'lt be.

Of honey eat not thou too fast
Lest it should make thee sick at last.

Human praise is sweet to our pride, but it should be accepted sparingly. The same is true of all earthly pleasures.

Of Lions white and red beware;
They always take the lion's share.

It is curious that these mythical animals should so often be selected as signs for houses of entertainment. Is it because the weary traveller will there find something to lie on ? Or because, by means of wines, white and red, many are apt to make beasts of themselves ? A lawyer's clerk in Manchester, being requested by his employer to show a gentleman the "lions," took him to all the public-houses designated by the titles of "The Red Lion," "The Black Lion," "The White Lion," &c. ; and the gentleman, enjoying the joke, "stood Sam" at each place ; the result being, that the clerk returned to the office anyhow but sober. The "lions" had proved too much for him.

Of little meddling comes great ease.

But even a little meddling may destroy all ease. "Hands off" is a good word. It is easier to keep out of a mess than to get out of one. Medlars are poor fruit, and so are meddlers.

Of pepper take none in thy nose,
However much thy friends oppose.

Friends mean well, even when they do not agree with us ; therefore, let us not take offence at them.

Of saving cometh having.

Yet you must "have" first. Some save nothing, and consequently have nothing in the hour of need. Others try to save everything, and even rob themselves of common comforts, and thus really have nothing. May we be saved from both extremes, and have what we have to the glory of God.

Of smoothsayers and soothsayers beware.

Those who prophesy smooth things, and those who prophesy future things at all apart from the Scriptures, are dangerous people. Modern prophets are unprofitable.

Of the dead say only what is good.

And if nothing good can be spoken, say nothing, but conclude—

> Seeing he is dead,
> No more shall be said.

Of wasting cometh wanting.

Some have wasted roast meat, and have come to long even for the smell of it. How gladly would they now eat the crusts they threw to the hogs! Waste first makes want, and then makes it bitter.

Of what use is a violin to a deaf man?

There must be a capacity for enjoying, or there will be no enjoyment. It is of no use casting pearls before swine. Here is an amusing instance of the usefulness of literature to the utterly ignorant. An agent for a new cyclopædia tells this incident :— " Among those to whom I have shown the volumes I found but one young man who did not need the work. He has a cyclopædia, a number of large volumes ; he did not know how many, nor did he know the name of the editor or publisher ; but they are very large, heavy volumes. Believing he did not frequently consult them, I asked if he ever used them. ' Certainly,' said he, ' I use them every day.' ' What can you possibly do with them ? ' ' Why, I press my trousers with them.' " There was some use in the encyclopædia ; but we wonder how the deaf man would use the fiddle.

Offenders never pardon.

It is strangely true that the man who wrongs you hates you far more surely and maliciously than the man whom you have injured.

> Forgiveness to the injured must belong ;
> For they ne'er pardon who have done the wrong.

Oil and truth will yet,
The uppermost get.

There is no keeping truth under. It is from above, and it tends towards its source.

> Despair not thou ! Though truth be beaten oft,
> In God's own time she shall be set aloft.

Old age is honourable, but youthful pride is abominable.

Yet there is far too much of the latter.

"Now every boy's the old man's teacher:
The father's a fool, the child a preacher."

Old age makes the head white, but not always wise.

Yet "with the aged is wisdom." If years do not teach, what will?

Old birds are hard to pluck.

Meddle not with others at all, but be sure not to take up the cudgels with those whose experience has taught them to take care of themselves. Lay not your hand on the mane of an old lion.

Old birds are seldom caught by chaff,
Old rats by wooden trap or gin;
And if you dig a pit, my friend,
The chances are you'll tumble in.

Old dogs are in no hurry to bark.

Old hounds do not begin yelping the moment they are out of the kennel, but they only get into full cry when they see the fox. Practised preachers do not commence with a loud voice, but wait till they warm to their subject, and then give it tongue.

Old foxes are caught at last.

And generally when they conclude that no one can catch such very sensible, wide-awake people.

Old foxes are not easily caught.

They are wary because of former mishaps;
And therefore they fight very shy of your traps.

Experience makes men open their eyes and keep them open, and they are not readily imposed upon after a good drilling in the consequences of believing all they hear.

Old foxes want no tutors.

They know too much already. One who has lived long in such a world as this knows a thing or two. "An old Parliamentary hand" knows his way about. Proverbs about foxes are very plentiful; the fact being that the creature so brings up the idea of sport that men like to talk about him. There is a love of animals innate in most people.

While the rich are hunting foxes,
Poor men mend their rabbit boxes.

Old gold, old hay, old bread,
Stand a man in good stead.

> He who is always taken with that which is new will soon be caught in a noose. Last year's stack of hay in the yard is a pretty sight to him who has horses to feed.

Old gold, old truth, and old friend,
These are treasures to the end.

> Satisfy yourself with the tried and proved, and let others have novelties if they choose.

Old head and young hand.

> A good combination : prudence and energy.

Old heads will not suit young shoulders.

> It would be hypocrisy for youths to speak with the certainty, caution, and experience of old men. It is neither natural nor desirable that grey heads should grow on green necks.

Old is the boat, but it still keeps afloat.

> It is pleasant to see the aged still trying to be useful. We say, "The old ferry-boat will carry us over the river yet once more"; and so the worn-out man may yet again serve his God.

Old Lawrence has got hold of you.

> Which means that the man is in the power of the demon of laziness, St. Lawrence being the patron of idleness. Surely that is not the Lawrence who was martyred on a gridiron! And yet perhaps it is; for lazy people will find things rather hot in these days, even if they do not go to the grill-room of utter bankruptcy.

Old men are as anxious to live as the young.

> Willingness to depart comes not with years ; in fact, the longer men live, the more they cling to life. The man has breakfasted, dined, and supped ; and yet he is in no hurry to go to bed.
>
> > The tree of deepest root is found
> > Unwilling most to quit the ground.

Old ovens are soon heated.

> Men long given to sin are soon excited to a repetition of their vicious practices.

Old oxen have stiff horns.

When a man of years makes up his mind, he is not easily prevented from carrying out his purpose.

Old reckonings breed new disputes.

Old accounts smell abominably. There is nothing like clearing up as you go.

> To-day and to-day we pay and we pay,
> And this from obstructions cleareth the way.

Old sacks want much patching.

Old bodies want nourishing and doctoring; old businesses need fresh methods to suit the times; old corporations need reforming.

Old shoes are easiest, and old friends are best.

We are used to them; they fit us; and we cannot bear to part with them. Bring me my old slippers when my feet ache, and fetch me my old friend when my heart aches.

Old sins breed new shame.

When they rise in the conscience, or when they are talked of in the world, they bring the blush to the cheek.

Old thanks do not suffice for new gifts.

Gratitude should spring up perpetually. Praises, though rendered a little ago, must be renewed as fresh benefits are received.

Old tunes are sweetest, and old friends surest.

Oh, for the old music, before the fly-away-jack tunes came in! Oh, for the like of the grand old men who are now in heaven! True as steel they were, though nowadays they call them narrow.

Old wounds soon bleed.

Well do I remember a grey horse falling, bleeding terribly, and cutting itself wofully. I could not understand why it was so grievously hurt till I learned that it had been down before, and was now injured in the same place. It is so with old sins. Men are apt to bleed in the old spot.

Omission of good is commission of evil.

In other words, "Omitted duty is committed sin." How this should humble us when making confession of sin! Who can measure what he might have done and should have done?

Omit ornament if it straitens strength.

A man had a plain strong bow with which he could shoot far and true. He loved his bow so well that he would needs have it curiously carved by a cunning workman. It was done; and at the first trial the bow snapped. We may make our style of speaking so fine that it loses its force. It is foolish to sacrifice strength to elegance.

Omittance is no quittance.

If your creditor does not call for the money, it is just as much his due. Pay it like an honest man ; and don't hint that "You thought he had given it to you."

> That is the brogue
> Of an old rogue.

On a good bargain think twice.

Or else leave it without a thought. It may not be all it looks ; and if you do not need the article, it may be folly to buy it at any price. Why should people sell you goods under cost price?

On a long journey even a straw is heavy.

Because of the length of time you will have to carry it. The less luggage the better, and the less care the happier you will be.

On his own saddle one rides safest.

Where a man is most at home, he has least fear, and least danger. In one's own line of things one is least apt to slip.

On Monday morning don't be looking for Saturday night.

It will be reached soon enough if you work your passage to its shores.

On some men's bread butter will not stick.

Ne'er-do-wells seldom remain in comfort long. If you were to put them into a river they would soon be high and dry in the bed of it. They attribute it to being born under a twopenny planet; but the fault, dear sillies, is not in your stars, but in yourselves.

On the heels of folly shame will surely tread.

Shame is the estate which is entailed on fools.

On the sea one hath not the sea in his hands.

You must put up with its changes, and manage your vessel accordingly. So in business, we cannot arrange circumstances. The storms of life we can neither raise nor lull.

On the sea sail, on the land settle.

Act as circumstances require, and utilize all opportunities.

On the spree still sober be.

But our London people can scarcely enjoy a holiday without a fiddle and a fuddle.

On their own merits modest men are dumb.

Praise of self from a man's own lips is loathsome.

Once bit twice shy.

Prudence forbids putting your hand a second time within reach of a dog. He who had his head bitten off by a lion had no chance of putting this proverb in action. A friend of mine had a little dog which had been bitten by a larger dog, and ever afterwards refused to go near the place where this happened. Another dog, which had been scratched by a cat, would not go within a couple of fields of the house where the cat lived. Are not dogs wiser than men?

Once cut the cheese, and the cheese will soon cut.

Householders find it so.

> Only change a pound,
> And it can't be found.

Once shot you cannot stop the arrow.

> "A word once spoken can return no more;
> A wise man sets a watch before the door.
> The bird in hand we may at will restrain;
> But being flown, we call her back in vain."—*Whitney.*

One action does not make a habit.

But it may be the beginning of it. We may not say, "Once is never," but we may hope it is not always. Yet there is fear that one sin may force on another, as *Dryden* says—

> "He that once sins, like him who slides on ice,
> Goes swiftly down the slippery paths of vice."

One always hits himself in a sore place.

Persons think that they are being alluded to, and even insulted in a discourse, when they are not even thought of. They have a sore place, and so they are always being touched upon it. Conscience makes cowards of men.

One barber shaves another.

An infidel critic generally practises his art by cutting up the man who followed the same craft before him.

One barking dog sets all the street a-barking.

" Lie down, sir ! " We can't afford to have all dogdom pouring forth its howls in our ears.

One beats the bush, and another gets the birds.

It is often so with inventors, originators, authors, and other persons of genius, who cannot produce their work without outside help. They have the labour, and others take the profit. The hen lays the egg, but the man eats it.

One body may as well have two souls, as one soul two masters.

One broken wheel spoils the machine.

One grave fault may ruin a character, one weak point may prevent the success of a scheme, and one bad man may hinder the prosperity of a whole church.

One can go a long way after he is tired.

Pluck will keep a man going long after his strength is spent.

One can't hinder the wind from blowing.

Nor gossips from tattling, nor fashions from changing, nor troubles from coming, nor heresies from spreading.

One day may be better than a whole year.

At any rate, there is no time like time present. At certain seasons more can be done in a single day, than at other times in quite a long period. Let us use each passing day energetically, and with a large hopefulness.

One dog can drive a flock of sheep.

One brave man may face a multitude without fear. *Alexander* said, " One butcher does not fear a herd of cattle."

One chick keeps a hen busy.

It will need all our care to bring up even a single child.

One drop of ink
May make a million think.

> Great is the power of the pen. How carefully it should be used!

One enemy is many too many.

> "The man who has a thousand friends
> Has not a friend to spare,
> But he who has one enemy,
> Will meet him everywhere."

One expense leads to another.

> The Sanscrit proverb says, "To protect his rags from the rats he got a cat, to get milk for the cat he bought a cow, to tend the cow he hired a servant, and to manage his servant he procured a wife." An insolvent said that he was ruined by a new sofa; and he thus explained the mode of his ruin :—"That sofa was the bad *beginning* —it was too fine for me. It made my old chairs and table look mean, and I had to buy new ones. Then the curtains had to be renewed. Then the furniture in the other rooms had to be sold, and new articles bought to correspond with the parlour. Soon we found the house was not good enough for the furniture, and we removed into a larger mansion. And now, here I am, in the Insolvent Court."

One eye of the master sees more than four of the servants.

> For he has greater influence and control. Trusting to others is not one quarter so effective as looking after the matter yourself. Where should the eye be but in the head?

One eye-witness is worth more than ten hearsays.

> Seeing is good evidence, and carries conviction with it.

One fact is worth a ship-load of opinions.

> We don't want to know how you think it ought to be; but tell us how it is. Religious opinions are fickle as the wind; but the facts of Scripture are firm as a rock.

One false move may lose the game.

> It is so in life, although it is no game. Hence the need of great caution. The Chinese have a proverb, which *Mr. Scarborough* has translated :—

> For one bad move, if you're to blame,
> Be sure that you will lose the game.

One father maintains ten children better than ten children will maintain one father.

For shame! Let us hope this is a calumny; yet have we seen sad instances of unkindness on the part of sons.

One fool in a house is enough in all conscience.

Say rather, "is one too many." Where is there a family without this piece of furniture? There is no need for us to increase the fraternity. The Ancient Order of Stupids is very large.

One fool makes many.

By his absurd actions he may win attention, and hold a gaping crowd. His folly may lead others into folly. Crazes are catching.

One foot is better than two crutches.

Better far to be independent and walk on your own legs, than depend on borrowed help. The power of extempore speech is infinitely to be preferred to the best notes.

One frog croaks to another, so doth sorrow to sorrow.

Troubles are many. "Deep calleth unto deep." Like the frogs of Egypt, they come into the kneading-trough and the bedchamber; but yet in the Lord's time they will all be swept away when their purpose is accomplished.

One good mother is worth a hundred schoolmasters.

The master's law *com*pels, but the mother's love *im*pels. He polishes, but she has the first hand in the fashioning. The man never forgets what he learnt at his mother's knee. When the conflict between Church and State in Piedmont was at its height, a deputation of noble ladies from Chambery waited on the king, imploring him to revoke the decree by which the nuns of the Sacred Heart were expelled from their city. They declared that they saw no prospect of having their daughters properly educated if the pious sisterhood should be removed. The king listened attentively, and at the close of their appeal most courteously replied: "I believe you are mistaken. I know that there are at this moment in the town of Chambery many ladies much better qualified to educate your children than the Sisters of the Sacred Heart." The ladies looked surprised, exchanged inquiring glances, and at length begged the king to point out the pious teachers of whose existence they were ignorant. "The pious teachers," replied Victor Emmanuel, bowing more courteously than before, "are yourselves; your daughters can have no persons better qualified to superintend their education than their own mothers."

One good stroke does not prove me a woodman.

One happy speech does not warrant a man in setting up as an orator. Balaam's ass spoke well once, but it never tried it again. Altogether it differed greatly from its brethren.

One good turn deserves another.

One good yawner makes two.

"The adage understates the case. I verily believe that one good yawner might make a hundred such, if he only had a fair field for his operations."—*C. J. Dunphie.*

One hair of a woman draws more than a team of horses.

Their tenderness subdues the stubborn heart, and for good or for evil has a mighty force within it. Who can resist its charms?

One half the world does not know how the other half lives.

But this is not the fault of Mrs. Tattle, for she has done her best to let them know. If without gossip we could know more of each other's trials it would promote sympathy and charity.

One hand washes another.

Many show kindness in expectation of getting similar help. "Sinners also lend to sinners that they may receive as much again." Yet it is surely nothing less than nature that those who are members of the one spiritual body should promote the holiness of others, and should be zealous to defend their character.

One hard word brings on another.

Do not open the ball. There is no credit in throwing the first stone, for you may be accountable for all that follow it.

One has need of much wit to deal with a fool.

Because he misunderstands you, and, if trusted, he will lead you into great blunders. It would seem that his folly is catching, for often if there is one fool in a business there is more than one.

One head cannot hold all wisdom.

Therefore we excuse mistakes in others, and do not dare to think ourselves perfectly wise. It is a marvel that some men know so much. Remember the schoolmaster and the peasants—

"And still they gazed, and still the wonder grew,
That one small head should carry all he knew."

One hour's sleep before midnight is worth two after.

This is often quoted to get young folks to bed; and we suppose there must be truth in it. One said, "One hour before midnight is worth two after." "Yes," said the other "that is why I sit up, for I don't like to be wasting the best of the hours in sleep."

One is never so rich as when one moves house.

Then you turn up such a collection of goods, which you had quite forgotten, that you wonder where you will put them all.

Old spoons and old rings,
And all sorts of things.

One keep-clean is better than ten make-cleans.

Frequent fouling leaves its mark, and the washing wears the material. It is with morals, as with linens.

One lie makes many.

One lie must be thatched with another, or it will soon rain through. Lies breed like fleas, or aphides.

One lie needs seven lies to wait on it.

And they will not be enough to keep its train off the ground.

Oh, what a tangled web we weave,
When once we venture to deceive!

One link broken, the whole chain is broken.

An illustration of the great truth, that he who breaks one commandment is guilty of the whole law.

If from a chain a single link you strike,
Tenth or ten thousandth, breaks the chain alike.

One log does not burn well by itself.

Fellowship in religion is a great stimulus to the heat of piety. Burning coals heaped together hold the fire, where separate portions die out. Union is force of fervour, as well as of strength.

One loss brings another.

In the Telugu we read, "First, he lost his horse, and then he had to pay for digging a pit in which to bury it." Merchants and traders know how one link of loss is part of a chain, and draws on other links. When one nine-pin falls it upsets others.

One man is worth a hundred, and a hundred is not worth one.

Many a time a solitary champion has won the victory, and far oftener a band of warriors has been scattered. The concentration of one may surpass the divided force of a hundred. One man with God on his side is more than a match for the whole world.

One man is no man.

Without followers the leader is nothing. One oar cannot win the boat race, even though it be the stroke oar. One man is invaluable as a captain, yet a captain can do nothing without his crew. It needs many men to man a ship, and many arms to make an army.

One man makes a chair, and another sits in it.

This is division of labour. He that sits in it may have less pleasure in it than he who made it, especially if he be the chairman of a noisy public meeting.

One man may better steal a horse, than another look over the hedge.

The first man has a character, and no one thinks that he will do wrong; the other is too well known to be trusted. No doubt also the world practises gross favouritism, and allows to one person liberties which it denies to another.

One man may lead a horse to the water, but twenty cannot make him drink.

We may preach the gospel, but only God's grace can lead a man to receive it into his heart. We may lead to the green pastures, but only the Good Shepherd can make the sheep to lie down therein.

One man may teach another to speak, but none can teach another to hold his peace.

The silent man must in this respect be self-made. He has mastered the greatest point of oratory. That is the true Chrysostom, or golden mouth, which can be kept closed at proper times.

> To use the tongue in speech is great,
>   But greater to refrain :
> Thousands have taught the art to prate,
>   Not one the tongue to rein.

One man with one eye sees more than twenty men without eyes.

Hence, one spiritually enlightened man knows more than a whole nation of worldlings.

One man's fault should be another man's lesson.

Instead of which it is too often another man's gossip.   The right use of an observed fault is to talk to yourself about it, and to say nothing to anyone else.

One man's meat is another man's poison.

Certainly it is so, if the old saws were ever true which describe the health-giving food of our ancestors ; for we should die on such diet.   Take, for instance, the West-country rhyme :

> Eat leeks in March, and garlic in May,
> And all the year after physicians may play.

After such odorous and odious food one might well find doctors and everybody else keeping as far off as possible.   Another proverb says :

> Eat an apple going to bed,
> Make the doctor beg his bread.

We should not like to try the prescription, unless the apple had been well roasted.   We prefer the notion that "fruit is gold in the morning, silver at noon, and lead at night."

One master passion in the breast,
Like Aaron's serpent, swallows up the rest.

One may buy gold too dear.

If you part with principle to procure it, or suffer spiritual loss to gain it.   It is not of every place that it could be said, "And the gold of that land is good."

One may have good eyes, and see nothing.

We have plenty of proofs of this, especially when people have no wish to see, or seeing do not care to perceive.

One may say too much even upon the best subject.

You may make a man sick with the honey which was intended to sweeten his mouth.   You may keep on hammering at a nail till you first drive it in, and then drive it out again.

One may tire of eating tarts.

Monotony is wearisome.   The repetition of the same thing is tiresome, whether it be in seeing, hearing, or tasting.

One may understand like an angel, and yet live like a
    devil.

> Sad fact. Light in the head may leave the heart in the dark. To
> know is little, but to practise is great. It involves a terrible re-
> sponsibility when a man is forced to confess,—
>> " I see the right, and I approve it too,
>> Condemn the wrong, and yet the wrong pursue."

One mild answer quenches more than two buckets of water.

> Blessed are those firemen whose gentleness is as a fire engine to
> the flames of strife. Soft answers are hard to answer. A man can-
> not quarrel alone. Anger cares not to sing a solo.

One millstone alone,
Of meal makes none.

> A bachelor is that one alone. Some say he is like one of the legs
> of a pair of scissors, or a pair of compasses—of no use without the
> other.

One must never put a hawk into a hen-house.

> Nor introduce a bad fellow to your daughters.

One must plough with the horses one has.

> It is wisdom to do our best with what comes to hand. Men and
> women are not perfect, yet God uses them : if they are good enough
> for him, why should we refuse to work with them?

One of these days is none of these days.

> Business for which there is no fixed time seldom gets attended to.

One of his hands is unwilling to wash the other for
    nothing.

> This is the mercenary principle in an extreme degree, and doubt-
> less it scarcely exaggerates the spirit of some who will do nothing
> unless they are to have a wage for it; and hardly then. It reminds
> me of an old man with a sluggish horse, who, as he struck it with
> the whip, would say, "Take that; you're just like a lawyer, you
> won't go an inch unless you are well paid."

One ploughs, another sows:
Who will reap no one knows.

> Yet it is ours to sow even if we do not live till harvest ; for others
> sowed, and we entered into their labours.

One pot of beer makes room for another.

Creates a craving for another. Till the first went down, the man was happy without the poison; but now he is not master of himself, and must have another pot to keep the first one company.

One potter loves not another potter.

Two of a trade will not agree. The above proverb is one of the very oldest on record; but we do not suppose that potters are any more cantankerous than other mortals. This is put into rhyme as follows:

> The potter hates another of the trade,
> If by his hands a finer dish is made;
> And thus his envy is betrayed.

One rotten egg will spoil a large pudding.

A grand life may be marred by a single evil deed.

One saddle is enough for one horse.

One office should satisfy one man; it is all that he can properly carry out. Some are saddled from head to tail, but carry little.

One seldom meets a lonely lie.

Lies go in droves. Truth can stand alone, but a lie needs a brother on the right, and another on the left, to keep it up.

One sheep follows another.

It is their sheepish nature; and men are even more sheepish than sheep.

> If one of them should go astray,
> Sure all the flock will tend that way.

Carlyle said that he would like to stop the stream of people in the Strand, and ask every man his history. On reflection he decided, "No, I will not stop them. If I did, I should find they were like a flock of sheep, following in the track of one another."

One sickly sheep infects the flock.

So spreading is an evil example.

One sin opens the door to another.

Satan puts a little sin in at the window to open the door for a bigger transgression.

One story is good till another is told.

> If it be not a good story at all, but a bad one, it is fair to hear what may be said on the other side. It is wonderful in how different a light the same actions may be seen.
>> Be slow to censure. Spare your blame;
>> Rash speech may wound the fairest name.

One swallow makes not a summer.

> Nor one woodcock a winter: but it prophesies the coming of it. One grasshopper makes many springs.

One thing at a time, if upward you'd climb.

> "A wag asked my lord, how it came to appear
> Such a great mass of work he got through in a year,
> Said Chesterfield promptly, 'You elderly dunce,
> By never attempting, sir, two things at once.'"

One thread of kindness binds more surely than ten bonds of steel.

> Yet men are afraid to try the bonds of love. How well will society be bound together when kindness shall bind man to man!

One to-day is worth a thousand to-morrows.

One tongue is enough for two women.

> Are not women unfairly judged in this matter? Are there not many male chatterboxes? It is the men who say these hard things. One of them dares to write—
>> "When man or woman dies, as poets sung,
>> His heart's the last that stirs; of hers the tongue."
>
> In our judgment there is little or no truth in the insinuation that the gentler sex talk more than the men. An old bachelor says—"A woman may be surprised, astonished, amazed, but never dumbfounded." But then he is a bachelor, and deserves to remain in that horrible condition during the term of his unnatural life.

One trick needs a great many more to make it good.

> Thus from one act a man seems forced to become a trickster. By-and-by one of his tricks fails him, and where is he?
>> Trick upon trick, like brick upon brick:
>> All comes tumbling down right quick.

One wears white linen, but another did the washing.

> The credit is not always, nor even generally, given where it is most deserved.

One would rather be bitten by wolves than by sheep.

Injuries inflicted by men whom we respect, are more keenly felt than those which come from bad men, of whom we expected evil.

One vice is more expensive than many virtues.

Think what lechery, gambling, drinking, and pride cost. All the virtues do not involve so much expense as one of these.

One volunteer is worth two pressed men.

It is certainly so in all holy service. Our God wants none in his armies who do not enter there with all their heart. Yet in another sense all the Lord's volunteers are conscripts by effectual calling, pressed into the Lord's service by his love.

One year of blow,
Makes three of hoe.

This appears to be an Essex proverb. If thistles and weeds are allowed to ripen, and their seed is blown about for one season, it will take three years to be rid of the mischief. If we allow bad habits to master us for a little while, it will cost us a long time to uproot them. Another form of the proverb is:

One year's seeding:
Seven years' weeding.

One's own hearth is gold's worth.

The lover of home is the wealthy man. God there gives us more of bliss than all the rest of the world could buy.

Only evil fears the light,
God will vindicate the right.

Open doors invite thieves.

Windows and doors badly fastened, or left open, practically say to a burglar, "Come in, and take what you please."

Open not your door when the devil knocks.

When he finds that he has no response he will go away. Alas! he hardly needs to knock twice in many cases, the door flies open at his first touch. It is not the prince of darkness, but the Lord of Love, who has to cry, "Behold, I stand at the door and knock."

Open thy mouth, and God will open his hand.

"We have not, because we ask not." A pleading heart on earth soon finds a yielding hand in heaven. The Lord is more ready to give than we are to receive.

Open thy mouth for the dumb.

Let every dumb animal find an eloquent advocate in every one of us. When men cannot speak for themselves, this proverb bids us act as their advocate.

Open thy mouth, that I may know thee.

Till then we can only see as far within a man as his teeth ; but speech lets us see further down his throat. We know no man till we have lived with him and heard his communications.

Opportunities do not wait.

We must seize them as they pass us. The tide remains not long at flood.
> The first occasion offer'd, quickly take,
> Lest thou repine at what thou didst forsake.

Orators without judgment are horses without bridles.

In such cases their tongues run away with them, and there is no telling where they will go, nor what mischief they will do.

Order well, that you may be well obeyed.

Be clear, thoughtful, and kind in your commands. When the master knows what he wants done, the servants are likely to do it.

Order your dog, but order not me;
For I was born before you could see.

A tart reply to one who takes too much upon himself, and would domineer over one older than he is, and independent of him.

Ornament an ass, but it does not make him a horse.

However fine the dress, the man is not altered thereby. An ass is still an ass even if you put on him a Mayor's chain, or cover him, ears and all, with stars and garters.

Our first breath is the beginning of death.

We have just that one breath the less to draw. "Our life is woven wind" and nothing more. "As a flower of the field, so he flourisheth."
> The sweetest flowers that scent the sky
> Are only born to blush and die.

Our greatest enemy is within ourselves.

With some especially it is so. We know a man of such ability that nobody hinders his usefulness except himself, but self stands in his way very sadly. Self-consciousness is a dreadful hindrance to a minister, missionary, or miss of any sort.

Our homes should be sweet, and airy, and light.
Our clothes should be clean, and never fit tight.

Our idle days are Satan's busy days.

> When our minds lie fallow, the wicked one sows them with weeds. "Beware of emptiness. Empty hours, empty hands, empty companions, empty words, empty hearts, draw in evil spirits, as a vacuum draws in air."—*Arnot.*

Our mercies are more than our miseries.

> Assuredly. God's deeds of kindness far exceed his acts of judgment. We can count the plagues of Egypt, but who can measure the manna which fell in the wilderness?

Our rust needs a rough file.

> Therefore we may expect many afflictions.
>
> > Till God hath wrought us to his will,
> > The hammer we must suffer still.

Ours is a duck of a climate—for a duck.

> And not always *that;* for one writes of a certain winter's day, "First it *blew,* and then it *snew,* and then it *driz,* and then it *friz.*" We have no climate, but only weather.

Out of one quarrel will come a hundred sins.

> On all sides angry tempers will be engendered, falsehoods uttered, hard thoughts indulged, peace broken, and holiness grieved. Will it not be better to let it pass?

Out of the frying-pan into the fire is no gain.

> To rush from one form of evil to another and perhaps a worse, is of no avail to salvation. That was a true song of Bunyan's :—
>
> > "What danger is the pilgrim in !
> > How many are his foes !
> > How many ways there are to sin,
> > No living mortal knows.
> >
> > Some of the ditch shy are, yet can
> > Lie tumbling in the mire :
> > Some, though they shun the frying-pan,
> > Do leap into the fire."

Out of time and place even wisdom is folly.
Out of the path of duty into the path of danger.

Outside the precept is outside the promise.

When we quit the King's highway of holiness, the King's protection is no longer guaranteed us.

Overdone is worse than underdone.

You can always do more, but it is not easy to undo what is done. The following story is told of *Dean Swift:*—It happened one day that his cook had greatly over-roasted the only joint he had for dinner. "Cook," said the Dean in the blandest possible tones, "this leg of mutton is overdone, take it back into the kitchen and do it less." The cook replied that the thing was impossible. "But," said the Dean, "if it had been underdone you could have done it more." The cook assented. "Well then, cook" said he, "let this be a lesson to you. If you needs must commit a fault, at least take care it is one that will admit of a remedy."

Over-dressed is ill dressed.

When garments attract the eye they disfigure the figure upon which they are hung. Neatness and plainness bear the bell, and make the belle far more beautiful than if gaudily arrayed. A young Grecian painter was rebuked by his master for having decked his Helen with ornaments, because he had not the skill to make her beautiful. It is possible that some think to atone for the want of beauty by their gorgeous attire, but they make a great mistake. Ugliness bedizened advertises its deformity.

Over-reachers over-reach themselves.

Before long the biter is bitten : the grasper of all is left with nothing but a shadow. He makes a dirt-pie, and has the pleasure of eating it himself.

Over shoes over boots.

So the man plunges deeper into the mire. He is reckless of the worse, because already so used to the bad.

Owls hoot, but the sun shines on.

None of the mole-eyed critics have robbed the Bible of its power or blessing, or Christ of his crown, or God of his glory.

Own thyself foolish, that thou mayst be wise.

Confession of ignorance is the doorstep of knowledge.

Ox, keep to your grass.

Be satisfied with your daily fare. Covet not those luxuries which are not fit for you.

Sayings of a more Spiritual Sort.

Offer weekly to the Lord,
Even as thou canst afford.

> See Paul's rule of church finance.   "On the first day of the
> week let every one of you lay by him in store, as God hath
> prospered him."—1 Cor. xvi. 2.   If this rule were followed,
> Christian people would be better off, and the cause of God would
> have no need of fancy fairs or other fancies.

On earth we roam,
Heaven is our home.

> May we keep our faces homeward, and, like horses, mend our pace
> as we see which way the road is going.

On Sinai we learn our duty, but on Calvary we find motives
    for doing it.

> The death of Jesus creates love in our heart, and so we come to
> obey the Lord.   That is not a bad verse :
>
>> Trust, for salvation comes by Faith alone—
>> But work, as though all Merit were thine own ;
>> Live as though Gospel light the world ne'er saw
>> But die as one who is not under Law.

One day in seven is due to heaven.

> And when reserved for heaven, it becomes the best possession for
> ourselves.   The Sabbath which is made for God, is the day which,
> above all others, is said to have been "made for man."

One hour's cold will drive out seven years' heat.

> It will do so in the body, and assuredly it has this effect upon the
> soul.   A temporary declension robs us of the advantage of years of
> earnest spiritual life.   Some believers have to complain that holy
> heat is so soon gone.   They go to bed warm and wake up cold.
> This is a sad experience.

One in a house, of grace possessed,
May win for Jesus all the rest.

> Get one candle lighted, and all the candles in the house may be
> made to shine.   Grace is not contagious, but yet it is of a spreading
> character, and brings a blessing to a man's family.

One touch of grace makes the whole church kin.

> The saints in prayer, praise, and any other gracious services and acts appear as one in word, and deed, and mind.

Only those who follow the steps of Jesus are walking with God.

> For the way of obedience which Jesus followed is the path of fellowship, and he that wanders from it loses communion with God.

Ordinances without the Spirit are cisterns without water.

> We go to them in vain, and return from them bitterly disappointed when the Holy Ghost does not bless them. But when he works by them they are the appointed conduits of the water of life, and it flows fully and freely through them.

Our churches must not become chapels-of-ease.

> " Woe to them that are at ease in Zion."

Our conversation need not always be *about* grace, but it should always be *with* grace.

> We may add, that books upon religion are needed, but works upon common subjects, written in a religious spirit, are still more needed.

Our God we praise
For Sabbath days.

> The rest they bring, and the holy occupations they suggest, are matters for constant thankfulness. God must have loved the poor working-man, or he would not have taken such care to give him rest.

Our graces are the children of free grace.

> The law did not create them, but they are the outcome of the mighty grace of God which works all good in us.

Our Lord's last will and testament is fine reading for his heirs.

> A man was one day walking to church, reading the New Testament, when a friend who met him said, "Good morning, Mr. Price." "Good morning, " replied he ; "I am reading my Father's will as I walk along." "Well, what has he left you ? " asked the friend. "Why, he has bequeathed me a hundredfold more in this life; and in the world to come, life everlasting." This beautiful reply was the means of comforting his Christian friend, who was at the time in sorrowful circumstances.

Our love to God arises out of our want: his love to us out of his fulness.

Our salvation begins with self-condemnation.

We must plead "guilty," or mercy has no ground upon which to deal with us.

Our Saviour has a salve for every sore.

Herrick wrote, in one of his better verses,

To all our wounds, how deep soe'er they be,
Christ is the one sufficient remedy.

Our sinful stains
Should cause us pains.

Till they are washed out we ought not to give rest to our eyes, nor slumber to our eyelids.

Our sufficiency is in God's all-sufficiency.

Self-sufficiency is mere self-deceit.

Over the bridge of sighs we pass to the palace of peace.

Repentance is the road to rest. The way to heaven is round by Weeping Cross. Tears are the water in which we take Christ's healing medicines.

ADDLE your own canoe.

Join the Help-your-self Society. Don't be loafing on your father, or brother; much less upon your wife, as some worthless wretches are doing.

Paddy doesn't kill a deer every time he fires.

Great successes are occasional, and it would be idle to expect them every day. We don't find a sovereign every morning.

Pain past is pleasure.

> When the shore is won at last,
> We shall smile at billows past.

Pains are the payment for sinful pleasures.

What pains they are! Not a few have endured a hell upon earth in consequence of their wicked ways.

Paint not thy nose
At the sign of the Rose.

The paint is expensive, and the nose, despite its rubies, is by no means more of a jewel. "What are you doing there, Jane?" "Why, pa, I'm going to dye my doll's pinafore red." "But what have you to dye it with?" "Beer, pa." "Beer! Who on earth told you that beer would dye red?" "Why, ma said yesterday that it was beer that made your nose so red, and I thought that—" "Here, Susan, take this child to bed."

Pardon great, and pardon small;
But pardon not thyself at all.

One who felt the evil of his sin exclaimed: "God may forgive me, but I can never forgive myself." Yet in another sense we do forgive ourselves, for we enjoy a sense of peace when we are assured of pardon through the precious blood of the great sacrifice.

Parents' blessings can neither be drowned in water nor consumed in fire.

So say the Russians; and there is truth in the saying. The blessing invoked on us by godly parents is a rich endowment. The paternal blessing is a patrimony.

Partnerships with men in power
Can't be built on for an hour.

> Great ones are apt to look down upon you, and to think that your share of the profit is so much taken out of their pockets. Join in partnership with a man of your own size, or else keep yourself to yourself. You cannot well yoke an ox and a goat together.

Party is the madness of many for the gain of a few.

> One would think that each party man was going to make his own fortune, whereas he is only toiling to get into office a certain set of men who are hungering after place. These gentlemen will do nothing whatever for the underlings whose sweet voices they now enlist in their favour. The outs and the ins are as like as two pins : they both want to stick in good places.

Party spirit is an evil spirit.

> It divides people who else might join together for the common good, and it makes men strive for power, rather than for the national benefit. Yet this spirit rules politics. Greed for office and its spoils is more potent than patriotism.

> > All their contentions are but these :
> > Which set of mice shall eat the cheese?

Passion doth unman a man.

Passion is a fever that leaves us weaker than it finds us.

> > All in a heat it makes you run,
> > But how you tremble when it's done !

Past and future seem most fair
When with present we compare.

> But the comparison is not correctly made. We feel our present pains, and forget those which have come, and will yet come.

Past hope, past shame.

> Despair breeds a defiant spirit, and, as he has no prospect of mercy, the man cares not what becomes of him, and dashes into still greater infamy of sin.

Patches and darns are better than debts.

> By the right use of the needle some are half-clothed. Their mends and darns, as the ensigns of industry, are an honour to them. Better a thousand darns than a single debt.

Patience and cowardice are very different things.

The patient man is the bravest of the brave, and bears evil usage, not because he dares not resent it, but because he means to repay it in God's way—by giving good for evil.

Patience and water-gruel cure many diseases.

Of all prescriptions this is the most reliable, and practically this is the point to which doctors are coming. A little starving is very useful treatment. Grantham gruel is recommended: nine grits and a gallon of water will not overload the stomach.

Patience is a bitter plant, but it has sweet fruit.

It sweetens other bitter herbs. Those who let it have its perfect work will become perfect themselves. Like the anvil, it breaks many hammers simply by bearing their blows.

Patience is sister to meekness, and humility is its mother.

Patience is the cheapest law, as temperance is the safest physic.

Patience with poverty is all a poor man's remedy.

But it is a good remedy. Patience is a patent Poor-man's Plaster. It is wise to say, " If I cannot get it I will go without it." To be jolly under difficulties is the mark of a noble heart; but Mark Tapleys are not common persons. When *William Chambers* was young, he endured great hardships. But he says: " Over the door-way of an old house which I passed several times daily was the inscription, carved in stone,

‘ He that tholes overcomes.’

I made up my mind to *thole*—a pithy old Scottish word signifying to bear with patience; the whole inscription reminding us of a sentiment in Virgil : ‘ Whatever may happen, every kind of fortune is to be overcome by bearing it.’ "

Patient waiters are no losers.

Everything comes to the man who is able to wait for it.

With patience I the storm sustain,
For sunshine still doth follow rain.

Paul Pry is on the spy.

The negroes say, " There are people who will help you to get your basket on your head, because they want to see what's in it." They would like to see how we pull on our stockings in the morning, and how we get between the blankets at night ; and yet they hope they don't intrude.

Pay as you go,
And nothing you'll owe.

And if you can't pay, don't go. Keep clear of debt, and then you will be like *Longfellow's* Village Blacksmith :

" He looks the whole world in the face,
For he owes not any man."

Gough once said, "If one steal a penny, he is a thief. Is he not a thief who will '*do*' a creditor, shirk payment of an honest bill, or act the part of a mean trickster? 'There goes a sculptor.' 'What do you mean?' 'Only that he chisels tailors, bootmakers, and all who trust him.'"

Pay beforehand if you would have your work ill done.

Men never like working for a dead horse, and that is the name they give to a job for which they have had the money, and spent it.

Pay down your rent
Ere cash is spent.

Don't leave this matter till there is a man in possession, but keep yourself in possession by paying promptly.

Pay good wages, or your servants will pay themselves.

By pilferings on a greater or less scale they will balance the account. When a man's wages are so small that he cannot live on them, he is apt to add to them by hook or by crook. Very dishonest ! True, but is it right to tempt men to such roguery ?

Pay the reckoning over-night, and you won't be troubled in the morning.

Especially when leaving your hotel get all things settled soon, that there may be no delay in your going away.

Pay thy tithe, and be rich.

So say the Rabbis. Nothing is gained by robbing God. It is my solemn belief that the dedication to the Lord of a portion of our substance, certainly not less than a tenth, would tend to prosperity. So have I found it.

Pay well when you are served well.

A good horse that works hard requires and deserves a good measure of corn ; and a faithful servant deserves to be fully and even generously remunerated.

Pay without fail
Down on the nail.

This is the happiest and most economical way. If you wait, the amount will not lessen. There may even be two nails to pay upon instead of one. There are other debts which ought to be paid. Give thy need, thine honour, thy friend, the church, and the poor, their due. Be not in debt even to posterity. "There is a significant entry in John Evelyn's diary of June 19, 1653 : 'This day I paid all my debts to a farthing. O blessed day!' One of Shenstone's paragraph essays opens with the note of exclamation, 'What pleasure it is to pay one's debts!' Gay writes to Swift : 'I hate to be in debt, for I cannot bear to pawn £5 worth of my liberty to a tailor or a butcher.'"—*Francis Jacox.*

Pay your share of the reckoning, like a true man,
Don't ever be scheming to shirk if you can.

Plenty are ready to feed or fuddle at other people's expense.

"They find a pleasure much more sweet
In being treated than to treat."

Very specially is this the case with the Lushington Club, who are always ready to drink any *given* quantity, and to do their duty with other folks' glasses. It is said of one of them—

"But though he likes his grog,
As all his friends do say,
He always likes it best
When other people pay."

Peace purchased by parting with principle is profanity.

There is plenty of it nowadays.

Peace is the price for which the Lord is sold.
And not for twenty pieces, as of old.

Pedigree won't sell a lame horse.

However famous the sire, people want speed in the steed himself. Many boast of their family connections, and conclude that they must be great because their great grandfather was somebody.

Mules deliver big discourses
Because their ancestors were horses.

Pelt all dogs that bark, and you will need many stones.

Answer all who slander you, and you will have a vocation for life. Prosecute every slanderer, and you will need a court to yourself.

But if all dogs upon this earth should bark,
It will not matter if you do not hark.

Pence well spent are better than pence ill-spared.

Pence were made to clear away expenses. Saving is sometimes a loss. When the time has come to spend, it is as injurious to withhold as it would be for the farmer to lock up the corn in the time of sowing. The street Arabs say, "Chuck out your mouldy coppers."

Penny goes after penny,
Till Peter hasn't any.

Little expenditures run away with a great deal of money; in fact, more is lost by small leakages than by great overflows.

Penny is penny's brother, and likes his company.

If there were two pennies in a bag, they would get together. He that hath shall have. Shillings, like starlings, fly in flocks.

Penny laid on penny,
Very soon makes many.

Economy in small matters leads to savings which are little in themselves, but tell up before long. James Lackington, who began business as a bookseller, in 1774, with a few old books on a stall not worth £5, retired in 1792, when the profits of his business amounted to £5,000 a year. He said he had realized all his wealth by "small profits, bound by industry, and clasped by economy."

Penny wise is often pound foolish.

People count up the faults of those who keep them waiting.

If we are unfairly detaining people, we shall be the subject of a discourse which is not likely to be biased in our favour.

People never should sit talking till they don't know what
to talk about.

Long before subjects are exhausted the tongue should be allowed a holiday. But so it is that, when all the yarn is gone, men spin the faster.

> Men chew not when they have no bread,
> Yet talk the more when nothing's said.

People take more pains to be lost than to be saved.

With resolute zeal some men go over hedge and ditch to hell; while others, in going to heaven, are as slow in their movements as a boy going unwillingly to school.

People throw stones only at trees which have fruit on them.

So the French say. Certainly, the attacks made upon good men may be treated as a diploma of merit. If they had been what the world makes them out to be, they would not have been worth the powder and shot spent upon them. Wasps go after sweet fruit.

People who live in glass houses should never throw stones.

For some one else may do the same and break our windows. Indeed some of the stones we throw may do ourselves damage. When *Charles Dickens* heard an empty and pretentious young author declaiming against the follies and sins of the race, he remarked, "What a lucky thing it is that you and I don't belong to it!"

Perfect men and perfect horses nobody ever sees.

We have heard talk of them, but could never get either man or beast with any such warranty. We have not found perfect men quite quiet in harness; but we have remarked that they are generally a good deal touched in the wind, and not free from a nasty habit of carrying their heads high in the air. "I have never known but two women that were perfect," said one French lady to another. "Who was the other one?" asked her companion.

Perform all your work without uproar and din :
When wisdom goes out then clamour comes in.

Those who do nothing generally take to shouting. The best work in the world is done on the quiet.

"Perhaps" hinders folk from lying.

By using this, and other qualifying words, truthfulness is preserved. Those who talk as fast as express trains are ever known to run should always have buffers to their engine.

Perpetual chatterers are like crickets in the chimney-corner.

Oh, that we could silence their perpetual chirping!
On, on, on, on ; for ever and a day :
Nothing but death will make their jawbones stay.

Perseverance wins.

"Hard pounding, gentlemen," said the Duke ; but by steadily bearing this hard pounding Waterloo was won. Only hold on long enough, and the day will be yours.

Persevere and never fear.

"All things must yield to industry and time :
None cease to rise but those who cease to climb."

Peter's in, Paul's out.

As much as to say, now that one person essential to the business is at home, another equally needful is away. We do not find all things working quite as we would like; but this is nothing new.

Petticoat government has proved good in England.

"God save our gracious Queen.   Long live our noble Queen."

"*A place under government,*
Was all that Paddy wanted :
He married soon a scolding wife,
When all he wished was granted."

Philosophers cover the pie of their ignorance with a Latin crust.

"Doctor," said an old lady the other day to her family physician, "kin you tell me how it is that some folks is born dumb?"   "Why, hem, certainly, madam," replied the doctor ; "it is owing to the fact that they come into the world without the faculty of speech !" "La, me !" remarked the old lady ; "Now just see what it is to have a physic edication !   I've axed my old man more nor a hundred times that ar same thing, and all that I could get out of him was, '*Kase they is.*'"   Still, spiflication is no explanation.

Physicians are joked at only when we are well.

Hence, when *Voltaire* was well, he said, "A physician is a man who pours drugs of which he knows little, into a body of which he knows less."   But when he felt in a more respectful, because more sickly, condition, he said, "A physician is an unfortunate gentleman, who is every day called upon to perform a miracle, namely, to reconcile intemperance with health."   One thing is clear, doctors do not bleed us in the arm as much as they did ; but they do bleed us in another place, and that without a lancet.

Piety is a greater honour than parentage.

It is of small use to have had a godly father if one is himself leading an evil life ; yet those who are a disgrace to their ancestors are often the loudest in boasting of their descent.   What a descent !

Those who on holy ancestry enlarge,
Produce their debt ; but where is their discharge?

Pigs grow fat where lambs would starve.

Evil men can flourish where the honest would perish.   The food of the wicked would be the poison of the gracious.

The talk which modern men adore
Would make me sick, and nothing more.

Pigs grunt about everything and nothing.

I think I must have heard some of these animals.

Pigs may whistle; but their mouths were not made for it.

Spoken of those who attempt performances for which they are evidently unfitted : a very common piece of uncommon folly.

Pigs when they fly go tail first.

They never do fly ; but the old saying means that when men aspire to things of which they are not capable, they always go the wrong way to work. Whistling oysters are always out of tune.

Pills should be swallowed, not chewed.

Many disagreeable things had better be accepted in silence, and not much thought about, or their bitterness will be all the more perceptible. Accept the inevitable, and don't dwell upon it.

Pinch yourself, and learn how others feel when they are pinched.

It would do many an employer good to live for a week on the small wage he pays his men on Saturday.

Pity fair weather should do any harm.

Pity without relief is like mustard without beef.

Very tasty, but not very nourishing. A man who had been in good circumstances was reduced to selling cakes in the street. One who knew him in wealthier days commiserated him at great length, till, his patience being exhausted, he exclaimed, "Bother your pity! Buy a bun." A pennyworth of help is worth a heap of pity.

Plain-dealing is a jewel, and he that useth it shall prosper.

Shall he? He ought to do so, but possibly he may not. But prosperity is not the greatest thing to desire. The plain-dealer will, at least, have a quiet conscience, and that is a pearl of great price. Diogenes would still need his lantern to find a plain-dealer.

Plant the crocus, but don't play the croaker.

It is said that crocus-growers in the olden time had a very precarious crop, and were called croakers, not from the frog, but from the saffron crocus which they cultivated, and which, for various reasons, tried them so much in its production. As farmers do not now grow saffron, they have of course left off being croakers (?).

Plaster thick,
And some will stick.

> A wicked piece of advice : belie a man's character very heavily, and some of the slander will be believed.   Surely Satan himself is at the bottom of such a malicious precept.   Speak evil of none.

Play, but do not play the fool.

> Be wise in your recreation as in all things else.   Follow Rowland Hill's advice : "Keep up the distinction between pious cheerfulness and frothy levity."   Play should be such as fits for work.

Play not with fire,
Nor with foul desire.

> For they are dangerous things, and must not be trifled with.   It is an infinite folly to make gunpowder in a smith's shop, and then try to persuade people that there is no danger in it.   Even when a man is not burned, he gets blackened if he meddles with hot coals.

Playful kittens make sober cats.

> May all our cheerful youth grow up to be earnest men and womer

Please ever, tease never.

> Unless it be the kind of teasing which is a form of pleasing, only flavoured with a little spice.   Tease only as you would wish to be teased yourself.

> > If you please,
> > Do not tease.

Please yourself, and you'll please me.

> We cannot often say this ; but when people are worrying about mere trifles, we thus give them *carte blanche,* and hope we shall hear no more of their chatter.

Pleasures are like poppies spread ;
You seize the flower, its bloom is shed.

> So *Burns* found them ; but then he was too apt to snatch at pleasures of a kind which wisdom would forego.

Plough deep while sluggards sleep,
And you shall have corn to sell or to keep.

> Here we have *Franklin's* wisdom, as he put it into the mouth o. Poor Richard.   It suits England as well as America.   Hard work is still the road to prosperity ; and there is no other.

Plough or not plough, you must pay your rent.

That will be demanded, and no mistake, for nothing is surer than death and quarter-day. Neither will landlords be content to go without their share because your share has been rusting in the furrow. If work does not pay, idleness will not.

Plough well if you plough slowly.

It will pay to take more time over it, rather than to do it in a slovenly manner. Do as little as you like, but do that little well.

Ploughmen on their legs are higher than gentlemen on their knees.

The independence of the working-man is more noble than the obsequiousness of the courtier or the tradesman who bows before others to get gain. Whatever you are, be a man.

Poach nothing but eggs.

Whatever we may think of the game laws, we don't intend to break them. Poached eggs are a family dish, but we don't get them from poachers. Stolen goods are too costly for honest purses.

Politeness is excellent, but it does not pay the bill.

Tradesmen would like more money even if they had less manners.

Poor, but honest.

"This reminds me of the reply of a wise man, whose son said to him, 'Father, I often hear people say, "Poor, but honest." Why don't they say, "Rich, but honest"?' 'Because, my son, no one would believe them.' But I was going to suggest whether we hadn't better make a change, and say, 'Poor, *because* honest.'"— *Dr. Philetus Dobbs.*

Poor folks are glad of porridge.

Therein they are rich; for their power to enjoy their food has a wider range than the taste of the epicure, who must have dainties, or he cannot make a satisfactory meal.

Poor folks must say, "Thank ye" for a little.

They must be grateful for small mercies. Some donors require a waggon-load of homage for a small basin of very thin soup. As for a blanket it can hardly be acknowledged by a century of curtseys and a billion of bows.

Poor in the midst of wealth is poor indeed.

Such is the miser in his self-inflicted penury. Such again is the poor relation in a purse-proud family, and the man who is unhappy, on account of fear, where others rejoice in hope.

Poor men seek meat for their stomach ; rich men stomach for their meat.

Thus things are somewhat equalized. Which is the worst, appetite and no food, or food and no appetite ?

Poor men's tables are soon spread.

And very soon cleared again. *Charles Wesley's* Elegy on William Kingsbury, a man who lived and died in extreme poverty, is very touching :
> " Toiling hard for scanty bread,
> Scanty bread he could not find."

Poor purse and dainty palate are ill met.

For you can't buy oysters with coppers, nor turtle-soup at a groat a quart. Beau Brummel, when asked if he took vegetables, replied, that he believed he had once tasted a pea. Poor Brummel ! Fancy this affected beau condemned to eat raw turnips.

Poor wages make poor work.

Of course no man will throw his heart into a task for which he is underpaid. If you are so unreasonable as to expect it, the workman will be reasonable enough to disappoint you. You may try to sweat a man, but he will not sweat for you.
> Give a fair day's wage for a fair day's work :
> Take a fair day's wages, and never shirk.

Positive men are oftenest in error.

Never are they more certain than when they are mistaken. No creature is more obstinate than a donkey ; no bird more dogmatic in his gibble-gabble than a turkey-cock.

Possession is nine points of the law.

And there is only one more point. Therefore, hold on like grim death, till lawful authority bids you be gone.

Possess your money, but let it not possess you.

" It is not the fact that a man *has* riches which keeps him from the kingdom of heaven, but the fact that riches *have* him."—*Dr. Caird.*

Pot by pot, Sam grows a sot.

He only took a drop at first; but he refused to drop it. Soon his drops came often. By-and-by he dropped into a habit of continual dropping ; and now he very often has a drop too much, and looks as bloated as if he had the dropsy.

Pot! Don't call the kettle black.

Kettle called Pot—
You know what.

It is generally so, that those who are themselves most full of fault are the quickest to cry out against others. It is an old plan for the thief, when he runs away, to cry "Stop thief" while he runs.

Potatoes don't grow by the side of the pot.

They must be worked for. Some are so lazy that one would think they expect the potatoes to fall upon their plates ready boiled ; but even in Ireland under Home Rule this will not happen on any of the seven days of the week.

Pots of beer cost many a tear.

Wives with children in hunger and nakedness weep because the man who should love them loves nothing but the drink.

Poverty breeds strife.

When all are satisfied the state is quiet, but great poverty foments rebellions.

Poverty is no crime and no credit.

It all depends upon how it comes. Lazarus did not go to Abraham's bosom because he was poor, or every sluggard would go there easily. There are the Lord's poor, who are rich in faith, and there are the devil's poor, who are good for nothing but to eat other people's bread.

Poverty is not a shame, but the being ashamed of it is.

For, if we are poor, why should we hide it? If we were rich, fear might make us conceal our wealth ; but as no one will rob us of our poverty, we need not cover it. If our poverty be not our fault, we may glory in being called to serve the Lord in the hottest part of the battle, and we should by no means blush at the fact.

Poverty is the mother of health.

In many cases the labour entailed by necessity creates and nourishes good health. Exercise exorcises diseases.

Poverty laughs at robbery.

The old story hath it : " There was a poor man, on a tyme, who said unto thieves who brake into his house at night, ' Sirs, I marvel that ye think to find anything here by night, for I assure you that I can find nothing here by day.' "

> By this tale plainly appeareth,
> That poverty little feareth.

Poverty tries friends and allies.

And too often in the trial they turn out to be base metal. Somewhat harshly a versifier puts it—

> If Fortune wrap thee warm,
> Then friends about thee swarm,
>   Like bees about a honey-pot.
> But if Dame Fortune frown,
> And cast thee fairly down,
>   Thy friends will let thee lie and rot.

Poverty wants some things, luxury many things, avarice all things.

So that the miser is the poorest man of all : you'll break your neck as soon as your fast in his house at his expense.

Practice makes perfect.

If that practice is careful, constant, and long continued.

**Practise not your art,
And it will soon depart.**

Out of work we lose the knack of working. After being in the marshes for a month the horse finds the collar galls him. He who would keep clever at his trade must keep ever at his work.

Practise thrift, or else you'll drift.

Whether you are rich or poor you will need management and economy. Go forward, or you will get backward.

> He that gets money before he gets wit,
> Will be but a short while master of it.

Praise a fool, and you water his folly.

And that folly will grow like willows by the water-courses. He will lift his head so high that it will go through the ceiling. His pride will rise over even a prophet's head, like the gourd which was the growth of a night. Let the green thing alone.

Praise from the worthless is worthless.

Worse: it is suspicious. A philosopher, when a base fellow applauded him, asked, "What have I done that such a fellow should speak well of me?" Praise is worthy from the praise-worthy.

Praise God more, and blame neighbours less.

Praise invigorates the wise, but intoxicates the foolish.

The sensible endeavour to do all the better because they are thought to have done well. Vain persons, by a little commendation, are first puffed up, and then puffed out. Few stomachs can digest the rich pastry of praise. Butter needs to be thinly spread.

Praise little, dispraise less.

Let your expressions be well weighed, so that value may be attached to them. He who is constantly expressing his hasty opinions will find that little regard is paid to him. *Andrew Fuller* tells of one, who, being much edified by the discourse of a popular minister, met him at the pulpit stairs with, "I really must not say what I think of your sermon, it might do you harm." "Not at all, my friend," was the rejoinder, "speak out, for I do not attach much importance to your opinion." More frank than flattering.

Praise makes good men better and bad men worse.

The unworthy grow proud, and the deserving become more humble. It is hard to live up to the good opinion of our friends.

Praise others far more than yourself.

A hearty word of commendation to others is generous and good; but self-praise is no recommendation. Be not your own publisher.

> If one hath serv'd thee, tell the deed to many:
> Hast thou serv'd many?—tell it not to any.

Praise Peter, but don't find fault with Paul.

Why should you run down one because you prefer another? This is a common and senseless habit. Praise John and Joan too.

Praise the hill, but keep below.

If you desire easy travelling take the lower road, although you may admire the scenery of the mountain way. Admire wealth, rank and office; but do not hanker after them yourself.

> There's wind on the hill, and the road is steep;
> It's warm in the vale, so here I shall keep.

Praise the bridge which carries you over.

Honour the man who gave you an education. Love the country which gives you shelter. Speak well of the trade by which you get a living. Extol the truth which bears up your spirit.

Praise the horse which has brought you so far.

With a lively sense of favours to come, hoping that he will carry you safely the rest of the way.

Praise the sea, but keep on land.

So said *George Herbert*, and the wise men before him. They knew that Britannia ruled the waves, but wished that she ruled them straighter. It is all up with some when they go down to the sea.

Prate is prate: work is the duck which lays the eggs.

Sam Slick says:—Work; earn your own pork, and see how sweet it will be. Work and see how well you will be. Work and see how cheerful you will be. Work and see how independent you will be. Work and see how religious you will be; for before you know where you are, instead of repining at Providence, you will find yourself offering up thanks for all the numerous blessings you enjoy.

Pray and stay are words for every day.

Good words and wise. Practise both. Worship and wait. God's answers are not always immediate. His delays are not denials. *Erskine* rightly says:—

"I'm heard when answered soon or late ;
And heard when I no answer get :
Yea, kindly answer'd when refused,
And treated well when harshly us'd."

Pray brighten each day with domestic delight, And bring home the wages on Saturday night.

Pray, do hold your tongue a minute : What you say has nothing in it.

Cease your chatter and mind your platter. Your tongue runs on like a mill-wheel disconnected from the machinery : clatter, clatter, clatter, but grinding nothing whatever. The wonder is your teeth do not shake out of their sockets through the continual motion of your jaws! Do be quiet for a change.

Pray for all, but prey on none.

How much difference one letter makes! Let us not imitate the bankers who commenced business with supplication and ended in liquidation.

Pray to God, but keep the hammer going.

> He gives us our daily bread by enabling us to work and earn it. Throw not your tools away because you trust in God; on the contrary, use them with braver heart.

Pray to God, sailor, but pull for the shore.

Prayer and pains
Bring best of gains.

> They should go together. Prayer without labour is hypocrisy, and labour without prayer is presumption.

Prayer and provender hinder no man's journey.

> Far rather do they speed
> Both the man and his steed.

Prayer is the key of the morning and the lock of the night.

> Let not your habitation be without it. It is ill living where this lock and key are unknown. As well have a house without a roof as a home without family prayer.

Praying without working is a bow without a string.

> There's nothing in it. If the man desired that which he pretends to pray for, he would be eager to labour for it.

Preach best in your own pulpit.

> The life at home should be even better than the conduct abroad. It is said that some would find it hard to stand on their own doorstep and preach; they find it convenient to go where they are not known. From such preachers may the Lord deliver us!

Preach your own funeral sermon while living.

> Prepare the material of an honourable and instructive memorial by an earnest and useful life.

Precious ointments are put in small boxes.

> We cannot expect great quantity where we have high quality. Of otto of roses a drop is precious, and it needs only a very small bottle to hold as much as pounds can buy. Little people are rather proud of this proverb, and no one would wish to take it from them. There are many good little bodies. God bless them! Valuable articles are generally done up in small parcels.
>
> > Mark inward worth, and you shall find it then
> > That lesser bodies make not lesser men.

Prejudice is a prophet which prophesies only evil.

Dr. M., an army surgeon during the American war, had a great contempt for a certain set of officers, whose education was defective. One day, at mess, a brave and accomplished officer, and a great wag, remarked to the doctor :

"Dr. M., are you acquainted with Captain G. ? "

"Yes, I know him well," replied the doctor ; "he's one of the new set. But what of him ? "

"Nothing in particular," replied Captain S. "I have just received a letter from him, and I will be bound that you cannot guess in six guesses how he spells ' cat.' "

"Done ! " said the doctor

"Well, commence guessing," said S.

"K, a, double t."

"No."

"K, a, t, e."

"No."

"C, a, double t, e."

"No."

"C, a, double t."

"No."

"K, a, t."

"No, that's not the way. Try again, it's your last guess."

"C, a, g, h, t."

"No," said Captain S. "You're wrong again."

"Well," said the doctor, with much petulance of manner, "how does he spell it ? "

"Why, he spells it c, a, t," replied Captain S., with the utmost gravity, amid the roar of the mess.

Prepare for sudden death, and it will not be sudden.

Soon come, soon go :
Thy life is so.

Prepare for the worst, and hope for the best.

Neither the best nor the worst come when they are expected. To be prepared is often to escape : to hope is sometimes to possess.

Prettiness makes no porridge.

That is to say, the handsomeness of the wife will not feed the family. In a woman domestic ability is needed even more than personal beauty. Still there is no proof that ugly women cook better than handsome ones do. Prettiness spoils no porridge.

Pretty and new,
Please not a few.

Fools care for nothing which they have seen before. Prettiness is the chief attraction with many. Well, well ; women are no worse for being handsome, and eggs are no better for being old.

Pretty children sing pretty songs.

Especially if they are our own children. "Music is the sound which one's own children make as they romp through the house. Noise is the sound which other people's children make under the same circumstances."

Pretty speeches will not sugar my gooseberries.

Yet they may be a spoon to hand out the sugar. For the sour things of life we need the loaf sugar of kindness, or the moist sugar of sympathy, or the saccharine of grace : when these come in the silver spoon of goodly words they are none the worse.

Prevention is better than cure.

The work of the Band of Hope, in keeping the children from ever touching the drink, is of even more value than temperance work for reclaiming those who have become drunkards.

Pride and poverty are ill met, yet often live together.

Pride only makes poverty more poor; yet some must seem "respectable" if they starve. They keep up show, and pinch for it. The Scotch wisely say : "A brass plate with a man's name on it is a pretty thing ; but a dinner plate with meat on it is much better."

Pride and scorn are briar and thorn.

Tearing both the proud man and those around him. These are two fine things to look at, but they are the fruitful source of misery.

Pride breakfasted with plenty, dined with poverty, and supped with infamy.

Where it went to bed we may very easily guess.

Pride costs more than hunger, thirst, or cold.

Note the expense of money in dress, in cutting a dash, and in keeping up appearances : then note the loss of love, the loss of truth, and the loss of grace ; and you will say that pride is a very expensive luxury. As it is worth nothing, it is indeed a costly thing. Pride will eat a man out of house and home.

Pride feels no cold.

Hence, ladies in the severest season will go out to parties less than half-dressed. Modesty should assist prudence, and make them dress decently ; but pride has such sway that they will die to be in the fashion. As martyrs burn for Christ, so ladies freeze for fashion.

Pride flies above the reach of love.

It asks to be feared, and cares not for affection. It makes no friends, but provokes enmity. Pride and love are strangers.

Pride goeth before, and shame cometh after.

King Louis XI. was wont to say : "When pride is on the saddle, shame sits on the crupper." All on earth, and all in heaven, and all in hell are united to pull down a proud man.

Pride had rather go out of the way, than go behind.

If the proud man can anyhow pass his neighbour on the road, and give him his dust, he does not mind running the risk of driving into the ditch. To be great, many cease to be good.

Pride in dress
Is foolishness.

It is unreasonable ; for of all the fine things which men wear, it must be said, "Alas, master ! they are borrowed."
"The poor sheep and silkworm wore
That very clothing long before."

Pride in prosperity turns to misery in adversity.

Pride is a moth which is soon bred in fine garments.

Pride is a peacock, all strut and show.

How hideous is its voice in the ears of the discerning ! It is a fine bird, but yet it was hatched in the straw-yard.

Pride is a weed which will grow on any dunghill.

A dustman may be as proud as a duke. Pride lives in the kitchen as well as in the parlour. When men go up in the world they don't know their own fathers. They
Forget the dunghills where they grew,
And think themselves they don't know who.

Pride is as loud a beggar as want, and a great deal more saucy.

It asks and will have. Its owner cannot refuse what his vanity craves, whatever the cost may be.

Pride of knowledge is a sign of folly.

"Knowledge is proud that he has learned so much ;
Wisdom is humble that he knows no more."—*Cowper.*

Pride of pedigree is great stupidity.

One man is said to have declared that when Noah was in the ark his ancestor had a boat of his own. Another placed Adam half-way down in his family tree. Far wiser was the good man who bade his heirs write on his gravestone :—

> John Carnegie lies here,
> Descended from Adam and Eve.
> If any one can go higher,
> I'll give him leave.

Pride owns no superior.

It must be king of the castle. Some men have a manner about them which gives you the idea that the world is not good enough for them, and that they are the only people for whom the sun rises and sets. *Churchill* thus denounced the arrogance of Bishop Warburton :—

> "He is so proud that should he meet
> The twelve Apostles in the street,
> He'd turn his nose up at them all,
> And shove St. Peter from the wall."

Pride wears humility's cloak.

The pride which apes humility is the most Satanic of all pride.

Pride went out on horseback, but came back on foot.

It had a come-down ; and nobody was sorry.

Pride with pride will not abide.

Nothing is surer than that one haughty man will fall out with another. They will fight like Kilkenny cats.

Pride's chickens have bonny feathers, but bony bodies.

Its doings are all show and emptiness.

Priestcraft is no better than witchcraft.

One grows indignant at the pretensions of men to confer grace, to work regeneration, to forgive sin, and so forth. Look at the way they go to work !

> With crosses, relics, crucifixes,
> Beads, pictures, rosaries, and pyxes ;
> Those tools for working out salvation
> By mere mechanic operation.

Private reproof is the best grave for private faults.

Probe not a wound too deep, lest you make a new one.

> Be gentle in dealing with a fault or a quarrel, lest there be more sinning and more quarrelling.

Procrastination is the thief of time.

> That is to say, in cases of delay of duty. In the matter of turning to God, procrastination is the kidnapper of souls, and the recruiting officer of hell.

Promise little and do much.

> Ring a small bell, and give a great dinner. Moderate those puffing advertisements. Let us have less brag, and more pudding in the bag. Let not your tongue be longer than your arm.

Promises may get friends, but only performances can keep them.

> People are attracted to a promising young man, but they do not like him long if he does not turn out to be a performer.

Promises should be given with caution, and kept with care.

> Hence, we should be slow to say "Yes" to all applicants. It is a very small matter for them to open their mouths and ask great things; but it will be a great matter for us to fulfil our promise if they manage to extort one. To be able to put off certain resolutely rude beggars we may quote these lines from *Martial:*—
>
> > "Tis a mere nothing that you ask, you cry:
> > If you ask nothing, nothing I deny."

Promising is not paying.

> "There, that's settled," said a fellow who had given a bill. He ought to have remembered this proverb. If promises were payments, nobody would be in debt. A boy at a crossing having begged a copper of a gentleman, the latter told him he would give him something as he came back. The boy replied, "Your honour would be surprised if you knew the money I have lost by giving credit that way."

Promote the truth, and the truth will promote thee.

> Though thou suffer with it for a season, thou shalt triumph with it in due time. Dishonour for truth's sake is true glory.

Prompt pay makes ready way.

> You can go all over the world with a sovereign in your hand. Pay at once, and any one will deal with you.

Prosperity's right hand is industry, and her left hand is frugality.

> The one produces, and the other preserves. A sensible writer gives the following rules for prospering in business :—
>
> > Early to bed, and early to rise ;
> > Wear the blue ribbon, and advertise.

Proud heart in poor breast :
Much fret and little rest.

> Proud looks lose hearts, but courteous words win them. This was a favourite saying of Ferdinand of Spain, and it is undoubtedly true. A game cock has more fight than flesh.

Proud men hate pride in others.

> Because it is a sort of defiance to their own pride. "I tread on the pride of Plato," said Diogenes as he walked over Plato's carpet. "Yes—and with more pride," said Plato.

Providence often puts a large potato in a little pig's way.

> We marvel at the way in which some men get on, who do not appear to have any particular aptitude for business. In this strange world we meet with people who find the biggest possible potatoes, and yet are the very smallest of piggies.

Providence provides for the provident.

> As for the lazy and drunken, providence soon provides for them rags and jags, and a place in the county gaol.

Prudence is good *before* the act, but courage *in* the act.

> > He saves the steed that keeps him under locks ;
> > Who looks may leap, nor fear his shins have knocks ;
> > Who tries may trust, nor flattering friends shall find ;
> > Who speaks with heed may boldly speak his mind.

Prudent youth is better than rash old age.

> One occasionally meets with the latter. Certain men grow older, but not wiser. To have furrows on the brow, and folly in the heart, is a sad mixture. Grey heads are not always wise heads.

Publish a Revised Version of your life.

Correct the errata, add a supplement, and alter the type.

Pull down the nests and the rooks will fly.

Thus John Knox would demolish abbeys to get rid of monks; and there was common sense in the advice. If drink-shops were abolished, should we be rid of drunkards?

Pull the cat's tail, and she'll scratch without fail.

If you annoy people you must not wonder if they turn upon you.

Punctuality is only common honesty.

For it is due to others that we keep due time. What right have we to rob a man of his hours? Might we not as well steal his money as steal minutes in which he could be earning it?

Punctuality is the hinge of business.

Except with lawyers, who give this praise to procrastination. Punctuality may be a minor virtue, but the want of it produces some of the major evils. Keep Greenwich time.

Punish your enemies by doing them good.

Pure water is good within and without.

Certain drinkers have never tried cold water : they have no idea what a delicate taste it has, nor how refreshing it is when it comes in contact with the skin. Try *aqua pura!*

Purses shrink,
While workmen drink.

A prudent man advised his drunken servant to put by his money for a rainy day. In a few weeks his master inquired how much of his money he had saved. "Faith, none at all," said he; "it rained so hard yesterday, that it all went."

Put a key on your tongue.

Do not have lockjaw, but yet lock your jaw.

Put glasses to thine eyes, not to thy lips.

Wear spectacles, but do not make yourself a spectacle by taking too much liquor. You will not take too much if you take none.

Put in with the loaves, and taken out with the cakes.

And so only half baked. Many are thus underdone as to common sense, and hence they remain for ever very soft and sappy.

Put not a ring of gold into the snout of a swine.

Do not pay honour to the base. Do not tell the sacred mysteries of the inner life to the profane. Ask not an unworthy person to minister in holy things. Observe the propriety of things.

Put not all your crocks on one shelf.

For if that shelf should fall, all your pottery would be smashed. Divide your ventures and risks. Trust not all your cash to one speculation. There is common sense in this proverb.

Put not milk into a leaky can.

Don't tell your secrets to a blab, nor invest your cash in doubtful companies, and questionable speculations.

Put the saddle on the right horse.

Adam blamed Eve; Eve blamed the Devil; they should have blamed themselves. This also applies to us.

Put the whip into the manger.

Give corn instead of cord. Feed, but do not flog.

Put what you like into your mouth, but mind what comes out of it.

If you like to eat dirt, that's your own concern; but if you speak dirt, others will be defiled.

Put your foot down where you mean to stand.

Be firm. Resolve, and resolutely stand to your resolution.

If well thou hast begun, press on for right ;
It is the end that crowns us, not the fight.

Put your hand quickly to your hat, and slowly to your purse, and you'll take no harm.

Be liberal with your courtesy, but be economical in your expenditure. Civility costs nothing, but earns much.

Sayings of a more Spiritual Sort.

Pardon is not properly prized without a solemn sense of the fount, folly, filth, and fruit of sin.

See how David felt all this, and set it forth in the fifty-first Psalm. *Tennyson* wrote—

"He taught me all the mercy, for he show'd me all the sin."

Pardoned sin makes peace within.

It is the first in the catalogue of blessings, "Who forgiveth all thine iniquities."—Ps. ciii. 3. *Stillingfleet* asks: "How can we be at peace with ourselves till we have reason to believe that God is at peace with us?"

Partners in sin are justly made partners in punishment.

Therefore, both body and soul will suffer the future punishment of unrepented sin.

Patience is the livery of Christ's servants.

In it they are known to be of the household of the Crucified. It requires more grace to suffer patiently than to serve laboriously.

Peacemakers are the children of God: peace-breakers are the children of the devil.

John Trapp says: "Peace-making is as sure and as sweet a sign of a son of the God of Peace, as the parti-coloured clothes were anciently signs of a king's daughters.—2 Sam. xiii. 18."

Penitent sighs bring forth exulting songs.

"Sin, repentance, and pardon, are like to the three vernal months of the year, March, April, and May. Sin comes in like March, blustering, stormy, and full of bold violence. Repentance succeeds like April, showering, weeping, and full of tears. Pardon follows like May, springing, singing, full of joys and flowers. If our hands have been full of *March*, with the tempests of unrighteousness, our eyes must be full of *April*, with the sorrow of repentance; and then our hearts shall be full of *May*, in the true joy of forgiveness."— *T. Adams.*

Perfect trust in a perfect Saviour brings perfect peace.

> " We may trust him solely, all for us to do :
> They who trust him wholly, find him wholly true."
> *R. F. Havergal.*

Pharisees and Publicans both pour out their hearts before
God, the one in bragging, the other in begging.

Plead for Jesus, for he pleads for you.

Please God, and you will please good men.

Please God in all you do, and be pleased with all God does.

> This would be heaven on earth if we could fulfil it.

Poor are they that think themselves rich in grace : rich
are they that see themselves poor.

> A clergyman once said to Mr. Newton, "Really, sir, what a
> beautiful tract that is of yours, 'The Progress of Grace'!   I never
> saw so clearly that I was in the full ear."   "Why," said Mr.
> Newton, "I put, or intended to put, as one mark of it, a humble
> opinion of ourselves."

Poor sinners have a rich gospel.

Poverty in the way of duty is to be chosen rather than
plenty in the way of sin.

> When Philip Henry was fined for holding services, and his goods
> seized, he said, " Ah, well ! we may be losers *for* Christ, but we
> cannot in the end be losers *by* Christ : praise his name."

Poverty of spirit is the riches of the soul.

> "Humility is not only a precious grace, but the preserver of all
> other graces ; and without it (if that could be) they are but as a box
> of precious powder carried in the wind without a cover, in danger
> of being scattered and blown away."—*Leighton.*

Practical holiness is the seal of personal election.

Pray against sin, but don't sin against prayer.

> We sin against prayer when we ask for what we will not seek, and
> pray one thing and act another.   To forget our own petitions, or to
> refuse their answers when they come, is an offence against the
> mercy-seat.   So also to pray holiness and live ungodliness is a
> crime against the throne of grace.

Pray David's prayer if you would sing David's song.

Pray for a blessing, and your prayer will be a blessing.

In the very seeking of a benediction grace is put into action, and is strengthened by the exercise.

Pray for those who do not pray for themselves.

Some one prayed for you when you were yet unsaved: return that effectual prayer to the treasury of the church by pleading for others. Plead hard for the hard heart which never pleads.

Pray for your minister, and you will be praying for yourself.

Whatever blessing he obtains will appear in his ministry, and you will be a partaker of it.

Prayer breathes in the air of heaven, and praise breathes it out again.

Thus we have heavenly respiration, and by it we live unto God.

Prayer and praise, with sins forgiven,
Bring down to earth the bliss of heaven.

Prayer bringeth heaven down to man, and carrieth man up to heaven.

Prayer is God's rod which fetches forth streams of blessing from the Rock of affliction.

Prayer knocks till the door opens.

Open it will, for so runs the promise of our faithful God, "To him that knocketh it shall be opened." "If the angel opened the door of the prison to let Peter out, it was prayer that opened the door of heaven to let the angel out."

Prayer moves the hand that moves the world.

"Prayer is a creature's strength, his very breath and being;
Prayer is the golden key that can open the wicket of Mercy.
Prayer is the magic sound that saith to Fate, 'So be it';
Prayer is the slender nerve that moveth the muscles of Omnipotence."—*Martin Tupper.*

Prayer must not come from the roof of the mouth, but from the root of the heart.

Prayer oils the wheels of the waggon of life.

Try the effect of it when the wheel begins to creak. A missionary in a heathen land had grown sadly weary and discouraged. He was going forth to his work with a joyless face, when his young wife called him back, went to him, put her hands on his shoulders, and, with tears in her eyes, said, "O Willie, Willie! much work and little prayer is hard work." Then she led him to a private room, and there, kneeling down, prayed with him as only one who loved with a true heavenly love could pray. From that room he went forth strong in the strength which never failed him; never again was he tempted to sever work and prayer.

Prayer rightly offered is richly answered.

"Prayer, like Jonathan's bow, returns not empty; never was faithful prayer lost. No tradesman trades with such certainty as the praying saint. Some prayers, indeed, have a longer voyage than others, but then they return with richer lading at last; the praying soul is a gainer by waiting for an answer."—*Gurnall.*

Prayer should be pillared on promises, and pinnacled with praises.

Prayer without words can win :
Words without heart are sin.

"She also prayed who touched Christ's garment's hem with reverent faith; ay, and was answered too, although no word escaped her."—*Partridge.*

Preach Christ to sinners if you would preach sinners to Christ.

Daniel Wilson suggested to a friend, as a text for a sermon, the word "Christ." "Begin with Christ, go on with Christ, and end with Christ, and I am sure your hearers will never be tired, for his name is as ointment poured forth."

Preachers are apt to think more of their own credit as God's messengers, than of the credit given to God's messages.

Faithful preachers will get little credit from men of the world, or from worldly Christians; for the religion of to-day leans to unfaithfulness :

> " It calls for pleasing pulpiteers,
>   Modern, and brilliant, and fast ;
> Who will show how men may live as they list,
>   And go to heaven at last."

Preachers often draw the bow at a venture, but the Spirit of God takes sure aim.

Preaching in pride is doing God's work in the devil's livery.

Precious promises are the provender of faith.

> *Dr. Gordon* says, "We would commend a faith that even seems audacious, like that of the sturdy covenanter Robert Bruce, who requested, as he was dying, that his finger might be placed on one of God's strong promises, as though to challenge the Judge of all with it as he should enter his presence. As we stand face to face with the Word we cannot be too bold."

Pride climbs up, not as Zacchæus to see Jesus, but to be seen itself.

Prize the doctrine of grace and the grace of the doctrine.

> Take care that these go together, for so hath God appointed.

Providence may change, but the promise must stand.

> The wheel of providence revolves, but the axle of divine faithfulness remains in its place. "He cannot deny himself."

Punishment usually bears upon it the image of the sin.

> Jacob deceived his brother, and his sons deceived him; David took another man's wife, and his own bed was defiled by Absalom. These are two instances out of thousands. The Lord makes his children see their sin in the smart which it brings upon them.

UACKERY has no friend like gullibility.

If none would swallow, none would make the pill. Persons invite deception by the eager way in which they snap at the bait. Advertise enough, and you may sell liquorice water at a guinea a gill.

Quality is better than quantity.

They do not often go together. Prefer to do a little well rather than a great deal in a poor style.

Quarrel only at twelve o'clock, and get it over at noon.

Which is much the same as—Never quarrel at all.

Quarrellers seldom grow fat.

They worry the flesh off their bones by agitation, waste their substance in litigation, and weary their minds in disputation.

Quarrelling dogs come limping home.

They give and receive hurts; and many a painful footstep they cause themselves by their fighting propensities.

> Since dogs delight to bark and bite,
> When they get hurt it serves them right.

Quarter on the enemy.

It is a wise thing to make missions and other good works as nearly as possible self-supporting. It has been done in several cases; and in the process many good purposes have been answered, for the people have been trained to independence and generosity.

"Queen Elizabeth is dead."

A sarcastic remark when stale news is reported.

Queries from queer quarters may be left to answer themselves.

If we are to answer all questions, we have our work cut out for the next thousand years. We are bound to tell the truth if we tell anything; but we are not bound to tell anything at all. Here is a neat answer which says nothing :—

> Said a mortgagee to a mortgagor,
> What do you want my money for ?
> Said the mortgagor to the mortgagee,
> Lend me the money, and then you'll see.

Quick and well seldom go together.

"Hurry and Cunning are the two apprentices of Dispatch and Skill; but neither of them ever learns his master's trade."—*Colton.*

Quick believers need broad shoulders.

To support the burden of all which they accept as gospel.

Quick believers will need wide swallows.

To take in all that is told them. Better be a little inhospitable when the story looks like a traveller; for if you take it in, it may take you in. The foolish believeth every word, but the wise man enquireth.

Quick removals are slow prosperings.

Two removals are as bad as a fire. He who shifts his place often, is like a tree frequently transplanted, whose fruit is very small.

" Change for spite and rue it,
And wish you could undo it."

Quick steps are best over miry ground.

When you come into a dangerous place, and must needs pass through it, use all speed, and be away as soon as possible. If in the course of your calling you must needs speak with bad men, have done with them as soon as ever you can, and be on your guard all the while. A person caught in a shower puts up his umbrella, and mends his pace; so should we protect ourselves, and hurry on.

Quick to borrow is always slow to pay.

Those, on the other hand, who will never borrow till they are driven to it, are the people who are eager to get out of debt.

Quickly come is often quickly go.

Easy gainings make easy spendings. Is this why a spendthrift is said to be *fast?* He came by his money on a sudden, and as suddenly he makes it vanish.

Quiet is sweet when riot is over.

Nobody values peace more than he who knows the evil of contention. "Then are they glad, because they be quiet."—Ps. cvii. 30.

Quiet sleep feels no foul weather.

Once off into the land of Nod, we are to the east of Eden, and care not whether it rains or snows. *Bed*ford is a quiet place.

Quiet sleep is the best patent medicine.

What a blessing to be able to enjoy it ! *Hood* calls bed—

> " That heaven upon earth to the weary head ;
> But a place that to name would be ill-bred
> To the head with a wakeful trouble—
> 'Tis held by such a different lease !
> To one, a place of comfort and peace,
> All stuffed with the down of stubble geese,
> To another with only the stubble ! "

Quit not certainty for hope.

Better a sure shilling than a sovereign in the clouds, to come or not to come. Never trust promising appearances so as to give up what you have realized.

**Quit your pots, and your potations ;
Yield to wisdom's exhortations.**

" Will you take something ? " said a teetotaler to a friend standing near a tavern. " I don't care if I do," was the reply. " Well," said the teetotaler, " let's take a walk."

Quizzing is pleasant, but it is a game which two can play at.

This is a bit of Judge Halyburton's humour, and he practically illustrated it in his own way. For a very clever fellow to be quietly taken in while he thinks he is showing his superiority to others, is a merited chastisement which is likely to do him good.

Quoth the dog to the Bishop, "Every man to his trade."

A capital specimen of impudence, cool as a cucumber. We have met with observations quite as cheeky from very small puppies.

Sayings of a more Spiritual Sort.

**Quick, quick, in holy things ;
For flying time has lightning wings.**

> Choose, O youth, the narrow way,
> Flee at once from sin and sorrow ;
> Say not, 'tis too soon to-day,
> Lest it be too late to-morrow.

Quickened by grace, quicken your pace.

AGGED colts may make handsome horses.

But they will need breaking in, and a good deal of curry-comb. Never despair of a boy because he has high spirits. This will sober down into quiet energy.

Rags are the livery of laziness.

They may come of blameless poverty, but they seldom do; for the industrious poor patch and mend.

> Thou barefooted lout !
> Why not cobble and clout ?

Rainbow at night is the shepherd's delight,
Rainbow in the morning gives the shepherd warning.

These weather signs vary according to the place, and do not apply universally. Other weather prophets foresee rain when—

> "Last night the sun went pale to bed,
> The moon in halos hid her head ;
> The boding shepherd heaves a sigh,
> For see, a rainbow spans the sky ! "

Rainy days will come; prepare for them.

Just as bees store honey against the coming of winter.

> Wise saving is not mean : the best of men may see
> That rainy day which surely comes to man and bee.

Rainy days will surely come;
Take your friend's umbrella home.

We see in the shops " *Umbrellas Recovered.*" We should like to recover those we have lent; but to return an umbrella is a lost art. A plain-spoken preacher delivered the following from his desk : " I would announce to the congregation that, probably by mistake, there was left at the meeting-house this morning a small cotton umbrella, much damaged by time and wear, and of an exceeding pale blue colour, in place whereof was taken a very large black silk umbrella of great beauty. Blunders of this sort, my brethren, are getting a little too common." There is nothing so rigidly Catholic as an umbrella, it keeps Lent the year round.

Raise no more devils than you can lay.

Do not provoke animosities which you cannot pacify, nor set in motion elements of disorder which you will be unable to control. It is easy to open the cages of wild beasts and let them loose ; but who will coax tigers back again ?

Rake not the bottom of an old canal.

Old quarrels and old charges are best left alone. Raise no unsavoury odours. If evil will die, let it die.

Rank folly is a weed which often grows in the ranks of fashion.

And elsewhere too. Whether the grass be long or short, this green-stuff is sure to grow. There is a rather rude verse which brings this matter very closely home :—

Of fools the world is full,
Whom if you would not see,
Follow one simple rule,
Effectual it will be.
Alone you must remain,
And, as you hate an ass,
Excuse my being plain,
Quick! Smash your looking-glass.

Rare birds are sure to be noticed.

More was at first made of a black swan than of all the royal birds on the Thames. Something eccentric and out of the common soon commands attention; yet wise men value not things by their rarity, but by their real worth.

Rash presumption is a ladder, which will break the mounter's neck.

Who climbs too high may break his neck:
Let this thy pert presumption check.

Rashness is not valour.

It has for a while led to the same sort of action as that which comes of true courage, but it will not bear the test of time.

Rather look on the good of evil men than on the evil of good men.

It is a great thing to have an eye for goodness everywhere; but it is a disease to be always spying out the faults of the truly excellent. See most of the least, and least of the worst in your fellows.

Rather the egg to-day than the hen to-morrow.

Present advantage is thus set above future gain. This proverb is true, or not true, according to its application.

Rats play a rare game
When cats are too tame.

If authority does not show its power, the lovers of disorder will play their pranks. Why have we cats if they are afraid of rats?

Raw leather will stretch.

There's a good deal of it in use for making consciences just now.

Awkward corners of truth away they will whittle ;
If their creed does not suit, they will stretch it a little.

Read men as well as books.

Or else the most interesting records will be unknown to you. Read man as well as manuscripts. Be not mere book-worms. "The proper study of mankind is man." There is wisdom in that sentence of *Hobbes,* "If I had read as much as other men, I should have been as ignorant."

Reading maketh a full man, conversation a ready man, and writing an exact man.

Ready money has the pick of the market.

Those whose pay is questionable will have questionable wares sent to them. Nobody is eager to press the best of his goods upon long-winded purchasers.

Ready money gets the first ;
Doubtful credit takes the worst.

Ready money is a wonderful medicine.

To the estate it is a balm, to the temper a calm, to no wise man a harm. Go thou with money in thy palm, it worketh like a charm. Another proverb is : Ready money works great cures.

Ready money is sweet as honey.

So says the tradesman : it enables him to replenish his stock, and turn over his capital. Credit is not creditable to those who have cash. Everybody is glad to get his money ; he calls it sugar.

Ready money is the secret of economy.

For people who pay know where they are, and are able to regulate their expenses by knowing how the money goes. Besides, they buy better. Yet true is the old proverb, " Ready money will away." Even on cash principles money evaporates very fast.

Reason governs the wise man, and cudgels the fool.

The wise obey reason, and so are rightly led ; but the fool refuses obedience to common sense, and therefore before long he endures remorse, which is repentance armed with a scourge of thorns and briars. Reason binds the man; but he is never more free than when he yields to its constraint.

Reason is most reasonable when it leaves off reasoning on things above reason.

This saying of *Sir Philip Sydney* deserves such frequent quotation as to make it proverbial, if it be not already so. The mysteries of faith are not contrary to reason, but they are so much above and beyond it that they can only be received by faith.

Reason lies between bridle and spur.

The medium between reserve and resolve, between restraint and energy, is hard to hit ; but it is the golden mean.

> Between the bridle and the spur
> How very apt we are to err !

Reason not with the great :
'Tis a perilous gait.

It requires much courage to argue with those on whom you are dependent : you may be proving away your bread and butter. Still, if truth requires it, we dare face a parliament of kings.

Reasoning often banishes reason.

Argument confuses where men are not anxious after truth. It is easy for reason to throw dust into its own eyes.

Rebukes ought to have a grain more of sugar than of salt.

Or else they may be rejected and resented. Yet it is not easy to sugar the pill of reproof. Let us try to do so, for rebuke is sharp enough in itself without the addition of needless severity. Rebuke with soft words and hard arguments.

Reckless youth makes rueful eld.

When the sins of youth lie in a man's bones in his later years, he has bitter cause to mourn his folly ; but his mourning cannot remove the consequences of his early faults. Wild oats sown in our young days make an awful harvest in the autumn of life.

Recklessness soon wrecks an estate.

Let us therefore act with thoughtfulness, be our estate little or great, for we don't want it wrecked.

> Though some men do as do they would,
> Let the thrifty do as do they should.

Red Lane needs watching.

That is to say, we must be careful of what goes down our throat. "Doctor," said a patient to one of the great hydropathic lights of Malvern, whom ill-health had obliged him to consult, "Do you think that a little spirits, now and then, would hurt me very much?" "Why, no, sir," said the doctor, deliberately, "I do not know that a little, now and then, would hurt very much; but, sir, if you don't take any, you won't be hurt at all."

Reform your wife's husband.

I mean your children's father. Try your level best to make your own roof-tree "the Reformer's Tree in the Home Park."

Regard the world with open eye,
For sure the blind eat many a fly.

This is not the world to be blind in. We need all our wits about us, or we shall be killed, cooked, and eaten before we know it. If we escape so dire a fate, still the clouds of flies will half choke us if we do not see them and brush them off.

Rejoice in little, shun what is extreme :
A boat floats safest in a little stream.

Relatives are best with a wall between them.

Else they take sundry liberties; these liberties are resented, and the fat gets into the fire. Family quarrels arise out of freedoms which are very naturally taken, but are not quite so naturally liked by those upon whom they encroach.

Religion is the best of armour, and the worst of cloaks.

As a defence it wards off ten thousand ills; but as a pretence it is the worst form of deceit.

Religion lies more in *walk* than in *talk*.

People should prefer the "w" to the "t." Words are all very fine, but character has far more weight in it.

Remove an old tree, and it will wither and die.

It is not well to make great changes in old age.

Remove not the ancient land-marks which thy fathers have set up.

A curse was solemnly pronounced by the law of Moses on those who did so. (See Deut. xxvii. 17.) Neither openly nor secretly were the boundary stones to be shifted. The old land-marks of truthful doctrine, holy practice, and lawful custom, should be kept in their appointed places. Mark the men who move land-marks, and move yourself away from them.

Renewed spirits can forego ardent spirits.

> Raised from the dead I quit my *beer;*
> My joys from canted *w(h)ines* are clear;
> Made free, I am no *brand(i)ed* slave;
> No *spirit* vault's my spirit's grave.

**Rent and taxes never sleep;
Up and earn them, lest you weep.**

No three letters are so remunerative to a tradesman as N.R.G. He must use them or run short of L.S.D.

Repair the gutter, or you'll have to repair the whole house.

The wet will run down the walls, or get through the roof, and the damage will be most serious. Remember the stitch in time in connection with every form of business.

Repentance costs dear.

That is to say, it is far better to avoid a wrong action than to do it, and have to repent of it. It is a great waste of time and labour to go the wrong road, even if you are happy enough to return from it into the right path. Do not buy repentance at a high rate by rushing into sin.

Repentance is never too soon.

It is a blessing that it is never too late, if it be but true. It is the heart's medicine, and the sooner it deals with the disease of sin the better. To delay repentance is sinful and dangerous.

> Repent, or God will break the thread
> By which thy doom hangs o'er thy head.

Report makes crows blacker than they are.

No doubt an ill story grows, and the worst are made out worse than they really are. They say that even the devil is not so bad as he is painted; but of *that* we have great doubt.

Report makes the wolf bigger than he is.

Thus men are needlessly frightened, and the wolf has all the more chance to worry the sheep. No good comes of exaggeration. Yet the wolves of the present day are able, by their sheeps' coats, to make themselves out to be no wolves at all; and our great danger is not from undue alarm, but from deadly indifference.

Reputation is commonly measured by the acre.

The multitude judge of a man's worth by what he is worth, and if he has a great estate he must needs be a great man. It is not always for what he has done, but for how much he owns, that a man is considered a man of mark. According to this, the best judge of character is a land-surveyor. Squire Broadacres shall be asked to take the chair at our next public meeting, though he is mute as a mackerel; for he speaks guineas.

Resist the devil, but flee from lust.

Fénelon makes Mentor say to his young disciple, in the island of Calypso, "Fly, Télémaque, fly! There remains no way of conflict, but by flight." By this means Joseph conquered. It is the only mode of conquest in this most seductive of conflicts.

Respect a man, that you may make him respect himself.

In this way some may be raised out of the gutter. Your generous treatment will make them feel their manhood. Treat them like men, and they will try to live up to your idea of them.

Respect yourself, or no one else will respect you.

Play the fool on your own account, and others will play the fool with you. Paul said to Timothy, "Let no man despise thy youth." Despise it they will if the young man despises it.

Rest and let rest; bless and be blest.

Rest, but do not rust.

Rest in order to future work; and so time and manage the vacation that it shall not make you vacant. When you are called to do nothing, do it heartily. Rest as hard as you can, that you may the sooner get to your work again, and do it better than ever.

Rest comes from unrest, and unrest from rest.

When the heart has been troubled for sin, it is driven to repose in Jesus; and, on the other hand, when the soul has for a while rejoiced in peace, it is too apt to grow carnally secure, and then it falls into distress almost as bitter as at the first.

Rest is honest when work is finished.

Then rest is deserved, and so it may be freely enjoyed.

" Toiling—rejoicing—sorrowing,
Onward through life he goes ;
Each morning sees some task begun,
Each evening sees it close ;
Something attempted, something done,
Has earned a night's repose."
Longfellow's " Village Blacksmith."

Rest is won only by work.

The lazy man idles away his time, but does not rest : even if he has a holiday, he is restless. The science of rest is quite beyond the reach of the non-worker.

Rest on the Sabbath, or you will be worse than a slave.

" A Sabbath well spent
Brings a week of content,
With rest for the toils of the morrow ;
But a Sabbath profaned,
Whate'er may be gained,
Is sure to be followed by sorrow."

Revenge is sweet when it avenges injury with love.

Any other form of revenge is bitter. Revenge of a wrong only makes another wrong. To heap kindness on an enemy is after the manner of God.

The sandal-tree, most sacred tree of all,
Perfumes the very axe which works its fall.

Rich enough is he who does not want.

" A man contented's greatly rich,
Possessed of e'er so small ;
But not contented, though most rich,
He poorest is of all."

Rich men have no faults.

Say, rather, they have no friend kind enough to tell them of their faults. Their spots are covered by their money, in the judgment of those who wish to get something out of them. Yet riches sometimes cause arrogance, and a man with a big purse is apt to grow purse-proud. This sort of bumptiousness is a fault of the most contemptible kind.

Riches adorn the house, but virtue adorns the man.

It enters into the very being of the man, and is a beauty of the highest order.   Yet *Herrick* very properly complains—

How rich a man is, all desire to know,
But none enquire if good he be or no.

Riches and cares are inseparable.

The care to get, to keep, to increase, to invest, to transmit : these and innumerable other worms gnaw at the heart which is the slave of wealth.   Riches are the shell, and the kernel is care.   High stations have heavy duties.   Why long to be burdened with a lump of clay, and a load of care?   *Isaac Walton* says : "Cares that are the keys that keep those riches hang often so heavily at the rich man's girdle that they clog him with weary days and restless nights, even when others sleep quietly."

Riches are not his who gathers them, but his who uses them.

Why starve yourself to feast an unknown heir?

Riches are often abused, but never refused.

Sages decry them and desire them.   They say, "Riches rule the roost"; yet all men wish them to roost on their tree.   *Colton* says, "Many speak the truth when they say that they despise riches and preferment; but they mean the riches and preferment possessed by *other men*."

Riches are unstable;
Beauty will decay;
But faithful love will ever last
Till death drive it away.

Brooks says, "Riches are like bad servants, whose shoes are made of running leather, and will never tarry long with one master. Love, however, suffereth long, and is kind; and where it fixes its abode it remains till death."   A Scotch proverb says, "Riches are got with pain, kept with care, and lost with grief."

Riches have made more men covetous than covetousness hath made men rich.

Riches, like manure, do no good till they are spread.

One wonders how men can find such pleasure in hoarding.   Surely it must be as one says, "They are manured to it."   Riches must be spread abroad.   Fork them out.   Dispurse and disperse.   What heaps now lie reeking up offensively to heaven!   If generosity does not use them, death will diffuse them.

Riches take to themselves wings and fly away.

Do not let yours thus depart. Clip their wings, and send the feathers to the Stockwell Orphanage, to feather the nest of the five hundred orphans. Address, C. H. Spurgeon, "Westwood," Upper Norwood.

It is a sweet thought, that while riches may take wings and fly *from* us, grace takes wings and flies *with* us to heaven.

Hugh Stowell Brown remarks most wisely: "Riches do often make to themselves wings and fly away; and they are not the wings of a goose, that can hardly fly over a hedge; nor the wings of a pigeon, that will return to its dovecote; nor the wings of any common or weakly bird, that might not fly fast, or might drop the prey from its bill; no, they are the wings of an eagle, a rapacious bird, a strong bird, a bird of swift and lofty and untiring flight, a bird not easily shot when flying, not easily reached when in its aerie; there is little hope of recovering what the eagle carries away; and thus riches lost are, as a rule, lost for ever."

Riches will ourselves abuse,
Unless we rightly learn to use.

If we hoard them for ourselves, they are like waters collected in a stagnant pool, breeding all manner of evils; but if by generosity we let them flow abroad they become a fountain of fertility. Wisdom is needed with wealth. The Greeks of old said—

"Abundance is a blessing to the wise:
The use of riches in discretion lies.
Learn this, ye men of wealth! A heavy purse
In a fool's pocket is a heavy curse."

Ride on, but look before you.

Go ahead, but know which way you are going, lest you rush to ruin. Keep your eyes in advance of your nose.

Right, if pulled too tight, turns to wrong.

Sometimes it is right to waive a right; especially when it would involve hardship to push your claim to an extreme. Rights should fit like bracelets, and not grip like handcuffs.

Right mixture makes good mortar.

Due proportion and thorough blending of various graces make up a good character. Also in forming a partnership a wise arrangement and a good spirit will secure lasting unity. In marriage a fit blend is almost everything.

Right wrongs no man.

He that is the gainer by right makes no man a loser, for no man can lose what is not rightfully his own. Right is right all round.

Rivers need a spring.

That they may begin they must have a source : that they may continue they must be supplied from flowing springs. A worthy course of life must have a holy motive to sustain it.

Rogues reckon all men rascals.

They know themselves, and they suppose none to be better than they themselves are. The dog who runs away with stolen meat thinks that every other dog would rob him of it. Men see themselves in other men's eyes. Innocence is not suspicious ; but guilt is always ready to turn informer.

Rome was not built in a day, but many are building it in the night.

Yet nobody seems to care. Protestants enter very faint protests, and Rome everywhere finds room enough for growth.

Roses fade away:
Thorns for ever stay.

This is a hard saying, and by no means true. Our sorrows pass away even as our joys. There is a Rose which never fades, and this takes away the sharpness of the thorns, both in life and death.

Rotten apples abide no handling.

When a matter is far gone in the wrong direction, people cannot bear you to mention it. "Let ill alone" is the motto of very many. The state of affairs is very bad, therefore you must not stir in it, nor even look at it. Remember who it was in the gospel that said, "Let us alone."

Rough nets are not the best bird-catchers.

And in the case of birds of the human order, the less of roughness the better. He that would win a soul must have a tender heart and a gentle tongue.

> Who scares the linnet
> Shall not win it.

Rub your sore eye with your elbow.

That is to say, don't rub it at all. So my father used to say to me at the dinner table, "Pick your teeth with your elbow"; that is, let them alone when in the company of others.

Rubs and snubs and drubs make the man.

They develop the hardier qualities, and prepare the man to bear prosperity should God be pleased to send it. As *Kingsley*, in his " Ode to the North-East Wind," says:

> " 'Tis the hard gray winter
> Breeds hard Englishmen."

Rue and balm grow in the same garden.

The sorrow and the succour, the cross and the comfort, are generally joined together.

> Our dangers and delights are near allies :
> From the same stem the rose and prickle rise.

Rule your children, or you'll ruin them.

Unruly children are not happy even as children, and when they grow up they prove a curse to all around. Break them in, or they will break out, and in the end break your hearts. An aged woman, speaking of the days when her children were all young and all around her, said, " *I let them be happy, but I aye keepit the crown on my head.*" In contrast to this it has been said that this is "the age of obedient parents."

Rule your temper, or it will ruin you.

No danger is greater than that which may come from an ungoverned temper. Better sleep on a bed of dynamite. This is harder for some than for others. " A grove of cactus in the tropics is almost sure to swarm with serpents ; and there are natures in which bad passions breed and multiply as if that were the law of their being. It is easy for a man who is free naturally from such pests to look down on the unfortunates, and scourge them with rebukes. 'I wish,' said a certain cool, phlegmatic old gentleman to his neighbour, 'that you would govern your temper.' 'My dear sir,' was the answer, 'I control more temper in five minutes than you do in five years.' "—*Dr. Willcox.*

Run! run! Here's a cockney with a gun.

You are likely to be shot if you get within range ; unless you can keep near the game, so as to be aimed at, in which case you are as safe as the Bank of England.

Rust consumes more than use wears.

Leave a knife outdoors sticking in the earth, and it will be eaten up a hundred to one more than if it had been in constant use.

Sayings of a more Spiritual Sort.

Reason makes us men, grace makes us saints.

Unaided reason never rises to saintship; and yet there is the highest reason for being saintly.

Religion without Christ is a lamp without oil.

"The foolish took their lamps, but took no oil with them." Jesus says, "Without me ye can do nothing."

Religion without head is fire without wood.

It runs to superstition and fanaticism; and after blazing with fury, it dies down into ashes, which the wind carries away.

Religion without heart is a dead formality.

The heart is the life, the essence, the joy of it; and that gone, all is gone but the mere shell. "The puffing system is an advertisement of hollowness. He whose religion is ever on his lips, has seldom any of that valuable treasure in his heart; it keeps watch, like a liveried porter at his door, but there is nobody at home, and there is nothing to steal; if it were well lodged in his soul, he would not be so afraid of its escape."

Remember the shame of sin when tempted by the sweet of sin.

Repentance looks upon the past with a weeping eye, and upon the future with a watchful eye.

Repentance must be universal to be effectual.

Every sin is to be bewailed, and forsaken: one sin reserved will ruin all our hope. One leak will sink a ship; one bullet in the heart will kill a man; one sin delighted in will ruin a soul. *Brooks* says, "He that turns not from every sin, turns not aright from any one sin."

Resignation is putting God between one's self and one's grief.

Thus one is shielded in the best possible manner. Accept affliction, and the sharpness of it is gone.

Rest not till you rest in Christ.

> For any rest, short of Christ, is like the deadly pause of Lot's wife, which sealed her destruction.

Rest the body and feast the soul,
And keep for God the Sabbath whole.

> *Chateaubriand* says that during the time of the Revolution, when an attempt was made to substitute decades for Sabbaths, the peasants of France were in the habit of saying, "Our oxen know when Sunday comes, and will not work on that day."

"Retire, and read thy Bible to be gay."

Righteous men believe themselves to be sinners, and sinners believe themselves to be righteous.

> So says *Pascal*, in his "Pensées"; and his saying is true. The late Dr. —— did not satisfy, by his preaching, the Calvinistic portion of his flock. "Why, sir," said they, "we think you dinna tell us enough about renouncing our ain righteousness." "Renouncing your ain righteousness!" vociferated the doctor, "I never saw any ye had to renounce."

ADNESS and gladness take turn about.

Sunshine and shower
Make up life's hour.

Safe bind, safe find.

Have everything legally correct, and so be free from anxiety and dispute. But specially make things sure for eternity; for a flaw in your title to a mansion in the skies will be serious indeed.

Deeds for your lands you prove and keep with care,
Oh, that for heaven you but as careful were!

Safer on shore in an old cart than at sea in a new ship.

Yet our brave sailors don't think so. When they are out at sea they glory that they are safe from falling tiles and chimney-pots, and the horse does not run away with the cart, or fall down.

Saint Francis shaved himself before he shaved his brethren.

Reform should begin with the reformer himself. Yet personal reformation is often most distasteful. *Charles Kingsley* said, "I don't deny, my friends, that it is much cheaper and pleasanter to be reformed by the devil than by God, for God will only reform society on condition of our reforming every man his own self; while the devil is quite ready to help us to mend the laws and the parliament, earth and heaven, without ever starting such an impertinent and 'personal' request as that a man should mend himself."

Saint Monday is one of the devil's saints.

Truly "Saint Monday maketh many sinners."

Saint Swithin's day, if it doth rain,
For forty days it will remain.

Sheer superstition; yet so commonly repeated when July 15th comes round, that we must needs mention it. In *Poor Robin's Almanack* for 1697, this silly prognostication is given at length:

" In this month is St. Swithin's day,
On which, if that it rain, they say,
Full forty days after it will,
Or more or less some rain distil.
This Swithin was a saint, I trow,
And Winchester's bishop also,
Who in his time did many a feat,
As popish legends do repeat."

Salt never cries out that it is salty.

> So say the Creoles. True virtue never boasts. Fire never cries out "I burn." Goodness has no need to proclaim its own qualities.

Salt spilt is never all gathered.

> When wrong is done, you cannot undo it all ; and when anger is excited, and ill words spoken, it is hard to clear it all up, and put a complete end to the scandal.
>
> > When out of bag the cat is let
> > Its tail inside you cannot get.

Salute, and be saluted.

> All the world over this is the rule. As you do to others, others will do to you ; at least, in matters of courtesy. Bow and be bowed.

Same clothes every day
Make clouts for Sunday.

> It is a sad lack of economy to go on all the week without change of garments, and have no " Sunday go-to-meeting coat " ; but it would seem that in the olden times there were wasters of this sort.

Samson was a strong man, but even he could not pay money before he had it.

> Yet he took care, when he fell into debt to those who found out his riddle, that they were not long without the reward which he had promised them. It is true we cannot pay money before we have it, but we ought not to come under obligation to pay unless we see the means of doing so.

Sands form the mountains, moments make the year.

> *Dr. Stoughton* says, " As in money, so in time, we are to look chiefly to the smallest portions. Take care of the pence, and the pounds will take care of themselves. Take care of the minutes, and the hours and years will take care of themselves. Gold is not found in California for the most part in great masses, but in little grains. It is sifted out of the sand in minute particles, which, melted together, produce the rich ingots that excite the world's cupidity. So the spare pieces of time, the shreds, the odds and ends of time put together, may form a very great and beautiful work."

Sanguine men are seldom safe men.

> They reckon as assets all that they hope to get. They are all very well as acquaintances for a little cheering up ; but, if you follow their advice they will soon let you down. They may be cheerful travelling companions, but they will never do for bankers.

Satan is a lion to those that fly him, and a fly to those that face him.

> Submit, and he roars ; resist, and he flees.

Satan is wiser than in days of yore,
And tempts by making rich, not making poor.

> Assuredly there are more perils to most men in wealth than in poverty. It is easier to keep your footing in the low dungeon than on the lofty tower.

Satan keeps school for neglected children.

> The schools and schoolmasters of the devil are very many: a book might be written about the Satanic method of instruction. When a lady once told Archbishop Sharpe that she would not communicate religious instruction to her children until they had attained to years of discretion, the shrewd prelate replied, "Madam, if you do not teach them, the devil will!"

Satan promises the best, and pays the worst.

> He is a liar from the beginning. The foolish are deceived by him. "I have read of King Canute," says an excellent minister, "that he promised to make him the highest man in England who should kill King Edmund, his rival; which, when one had performed, and expected his reward, he commanded him to be hung on the highest tower in London. So Satan promises great things to people in pursuit of their lusts, but he puts them off with great mischief in the end. The promised crown turns to a halter; the promised comfort to a torment ; the promised honour into shame; the promised consolation into desolation ; and the promised heaven into a hell."

Satan shows the bait, but hides the hook.

> He is far too crafty to let men see the naked sin, or the unveiled punishment. He covers the hook with the bait of pleasure, or profit, or philosophy, or progress, or even piety.

Satan's palace—the gin palace.

> Doubtless he is the real king of the place where evil spirits are retailed. His is the blue ruin, his the fire-water, his the reeling brain, and the delirium tremens. A pamphlet having been written to prove that temperance and other societies were the seven last plagues predicted by John, a tavern-keeper in America got a supply, and in front of his bar posted a bill bearing this inscription— "*The Seven Last Plagues sold here.*" Some of his customers took the hint, and bought no more of them.

"Saturday night is my delight,
    And so is Sunday morning;
But Sunday noon comes round too soon,
    And so does Monday morning."

Either this is the song of the lazy man who loves to escape from work, or of the truly devout man, to whom even the eve of the Sabbath is precious. The Lord's day should begin on the previous evening if possible, for the blessing on the seventh day has never been withdrawn. Never is the Sabbath too long: we would like to clip the wings of time to cause the holy hours to linger. We dread to go back into the cold world again.

Sauce for the goose is sauce for the gander.

What is fair for women is fair for men. Our laws should be equal, though they are not. In social life we should deal evenly with both sexes. Women and men are very much alike in goodness, especially women. Let us hope that men and women are not both geese, as the proverb insinuates.

Save a thief from prison, and he'll pick your pocket.

He is incapable of gratitude from his very nature, and will prey upon his benefactor as soon as upon anyone else. Warm a viper in your bosom, and its first act is to sting you.

Save me from a boar, a boor, and a bore.

Three dreadful creatures, alike in name, and equally objects of dread to those who know them.

Save me from my friends.

These are often more injurious than enemies. Some through their flattery, others by implicating us in their imprudence, and others by what they call their candour—a smiling cruelty which reminds one of threading a worm on a hook tenderly, as if you loved it.

"But of all plagues that heaven in wrath can send,
    Save, save, oh, save me from the candid friend!"

Save sixpence, and lay the foundation of a fortune.

Most great fortunes have been commenced by littles, and have grown by slow degrees.

Come to London with half-a-crown;
And by-and-by you'll own a town.

Save something for the sore foot.

For yourself, when you cannot move in so lively a way as you now do ; and for others, that you may help those who are incapable of work.   In order to achieve a fair measure of saving, old writers warn men against the three B's :—Back, Belly, and Building. Fine clothes, fine tables, and fine houses cause heavy expenses. Wastefulness is a sin against that providence of which thrift is a humble imitation.

Save while you have, and give while you live.

It is too late to begin saving when all is gone, or to become a generous giver after you are dead.   Be your own executor ; for very frequently, if money is left for a good purpose, the purpose gets no good from it.

Save yourself pains by taking pains.

To do a thing thoroughly well is the easiest plan after all ; for if you have to do it over again, you will wish you had done it well at first.   Take trouble that you may be saved trouble.

Saved pence make men rich, but saved minutes make them wise.

It is more needful to be economical of time than of money.   We may get more money, but we cannot buy more time : it is not in the market.   Goldsmiths save even the sweepings of their shops : utilize the fragments of your time.   Great things can be accomplished by the persevering use of odd minutes.

Saving is a greater art than getting.

Professor Bluntschli, the famous jurist, celebrated his seventieth birthday by sending a present of seven hundred francs to Zurich, his native city, which was to be expended in buying money-boxes for the children of the working-classes in the schools, "in order to train them," as he says, "by the regular laying by of their little savings, to begin the collection of a small capital early in life."

Say " God help me " ; but don't lie on your back.

Remember how Hercules advised the rustic to put his own shoulder to the wheel, and get the cart out of the slough.

Say less in thy promise than thou dost intend ;
Surprise with thy bounty, and gladden thy friend.

This is much better than promising acres, and giving only the scrapings from your muddy boots.   He who is better than his word, is better than the man whose words end in words.

Say little, write less, print least.

Or better, print none at all. It would be a great relief to this press-ridden nation if this advice could be enforced. The following motto for a "waste basket" appeared in the *Atlantic's* "Contributors' Club" :—

" If all the trees in all the woods were men,
And each and every blade of grass a pen ;
If every leaf on every shrub and tree
Turned to a sheet of foolscap ; every sea
Were changed to ink, and all earth's living tribes
Had nothing else to do but act as scribes,
And for ten thousand ages, day and night,
The human race should write, and write, and write,
Till all the pens and paper were used up,
And each great inkstand was an empty cup,
Still would the scribblers clustered round its brink
Call for more pens, more paper, and more ink."

Say " No," before you know it to your cost.

Little by little men are drawn on by seductive arts, till they are seriously involved. If they had but manliness enough to say " No," they would not be drawn in by schemers.

"Nay," *John*, "Nay," *John*, that's what you must say, *John*,
Whenever you are asked to drink, or you'll be led astray, *John*.
Say that though you are not old,
Nor yet so very wise, *John*,
Yet what is right, and good, and true,
You're old enough to prize, *John*.
Let the people drink who will,
But when they come to you, *John*,
Boldly say, "I've signed the pledge,
And mean to keep it too," *John*.

Say not all the say;
Let others share the day.

Do not imitate Dr. Johnson, who would have all the talk for two hours, then rub his hands and say, "What a splendid conversation we've had !" Treat your friends in conversation as you would at table, when you are carving :—

"Give no more to every guest,
Than he's able to digest :
And that you may have your due,
Let your neighbour carve for you."

If they listen to you, take your turn in listening to them. Most people like the sound of their own voices better than that of others ; at least, let them have a sandwich of your meat and their bread.

Say not all you know; do not all you can.

Keep a reserve. Always have a shot in the locker. If you fire all your cartridges, you will be out of the battle. Never talk yourself dry, nor run yourself lame.

Say, say; but you cannot unsay.

Therefore do not "say, say," without a good deal of consideration. Think twice before you speak once; and once having spoken, stand to your word as a brave soldier stands to his guns.

Say well when you may, but do well all the day.

Say-well and Do-well end with one letter:
Say-well is good, but Do-well is better.

Saying and unsaying
Are truth's decaying.

A sort of playing fast and loose with truth is the ruin of the mind's honesty. Say what you believe, and believe what you say.

Saying is one thing, doing is another.

Alas! with many there are miles of distance between their tongue and their hand. They promise you fairly, but they act foully, for never a word do they carry out as you understood it.

Scalded cats dread cold water.

Having felt the power of water when it is boiling, they are afraid of it in all conditions. A dog that burned his mouth with a hot pancake, was henceforth terrified at the sight of the frying pan, even when cold. Men would be more safe if they learned caution as readily as cats and dogs learn it.

Scandal is a serpent with wings.

It grovels, it stings, yet it flies as with wings.

" There is a lust in man no charm can tame,
  Of loudly publishing his neighbour's shame;
  On eagle's wings immortal scandals fly,
  While virtuous actions are but born and die."—*Harvey.*

Scandal will rub out like dirt when it's dry.

Let it alone, and never try to answer it. The more you meddle with it, the more will the wet mud be spread. Wait till you can use the clothes-brush with real effect.

Scorn no man's love,
'Tis from above.

Whatever the degree of the person who loves you, value the love itself as a true jewel. A dog kindly fawned on a person, but he did not notice him ; and when another day the dog bit him, it was no great wonder. Kindness despised curdles into ill will. The lion may yet need the mouse ; let him value his little friend.

Sea and air are common to all men.

So said *Queen Elizabeth.* But without something more, men would only have a flood to drown in, and a place to starve in.

Search in a hurry, and you'll have to search again.

It is wasted time to scamp the search. Examine drawers and boxes with care. To do your work thoroughly at once is the easiest and the cheapest method in the end.

> Yet 'tis a truth well-known to most,
> That whatsoever thing is lost,
> We search it, ere it come to light,
> In every corner but the right.

Search the Scriptures, and let them search you.

In the Word of God you have a search-warrant for the whole Bible : " Search the Scriptures." From the Court of Conscience let us issue a warrant for the sacred Scripture to search our inmost souls.

Search thy friend for his virtues : thyself for thy faults.

The first is generosity, the other is faithfulness : both are justice.

Season should weigh with reason.

The occasion has much to do with the fitness of things. That which is good to-day may.not be so good to-morrow. There is a time for every purpose under heaven, and, out of the proper time, the purpose may be improper. Marriage in old age is like spring flowers in autumn.

> Fruit out of season,
> Gripes out of reason.

Season thy tongue with salt, not with pepper.

With cool truth, and not with hot wrath. Be sincere and sensible ; but not fierce and sarcastic. Too many use cayenne. A leading member of a church was talking with his pastor about an excellent, but somewhat aggressive lady of the parish. After descanting at length on her virtues, he concluded by saying : " In fact, she may be called the salt of the earth." " Yes," responded the clergyman, quickly, " and the pepper too."

Seat yourself in your place, and you will not be made to quit it.

Right will be on your side ; but if you seat yourself too high, you may be forced with shame to take the lowest room.

Second thoughts are best.

This is not always true. Generous impulses, which are often the first thoughts, are much to be preferred to the hard second, and second-class thoughts of selfish prudence, which smother the man's better self. The first thoughts of the generous are best; but, in the case of the rash, we would prefer the second and revised edition.

Secrets had better remain secrets.

The countryman in *Plutarch* was asked, by an inquisitive person, what he carried so closely covered in his basket. To this he wisely answered, "If I wished you to know what it is, I should not so carefully have covered it up." Why wish to see what thy neighbour desires to conceal ?

See, hear, consider, and say nothing.

Then you may hope to live in peace ; but is this the only thing worth considering ?

See to the carrying out of your dying will while you have a living will.

Be your own executor, and save both duties and disputes.

> Silver from the living
> Is gold in the giving :
> Gold from the dying
> Is but silver a-flying.
> Gold and silver from the dead,
> Turn too often into lead.

So said old *Fuller*, and he spake the truth. What infinite trouble has been made through wills which looked well enough, but turned out ill enough ! Mortmain is a mortifying foe to charitable legacies. Better give a thousand than bequeath a hundred.

See with your eyelids as well as with your eyes.

"Let thine eyes look right on, and let thine eyelids look straight before thee."—Prov. iv. 25. Sometimes see, and do not see. God has given you eyelids as well as eyes.

See what you see, and know what you know.

Don't be in doubt. Make sure, and be sure. Arouse your five wits to be undeniable witnesses for the truth.

See yourself in other men.

Especially in other men's faults and failures.

Seeing is believing.

But it is not those who stare most who see best. Eye-witness is the best of witness. In the Scriptural use of terms seeing is *not* believing, but believing is seeing.

Seed must be sown,
If crops are grown.

We shall get nothing without using the proper means.

Don't expect to gather corn,
If from sowing you've forborne.

Seek not a physician for every qualm.

He who must be physicked for every pain will soon be ill indeed. He that must see a doctor every time his stomach aches, will have a consumption in his purse, and in his body something worse.

Seek not a name, but have an aim.

Have a noble aim in life, but let it not be merely to get thyself renown among men. "What's in a name?"

Seek that first which is first.

That which is real substance should have the preference of the shadows of time.

Some there be that shadows kiss :
Such have but a shadow's bliss.

Seek the love that hath no wings ;
Follow pleasures without stings.

Sensual pleasures are like to those locusts mentioned in the Revelation ix. 7, the crowns upon whose heads are said to be only "as it were crowns like gold." In everything they were but as this, and as that, till we come to verse ten, and then we read, "there were stings in their tails." These were not "as it were," but they were killing facts. There is nothing real about the pleasure of sin, the reality lies in the punishment of it.

Seek till you find, and you'll not lose your labour.

If the search is worth beginning it is worth continuing. Perseverance is the practical way of expressing our conviction that we have been acting wisely. To give over is to lose what we have wrought. Stick-to-it finds the hidden treasure.

Seen or unseen
Always be clean.

>A dirty child of God !   How can it be ?

Seethe stones in butter the broth will be good.

>That's all : the stones will be hard as ever.   Surround bad men with wealth and honour, and their possessions and glories will be desirable ; yet the men themselves will contribute nothing to the goodness of their surroundings, but remain base and ignoble.

Seldom at church, he'd such a busy life ;
But duly sent his family and wife.

>A common practice.   The man is self-condemned : he owns that the worship is good by sending his family ; but for staying away himself he is without excuse.

Seldom poke another's fire,
Or you may rouse his burning ire.

>One must be very much at home indeed before he may venture to use the poker in another's house.   Unwise persons who rush in where their betters fear to tread, deserve to overhear the remarks made by the housewife when they are gone.

Seldom seen, soon forgotten.

>One must keep himself in evidence if he desires to be favourably remembered.   If you advertise, do it on a liberal scale.

>>If you would boil your business pot,
>>Advertisements must keep it hot.

Self is always at home.

>Yes, a man is always alive to his own interest.   You can always get his attention to this important point.   One minds number one.

Self loves itself best.

>" What must I do to get a picture of the one whom I love best ? " said a mean man to a friend who knew him only too well.   " The easiest way," was the reply, " is to sit for your own portrait."

Self-conceit is self-deceit.

>He who thinks much of himself thinks too much of himself : he mistakes his new farthing for a sovereign ; but it is worth none the more for his silly opinion.

Self-preservation is the first law of nature.

This makes men bear the ills of life. Alas! this law sours into selfishness, and makes men careless how they tread down others so that they can take care of themselves.

Self-seekers are self-losers.

" Whosoever will save his life shall lose it."—Matt. xvi. 25.

Self-will cannot please itself.

A man who is doggedly determined to do whatever he likes, does not even like to bow to his own will, but hesitates for fear that, in having his own way, he should be forfeiting his liberty to take twenty other ways. It reminds us of the verse about the English-man's dress : he is represented as saying ;

> " I'm an Englishman, and I stand here,
> And I don't know what clothes I will wear ;
> Now I will have this, now I will have that,
> Now I will have I don't know what."

Sell honestly, but never sell honesty.

If a profit can be made, never mind what you deal in ; but never part with a grain of principle, even if the world could be gained by it.

Sell not your fowls on a rainy day.

Then they look wretched and draggled. One may as well present one's goods at their best; and when they are undergoing a necessary process which injures their appearance we had better wait a while.

Sell your wheat at market price,
And keep it not for rats and mice.

Hoarding of wheat is senseless ; and is sure to bring a bad name with it. " He that withholdeth corn, the people shall curse him." The Africans say, " Mice eat the miser's corn." Mice are the miser's misery.

Selling at a great sacrifice usually means sacrificing the customers.

There may be genuine sales of goods greatly at a loss, but it does not look very likely, and the probability is that the buyers will be sold as well as the goods. On the other hand, it is hardly the right thing to be looking out to get articles at less than their worth. Is it not a sort of stealing ? Are not under-price buyers as bad as the sweaters who have to supply their greed ?

Send a portion to the needy,
Lest through wealth thy soul grow greedy.

> Men cannot safely and healthily possess large properties unless they habitually give away considerable amounts to the poor and to the cause of God.

Send hearers away, not loathing, but longing.

> Long sermons only make people long for the end of them; the best discourses are those which leave us longing for more of the same matter.   Hear what a sermon should be:

> > " It should be brief : if lengthy, it will steep
> > Our hearts in apathy, our eyes in sleep.
> > The dull will yawn, the chapel lounger doze,
> > Attention flag, and memory's portals close."

Send not for a hatchet to break an egg.

> Don't deal with trifles in the grandiose style.   Don't alarm yourself and summon an army to attack a maggot.   Adapt means to an end, and let not the labour be worth ten times more than the result.

Send you to the sea, and you'll not find salt water.

> You are so utterly blind and stupid, that you cannot discover that which is all around you.   If you were surrounded by reasoning, you would not see an argument.   If you had your Bible before you, you would not see the Lord Jesus Christ in it.

Separation is hard; but every two must come in two.

> Happy are they who live together in perfect harmony through a long life : but even these must be divided.

> > One in purpose, one in heart,
> > Yet the mortal stroke must part.

September blow soft
Till the fruit's in the loft.

> Lest the fruit should be blown off from the trees, and in falling be bruised so that it cannot be stored for winter use.

Seriousness should not be a covering for foolishness.

> Some people are as solemn as owls, and about as stupid.   *Cowper* wrote of one in his day :—

> > " A shallow brain behind a serious mask :
> > An oracle within an empty cask."

Service unrequested is generally unrequited.

> For proffered service stinks. Men begin to inquire why it is thus presented; and, not perceiving a reasonable motive, they imagine evil. Yet I, for one, have not found the proverb true; but, on the contrary, having gratefully accepted spontaneous help, have felt very thankful for it, and have been justified in my gratitude.

Set a beggar on a horse, and he'll ride it to death.

> Some say to a worse place still. No doubt those who are the least acquainted with luxury go in for it with a vengeance whenever they have a chance. Nobody is so extravagant as a pauper when he once gets a little money to lay out.

Set a frog on a golden stool,
Away it hops to reach the pool.

> It is out of its element, and returns to its proper condition as soon as it can. Official etiquette is terribly irksome to certain humans as well as to froggies, and persons with simple tastes, and natural habits, are glad enough to get off their golden stools.

Set a stout heart to a steep hill.

> Say, I mean to climb it, by the help of God. It is wonderful how little hill is left when faith has resolved to reach the top. Everything gives way before a steadfast purpose.

> > Pluck made the gap,
> > Push got through it;
> > Plod had good hap,
> > Pith stuck to it.

Set a thief to catch a thief.

> He knows where to look, and when to expect the rascal. Yet one does not like this sort of thief-catching: it is too much like taking the devil into one's pay.

Set hard heart against hard hap.

> There is nothing so hard but it may be cut by something harder. A resolution like a diamond would bore through a mountain, even if it were all of granite.

Set not thy foot to cause the blind to fall;
Nor daub the dead with slander's bitter gall.

> These are two inexcusable offences. We are to protect the blind, and guard the reputation of the departed.

Shall goslings teach the goose to swim?

Often enough they try it. Just out of the egg, with bits of shell on their heads, they open school for the old birds, and talk of modern natation and the progress of aquatic locomotion. The Africans say, "Every monkey's grandmother was a fool," and no doubt most young monkeys think so; but their grandmothers see that the folly is pretty plain further down in the family.

Shall the devil have the wine, and God the lees?

'Tis often so: the best part of life is wasted in sin, and only the declining years are spent for the Lord.

Shallow streams make most din.

The less there is in a man the more noise he makes about it. Perhaps he is afraid that no one will think anything of him unless he calls attention to himself. Bang! Bang! It's only powder.

Shame comes to no man unless he himself help it on the way.

Nobody can be truly put to shame unless he has done something shameful. The innocent man may hold his head up and defy all the abuse that can be heaped on him.

Shame take him that shame thinks.

Honi soit qui mal y pense.

He that smells evil where there's none,
Will smell himself before he's done.

Share alike to-day, and share again to-morrow.

This is the leveller's motto. If we were all equal at this moment, one would spend all, and another would labour to increase his stock, and so the demand would arise for sharing again. Very just that!

What is a Communist? One who hath yearnings
For equal division of unequal earnings.
Idler or bungler, he's one who is willing
To fork out his penny and pocket your shilling.

Sharp appetites make clean tables.

None of your picking over the food, and cutting out little bits of fat and gristle when a fellow is hungry. It is a pleasure to see fellows eat who are sharp set: there's no nonsense about them.

She hath goods enough if she is good enough.

Property is not the main thing in a wife, but a good and amiable character. Neither is beauty the main consideration, for another saying is—"She is fair enough if she is good enough." Happy is the man who has found that measure of goodness in his partner of life which will secure blessedness to him and to his family.

> If fair of face be scant of grace,
> I find no grace in that fair face;
> But if the grace of God be there,
> Though plain the face, to me 'tis fair.

She that marries secretly is defamed openly.

People will have it that there was a reason for the concealment, and you need not wonder that they think so. When wedded people fear to have their marriage known they have concealed their own honour, and people doubt if all is right.

She would not have the walkers, and the riders have gone by.

The poorer sort of admirers were not good enough for her, and she was not good enough for the richer ones, and so she remains without a husband. She waited for Mr. Right, and she remains Miss Left, and will probably join the Woman's Rights Society.

She's better than she's bonny.

It is well when the character is more beautiful than the face. "She's black," said one, "but she has a sweet smack." If a woman cannot be said to be good-looking, yet it is better if we may say that she looks good. The Highlander blundered over our proverb, and said that his wife was bonnier than she was better.

Sheathing the sword does not heal the wound.

Or in another form, "Shutting up the knife does not cure the cut." To cease from slander is well; but this does not undo the harm which has been done. Who is to restore what has been burned? Even if you put the fire out, that question remains.

Sheep may fall into the mire; swine wallow in it.

Herein is a great difference between a fallen believer and a sinner acting according to his evil nature. The swallow may touch the stagnant pond with his wing, but he is soon up in the air: the duck revels in the foul element, for he is another sort of bird.

Shine like a light, but do not flash like lightning.

Be not ambitious to dazzle. A steady light is far more valued than the brilliant flash which startles and astounds, but goes out as soon as it comes out.

Ships fear fire more than water.

Water bears them up, but fire burns them up. It seems strange that a vessel should burn in the middle of the sea. It is sadly singular that men should perish with salvation all around them.

Ships leak: some amidships, some in the bows, some in the hold.

Men have faults of different orders; but a man quite without failing you have not yet met with.

Shirt sleeves are a noble uniform.

Industry bears for its coat of arms, a coat without arms.

Shoot me sooner than put me in a damp bed.

To put a man in a damp bed is little short of murder: nay, in some respects it would be better to kill a man outright than to injure him for life. Those who are itinerant preachers endure, among other imminent perils, "perils of damp beds."

Short cuts are often the longest way.

Especially short cuts to wealth: they usually end in the mire.

Short hair is soon brushed.

A little property is soon looked over; a small wage is soon laid out. Slender knowledge is speedily arranged, and a short speech is soon delivered.

Short pleasure may cost long sorrow.

And if we are delivered from the sins themselves, yet they often involve long and bitter repentances. Sinful pleasures are always dearly bought. Short the sin, but long the shame.

Short reckonings make long friends.

Towards men it will be wise to settle up at brief intervals, for then we shall feel free and independent. Towards our God it is needful to make frequent confession, and exercise constant faith. Daily we incur guilt, daily let us seek cleansing.

Short tempers often go with long tongues.

Then both the short and the long of it are hard to bear. "Double up your whip," said one to an angry talker. The tongue goes nineteen to the dozen when a man's monkey is up.

Show me a liar, and I will show you a thief.

The same evil of heart which makes a man false with his tongue, makes him false with his hand.

> He that to a lie will stick
> With pleasure would a pocket pick.

Show me a man without a spot,
I'll show a maid without a fault.

But not till then. In man, and maid, of human kind, no perfection we shall find.

Showers of repentance breed flowers of rejoicing.

Blessed drops which fall from the eye of penitence! Sweet flowers which spring in the garden of faith!

Shrouds have no pockets.

We brought nothing with us into the world, and it is certain that we can carry nothing out.

Shut up your mouth, or it will shut you up.

In certain cases it is sadly so. If some people could be gagged, they would get on, for silence catches the mouse; but with so much jaw they must ruin themselves, for open doors let out prosperity. Talk takes the value out of a servant. Who cares to hire a horse which keeps on neighing throughout the journey?

Sickness tells us what we are.

Then the very good-tempered man becomes touchy; patience, which was so assured, gives way to complaining; and courage yields to depression. See a man when he is ill to know how little a man he is. Great Cæsar cries for drink like a sick girl.

Sift him grain by grain, and you will find him all chaff.

Poor creature! There are some such, no doubt; but it is rather hard judgment. Is there no grain of hopefulness even in the worst we have ever met? Don't let the chaff blind our eyes.

Sighs fill no sails;
But prayer prevails.

Fretting and stewing do no real good, but prayer does wonders.

Sign nothing without reading,
Or else you'll soon be bleeding.

You may, without knowing it, sign away your estate, or become surety and have to pay, or you may slander a friend. Read carefully, and sign cautiously. Don't swallow the pudding while it is tied up in a bag.

Silence and reflection,
With circumspection,
Save from dejection.

Silence cannot be put in the papers.

Nor can it even be written down for private circulation. To say nothing, is to tease the slanderer, and baffle the gossip.

Silence is a fine ornament for a woman.

Or for a man either. He that can hold his tongue can hold his peace; and nothing is more worth holding than peace. A quiet spirit is said by the apostle to be of great price. "Do you love her still?" asked a judge of a fellow who applied to be divorced from his wife. "Yes, sir, I do; but the trouble is that she is never still for a moment." Query: Would he let her be still?

Silence is consent.

Not from a dumb man; nor of a surety from any man. Many a man is silent, not because he consents or dissents, but because he treats the whole question with utter contempt.

Silence is not golden when it is guilty.

He who stood speechless did not therefore escape. If a man is silent because he knows he is guilty, his silence is not commendable. Well may he be silent who has nothing to say. "We must give an account of idle silence, as well as of idle speech."

Silence scandal by silence.

It is the surest way. "Where no wood is, the fire goeth out." If you make no defence there is the less for the assailant to work upon. Dr. Henry Rink, the learned Dane, who has written the best book about the Eskimo, says that they show annoyance at an offence by silence. Let this Eskimo fashion prevail everywhere.

Should envious tongues some malice frame,
To soil and tarnish your good name,
Live it down!

Rail not in answer, but be calm;
For silence yields a rapid balm,
Live it down!

Silent sense is better than fluent folly.

> A quiet man is worth a dozen chattering monkeys.

> > Silence seldom causes harm :
> > Gossip raises great alarm.

Silken cords are fast binders.

> The cords of love outlast the bonds of force, the chains of interest, the ties of party, and the fetters of fear.

Silken tongue and hempen heart often go together.

> That is to say, in hypocrites, who would both hug you and hang you, butter you and eat you.

> > They give a kiss,
> > But mean a curse.

Silly birds eat the seed, but see not the net.

> So are the foolish beguiled by the pleasure of sin, and see not the deadly consequences which will surely follow.

Silly lasses linger long at looking-glasses.

> When there is nothing whatever to be seen but their own silliness, why should they be so long in seeing so little?

Silver keys open iron locks.

Simple must always serve.

> He is fit for nothing else, and, though he may be a fair servant, he will fail as a master.

> > From wit and wisdom wholly free,
> > Dog to another thou must be.

Sin begets sloth, and sloth begets sin.

> Thus they take turns in the parentage of each other. Vice leads to idleness, and idleness leads to vice.

Sin has many tools, but a lie is a handle which fits them all.

> By this it works its devices. Virtue and truth fit well, and so do vice and falsehood. Because there is a lie in his right hand, a man becomes dexterous in evil.

Sin is learned without going to school.

> It is the natural behaviour of the natural mind, the mother-tongue of the sons of Adam.

Sin is sin even if it be not seen.

> Secrecy does not screen, nor even diminish its wickedness. Yet many are sorry for being found out, who were never sorry for the sin which was found out.

Sin kisses, but kills.

> It is a sweet poison. Like a glittering sword, it is brightness to the eye, and death to the heart.

Sin, which drowned the old world, will burn this.

Sipping sour milk with a fork is the height of nonsense.

> *Punch* awards the palm of folly to the man who spends his very last shilling in buying a purse. There are others quite as bad, and one is for a dying man to live as if he were immortal.

Sir Hobbard de Hoy, be no longer a boy!

> Prove yourself a man, by manly deeds; put away childish things. Get wisdom within now the down's on your chin.

Sir John Barleycorn is not the working-man's friend.

> He professes to give the man strength, but makes him so that he can neither walk nor stand. He drains the man's purse, by making him say, "Let us have a drain." Sir John very often makes work for the surgeon.

Sit still rather than rise and fall down.

> Be quiet sooner than talk to your own confusion : keep in a small way of business rather than launch out and come to bankruptcy.

" Six days shalt thou labour " :
Mind that, lazy neighbour!

> This is as much a part of the commandment as resting on the seventh day. Many an idler forgets this. A missionary from the Congo says of the natives, " Six days' labour, and one day's rest, is not exactly the proportion to their minds ; more the other way round. The only piece of higher criticism in which they indulge is to say that one day's rest, and six days' labour, is manifestly not the Word of God."

Six feet of earth make all men equal.

> Death is the great leveller. The worm has no respect for knighthood or nobility.
>> The mighty monarch and the slave,
>> Find common bed within the grave.

Skin-flints and split-plums would rob a workhouse child of his breakfast.

> "Bless you, man!" said a woman, concerning a certain tanner, "He'd flay two devils to get one skin." To this I had no objection, for those evil spirits are too plentiful. I knew the style of man, and abhorred him: he lived at Greediton, the abode of those very respectable families, the Pinchpoors, the Closefists, the Hoarders, the Graspalls, the Squeezers, and the Grinders. Nice people to work for—any one of them!

Slake your thirst with Adam's ale.

> There is not a headache in a hogshead of it.
>> Pure water for me! Pure water for me!
>> 'Tis the drink of the wise; 'tis the wine of the free.

Slander is a coward's revenge.

> He dares not strike with his fist, and so he stabs with his tongue. He has nothing to say that is true, and so he lies like a Cretan. He loses his revenge if no notice whatever is taken.

Slander is the devil's daughter, and speaks her father's language.

> Yes, and speaks it with a more diabolical accent than her sire The devil is Abaddon, but slander is fifty bad ones.

Slander is tongue-murder.

>> A poison, neither mineral nor herbal,
>> But a much deadlier—a poison verbal.

Slanderers are best let alone.

> It is so difficult to deal with the creatures:—
>> "However thou the viper take,
>> A dangerous hazard thou dost make."

Slanderers are the devil's bellows to blow up strife.

> And what a fire they can make! What a vice is this habit of backbiting! One has truly said, "A foul breath is a calamity; but a foul mouth is a criminality."

Sleep not too little nor too much.

Our old proverbs prescribe too little sleep : they are more suitable for the strong than for the weak. All time is not lost which is spent in bed : sometimes it is true economy to be well rested before getting to work. The stern discipline of our fathers said concerning the hours of sleep :—

> " Nature requires five, custom takes seven,
> Laziness takes nine, and wickedness eleven.

Sleep over it, or you may weep over it.

Sleep upon it, and pray before you sleep.

> "A good night's rest
> Will counsel best."

Sleeping cats make saucy mice.

When masters and magistrates tolerate evil, evil ones take great liberties, and iniquity abounds.

Sleeping dogs catch no hares.

In another form we have it : Sleeping foxes catch no chickens. One had need be wide awake nowadays to catch anything unless it be the measles.

Sleepy hearers make sleepy preachers.

Preachers and people act and react upon each other. The pulpit can mesmerize the pew, and the pew can electrify the pulpit, or *vice versâ*. In England all places are liable to rates and taxes if anybody sleeps on the premises. Query : Should not many churches and chapels be called upon to pay ? A clergyman remarked that none could sleep in his church, for he had instructed the sexton to wake them up. He was wisely asked if it would not be better for the sexton to wake *him* up. Wakeful preachers have wakeful hearers. Some preachers are great mesmerizers.

Slippery is the stone at the rich man's door.

He is apt to trip who goes there begging and cringing, and the owner himself is apt to slip when he comes out with his head up.

Sloth begat poverty, and poverty begat fraud.

So runs the genealogy of many another sin : idleness is usually the grandfather of the crime, whatever the father might be.

Sloth is the key of poverty.

> If thou wouldst know where want doth dwell,
> Sloth will conduct thee to its cell.

Sloth makes all things difficult, industry all things easy.

The least exertion fatigues an idle man, and he is glad of the excuse of difficulty, that he may shirk work. The difficulty lies in his own lazy bones. He is loth to carry his meat to his mouth. Diligence does not *take* things easy, but it does *make* them easy.

Sloth shortens life and lengthens sin.

> " Fly sloth, which body tires and mind benumbs :
> It is a taste of death before death comes."—*Sir R. Baker.*

Slothful men never have time.

You would fancy that they were working like niggers, while they are just throwing time away in doing nothing. That was a smart old lady, who, to a man's complaint that he had "no time," replied, " You have all the time there is."

Slow and sure.

On one occasion, at a council of war, during a siege, General Wolfe complained greatly of the slowness of the approaches. " My maxim," said the engineer, " is slow and sure." " And mine," replied Wolfe, " is quick and sure—a much better maxim."

Slow and sure will long endure.

The offspring of an hour dies in the next hour ; but that which comes of thought and plodding stands firm as the hills. Better an oak of ages than a mushroom of minutes.

Slow fires make sweet malt.

Quiet, thoughtful action is best. Thoroughly good work comes out of deliberation. Good temper promotes a loving, amiable conversation. Steady, patient perseverance makes happy life.

Slow in choosing, slow in changing.

Apply this especially to friendship, and even more emphatically to courtship ; for once married, it is for better or worse. True love neither ranges nor changes. Among old ring-posies we find :

> " Let love abide till death divide."
> " God did decree our unity."

Sluggards grow busy when the hours grow late.

They wake up when it is time to go to sleep. It is their nature to run contrary to nature.

> Ever is it sluggard's guise :
> Loth to bed, and loth to rise.

Small bags hold large diamonds.

Little bodies often contain great souls. Five feet of sense is better than six of folly. Wilberforce was a very small man. *Boswell* says of his appearance at the election for York county : " I saw what seemed a mere shrimp mount on the table ; but as I listened, he grew and grew, until the shrimp became a whale."

Small beginnings may have great endings.

Sparks set the prairie on flame. Little springs begin the mighty Thames. Two or three praying men may bring down a great revival for a whole nation.

Small birds must have meat.

The least must be fed as well as the greatest. Should not the big birds leave a little more room for the sparrows and the finches ? Should not great monopolists think of the hundreds whose livings they absorb ? Live, and let the little folk live.

Small differences make great discords.

It is wonderful how little a thing will cause grievous quarrels. Outsiders can hardly see the point. It looks like the division of the Lilliputians into Big-endians, and Little-endians, all arising out of their views as to how an egg should be eaten. We may say, as another did on another subject :—

> Strange that such difference should be
> 'Twixt tweedle-dum and tweedle-dee.

Sma' fish are better than nae fish.

Quite true, Scotch friend ! Better to keep on earning pence than lose your place, and be without a penny to bless yourself with.

Small habits, well pursued betimes,
May reach the dignity of crimes.

Bad habits soon grow to something worse, and these corrupt into villainies, and make the man too bad to be tolerated in society.

Small profits are sweet.

Especially if often repeated, and long continued. Those who reach after rapid riches miss many pleasures, and run ruinous risks.

Small should be content with small.

So *Herrick* sings :—

> " A little seed best fits a little soil,
> A little trade best fits a little toil ;
> As my small jar best fits my little oil.
>
> A little bin best fits a little bread,
> A little garland fits a little head ;
> As my small stuff best fits my little shed."

Small rain lays great dust.

Gentle words end great quarrels. Loving tenderness removes irritation. Many like kicking up a dust ; let us try to lay it.

Smooth bullets fly farthest.

Kind words, and arguments courteously advanced, have greater currency than uncouth denunciations.

Smooth words make smooth ways.

An atmosphere of gentleness is created, and roughness and unkindness are banished where all have learned to speak tenderly.

Snakes may have fine colours, and yet have deadly stings.

So many lusts, so many lords.

For every evil passion strives for the mastery, and holds the mind in subjection. He that would be free from bondage must wear the yoke of Christ, and deny his own passions.

So many skulls, so many schemes.

Every man has his own plan, and each one believes that his method is preferable to every other. Specially is this true in medicine : so many skulls, twice as many pills. Liniments are as varied as the lineaments of the doctors' faces.

So much meal cannot all have come from your own sack.

You must have borrowed some of that discourse : it is too full, too deep to be all your own. Thus men overdo their borrowings, and are found out. The excellence of what they steal is the plague of plagiarists.

So rejoice that you can rejoice over your rejoicing.

Wine that you can drink when you have made it, and think of with pleasure after you have drunk it, is alone worth making and drinking. A joy fit to be looked back upon is alone a real joy.

" So to the dust
Return we must."

For out of it we were taken, and our dust longs to be back with its brother.

Soap and water, soap and water!
Wash yourself, and wash your daughter.

A lady in Utica took a child to a physician to consult him about its health. Among other things, she inquired if he did not think the springs would be useful. "Certainly, madam," replied the doctor, as he looked at the child. "I advise you to try the springs at once." "You really think it would be good for the poor little thing?" "Decidedly I do." "What springs would you recommend, doctor?" "Any will do, madam, where you can get plenty of soap and water."

Sobriety is the door of prosperity.

Not only in the health it brings, and in the sin it prevents; but in the saving it involves, the thrift it promotes, and the industry it encourages. A prosperous drunkard is a rare bird.

Soft and fair goes long journeys.

A staying pace is what is desirable. Begin as you hope to go on; and mind you do go on. Rush and dash make headway for a short time, and then there comes a fall or a stop.

An early start and a steady pace
Take the slowest through the race.

Soft words scald not the mouth.

You may talk any quantity of them without needing to regret their use. Ugly expressions are like boiling water, as well to those who use them as to those who hear them.

Soft words win hard hearts.

Many a man yields to loving entreaty who cannot be touched by threatening. Soft words break no bones, but they break hard hearts. Kindness wins where roughness fails.

"Softly! softly!" caught the monkey.

So say the negroes; and these darkies know a thing or two. Sambo very sensible! Gently gets the game.

Solid arguments are lost on shallow minds.

Yet what else are we to use? We are bound to give them reasons; but we are not called upon to give them understandings.

Solitude is often the best society.

Yet the Italians say, "One would not wish to be alone even in Paradise." If it were to last always there would be no charms in solitude, but an occasional interval of it is the joy of good men. To be alone with God is to be in the best company.

Solomon made a book of proverbs; but a book of proverbs never made a Solomon.

Even the present book may fail with here and there a reader. Friend, it may be you are a Solomon already; and in that case, there remains no hope for our book of proverbs.

Some are always doing, and never do anything.

Like a dog in a fair, they are in and out everywhere, and they do no more than a dog would do, who seems to be always busy, but what his business is no man knoweth.

Some are made ill by trying to be cured.

So we have read an epitaph, which we look upon as a sheer invention—

Here lie I and my two daughters
All through drinking mineral waters;
If we'd been contented with Epsom salts,
We shouldn't have been lying in these here vaults.

Some are mated who are not matched.

Every couple's not a pair;
Wife a mule, her man a bear.

For such a couple the following epitaph might be appropriate: "Here lies the body of James Robinson, and Ruth his wife"; and underneath is this text, "Their warfare is accomplished."

Some are too ignorant to be humble.

It needs a measure of self-knowledge to take down pride. Many carry their heads high because there is nothing in them.

Some are wise, and some are otherwise.

Some are wise, and others are like-wise by associating with them; but the otherwise people grow without watering in anywise.

Some boys have too much rope, and too little rope's end.

They are allowed to take great liberties, and are never corrected for their faults. Abstinence from correction is a patent method for growing bad men.

Some chop at every tree and fell none.

They attempt many things, and, therefore, succeed in nothing.

Some dangers are avoided by facing them at once.

It is only timidity which makes them dangers. Go straight on, and they vanish like the mere shadows which they are.

Some defy the devil with their lips, but deify him in their lives.

In fact, those who talk most flippantly about the arch-enemy are generally his friends. Those who have really fought with him have a salutary horror of his very name.

Some do not bite because they have no teeth; Some give a kiss, but hate is underneath.

Hatred has been often veiled where it still prevailed. In other cases it is held back by inability, and not by amiability.

Some dog or other will be barking to-day.

Expect to be spoken against, and when it comes it will not surprise you. Who can stop all mouths? A dog may as well bark at you as at anyone else. Bitter bark is a good tonic.

Some drink healths till they drink away their own health.

An Irishman used often to come home drunk; and once, when he was watering his horse, his wife said to him, "Now, Paddy, isn't the baste an example to ye? Don't ye see he leaves off when he has had enough! the craythur, he's the most sensible baste of the two." "Oh, it's very well to discourse like that, Biddy," cried Paddy, "but if there was another baste at the other side of the trough to say, 'Here's your health me ould boy!' would he stop till he drank the whole trough, think ye?"

Some earn a farthing, and get two pennyworth of thirst.

So that with their parched throats, they are forced to hurry to the drink. Pity the sorrows of such little-working and much-thirsting men ! They hardly earn enough to keep their throats oiled.

Some ears are left after the cleanest gleaners.

Still is there truth unnoticed in a text. Still are persons overlooked in the best visited district. Still is a living to be picked up, though many have traded in the place.

Some go to church to take a walk ;
Some go there to laugh and talk ;
Some go there to meet a friend ;
Some go there their time to spend ;
Some go there to meet a lover ;
Some go there a fault to cover ;
Some go there for speculation ;
Some go there for observation ;
Some go there to doze and nod ;
The wise go there to worship God.

Some have milk in their mouths, and gall in their hearts.

Dreadful is it to have to deal with these double-distilled wretches. Happily we are able to discover their false-heartedness, and then we despise them, and give them a wide berth.

Some men die before they begin to live.

" He lives who lives to God alone,
And all are dead beside ;
For other source than God is none
Whence life can be supplied."—*Cowper.*

Some men follow their consciences as navvies follow the wheelbarrows which they push before them.

It is all very fine to be pleading " conscience," but we are responsible *for* conscience, as well as responsible *to* it. If we keep conscience in the dark, or render it morbid, it will not excuse us in wrong-doing. If a captain falsifies his compass, and then steers by it, his shipwreck will be his own fault.

Some men go through a forest and see no firewood.

They are unobservant. That which is everywhere for others is nowhere for them. In the holiest church some see no virtue, and in the Bible no divine utterances.

Some men have no heads, but every man has a heart.

For this reason intellectual preaching can only impress a few; but warm, loving discourse will have power with everybody.

Some men have rats in their mouths, and mice in their heads.

Their talk is larger than their real intent: the brag is bigger than the brain. They thunder with their tongues, but squeak in their thoughts.

Some men would skin a grindstone if they could.

Nothing is too bare for them to get something out of it. They would shave an egg, and make soup of a stone.

Some men's principles follow their interests.

Interest should arise out of principle; principle must never be subordinate to interest. There is a pun here, but a truth also.

Some people are little and loud.

There is not much of them, but they make much more noise for their size than you might expect.

Some people's words go many to a pound.

They seem resolved to make up for the quality by the quantity. Though their words are light as air, it is heavy work to hear them, for they heap them on in such superabundance. When we suspect a man's truthfulness his words are wind. He who looks one way and walks another, may talk a horse's hind leg off, but his chatter is of small account.

Some stumble at a straw, and jump over a stack.

They "strain out a gnat, but swallow a camel."

Some swim in wealth, yet sink in tears;
Some rise in state, yet fall in fears.

Rich men have often described themselves as specially miserable. There is nothing in rank and station which can ensure happiness to the mind. It is very cold on the high Alps. Not where we are, but what we are, determines our happiness.

Some take so much time in getting advice, that no time is left in which to carry it out.

Delaying and delaying, they break while learning how to prosper, and die learning how to live.

Some women conceal only what they do not know.

Mrs. Blab, for instance, tells all her secrets over a cup or two of tea. You can only be sure that she will never say what she does not know, and cannot make up.

Some would eat a house, and still be hungry.

Their greed is so great that the world itself would not content them. An old gentleman once asked a lad—When was a covetous man rich enough? "When he has a thousand pounds," was the reply. "No." "Two thousand." "No." "Twenty thousand." "No." "A hundred thousand," said the lad at last, in desperation; and still being told "No," he confessed that he could not say. His questioner then informed him—"When he has a little more than he has, and that is never."

Some would play a tune before you could tune your fiddle.

Like the Welsh preacher, who sets the world on fire while the Englishman is looking for a match.

Some would see faults if their eyes were out.

Their minds are made up to carp and cavil; and in the dark, with their eyes out, they can see what never existed.

Somebody will grumble at the weather to-day.

Probably you will yourself. Englishmen are always criticizing the weather; but the weather takes no notice of their remarks.

Something is better than nothing.

Therefore, hold on to your employment, however poor the pay, and don't plunge into utter poverty because you are dissatisfied. This proverb sometimes runs, "Something *tastes* better than nothing." Dry bread is sweeter than fried nothing.

"Something short"—a drunkard's sense.

If this were not true he would never ask for this "something short;" which is apt to make him short of money, short of health, and short of character before very long.

Sometimes the best gain is to lose.

Young men beginning to gamble, or to speculate, have been saved by making an ugly loss at the very beginning. Had they gained a pound or two they would have been lured on, and would have been utterly, and perhaps, eternally ruined.

Sometimes 'tis wise
To shut one's eyes.

> When you can do no good by seeing, it is well to remember that an unseeing eye leaves us an unruing heart.

Soon ripe, soon rotten.

> Precocious children often make silly men. Those who soon come to perfection are soon past their prime. He who is a man when a child, is in danger of being a child when a man; but it is by no means always so. If the rule were invariable some of our friends would be able to tell us very startling stories of their own early wisdom.

Sorrow and trouble break many a bubble.

> Airy notions in religion are soon destroyed by the rough hand of real trouble. If adversity should once get hold of some of our cultured bodies it would shake them like a rat, or say, as a child shakes all the inside out of a bran doll.

Sorrow and worry wear us more than hard work.

> Assuredly this is very true. These turn the hair grey, and plough the forehead with furrows.
>
> > Sorrow and strife
> > Soon age a wife.

Sorrow is fit sauce for sin.

> Many have had to dip their sin into it; and if they had not done so, evil would have poisoned them. Take heed that you do not have to taste these bitters to all eternity.

Sorrow is the cloud; tears are the rain.

Sorrow rode in my cart.

> Yes. We unwittingly bring home grief in our own waggon. We pick up a trouble on the road, and give it a seat in our cart, and thus bring it home. Trade brings trial, pleasure leads to pain, friendship breeds grief, and wedlock has its woes. Never mind. Let us be glad we have a cart to ride in.

Sorrow will pay no debt.

> "I'm very sorry," said the lady when a dog had bitten a man in the leg. "Sorry won't heal my wound," said he. Nor would it.

Sounding professions are seldom sound.

> They are often all sound, and there is nothing solid about them.

Sour grapes, as the fox said when he could not reach them.

Sour grapes can ne'er make sweet wine.

> Unless they are left to ripen. In their sour state they cannot yield sweetness. Neither can bad motives, and bad principles, bring us peace and happiness.

Sow an act, reap a habit;
Sow a habit, reap a character;
Sow a character, reap a destiny.

> Thus an act may decide destiny. "There was an abbot of this land who desired a piece of ground that lay conveniently for him. The owner refused to sell it, yet, with much persuasion, was contented to let it. The abbot hired it for his rent, and covenanted only to farm it for one crop. He had his bargain, and sowed it with acorns—a crop that lasted three hundred years. Thus, Satan begs but for the first crop; let him sow thy youth with acorns, they will grow up with thy years to sturdy oaks, so big-bulked and deep-rooted, that they shall last all thy life."

Sow beans in the mud, and they'll grow like wood.

> So our gardening forefathers thought. Do the moderns find it so?

Sow cockle, and it will not yield corn.

> What folly to sow it! How many work hard at this bad sowing!

Sow ill, reap ill.

Sow the seeds of heart's-ease.

> Get a packet of kindly actions, a handful of old honesty, a bag of peace, and a selection of sweet herbs, and you will find that heart's-ease will spring up naturally among them.

Spare dinner, spare doctor.

> Sparingly feed,
> No doctor you'll need.

Spare when you're young, and spend when you're old.

> Often the reverse is done: the youth squanders, and the old man hoards. This is folly writ in capitals.

Spare your bait, and lose your fish.

> Economy in advertising is no economy. Want of preparation before preaching is extreme folly in one who would hold the attention.

Sparrows fight for corn which is none of their own.

So do the rank and file engage in battle for that which does not concern them an atom. Men will discuss doctrines in which they have really no personal concern. Why dispute about a heaven to which I am not likely to go?

Speak as wisely as you list,
Some will still your language twist.

It is the nature of the beast. The twister makes a man an offender for a word which he did not utter.

Speak as you find, says Old Suffolk.

And he was by no means "Silly Suffolk" when he made the observation. Go not by common report, but by your own actual experience.

What others are saying never you mind,
Do me the justice to speak as you find.

Speak fitly, and then you may speak freely.

Speak of a man, and his shadow falls on you.

So does it often happen according to the chapter of accidents.

Speak of the wolf, and you'll see his tail.

And speak of the devil, and one of his imps will be near. Often have we noticed that just as we were talking about a matter the individual concerned in it put in an appearance.

Speak only that which is worth speaking.

It will be well to make a selection rather than a collection of themes for conversation. It is well in helping others to our thoughts, to remember the rule in carving for a guest:—

" Give him always of the prime,
And but little at a time.
Carve to all but just enough,
Let him rather starve than stuff."

Speak up for the absent.

Alas! few do this: the absent are set in the stocks. The Arabs say, "Fellows rail at the Sultan himself when he is not there."

Speak well of your friend; of your enemy speak neither well nor ill.

Speak plain English.

Dr. *Taylor* says, "Never say 'hebdomadal' when you mean 'weekly'; and do not lament that men have 'perverse proclivities to prevarication,' when you might express the same thought in Falstaff's words, 'How this world is given to lying!'" Don't go roundabout to conceal your meaning. If you want to be forcible use pure Saxon. It will take a man a lifetime to speak our language correctly, and that advice is not bad which is given in the rhyme:

> Leave all the foreign tongues alone,
> Till you can spell and read your own.

Speak when ye're spoken to,
Do what ye're bidden,
Come when ye're called,
And ye'll not be chidden.

Good advice for children. It will be well for families if the youngsters will heed it.

Speak your mind,
But still be kind.

In being frank some are rough, and this is by no means needful. Speak the truth in love.

Speaking silence is better than senseless speech.

"Some feel it a cross to speak, and others feel it a cross not to speak; I would advise both to take up their cross," was the remark of a shrewd writer quoted by *J. B. Gough.*

Spears are not made of bulrushes.

Strength is wanted in those who have stern work to do. Poor, vacillating mortals are out of place when a fight is on.

Speculation is jumping out of the window to get upon the housetop.

The man takes a desperate leap, and, in the vain hope of rising, he plunges into the abyss.

Speculation leads to peculation.

Not always, but often it is so. He who would grasp a fortune all at once seldom waits to see whether it can come honestly. When a man goes up in a balloon, there is generally foul gas about.

> Gambling's grown to such a pitch
> In all quarters of the nation,
> Some get poor and others rich
> By mere daily speculation.

Speech is silver, but silence is gold.

It is an old saying that few words are best,
And he that says little shall live most at rest.

Spend not all, or want may befall.

Seldom live up to the full height of your income, and never over-run the constable. Let not all the roast meat of thy wealth run away in the dripping of little wastes, and let none of it burn in wantonness. Be a good steward, and act with thy substance as one who has to give in an account to his lord.

Spend not when you ought to spare, and spare not when you ought to spend.

They said of a certain poor economist that he never tapped his beer till it was sour, nor cut his cheese till it was mouldy, nor ate his meat till it was putrid. This is the reverse of thrift. One refused to pay for a pane of glass in a window, took cold from the draught, and had to pay the doctor, and lose a fortnight's work.

Spend with great glee
When the time be :
Save with firm hand
When times demand.

Spend not your money before it be got : Speak not your mind before you have thought.

A stock-broker's rule was also wise : "Never sell what you have not got, and never buy what you cannot pay for." On the last line of our old saw, we would say, Do not take down the shutters till there is something in the shop. There can be no need to display the nakedness of the land.

Spend nothing on silk Till you've paid for your milk.

It is a sort of thieving to buy luxuries while bills are running. To let small sums accumulate to great ones by long delay is a cruel wrong to the little dealer who is standing out of his money. No wonder the milk looks blue when it has not been paid for week after week.

Spend your evening at the sign of "The Teakettle."

Sing as the kettle does, "Hum, hum, sweet hum."

Spending your money with many a guest, Empties the larder, the cellar, and chest.

Spin not too fine a thread, lest it break in the weaving.

If the discourse is too fine people will not understand it, and if the theory is too subtle it will go to pieces in the discussing. Many sermons are too grand: they will be of no more use to common hearers than the Requiem of Mozart to a field of cabbages.

Splitting plums is a beggarly business.

The tin-pot economy habit in trade does not pay. People grow disgusted with the farthings and mites, and half-inches; and deal with a more liberal shop-keeper. It seems silly to lose a large profit because you will not lower your price a very little. Some men might have been rich if they had not been so mean-spirited.

Squeaking will not get the pig out of the ditch.

Complaining will not alter the trial into which providence has brought us. No hog ever grunted the ring out of his nose.

Stability is ability.

He that can put his foot down and stand firm has force with which to lift the load of life. To be unstable is to be unable; but to be well established is to possess influence.

Stake your dahlias, but don't bet.

Leave betting to fools and knaves: it is the peculiar delight of these two sorts of gentlemen. They know where the active pea is hiding, and you do not; therefore, bet nothing whatever.

Stand fast, but do not stand still.

Stand fast, stand firm, stand sure.

> Still for the good old cause stand buff,
> 'Gainst many a bitter kick and cuff.

Stand on your head, and the world will be upside down.

Your own position affects your view of things. If you will turn yourself upside down, everything around you will appear to have done the same.

Standing pools do quickly putrefy.

Stay a little, that you may make an end the sooner.

This was a favourite saying with a statesman when he found people in a great hurry to decide a question.

Stay a while, sir! Stay a while!
Help a lame dog o'er a stile.

>Be not in such haste that you cannot help the needy. You will make all the greater headway for lending a hand to the distressed.

Stay not at a friend's house too long, lest thou overstay thy welcome.

>Go before they want you gone. Why should you become stale where once you were so much desired? Yet there are exceptions. Dr. Watts was invited by Sir Thomas Abney to stay a week at his house; and though this week extended to thirty-six years, it was none too long. The old distich says:—
>
>> "Fish, and the friend who comes and stays,
>> Don't do to keep beyond three days."

Steady toil and earnest prayer
Often prove a cure for care.

Steal eels and they'll turn to snakes.

>Reckon that a fishy transaction will turn out badly.

Steal not from the closet to pay the kitchen.

>Do not neglect prayer because of household duties. Domestic and secret claims should both be met.

Steel whets steel.

>Or, as Solomon saith, "Iron sharpeneth iron."

Step by step the hill will be climbed.

>Don't dream of doing all at once; but divide the labour and conquer the difficulty bit by bit.

Step by step one goes far.

>The Burmese say, "A wise man takes a step at a time: he fixes one foot firmly before he moves the other." An old place is not to be left till another is secured.
>
>> " One step, and then another,
>> And the longest walk is ended;
>>   One stitch, and then another,
>> And the longest rent is mended;
>>   One brick upon another,
>> And the highest wall is made;
>>   One flake upon another,
>> And the deepest snow is laid."

Step not on a sleeping serpent.

> Do not arouse hostility. If the bad man is quiet let him keep so. Never stir up a hornet's nest, nor wake a kennel of hounds.

Stick well to your trade,
Or profits will fade.

> These are not times for sloth or sudden changes. If a man does not look after his business while he has it, it will run away, and then he may look after it in vain. Where? Where? And O where is the bonnie business gone?

Sticks and stones may break my bones, but names will never hurt me.

> Therefore let us take patiently the nicknames which ridicule may append to us, which usually, before long, mellow into titles of honour.

Stolen grapes give woful gripes.

> *Tom Fuller* says:—"Upon the question, What is the worst bread that is eaten? one answered, in respect of the coarseness thereof, Bread made of beans. Another said, Bread made of acorns; but the third hit the truth, and said, Bread taken out of other men's mouths who are the proprietors thereof. Such bread may be sweet in the mouth to taste, but it is not wholesome in the stomach to digest."

Stoop to conquer. He who yields wins.

> It is so in Christian life. We are to be anvils, and overcome the hammers, not by striking again, but by patiently bearing the blows. Non-resistance and self-sacrifice will conquer all the world.

Stories grow as they flow.

> *De Quincey* says, "All anecdotes are false"; and this comes of their shape being altered as they pass from mouth to mouth. They not only grow as they flow, but change as they range.

Storms make oaks take deeper root.

Stout makes many men lean.

> But the leaning is against the lamp-post. A quaint versifier says:—

> > "Leave stout alone if you should ail,
> > And ale if you are stout;
> > A drinking bout won't make you well,
> > Mind well what you're about!
> > Be doctored, if you please, with stout,
> > The stout is *doctored* too."

Straightforward is the nearest way.

Go to the man himself if you have anything to complain of, or to ask from him. A straight line is the shortest distance ; and plain, personal speaking is the wisest method. Don't be always sneaking up the back-stairs. Leave crooked ways to crooked men.

Straightforward makes the best runner.

Run at once to the Lord with your wants instead of going round about to friends and neighbours. He must help, even if it be by human agency ; and if we go to him first of all, we shall be going in a sure way and a short way, thus saving both time and honour.

Straws show which way the wind blows.

Straying shepherd makes straying sheep.

The people follow the pastor, and his going aside is therefore all the more lamentable. If a private man's watch does not keep time he will himself be misled ; but if the church clock is wrong, the whole parish will be unpunctual.

Strike while the iron's hot.

But don't keep on striking till it's cold. Don't preach the people into a good state of mind, and then preach them out of it. Speak while people delight to listen, and there and then endeavour to work them to decision.

Strip not before you reach the water.

Some give up their property before death ; but as it is unwise to take off your clothes till you go to bed, or to undress for the bath when you are a mile off it, so is it foolish to part with property which you may yet need. While you keep on living keep something to live on.

Strong drink is the devil's way to man, and man's way to the devil.

Both portions of this saying are equally true, and so we have a double reason for leaving strong drink alone. If we will put evil spirits into our bodies we may not marvel if we go where evil spirits dwell. Those who have a strong weakness for strong drink are making a short journey to their long home.

Strong is the vinegar of sweet wine.

When good-tempered men grow angry, it *is* anger. When mercy kindles into wrath, it is terrible indeed. When persons, who were very loving, disagree, the quarrel is often very sharp. "Spoons before marriage may become knives and forks afterwards."

Strong reasons make strong actions.

> Sure that he is right
> Man puts forth his might.

Study yourself to death, and pray yourself alive again.

Adam Clarke's advice to students. Let them carry it out.

Subtlety set a trap, and was caught itself.

Success is the blessing of God on a good cause, and his curse on a bad one.

Thoughtless people consider that success always proves that their course is right. The true man, when defeated in a right cause, is by no means daunted, but fights on expecting victory in some form or other. Success in evil is a terrible calamity.

Such as ye give, such shall ye get.

Your chickens come home to roost. The echo repeats your own words. As you have measured, it will be meted back to you.

Such mistress, such Nan;
Such master, such man.

Like strangely calls its like to itself. Difference in rank does not prevent similarity in character. The head of a household gives a tone to all in it down to the scullery-maid.

Such the mind, and such the man.

Not his bodily condition, but the state of his mind, makes the man's happiness or woe.

> The mind, by its own force, as by a spell,
> Could make a hell of heaven, a heaven of hell.

Sudden friendship, sure repentance.

At least, it is often so :—

> We give our love without a test
> To those whom we shall soon detest.

Sugared words generally prove bitter.

A French priest praising the soft word that turns away wrath said, "It is with honey that we catch flies." A listener replied, "Yes, to kill them !" Beware of men made of molasses.

Sunday newspapers are Satan's sermons.

In London they command enormous congregations. It is sad to see religious people supporting such things. It was not always so.

Sunday oils the wheels of the week.

Its bodily rest is useful, but its spiritual anointing is far more so. Let us go on the Sabbath where there is oil in the ministry.

Sunday profits in trade
Are the worst ever made.

They come out of the life-blood of the Sabbath-breaker's soul. What can it profit him? His Sunday gains are cankered money which will defile all the takings of the week.

Surety for his borrowing friend,
Sure tied to trouble without end.

When a young man cannot afford to give his needy friend the money, it is not honest to become security for the amount. Never promise to give what you have not got. The surety will be sure to be called upon to pay; and what then? He that is surety shall smart for it. Yes, and his wife and family with him.

Surgeons should have an eagle's eye, a lion's heart, and a lady's hand.

They should be quick to see, brave to operate, and tender in every touch. Not one of these points may be absent in a skilful surgeon.

Suspect suspicion, and trust trustfulness.

Suspicion is ruinous to peace. Those who are most quick to excite it, are generally persons who deserve no confidence. Better far to see a thing through to the end, than to be tortured with continual suspicion. In the darkness of ignorance the vampires of suspicion fly abroad. Let in the light upon them, and they will no longer be seen. Better trust too much, and suffer the consequences, than pine under the withering blast of perpetual mistrust.

Swearers use oaths because they know their words will not be taken.

But if a man is not to be believed upon his word, we shall be very unwise to trust him when his profane expressions declare the rottenness of his heart. He that will blaspheme God will cheat me.

Sweeping judgments are unjust judgments.

For thus are the innocent condemned with the guilty. There are exceptions to general iniquity, and those exceptions deserve our sympathy all the more because of the difficulty which surrounds them. Confound not the righteous with the wicked.

Sweet May, how short thy stay!

Like every other pleasure, it is short and sweet. We no sooner reach the merry month than it is gone.

Sweets to the sweet.

This is an appropriate distribution. How much will the reader get? I hope a lapful. Let him take home much to his wife, if he has one ; and if he lives in single wretchedness, let him carry home the sweets to his mother, or his sister.

Sweetest nuts have hardest shells.

As if to bring forth and reward our diligence everything worth the having requires of us pains and strains.

Sayings of a more Spiritual Sort.

Sabbath-breakers are their own enemies.

They rob themselves of earthly rest, and of the sweet hope of rest in heaven. No enemy could do them a worse turn. A traveller in Pennsylvania says, that passing a coal mine he saw a small field full of mules. The boy who was with him said, "These are the mules that work all the week down in the mine, but Sunday they have to come up into the light, or else in a little while they would go blind." Are not many men blinded by never quitting the darkness of worldly care?

Saints are blessed when they are cursed.

It is with them as with Israel when Balaam sought to curse them : "Howbeit our God turned the curse into a blessing."

Saints are never far from home.

In the remotest places they are in the dominions of their Father, and on the borders of heaven.

" The earth is God's, and in his hands
Are all the corners of the lands."

Saints cannot fall without hurt, nor rise without help.

Saints may feel the stroke of death, but not the sting of death.

Isaac Walton, speaking of the death-bed of Dr. Donne, said : " He lay fifteen days earnestly expecting his hourly change, and in the last hour of his last day, as his body melted away, and vapoured into spirit, his soul having, I verily believe, some revelation of the beatific vision, he said, ' I were miserable if I might not die ' ; and after those words closed many periods of his faint breath by saying often, ' Thy kingdom come, thy will be done.' "

Saints' tears are better than sinners' triumphs.

Saints would rather have holiness without comfort than comfort without holiness.

Salvation comes by faith, not by feeling.

Salvation by feeling would be variable as the weather. Faith embraces Christ, and in him finds salvation.

Salvation is a helmet for the head, and armour for the heart.

"Let us ascertain whether we have this helmet of hope on our heads or not. As for such paltry ware as most are contented with, it deserves not the name of true hope, no more than a paper cap doth of a helmet. Oh! look to the metal and temper of your helmet in an especial manner; for at this most blows are made. He that seeks chiefly to defend his own head (the serpent, I mean) will aim most to wound yours."—*Gurnall.*

Salvation is all of grace, but destruction is all of sin.

Both these statements are true, though some represent them as opposed. Sovereign grace and human responsibility are both true.

Sanctification is the best decoration.

Watson says, "Sanctification is the spiritual enamel and embroidery of the soul; 'tis nothing else but God's putting upon us the jewels of holiness, the angels' glory; by it we are made as the king's daughter, *all glorious within.*—Ps. xlv. 13."

Sanctified afflictions are spiritual promotions.

A choice sentence, full of consolation to those who seek that every twig of the rod may be made a blessing to them.

Satan as a master is bad, his work worse, his wages worst of all.

This is the worst form of Down-Grade: everything runs down to the lowest deep. In a sermon by *Tauler*, who lived and preached in Strasbourg, in the fourteenth century, occurs the striking expression, 'The devil's martyrs'! Such are many sinners, suffering both here and hereafter in Satan's service.

Satan cannot constrain, if we do not consent.

He tempts with a crafty bait, but he cannot compel us to bite at it. The will of the weakest, if helped to resist by grace, can lock the devil out of the heart. *Brooks* says, "As Satan must have leave from God, so he must have leave of us. That is a remarkable passage in Acts v. 3: 'Why hath Satan filled thine heart to lie to the Holy Ghost?' Peter doth not discuss the matter with Satan; he doth not say, 'Satan, why hast thou filled Ananias's *heart* to make him lie to the Holy Ghost?' but he expostulates the case with Ananias. He said, 'Ananias, why hath Satan filled *thine heart* to lie to the Holy Ghost?' Why hast thou given him an advantage to fill thy heart with infidelity, hypocrisy, and obstinate audacity, to lie to the Holy Ghost? As if he had said, Satan could never have done this in thee, which will now for ever undo thee, unless thou hadst, thyself, given him leave."

Satan doth more hurt in a sheepskin than when he roars like a lion.

Subtlety is ascribed to the serpent in Genesis, and it is still the main strength of our arch-enemy. Better by far a roaring devil than a canting one: the first we overcome, the second comes over us.

Satan sometimes accuseth *us* to God, and sometimes accuseth *God* to us.

He would make us think hard things of divine providence, and wicked things about divine grace. Let us not believe his slanders of our heavenly Father, for our Father does not heed what he says against us.

Satan tempts in life, and taunts in death.

After recklessness comes remorse, and both are the creation of the same evil hand. He makes men live without fear, and die without hope. Let us flee from the seducer to the Saviour.

Scarlet sinners may become milk-white saints.

"Wash me, and I shall be whiter than snow."—Ps. li. 7.

Scripture silence speaks solemnly.

It becomes us to be silent where God speaks not. We must not venture to rush in where God hath hung a veil.

Secret meals make the soul fat.

Private communion with God, and secret study of Scripture, cause the soul to grow exceedingly, and become strong in the Lord.

See the face of God before you see the face of man.

First speak with God in prayer in the morning before you have a word to say to your fellow mortals.

Seek all in Christ, and Christ in all.

Seek the Lord on earth, and you shall see him in heaven.

Sermons are not made for critics to look at, but for Christians to live upon.

The critic stands outside the window and judges the meat, but the hungry man enters and enjoys the food. We don't keep shop for lookers-on, but for such as will "buy and eat."

Sermons should be weighty, but not heavy.

> We fear they are frequently heavy, but not weighty; ponderous, but not persuasive.
> *Lady*—"Mr. —— is really a wretched preacher."
> *Husband*—"My dear! Mr. —— is one of the most sound, orthodox preachers I know."
> *Lady*—"He may be very orthodox, but he is very heavy."
> *Husband*—"Gold is heavy."
> *Lady*—"Yes, but gold is bright."

Signal piety shall be crowned with signal power.

> *George Whitefield's* prayer was, "O Lord, make me an extraordinary Christian." He sought extraordinary grace, and he was answered by extraordinary usefulness.

Simple faith in God is worth
More than all the gains of earth.

> Faith makes us possess the Most High God, who is the possessor of heaven and earth.

Sin always ruins where it reigns.

> Therefore it must be dethroned; and none can do this but the strong Lord of love, who casts it down, and breaks its reigning power in the heart which he enters.

Sin and shame came into the world together, and they are fit companions.

Sin dies most when faith lives most.

Sin forgiven
Is dawn of heaven.

> The shadows flee away, and the eternal light breaks in upon the soul, when free grace blots out our sins.

Sin hath turned our houses into hospitals.

Sin is a sovereign, till sovereign grace dethrones it.

Sin is honey in the mouth, but gall in the belly.

> *Secker* wrote: "Though Satan's apples may have a fair skin, yet they certainly have a bitter core."

Sin is like a river, which begins in a quiet spring, but ends in a roaring sea.

Sin keeps no Sabbaths.

It has no holidays, but works day and night.

Sin may sleep long, but it will wake at length.

If it is only lulled asleep by reformation, it is still there. It needs to be slain, and only the two-edged sword, which goeth out of Christ's mouth, will do it.

Sin puts hell into the soul, and the soul into hell.

Sin, the worst disease, needs the best physician.

> " Lord, I am all diseases : hospitals,
> And bills of mountebanks, have not so many,
> Nor half so bad.   Lord, hear, and help, and heal me.
> Although my guiltiness for vengeance calls,
> And colour of excuse I have not any,
> Yet thou hast goodness, Lord, that may avail me.
>   Lord, I have poured out all my heart to thee :
>   Vouchsafe one drop of mercy unto me."
>
> *Christopher Harvey.*

Sin's misery, and God's mercy, are beyond measure.

Thus the latter exactly meets the need of the former.   As *Bunyan* said : "It must be great mercy, or no mercy, for little mercy will never serve my turn."

Sin's service is slavery.

"An exiled king had learned this truth; for James II., on his death-bed, thus addressed his son : 'There is no slavery like sin, and no liberty like God's service.' Was not the dethroned monarch right?   What think you of the fetters of bad habits?   What think you of the chains of indulged lust?   The drunkard who cannot resist the craving for the wine, know you a more thorough captive?   The covetous man, who toils night and day for wealth, what is he but a slave?   The sensual man, the ambitious man, the worldly man—those who, in spite of the remonstrances of conscience, cannot break away from enthralment—what are they, if not the subjects of a tyranny than which there is none sterner, and none more degrading? "—*Melville.*

Sincerity is the salt of the sacrifice.

Without it the offering can never be acceptable to the Lord.

Single coals do not burn well.

Holy company increases the warmth of piety.   Join a church, and speak often with holy men, that you may be helped to greater earnestness.

Sinners fare the better for saints.

Laban confessed that he had learned by experience that the Lord had blessed him for Jacob's sake. So we read "The Lord blessed the Egyptian's house for Joseph's sake." As *Bishop Hall* says, "His very presence procures a common blessing; a whole family shall fare the better for one Joseph."

Sinners, spider-like, suck poison out of the sweet flower of God's mercy.

Whether spiders do get poison out of flowers we know not, but assuredly he is a sinner indeed who perverts mercy into an argument for further sin.

" None shall in hell such bitter pangs endure
 As those who mock at God's way of salvation.
 Whom oil and balsams kill, what salve can cure?
 They drink with greediness a full damnation."—*Herbert.*

Sleepy Christians never awaken dead souls.

God uses suitable instrumentality. He gives life by the living. We cannot snore men into the kingdom.

So let me live, so let me die,
That I may live eternally.

This answers to the precept. So live that thou mayst live for ever. Let your life be the life which is life indeed.

Some men speak two words for Christ, and ten for themselves.

Those fine passages and poetical perorations must be for their own glory among men, for they serve no other end. Truth, which glorifies the Lord Jesus, is often kept back.

Some preach the gospel as donkeys eat thistles—very cautiously.

Fearful lest the guilty should be too easily comforted, or wicked men should invent excuses for continuing in sin, they handle the word with trembling, rather than with boldness. Yet men always will pervert the gospel, and it is ours to preach it none the less freely because of this evil habit.

Some would wear Christ's jewels, but waive his cross.

This cannot be : the cross goes ever with the crown.

Sorrow for sin as long as you have sin to sorrow for.

Do not part with that fair friend, repentance, till you reach the gate of paradise. *Rowland Hill* said : "If I may be permitted to shed one tear, as I enter the portals of the city of my God, it will be at taking an eternal leave of that beloved and profitable companion—Repentance."

Souls need care after they receive cure.

It is not enough to seek or even to find lost sheep, they must afterwards be tended, led, and fed.

Sport not with time, for there is no sporting in eternity.

Life should be cheerful, but at the same time earnest. Those who make life a comedy will land themselves in a tragedy.

Strength in prayer is better than length in prayer.

Long prayers may send people to sleep, but a strong prayer tends to arouse the listener. God does not measure our pleadings by the yard. Prayer must be estimated by weight, not by length.

Suffering is better than sinning.

"There is more evil in a drop of sin than in an ocean of affliction." Better burn for Christ, than turn from Christ.

Sunday is the spiritual market-day of the week.

Lay in store holy thoughts and feelings. Let the first day set the tune for the whole week.

Sunday is the summer of the week.

How are we when it comes round with its time of singing, flowering, and fruit bearing ? Happy Sunday !

Suns have their spots,
And saints their blots.

" As if to stain the pride of man, the most eminent saints have, in some flagrant instance, failed in the very grace for which they were most renowned. In hours of darkness Abraham, the true, equivocates ; Job, the patient, is insubmissive ; Moses, the meek, strikes the rock in anger ; Elijah, the fearless, hides in the desert from his foe ; David, the seraphic, plunges into the sins of the senses ; Simon, called Peter, 'a rock,' for his strong and stern decision, has to be reminded that he might rather be called Jonas, 'a dove,' for the weak, scared, fluttering spirit he displayed in the storm of temptation."—*Dr. Stanford.*

AKE a horse by his bridle, and a man by his word.

If every man would follow his word as readily as a horse follows his bridle, it would be well; but if a man is not to be led by his word, it is hard to know how to hold him at all. Perhaps the other saying, "A man by his word and a cow by her horns," hints at a measure of difficulty. A word should be sufficient between man and man; but it is so frequently otherwise, that it is better to have an agreement in black and white.

Take a joke as a joke, and it will not provoke.

"When the loud laugh prevails at your expense,
All want of temper is but want of sense.
Would you disarm the sneerer of his jest,
Frown not, but laugh in concert with the rest."

Take a man's judgment for what it is worth.

Give it due weight, but not more. All will depend upon who the man is, and what he knows about the matter under consideration.

Take a woman's first opinion, and not her second.

She is very apt to come to a right conclusion by a leap of instinct; but when she corrects that instinctive judgment by reasoning, she may possibly be mistaken. This proverb does not always turn out to be correct: second thoughts of women and men are often their best thoughts; indeed, they should be.

Take away fuel, take away flame.

If we say nothing upon which strife can feed, its evil fire must die down. In all disagreements, silence is the friend of peace.

Take care of coppers, and beware of pewters.

Too often the pence are lost in the pewters. Cool pewters at night do not make cool coppers in the morning. Spend no pence to buy regrets.

Take care of the minutes; the hours will take care of themselves.

Economy of time on a large scale will grow out of careful use of the odd five minutes. Many valuable books have been produced by their authors during intervals which others would have wasted.

As the watch crieth tick,
Each minute flieth quick.

Take care of your lambs, or where will you get your sheep from?

If we do not win the hearts of the young, where shall we get another generation of Christians? Those who speak of them as "a parcel of boys and girls" are not wise. A Highland shepherd, when asked how it was that he took the prizes so frequently at the cattle-shows for the best flock, replied, "I look weel to the lambs."

Take care of your plough, and your plough will take care of you.

Thus you must share with your share. If you keep the plough going, it will keep you going. Those who would have cash must earn it.

**Take very great care
Of your own grey mare.**

Watch lovingly over your wife, who is to you as your own self.

Take heed of speedy friend and slow enemy.

The first is hasty, and may fail you; the other has weighed matters, and is not likely to alter, and, therefore, he is to be feared because of his determination. If your foe is deliberate, so much the worse for you; for he will persevere in his attack till he gets you in his power. Malice in cool blood is the bitterest form of it.

Take heed when thou seest no need of taking heed.

Moments of self-security are moments of great peril. A sleeping devil is dreaming of deadly mischief. Watch most when there seems least cause for it.

Take heed you find not what you do not seek.

Many by their unjust suspicions have made for themselves life-long sorrows. Why thrust in your hand among burning coals?

> While poking their noses
> Into other men's roses,
> Paul Prys have been pricked by the thorns:
> And no one supposes,
> That o'er the proboscis
> Of Pry any one of us mourns.

Take me upon your back, and you'll know what I weigh.

Carry my sorrows by actively sympathizing with me, and you will then have some idea of the burden of my life. If you wore my boots you would know where they pinch.

Take more time, and you'll be done the sooner.

No doubt a steady careful mode of working leads to a speedier end than a hurried superficial method, which does nothing thoroughly, but only seems to do it. *Punch* says, "What is the best thing to do in a hurry? Answer, Nothing." Go slowly to make haste.

Take no man's talk out of his mouth.

It is a shame to have to eat your own words, and it is not good to eat another man's words out of his mouth. It is as great a pleasure to another to speak as it is to you; let him have his turn, and do not forestall him.

> Let every man say what he meant to have said,
> Don't rob him of words any more than of bread.

Take no more on your back than you can carry.

Attempt as much as you can compass, but do not overtax yourself, lest all your work suffer. Undertake only what you can overtake. Be temperate in business as well as in drink.

Take not a musket to kill a butterfly.

The creature is too insignificant to be thus overwhelmingly assailed. Adapt the means to the end. Some theories do not. deserve to be argued down, a jest may suffice to crush them.

Take not a wife from a wicked household.

Look to her parentage. You cannot expect to find grapes among thorns. If the well-head be foul, the stream will not be pure. Yet this is not always true; for the providence and grace of God have made some of the loveliest characters to grow up in the most degraded families, and it would be a shame to think ill of them because of a parent's sins.

Take not advice from a man who never takes advice.

If he is not wise enough to know his own need of counsel, he is not wise enough to counsel you. Who will not learn cannot teach.

Take not offence at the arrow, but look to the archer.

A dog bites the stick, and forgets that it could do nothing if it were not in a man's hand. Quarrel not with the second cause of your sorrow, but humbly cry to the Lord, "Show me wherefore thou contendest with me."

Take not the baggage for the sake of the bag.

Marry not a good-for-nothing woman to get her goods.
    If she be base, though she be rich,
    Keep thyself clear of such a witch.

Take pepper, but do not be peppery.

Very hot-tempered people are hard to live with. Some are as
hot as the very strongest black pepper, with which they say hogs
can be killed. Your eyes will ache if the smallest grain of them is
in the air. Be not a Hotspur yourself.

Take the bit, and the buffet with it.

Accept a little buffeting for the sake of a livelihood. We must
all put up with something. When a man intends real kindness, we
must not notice the roughness of his manners.
    Though smitten sorely by thy God,
    Yet with the covenant take the rod.

Take the chestnuts out of the fire with a cat's paw.

We do not advise any such mean course of procedure ; but it is
a very general practice. Monkeys generally imitate men, but in
this thing man imitates the monkey, if the fable be fact.

Take the cotton from your ear
When the gospel cometh near.

We have read that when Queen Elizabeth compelled all her
subjects to attend the Parish Church, the Romanists put wool in
their ears that they might not hear. It is to be feared that Satan
does this for many nowadays ; but it is an unpardonable thing to
go to the place of hearing determined not to hear.

Take the pledge, and leave off pledging.

The temperance pledge, and absence from the pledge-shop,
usually go together. It is not the total abstainer that keeps the
pawnshop going.

Take the tide, it will not bide.

The tide will not be tied. Take it at flood, or lie high and dry
while it ebbs. One to-day is worth a hundred to-morrows.

Take the world as it is, and try to make it what it ought to be.

Use men and things as you find them. Do not despair because
they are not so good as they might be and should be ; but set to
work to improve rather than censure.

Take thou good heed,
And thou wilt speed.

At least, it is one of the ways of doing so. Nobody fails through being too careful. Mind, or thou wilt be behind.

Take time by the forelock.

He is said to be bald behind, so that when time is past we can no longer seize upon it, and turn it to account.

"Shun delays, they breed remorse ;
Take thy time while time is lent thee ;
Creeping snails have weakest force ;
Fly their fault lest thou repent thee ;
Good is best when soonest wrought,
Ling'ring labours come to nought."—*Southwell.*

Take time in turning a corner.

Or you may run into something, or be run into by something. When making a change in the manner of your life, consider all the bearings of it, and be in no haste to wheel about and turn about.

When thou a dangerous way dost go,
Walk surely, though thy pace be slow.

Take time while time is, for time is flying.

" Complete what wisely you've begun,
Or you may live to rue it ;
When once you know what should be done,
Proceed at once to do it.
" Those who with time will sport and play,
Find often to their sorrow,
The birds that might be caught to-day,
Are fled before to-morrow."

Take you care, or care will take you.

And then it will be care indeed, of that black sort, which darkens all the skies of life.

Take your own case in your own hands.

Don't be for ever making other people into crutches for yourself. Why come to me ? I am neither your father-in-law, nor your mother-in-law, nor your brother-in-law, nor your dear old aunt.
" I've travelled about a bit in my time,
And of troubles I've seen a few ;
But found it better in every clime
To paddle my own canoe."

Taken to excess, even nectar is poison.

> In all human things you must draw a line, and say, "So far is good, and all beyond is evil." In meats, and drinks, and recreation, this is specially true.
>
> > Take not more than enough
> > Of the wholesomest stuff.

Talk and tattle
Make blows and battle.

Talk is talk; but it takes money to pay bills.

> Blandly, with a great show of politeness, the gentleman shows the best of reasons for not being able to settle the little account to-day. All very fine; but there stands the debt. A little of the precious metal would be better liked than a cart-load of this precious talk.

Talk like Robin Hood when you can shoot with his bow.

> But to use big words and swelling phrases, when you have nothing to show for your greatness, is absurd.
>
> > Frogs may not bellow like the ox,
> > Nor robins crow like farmyard cocks.

Talk much, sin much; pray much, have much.

Talk of what God does for you, not of what you do for God.

> For this last is too small a subject; and, indeed, if it were greater, it would all be wisely comprehended under the first head. God works in us what we work for him.

Talk, talk, talk, and it brings in nought;
Work, work, work, and the bread is bought.

> Thus *Thomas Spurgeon* describes that perpetual chatter which is so useless and wearisome:
>
> > "Bibble babble, gibble gabble, rattle, prattle, prate,
> > They jabber, chatter, cackle, clack, at ever such a rate.
> > Talk about the magpie, the parrot, and the jay,
> > I'm very sure these gossips talk ten times as much as they.
> > Talk about your talkabouts—the gift of g, a, b,
> > Loquacity, verbosity, and volubility;
> > The beasts, the birds, the fishes, if all of them could speak,
> > Would say no more in fifty years than these folk in a week."

Talking comes by nature, silence by wisdom.

Talking pays no toll.

> If it did, the County Councils would need no help from the Van and Wheel Tax. If only a penny a line could be charged, the Panama Canal could be finished with the money which would have to be paid in less than a week.

Tall trees catch much wind.

> Eminent persons are sure to be criticized, envied, and abused. Let no tree aspire to be a poplar, and no man aim to be popular.

Tarry, tarry, tarry, tarry,
Think again before you marry.

> One might push this tarrying too far, but we seldom meet with such a case. They rush at matrimony like a dog at a piece of meat. A quaint writer says, "I have seen women so delicate that they were afraid to ride, for fear of the horse running away; afraid to sail, for fear the boat might be upset; afraid to walk, for fear they might fall; but I never saw one afraid to be married, which is far more riskful than all the others put together."

Taste and try before you buy.

> This is the costermonger's invitation. As a piece of advice it applies to many more things than fruits.

Teach your boy a trade
And his fortune's made.

> But a clerkship, or a roving commission, or the genius which can do everything, will leave him in risk of poverty. He that hath a trade hath a settled estate, which no man can take from him.

Teachers' sins are teachers of sins.

> Children, and indeed all sorts of people, follow the examples of their teachers if there is anything wrong about them. Thus faults are reflected and repeated if seen in men of light and leading.

Teaching others teacheth yourself.

> A young man at Cambridge spoke to a wise man about taking a tutor to coach him, but the other said, "Rather take a pupil." To learn, and then to teach, is to engrave one's learning on the heart and memory.

Tears are powerful orators.

> This flowing eloquence melts the heart. Lions' teeth, and bulls' horns, are nothing in power to women's tears.

Tears are liquid eloquence.

"Tears have tongues"; and as these appeal to eyes rather than ears, they have greater power than words.

> Tears are the noble language of the eye;
> And when true love of words is destitute,
> The eyes by tears speak while the tongue is mute.

Tease a dog till he bite you, and then blame yourself.

Worry servants or children till they rebel in their anger, and with whom will the fault lie? The same Scripture which bids children obey their parents, also says, "Ye fathers, provoke not your children to anger, lest they be discouraged."—Col. iii. 21.

Tell-all is thought a fool, And everybody's tool.

They pump him for information, serve their own purposes by his tattle, and then laugh at him. Note this, Mr. Blabs.

Tell me the moon is made of green cheese.

I shall believe that fable quite as much as the silly tale which you are trying to palm upon me.

Tell me with whom thou goest, and I will tell thee what thou art.

> When I see thy company
> I will tell thee what thou be.

Tell the truth, and shame the devil.

If, indeed, he can be shamed. Nothing is less to his taste than the undiluted truth. His kingdom rests on falsehood.

Tell your affairs in the market-place, and one will call them black, and another white.

Every one will have an opinion. You thought everybody would agree with you, and see your wisdom. Alas! none see with your eyes, and therefore they neither see *as* you see, nor *what* you see.

Temperance is the best medicine.

For it is a preventive and a preservative, as well as a cure. Some do not like it any better than physic.

Ten children have eleven dispositions.

This is a Hindoo proverb, and sets forth the variety which can be found in a single household. Should not the training of each child be adapted to its special character?

Ten fingers ought to be able to feed one mouth.

And as a rule they will. Able-bodied persons without families ought not to be dependent upon charity. He who will not work for himself will not work for anyone else.

> " Far, far before the slave of pelf,
> Give me the son of labour:
> The man who rightly serves himself
> Will rightly serve his neighbour."

Ten honest "noes" are better than one false "yes."

Yet people will go on begging of us for a promise when we tell them that it is not in our power to do what they wish. We persist in our "no," though "yes" would, for the time, be far more pleasant. Why cannot people take our "No," and have done?

Ten measures of talk were sent down from Heaven, and woman took nine.

Shameful statement! It was invented by some horrid man! Was it the same cynical wretch, who, being requested to propose the toast, "To the ladies," said, "They require no eulogy; they speak for themselves"?

Tenderness matches well with manliness.

> " Use a woman tenderly, tenderly;
> From a crooked rib God made her slenderly.
> Straight and strong he did not make her,
> So if you try to bend you'll break her."

Test the truth, and then testify the truth.

No testimony can equal that of a man who has by personal experience certified his own soul of the truth to which he bears witness. Experience is the best college tutor. It is the sinew of the arm of persuasion, and the marrow of the backbone of confidence.

Thank God that hath so blest thee, And sit down, Robin, and rest thee.

Spend not all your life in getting, and none in enjoying. Some are so eager to get a living that they never live. Surely God meant us sometimes to sit down and enjoy life, and be thankful.

" Thank you, pretty pussy," was the death of my cat.

Compliments and flatteries do us more harm than good.

Thankfulness makes much of little.

> Be the meal of beans and peas,
> God be thanked for those and these.
> Have we bread or have we fish,
> All are fragments from his dish.

Thanksgiving is a good thing, thanks-living is a better.

The one may die in words ; the other lives in acts.

That cake came out of my oven.

It is amusing to see on another man's table some of your own cakes ; and so it is to see in a person's book or sermon a dose of your own thoughts, coolly taken, and never acknowledged.

That cat won't jump.

You need not try on that trick with me ; for I am not to be taken in by it. You can't lodge here, Mr. Ferguson.

That cruse of oil will not be less
That helps a brother in distress.

The widow fed the prophet, and the prophet's Master fed her.

That fish will soon be caught which nibbles the bait.

> The fish that nibbles at the bait
> Is very soon upon the plate.

Toying with temptation is extremely dangerous work.

That head is very sound that has no soft place.

There is a boggy spot on all headlands, and it is well for each man to know where his marshy places lie.

That is a good war in which no blood is shed.

> That was of all the very best fight,
> When never a man was slain :
> They ate their meat, and drank their drink,
> And then went home again.

That is vain which vanisheth.

Therefore fix thy heart on nothing but that which is eternal.

That is well spoken that is well taken.

Much depends upon the mind and spirit of the audience. That which was accepted as overwhelming eloquence when spoken, may be dull enough when read in cool moments at home. In private talk we give offence at one time by that which would have been right enough at another, because our friend is in a bad humour.

That lawyer is honest who has hair on his teeth.

This was in the olden times said of millers who tolled the corn brought to them for grinding. We dare say it was quite as true of the gentlemen of the sack as of the gentlemen of the long robe ; or quite as false.

That man is lost indeed who is lost to shame.

There is nothing left to work upon. The creature's hide is too thick for us to make him feel. We shall have to let him run away, for he has become too hard in the mouth for our bit.

That man is surely badly bred,
Who's strong in the arm, but weak in the head.

Of this bad breed there are many. Giants in muscle, and dwarfs in mind. Men weak in the head are generally head-strong !

That man most justly fool I call,
Who takes to scribbling on a wall.

Cutting initials on trees, and writing on public seats, and so forth, is a vulgar habit, against which all decent men should set their faces. Quote this rhyme till it becomes a common saying, and something will have been done to mitigate the nuisance.

That quite alters the case.

When it is yourself or a relative that is concerned, you are apt to alter your opinion upon the business. *Morton*, in his "Bengali and Sanscrit Proverbs," gives the following :—

> "Said a clown to a Brahmin, 'Sir, tell me, I pray,
> For crushing a spider, what fine must I pay ? '
> 'Why, friend,' he replied, ' 'tis a grievous offence,
> And demands an atonement of serious expense.'
> 'Indeed—then, alas ! with deep sorrow I'm filled ;
> Your son, sir, a poor little spider has killed.'
> 'Out, fool,' cries the Brahmin in anger—'away !
> For killing a spider there's nothing to pay ! '"

That thou mayest injure no man, dove-like be;
And serpent-like, that none may injure thee.

"When the fellow will not mind your dove," says one, "set your serpent at him"; but that is hardly the correct thing. Keep your serpent, not for offence, but only for defence.

That tongue which every secret speaks
Is like a barrel full of leaks.

There cannot be much in it; but it makes a great mess, and causes great loss.
> The blab no secret can retain;
> But what he hears he tells again.

That which a man causes to be done he does himself.

Masters cannot innocently take the profit of that which is done by those they employ in an evil trade. How can you have your barmaids serving out liquors while you yourself are at church?

That which comes with sin goes with sorrow.

Or, if it stays, it brings a curse with it. That which is hatched under the wing of a raven will peck at its owner's eyes.

That which covers thee discovers thee.

A man is known by his clothes, and a woman still more.

That which humbles us is always for our good.

That which is born of a hen will take to scratching.

Everything is according to the birth. That which is born of the flesh is flesh, and nothing better in the best of cases.

That which is evil is soon learnt.

And when learned, it so suits the disposition of the learner that he never forgets it. All the scholars in the school of sin are quick in getting hold of their lessons.

That which is got over the devil's back is usually spent under the devil's belly.

It goes as badly as it came, and usually in some form of worship of the belly god. *Nathaniel Bailey's* explanation of this proverb is, that "it is used of such covetous persons, who have, by unjust, fraudulent, and oppressive methods, amassed to themselves worldly riches. It intimates that such ill-gotten wealth is commonly wasted by a profuse heir, in riot and luxury, and seldom descends to the third generation."

That which is learned early is remembered late.

In our last days our memory is stronger concerning the facts of childhood than in reference to the events of yesterday.

That which is sharp is generally short.

This is comfortable to remember when in pain, or under slander, or in a thunder-storm, or when buffeted by a passionate man.

That which looks like a mountain may melt like a mist.

Have courage, and press forward ; for tremendous difficulties will vanish as you advance.

That which lowers itself is beginning to fall.

When a man inclines to low company and questionable ways, he is likely to go into gross faults. When a tradesman stoops to trickery, he is probably on the road to bankruptcy.

That which will not be butter must be made into cheese.

If a thing cannot be used in one way, we must use it in another, and suffer no waste. We must also make ourselves of use to the good cause by ingenuity of earnestness.

> In some way or other, help, if you please :
> If you can't be butter you must be cheese.

That you may be loved, be lovable.

Else you cannot expect people to love you, nor should you even desire them to act in so unreasonable a way as to love that which is not worthy of love. Love, and be loved : being loved, love.

That's my good which does me good.

That's not good language that all understand not.

The proverb refers to the language of preachers of the gospel ; they must not speak in an unknown tongue, but use market language. *Old Cobbett* said, "I not only speak so that I can be understood, but so that I cannot be misunderstood."

Thaw reveals what has been hidden by snow.

So, changes in nations and families bring many things to light. Injured reputations are often thus restored. On the other hand, when a man's riches melt away, many dirty things are seen which his wealth concealed.

The accomplice is as bad as the thief.

Sometimes he is worse. Jonathan Wild was a worse black than Jack Shepherd and the rest of the gang whom he protected, fleeced, and betrayed.

The account is correct, but not a sixpence appears.

Accuracy of accounts is most commendable; but when there is no income, no correctness of accounts can fill up the vacuum. However good the account, the estate is of no account when there is nothing to be counted. However, even if the balance is on the wrong side, keep the books correct to a farthing.

The adviser is not the payer.

That is to say, he who gives advice, as a general rule, has nothing to lose in the matter. Be chary of the counsel of one who carefully keeps on shore, but exhorts you to go to sea.

The ale jug is a great waster.

Toby Fill-pot fills his own pot, but he often empties the tea from the teapot, and the flour from the kneading trough. A drunkard's purse is a bottle, and everything runs out of it.

The ancients have run away with all our new ideas.

" I pine to be original,
But this I cannot be;
For ev'ry one's done ev'ry thing
In long advance of me.
I've come into the world too late—
I fear it must be so:
Oh, could I but be born afresh,
A thousand years ago ! "

The anvil fears not the hammer.

In patience it stands still and bears,
Till all the hammers it outwears.

The arm is the stronger, but the tongue is the longer.

When the strong arm is weary, the nimble tongue still runs its race. The more's the pity.

The ass that brays most, eats least.

Moral :—

If you would be largely fed,
Keep a still tongue in your head.

The back door is the one that robs the house.

There is an unknown leakage going on out of sight. Little lots of goods go off to other houses. Back doors for going out, and back stairs for going up, are of little use to honest men.

The beadle of the parish is always of the vicar's opinion.

Of course. Would you have the good man quarrel with his beans and bacon? He is bound to order himself lowly and reverently to his spiritual pastor and master.

The bear is not so bearish as folks make him.

Often when we come to know a man who has a reputation for roughness, we find him quite amiable: he "roars like a sucking dove." If you are not a bear, why wear a bear's skin?

The beaten road is the safest.

Keep to it, and let foolish speculators go over hedge and ditch, and meet with tumbles, and thieves, if so it pleases them.

The beginning prophesies the end.

So Christiana sings of her setting out upon the spiritual life:—
"Our tears to joy, our fears to faith,
Are turnèd, as we see;
Thus our beginning, as one saith,
Shews what our end will be."

The bell does not go to service, and yet it calls everyone to it.

This is very right in the bell, but it should not be told of a belle, or any other of man or woman kind. Where we bid others go, we should lead the way, lest the following rhyme be applicable to us:
The sign-post duly points the way,
Yet standeth still from day to day.

The best cause requires a good pleader.

Such a cause as that of the Saviour and his cross deserves our best efforts; and so long as men are desperately set on mischief, we shall need to plead with them on truth's behalf, as for our lives.

The best colt needs breaking in.

Your own delightful son requires it as much as other people's much inferior offspring. Perhaps if you knew all you would attend a little more to this very needful business. He that cockers his child makes a rod for his own back.

The best dog leaps the stile first.

All the pack will follow, but one hound leads the way, and, of course, he is the strongest and most daring. Those who aspire to leadership should take the first place in danger and in self-sacrifice. The holiest man will be first in protesting against evil.

The best eyes look inwards and upwards.

The best fish swim near the bottom.

Go deep into truth. Be not content with the surface of it; for in the depths lie the most precious thoughts. In soul-winning deal with the very worst, and you may bring to light, in many an instance, originality, force, fervour, and intense gratitude.

The best go first, the bad remain to mend:
Let bad beware, for patience hath an end.

Spared by long-suffering, we must improve, or else the God who has taken his saints home will send us to our own place.

The best ground bears weeds as well as flowers.

The best families have their " aunt-eaters and uncle-suckers."

The best harvest is the longest in being reached.

Archbishop Whateley said : "The man who is in a hurry to see the full effects of his own tillage, must cultivate annuals, and not forest trees." Only children will be in such foolish haste.

The best is the cheapest.

Because it lasts out so many of the sweater's good-for-nothing goods. Cheap is dear, and dear is cheap. We ought not to beat down the prices of first-rate articles : it is grinding down the workman, and forcing down the quality of the goods.

The best knowledge is to know God.

The best merchants never best each other.

They do not take each other in, but they deal fairly. If a man cannot become eminent by fair dealing, he had better keep in the background. Only small and mean traders look out for opportunities of taking undue advantage ; and such people never prosper.

The best of all acids is assiduity.

Use this wonderful chemical. It will eat its way through every difficulty. A great reduction upon taking a quantity.

The best of cloth
May harbour moth.

> The moth is no respecter of qualities. Sin assails the purest of men, and will work them mischief if it can.

The best of days for mending your ways.

> This very day is the best. Every moment you remain in sin you sin again. Till your debt is paid, your debt increases.

The best laid schemes o' mice and men gang aft a-gley.

> Because neither mice nor men can foresee all contingencies, and something happens which puts them out in their calculations. We do not wonder that mice fail : are men at all surer of success ?

The best of men are but men at the best.

> When trial comes it is seen to be so. What fault one man commits another may commit. Those are not the best of men who forget that they are only men.

The best physic is fresh air ;
The best pill is plain fare.

> It is well to remember this, for else we may fly continually to medicine, and end like the man who put on his tomb, " I was well, I wanted to be better, took physic, and died."

The best surgeon is he that has been well hacked about himself.

> He knows how to sympathize, for he has felt the smart. What a physician we have for our souls in the Man of Sorrows !

The best swimmer is often the first to drown.

> Because he is venturesome, while others avoid the water, since they know they cannot swim. Another proverb says, " The strongest swimmer was drowned at last." Nevertheless let us all learn to swim.

The best throw of the dice is to throw them away.

The better thou be, the more careful must thou be.

> The proverb books add, "quoth Hendyng." Whoever that worthy may have been, he spoke sound truth. It is hard to live up to a noble character : it is like keeping up a great house where the expenditure is large.

The Bible is the book which has no errata in it.

Neither in matters historical nor scientific does it blunder, any more than in matters theological. The worst mistake is with the man who thinks the Holy Spirit can be mistaken.

The big fish eat the little ones.

This is the mischief of it, for then one fish devours quite a number of small fry. Now, if the little fish ate the big fish, one of them might satisfy the hunger of hundreds. It is not an economical system, but so it is. Please, don't eat me up as yet.

The biggest horses are not the best travellers.

In fact, the little ones have the reputation of keeping on long after the big horses are knocked up.

> The biggest ox may do least work ;
> Yet little ones know how to shirk.

The biggest pears are not the best.

On the contrary, those fruits which exceed in size generally fail in flavour, and a big pear when eaten reminds one of a turnip.

The bird that can sing, and won't sing, must be made to sing.

The birds see the bait, but not the net.

So men see the present pleasure of sin, but not its fatal result.

The black ox treads on all our toes,
And every man his burden knows.

Care and trouble come to all. We should be glued to this world if this were not the case.

The blade oft used no rusting frets :
The running stream no filth begets.

Activity is health to the mind as well as to the body. Neither for our holiness nor our happiness is idleness helpful.

The blind lead the blind, and both fall into the ditch.

Our old-fashioned fathers were wont to sing :—

> " The Pope, that pagan full of pride,
> He hath us blinded long ;
> For where the blind the blind do guide,
> No wonder they go wrong."

The blind man sees his neighbour's faults.

The blood of the martyrs is the seed of the church.

> From the ashes of the martyrs springs a new race of confessors.
> The policy of cruelty has failed altogether.

> > The church of Christ is like a camomile bed :
> > The more it is trodden, the more it will spread.

The "Blue Boar" is a great devourer.

> Romeo would never have asked, "What's in a name?" if he had
> but lived to take a tour in England, and become acquainted with
> the nomenclature of some of our inns. To us there is hardly a
> sign in the kingdom which is not thoroughly significant; and any
> traveller, we should think, who has his mental eyes about him, may
> see at a glance outside the way in which he will be taken in. Who,
> for instance, would expect to enter the jaws or doors of a *Lion*
> without being bitten, or to get away from an *Eagle* without con-
> siderable bleeding? A little matured, the *Lamb* becomes decidedly
> indicative of fleecing; while every *Bear*, we know, is naturally
> prone to squeeze as many as he can lay his paws on. Roguery in
> the *Fox* is what everybody looks for, and plucking and roasting are,
> of course, inseparable from a *Goose and Gridiron*. Nor is the *Blue
> Boar* an exception to the rule, for it most aptly symbolizes your
> complexion when you leave it; and no one, we should think, would
> enter a *Green Man*, when reminded on the threshold of his verdancy
> in doing so. Of all our signs, however, perhaps there is none more
> suggestive than the *Magpie and Stump*, which anyone may see is
> merely a contraction for the far more significant *Magpie and Stump
> Up.*—*Punch* (more than twenty-five years ago).

The board slays more than the sword.

The boaster counts his penny silver.

> As for himself, he is a wonder. If you would but believe it, he is
> the greatest man that ever honoured the race by being born into it.

> > Of all speculations the market holds forth,
> > The best that I know for a lover of pelf,
> > Were to buy up our John at the price he is worth,
> > And sell him—at that which he sets on himself.

The body has two eyes, the soul must have one only.

> A single eye to the glory of God is essential to a holy life.

The bone of contention is the jaw-bone.

The bottle and the glass make many cry "Alas!"

"The bottomless pit is in Chancery Lane";
So said a man; and he spake very plain.

> Law is not good news, its agents are not angels, and it does not lead to bliss. The place where the legalities abound is not likened to the highest heaven. It's an ill chance which leads to Chancery.

The boughs that bear bountifully bow low.

> "Trees are bowed down with weight of fruit,
> Clouds big with rain hang low;
> So good men humbly bear success,
> Nor overweening grow."

The bow must not be always bent.

> When life's all labour, and has no intermission, it becomes slavery. Work without rest is like an unstuffed saddle, and cuts the rider to the bone.

The brain is ever sowing corn or cockle.

> It cannot be still. If you want to keep out bad thoughts, fill up the mind with good considerations.

The brains don't lie in the beard.

> Age goes before honesty, but not always after wisdom.

The bread of idleness should never be eaten.

> *Judge Haliburton* says, "The bread of idleness in a general way is apt to be stale, and sometimes I conceit it is a little sour." None but the meanest of the mean will eat a crumb of it. It ferments within a man, and breeds vice, roguery, and lechery.

The butcher looked for his candle, and 'twas stuck in his hat.

> He could not have seen except by that candle's light; and by that light he looked for the light! So, many are carefully looking for the grace of God in their hearts, though they would never have a desire to possess it unless grace had wrought that desire.

The cask is sure to smell of the wine it has held.

> Habits leave their impress upon the mind, even after they are given up. You cannot pour sin into the soul and out again without a taste remaining. The ill savour abides, though the sin is forgiven.

"The cat did it"; but the puss had only two legs.

> Alluding to the general explanation of breakages. There is a cat in every catastrophe of a domestic kind.

The cat invites the mouse to a feast.

> So the strange woman solicits the unwary youth.
>
> " Will you walk into my parlour ? said the spider to the fly,
> 'Tis the prettiest little parlour that ever you did spy."

The cat knows more than the kitten.

The cat settled the dispute between the birds.

> By eating them both up.
>
> > Does this differ a straw
> > From the action of law ?
>
> It is thus described :—
>
> > " Then take, says Justice, each of you a shell ;
> > We live at Westminster on folks like you.
> > 'Twas a fat oyster. Live in peace. Adieu ! "

The cat that killed the rat is the cat for me,
Whatever colour that cat may chance to be.

> Utility is in many matters the test of value. Whether a cat be white or cherry-coloured, that is to say, black, if she catches mice, she is worth her milk.

The cat thinks one thing, and the mouse another.

> The mouse plays, but the cat preys. The mouse seeks the corn, but the cat seeks the mouse. Hence :—
>
> > The cat's advice
> > Is bad for mice.

The cats that drive away the mice are as good as those that catch them.

> The one object is to save the corn, and the way in which this is done is not material. The policeman who keeps thieves away is quite as useful as another who arrests them.

The chamber of sickness should be the chapel of devotion.

> But devotion should not be confined thereto. It would be a pity that a man should need to be sickly to be saintly, and that the best promoter of devotion should be disease.

The chapter of accidents is the Bible of the fool.

He directs his course by his circumstances, and estimates the pleasure or anger of God by the incidents of Providence: this is a grave error. He believes a statement because others profess to believe it, but the Word of the Lord has no weight with him.

The charitable give out at the back-door, and God puts in at the window.

They give in secret, but receive in public. The rich are trustees for the poor, and if they execute their trust faithfully, the Lord often sees fit to put more into their hands; or, on the other hand, when he judges that their trust is fully discharged, he may see it best to release them from further worry and responsibility by allowing them to retire contented with a little.

The chicken is fed in the country, but eaten in the city.

One man has the labour, and another the enjoyment: let us hope that both are satisfied. One feeds the bullock, and another feeds on the beef: let us hope that neither of them finds it tough work.

The child is sure to hate the man unwise,
Who gives him everything for which he cries.

He has spoiled the child, and in due time his child will spoil him.

The child of the rabbit soon learns to burrow.

In all cases the offspring takes after the parents. How can we greatly blame our children for being faulty like ourselves?

The child says what he heard his mother say.

Of course he speaks his mother tongue. Let his mother mind what she says, or her talk will be her bairn's bane. A gracious mother writes: "Something having annoyed me one day, I said impatiently, 'botheration,' when immediately I heard the child-voice repeat clearly, 'bo-ther-a-tion.' I was greatly shocked, so dreadful did it sound on his little lips, that I felt as though I had thus heedlessly dropped into *his* soul the possible seedling of future blasphemy." Oh that all mothers were thus conscientious!

The chimney catches fire from within.

It would be hard to set it alight from the outside; but when the soot has accumulated, it is apt to burn. So temptation from without would be a very small danger to us if it were not for the soot within. Our corruptions are a greater danger than our temptations. How wise to keep the chimney well swept!

The cleaner the linen, the plainer the spot.

Or, "The fairer the damask the worse the stain." The faults of very good men are more noticeable than those of persons of inferior morals.

> Keep thy snow-white garments clean,
> For stains on such are quickly seen.

The coaches won't run over him.

He has got into jail, and is quite beyond fear of the accidents of the road. He has more to do with the turnkey than the turn-pike. The wheel will not go over him, for he is over the wheel.

The coalheaver is king in his own cot.

So he ought to be. Shall we call him Old King Coal? Take no liberties in his majesty's dominions, but treat him with due respect, lest the coalheaver heave you out of the house.

"In England every man's cottage is held to be his castle, which he is authorized to defend, even against the assaults of the king; but it may be doubted whether the same privilege extends to Ireland. 'My client,' said an Irish advocate, pleading before Lord Norbury, in an action of trespass, 'is a poor man; he lives in a hovel, and this miserable dwelling is in a forlorn and dilapidated state; but still, thank God! the labourer's cottage, however ruinous its plight, is his sanctuary and his castle. Yes, the winds may enter it, and the rains may enter it, but the king cannot enter it.' 'What! not the *reigning* king?' asked the joke-loving judge." — *The Tin Trumpet.*

The cobbler's wife is badly shod.

Usually those who sell an article are ill supplied themselves. They say the doctor's wife takes no physic. It is bad when ministers' families are the worst brought up in the parish; and when the teacher of other people's children spoils his own.

The cock doth crow to let us know,
If we be wise, 'tis time to rise.

If we went to bed earlier, and then rose at cock-crowing, we should enjoy the best part of the day, which now we never see.

The cock shuts his eyes when he crows, because he knows it by heart.

Many a preacher might do the same; but probably he does enough of eye-shutting upon other people.

The coddled child is the sickly child.

Mother is afraid the wind should blow on her darling, and so she keeps the fresh air away from him. Poor dear! "Do him up in lavender." Take care that you do not soon have to do him up in elm!

Who killed poor Sam?
His *Ma* called him "lamb"; and with treacle and jam,
She killed poor Sam.

The common people
Look at the steeple;
But the joy of the place
Is the gospel of grace.

What is architecture compared with the glad tidings from heaven? A fine church without the gospel is like a silver cover and no beef under it, or a golden pump without a drop of water.

The constant drop will wear the hardest stone.

Let it keep on long enough, and even the most despised of holy influences will tell upon the most stubborn mind.

The course of true love never did run smooth.

It is,

Like new-laid pavement, rather rough;
Like trade, exposed to losses;
Or like a Highland plaid, all stuff,
And very full of crosses.

The cow in the meadow would like to be on the common.
The cow on the common would like to be in the meadow.

We are never content with our position, whether we be cows or men. The ins would be out, and the outs would be in. Apprentices would be journeymen, and journeymen would be masters. The unmarried would like to be wedded, and some of the married wish they were single.

The cow little giveth that hard liveth.

We must feed her well if we expect much milk. Nothing comes out which is not first put in. Even Ayrshire cows can't live on air, and short-horns will not thrive on short commons.

The crop will show how the field was tilled.

The crow calls the rook black.

He looks at his friend's blackness, and quite forgets his own.

The cut that is worst
Of a leg is the first.

> This alludes to a leg of mutton, where the first cut is simply a great gaping gash. He who is content with the first cut of a shoulder of mutton has no appetite. In trade the first cut is nothing : most men lose at first. It must be all out-going at the beginning, and for some little while after ; the next cut is better.

The darker the day, the more we must pray.

The darker the days, the more we should praise.

The daughter of a good mother will be the mother of a good daughter.

> If she meets with a good husband. There is a great deal more in the stock from which a child comes than some suppose. Marry a daughter of a good daughter, and hope to have a good daughter.

The day hath eyes, and the night hath ears.

> Thus we are always under observation, and must not dare to sin.

The day is short, and the work is long ;
To waste a moment would be wrong.

The day may be foggy ;
You need not be groggy.

The day you do not clean the house some special friend will call.

> Mind this, Mrs. McTorker. It is always so, that when things are awkward, folks most respected, but quite unexpected, drop in.

The dead all slumber in the same bed.

> " Cover his head with turf or stone,
> It is all one ; it is all one."

The dead, and only they, should do nothing.

> While there's life in us let us live to purpose. He who has nothing to do may as well die.

The devil can cite Scripture to suit his purpose.

> But it is always with a twist of omission or addition. He cannot really support lies with truth ; but the language of truth makes falsehood go down with the unwary.

The devil comes to us across the fields.

Just when and where we think he cannot get at us, his temptations are sure to find us out.

> The devil will be where we think he's not;
> Security's vale is his favourite spot.

The devil does most when men are doing least.

Idleness gives the evil one a great advantage : he gets into the train while it waits at a station. The Turks say, "A busy man is plagued with one devil, but an idle man with a thousand."

The devil entangles the youthful with beauty, the miser with gold, the ambitious with power, the learned with false doctrine.

He has his peculiarly adapted temptations. How true it is that the learned are specially inclined to heresy ! You cannot get up a false doctrine without a D.D. to doctor the gospel for you. This is the case when their knowledge puffeth up, and they have not the love which buildeth up.

The devil falls in when saints fall out.

Times of contention are great opportunities for Satan. He is the spirit of hate, and feels much at home where ill-will is rampant. Yet when saints fall out with error and worldliness, the evil one has his nest disturbed, and he likes it not.

The devil first plays the fox, afterwards the lion.

First deceives, and then destroys. Thus error first pleads for liberty, and then lords it over truth, and rages at those whom at first it flattered.

The devil in a sheep's-skin is a devil indeed.

His deceitful nature thus finds a fit incarnation, and he riots among those whom he delights to worry, and desires to devour.

> Oh, what may man within him hide,
> Though angel on the outward side !

The devil is a bad master, and he has bad servants.

Yet his bad servants are obedient to him, zealous in his cause, and obstinate in following his ways. This evil master and his servants grow more and more alike the longer they are together.

The devil is a busy bishop in his diocese.

Nobody can ever complain that he does not hold Visitations and Confirmations. He is all over his diocese, and puts forth all his energy. Hugh Latimer has a pithy piece upon this "most diligent bishop and prelate in all England."

The devil is neither dead nor lame.

Of *Mr. Haynes*, the coloured preacher, it is said that, some time after the publication of his sermon on the text, "Ye shall not surely die," two reckless young men, having agreed together to try his wit, one of them said, "Father Haynes, have you heard the good news?" "No," said Mr. Haynes, "what is it?" "It is great news indeed," said the other, "and if true, your business is done." "What is it?" again enquired Mr. Haynes. "Why," said the first, "the devil is dead." In a moment the old gentleman replied, lifting up his hands, and placing them on the heads of the young men, and in a tone of solemn concern, "O poor fatherless children! What will become of you?"

The devil is old, but not infirm.

On the contrary, his age has sharpened his cunning to an intense degree. Thousands of years he has been tempting men, and who can hope to be a match for him?

The devil leads him by the nose,
Who the dice so often throws.

Gambling is so silly a vice, that it is fair to say that its votary is led by the nose; and it is so ruinous, that surely Satan must have a special hand in it. The ancients say, "The devil goes shares in gaming"; and yet again, "Play hath the devil at the bottom of it." Yet the devil does not demean himself to play.

The devil likes to souse what is already wet.

Where evil is already abundant, he sees good soil for the growth of more. The worse a man is, the worse he may become; and therefore Satan attends carefully to his education in immorals. Evil is not evil enough for him; he would increase it without measure. Every sin is excess, but he would make it more excessive.

The devil takes ill-care of his own servants.

For a while he seems to reward them, but it is to mock them. What is called "the devil's luck" is only disguised ruin. Satan has no gratitude; but those who serve him best are the greatest sufferers in the long run.

The devil was sick—the devil a monk would be ;
The devil was well—the devil a monk was he.

> Sick-bed repentance is generally sickly repentance, and dies as the man recovers.

The devil will not drive out the devil.

> Else would his kingdom fall. Anger is not the way to drive evil out of your wife or your servant. Those who beat children unmercifully may drive one devil out, but they drive ten devils in.

The devil's apple has a bitter core.

> Beware of his tempting fruit. When he says "*Ave*," think you hear wisdom saying "*Cave*." Every child of Eve should sicken at the sight of the serpent's apple.

The devil's journeymen never want work.

> He makes work for them, and makes them work for him.

The devil's meal is all bran.

> His gains and profits are not what they seem, but dwindle down to the small end of nothing.

The dew of the morning sparkles with health.

> Those who have it often on their brows speak highly in its favour.
>
> Wash thy face in morning dew ;
> Thou wilt thus thy health renew.

The difficult thing is to get your foot in the stirrup.

> To begin is the difficult matter. Once mounted, riding will be simple enough. To get some men really into the stirrups is the hard matter: they hesitate and remain undecided. To get a livelihood, it is a great thing for a young man to get his foot on the ladder, even if it be the lowest rung.

The dog does not get bread every time he wags his tail.

> He would be far too fat if he did. We must not expect to have all our wishes granted us. Children ought not to have every whim gratified, or they will be ruined.

The dog is a better friend to man, than man to the dog.

> It should never be so. He is a cruel cur indeed who is cruel to his dog. They say, "Love me, love my dog"; but in some cases the difficulty would not be to love the dog, but the brute that owns him. "Is thy servant a dog?" No, he is nothing half so noble.

The dog that minds not your whistle is good for nothing.

Without obedience what is the value of the creature you keep? From the dog up to the servant and the child, the master has a right to expect attention all round.

The donkey's gallop is short.

Some say, "short and sweet." Many men are soon over with their little game. They take up work fast enough; but they drop it quite as fast. There is no depending on them for half-an-honr.

The double-shuffle is the devil's dance.

He practises, inspires, and admires the arts of deceit.

The dove hates the least feather of the hawk.

Every pure-minded man will hate even the appearance of evil.

The drunken man's joy is the sober man's sorrow.

He wastes the substance of the family, and degrades its name; and for this, father, brother, and specially wife, have grey hairs on heads which should not so soon be thus whitened.

The ducks fare well in the Thames.

Where there is plenty of room, and an ever-flowing stream. They are not alarmed by the fear of Cookham or Eton; but they disport themselves in the green and peaceful streams, and nobody hears of their being injured by the abundance of water. Where there is "enough and to spare" is the place for me also.

The Dutch have taken Holland.

Wonderful! And an ass has eaten thistles! A dog has gnawed a bone! A "modern thought" apostle has denied the gospel.

The ear tires sooner than the tongue.

Few are tired of talking, but very many are wearied with hearing. And well they may be when we think of what they have to hear. Many sermons exercise the patience of the saints.

The emperor rules the empire, but the empress rules the emperor.

Oftentimes some favourite son rules the empress, and then the land is unhappy, for it is really governed by a child. It is wonderful with how little wisdom kingdoms are governed.

The empty cask sounds most.

It is a common remark that men talk most who think least. When knowledge comes, chatter stops, just as frogs cease their croaking when a light is brought to the water's side.

The envious die, but envy lives.

The eye of charity should be open, as well as its hand.

To give indiscriminately may be almost as mischievous as not to give at all. Charity must never be blind; but it may see too much, and therefore close its hand. Keep the middle way.

The eye of the master does more than both his hands.

He may do but little manual labour, but his oversight of the work gets it done in quicker and better style than if he were away. The more servants a man has, the more will he need to stay at home and look after them.

The farmer's care makes fields to bear,
Yet God, we know, makes harvests grow.

How the omnipotence of God works through the labour of man we know, for we see it before us every day. We work as if we did all; but we trust in God, knowing that all power belongs to him.

The farther from Rome, the nearer to God.

And it even seems as if there were less Popery in Rome than thousands of miles away from the Vatican. Even the imitation of religion does not flourish in that harlot city.

> They truly say the Pope of Rome
> Is little thought of nearest home.

The farther in, the deeper.

The more we press into the centre of true godliness, the deeper shall we find its mystery, its power, its joy. Those who are up to the ankles in the river of life should go further in till they reach "waters to swim in."

The feet are slow when the head wears snow.

Old age must be content to leave running to youth and middle age.

The fewer to stare, the better the fare.

It is, to some of us, impossible to eat at banquets. We feel like the wild-beasts, whose feeding is a thing for the public to stare at.

The finest diamond must be cut.

Because it is so precious it must undergo this ordeal. God tries the heart he values. The more dear we are to him, the more shall we be chastened. Pebbles lie undisturbed, but jewels do not.

The fire that burneth taketh the heat out of a burn.

It is so on homœopathic principles. That grace which burns us with conviction of sin taking the fire out of the burns of sin. We are judged in conscience that we may not be judged.

The first dish pleaseth all.

In the beginning, appetite is not satiated: everyone is prepared to start fair. The first speaker at a meeting is borne with because the people are not yet wearied.

The first hour of the market for me.

When I am fresh, and my customers have not yet spent all their money. When the goods are fresh and I can have the pick of them as a purchaser.

The first three men in the world were a gardener, a plough-man, and a grazier.

Honourable employments these! Let no man think little of the various forms of husbandry. They are the most healthful and enjoyable of callings. Being made of the earth, we are earthy, and thrive best in those employments which take us back to the ground whence we were taken.

The first to end a fray
Is the best man, I say.

He who is the least to blame is the first to desire reconciliation.

The first who speaks of a suit at law is not therefore in the right.

No, he is frequently a bully, who wants to frighten his opponent. "I'll bring an action" is his frequent threat. "I don't care a fraction" is the answer which usually silences him for the time.

The fish which we did not catch is a very large one.

That which gave us a nibble was immense! That which ran away with the hook was simply enormous! Thus do we make capital out of our failures. What might we not have done if—— !

The flawed pot lasts longest.

When things are a little cracked it is wonderful how long they last, and the like long continuance is proverbial in sickly people. And yet if ever a dish is broken it was cracked before ; and that wicked Mr. Nobody did it, or possibly the cat.

The flesh is master when the mind is idle.

An awful tyrant it is. O sleeping mind, wake up and claim thy proper sovereignty !

The fly that playeth with the candle singeth her wings.

How many do so until they perish ! We know many moths and flies in the shape of young men and women who are already feeling the flame. Fly away, poor creatures!

The fool is fond of writing his name where it should not be.

When I see a person's name
Scratched upon the glass,
I know he owns a diamond,
And his father owns an ass.

The fool saith, "Who would have thought it ?"

When the reply might be, "Who would *not* have thought it ?" When simple souls run into evil, *they* may be surprised at the consequence, but no one else is.

The foolish alchemist sought to make gold of iron, and made iron of gold.

So it is with those who deal with outside brokers, and go in for "cover, and options," and so forth. They were going to turn their little savings into a fortune, and instead thereof they turned them into smoke. Keep out of the stocks, or you will lose your stock.

The foolish and perverse
Fill the lawyer's purse.

There be many people so given to strife,
That they'll go to law for a twopeny knife.

The fools do more hurt in this world than the rascals.

So it would seem. Our own worries come not so much from the wicked as from the weak. A defence of you by a fool may do you more harm than a slander. Save us from a fool's enthusiasm !

The fowler catches old birds as well as young ones.

The fox barks not when he would steal the chickens.

> No, he is as cautious and silent as a modern theologian who is scheming to mislead an orthodox church.

The fox of Ballybotheram was caught at last.

> He worried both dogs and men, led them a fine dance, and got away every time : but the hounds devoured him at length.

The fox praiseth the cheese out of the crow's mouth.

> Let the crow suspect the praise, which is not given for her own sake, but for her cheese sake. You know the fable : it is the picture of that which happens every day.

The friend of the table
Is very variable.

> So say the French, and many English have proved it to be true. He is a wooden friend who owes his friendship to your mahogany.
>> The friend who serves for feasts and gain,
>> And follows but for form,
>> Will pack when it begins to rain,
>> And leave thee in the storm.

The full man does not believe in hunger.

The game is not worth the candle.

> The Hindoos speak of a leaf falling into a well, and seven men falling in while looking for it. It is a mad world, and exhibits many instances of hunting mud rabbits with golden hounds. For a homely instance, let us note that when a woman went out to work and earned a shilling, but left her children to do and suffer ten shillings' worth of damage, her game was not worth the candle.

The getting out of doors is the greatest part of the journey.

> With some it seems the hardest thing to start. Once off, they go well enough. It is a task indeed to get them into going order. Nothing will ever be attempted if all possible objections have first to be overcome; and with many timorous people this is very much the case. They will get on if they get off.

The girl with a settlement will soon be settled.

>> That opposite effects may flow
>> From the same cause, 'tis clear's no hum ;
>> For money makes the *mare* to *go*,
>> And also makes the *men* to *come*.

The girl with a sneer
Shall never be my dear.

> I should think not. What if she should sneer *at me* after I had courted her? She might, but she shan't.

The glutton's temple is the kitchen, and his belly is his god.

> His sacrifice is his health. His reward is early death. Gluttony kills more than war. The epicure heaps suppers upon dinners, and breakfasts upon suppers, and lunches upon breakfasts, without intermission, till it costs him more to choke up his interior than it would to keep a dozen healthy men and women. The following lines were written by *Lord Francis Hervey* in a pastrycook's shop:
>
> > " Be sure that when you've had your fill,
> > You beat a swift retreat ;
> > For Satan finds some dainties still
> > For idle mouths to eat."

The good are better made by ill,
As odours crushed are sweeter still.

The good-man is the last who knows what's amiss at home.

> He must be a singularly absent-minded husband who would allow everybody else to see what he cannot see himself. No doubt it is sometimes so : the man is long-sighted outside in the world, but sees not that which is just under his nose.

The goodness of news half lies in the hearer's ear.

> When people are anxious, and longing for tidings, they think every word precious.

The grace of God is gear enough.

> He that hath grace shall have all other things added to him. "Man wants but little here below" ; grace will secure us that little, and much more. This is a good wish for a friend—
>
> > A little health, a little wealth,
> > A little house, and freedom ;
> > And in the end a little friend,
> > And little cause to need him.

The great ship has also great dangers.

The greatest art is to conceal art.

> It is well to do a thing so naturally that no one would dream that you had followed any rule, or had even taken thought.

The greatest learning is to be seen in the greatest plainness.

This is so with a preacher. If a man cannot make you understand what he is saying, he probably does not understand the matter himself. Ignorance conceals itself behind hard words : true learning expresses itself with careful clearness.

The greatest man must be put to bed with a shovel.

From the graves of the cemetery comes this voice :—

Princes, this clay must be your bed,
In spite of all your towers ;
The tall, the wise, the reverend head
Must lie as low as ours.

The greatest of all faults is to be conscious of none.

For this will prevent all hope of mending by making a man think that he is perfect. That must be the greatest of faults which protects all the rest.

The greatest things are done by the help of small ones.

The hand that gives gathers.

May God make it so to every generous giver ! Giving is sowing.

The hard man gives no more than he that hath nothing.

Miserly persons, if they have wealth, are more looked after than beggars ; and yet they are not worth a penny more to anybody.

The hard-hearted man is the first to complain of unkindness.

He feels for himself because he feels for nobody else.

The hasty angler loses the fish.

He must have patience, and bide his time, and let his fish have a run, or else he will go home with a bare basket. Let him go, that he may not be gone. Let him pull out, that you may pull him in. Humour men and women in much the same way.

The head grey, and no brains yet !

This expression of wonder might apply to a very large number. Better not let them hear it, or a part of their head may grow red. *Dr. Chatfield* has the following :—" I wish to consult you upon a little project I have formed," said a noodle to his friend. " I have an idea in my head "—" Have you ? " interposed the friend, with a look of great surprise, " then you shall have my opinion at once : *keep it there !*—it may be some time before you get another."

The heart of a fool is in his mouth; but the mouth of a
  wise man is in his heart.

When the heart is in the mouth, too much comes up; but when the
heart controls the mouth, communications will be wise.

The heart that trusts for ever sings,
And feels as light as it had wings.

That is to say, when the trust is rested upon God alone the rest
which comes of it is true and gladsome.

The hen that laid the egg ought to hatch it.

Those who commence a scheme should see to its development,
and other people should defer to them, and give them the option of
working out their own methods. The "ought" in this proverb
may mean either duty or privilege, or both.

The herbs in our own garden will not do for medicine.

No, we must fetch plants from India. Herbs are not prophets in
their own country. Our own mineral springs are just as good as
those in Germany, but no one drinks such common and vulgar
waters!

To German *bads* our sick ones roam:
Our water's quite as bad at home.

The higher the fool, the greater the fall.

Fall he will, sooner or later; and what a smash there will be!

The higher the head, the humbler the heart.

It should be so; but very often the opposite is the case.

The highest branch is not the safest roost.

For there the bird is soonest seen,
And shot at by some sportsman keen.

The hog that is filthy tries to make others so.

He hastens to rub against his fellows, and foul them with his own
mud. Bad fellows cannot bear to see innocence. By example or
by slander they will either make others wicked, or cause them to
appear so. By all means keep clear of swinish men.

The home may soon be full of gear,
If you will learn to save the beer.

The beer-money looks little enough as you drink it away; but
when it is saved it is wonderful how rich you seem, and how much
you can buy. Going without the beer makes all the difference.

The horseshoe that clatters is a nail short.

> The clatter of the tongue in many a head indicates the same melancholy shortness with regard to the mind ; only we generally say, "there's a button short," or "a slate loose." The worst of it is, that you cannot keep a cracked bell still.

The hour of idleness is the hour of temptation.

The house gives the wife a character.

> According to its cleanliness and order she will be esteemed. An ill-kept house will damage her good name, and make the neighbours speak lightly of her.

The improvident fight against providence.

> They may say what they please about their faith ; but as a provident man is not pleased with improvident children, so our Father in heaven loves not prodigality. Those fly in the teeth of providence who squander the provisions of God's bounty.

The jawbone does the mischief.

> Whether by too much talking or by too much eating. Much jaw much jeopardy, and much meat much malady.

The joking of wits, like the playing of puppies, often ends in snarling.

The King of Terrors is a terror to kings.

> Hence Louis XIV. built his palace at Versailles, since he could not endure that of St. Germains, because from the terrace he could see the tower of the abbey of St. Denis, where the French kings are buried. Death is a dreadful leveller. What cares he for crowns?

The king may bestow offices, but cannot bestow wit to manage them.

> To the misery of the parties concerned, this has been proved true in sadly many cases. Desire to be fit for a post before you desire the post itself. If you cannot ride, why seek a horse?

The king must wait while his pudding's boiling.

> Or some say, "while his beer is drawing." Like other mortals, he must have patience, for he cannot eat pudding till it is cooked. The Queen herself cannot drink tea till the water is made hot. She who is waited on must wait. Should not we wait also?

The knot you knit
Think well on it.

> Before you make the thing binding, consider and reconsider.

The last drop makes the cup run over.

> Just as the last ounce breaks the camel's back, and the last cruel word breaks the heart. We receive many good things as a matter of course, though we ought not to do so; but some little extra blessing makes us pour out our hearts in gratitude.

The latest fashion is often the latest folly.

The law of love is better than the love of law.

The lawyer grows fat, but his client is lean.

> "A country carter, driving his team, upon a time, along the highway, the foremost horse, it seems, was in very good case, and the rest could hardly crawl after him without the crack of the whip. 'Why, how now, honest man,' cries a counsellor, 'how comes it that your first horse is so fat, and the others so lean?' 'Ho, sir,' says he smartly enough, 'the leader is a lawyer's horse, and those that follow him are but his clients.'"

The lazy begin to be busy when it's time to go to bed.

> Just when the season is over, he proposes to work; and just as he might prosper, he dies. Many a man has gone to the grave when he expected his great baking of bread to come out of the oven.

The lazy man is the beggar's brother.

> Even the beggar is by no means proud of him, but bids him go and sing for his supper, like the rest of the gang.

The lazy man's dessert—roast nothing and no turnips.

> Scant is the table of sloth, and scant it ought to be.

The leanest pig squeaks most.

> Generally. If there is one man worth less than another, he is the fellow to agitate for more wages, or shorter hours.

The least said the soonest mended.

> Every ill-word makes a breakage. If there has been no tittle-tattle, matters can soon be set right.

The less men think, the more they talk.

The less brain, the more jaw. It was said of one verbose preacher—

"Ten thousand thousand are his words,
But all his thoughts are one."

The less the fire, the greater the smoke.

Frequently it is so: a little smothered fire makes huge volumes of smoke, where a vehement flame scarcely makes a puff. The less grace the more boast. The less solidity the more pretence.

The less the temptation, the greater the sin.

For it is the more wanton, deliberate, and personal. If we run after sin, and are not drawn into it, we show great depravity of heart. Adam's offence had a great aggravation in it, since he did not sin by depravity, or habit, or example, or from poverty, or persuasion, or force of fashion.

The less wit a man has, the less he knows his want of it.

In fact, where there is very little wit, the man sets up for a sage, and out of his empty skull brings forth oracles of wisdom.

The less you have of goods, the more you need of God.

But it is equally true, "The more you have of goods, the more you need of God." Viewed from different points, positions of poverty or wealth are equally perilous, unless unusual grace be granted us. We may be poor and envious, or rich and proud. From each of these may grace deliver us !

The life of love is better than the love of life.

The love of life is natural, the life of heavenly love is supernatural, and is created in us by him whose name is LOVE.

The longest life is a lingering death.

This is a pessimist's view of things. A man with a bad liver made this estimate : the worth of the life depends on the liver.

The loosest spoke in the wheel rattles most.

Those who are quietly doing their duty make no fuss, but the blameworthy are always in evidence.

The loudest are not the wisest.

But, on the contrary, the louder the bray, the bigger the ass.

The loudest bummer's not the best bee.

In fact, he is no true bee at all, but only a bumble-bee.

The loudest to threaten are the last to thrash.

The love of money is worse than the lack of money.

One can go to heaven without gold in the purse, but one cannot get there at all with gold in the heart. Not money, but *the love of it,* is the root of all evil. *South* says, "Mammon has enriched his thousands, but damned his ten thousands."

The love of the wicked is more dangerous than their hatred.

They can flatter to evil, where their frown would have no effect.

The lowliest Christian is the loveliest Christian.

No virtue adds such grace to a fair character as humbleness of mind. The lily of the valley is a lovely flower.

The mad dog bites his master.

He is often the very first person he flies at. When persons are out of their minds, they often hate those most whom once they loved best. It is a token of great folly and wickedness when a man turns round upon the person who was his benefactor and his leader.

The man is what his wife makes him.

> The man who weds a loving wife,
> Whate'er betideth him in life,
> Shall bear up under all;
> But he that finds an evil mate,
> No good can come within his gate,
> His cup is filled with gall.

The man of courage knows not when he is beaten.

Like the English drummer-boy, he does not know how to beat a retreat. He may be crushed down, but never crushed out.

> The good man, like a bounding ball,
> Springs ever upward from his fall.

The man of loose life
Shan't have me for a wife.

Sensible woman ! Mind you stick to that resolution. If you do not, you will have yourself to blame when misery comes upon you.

The man that once did sell the lion's skin
While the beast lived, was killed with hunting him.

He made too sure of destroying the enemy, and so became himself the prey. Also : never sell what you have not got.

The man who does not trust his own judgment is a man of good judgment.

No man but a fool is always right. A wise man knows this, and fearing that he may err he is willing to be advised. On the other hand, the first degree of folly is to think one's self wise, the next to tell others so, and the third to despise all counsel.

The man who is everything is nothing.

He resembles the man whom *Dryden* describes as—

"Stiff in opinions, always in the wrong,
Was everything by starts, and nothing long ;
But in the course of one revolving moon,
Was chemist, fiddler, statesman, and buffoon."

The man who knows most, knows most his own ignorance.

When one ventured a compliment to the great philosopher and naturalist, Louis Agassiz, upon the extent and variety of his investigations into the secrets of nature, the Professor's ready and modest reply was, " My dear sir, the longer I live, the more I find I know nothing."

All things I thought I knew ; but now confess
The more I know, I know I know the less.

The master's eye puts flesh on the horse's bones.

" A fat man riding once along the road, upon a starved and bony jade, was asked, in a banter, why he himself was so jolly and good-like, and his pad so scragged and lean ? He replied very pat to the purpose, ' Why, I feed myself, you must know ; but my servant looks to my horse.' "

The master's presence is the field's profit.

His foot fattens the soil. When things are well looked over they are not overlooked. Who lives in his business will live by his business.

The meanest reptiles crawl up the highest pillars.

You cannot, therefore, judge of a man by his position in society.

The meekness of Moses is better than the strength of Samson.

Moses conquered himself, which Samson could not do.

The middle course is usually safest.

Not that which lies between truth and error, or right and wrong; but that which lies between violent extremes. Desire neither riches nor poverty; be neither sceptical nor credulous; spend neither with prodigality nor with meanness. Follow the golden mean.

The mill goes click, click; but where's the meal?

Plenty of resolving to do, and boasting of what is doing; but what really comes of it all?

The mill will never grind with the water that is past.

> " Listen to the water-mill
> Through the livelong day
> How the clicking of its wheel
> Wears the weary hours away.
> And a proverb haunts my mind,
> And as a spell is cast:
> 'The mill will never grind
> With the water that is past.' "

The mistress's eye keeps kitchens clean.

Let her leave the maids to themselves, and she will soon see more dirt than there is dust in March, or rain in April.

The more a donkey grows, the more of a donkey he is.

Even growth in knowledge does not remove the folly of a fool. We have heard of a man who went to two colleges, but he was likened to a calf which sucked two cows, and the more it sucked, the bigger a calf it grew.

The more a fool has, the more a fool he is.

He has the more opportunity of developing and displaying his folly. He is able to spend money on his whims, and so he multiplies and magnifies them. Who does not remember a "Smith's Folly," or a "Robinson's Blunder"?

The more coin, the more care.

Yet most men will run that risk; for they hold, on the other hand, that

> To have no coin,
> Is more annoying.

The more cooks, the worse custards.

Indeed, it is possible that you may get none at all. One would not be surprised to learn that one had left it to the other, and the other to a third, and so the custard was forgotten altogether, or that mustard was sent to table instead.

The more froth, the less beer.

Those who foam, and fume, and fuss, have so much the less of real worth in them.

The more haste, the worse speed.

Four things only are well done in haste : flying from the plague, escaping quarrels, catching fleas, and forsaking sin.

The more laws, the more offences.

This statement is true upon the face of it ; and it illustrates the Scriptural doctrine, that the commandment, however good, works sin in our corrupt nature, exciting desire by its prohibition.

The more noble, the more humble.

It is usually so. A proud man has nothing to be proud of ; with the lowly is wisdom, and wisdom makes a man noble.

The more one has, the more one wants.

Sad truth, that in many cases the wolfish hunger of covetousness increases with the quantity which it has devoured.

The more servants, the less service.

Rather a petulant declaration, like that other saying, " the more servants the more plagues." Yet was a man ever better served than when he had one " gyp " to do everything for him ?

The more the good tree grows, the more shade does it afford.

When a good man's estate increases, he diffuses the grateful shadow of comfort all around him.

The more the merrier, the fewer the better cheer.

This is at a feast. The generous like to see many guests ; but those who are hankering after a great feed for themselves, calculate that the fewer the eaters, the more will remain for each one.

The more thou doest, the more thou canst do.

And the more thou wilt have to do ; for in this world willing workers are driven most mercilessly.   If thou wilt thou shalt.

The more understanding, the fewer words.

When a man knows his subject well he is able to give a brief description of it.   A great preacher desired more time in which to study his sermon, that he might make it shorter.   A few drops of otto of rose are worth a ton of leaves.

The morning hour has golden minutes.

All the day is the richer for a man's beginning it in good time. Another proverb says: "The morning hour has gold in its mouth."

> Up at five all alive—
> That's the way to live and thrive.
> Up at nine, the day is gone,
> Will not do to think upon.

The most positive are often the most mistaken.

Cromwell, writing to the Presbyterian ministers of Scotland, once said, "I beseech you, dear brethren, think it possible that you may be wrong." But we are too wrong to think we are wrong.

The mouth is the door of mischief.

Both for entrance and exit.   Mischief goes into the mouth in the form of strong drinks, and comes out in the shape of weak words.   He was wise who prayed, "Set a watch, O Lord, before my mouth ; keep the door of my lips."—Ps. cxli. 3.

The myrtle among brambles is still a myrtle.

Even as the lily among thorns is a lily still.   Where there is the grace of God in the heart, the necessary associations of this evil world shall not destroy the beauty of the divine creation.

The nearer the church, the further from God.

It is sad when this is the case.   It is worst of all when those who serve in the temple are themselves ungodly, and when ministers' children are children of the devil.   Yet it is too often so, that those who are almost in the church are yet leagues away from it, and nobody thinks of looking after them.

> The cobbler's wife, and blacksmith's mare,
> Among the barest go most bare.

The new-made knights
Have great delights
To hear the people call them "Sirs,"
And mark the jingle of their spurs.

The novelty of their promotion pleases the little men, as new toys charm little children. The new-made D.D. grows so vain that some think him M.D., with an A. between.

The north wind finds out the cracks in the house.

Affliction tests our religion, and lets us see our failures of faith, patience, and temper. Blame not the wind, but the wall.

The old gospel is the only gospel.

As there is but one God, one Saviour, and one Spirit, so there is but one gospel.

The older the crabtree, the more crabs it bears.

Does it? Well, we fear it is so with human crabtrees. Age does not temper some tempers.

The only way to have a friend is to be one yourself.

And this is the way to keep a friend when you have him. This reminds us of an old country health, which a farmer gave at the house of a neighbour who had helped him to get in his crops :—

> Here's health to you and yours,
> Likewise to us and ours;
> And if ever you and yours
> Need help that's in our powers,
> We'll do as much for you and yours,
> As you have done for us and ours.

The other man is to blame.

He is in the country now, and not to be got at. Jack says "Harry did it"; and Harry says "'Twas Jack."

The other side of the road always looks cleanest.

Who has not noticed this? So we think that others are free from trouble, when it is possible that they are even worse off than we are. "It is common," says *Tacitus*, "to esteem most what is most unknown."

The owl of ignorance lays the egg of pride.

A very fine egg, but of coarse flavour.

The owl thinks all her young ones beauties.

And so don't we! How often parents are the only admirers of their own offspring! Happy partiality! " A beetle is a beauty to its mother."

Where was ever seen the mother,
Would change her booby for another?

The ox ate the corn, and they beat the donkey for it.

Certain persons seem ordained to be the scape-goats for others. One boy does the wrong, but sneaks out of it; and another seems always to be caught in the act, and yet is innocent.

The ox ploughs the field, but the man eats the grain;
One does the work, and another gets the gain.

This comes from the Chinese, and shows that there is injustice everywhere; and where there is none, there is still grumbling.

The paleness of the pilot is a sign of a storm.

The parings of a pippin are better than the whole of a crab.

Yes, a few cheery words from a genial friend are far better than an hour's scolding from a churl.

The parson's pig is as hard to drive as mine.

The lot of the very best is not free from crooks.

The penny in the purse is sometimes handier than the pound in the bank.

For immediate purposes, a little ready knowledge may be more serviceable than a mass of learning which cannot be used.

The perverting of words is the subverting of peace.

Because misunderstandings are thus created. The man whose words are twisted is aggrieved; and so are those against whom those words are supposed to have been uttered.

The philosopher's stone is " Pay as you go."

It does not turn all things into gold, but it is the best way of preserving what gold you have. Do as little as possible with borrowed money. Even in building a house remember the lines: —

The man who builds and wants wherewith to pay,
Provides a home from which to run away.

The pink of gentility is often the poppy of pride.

The place to spend a happy day—Home !

The pleasure of love is in loving.

> Not altogether : one is pleased to be loved in return.

The plough goes ill when one ox pulls one way, and the other another.

> When husband and wife are not of one mind, family arrangements are disarranged, and specially when there is a difference about religious matters. "Be ye not unequally yoked together with un-believers," is a wise precept, which should in no case be disregarded.

The poor man fasts because he has no meat,
The rich man fasts because he cannot eat.

The poor man no one kens ;
The rich have many friends.

The poor man's budget is full of schemes.

> His plans are wonderful, but they end in plans.

The poor man's hand is Christ's treasury.

> Fill it.

The poorest truth is better than the richest lie.

The pot boils best on its own hearth.

> The writer cannot study well except in his own den. Men are cleverest in their own sphere. Home has a developing power ; for when men are at their ease, they are able to bring forth things new and old. The proverb is a good reason for declining either to lend or borrow a pot, or kettle. Your own goods are best at home.

The price of mercy is to prize it.

The prodigal robs his heir, the miser robs himself.

> It would be hard to say which is the bigger fool of the two, but surely the second in order is not second in degree.

The proof of the pudding is not in chewing the bag.

> No : nor does the proof of soundness in the faith lie in using the phrases of orthodoxy, and harping on mere words.

The proud man has no God ;
The envious man has no neighbour;
The angry man has not himself.

The proudest nettle grows on a midden.

That which grows out of a dunghill is apt to smell of pride. The lower the extraction, the more offensive the exaltation. He who has gained his wealth by unsavoury means seems all the more conceited because of his money-bags.

The quarrels of professors are the reproach of their profession.

Let us contend for nothing but the faith once for all delivered to the saints. All other contention should end at conversion.

The quart pot helpeth not.

Yet it is a notion with many that they cannot work till they have seen the bottom of it.

> The thatcher said unto his man,
> "Let's raise this ladder, if we can."
> "Nay," said the man, "but first let's drink,
> And then mayhap we can, I think."

The receiver is as bad as the thiever.

Often he is the cause of the theft ; for few would steal if they had no "fence" to conceal the goods. Some men can be both thieves and receivers. We heard of one concerning whose honesty it was said, "It would not be safe to leave him in an empty house if there were any soot in the chimney." What can be blacker ?

The reward of one duty is the power to do another.

He that carries out one work well, shall be entrusted with another. Even heaven is after this order: "Thou hast been faithful over a few things, I will make thee ruler over many things."—Matt. xxv. 21. It is so in nations : the general who won in Asia shall fight in Africa.

The rich and ignorant are sheep with golden wool.

But they are sheep and nothing more, however much their fleece may fetch. Yet a prize sheep attracts attention.

The right way leads to the right place.

Wrong roads can never do this, however much they may appear to do so. Beware of the green lanes which lead to destruction.

The road to ruin is as smooth as a bowling-green.

> Hence the travelling along it is very rapid. When ready-money
> horses the coach, the prodigal makes a very rapid journey; and the
> old rhyme is scarcely an exaggeration:—

> Tom Goodfellow came to his fortune on Sunday,
> And *friends* came to see him in dozens on Monday!
> On Tuesday were with him to dinner and sup;
> On Wednesday in honour of Tom kept it up!
> On Thursday his *friends* set the dice-box afloat!
> This game pretty soon strips a man to his coat.
> On Friday, by some means, Tom lost his last guinea,
> And Saturday—Saturday ended the ninny.

The rougher March the fairer May.

> Of this we are not sure as a matter of weather: but, as a rule,
> after a period of trial comes a season of repose.

The rule of the road is a paradox quite,
  In riding or driving along;
If you *go to the left* you are sure to be right;
  If you go to the right you are wrong.

But the rule of the footway is clear as the light,
  And none can its reason withstand;
On each side of the way you must *keep to the right*,
  And leave those you meet the left hand.

Or—

But in walking the streets 'tis a different case,
  To the right it is right you should bear;
To the left should be left quite enough of free space
  For the persons you chance to meet there.

The saddest dog sometimes wags his tail.

> Poor Tray! We will not portray his grief, but let us be glad
> that even he has his day, and when that day comes he rejoices, or,
> at least, his tail does. It is an exemplary trait in Tray's character
> that he freely gives you a wag of his tail.

The sea, great as it is, grows calm.

> So say the Italians. Why should not we little folk be at rest?
> What good can come of our storms?

The seeds of great things are often small.

The serpent's eye is an ornament when placed in the dove's head.

The wisdom and sharp-sightedness of the serpent make a fine blend with the tenderness and modesty of the dove.

The sheep look not at the hedge, but at the turnips.

Not the arrangement of the sermon, but the spiritual food in it is what hearers care about. "What is a hedge," said a rustic philosopher, "but that which joins one field to another?" Such are the divisions of a discourse.

The ship does not go without the boat.

The great carry the small with them. The glorious Lord bears with him his poor people.

The shorter the tongue the sweeter the speech.

Especially when the speaker is in a bad temper. So those have said who have been subjected to the wifely discipline of the curtain lecture. No doubt, many husbands deserve it, but none of them like it. One of them wrote:—

" That marriage is an enterprise,
Experience doth show ;
But scolding is an exercise
That married men do know."

The shortest day is too long to waste.

The shovel makes game of the poker.

But why? They stand in the same fender, work about the same fire, and are very nearly related. Why does one worker make game of another?

The silent cat catches the mouse.

If she were always mewing, her little game would be up and away.

The silver arrow hits the white.

It is too true that a tip is the tip-top way to succeed where even justice fails : hence one says—

Fight thou with shafts of silver and o'ercome,
When no force else can get the masterdom.

The slowest insects have most legs.

Those men often do the least who seem to have most abilities and opportunities. They are all leg, and have no heart.

The slut forgets to mend the slits.

Therefore they grow bigger, and her dress comes very soon into the rag-bag. It is slovenly to allow little faults to grow.

The smaller the house, the sooner cleaned.

The smallest boy often carries the biggest fiddle.

Little men aspire to big works; and they always try to carry the big fiddle, even if they cannot play it.

The smallest fishes bite the fastest.

Little minds take up with the last absurdity. Many are waiting to be taken in, and would be unhappy if some new nonsense were not dangled before them. This proves the littleness of their minds.

The smith and his penny are both black.

So are the sinner and his righteousness.

The smith's dog sleeps while the sparks are flying.

Use is second nature. Our hearers learn to sleep while the law is hammering and the sparks of wrath are flying in their faces.

The smoke of my own house is better than the fire of another's.

Not always true. Only a home-bird will say quite so much. And yet most assuredly I would sooner see my own chimney smoking than see another man's house on fire.

> My home with houseleek on the thatch,
> Against a palace I will match.

The son of an ass is sure to bray.

Should he not follow his father? Do some people wonder that their offspring talk foolishly? What other style of talk do they hear? Alas! certain sons of wise fathers exhibit a folly which is not hereditary. Rehoboam was the son of Solomon.

The sooner the better;
Delay is a fetter.

In all good things, promptitude is a valuable element. If hard to-day, a holy act will be harder to-morrow.

The soul lives where it loves.

> A religious man who does not love religion is irreligious. Life is where the heart is; and when the heart is in heaven, our life is in heaven. Life without love is day without the sun.

The sourer the gooseberries the more need of sugar.

> Bad tempered people must be treated with great kindness. When you have a sharp thing to say, mix much love with it.

The south wind brings wet weather,
The north wet and cold together;
The west wind always brings us rain,
The east wind blows it back again.

> So that, according to this venerable saw, it must always be raining. We think this saw is rusty through too much wet, and needs re-setting. Yet some years it does seem as if the weather, like the Queen, was always reigning, or say, raining. Still, we do have dry days even in England.

The spur won't hurt where the hide is thick.

> We know persons who have a thin skin, and we have pitied them; but, having lately come across persons with no sense of honour or shame, we have altered our mind. Give us the grace to be sensitive rather than the coarse nature which feels nothing. They say, where there's sense there's feeling; and certainly men who have no feeling have seldom much sense.

The stone is hard, and the drop is small,
But a hole is made by the constant fall.

The stone that lieth not in your way need not offend you.

> Don't go out of your road to find something to stumble at. What is the good of looking out for a grievance?

The string slips where the knot's loose: tie tight.

The sun moves on, whoever hides its light.

> It were great folly should it stop. What end would it serve? Its answer to dark bodies is to shine on them. My son, imitate the sun.

The superfine gentleman is nobody's money.

> " The son of toil will gain the spoil,
>   While delicacy lingers :
>   That man's unwise, whoe'er he is,
>   Who fears to soil his fingers."

The surety is sure to be sued.

"He that is surety for a stranger shall smart for it" (Prov. xi. 15). Mark this, and save yourself many a mark.

The sweet and the sour,
The nettle and flower,
The thorn and the rose,
Our life-time compose.

Like the year, life has its changeful seasons. It wears a Joseph's coat of many colours. He that knoweth it through age and experience, may say of it, "I will sing of mercy and judgment; unto thee, O Lord, will I sing."—Ps. ci. 1.

The tailor that makes not a knot loseth a stitch.

The time that we take to make our work sure and lasting is by no means lost: in fact, it is an economy of time to do things thoroughly well. Yet in these days, such is the evil force of competition for cheapness, that tailors would not only sew with a red-hot needle and a burnt thread if they could, but they would prefer to throw the pieces of cloth together, and let them hold on by their edges as best they could.

The tale-hearer is as bad as the tale-bearer.

A witty divine once said that the tale-bearer should be hung up by a nail through his tongue, and the tale-hearer by nails through his ears. So, too, those who tell you stories, will tell stories of you. The dog that fetches is of the same breed as the dog that carries: they are much of a muchness, and would both be the better for being muzzled.

The tallest trees
Feel most the breeze.

Don't grow up aloft, for there you feel the full force of the hurricane. Wisdom would suggest that we keep near the ground, and run to fruit rather than to wood.

The tankard robs more than the thief.

It steals a man's senses, character, and hopes: in fact, it steals the man himself, and robs him both of the happiness of this life, and the eternal felicities of the life to come.

All his life was cankered,
Since he ever hankered
For the flowing tankard.

The tears of the oppressed plead hard with God.

Those pence earned by ill-paid labour, with tears, and sweat, and life-blood, are memorials before the Lord which he will not forget: the sweater shall find another sort of sweat upon his brow when God deals with him.

The thief can steal in a moment, but the watchman must watch all night.

Temptation calls for constant watchfulness: sin may undo in an unguarded second the character which needed years to form.

The thief comes when the candles are out.

Darkness suits all ill designs. Ignorance is the worst of darkness, and spiritual ignorance the worst of ignorance. Let us light up many a candle in our own beloved land, and drive the thieves away. Does not the proverb remind you of certain altars with unlighted candles on them? It would be well to carry light there also, not to light the candles, but to enlighten the men.

The thin end of the wedge is to be feared.

The big end cannot do mischief till the thin end has made way for it. Avoid the beginnings of evil. Alas! the many take no heed to minor errors, and so invite the greater heresies.

The thorn serves well to guard the rose.

The thread breaks where it is thinnest.

We fail where we are weakest: but where are we not weak?

The times be good when men are good betimes.

To the like effect is the other sentence, "The times would mend if men would mend betimes." Some are always crying out for "the good old times"; but these are the "old times," for time was never older than now, and the times would be good enough if we were so. *Sydney Smith* used to say:

> "The good of other times let others state:
> I think it lucky I was born so late."

The tongue bites sharper than the teeth.

The tongue cuts where the teeth cannot bite. The teeth cannot get at the heart, but the tongue can. Moreover, the tongue bites miles away, and the teeth must be near. What awful wounds a cruel tongue can inflict! and yet who can protect himself from it?

The tongue does more mischief than all the other members.

For its range is wider, and its power is more penetrating than that of hand or foot. It is a world of evil when it is evil.

The tongue is in a wet place, and easily slips.

Slips of the tongue may be as harmful as slips of the foot : we must guard well the movements of that powerful little member.

The tongue is not steel, but it cuts.

And its worst wounds are not with its edge, but with its back.

The tongue of idle persons is never idle.

Yet is it always idle : idly making a noise, and doing damage. *Peraldus* reckons up four-and-twenty different sins of the tongue ; one for every hour of day and night.

The tongue turns to an aching tooth.

Sympathy moves it. Thus should all Christians feel for each other, and instinctively render what relief they can to those who suffer ; for we are members one of another. Yet, I pray thee, Mr. Talkative, turn not thy tongue to me, however much I ache.

The tongue which slanders is worse than the hand which strikes.

Knock me down if you will, but don't injure my character. I can rise after a blow, but who can restore a blighted name ? "What shall be done unto thee, thou false tongue ? "—Ps. cxx. 3.

The tools to him who can use them.

And if he cannot use them he ought not to take them to play with them and spoil them. Books, pulpits, seats in parliament, pens and ink, and so forth, should only be trusted to those who can use them to good purpose.

The tree is sure to be pruned before it reaches the skies.

No man will always rise. Something will occur to keep him within due limits. Envy will gnaw his root if nothing else happens.

The tree of knowledge has often flourished where the tree of life never grew.

One may have all knowledge, but without grace what a vain thing it is ! Alas, if knowledge bring not good, how it works evil !

The truly great man would not trample on a worm, nor tremble before an Emperor.

He is neither crouching nor crushing.

The very name " husband," what does it say?
Of wife and of household, the band and the stay.

The vicar of Bray will be vicar of Bray still.

Amid the changes of religion in different reigns, from Popish to Protestant, and back again, this ecclesiastic still held his post; for his doctrine was expressed in the chorus of the old ballad:

And this is law, I will maintain,
Until my dying day, sir,
That whatsoever king may reign,
I'll be the vicar of Bray, sir.

The vulgar count not your hits, but your misses.

This is only fair after all; for you yourself will record your hits, but not your misses, and thus a complete chronicle becomes possible.

The waggon must go whither the horses draw it.

So will national affairs, parish matters, ecclesiastical policies, and domestic arrangements, go in the way in which the most energy is displayed. It is a sad pity when the horses are head-strong, and take to the wrong road.

The waster delayeth, and lets the debt lie;
The prudent man payeth, the cheaper to buy.

Doubtless prompt payment gives a man great advantage in the market. The small tradesman cannot afford to be in debt.

The way to be safe is to take nothing for granted.

See it right yourself, with your own eyes.

The Welshman keeps nothing till he has lost it.

Surely this is Irish! We suppose the Welshman is impulsive and generous, and only learns economy when he perceives that he has given more than he could afford.

The whole truth is wholesome.

But a part of the truth may mislead, and cause us to make as great errors as if we had believed a falsehood. Half the truth is a lie; or say, "a half-truth may be a falsehood." Therefore, let us endeavour to have a fair full-faced view of matters.

The wife can throw away more with a spoon than the husband can bring in with a shovel.

Little wastes can prevent the accumulation of large earnings. Still, the greatest danger is not from the wife's spoon, but from the husband's cup.

The wife must prepare what the husband provides.

> " John's wife and John were *tête-à-tête;*
>   She witty was, industrious he.
> Says John, 'I've earn'd the bread we've ate.'
> 'And I,' says she, 'have *urn'd* the tea.'"

The wife that loves the looking-glass hates the saucepan.

Not always true; yet the fear is that the folly which shows itself in dress and self-admiration should lead to neglect of household duties. Blessed is the wife that can cook well, for she shall have her husband home to dinner. Well was she commended of whom it was said :

> " Tell me a thing she cannot dress :
>   Soups, hashes, pickles, puddings, pies,
>   Nought comes amiss, she is so wise."

The wind in one's face makes one wise.

We wish it did. Still we know what the proverb means : it is by opposition and trial that we learn. There is an old saying that "The Tracys always have the wind in their faces" : we don't know the gentlemen, but we heartily rejoice with them, for nothing is more refreshing than a bracing breeze.

The window opened more and more
Would keep the doctor from the door.

How long will it be before people will believe in fresh air?

The wing with the liver
To him who's the giver.

Let him have the best part of the fowl, since he placed it on our table. Let anyone who has fowls to give away try us, and see if we will not carve him the liver-wing.

The willow will buy a horse before the oak will pay for a saddle.

Willow branches are quick in growth, and bring in more by far than the slow-growing oak. Men of small parts may do more by speed and perseverance than greater men who are slow.

The wise man gets learning from those who have none themselves.

Therein showing what a wise man he is. Wise men learn more from fools than fools learn from wise men.

The wise man keeps on good terms with his wife, his conscience, and his stomach.

Either of these three can make his life a misery to him, and therefore he would keep them all in good humour.

The wise man knows the fool, but the fool doth not know the wise man.

Yet he must be a very wise man who thoroughly knows a fool, for the ways of folly are inscrutable. The proverb is true in its own sense; but, like others, it needs a pinch of salt.

The wise with a tick,
The fool with a kick.

A wink is enough to make the sensible understand, but the stupid need more impressive instruction. So some think. We kick no one : it wears out our boots.

The wisest are not always wise.

The wisest man does not think himself so.

A famous Eastern judge, on one occasion, after a very patient investigation of facts, declared that his knowledge was not competent to decide upon the case before him. "Pray, do you expect," said a pert courtier, who heard his declaration, "that the Caliph is to pay your ignorance?" "I do not," was the mild reply ; "the Caliph pays me, and well, for what I do know. If he were to attempt to pay me for what I do not know, the treasures of his empire would not suffice."

The wisest mouse keeps farthest from the trap.

The most prudent man is most careful to avoid temptation, and the sin which comes of it.

The wittiest man laughs least.

Because he has a high standard of wit, and is not affected by much which pretends to be facetious. Wit is not always grinning.

The wolf does not weep over the death of the dog.

No, for he has now more liberty to prey on the sheep. A faithful minister's death is joy to the heretic, and his leader, the devil.

The wolf loses his teeth, but not his inclinations.

Old age leaves him still a wolf. He retains his taste for mutton, though he cannot now leap into the fold to help himself thereto. Apply the proverb to wicked old men.

The wolf offered to watch the flock for nothing.

But he meant to pay himself in mutton. Always suspect that those who offer to do work for nothing intend to do it for something. Errorists are seemingly generous till their ends are served.

The workman makes the work, but the work also makes the workman.

This reminds us of William of Wyckham's inscription upon a building erected for the king. THIS WORK MADE WILLIAM DE WYCKHAM. When the royal owner objected to it, he explained it to mean, not that he made the work, but that the work made him. Both readings were true.

The world at its best is a handful of shadows.

No, not even a handful; it fills nothing : it is altogether emptiness. The world's ALL is nothing at all.

The world is governed with little brains.

History often forces this reflection from its readers. It would even seem as if madness had been more common in rulers than in the governed. Many a crown has no head beneath it.

The world is too narrow for two fools quarrelling.

If they could shove each other over the edge of the universe, society would not suffer much. For two such big men an extra world or two would be convenient, that they might swing their big swords, and fulfil their terrible threats without harm to others.

The world over, crows are black.

Meaning that men are sinful everywhere.

The world owes me a living, providing I earn it.

Those last words are a qualifying clause, which many forget. What right can we have to live on other people's earnings ? Yet many fancy that all the world is in debt to a lazy fellow who puts nothing into the public purse.

The world was not made in a minute.

London was not built in a day : great things are not accomplished in a hurry. We must learn to labour and to wait.

The world would be better if you were.

> The world is as you take it;
> It will be what you make it.

The worse the carpenter, the more the chips.

He who does his work well, makes little fuss about it; but the incapable workman buries himself under the rubbish he creates.

The worse the passage, the more welcome the port.

"Then are they glad because they be quiet." What music is made when the ship is in the harbour, and the chain of the anchor runs out! He that was most sick is the gladdest to land.

The worst argument is an ill-name.

Bishop Horne says, "It is too frequent a custom to give ill names to those who differ from us in opinion." *Dr. Hammond* mentions a humorous instance of it, that when a Dutchman's horse did not go as he would have him, he, in a great rage, called him an "Arminian."

The worst wheel rattles most.

Always. Those complain most against whom most complaints could be laid.

Their fears are most who know not what they fear.

Belshazzar saw only a hand writing on the wall, and this mystery appalled him. The unknown is the terrible. Ungodly men flee when no man pursueth, for at bottom they are superstitious.

> The wicked walk in fear of bush and brake,
> Yea, oftentimes their shadow makes them quake.

Then's then, but now's now.

Then let your now be now. What you resolve to do one day do this day. To-day is *the* day.

There are calumnies against which even innocence loses courage.

Slanders may be too foul to be met except with tears; or, they may be told with such an appearance of truth that they gain instant belief. When a man is so stunned by a wicked charge that he cannot contain himself, or make a reply, it is an argument for his innocence. The Lord save us from the arrow which flieth by day!

There are forty men of wit to one of sense.

> Without sense men can talk nonsense. Smart witty people are far more common than thoroughly sensible persons.

There are good dogs of all sizes.

> Condemn not this dog for being too large, nor that for being too small. If you know where to look for them, you may find good little men, and even good great men.

There are many things much in use, which are not of much use.

> Such as the excrescences of fashion in dress, and so forth.

There are more ways of killing a dog than hanging him.

> If a fellow cannot be overcome in one way, he may be ruined in another. Let the poor dog look out and sharpen his teeth, or his enemy will compass his death one way or another.

There are no fans in hell.

> So say the Arabs. It is a terrible proverb ; but how true ! Misery without mitigation is of the essence of future punishment.

There are other thieves besides those who are locked up.

> A worthy divine was robbed of his portmanteau in which were a number of his discourses. Some one wrote for him as follows :—
>
> > " The thief who stole my sermons,
> > On which I set such store,
> > May safely bring them back again ;
> > They were stolen long before."

Another version of this story is more circumstantial, and savours more of slang. The Rector of Kingston-by-Sea, on his parsonage being entered and robbed, is credited with the following :

> " They came and prigg'd my stockings, and my linen, and my store ;
> But they could not prig my sermons, for they were prigg'd before."

There are toys for all ages,
For fools and for sages.

> The man's toys are the most expensive, and the sage's are the most mischievous. There are the Evolution humming-top, and the New Theology penny whistle, and a number of other childish things.

There are wedges for all woods.

If we will use our wits, we can conquer all difficulties, even as all logs can be split if we get the right beetle and wedge.

No man may grow carnally secure; for God knows how to bring him down. Who can stand before his wrath? The proverb may also mean that there are temptations for all men, and if they do not yield to one they may to another.

There is a devil in every berry of the grape.

So says the Koran. It is a striking way of setting forth the evils of intoxicating drink. It will not frighten English wine-bibbers, for their stuff does not flow from grapes.

There is a religious way to perdition.

And it is none the less sure because smoothly rolled with ceremonies and professions.

There is a remedy for all evils but death.

I have known two persons who boasted that they would never die; but I hope they are dead, for I am sure they are buried.

There is a salve for every sore.

The thing's to find the ointment out,
And that you should be quick about.

There is a snake in the grass.

Where? Well, just where you do not think there is one. Who is he? Well, he is one whom you could not suspect; therefore don't suspect anybody. The "he" may be a "she."

There is a special providence in the fall of a sparrow.

The same law governs the small as well as the great. This is noticeable in all the laws by which the Lord governs nature and providence; they affect the minute as well as the magnificent.

The very law which moulds a tear,
And bids it trickle from its source,
That law preserves the earth a sphere,
And guides the planets in their course.

There is a time to fish, and a time to dry nets.

Happy is he who knows when his hour is come, and does the work appropriate for that hour. To rest when rest is due is as wise as to labour when the hour arrives.

There is a time to wink as well as to see.

Some things are best unseen, especially personal slights.

There is a world of meaning in a little text.

One who tried to expound a passage said : "There's a wonderful deal in it, my friends, if I could only get it out."

There is more bitterness in beer than comes from the hop.

Don't try it to see. Ask the publican ; or, better still, see some of his work taken home, or carefully laid by in the police cell.

There is more disputing about the shell than the kernel.

Controversy often concerns minor points ; it seldom touches vital matters ; but when it does, it is serious work.

There is no banquet, but some dislike something in it.

For it is said, "There is no feast without a fool at it." It is said that one, at least, goes away unfed from every feast. The only exception is the Lord's festival of grace.

There is no benefit in a gift that sticks to the fingers.

If you give grudgingly, or taunt a man with it afterwards, the grace of the gift has gone like smoke.

> He gives as if his blood he shed ;
> Indeed, he would be sooner bled.

There is no better patch than one off the same cloth.

The deceased wife's sister will often supply the place of the deceased wife better than anyone else, *unless she is a cross patch*. It is a pity that bishops have no deceased wives' sisters. They would then see beyond their sees, and read Leviticus with clearer eyes.

There is no corn without some chaff.

Nothing is absolutely free from imperfection. Wisdom is mixed with folly, truth with error, holiness with imperfection.

There is no going from Delilah's lap to Abraham's bosom.

Shorn locks, blinded eyes, imprisoned lives, and cruel shame come from the lap of the strange woman. Even a Samson is vanquished there. The young man must, above all things, keep himself clear of all wantonness if he would lead a happy life here and hereafter.

There is no larder but may have its mice.

However large or small, it needs watching; for where the cheese is, thither will the mice be gathered together.

There is no law but has a hole in it for those who can find it out.

You can drive a coach and four through any Act of Parliament. A keen lawyer can find a way through every law but Mortmain.

There is no stripping a naked man.

He that has nothing cannot be fined or robbed. But if he can't be stripped he can be whipped. He that cannot pay with his tin must pay with his skin.

There is no such flatterer as a man's self.

How delicately he pleases his customer! He hates flattery; he is so humble! The dear old stupid, how he drinks it in, and leaves no heel-taps in the cup!

There is no use in blowing a fire that burns well.

Exhorting those to liberality and industry who are already doing their best, is not the wisest way of using one's oratory.

There is no use in preaching to the hungry.

Give them a dinner of at least one course, and then give them a discourse. Theology is cold stuff on an empty stomach. The belly hath no ears when it hungers.

There is nothing so like a good shilling as a bad one.

Except it is another good shilling. Of course, hypocrites imitate true believers as far as they can, or they would get no gain by their hypocrisy. No wonder that we are deceived! Yet the existence of hypocrites does not prove the non-existence of true believers, any more than bad sovereigns prove that there are no good ones. The proof is all the other way.

There never was a five-pound note but there was a ten-pound road for it.

One never has money without having ways of spending twice as much. It may not be so with millionaires, but so we find it.

How doth our little careful wife,
And children all alive,
Demand our money all through life,
And soon devour a five!

There never was a looking-glass that told a woman she was
ugly.

It was never plain to a woman that she was plain. In fact, from
some point of view, every woman has her beauties, and she has the
art of seeing herself from that stand-point. Bless the dear mirrors
of perfection; no wonder they admire themselves. It shows their
good taste and ours also.

There will be no Mondays in heaven.

No weary Mondays for pastors; no wicked Mondays for drunkards;
no worldly Mondays for the outwardly religious.

There would be fewer open mouths if there were fewer
open ears.

Just so. If there were not a market for scandal, nobody would
be a scandal-monger. Where there are heads on one side, there
will be tails, or rather tales, on the other.

There's a way to heaven from the gates of hell.

The worst of sinners may be saved.

There's a way to hell from the gates of heaven.

The proudest professor may be lost.

There's always room at the top.

The best men are always wanted, and there's always a scarcity of
them. One could find ten thousand middling workmen; but where
shall we look for a first-class hand?

There's always water where a calf is drowned.

One would think so. If there is sufficient of anything to do
mischief, there must be enough for a better purpose. The man who
has wit enough to be a thief, might earn a good living.

There's crust and crumb in every loaf.

We must take them together. The rough and the smooth, the
soft and the hard, make up life, and there's no use hoping to see it
altered. The best bred are not all upper crust.

There's gold in quartz, I hear:
Mine's gone in quarts of beer.

This confession is seldom heard, but in many instances it is true
as the Confession of Faith.

There's little roast
Where braggarts boast.

There's little tale-bearing on the right side.

A good deed in common life gets no corner in the newspaper, and no gossip busies herself with informing her neighbours of it. Yet surely it should pay as well to hawk sweet fish as stinking ones.

There's mischief brewing when the wolf licks the lamb.

Extraordinary displays of affection have their motive—a motive which means no good to the victim of their effusive love. Young women should note this proverb. Affectionate wolves are common.

> Whose manner is so over-sweet,
> Has cheated or intends to cheat.

There's more room without than within.

A young preacher once told me that he had a great congregation, and, he added, "There were more people outside than in." I answered, that I fully believed it. He saw my drift. Old houses had the chimney built outside the house; was this because there is more room outside than inside? There is more liberty outside of some societies than you can expect within.

"There's ne'er a best among them," as the fellow said by the fox cubs.

Among certain sets of men all are so bad that the question is, "Which is the worst?" and never, "Which is the best?"

There's never any cake
But there's some of like make.

Nobody is so odd, or so bad, or so good, but what there are others to match, if you know where to look for them.

There's no evil, but it might be worse.

There's no flying without wings.

Trading on credit, preaching without ability, and the like, are vain attempts. They all end in a downfall.

There's no garden without weeds.

No character without faults; no church without false professors; no family without troubles. Weeds come without inviting.

> In the garden much more grows,
> Than the busiest gardener sows.

There's no getting oil out of a mill-stone.

> Nor wine out of a wall, nor money out of an outside broker. Extracting feeling from some men is quite as difficult as getting blood from a turnip. To get money out of misers is about as hard as getting butter out of a dog's mouth.

There's no happiness where there's no occupation.

> Want of something to do is downright misery. It is long since some of us could complain of that affliction.
>
> > The want of occupation is not rest,
> > A mind quite vacant is a mind distressed.

There's no making omelets without breaking eggs.

> We must go to some expense to effect our purpose.

There's no mother like my mother.

> No, not even the Prince of Wales's mother! "No, sir," said a child when he heard a visitor quote Pope's familiar line, "An honest man's the noblest work of God." "No, sir, my mother is the noblest work of God."

There's no need to fasten a bell to a fool; everybody will know where he is.

> If his tongue wags he will not need to be looked for.

There's no need to grease a fat sow.

> Yet many are eager to do it : everybody helps the man who does not need it. Somewhat bitterly one writes—
>
> > By all observers it is known,
> > And daily seen on every hand;
> > The prosperous in life alone
> > Have proffer'd service at command.

There's no place like home.

> It is a great pity when either husband or wife is forced to answer, "I'm glad there isn't."

There's no piety where there's no morality.

> He that has not the pence of morality cannot possess the pounds of godliness. Sir J. Lubbock says of the aborigines of Australia, "They do not believe in a supreme Deity, or in the immortality of the soul ; nor is morality in any way connected with their religion." Alas, that this should be true of so many nearer home !

There's no profit in teaching a pig to play the flute.

> Even if the pupil could learn, others would do the business better. There are persons who have no capacity for learning a certain art, and teaching it to them would be lost labour.

There's no reaping where there's no sowing.

> Thou canst not gather what thou dost not sow :
> As thou dost plant the tree, so will it grow.

There's no remedy for consumption of the purse.

> Why not ?   Brace the economical system by pulling the strings tighter.   Administer an elixir of extra earnings.   Try thrift.

There's no riding to heaven on a feather bed.

There's no security where there's a Committee of Safety.

> Though in the multitude of councillors there is safety, it lies in the direction of their never doing too much—if they ever do anything.   A committee is like armour, an excellent device to preserve a society from harm, and to prevent its doing much of either harm or good.

There's no taking snakes with sugar-tongs.

> Hitting them over the head is far more effectual.   Had Luther handled error daintily, the Reformation would never have come off.   Some bad things need vigour and rigour rather than daintiness.   Luther threw an ink-bottle at the devil's head, whereas another preacher, when Satan tempted him to doubt, set a chair for him, and bade him sit down and have it out : a rash experiment.

There's nothing impossible to perseverance.

> We copy the following from *Aunt Rachel's Advice to her Niece:*— "Mr. Medhurst, who was formerly a missionary in China, gives in his book a curious story—which reads more like a fable than a fact —of a woman, whom he saw one day rubbing a small iron crowbar on a stone, at which she had been engaged for a very long time.   And when he asked what she was doing it for, he was informed that she wanted a needle, and not being able to meet with one, she was grinding the crowbar down to the proper size ; a singular instance, *if true,* of energy and perseverance."

There's nothing like leather.

> Pardon me, good sir ; that beef-steak upon which I wearied my teeth the other day was extremely like it.   Every man cries up his own wares, and hence the tanner cries " Nothing like leather."

There's poor profit in flaying flints.

> Don't attempt to get money from the very poor. Some people seem to live upon what they can extract from the dregs of poverty : it must be a wretched business. The miserly are, however, worse to deal with than the very poorest : they are flints of the hardest kind, and are neither to be flayed nor chipped.

There's time enough where there's will enough.

> At any rate, good sir, you have all the time there is ; and when you have made up your mind to use it, there will be more. "I have no time" should frequently be interpreted "I have no will."

There's too much weighing meat about it.

> Spoken of trades and transactions in which there are a great many things upon which a loss will be sustained. It comes from the former habit of butchers, when selling prime joints, to throw in a bit of an inferior part, or perhaps a bone, under the idea that nobody could expect to have all the best of the meat, and none of the rougher portions.

These evil days bring sorry jokes
To simple men like Johnny Nokes.

> "*John a Nokes* was driving his cart toward Croydon, and by the way fell asleep therein. Meantime, a fellow came by and stole away his two horses, and went fair away with them. In the end, John, awaking and missing them, said, 'Either I am *John a Nokes*, or I am not *John a Nokes*. If I am *John a Nokes*, then have I lost two horses ; and if I be not *John a Nokes*, then have I found a cart.'" Simple persons need a friend to look after them, or they will be sorely troubled.

They are like a ha'p'orth of soap in a wash-tub.

> Or like a chip in the porridge : of no great consequence : too little to be of use. Like the gospel in certain modern sermons.

They love but little who can tell how much they love.

> In no case can love be subjected to either the rod or the scale. It is too ethereal for inches and ounces. No real lover of the Lord can measure his love ; but he wishes it were far more.

They may point at a star, but they cannot pull it down.

> Evil persons may ridicule a truly good man, but they cannot pluck him from the position wherein providence has placed him.

They never wrought a good day's work who went grumbling about it.

No one can work well when his heart is not in his labour: he is sure to fail in quantity or in quality. Give me the man who works with a will, and is not always looking for six o'clock.

"They say so," is half a lie.

Because it may be that we lead people to think that it is the universal opinion, when, perhaps, "they" means only myself and another fool.

> If thou wouldst tidings understand,
> Take them not at second-hand.

They say there is a skeleton in every house.

I have added "they say" to this proverb, because otherwise it is far from true. There are Christian homes which have nothing to conceal, no shameful secret, no Blue-beard cupboard.

"They say, they say," and donkeys bray.

Common talk is really no more to be regarded than the braying of asses. The theoretical talk of infidel scientists may be put in the same category. Think of this as taught by science :—

> Man was an ape in the days that came early ;
> Centuries after his hair became curly :
> Centuries more gave a thumb to his wrist,
> Then he became man and a Positivist.

They should be more thankful that give an alms, than they that receive it.

Certainly they are the more favoured of the two, and most in- debted to the goodness of God. A worthy Quaker would hear nothing of thanks for money given by him to charitable objects. His reply to those who thanked him was: "Friend, I am much obliged to thee for thy trouble in applying this money to good use."

They that hide can find.

As a rule this is a truism. But he that hides his religion may one day find that he has none to hide.

They that walk much in the sun will be tanned at last.

Exposure to evil influences tells upon the character, and before long the result is visible in the conduct.

They that wash on Monday have all the week to dry ;
They that wash on Tuesday are not much awry ;
They that wash on Wednesday there's no need to blame ;
They that wash on Thursday wash for shame ;
They that wash on Friday wash for need ;
They that wash on Saturday—oh, they are sluts indeed !

These rude lines are a warning against putting off things to the very last day. The habit of delay begins with some when children, and then they are assailed with—

"Dilly, Dilly, dollar,
Ten o'clock scholar."

This continues through life, and leads to Saturday washing and general tardiness. If those who "first come are first served," dilatory persons are served right when never served at all.

They who cannot have what they like should learn to like what they have.

A tough lesson, but well worth learning.

They who have money are troubled about it,
And they who have none are troubled without it.

So that neither poverty nor riches will ensure perfect repose.

They who will not be counselled cannot be helped.

Refusing to be guided, they must even "gang their ain gate." It is said, "If you have your own way you won't die in a pet "; but on the other hand, such are very likely to fall into the pit.

They wonder at the cedar when it is fallen.

They had no idea that the man was so good and great until he was dead ; and then they knew the miss of him, and regretted that they had allowed him to be among them, and to be so little esteemed.

They wrangle about an egg, and let the hens fly away.

Too often in disputes between master and men, trade is ruined, and so the hen flies away. In controversies over trifles, the spirit of love is driven away from a church, and the main thing is thus lost.

They wrong themselves, that wrong others.

At some time or other the evil done falls upon the doer of it. The ball thrown against the wall comes back into the sender's hand. He that watereth a path with vitriol to kill the grass, is pretty sure to burn his own boots.

Thick sown and thin come up.

In some places the gospel has been faithfully preached by many ministers, and yet few are converted. On some men much teaching has been expended, but they know nothing. Their fathers spent much money upon them at college, but they are forced to cry, "We put gold into the fire, and there came out this calf."

Things forbidden have a secret charm.

This is sadly true. "I had not known lust, except the law had said, Thou shalt not covet." Adam might not have cared for the fruit of that one tree had it not been forbidden. In a smaller way, this is the cause of smuggling, poaching, and many other offences.

Think and thank.

There is only a letter of difference between the two words. Surely we should never do much thinking without rising to thanking.

Think kindly of the poor
When it's cold out of door.

But let your thoughts be practical. A hundred thoughts will not warm them half so much as half-a-hundred of coals.

Think not, the husband gained, that all is done—
The prize of happiness must still be won;
And oft the careless find it to their cost,
The lover in the husband may be lost.

What a pity it is when people leave off their courting manners as soon as they are married! Should they not take more pains to be agreeable when they see each other all day, than they did when they had only occasional meetings?

Think of ease, but work on.

So long as there is any life in the old ox, let it keep to the plough. It is more easy to think of ease, than to make yourself easy with nothing to do. Work for amusement if not for emolument.

Think thrice before you marry once.

Let the thinking be on both sides. Then the verse we are about to quote may come true.

> Abel wants to marry Mabel;
> Well, that's very wise of Abel.
> But Mabel won't at all have Abel;
> Well, that's wiser still of Mabel.

Think twice before you speak once.

> Then you will speak twice as well, or possibly you will do better, and not speak at all.

>> Wise men reflect before they speak,
>> Fools speak, and then think after.
>> Wise men's words are full of light,
>> But fools' are full of laughter.

Think twice over a great bargain, and then leave it.

> For in what seems a great bargain the chances are that we are taken in, or else we are making a market out of some poor man's pressing necessities. Beware of painfully cheap purchases.

Think well before you tie what you cannot untie.

> Enter upon marriage with courage, but with caution. Yet no one would go so far as the old bachelor of Elizabeth's days, who said—

>> If that a bachelor thou be,
>> Thou wilt keep so if ruled by me,
>> Lest that repentance all too late,
>> Reward thee with a broken pate.

Think well of a man
As long as you can.

> Frequently the rule would seem to be—

>> Think ill of each man,
>> The first time you can.

Think well of men if you would mend them.

> Nobody will let you suggest an improvement in his conduct if you begin by abusing him, or if he can see that you despise him.

Think when you speak, but speak not all you think :
Drink when you thirst, but thirst not after drink.

> Some are troubled with a constant running at the mouth; others with a constant drought in the same place. Of the latter, *Livingstone* wrote :—" The Ptolemaic map defines people according to their food—the Elephantophagi, the Struthiophagi, the Ichthyophagi, and the Anthropophagi. If we followed the same sort of classification, our definition would be by their drink, thus: the stout-guzzlers, the roaring potheen-fuddlers, the whisky-fishoid drinkers, the vin-ordinaire bibbers, the lager-beer swillers, and an outlying tribe of the brandy-cocktail persuasion."

Thirst grows by that it feeds on.

> The more drink, the thirstier is the drinker. The mouth is never satisfied with liquids. One glass makes room for another. Some soak in beer, some swim in wine, some splash in spirits; and all of them are apt to complain of being very dry. Some men are mere funnels.
>
> > According to this kind of taste
> > Did he indulge his drouth;
> > And being fond of port, he made
> > A *port*-hole of his mouth.

Thirty days hath September,
April, June, and November,
February has twenty-eight alone;
All the rest have thirty-one,
Except in leap-year, then's the time,
February's days are twenty-nine.

> By this rhyme John Ploughman has been able always to know the length of the month. He recommends it to Sam Straw, and Hob Carter, and other country gentlemen.

This gift is small, but love is all.

> This line is a posy for a ring. Another is, "Love the giver"; and another, "Not the gift, but the giver."

Thistles and thorns prick sore,
But evil tongues prick more.

> Many hearts have been pierced, and lives rendered wretched, by the cruel words of slanderers. He that will stab a man with his pen would stab him with his penknife, if he dared.

Thistles would never become roses, even should you plant
them in Paradise.

> Position will not change disposition. A thistle in a garden is only so much the bigger by the richness of the soil in which it is planted. Bad men in high places become all the worse.

Those are very poor whom nothing will satisfy.

> For their poverty is in their soul rather than in their pocket, and there is no filling such a great gulf.
>
> > When want is in ourselves begun,
> > Then whither from it can we run?

Those beans won't boil in my pot.

So say the Telugus. They mean much the same as when we say, "That cock won't fight," or "That game won't pay," or "You can't come over me."

**Those on whom you most rely,
Can do you greatest injury.**

In this respect we need to be saved from our friends even more than from our enemies.

> The man whom we fear and suspect for a cheat
> Can hardly delude us with art and deceit ;
> But he in whose faith we sincerely confide,
> May come round with impunity on our blind side.

Those who are hot-headed should keep in the shade.

Yet they generally put themselves very forward, and threaten to set every business on a blaze with their heat.

Those who are in the same boat should row together.

If they don't, they will be likely to be upset, or the boat will turn round and round, and make no progress, People who do not row together are very apt to *row* together.

Those who are past caring are past curing.

Those who are soon hot are soon cold.

Those who are soon wound up soon run down.

Yet among speakers, those who prepare least usually keep on longest. In other matters, the man who would do everything on a sudden, has done his everything quite as suddenly.

Those who do ill, dread ill.

Very naturally they do so. Judging others by themselves, they expect to be lashed with their own whip. They expect that when their dogs come home they will eat their masters.

Those who do nothing will soon do worse.

The preparatory school for rascals is idleness ; and well they bring the youngsters on in that academy.

Those who do well themselves think well of others.

Familiarity with good work makes them expect to see it in other men's shops. They are so busy in keeping their own work up to the mark, that they have no time in which to pick holes in others, but take it for granted that others are doing their level best.

Those who eat most are not always the fattest.

So those who read most have not always the most knowledge; they may even overload their minds with ideas, as men may fill their stomachs too full of food; and this may lead to mental dulness, as, in the case of the body, it causes indigestion.

Those who expect what in reason they cannot expect, may expect.

They have liberty to range the world in their idle fancies, but their dreams will never be realized. This is a poor way of deceiving one's self.

Those who fry in words often freeze in deeds.

Those who itch to know will ache to tell.

Curiosity has talkativeness for its vis-à-vis.

Those who know nothing are generally very knowing people.

It is disagreeable to see the airs of superiority they give themselves. The blind man said, "Stand back: let me see!"

Those who learn much should teach much.

Else they will be mere hoarders of information, and before long their heaps of knowledge will ferment, and be good for nothing. So, too, we may say that those who teach much must learn much, or their teaching will soon be lean as a gridiron.

Those who love you for little may hate you for nothing.

We flatter ourselves by forgetting this evident fact, and hence we are surrounded by a set of flies whose affection for us is really *nil*, but their buzzing around us is incessant while the warm weather lasts. That love which blazes soon, like straw, is very apt to die out as the fire of straw does.

Those who love you for silver may leave you for gold.

When once the sordid motive enters in,
Such friendship is not worth a headless pin.

Those who paint you before will black you behind.

Those who flatter will slander.

Those who promise mountains perform molehills.

Those who shift often, will often be put to shifts.

Changing so often they cannot get on. Moving costs them as much as their goods are worth. The time wasted in learning a little of a new trade would have made them perfect in their old business.

Those who take offence, usually make offence.

Those who talk always, think seldom.

Those who think to catch are often caught.

Those who thunder in preaching, should lighten in living.

None of us must say, "Do as I say, but not as I do." The real force lies in the man's personal character; apart from this, his words are only words; and words are wind.

Those who will not hear reason have no reason.

Thou must get thee some pelf by fifty and three,
Or reckon thyself a drudge for to be.

By fifty-three a man should have something, or he may conclude that he will finish his days in poverty.

Though a lie have seven-leagued boots, truth will overtake it.

Not always soon enough to undo all its mischief, but in time to expose it to the contempt of those whom it has duped.

Though an ass shakes his head, his ears don't come off.

He does not lose his donkey characteristics by shaking his head after the manner of learned divines. "Ah!" said one, "how wisely he shakes his head!" "Yes," said another, "he may shake his head as long as he likes, but there's nothing in it."

Though I'm down in the dust,
Yet in God I will trust.

Though old and wise, yet still advise.

Though one grain fills not the sack, it helps.

Though the cat winks, she is not blind.

We can see more than they think we see; and very impertinent mice should remember that even when the cat sleeps she has one eye open. Presume not upon the incapacity of your superiors.

Though the heavens be glorious, yet they are not all stars.

In the happiest life there are special days of bliss. Among the best of men some are peculiarly holy. Even in the Scriptures certain passages convey to us more gracious instructions than others.

Though the serpent has little eyes, he sees very well.

The small eyes of the envious are terribly piercing. Craft, also, is like a weasel for penetrating into secrets.

Though the speaker be a fool, let the listener be wise.

The rampant orator may say what he likes, but you must sift it, and be all the more judicious because of the wildness of his talk. Many open their mouths and shut their eyes, and swallow all that is put before them. No wonder their minds are poisoned.

Though the sun shines, don't give away your coat.

You will need it yet. Do not in a hurry part with your business, or other source of income, because you are very flush of cash.

Though thy hands be rough, let thy manners be gentle.

Courtesy will raise the poorest to the highest rank. The king returned the bow of the sweep, rightly observing, "Would you have a sweep more polite than a king?" "My boy," said a father to his son, "treat everybody with politeness, even those who are rude to you. For remember, that you show courtesy to others, not because they are gentlemen, but because you are one."

Though you dip in the sea, you take up only as much as your vessel will hold.

Great as the gospel is, we can but grasp a part of its fulness.

Though you've lost the ring, you have the finger.

The garnishing may be gone, but the essential member is left. We sorrow if we lose our estates, but this is little if our souls are saved. We add another consolation—

'Tis this—a line that does not need a verse;
Nought is so bad but that it might be worse.

Three helping each other are as good as six.

They double their results by division of labour and mutual support. Christian workers pulling together accomplish far more than if they were mere units.

Three removes are as bad as a fire.

So much damage is done in the removal both to the business and the furniture. *Poor Richard* says :—

> " I never saw an oft-removèd tree.
> Nor yet an oft-removèd family,
> That throve so well as those that settled be."

Through being too knowing the fox lost his tail.

Throw a stone into mud, and it will splash your face.

Of course it will. Why not let the mud alone? If people must needs interfere they will get bespattered.

Throw no stones at thine own window.

Thy friend has a friend, and thy friend's friend has a friend : be quiet.

Thy secret is safe with thyself, but not with thy friend and his friend, and his friend's friend's friend *ad infinitum.*

Thy hand is never the worse for doing thy own work.

" In London no man thinks of blacking his own boots," said a haughty Briton once to the late Mr. Lincoln, whom he found polishing his calfskin gaiters. " Whose boots does he black?" quietly responded Uncle Abe.

Thyself accuse ; thy friend excuse.

A great preacher said, " Every excuse a man makes for himself is something taken from his manhood; and every excuse he makes for his fellow-men is something added to his manhood."

Thyself know, that thou mayest know others.

Time and patience turn mulberry leaves to satin.

In time the mulberry leaf becomes a silk gown, and a silk gown becomes a lady.

Time and trouble try the truth.

Whether a man is really good or not is discovered by his perseverance in a good way. It is easy to run well just for a spurt, but to keep up the pace for years is the difficulty.

> Long journeys prove a horse's strength ;
> And life is tested by its length.

Time and words can never be recalled.

Therefore be careful of them. Be wise at once, and lose no time. Play not so late that thou hast to go to bed in the dark. Thou canst not recall a lost moment, much less a lost life. Time is but a part of eternity; live so in time as thou wilt wish to live in eternity. As to words, speak advisedly; for thou canst as soon call back a bullet which has been shot from a gun, as a word uttered from thy mouth.

Time covers and discovers everything.

We need not have everything decided in the next five minutes. If we can wait a little, the hidden truth will come to light.

Time enough is little enough.

He that lives longest has no time to spare. No one has more than the present hour.

Time flieth away
Without delay.

Time is a file which works without sound.

Shakespeare makes one say, " I wasted time, and now doth time waste me." It works away at our bones, and undermines our constitutions. The tell-tale of its doings is frequently seen upon the head. One facetiously said :

" My hair and I are quits, d' ye see ;
I first cut it ; it now cuts me."

Time is a ship that never anchors.

Time is long enough for him who has grace enough.

Time is quite long enough, for all useful ends ;
He who labours for God, its limits extends.

Time is not tied to a post, like a horse to a manger.

Time is not wasted in sharpening the scythe.

Time moves slowly to him whose employment is to watch its flight.

Time is too long for the doing of nothing, and too short for the doing of something : but to sit and watch it dribble from an hour-glass is dreary work indeed. As good have no time as have nothing but time.

Time passes slowly when sorrow presses heavily.

> " How like the fleeting wind, away
> Whole years of joy depart !
> But, oh ! how slowly does the day
> Move to the mournful heart ! "

Time, tide, and train, for no man will remain.

> Pursue thy work without delay,
> For the short hours run fast away.

Time trieth truth, but truth outliveth time.

Time will bring the roses,
Though cold bites our noses.

> Have patience : the snows will soon be thawing, and the cuckoo
> will be back again.   Sorrow endeth, joy cometh.

Tin plates don't mind dropping on the floor.

> A man prepared for rough usage puts up with a great many
> things which would break other people in pieces.

Tired men are quarrelsome.

> Tired men tread hard, and tried men feel hard.

'Tis a good fish if it were but caught.

> Many a scheme is first-class, but it is not practicable.

'Tis a good knife ; it will cut butter when 'tis melted.

> What must a bad knife be ?   Some people fix their standard of
> good knives and good men very low indeed.

'Tis a good penny that earns a groat.

'Tis a thriftless thing to be sad.

> Because it mends nothing, and does not bring in a penny piece.

'Tis a very good world to live in,
To spend, or to lend, or to give in ;
But to beg, or to borrow, or get back your own,
'Tis the very worst world that ever was known.

> This is the witness of many ; and we have heard it given with
> savage emphasis.   It is a pity that it should be so sadly true.

'Tis better to buy love than law.

> But how is it to be done? Here, you sir, let me have the equivalent to this five-and-four-pence in downright love, and you may give the law to the dogs.

'Tis better to sit with a wise man in prison than with a fool in paradise.

'Tis education forms the youthful mind;
Just as the twig is bent, the tree's inclined.

> "Spare me a little longer," said the young vine to the gardener, as he laid hold of one of her tender branches, to guide it to the prop he had provided. "I'll grow any way you like next year, if you'll only let me have my own way now."
> But the gardener shook his head.
> "Why not?" murmured the vine; "it's hard I may not have my freedom a little longer; it will be time enough, when I am older, to be guided and trained." "Ah!" said the gardener, "that only shows how little you know about it. Each year your branches will grow harder and less flexible, and where one nail will hold you now, it would take a dozen in a twelvemonth's time."

'Tis good buying wit with another man's money.

> How is it good to be mean? Some learn nothing from anybody.

'Tis good to be merry and wise;
'Tis good to be honest and true;
'Tis good to be off with the old love
Before you be on with the new.

> None of our readers will, we hope, need this warning. Very, very awkward it is to hang one's hat on two pegs at once, or to have two bonnets on your peg. Breaches of promise are bad, but a pair of breeches of this sort will prove very ugly wear.

'Tis good going on foot when you lead a horse by its bridle.

> You don't mind walking when you know that you can ride when you like. We are willing to do without a luxury if we feel that we could have it if we very much wanted it.

'Tis grievous to be poor in purse,
But poor in love is greatly worse.

'Tis hard to sail over the sea in an egg-shell.

> To speculate without capital is very unwise. To attempt to reach heaven by our own works and unaided strength is a notable instance of full-blown folly.

'Tis harder to unlearn than to learn.

How difficult to forget evil! How well-nigh impossible to be rid of an ingrained habit! To pick up Parisian French is rendered hard by the French of the school of Stratford-at-Bow, which was drilled into us in youth. Better learn nothing than learn wrongly. Blank paper suits an author; but to write over old manuscript is very unpleasant and unsatisfactory.

'Tis merry in hall when beards wag all.

When they are all eating and drinking, and otherwise agitating the lower jaw, and so causing the beard to move, of course, the whole of the jesters are in a merry cue. It was not quite so merry
When black-jacks all drained,
Each other they brained.

'Tis not all saved that's put in the purse.

It may be the occasion of loss, especially to men in trade; for as the Chinese say, "If a little cash does not go out, much cash will not come in." I knew a farmer who did not cultivate his fields because he thus saved the wages. His farm soon saw him saved all further trouble in husbandry.

'Tis not every question that deserves an answer.

We heard one say to an inquisitive person, "I move the previous question." The interrogator said, "And what is that?" "Well," replied the other, "the previous question is, 'Ought you to ask such a question?'"

'Tis not the food, but the content,
That makes the table's merriment.

'Tis said, that from the twelfth of May
To twelfth of July all is day.

The light never quite ceases during that time.

'Tis skill, not strength, that governs the ship.

Rule skilfully rather than wilfully. Tact is master.

Tittle-tattle, give the goose more hay.

That is, say and do any silly thing, those of you who are given to frivolous talk. We do not endorse this sarcasm: still, one is provoked to make some such remark when small talk annoys.
Pretty little damsels, how they chat!
Chit-chat, tittle-tattle-tat:
All about their sweethearts, and all that,
And chit-chat, tittle-tattle-tat.

To Adam, Paradise was home; to us, home is Paradise.

> And this, we boldly assert, is usually the case with Christian people, notwithstanding the trials of our lives, and the faults of our characters. We do not believe the old satire—
>
>> "Ah, madam! cease to be mistaken,
>> Few married fowl peck Dunmow Bacon!"

To advise a fool is to throw water on a goose.

> Still we would say as much as this to him: You have no right to make a fool of yourself so long as you have a mother or a sister to be put to the blush about you.

To angle all day, and catch a gudgeon at night.

> Some don't even catch that. This gives point to the definition of an angler—"a long pole, with a worm at one end and a fool at the other." Such a fool have I been, and would like to be again.

To all give ear, but do not all believe,
For some there be who would a saint deceive.

To all good wives we wish long lives.

> At home each happy husband sings:
>
>> "God bless my gracious Queen,
>> Long live my noble Queen!"

To and fro, come and go;
All our earthly life is so.

> "Here we have no continuing city, but we seek one to come."—Heb. xiii. 14.

To be angry with an angry man makes two angry men.

To be good among the bad is commendable;
To be good among the good is pleasurable;
To be bad among the bad is horrible;
To be bad among the good is abominable.

> Of course a man's character must be measured in connection with his difficulties or advantages. There is more virtue in some men's being a little good than in others being greatly so.

To be hale in October drink no October ale.

To be idle is to be evil: diligence nourishes delight.

To be proud of your learning is to show your ignorance.

To be secure never be security.

To be washed white and to be white-washed are very different things.

One longs for the first, but loathes the second. When washed white, we are alive unto God; but the white-washed are sepulchres full of corruption.

To believe a business impossible, is the way to make it so.

If a thing is right, the word "impossible" must not be in our dictionary. Believe that it can be done, and it will be done.

To boiling pot flies come not.

When a man is busy and earnest, he takes no notice of trifles. This is much the same in meaning as "Running dogs feel no fleas."

To bowl down hill is easy.

I heard of one who threw a stone half-a-mile, but the reason was that he stood on a hill where there was a continuous descent, and nothing to stop a falling object. One might easily throw a stone five miles if he cast it over a boat's side into the depths of the ocean.

To brew in a bottle, and bake in a bag.

Very little brewers and bakers these ! They are emblems of little minds, which do everything on the very smallest scale, and are quite content to have it so. One convert in a century delights them.

To build high, dig deep.

Nothing is like a good foundation. In religion, deep repentances contribute largely to stability and elevation of character.

To catch a Tartar.

This is a bad thing in matrimony. You look for a Celestial to make your tea, and find a Tartar to make you a pickle.

> Better be a lonely martyr
> Than be married to a Tartar.

To change and to mend are two different things.

We read of King Saul, that he had "another heart"; but what he needed was a new one. Some men when converted are like fair weather, when it changes for the worse.

To come out of "the shires."

> This is how eastern counties people commonly talk of those poor folk who come from other parts of the country. They emerge from those barbarous and uncivilized regions called "the shires." Essex, Suffolk, Kent, and so forth, are real counties, of considerable account; but East Anglia seems to think it sheer folly to expect much from those divisions of the country which are merely "shires."

To covet more,
Makes rich men poor.

> It is easy to be really rich! Do you think me trifling with you? Be contented, and you have it.

To cry with one eye, and laugh with the other.

> This is a queer condition; yet have we been in it. The comic side of the terrible, and the awful side of the mirthful, will sometimes turn up, and the mind cannot tell to which to yield.

To-day man lives in pleasure, wealth, and pride,
To-morrow poor—or life itself denied.
To-day married, to-morrow harried.

> Of course you shall have trouble in the flesh. Does not Scripture say so? At the same time, one does not want trouble in a wife: no one wishes for nettles in his bed.

To *do* good, one must first *be* good.

> "A corrupt tree cannot bring forth good fruit."—Matt. vii. 19.

To every bird its nest seems fair,
My home's a palace rich and rare.

To fall in love and to be wise are very different things.

> An old writer, under the heading LOVER, says, "See lunatic. A lover is a man who in his anxiety to possess another, has lost possession of himself." This is rather too bad.

To follow crowds but death I deem:
The live fish swims against the stream.

> Drifting with the multitude down the broad way is commonly chosen; but to go singly along the narrow road, and push aside all obstacles, is the gracious choice of the gracious man.

To fool the world tell the truth.

So accustomed are men to chicanery, that plain honesty appears to them to be the subtlest form of deceit. *Bismarck* has the credit of this proverb; and it shows his shrewdness.

To forget a wrong is the best revenge.

Lord, teach us to forgive : to learn of thee !
How very little to forgive have we !

To fry in his own grease.

By no means an elegant expression. Did not the Prussian speak of "Paris stewing in its own juice"? No bad man can have a worse doom than to be left altogether to himself.

To get by a thing, as Dickson did by his distress.

We must surely know this Dickson. He made quite a fortune out of the decease of a venerable horse. By petitions and begging letters, he gathered in enough to horse the Brighton coach. We must set the Charity Organization Society upon Dickson.

To give is honor,
To ask is dolor.

He who gives has abundantly more cause for gratitude than he who receives. He who refuses to give ought to come to begging.

To give one a mouthful of moonshine.

A very common thing. Attend a lecture upon a scientific fad, listen to a political schemer, or hear a "modern thought" divine, and you will have a clear idea of a mouthful of moonshine.

To give to the poor increases our store.

Others say, "To give to the poor will bless your store." Both proverbs have truth in them. None of us can afford to cease giving. The rich should give that they may remain rich, and the poor that they may not be poorer. Want of generosity is unthrifty.

To go rabbit hunting with a dead ferret.

Working with useless tools or lazy servants, is a dreadful business. To have a friend to help you who is quite useless, is like working with a broken arm. Better alone than with an inefficient partner.

To go to law is to go to sea.

When will you come to shore again? You will soon be sick of it. When you see the sharks around your estate, you will wish yourself on land again.

To grin like a Cheshire cat chewing gravel.

I have never seen the domestic pet in this condition.   I know how one stone in my teeth serves me, and a cat chewing gravel may very well grin if her sensations are like mine.

To harbour enmities is to plant miseries.

This is from the Chinese.   Put it in your tea, and drink it.

To have a wolf by the ears.

"When a man hath a doubtful business in hand, which it is equally hazardous to pursue or to give over, as it is to hold or let go a wolf which one hath by the ears."—*Ray.*

To have an M under your girdle.

To treat a person with proper respect, to call him *Master* so-and-so. People forget to do this.   There is a Creole proverb, "Behind dog's back, it is 'Dog'; but before dog, it is 'Master dog.'"

To have slanders forgotten by others, forget them yourself.

If you remember them, and continue to advertise them by answering them, they will live for years.   Let them die a natural death.

To hear as hogs do in harvest.

That is, not at all.   They are in fine feeding order, and they do not wish to hear the orders to quit the field.   They have on their harvest ears, and can hear nothing.

To keep the sea back with a pitchfork.

A very absurd enterprise : yet not more so than attempting to stop the will of the people by the use of force.

To kill little birds is to multiply caterpillars.

No doubt; and yet farmers, both here and in America, are of opinion that there may be too many sparrows.   One would think that even these must be better than worms and grubs.

To kill two birds with one stone.

Occasionally a person is able to accomplish two objects by one act. One would rather like the proverb to run, " To feed two birds with one hand," or, " To move two stones in one barrow."

To know little is bad; not to wish to know more is worse.

> *Bishop Ames* was once presiding over a certain conference in the West, when a member began a tirade against universities, education, &c., and thanked God that he had never been corrupted by contact with a college. After proceeding thus for a few minutes, the Bishop interrupted him with the question, "Do I understand that the brother thanks God for his ignorance?" "Well, yes," was the answer, "you can put it that way if you want to." "Well, all I have to say," said the bishop, in his sweet musical tones, "is, that the brother has a great deal to thank God for."

To know right, and to do right, are different things.

> As different as a *menu* and a dinner.

To live in peace, hear, see, and say nothing.

> Another form of it is: "To live in peace, we had need be blind, and deaf, and dumb." We do not go all this length; but, certainly, one can be too quick of observation, and fall into bickerings thereby. To prevent shying, wear blinkers.

To look for a needle in a bottle of hay.

> Rather hopeless work. "Bottle" is the old word for bundle. A needle in a haystack would be hard to find.

To mad words turn a deaf ear.

To marry a woman for her looks, is like eating a bird for its song.

> Since you do not marry her to look at, but to have as a companion and help-meet, observe the formation of her mind as well as the features of her face.

" To-morrow "—the day on which idle men work.

> But it never comes. The work they are going to do is wonderful. These gentlemen take three weeks' holiday every fortnight, and work hard in the time which remains.

To nought it goes that comes from nought.

> " *Sir James Macintosh* had no fewer than sixteen proofs of one of his works before he would allow it to go to press. The biographer of John Foster shows us through what agonies the perfection of style in his essays was attained. They say that Tennyson has spent days in the composition of a single line of poetry. A great musician was asked why he insisted on devoting so much time to the preparation of an apparently simple piece. He replied that, *without such care, nothing whatever could be expected to live.*"

To publish another's obligations, is to discharge him from them.

This is not the rule with good and grateful men; but it is the rule of the world, and there is a rough justice in it. When a man twits me with what he has done for me, he withdraws his claim upon my gratitude.

> To John I owed great obligation :
> But John unhappily thought fit
> To publish it to all the nation :
> Sure, John and I are more than quit.

To read without reflecting, is to eat without digesting.

It is one good point in *this* book that it would be hard to read page after page of it mechanically. But, perhaps, someone has already done so, as another read the Dictionary, and observed that it was a very nice book, but he could not quite see the connection.

To revenge a wrong, is to do a wrong.

> How hardly man the lesson learns,
> To smile, and bless the hand that spurns :
> To see the blow, to feel the pain,
> And render only love again !

To rob Saint Peter to pay Saint Paul
    Is shameful work for man to do ;
But surely it is worst of all
    To rob both Paul and Peter too.

Yet we know fellows who neither pay Peter nor Paul nor anybody else, but rob all saints and all sinners alike. As they have opportunity, they do harm unto all men.

To scare a bird is not the way to catch it.

Fierce, threatening preaching will not win men for Jesus.

To search for truth is commendable, but to enjoy truth is more comfortable.

One said that he loved the search for truth better than the finding of it : there is no accounting for tastes. We suspect that he was not over-fond of truth, but loved it best at a distance.

To see the sun rise is good for the eyes.

It is to be feared that many Londoners have never tried this golden ointment. Even lie-a-beds commend early rising.

To set up shop on Goodwin Sands.

Does it mean that the shop-keeper is to win good as the sands of time run out? Or, does it mean that a certain person has so little capital that he builds his trade on the sand, and will be shipwrecked by being shop-wrecked?

To speak to purpose, one must speak with a purpose.

To spin a yarn to fill up space is wretched work. He that speaks against time will find time speaking against him.

To spend and spend
Brings cash to end.

Stop spending, then, if your purse is getting low. But what is the use of money if it is not spent? It is the circulating medium, and was meant to flow out as well as in.

To stop the tongue of slander, stop your own.

We greatly question whether slander will ever cease till the last gossip is in her grave, or say, in *his* grave; but if anything will quiet it, it will be the silence of the person assailed.

If on the spark you do not blow,
Out, of itself, it soon will go.

To stroke with one hand, and stab with the other.

Often done by cruel dissemblers. They praise the gospel and undermine it. They call you "fine gentleman," and cut your throat. This is what is done by strong drink; in fact, some drinkers, when they have wished the bottle passed, have cried, "Stab yourself, and pass the dagger!" Significant, is it not?

To subdue the passions is hard: to satisfy them impossible.

To swallow an ox, and be choked with the tail.

This is done when men commit a great crime, and stickle over details; or when they embrace a huge error and boggle at a word.

To sweeten your morsel, share it.

Selfishness turns sugar into sickly lusciousness; but generosity changes the quartern of bread into a sugar-loaf.

To take the wrong sow by the ear.

Don't do that: better let the right sow escape you. Charges must be accurately laid, or not at all.

To talk without thinking, is to shoot without aiming.

To the wasp say, " Neither your sting nor your honey."

Half measures will not answer with malicious minds.

To think is well, but to know is better.

To wash an ass's head is waste of soap.

And it wins a chance of feeling the ass's heels. To correct some men is labour in vain, for it only provokes them.

To win a cat you lose a cow:
It may be wise ; I see not how.

To risk a great deal to gain little is the height of folly.

Tom Timid was drowned in a teacup.

He went in as a spoon, made a little stir, and was never heard of more : he is generally supposed to have sunk in matrimony.

Tongue breaketh bone,
And herself hath none,
    Quoth Hendyng.

Some make no bones about telling lies : in many cases there is nothing solid about what is said, but all is oily, slippery, worthless. I have heard that a well-dressed tongue needs five hours' boiling : I would like to see what half-an-hour would do with some tongues I wot of. They make my blood boil often.

Tongues are the best and worst meat in the world.

So *Æsop* taught. We add a selection of proverbs referring to the tongue.

" The boneless tongue, so small and weak,
Can crush and kill," declared the Greek.
" The tongue destroys a greater horde,"
The Turk asserts, " than does the sword."
The Persian proverb wisely saith,
" A lengthy tongue—an early death " ;
Or sometimes takes this form instead,
" Don't let your tongue cut off your head."
" The tongue can speak a word whose speed,"
Say the Chinese, " outstrips the steed."
While Arab sages this impart,
" The tongue's great storehouse is the heart."
From Hebrew wit the maxim sprung,
" Though feet should slip, ne'er let the tongue."
The sacred writer crowns the whole :
" Who keeps the tongue doth keep his soul."

Tongues run all the faster when they carry little.

Like every other machine, what the tongue gains in speed it loses in power. Great talkers not only *do* the least, but they even *say* the least, if their words are weighed instead of being counted. Talkative tongues are like the plague of frogs in Egypt: those creatures did not bite, but they wearied by their endless croaking.

Tongues seldom ache through lying still.

Paul Chatfield tells us of a chatterbox who said, " I talk a good deal, but then I talk well." " Half of that is true," said one who knew him. When a man has learned to keep silence he loves it.

Too far East is West.

Your nice man is nasty, your severely righteous man is unfair, your ultra-democrat is a tyrant, and your liberal thinker is a bigot.

Too late to spare when all is spent.

Too little for one, may be too much for another.

Too many cooks spoil the broth.

Or *spill* the broth; or forget to make any.

Too many " night-caps " make a man's head ache.

The night-caps we refer to are of a spirituous kind.

Too much breaks the bag.

Too much courtesy, too much craft.

Too much may be said on the best of subjects.

Let " Finally " stand within measurable distance.

Too much of a good thing is not a good thing.

Too much of one thing, too little of another.

Sam Slick wisely said : " Them that have more than their share of one thing, commonly have less of another. Where there is great strength, there ain't apt to be much gumption. A handsome man, in a general way, ain't much of a man. A beautiful bird seldom sings. Them that has genius have no common-sense."

Too much oil puts out the lamp; too much wood puts out the fire.

Too much book-learning puts out the man himself. He has no room for his mind to turn in, for he has blocked up the space with books. Too much fluency may be the death of eloquence.

Too much palaver, too little honesty.

You know the gentleman—all smiles and blarney; and as a dentist extracts your teeth under gas, so has he extracted your sovereigns by his empty pufferies.

Too much pudding will choke a dog.

So, one may be lectured till he cannot endure it. Is it not so, Mr. Caudle? And one may be dunned with the same subject till you wish yourself deaf. The proverb is rather a currish one, and may have been started by some young dog who had been over-done with stick-jaw pudding at Dotheboys Hall.

Too much sail suits not a small boat.

Too much sugar may spoil the pie.

A man who is all molasses, and "dearie, dearie," is a little too too, and we get sick of him.

Too much taking counsel ends in doing nothing.

The Committee sat, and sat, and sat, till every sensible plan was crushed as flat as a pancake.

Too soon is easy mended ;
Too late can't be defended.

If a person gets to an appointment before his time, a little waiting puts him right; but if he comes after the hour, he is unjust to the person whom he promised to meet.

Too too will in two.

Don't test the fabric with too hard a pull, and don't select too tender a material. Don't test friendship too severely, or it may fail. Don't try temper too often, or it may give way.

Touch a galled horse and he'll kick.

See how certain people lash out when you touch on a point about which their conscience is tender. Touch me not on my sore heel. Do not remind me of an unpleasant fact.

Touchwood! Touchwood! Mind the fire.

Touchwood soon takes fire. Where there is peculiar susceptibility to a sin, there should be a careful avoidance of all that leads to it. Don't put your cat in the pigeon-house, nor your dog among young rabbits; and don't put yourself into the kind of company which has aforetime led you astray.

Tough meat needs a sharp knife.

When fellows will not attend, sharp words become needful.

Towers are measured by their shadows, and great men by those that are envious of them.

Tradesmen may be like bad eggs, which look very well till they break.

But when the breaking comes, the tradesman is not in good odour, and his composition is not much admired.

Train up a child in the way you should have gone yourself.

Tread on the ball, live to spend all;
Tread on the heel, spend a great deal;
Tread where you may, money won't stay.

The wearing out of shoes by wearing them most in this place or in that, causes a portion of those expenses by which we are kept up, and our savings are kept down. In olden times men changed their shoes from day to day from foot to foot, to secure an equal wearing of them in every part. An old gentleman of our acquaintance, having a gouty foot, was ordered by his doctor to cut the shoe, and he did so. The next morning he was found with the uncut shoe on the sore foot, and nothing could induce him to forego the long habit of changing the shoes. So both had to be cut. Dear old Tory!

Trials are the ballast of life.

The burdened vessel may sail slowly, but she sails safely. Without the ballast of trial men are apt to blow over. Ballast yourself with sympathy, if you have no trials of your own.

Trickery is a dog which comes back to its master.

Dishonesty comes home to men. The knave outwits himself before long, and gets tarred with his own brush.

Trifles are only trifles to triflers.

Think nought a trifle, though it small appears:
Sands make the mountains; moments make the years;
And trifles, life. Your care to trifles give,
Else you may die ere you have learned to live.

Trifling with truth is like fooling with fire.

No one can guess what mischief may come of it.

Trinkets and trash run away with the cash.

Boys and girls had better leave flash jewellery to fops and flirts.

Trouble is soon enough when it comes.

Do not go forth to meet it by timorous apprehensions of its coming. Believe that with the trial suffi.ient grace will come.

Trouble often shows the man.

Until the steel the flint shall smite,
It will afford nor heat nor light.

True blue will keep its hue.

True blue will never stain.

The colours of pretence soon fade in shower and sun, but faithful honesty defies all circumstances and oppositions.

What is dyed in the grain
Will not run in the rain.

True fame is neither sold nor bought;
She sometimes follows where she is not sought.

A man's reputation is like his shadow : if it follows him, he will never leave it behind him ; if it goes before him, he will never go beyond it. It is best to take no note of it, but to be what you would be thought to be.

True friendship's laws are in this line expressed,—
Welcome the coming, speed the parting guest.

True *hospitality* is meant. Be as particular to see your guest off in good time, as you were to receive him ; and do not importune him to stay when he has once said that he must needs go.

True love never grows old.

Trust in God, and keep your powder dry.

This Cromwellian sentence has grand common-sense in it.

Trust is dead : bad pay killed him.

This is a sentence which I have seen written up in shops where the poor are wont to deal. *Willis*, in his "Current Notes," says that he saw in a public house, at Chichester, the following verse :—

"Since man to man is so unjust,
No man can tell what man to trust.
I've trusted many to my sorrow :
Pay to-day, take trust to-morrow."

Trust no fox with the care of your young ducks.

Send not your boys to a school taught by Father Roman, nor your girls to a parson who has a confessional. Trust not your young lambs to the care of the wolf, unless you really want them destroyed. Leave no gambler to play with your boys.

Trust not a boy with a sword.

Sooner or later he will hurt himself, or somebody else. High offices and mysterious discussions are dangerous in the hands of inexperience and incompetence.

Trust not a horse's heel, a dog's tooth, or a gossip's tongue.

Trust the last least. Mad dogs and kicking horses are better than slanderous tongues.

Trust not a smooth sea, nor a smiling world.

Few men in the world can be relied upon. " Put not your trust in princes." The sea has its sharks, but the land has its deceivers.

> To safe-guard man from wrongs, there nothing must
> Be truer to him than a wise *distrust ;*
> And to thyself be best this sentence known,
> Hear all men speak, but credit few or none.

Yet, at the same time, suspicion is but a cowardly virtue.

Trust not the man who promises with an oath.

He swears too glibly for his oath to be worth anything.

Trust not the ship to one rope.

Divide the risk, and have more than one earthly confidence.

> Good riding at two anchors men have told ;
> For if one break, the other still may hold.

Trust self, and lose all; trust God, and win all.

> Man who on himself
> Dareth to rely,
> Is like a frail reed
> When the wind passes by.

Trust to Providence, but lock the stable door.

This reminds us of Mahomet's observation, when one of his followers said that he would turn his camel loose, and trust it to Providence. " Nay," said Mahomet, " tie it up as best you can, and then trust it to Providence."

Trust when you can ; but know your man.

Men nowadays want a deal of knowing : when you think you are at the bottom of them, a trap-door opens.

> When man is practised in disguise,
> He cheats the most discerning eyes.

Trust your eyes rather than your ears.

See for yourself : your ears have to trust to other men's eyes, and tongues also : you will do well to put your own optics to work.

Truth always comes by the lame messenger.

After liars have told their tale, in comes honest truth to their confusion. Yet truth's messenger in another sense is by no means lame. His feet are beautiful upon the mountains.

Truth and time against the world.

Philip of Spain used to say, "I and time against any two." The man who defends God's truth can afford to wait; for both time and eternity are on his side. God and his truth have great leisure.

Truth cannot be bound nor drowned.

> Truth may go down
> But will not drown.
> This challenge, then, be boldly hurled,
> "The truth alone against the world."

Truth finds few that love her *gratis.*

People will look about and calculate the consequences. Faithful men not only seek no gain by truth, but are willing to lose all for her sake. Yet are these the greatest gainers.

Truth gives a short answer; lies go round about.

Truth needs not many words, but a false tale needs a large preamble. Some in their roundaboutness make us feel that there is some bamboozlement intended. Yet to certain minds the curvilinear mode appears to be as natural as the straight line is to others. There is a tale in Kashmir about a man who was once asked where his nose was. He did not reply by at once putting his finger on that organ, and saying, "Here it is"; but he pulled up the right sleeve of his long cloak, and passing his right hand around his head, eventually and with great difficulty, touched his nose with it. We know more than one friend who must have been a pupil of this Kashmiri gentleman.

Truth never grows old.

In the sense of decaying, or being out of date.

Truth in faith works holiness·in life.

Errors in the life breed errors in the brain,
And these, reciprocally, those again.

Truth is beautiful, but men scratch her face.

Truth seldom goes without a scratched face, for men love her not.

Truth is the best buckler.

Carry it with you, on you, within you.

Truth is truth till time shall end.

Truth lies at the bottom of a well.

Douglas Jerrold said, "I've heard people say, 'truth lives in a well,'; if so, I'd advise you to take an early dip in the bucket." A very good verse has been written on this saying of the Latins.

"Truth's in a well!" To get it out
You'll find there's this impediment,
That if you, blundering, probe about,
You'll stir up *doubt*—the sediment.

Truth, like oil, comes to the surface.

Truth may be blamed, but can never be shamed.

Yet some would blame it because it blames them. They are like the lady in the American story. Eli Perkins tells of an old maid with her face covered with wrinkles, turning from the mirror, saying, "Mirrors nowadays are very faulty. They don't make such mirrors as they used to when I was young."

Truth may come out of the devil's mouth.

And then it is truth still; but he puts it in such a fashion that he means it to support a lie, or look like a lie.

Truth needs nothing to help it out.

Truth oft oppressèd we may see ;
But quite suppress'd it cannot be.

A modern form of putting the same cheering sentiment is found in *W. C. Bryant's* verse :

"Truth, crushed to earth, shall rise again—
The eternal years of God are hers ;
But error, wounded, writhes with pain,
And dies among his worshippers."

Truth seeks no corners, and fears no scorners.

Truth should not swim in the brain, but sink into the heart.

Truth will in the end prevail,
Though it creepeth like a snail.

> Its slow progress in a false world is not wonderful; but God is with it, and its victory is sure. It is not a snail, but a mighty angel of God. *Magna est veritas, et prœvalebit.*

Truth will sometimes break out in unlooked-for places.

> As it did in the monastery with Luther.

Truths, like roses, have thorns about them.

> Hence one says, "Follow not truth too near at the heels, lest it dash out your teeth"; but this is evil advice. When the thorns of truth prick a man, they act as salutary lancets, and he may be thankful for the wholesome pain they bring.

Try and *Trust* will move mountains.

> Say rather—God will move the mountains if we truly trust him.

Try before you trust.

> "Take no man to your heart at sight,
> But prove his friendship strong;
> The man who often says you're right,
> May oftenest think you wrong."

Try to suffer with such patience, that those around you do not suffer.

> As they will certainly do if you grow peevish and exacting. This precept is not so easy as it looks. It is well to be ill well.

Turn away from sin before sin turns you away from God.

> Say to its pleasure, "Gentle Eve, I will have none of your apple." To hesitate is to yield; to yield is to go into bondage.

Turn over your store, and give to the poor.

Turn stumbling-blocks into stepping-stones.

Turn the cake in the pan.

> Cook one side as well as the other. Attend to the whole of your business. Change the topic of conversation. Don't keep always in one strain. As for yourself, be not as Ephraim, whom the prophet calls "a cake not turned." Be gracious in all ways.

Turn your tongue seven times before speaking.

Two blacks don't make a white.

> If the other party is wrong it will not make your wrong right. Mind this, and don't defend yourself by defaming others.

Two cannot quarrel if one won't.

> A coloured man related to a friend his plan for avoiding family jars in the following words: "I telled Betty, when we was wed, dat, if she saw me getting angry like, she must go to the bucket, and fill her mouth wid water; and if I saw her getting out of herself, I'd go to the bucket, and fill my mouth wid water. So we never had any quarrels, for one can't quarrel alone, and anoder can't quarrel wid you when his mouth's full of water."

Two cats and one mouse,
Two women in one house,
Two dogs to one bone:
These I let alone.

> We don't believe in this old saw, except in a special sense: and in that sense no good man would wish to have two women in one house. "No man can serve two masters."

Two cocks on one dunghill will not long agree.

> So that males as well as females fall out. Two big crowing men are best apart, for they are sure to fight. It would be well if they ceased from being so high and mighty, and then they might agree.

Two eyes are not sufficient to choose a wife by.

> Not even if the ears and heart co-operate. We have need to consult the sacred oracle, and use our coolest judgment.

Two eyes, two ears, only one mouth.

> See and hear twice, and speak but once.

Two fools in one family are two too many.

Two glasses of grog are two too many.

> If you can stand them, you can stand better without them.

Two halves do not always make one.

> A half and a better half ought to make one, but they do not. The fight is at times which one it shall be, and then things go to pieces.

Two heads are better than one, even if they are only sheep's heads.

Two feeble minds may keep right by mutual advice where one strong-minded person hurries into folly. Speaking of sheep's head reminds us of Douglas Jerrold. At a supper of sheep's heads an enthusiast cried out, "Sheep's heads for ever," and the wag replied, "What egotism!"

Two of a trade seldom agree.

Competition is too apt to breed contention; but it must not be so among Christians. Paul dwelt with brethren of his trade, "for they were tent-makers."

Two strings to your bow, and you'll miss the target.

Have two strings to your belle, or two belles to your string, and you will not very readily get so far as the ring; though you are far more likely to get wrung by some indignant father or brother.

Two to one in all things against an angry man.

We do not insert this as a bet, but as a fact. He is too hot to be of cool judgment: his temper will lose him friends.

Sayings of a more Spiritual Sort.

Tears of repentance are good for the eyes.

> But more certainly good for the heart.
> The tears of saints more sweet by far
> Than all the songs of sinners are.

Tell thy God thy wish and care :
Turn thy sorrow into prayer.

> So shall every want and wish become a way of approach to God,
> or at least a motive for communing with him.   The supply of those
> wants will also be a way in which thy Lord will come to thee.

Temptations, like foul weather, come before we send for
them.

> Therefore, we should pray, "Lead us not into temptation";
> and as that petition will not be universally and absolutely answered,
> we must add, "But deliver us from evil."

That garment which was worn to shreds on Adam's back
will never make a complete covering for mine.

> Human righteousness soon dropped to shreds on the back of one
> whose nature was unfallen ; therefore it will never suit us who are
> already sinful, and dwell in a sinful world.

That is best for us which is best for our souls.

> For our souls are the best part of us.

The ark of God always pays for its entertainment, wheresoever it dwells.

> Every Obed-edom will bear witness to this.   Lot let angels in,
> and the angels led him out.

The armour-bearer of sin is self-confidence.

The best way to live in the world is to live above it.

> Old Romish pictures represent saints in prayer as lifted up from
> the earth.   This is true spiritually.   Prayer and fasting produce
> an elevated condition of heart ; and if this can be maintained, we
> escape the injurious tendency of our surroundings, and in a sense
> this corruptible puts on incorruption.

The cross of Christ is the key of Paradise.

The curse of the serpent rests on the seed of the serpent.

> *Leighton* writes: "Earthly men are daily partakers of the serpent's curse; they go on their belly, and eat the dust."

The death of carnal hope is the beginning of spiritual life.

The death of Jesus is the ground of the believer's life.

> Let him stand upon it, and upon it only. If he shifts his ground, and relies upon his own experience, it goes ill with him.

The dew falls in due season.

> Let us pray the Lord to send it on all holy ministries.
>
> " If not full showers of rain, yet, Lord,
> A little pearly dew afford;
> A little, if it come from thee,
> Will be of great avail to me."—*Christopher Harvey.*

The earth will hide
Bright eyes and pride.

The excellent of the earth can see no excellence in the earth.

> " My soul, what's lighter than a feather? Wind.
> Than wind? The fire. And what, than fire? The mind.
> What's lighter than the mind? A thought. Than thought?
> This bubble world. What, than this bubble? Nought."
>   *Quarles.*

The fear of man weakens; the fear of God strengthens.

The gem cannot be polished without friction, nor man perfected without trial.

The gospel breaks hard hearts and heals broken hearts.

The gospel is sweet music in a sinner's ears.

> Well it may be, for it brings life for death, pardon for guilt, peace for terror, and heaven instead of hell.

The great God sees even a little good.

> His mercy makes him interpret hopefully every sign of grace. He spies out the first spark of desire, and fans it. If there be only a sigh of sorrow for sin it will be heard in heaven.

The heart must be broken *for* sin and *from* sin.

There is a beautiful Persian aphorism to this effect : " Nothing that is broken bears any value, except the heart, which becomes more valuable the more it is broken."

The hope of the hopeless is Jesus our hope.

Blessed be his name ! We do well to put into his mouth those words :—

" The foolish, the feeble, the weak, are my care ;
The hopeless, the helpless, I hear their sad prayer."

The key of prayer can open any lock, and deliver any Peter from prison.

Four fours of soldiers cannot keep the man whom God sets free in answer to prayer; nor could four armies succeed any better. The iron gate opens of its own accord when prayer opens the hand of God. It is harder for us to pray than for God to answer.

The least sin should make us humble, but the greatest sin should not make us despair.

The less of man, the more of God.

" None of self " is sweetly joined with "all of thee." God uses weak instruments, that we may the better see his power.

The life of sin is the death of the sinner.

" In South America there is a creeper which climbs, and enfolds, and hangs in pendant festoons about certain trees, poisoning as it goes ; it drinks the sap, sheds its destructive seeds, and multiplies its power of injury and death. It is called ' The Murderer,' for its well-known and fatal qualities. We cannot fail to think of the destroying power of sinful habits, how they commence in little things, yet creep and grow, spreading and hanging about character and life, drinking the strength, and poisoning vital energies."
M'Michael.

The Lord will never help us to catch fish with dirty nets.

He will have his work done in a cleanly style. " Be ye clean, that bear the vessels of the Lord."—Isa. lii. 11.

The Lord's-day is the lord of days.

Regard it as a right royal day. The head of seven is crowned from heaven. The day of the Lord is the lord of days.

The loss of gold is great, the loss of health is more ;
But the loss of Christ is such a loss as no man can restore.

> A good verse to be printed on a card, and put into the hand of the careless.

The minister's life is the life of his ministry.

> People will not mind his words unless there is a holy life at the back of them. We must burn in our acts, and shine in our sermons.

The ministry is the best calling, but the worst trade.

> To preach for a living is wretched hypocrisy ; to preach for the living God is noble service. A prostituted pulpit is an awful sight.

The more you draw from God's Word, the more you will find in it.

> "I see the oil of thy word will never leave increasing whilst any bring an empty barrel. The Old Testament will still be a New Testament to him who comes with a fresh desire of information."
> *T. Fuller.*

The only way to keep our crowns is to cast them down at Christ's feet.

The prayer of the heart is the heart of the prayer.

> The language of the heart cannot be imitated. Talma, the famous actor, hearing of the death of his father, uttered a loud cry of distress. Soon after he murmured, "Oh, that I could cry like that on the stage !" Too many prayers are but stage performances ; the voice of the heart is not heard in them.

The promises, like a well-drawn picture, look on all that look on them with an eye of faith.

The reading of the Scriptures is the terror of devils.

> "It is written" is a weapon which the prince of devils dreads ; but a man cannot readily quote or use what he never reads. "What's wrang wi' ye noo ? I thocht ye were a' richt," said a ragged boy, himself rejoicing in the Saviour, to another, who a few nights before professed to be able to trust Jesus, but who had again begun to doubt. "What's wrang wi' ye noo ?" "Man, I'm no richt yet," replied the other, "for Satan's aye tempting me." "And what dae ye then ?" asked his friend. "I try," said he, "to sing a hymn." "And does that no' send him away ?" "No ; I am as bad as ever." "Weel," said the other, "when he tempts ye again, try him wi' a text ; he canna staun that."

The same sun that melts wax, hardens clay.

The holy influences which accompany the gospel produce in some greater hardness of heart. As the man is, such is the influence of preaching upon him, till the Spirit comes with power.

The sermon is not done till the hearer does it.

Coming home from the kirk a little sooner than usual, the good wife was asked by her husband, " What! is the sermon all done ? " She wisely answered, " No, Donald, it is all *said*, but it has not begun to be *done* yet." Many sermons are done with, but not done.

The Son of God makes us sons of God.

This is the true sonship. That universal fatherhood which is so much cried up gives the lie to the great doctrines of adoption and regeneration, and it is itself a lie of the first magnitude.

The soul is the life of the body.
Faith is the life of the soul.
Christ is the life of faith.

The strongest objection to the Bible is a bad life.

The tear of repentance beautifies the eye of faith.

The tears of the congregation are the hope of the minister.

But they are disappointing. Men weep at the theatre at the sight of a tragedy, or at a funeral in the presence of death, but they wipe their eyes and forget all. It is much the same under sermons. Broken hearts are better than flowing eyes.

The thorough Christian is the true Christian.

A man who was in the habit of saying that although he was not what he should be, still, upon the whole, he was a good average kind of Christian, had given orders to a Christian man to construct a fence around his property. Meeting this man some days afterwards, he asked him if he had made a good fence. "Well," was the reply " the fence is not as it should be — it is not very strong in certain parts, and there are gaps here and there ; but it is a good average kind of fence." The man at once, with great indignation, said, " What do you mean ? Why, a fence of that kind is useless ! " " Quite true," was the answer, " and the man who is only a good average kind of Christian is not very much use either."

The true Sabbath is to rest in Christ,

His is that finished work which brings us endless rest. In him we ease from our own works as God did from his.

The water without the ship may toss it; but it is the water within the ship which sinks it.

> Therefore, let not care leak into your soul. "Let not your heart be troubled," even though your house may be.

The way to Canaan is through the wilderness.

> Where there is no way God leads his people by a right way.

The way to heaven is by Weeping-Cross.

> Repentance, with her clear wet eyes,
> Leads her children to the skies.

The will is no more free than it is made free by grace.

> The free-will of a man who is under sin is sheer slavery; he that doth the will of God from the heart is free indeed.

The worst want is want of faith.

> Faith will supply every other want, but what shall we do should faith cease to draw from God All-sufficient?

There is an infidel in every man's bosom

> An *honest* doubter is rare enough; but we are all born doubters of God, and of that holy truth which troubles us in our sins.

There is no reason for grace but grace.

> God's motive for mercy lies within himself. He loved his people because he would love them.

There is no water till God strikes the rock.

> Often all is dry as the desert till the Lord interposes in his providence, and then he turns the thirsty land into a pool. So, too, there are no streams of repentance till the touch of grace creates a fountain in the heart of stone.

There's a mountain of matter in every line of Scripture.

> The moderns will not believe it; but the spiritual know that it is so. One of the fathers rightly said, "I adore the infinity of Holy Scripture." There is little fear nowadays that men will make too much of the Bible: the most of them make too little of it.

They are well kept whom God keeps.

They that feel themselves lost are soon found.

> This is one of the earliest signs of a work of grace in the soul. Nothing can be truly found which was not first lost. Christ himself does not go after those sheep which have never gone astray.

They who sin the sin must bear the shame.

They who trust Christ's death must copy his life.

> We may not divide Christ. "Not a bone of him shall be broken." He must be our Exemplar, or he will not be our Saviour.

Those who are alive to God's glory are dead to vainglory.

> Thus to seek earnestly the glory of God is the best preservative against pride and self-seeking.

Those who believe are those who receive.

Those who deal with God must deal upon trust.

Those who have heaven in their hopes should have heaven in their lives.

Those who love God love God's Word.

Those who seek God, find him; and those who find him, seek him.

Those who think much of themselves, think little of Christ.

Those who welcome Christ may welcome death.

Those who wish to cross the seas
Must not lose the favouring breeze.

> Those who would enter heaven must use the blessed influences of the Holy Spirit. He bloweth when and where he pleases, and we must not neglect a single favourable opportunity.

Those who would get to heaven must get to Christ.

Though God may frown in the providence, he always smiles in the promise.

Though love will perfect fear remove,
Yet most I fear when most I love.

> This is not that slavish fear which has torment; but filial fear, which grows out of love, and is no enemy to joy.

To ask amiss is to ask and miss.

To be much like Christ, be much with Christ.

> A painter in Rome was forbidden to copy a famous picture. Determined not to be balked, he sat down in front of the painting and looked closely and steadfastly at it for half an hour every morning. He then hurried home and transferred one line or feature to his canvas. So he attained his object. If we would spend but half an hour each day in contemplating the grace and beauty of our Divine Redeemer, by a spiritual process there would be a transference of those lines of grace and beauty into our characters.

To broken hearts Christ brings unbroken peace.

To die *in* the Lord, we must live *to* the Lord.

To God keep near throughout the year.

To have a portion in this world is mercy; but to have the world for our portion is misery.

To look upon a promise without a precept is the high road to *presumption;* to look upon a precept without a promise is the high road to *desperation.*

To see the King is better than to see a thousand of his servants.

> Make it your desire, in going to the house of God, that you may behold the beauty of the Lord while you enquire in his temple.

To win Christ is the greatest gain.

TOO LATE is written on the gates of hell.

Trifling with sin is no trifling sin.

Trust not in the ordinances of God, but in the God of ordinances.

Trust God where you cannot trace him.

> Especially leave the unknown future in his hands. What is the use of fretting beforehand?
>
> > If evils come not, then our fears are vain,
> > And if they come, our fears augment the pain.

GLY women, finely dressed, are the uglier for it.

Are there any ugly women? We cannot say; but some evidently think themselves so, for they put on showy apparel to hide their plainness. Their gaudy trappings advertise their want of comeliness. The plainer the dress, the more conspicuous the beauty of the wearer.

Unborn pups are doubtful dogs.

To the same effect is the other proverb: "Unlaid eggs are doubtful chicks." It is idle to reckon upon the uncertain future.

Uncle pays for all.

In America it is Uncle Sam, and here it is Uncle John Bull, so far as the nation is concerned. "Never mind the expense, Uncle Bull will clear the bill." The Italians say that public money is like holy water, everybody helps himself to it. In families, also, the principle comes into action, and economy ceases when a rich friend "stands Sam." A bachelor uncle is almost as good as a maiden aunt; and in some respects better. It must be nice to be uncle when all the youngsters reckon on your paying for all they choose to buy.

Under a cloak the devil is two devils.

He is able to do double mischief when disguised.

Under golden sheath leaden sword.

Too often true; great show and poor substance. "Under silk hat a soft head," and "under a coronet no head at all." These may both be true; and yet all are not wide awake who wear wide-awakes.

"Under the rose."

That is, secretly. Let us do nothing which requires to be hidden. "*Sub rosâ*" is a state of things which makes honest men afraid.

Under white ashes lie glowing embers.

Men may seem very gentle, and yet be indulging the fiercest passions. Courtesy may conceal furious malice.

Underhanded dealing
Stirs up angry feeling.

Do everything above board; for no man likes to feel that he has been taken in and done for.

Unfit to die, unfit to live.

That which is necessary as a preparation for the next world is equally needful for this present life. If we live as we should, we shall die as we would.

Unfortunate and imprudent are often two words for the same thing.

When a man is incorrigibly stupid, he lays his failure upon his bad luck. Providence may arrange matters mysteriously at times; but, as a rule, when men cannot succeed, there is a reason for it. Those who are long out of work are generally out *with* work.

Unkind words fall easily from the tongue, but a coach and six horses cannot bring them back.

Unlooked-for often comes.

It is the unexpected that happens.

Unready and Unsteady are two Ne'er-do-wells.

Unsaid may be said, but said cannot be unsaid.

Therefore, prefer to err by silence rather than to sin by speech.

Unthankful men are unnatural men.

The unthankful and the evil are leashed together in Scripture, like a couple of hounds of the worst breed. No Billingsgate woman could give a man a worse word than to call him ungrateful. Nature is grateful: all the rivers run into the sea, and the clouds repay the earth for its mists by heavy rains. The flocks and the herds repay their keeper; and he is worse than a brute who hath no gratitude.

Until the physician has killed one or two, he is not a physician.

So say the Kashmiris; but those poor, ignorant people, have no acquaintance with our allopathic practitioners, and intend no allusion to those worthy gentlemen.

Unused advantages are no advantage.

He that hath fields he doth not weed,
He that hath books he doth not read,
He that hath ears but doth not heed,
Of common-sense hath grievous need.

Unwilling service earns no thanks.

Unwise people learn nothing from the wise.

> As the Burmese say, "A fool is like a wooden spoon, which does not perceive the flavour of the curry-gravy in which it is placed." Solomon says, "Ye fools, when will ye be wise?"

Up in the morning early,
And leave off being surly.

> Beds make beggars. Lazy lovers of sleep find all things going wrong, and they are on the grumble all the day. Getting up late, they get out on the wrong side of the bed, and are all day as surly as bears with sore heads.

Up like a rocket, and down like its stick.

> A gradual rise is likely to prove a permanent one ; but a sudden rise is often temporary. This proverb has been applied by ill-will to many who have not yet dropped like a stick.

Up hill spare me, down hill forbear me.

> This is a part of the good advice which the horse is supposed to give to his driver.

Upon an egg the hen lays an egg.

> To him that hath shall be given. Get a nest-egg and more will come. The difficulty of saving lies in the first ten pounds.

Use as little vinegar as possible in talking of others.

Use friends as you would have them use you.

> Expect no more from them than they might reasonably expect from you. Many people have no thought except for themselves.

Use is second nature.

> It is said that a man might live up to his neck in a horse-pond if he once grew used to it. But there is a limit to the influence of habit ; for when the miser was getting his horse to be used to live on a straw a day it died.

Use is the best estimate of value.

> That learning and talent which cannot be put to any service is not much esteemed.

> > A candle that affords no light,
> > What profits it by day or night?

Use legs, and have legs.

Those who walk can walk. It is the same with other things : the exercise of a faculty or ability is the making of it. Many a man has capacities which he has not discovered, because they have not been called into exercise.

Use more wit, and less sweat.

Many things which cannot be wrought by violent exertion are easily brought about by using a little common-sense. In public speaking let no man mistake perspiration for inspiration.

Use neither too much bridle, nor too much spur.

Good counsel as to horses, and equally wise as to young people under training. Neither curb too much, nor demand too great exertion of the mental powers.

Use pastime so as to save time.

Amusement is useful when it causes the mind to be rested, so that it is able to do all the more when you return to work.

Use soft words, but hard arguments.

Suaviter in modo : fortiter in re. The suaviter and the fortiter should be mixed in equal proportions. Be gentle. The sea is held in check, not by a wall of granite but by a beach of sand. Many think strong language strengthens a weak argument ; but it does not. A bully is by no means a conclusive reasoner.

Use sugar more than vinegar.

Be good-tempered. Be placid, and not acid. Don't show a litigious spirit. There is no surer way of setting everybody against yourself than that of setting yourself against everybody.

Use words with care, or ill you'll fare.

If one had arranged to dine at the "Green Man, Dulwich," and told the coachman to drive to the "Dull Man, Greenwich," he would miss his dinner. One may lose the habit of truth, and even of reasonableness, by being careless in the use of language.

Use your eyes if you would be wise.

Use your shoulders as well as your knees.

Work as well as pray.

Sayings of a more Spiritual Sort.

Unbelief is giving God the lie.

> That's the plain English of it. If a man has "honest" doubt, he will at least grant that God is honest too.

Undone duty will undo our souls.

> "Unprofitable servants" when we have done all; what are we when we have left all undone?

Uneven conduct makes uneasy conscience.

"Upward and heavenward" be always your motto.

Use not your Best Friend worst.

> Nay, use him better than your best has yet reached.
>
> > The glory of my glory still shall be,
> > To give all glory and myself to thee.

Use temporal things, but prize eternal things.

Use the world by making it thy servant; abuse it not by making it thy master.

Use what you have, that you may have more to use.

Utter to your utmost unutterable love.

AIN thoughts are vagrants, and must not be lodged.

> "How long shall thy vain thoughts lodge within thee?"—Jer. iv. 14.

Vainglory blooms abundantly, but fruits sparingly.

Vanity has no greater foe than vanity.

> In this case dog eats dog: one proud person hates another.

Vanity is a blue-bottle, which buzzes in the window of the wise.

> *Aristotle* once said to a conceited fellow, "Young man, I wish I were what you think yourself to be, and my enemies what you really are." Even so great a sage was annoyed by a fool.

Velvet paws hide sharp claws.

> Very soft and pretty speeches are often intended to cover hard and cruel meanings.

Venture a sprat to catch a herring.

Venture not on one night's ice.

> It will rarely be strong enough to bear you. New schemes and methods should not be trusted hastily. See whether they are safe.

Very cheap is mostly very dear.

Very few herrings are caught on Newmarket Heath.

> We must look for things in their proper places. We shall never find true pleasure in sin, nor rest in self, nor gain in gambling.

Very hard times in the wood when the wolves eat each other.

> When men who live upon the public take to devouring each other, things are probably going very badly with them.

Very like a whale in a butter-boat.

> Something very wonderful; too much cried up to be true.
>
> > When any tell a mighty tale,
> > I answer, " *Very like a whale.*"

Vexation treads on the heels of vanity.

Vice is learned without a schoolmaster.

> Yes, and all the more surely without schooling.

" Virtue in the middle," said the devil, when seated between two lawyers.

> A very old proverb, referring to lawyers centuries ago (?).

Virtue is a jewel of great price.

> No doubt. But how do the poor come by it ? It is neither to be bought nor sold : but it is the work of God.

Virtue is the reward of virtue.

> By doing well we learn to do still better. Virtue ranks above rank.
>> Virtue will homage gain in humble shed ;
>> While vice enthroned becomes a nation's dread.

Virtue soiled is virtue spoiled.

Vows made in storms are forgotten in calms.

Vox Populi, vox Dei.

> The voice of the people is the voice of God. By no means certain, for the people cried, " Crucify him." Yet that which is generally desired by the people is pretty sure to come to pass sooner or later.

Sayings of a more Spiritual Sort.

Vainglory easily creeps in even at the door of mercy.

> "One says, such a nobleman drank to me, shook me by the hand, discoursed with me ; and hereby he insinuates to the hearers some worthiness in himself, for which he was so graced. So some, in declaring God's works and favours to them, have a conceit of merit in themselves, deserving such respect."—*Thomas Adams.*

Verity is of God, and vanity is of man.

AGERS are the last arguments of fools.

> Yet how common it is to hear a man clench an assertion with, "I'll bet you ten to one on it!"
>
> Men, till losing makes them sager,
> Back their judgments with a wager.

Yet there is no argument whatever in this swagger. Men bet because they have no better proof of what they say.

"Wait and see," as the blind man said.

> An answer to one who wants to wait and see, when the case is obvious and urgent. His plea for delay is absurd.

"Wait" is a hard word to the hungry.

Wake not a sleeping tiger.

> By no means. When a passionate man is quiet, pray let him be. Don't start a discussion with a contentious individual.

Wandering lights deceive.

> He who is not fixed in his teaching cannot be true in it; for truth never alters. Wreckers' lights shift: lighthouses are stable.

Want is no friend to wit.

> It drives some men out of their wits. It is hard to be witty when you are hungry. Even when the poor man is really witty, few care to notice it; for truly does *Juvenal* say :—
>
> Want is the scoff of every wealthy fool,
> And wit in rags is met with ridicule.

Want makes strife
'Twixt man and wife.

> Too often when cruel need is in the house, love is soured into mutual disgust. Love lives on, but none can live on love.

Want of common-sense is a fatal want.

> Learning and grace may be had; but if a man has no common-sense, where will he find it? We mean
>
> Good sense, which is the rarest gift of heaven,
> And though no science, fairly worth the seven.

Want of money loses money.

Without capital the man has no chance of buying well. Without means he is hard pressed, and cannot avail himself of opportunities by which he might have profited if he had paid cash.

Want of punctuality is want of politeness.

And want of honesty. As to politeness : I ought not to insult any one by supposing that his time is worth nothing, and that he himself is a nobody, who may as well wait for me as not.

Wanton jests make fools laugh and wise men frown.

One should be very sorry if he finds himself overpowered by his sense of the ludicrous when the joke is not clean. Smut is not to be smiled at, but to be denounced in the plainest manner.

Wash a pig, scent a pig, still a pig's but a pig.

Wasps attack the ripest fruit.

Slander assails the sweetest characters ; and frequently all the more so because of their excellence.

Waste not a second : time is short.

Even those who would detain the traveller at their tavern disclaim all intent of causing delay. Outside a country inn hangs the sign of a gate, with this inscription—

> This gate hangs high, and hinders none :
> Refresh and pay, and travel on.

We question the assertion that none have been hindered.

Watch little expenses, or they will eat you up.

Observe how articles are consumed in the house, or there will be much waste unaware to yourself.

> Keep you your keys,
> And be at ease.

Water is strong drink ; Samson drank it.

It drives mills, floats navies, creates harvests. What is there which water cannot do ? Water never floated a man into the lock-up ; but wine and beer have ruined thousands. It was said of one —

> All his life was cankered,
> Since he ever hankered
> For the flowing tankard.

Water plants before they wither.

Look after those in whom there are the first signs of grace. A kind word may cause the weakly plants to flourish and bear fruit. Once let them wither, and watering may come too late.

Waters all run to the sea.

It seems as if wealth went to the wealthy. Using the saying in another way : All our love should flow to God, who is love ; and all our grace should bear us back to God, from whom it came.

We all row in the same boat.

Said by those who are agreed about a matter. It is a pity when the boat goes the wrong way, and all the crew agree therein.

We are bound to be honest, but not to be rich.

We are not infallible, not even the youngest of us.

A neat touch of sarcasm for the positive youth.

We buy the news to see that nothing is new.

We fall on the side we lean to.

No one does good by accident, because that is not the way nature inclines ; but if we fall, we fall into sin. Oh, for a new nature !

We know what we are, but we know not what we may be.

We may be happy yet. Another saying is, " We know what we have, but not what we may get." He who has the bag may get the sack. Let us live in hopes, if we die in a ditch.

We must all eat a peck of dirt before we die.

That may be ; but we would like to have it very little at a time, and as the negro said, " If I must eat dirt, let it be clean dirt." We must endure a good deal that we don't like ; but we will not bear sin and falsehood.

We must let you speak if you cannot hold your tongue.

Some cannot be kept quiet any more than a bag of fleas can be made good neighbours. To them we must say :

> You are not dumb-driven cattle :
> Still you must go rattle, rattle.

We must not lie down and cry, " God help us ! "

No, no : God helps us to help ourselves. " Up, guards, and at 'em."

We never know the worth of water till the well is dry.

> What a folly! Will men never value health, and opportunity, the gospel and grace, till they are lost beyond recall?

We ought to be doing, and to be doing what we ought.

We remember what we would forget, and forget what we would remember.

We should eat to live, not live to eat.

> "For if we make the stomach a cemetery for food, the body will soon become the sepulchre of the soul. One-half of mankind pass their lives in thinking how they shall get a dinner, and the other in thinking what dinner they shall get; and the first are much less injured by occasional fasts, than are the latter by constant feasts."

We should play to live, not live to play.

> When men make amusement their avocation, they are childish, if not worse. Play should help us to work; and if it does not, it is a wicked waste of time. Men should put away childish things.

We think our fathers fools, so wise we grow;
Our wiser sons, no doubt, will think *us* so.

> Secretly, we fear that in this opinion they may be justified; but we have also a conviction that, in some things, they might be wiser if they would follow their fathers, and leave well alone.

> > "The silver heads of wisdom, lassie,
> > Are wearing fast away;
> > Will the green anes coming up, lassie,
> > Be wiser than the grey?"

"We two have much to think about," said the fly on the head of a philosopher.

> "How well we played to-day!" said the blower to the organist. Yet all this is not so ridiculous as when we imagine that our thoughts are necessary to carry out the thoughts of God.

"We'll wait a bit and see," as the puppy said when he was a week old.

Wealth and worth are different things.

> Yet most people think, that if a man is worth fifty thousand pounds, he must be a man of worth. He might have all that, and yet be worth less; or even worthless.

Wealth is timid.

As soon as a man has a five-pound note in the savings bank, he looks with apprehension upon all changes in politics. He who has nothing feels that a revolution could not make him poorer; and possibly he hopes that if there came a smash, he might pick up some of the pieces. Consols are very consolidating.

Wealth makes wit waver.

Pounds sober puns, and silence satire. Who dares poke fun at a man who could buy you up, and twenty like you? There have been sensible men who were not minded to worship the golden calf; but even these feel some awe in the presence of half a million.

Wealth of wit makes stint of words.

It is not easy to find words for deep thoughts, and so a wise man is often slow of speech. Moreover, a sensible man often says little because he knows his company deserves no more.

Wear like a horse-shoe, the longer the brighter.

Not like a shoddy suit. Of such wear beware.

Wear your greatcoat till May,
For fickle is the day.

Wedlock is a padlock.

A padlock is a very useful thing to preserve treasure; but a thing much disliked by the very rogues who most need locking up.

Wedlock is either kill or cure.

If a man is not made sober by marriage, what will become of him? But to give a man a wife as a medicine is scarcely the right thing. Oh, that in every case the old service of the Greek Church expressed a fact! The priest says, "The servant of God marries the handmaid of God."

Weed your own garden first.

And your neighbour's when he asks you, and pays you for it.

Weep more for the lives of the bad than for the deaths of the good.

Well begun is half-done.

So much depends upon the start. A bad beginning may involve double trouble before the end is reached.

Well-earned wealth may meet disaster;
Ill-got goods destroy their master.

Well-laid out, is well-laid up.

When the right thing has been done with the money, no man is the poorer for what he has wisely expended.

Well may she smell, whose gown is burning.

No wonder that persons are in ill odour whose lives are not right.

Well won should be well worn.

Not proudly, nor wantonly, but with gratitude to God, and in obedience to his laws, should we enjoy the reward of our industry.

Were he to toss up a penny it would come down a pound.

Some persons appear to be favoured by fortune; but the general explanation of good luck is hard work, common sense, and frugality.

Were it a wolf it would bite you.

Said of a thing which is very near, and yet is not perceived.

What a day brings, a day may take away.

If trouble comes on a sudden, it may go away as suddenly as it comes. Great comfort this!

" What a dust I raise! " quoth the fly on the coach.

We know that fly: he buzzes in our parish.

What a man has done, a man can do.

The speech of a man of pluck. " Can you read Greek? " said a lawyer to Hodge. " I don't know," said Hodge. " Why," said the legal gentleman, "you know you can't." But Hodge coolly answered, " I don't know; for I've never tried." We will believe we can till we have proved that we cannot.

What a pity it is marrying spoils courting!

After-life ought to be a long sermon upon the text of the honey-moon, and those who discourse it should stick to their text.

What a weary traveller eats, tastes well.

So say the Africans, and experience proves the truth of the observation. Even dry bread is fine when hunger is fierce.

What can you expect from a hog, but a grunt?

What can't be cured must be endured.

What children learn abroad they tell at home.

> Yes, and what they learn at home they tell abroad.

What comes by the devil will go back to him.

> Gained by dishonesty, it is often spent in debauchery. The devil, like everybody else, takes his own when he finds it.

What comes from the heart goes to the heart.

> This is the secret of true eloquence.

What costs nothing is worth nothing.

> As a general rule, that which is not won by honest labour or fair purchase turns out to be a bag of moonshine.

What does the moon care if the dogs bark at her?

> Why should she care? Why should *you* care if men slander *you*?

What God makes he never mars.

What good is it to an ass to be called a lion?

> It only makes him the more ridiculous. Even in a lion's skin his ears and his voice betray him. Though you dub him F.R.S., men do not revere him if they clearly see him to be an A.S.S.

What greater crime than wasting time!

> It is a sort of murder, for in killing time it destroys the stuff of which life is made. Yet there are many who do so little, that if they were tied up in a sack and cast into the Atlantic, nobody would miss them. Is not this crime enough?

What has not been may be.

> It has not had its turn yet, and therefore we may look for it in due time. Gentle reader, you may yet be taken in.

What I *was* is passèd by,
What I *am* away doth fly,
What I *shall be* none do see,
Yet in that my beauties be.

> Here, then, is room for faith, that we may enjoy by anticipation the joys which are yet to be revealed.

What is bought is often cheaper than what is given.

> Because a gift involves an obligation, and to discharge this, one may have to spend ten times the worth of the gift.

What is bred in the bone will come out in the flesh.

> Nature, despite nurture, will show itself. The inner man is never quite concealed, even by the finest garments of propriety.

What is done can't be begun.

> It might be greatly improved upon if we could begin again in better style; but it is too late now: we must do our best with it.

What is God's will, can ne'er be ill;
In darkest night, he makes it light;
For those who trust, help them he must.

> These thoughts may render comfort to some poor soul by the cottage fireside. Learn them, and repeat them.

What is in another's pot,
This deponent knoweth not.

> And does not want to know. Yet I wish every man had a chicken in the pot once a week, and a pudding at pudding time.

What is learned in the cradle, lasts till the grave.

> The first impressions remain to the last, both in the memory and on the mind. Let every teacher of the very young ask for grace to be very wise.

What is not wisdom is danger.

> Folly is foolhardy. Even after wise thought, danger may remain; but if a thing is imprudent, it is certainly unsafe.

What is rotten will rend.

> When the time comes, every evil will come to its climax: the impecunious will be bankrupt, the untruthful will be called a liar, the hypocrite will be put to shame, and "modern thought" will develop into infidelity.

What is sport to the cat is death to the mouse.

> Quoted when persons make mirth without respect to the feelings of the victim of the jest. It is like the saying of the frogs to the boys in Æsop: "What is sport to you, is death to us."

What is the use of running when we are not on the right road?

The faster you go, the more astray you get. Earnestness in a bad cause makes a man's action all the worse.

What is true is not always probable.

Indeed, it is the improbable which occurs. I read, the other day, a Hindoo legend, and not long after, I saw in the daily paper a statement of fact which was in all respects a parallel to it. Those pictures which we think to be overdrawn are often truest to what the artist actually saw.

What is worth doing at all, is worth doing well.

Do thoroughly what you set about :
If you kill a pig, kill it out-and-out.

What is wrong to-day will not be right to-morrow.

Moral principles are fixed, and so are doctrinal truths ; but this age loves perpetual change. Men have windmills in their heads.

What lies nearest the heart is first in the mouth.

That which is in the shop is seen in the window. When a man loves onions, his breath smells of them. "Out of the abundance of the heart the mouth speaketh."—Matt. xii. 34.

What matters it to a blind man that his father could see?

Or to a fool that his father was wise? Or to a scamp that his father was honourable? Hence the inconsistency of making men hereditary legislators. The tenth transmitter of a foolish face is not necessarily qualified to be a ruler over wise men.

**What must be must ;
Man is but dust.**

Death is inevitable. Other decrees of God will also stand, whatever man in his puny wisdom may determine to the contrary.

What owl will not hunt mice?

What man will be averse to getting money?

What should we do if we had nothing to do?

We should feed the worms in the cemetery; at least this would be better than to imitate the social man, who has nothing to do but to go about wasting the time of those who are busy.

What small potatoes we all are compared with what we might be!

Or might have been. Yet we do not think small potatoes of ourselves. Do we?

What soberness conceals, drunkenness reveals.

What decency would have kept from mortal ears, the madness of drink blurts out. Hence alcohol is the picklock which opens drawers which had better have been shut.

What the eye does not see, the heart does not rue.

It is a blessing that many things escape our knowledge, and so do not vex us. It is a blessing not to see too much.

What the puppy learns the dog will do.

What thou givest forget; what thou receivest remember.

What tutor shall we find for a child of sixty years old?

He must be able to fetch him along quickly, for his pupil's time is short. Will the old boy stick to his book? If not, who is to appoint him impositions, or keep him in after school-hours?

What use is it to read the Vedas to a wild buffalo?

The best of books are lost on the profane: it is preaching to a mad dog. Cast not your pearls before pigs

What was worth borrowing is worth returning.

Unless the fellow has kept it so long as to have worn it out. Even if only an umbrella or a book, we are thieves if we keep it. Alas! we find that whatever sort of accountants our friends may be, they are very sure bookkeepers.

Not that imparted knowledge doth diminish learning's store;
But books, I find, when once they're lent, return to me no more.

What we are afraid to do before men, we should be afraid to think before God.

What we dinna ken we shouldna speak.

What we doat on by day we dream of by night.

The lawyer dreams of law's delays, the policeman of the cook and cold mutton, the student of his tutor (?), the British workman of his conscientious toil.

When sportsmen in the night do fall asleep,
Their fancies in the woods still hunting keep.

What will not a pig eat, or a fool say?

What fools say should not much trouble wise men. What can it signify? Yet sensible people are often sensitive people, and are as much worried by idiotic remarks as fair ladies by a wasp.

"What will you stand?" I'll stand outside the public-house.

Stand your ground, and stand nothing else. Treat your friend, but not to a pot of cold poison.

What you don't want is dear at a farthing.

Even as a gift it will only be lumber, and cumber.

What you put in the dough you'll find in the cake.

Mistakes made in the conception and rough hewing of a design will appear further on in the business. Sins of youth crop up in old age. Bad example seen by the child comes out in the man.

Whatever a man delights in he will do best, and that he had best do.

Follow the bent of your genius. Let not the man who would have been at home with the tailor's goose make a goose of himself by setting up for an orator. Whether to mould a pill, or watch a mill, or melt a bar, or drive a car, be your chosen pursuit, keep to it till you are the best hand at it in all the country side.

Whatever sea-room a shrimp gets it will never be a whale.

Give a little man all the chance and the sphere which he can desire, and he will be none the greater. In fact, his shrimpship will seem all the smaller in so wide a space.

What's a table richly spread,
Without a woman at its head?

It lacks its chief ornament, its life, its light, its music, its queen.

What's everybody's business is nobody's business.

But when every one minds his own business, work is done.

What's not your own,
That let alone.

A world of mischief and misery would thus be prevented; but fools will be meddling, and knaves will be pilfering.

What's the use of doing what is already done?

Enough of necessary work comes in our way without attempting to do what is already accomplished by somebody else.

> Why fight your battles o'er again,
> And three times over slay the slain?

What's the use of jumping high, and coming down on the same place?

Tremendous efforts made, and no consequent rise, are by no means remunerative. Sit still, or move for the better.

" What's the way to Beggars' Bush?" Ask at the first Gin Palace.

And when you have your answer, go in the opposite direction, down Water Lane, and up the hill of Thrift.

When a beggar grows rich he is apt to grow proud.

Have we not seen it? We must all go on our knees to the Duke of Ditchwater; so his grace seems to think, but we think otherwise.

> " When beggars on their horses ride,
> Their saddle's always stuffed with pride."

When a cow dances she does it in style.

It is so out of her line, that if she does go in for it, she must needs go for it all fours. Men overdo what they are not fit to do.

When a good man thrives, all around him thrive.

He is liberal in his payments, and promotes merit; he is kind to the poor, and does not run down weaker tradesmen. As he rises, he raises others and crushes none.

When a goose is fat it is still a goose.

Riches do not turn a fool into a wise man.

When a goose is in fine feather it is still a goose.

Those who trust to their fine clothes are all the more foolish because of their finery.

> A dandy is a thing that would
> Be a young lady if it could;
> But as it can't, does all it can
> To show the world it's not a man.

When a man is a fool his wife will rule.
When a man is a fool his wife *should* rule.

> These two oracles balance each other. We know a lady who rules, and we know her husband who is ruled, and it is our opinion that the thing is arranged by Providence for *his* good, if not for hers. He who is second is best in the second place.

When a man is going down hill, somebody is sure to give him a push behind.

> This is of a piece with the usual cruelty of man to man. The poet says of them :
>
> " Those that are up themselves keep others low ;
> Those that are low themselves hold others hard,
> Nor suffer them to rise, or greater grow ;
> And every one doth strive his fellow down to throw."
> *Thomson.*

When a man is half a fool he is worse than a whole fool.

> Fools and sensible men are equally harmless : it is in the half fool and the half wise that danger lies.

When a man is in a ditch, his first work is to get out.

> He may put on his gloves and brush his hat afterwards. Till our souls are saved, salvation should be our sole concern.

When a man is in the mud, the more he flounders the more he fouls himself.

> If he has got into a scrape, he makes matters worse by his excuses of himself and accusations of others.

When a man is wrong, and won't admit it, he always gets angry.

> This is to turn the scent. It's the old story of "No case : abuse the plaintiff." Make a dust that others may not see your weak point. Get angry, for fear the injured should get angry first, and get the whip-hand of you. This seems to be the notion.

When a mouse is in the meal-sack he thinks himself the miller.

> Those who profit by the brains of others are apt to impute the wisdom to themselves. He who has bought the invention of a poor man for a mere song thinks himself by far the cleverer person.

When a promise is made, let it be paid.

When a rogue kisses you, count your teeth.

For he may have stolen one of them. Another form of the proverb says that he counts your teeth. He is looking out for a chance of theft. You'll want all your eyes to match a rogue.

When a thing is plain, don't make a mystery of it.

Some people like to have a truth confounded, rather than expounded. They look for bones in an egg, and when they have cherries, they swallow nothing but the stones.

When a will's to be read, the sick leave their bed.

Of course they make an effort to assist in that important ceremonial. Out of pure esteem for the dear departed they wish to hear his very last wishes. Their interest is touching.

When all is right, a man will be
Himself his own best company.

Make a generous, educated gentleman of yourself, since you are bound to spend a great deal of time in his company.

When an ignorant man knows himself to be ignorant, he is no longer ignorant.

When an old dog barks, a wise man harks.

For there's something in it. Pups yelp for nothing; but the old dog sees a thief, or he would not make a noise.

When April blows his horn,
It is good for hay and corn.

This is a saying of the ancients, but it must be taken with a considerable quantity of salt. As a general rule, seasonable weather must be the best weather for crops.

When cat and mouse agree it is bad for the larder.

If policemen are in league with thieves we shall have a bad time. So in all similar cases the two parties are best apart.

When cats grow fat
They catch no rat.

Some men, when they make a purse, are of no more use for work. When parsons marry rich wives their throats are frequently affected, so that they quit the pulpit, or go to Jerusalem.

When caught by a tempest, wherever it be,
If it thunders and lightens, beware of a tree.

> Better get wet through than run to objects which attract the lightning, as trees so often do. Better damp than danger.

When Christ blesses the bread, it grows in our hands.

> Where God doth bless, in time abundance springs,
> And heaps are made of many little things.

When couples fall out they had better fall in again.

> And the sooner the better. If we clear up as we go on, and leave no back reckonings, we may live together for a century with growing love.
>
> > The kindest and the happiest pair
> > Will find occasion to forbear;
> > And something every day they live
> > To pity, and perhaps forgive.

When cracked is the bell
It soundeth not well.

> Evil comes out in the communications of the evil man. What a nuisance is a bell which is cracked, and yet keeps for ever clacking! A cracked man is worse than a cracked bell.

When dry as a herring, of publics beware,
And never go home as cross as a bear.

> Two good counsels; worthy of wide acceptation. Drinking beer will not improve the temper, nor long quench the thirst.

When every one minds his own business the cows get fed.

> The necessary duties of life are forgotten when no one is appointed to see to them. Nothing is worse for a family than muddle; even the cows suffer when personal work is neglected.

When everybody talks, nobody hears.

When everyone treats him as a pig, he is apt to go into the sty.

When fools go to market pedlars make money.

> Have your wits about you in transacting business, lest this proverb be remembered, and proved.

When fortune wraps thee warm,
Then friends around thee swarm.

> Who has not found it so? The sugar attracts the flies.

When foxes preach, geese should not be allowed out to late meetings.

Indeed, our young people and our old people also are safest when they do not hear the teachers of false doctrine, such as the advocates of superstition on the one side and of scepticism on the other. These are both foxes.

There be many foxes that go on two legs,
And steal greater matters than cocks, hens, and eggs;
To catch many gulls in sheep's clothing they go;
They might be destroyed; but I know what I know.

When good cheer is lacking,
Friends will be packing.

When good men quarrel, the devil cries, "Bravo!"

When Greek meets Greek, then comes the tug of war.

"You stout and I stout;" there will be a great struggle for the mastery. Neither will give way, and so they must fight like the two dogs, of whom nothing was left but half a brass collar.

When heads are hot, brains bubble.

And many things boil over which scald the hearers, or envelop them in steamy clouds. Keep your head cool.

When hogs fly, drunkards will prosper.

That is to say, when you can roast snow in a furnace, or fat pigs on pebbles, or teach a fish to dance a hornpipe.

When honest men fall out, rogues come by what is not their own.

No doubt: even as, on the other hand, when rogues fall out, the honest have a better chance of getting their own.

When Honesty is married to Poverty, they take Self-Denial to be their housekeeper.

Then love sweetens dry crusts, and puts a delicious flavour into a dinner of herbs. But this said self-denial is mainly practised by the wife, if ever practised at all; and yet those male wretches make it out that the women are expensive, and they call them "*dear* creatures." Here is a pretence at verse by one of these monsters.

"Heaven bless the wives, they fill our hives
With little bees and honey!
They soothe life's shocks, they mend our socks,
But—don't they spend the money!"

When I'm dead everybody's dead, and the pig too.

So far as this world is concerned. This is the reverse of Paddy's reason for insuring his life, because he would thus become a rich man as soon as he was dead.

When I'm rich, friends ask assistance ;
When I'm poor they keep their distance.

When Jack is in love, he is not a fair judge of Jill.

Wisdom and passion very seldom meet,
Hence lovers' bargains seldom are discreet.

When jokes give pain,
The wise abstain.

When joy abounds, grief is within hail.

Nothing on this earth can be the ground of settled confidence, for it is so uncertain. Like English weather, nothing lasts so as to be reckoned on an hour. Sorrow is the footman of mirth.

When joy is in the parlour, grief may be in the passage.

When man and wife fall out, none but a fool will interfere.

They would be pretty sure to unite their forces upon the intruder ; hence the wisdom of the verse :—

"When man and wife at odds fall out,
Let syntax be your tutor,
'Twixt masculine and feminine,
What should one be but neuter ? "

When mirth comes in, beware of sin.

Sin is so apt to mingle with our merry-making, that we need be doubly watchful. The house of feasting attracts evil spirits.

When musing on companions gone,
We doubly feel ourselves alone.

When one goose drinks, all drink.

Very true, both in natural history, and in the history of naturals.

When one horse will not go, all the team are hindered.

A whole factory may be thrown out of order by one man. No fellow has a right to interfere with the rights of others by hindering them in their work. In a family one person may upset all.

When one man's beard is burning, another lights his pipe at the flame.

This is the Oriental method of describing the total absence of sympathy among men of the world. There is a measure of truth in this description. The Bengali has it, "While one man is being impaled, another counts the joints of the stake."

When our vices leave us, we flatter ourselves we leave them.

Even as the Turks have it, " 'It is fast-day to-day, and I must not eat,' says the cat when she cannot reach the liver." It is a poor virtue which we follow because we have lost the power to be vicious. Some stoop down because they cannot sit upright, and others keep their ground because their legs will not let them run.

When peace goes to pieces it is hard to piece it.

A thousand difficulties arise when trying to settle an old quarrel. Cement and rivets are hard to apply to broken friendships.

When prosperity smiles, beware of its guiles.

More men are bribed to hell than are frightened thither. The Sirens are more terrible wreckers than the Furies.

When Satan goes to church, he goes to prey.

And when he leads any there, it is that he may make them more surely his own. A gospel-hardened sinner makes a fine armour-bearer for the great enemy.

When Satan goes to prayer, mischief is in the air.

The old form of it is, "When the devil says his paternoster he means to cheat you." If he patronizes religion it is to betray it.

When Satan talks of peace, double bolt the door.

The worst of war is in his heart when honeyed words are on his lips. The vilest enemies of Christ are those who praise his ethics, and undermine his doctrines.

When sorrow is asleep, wake it not.

When suspicion enters the family, affection departs.

When table-talk is stable-talk, 'tis time to stalk away.

By being in low company you suffer moral defilement, and you appear to countenance impure language. Part and depart.

When the beam is low, stoop your head.

> Or you may get a knock. Mark how the ducks never go through a barn-door without ducking their heads. There is not much need; but they do it in case there should be. Few are too humble.

When the cat joins the weasel, there's mischief a-brewing.

> Some cruel motive has brought these rivals into conjunction. When Herod and Pilate are friends, Christ is crucified.

When the cat's away, the mice will play.

> To this may be fitly joined, the other old saw,
>
> > When the cat has gone to sleep,
> > Out of holes the mice will peep.

When the cock crows, the fox knows.

> He is on the watch for him and his hens, and observes all their movements : besides, he knows by the cock-crow that day is dawning, and that foxes will be safest at home in the daylight.

When the cow dies, we hear how much milk she gave.

> "What a dear, good man he was!" Why was this never said while he yet lived? If a tithe of the love expressed when the man is dead had been shown to him in life, how happy it would have made him! Was it not his due?

When the curate clears the platter, there's not much left for the clerk.

> If you take all or talk all, what is anybody else to do?
>
> > For the clerk there's little fish
> > When the parson clears the dish.

When the devil is landlord, be not his tenant.

> Not even with the view of living cheaply, and doing good. Be not thou a lodger where thou canst not invite thy God to visit thee.

When the dinner's done, the spoon is forgotten.

> When we have served a man's turn, he forgets us.

When the earth is driest, look you out for rain.

> Another form of, "Man's extremity is God's opportunity."

When the fat is in the fire,
Keep thou clear, and come no nigher.

Never go where mischief and discord are afoot. The best conduct in a quarrel is not equal to being altogether out of it.

When the fields yield not, the saints have not.

This refers to matters years ago; but now our saintly clergy must have their tithes whether the fields yield or not. When the farmer's profit is nothing, can the parson's fair tithe be much?

When the fool has made up his mind, the market is over.

He is so slow in deciding, that his chance has made off and gone before his mind is made up. Even this may not involve so much loss as undue haste, but it effectually bars all hope of gain.

When the fountain is full it will overflow.

That which is greatly in a man's heart will before long show itself in his talk and life. The affluent of thought should be fluent.

When the fox dies, the fowls never mourn.

One would think not. The death of Bonner was the cause of joy to the good Protestants of his day; for by his death they escaped death, and did not become Foxe's martyrs. When a deceitful system is abolished, honest men wear no hatbands. I know several things which will not cost me a tear when I see them no more.

When the glass rises expect bad weather.

We expect good weather when the weather-glass rises, but the proverb refers to another glass, which we would see fall never to rise. After a glass or two some men are very stormy.

When the good wife is away, the keys are lost.

Nothing is to be found when she is out. She keeps all in order; and without her the little kingdom is in a state of anarchy.

When the harvest is ripe it will be reaped.

Corn fully ripe is reaped, and gathered in;
So must we be when ripe in grace or sin.

When the helm is gone, the ship will soon be wrecked.

He that is not guided by discretion, will make a failure of life.

When the hen crows, there's trouble in the yard.

The general arrangements are out of gear: one member of the family is where another ought to be, and the result is not desirable. Then we remember the old verse:—

" A jolly shoemaker,
    John Hobbs, John Hobbs,
He courted Jane Carter,
No damsel looked smarter,
But he caught a tartar,
    John Hobbs! John Hobbs!"

When the house falls, the windows are broken.

No doubt. When all goes, we may be sure that the weakest parts do not escape. Art, and science, and religion suffer in the ruin of a great commonwealth.

When the house is finished, the hearse stands at the door.

How often true! Great expectations and ambitious projects are at last realized, and in the moment of gratification the man dies. I knew a good man who had for years longed for a certain honourable position: it came, and with it a stroke of paralysis which made it of little worth. How vain are all things beneath the moon!

When the joke is at its best,
Then's the time to let it rest.

When the man will lie, never rely on the man.

One leak may sink a ship, and one lie may wreck a man's character for trustworthiness.

When the mistress sleeps, the servant creeps.

When the monkey reigns, dance before him.

Bad counsel. This is the policy of mean selfishness. No doubt it is prudent to keep on good terms with the powers that be. But think of dancing before Chimpanzee the First!

When the morn comes, the meal will come with it.

God gives the daily bread for which he bids us pray.

When the mouse laughs at the cat, there is a hole near.

Or she would be moved by very different feelings. When some people are saucy to their employers, it is because another place is open to them.

When the oven is hot, put in your bread.

> Seize on favourable occasions : success comes that way. If you don't bake your pie when the oven is hot, when will you?
>> The active man will catch the ball
>> Before it cometh to a fall.

When the pear is ripe it falls.

> If we exercise patience we shall have the blessing when it is meet.

When the pig has a bellyful, he upsets the trough.

> Which is very malicious of him ; but wonderfully like a pig. May not others feed also? What harm has the trough done? We know evil persons who spoil the trade by which they have lived, and thus knock down the ladder by which they rose.

When the prior plays cards, what will the monks do?

> They will take liberty to gamble in any way they like : the leader's example is always excuse enough for the underlings.

When the shepherd is a sheep,
All the flock will go to sleep.

> Lacking power to lead, because there is no leadership in him, the people will either quarrel with their feeble minister, or everything will drop into spiritual lifelessness. Oh, for men ! Oh, for men of God ! But these are almost as rare birds as white crows.

When the ship is sunk, everyone knows how she might have been saved.
When the ship went down, the story ended.

> The catastrophe did as the Frenchman said, " cut his little tale off short." It might apparently have gone on till now if the ship had not foundered. A great many other things come to an end when death cries "Finis."

When the shoulder of mutton is going, it is good to take a slice.

> Not if it does not belong to you. Under the impulse of such a knavish notion, many have helped themselves out of the general wreckage of a great estate, and have been guilty of utter villainy.

When the sky falls we shall catch larks.

> Numbers of little consequences come out of a great event. It is an ill wind which does not shake apples into somebody's lap.

When the spider's web is broken, he mends it again.

Well done, spider! Persevere, and you will yet catch the fly. The French say, "Bad luck will tire if you don't."

When the stars set, the sun will shine.

Lesser comforts may go, but our God will come nearer.

When the sun is shining all around, some notice nothing but the shadows.

When the sun shines, nobody minds him; but when he is eclipsed, all consider him.

A man may spend any number of years in holy living, and be unknown; but let him transgress once, and all will note it. Again, God may shine on us all the day, and we forget him; but if he withhold his light for a while, we cry out in anguish.

When the tale of bricks is doubled Moses appears.

So it is said, "When the night is darkest, the morning is nearest." When things are at the worst, they must mend.

When hope seems drooping to the tomb,
The withered branch shall freshly bloom.

When the thief cannot steal, he takes to honest ways.

Yes, and goes out lecturing upon the rights of property.

When the waggon is tilting, everybody gives it a shove.

Few will help you up, but a crowd will help you down.

When the weather is stormy, we must weather the storm.

When the wheat is ripe, the sparrows peck at it.

When the will is present, the legs are lively.

The Germans say, "Will is the soul of work."

When the wine is in, the wit is out.

The counsels that are given in wine
Will do no good to thee or thine.

The negroes say, "Liquor talks mighty loud when it gets out of the jug." By such talk folly gets wind. But there must have been very little wit in the man at first, or he would not have let the wine in. When wit is in, wine is kept out.

When there's no fire in the grate, there's no smoke in the chimney.

Without grace in the heart, there will be no sign of it in the life. On the other hand, when there's fire in the soul, there will be sparks in the speech.

When thy neighbour's house is on fire, it is time to look about thee.

It will come to thy house next. When thy neighbour dies, prepare thy grave. He yesterday; I to-day.

When thou hast done piping, they will cease dancing.

We must not conclude that all our converts will last: some of them are dependent upon our personal influence, and when we have done preaching they will have done professing.

When thou hearest, hear for thyself.

My friend, be sure you wear the caps
 You try to fit on others;
Take to yourself the preacher's raps,
 And no more blame your brothers.

When three know it, all know it.

Or very soon will. One man can hold his own tongue, but he cannot hold the tongues of the other two.

When tongues do clack, I turn my back.

Especially if I can't get a word in edge-ways myself.

When two quarrel, there's two in the wrong.

When war begins, hell opens its gates.

Another form of it is, "When war begins, death feasts, and hell holds carnival." What evil can be worse than even the best war? Is there any best about wholesale murder?

When waste is in front, want comes on behind.

When wife will gad,
Then home is sad.

She must keep within and look to her home carefully, or disorder will vex her husband, injure the children, and make the family miserable. Dear Mrs. Trotabout, stop at home for a change!

When wise men play the fool, they do it with a vengeance.

Solomon, who was the wisest of men, showed gigantic folly.

When with neighbours we deal,
Ourselves we reveal.

When women consume gin, gin soon consumes them.

When you can see no way to go, go no way.

When you don't know what to do, it is a clear indication that you are to do nothing. "Their strength is to sit still."—Isa. xxx. 7.

When you have a good name, keep it.

If you can do so ; not by truckling to others, but by walking in your integrity. Do not lose it by forming bad associations.

Avoid a villain as you would a brand ;
Which, if it burn you not, will smut your hand.

When you have nothing to say, say nothing.

But few observe this rule : they explain why they have nothing to say, and how glad they are that others are there who can speak so well, and all sorts of rubbish. They fancy that they hide the nakedness of the land, whereas they publish it abroad.

When you see a snake, never mind where he came from.

Kill him first, and then discover the origin of the evil.

When you take another man's hoe to work with, you must clean it, and put it back in its place.

This is sound African logic. Reasonable and fair is the dark man's demand. We press it upon white fellows, especially "the mean whites." Return a borrowed thing in good condition.

When you try to warm, mind you do not burn.

Observe a medium in all things. When you mean to arouse people to energy, don't drive them to fanaticism.

When you turn over in bed, turn out of bed.

So said the Duke of Wellington, a strong man who needed no indulgence. He may have been too hard. Do we not too often err in the other direction of sloth ? A verse says :

Six hours of sleep the human frame requires ;
Hard students may to seven incline ;
To eight the man whom toil or trouble tires ;
But lazy folks will all have nine.

When your head is broken you'll run for a helmet.

> Put the helmet on at once, and go to Paul's armoury for it. See Ephesians vi. 17. Go no more out with head unguarded.

When you're paying through the nose,
Very fast the money goes.

> There's no stopping this sort of bleeding. No agreement being made, and everything left to others, no estimate of the expense can be even guessed at. A house built on such terms will become the tomb of a man's estate. Always know what you are spending.

When you've drunk swallows' milk, but not till then.
You may expect good deeds from wicked men.

Where a man never goes, he will never be robbed.

> Neither can he be injured by company he never enters.

Where all are poor, it don't take much to make a rich man.

> If you retire into a village, you are quite wealthy on an income which, in a large town, would be called a miserable pittance.

Where gold avails, argument fails.

> Appeal to the man's palm, and you will gain his hand.

Where hens do crow I would not go.

> For there there is not much peace. Our forefathers were more eloquent about usurping women than against tyrannical men. Here is an old distich :
> > Wife a mouse, quiet house.
> > Wife a cat, dreadful that.

Where ignorance is bliss, 'tis folly to be wise.

> " I was a happy man," said one who looked very ill, " until my last birthday, when my wife made me a present of a microscope. In an evil hour I took it, and began examining the articles of food we eat and drink. I have been living for a fortnight on distilled water , it is the only thing that is not full of nameless horrors."

Where love is, there the eye is.

> The beloved object draws the glance, and before long fixes the gaze. Mind the eye of your mind. If we loved our Lord more, we should be more eagerly looking for his glorious appearing.

Where might is right, right is not upright.

Where rosemary flourishes, the lady rules.

> Seeing the rosemary growing luxuriantly in a certain garden, I somewhat accidentally quoted this old saying to mine host. He said nothing; but when I went into his garden a short time after, *the rosemary was dead.* Then I drew an inference. Ahem! Ahem!

Where sin dines, sorrow sups.

Where the bee sucks honey, the spider sucks poison.

> We do not know if this is good natural history, but it illustrates the undoubted fact that from precious truths some gather grace, and others wrest them to their own destruction.

Where the best wine grows, the worst is drunk.

> It may be so. Who can get good milk in a village? Who expects patience or charity from a Perfectionist? Who looks for extraordinary spiritual edification from a Doctor of Divinity?

Where the bird was hatched it haunts.

> We retain a love to old dwellings, and old habits. A man loves to worship where he was converted.

Where the cat caught a mouse she'll mouse again.

> They say that thieves love to go to the spot where they made a great haul. Where a man enjoyed an evil pleasure, the temptation is to make a frequent pilgrimage.

Where the devil cannot go himself he sends drink

> He could not send a more effective substitute. Ardent spirits do the work of the evil spirit in a terrible manner.

Where the heart is past hope, the face is past shame.

Where the wasp has pass'd,
The gnat sticketh fast.

> One may force his way by his weight and energy, where another is hindered by his own feebleness and want of character.

Where the wolf gets one lamb he looks for another.

> If one poor creature has fallen into sin, the great enemy will labour hard to get another of the same sort.

Where there are hooks, there may not be bacon.

Show may be without substance. A man may carry a horsewhip and never ride; he may cut a dash and have no dollars; he may be a deacon, or a minister, or a bishop, and have no grace.

Where there are geese, there are usually goslings.

Provide for them. Take earnest care of the young. Let no population be without its Sunday-school.

Where there are lambs, there will be bleating.

"The next sight that we get into the cares and troubles that married life is heir to, is through the remonstrance of a Hibernian paterfamilias, who declares to his wife that he really wishes that the children could be kept in the nursery while he is at home, 'although,' he considerately adds, '*I would not object to the noise if they would only keep quiet.*'"

Where there are rings on the water a stone has fallen.

These are the outward signs of an invisible presence. We see by the movements of the face what is felt in the heart.

Where there is loud cracking, there are few nuts.

And those are mostly rotten.

Where there's a mouse hole, there'll soon be a rat hole.

The tendency of things is to grow worse and worse. We may tolerate evil till it becomes intolerable.

Where there's a will there's a way.

Where there's drink there's danger.

> Write it on the liquor store,
> Write it on the prison door;
> Write it on the gin-shop fine,
> Write, oh, write this truthful line—
> Where there's drink there's danger.

Where there's no sore, there needs no plaster.

There's no use in comforting the careless, or in bringing the gospel to the self-righteous.

**Where there's very much clack,
Sense is sure to be slack.**

Where there's whispering there's lying.

> In general, that which is not meant to be heard is not fit to be heard; and what is not fit to be heard should never be spoken even in a whisper. Whisperers ought to be shut up in the Whispering Gallery.

Where they cannot climb over, they will creep under.

> Anything to get along. Dogged perseverance finds a way, or makes one. Self-seekers are not particular about methods: they can cringe and crawl where no upright man could go.

Whether or no the weather'll be fine,
No living man can always divine.

> Almanacks know nothing about it, and those who pretend to be weather-wise are generally otherwise. In one of the Percy Society's volumes there is a rhyme by one Duncomb, of Houghton Regis, which shows how little there is in the forecasts of rustics :—
>
> > " ' Well, Duncomb, how will be the weather ? '
> > ' Sir, it looks cloudy altogether,
> > And coming 'cross our Houghton Green
> > I stopped and talked with old Frank Beane :
> > While we stood there, sir, old Jim Swain
> > Went by, and said he know'd 'twould rain.
> > The next that came was Master Hunt,
> > And he declared he knew it won't.
> > And then I met with Farmer Blow ;
> > He plainly told me he didn't know.
> > So, sir, when doctors disagree,
> > Who's to decide it, you or me ? ' "

Which is the high road to Needham? Turn to the left, at the sign of the Quart Pot.

> So also the way to heaven is plain—" First turn to the right, just by the cross, and keep straight on."

Which way the wind blows, the dust flies.

> Persons of no character and mind go before the prevailing wind of opinion. But then they are but dust.

Whichever way the wind doth blow,
Some heart is glad to have it so :
Then blow it east or blow it west,
The wind that blows, that wind is best.

> This is optimism; and a grand faith it is. For some one or other, that which is an ill wind for others blows good. God's winds are the best he thinks fit to send to such a world as this.

While debts I owe, I sink in woe.

Unless you have been long a debtor, and in that case you try to borrow of somebody else, and are as bold as brass when thus trying to steal from your best friend. Without debt, without care.

While foxes are so common, we must not be geese.

While still at sea we must keep watch.

For as long as life lasts danger will be around us ; and even the wisest and most experienced must be on their guard. At the very entrance of the Fair Havens there are rocks.

> The seaman's greatest peril's near the coast .
> When we are nearest heaven the danger's most.

While the big girl was stooping, the little girl swept the rooms.

Spoken in praise of little people : but it is hardly fair thus to undervalue tall girls. At any rate, they are more likely to be able to whitewash the ceilings without having a scaffold put up. Of course tall people lie longest in bed, but little people are often the biggest when they are up—in their own opinion.

While the cat winks, the mouse is gone.

Much more is it true, that " while cats play, mice run away." We must be very wide awake to catch anything nowadays, unless it be a cold. While we think to catch we are caught.

While the dogs are fighting, the wolves are rending the sheep.

A good reason for hearty union among lovers of truth and grace.

While the grass grows, the steed starves.

While the great bells are ringing, no one hears the little ones.

Yet their music may be very sweet. Let the less man wait his time, and his voice may yet ring out o'er hill and dale.

While the medicine is coming the man dies.

While we live we hope, for while we hope we live.

Whisky drinking is risky drinking.

This is too charitable to the evil spirit.

Whisky is very harmless—if you don't drink it.

We remember one who poured it into his boots; and though we thought him foolish, we were glad he did not pour it into his legs.

Whisky whisks many to the grave.

Dr. Guthrie said, "There is nothing in this world like whisky for preserving a man when he is dead; but it is one of the worst things in the world for preserving a man when he is living."

White flour comes not out of a coal-sack.

A man of evil life cannot yield holy influences.

White walls are fools' copy-books.

They need not sign their names, we know who they are.

Who begins amiss, ends amiss.   Mind this, miss!

Who borrows, sorrows; who lends, learns.

Who brews a quarrel may bruise his head.

Let quarrels be brewed in some other party's boiler, but not in your teapot.   Keep away from strife.

> Leave foes alone, and give thine heart
> To such as will like love impart.
> The silly goat, so I have heard,
> Once kissed the fire, and lost his beard.

Who builds too fast builds not to last.

We have been inclined to christen certain rows of houses by the name of *Jonah's Gourds;* they are up in a night, and look as if they would perish in a night.

Who dainties love shall beggars prove.

The kitchen is the burial-place of the epicure's health and fortune. Queen Elizabeth, after going over a handsome mansion, observed, with her usual delicacy, "What a small kitchen!" The owner wisely replied, "It is by having so small a kitchen that I am enabled to keep so large a house, and entertain your majesty."

Who doth sing so merry a note
As Jack that cannot change a groat?

So it happens that many poor hearts are merry where the rich are burdened with care.

Who cannot sing may whistle.

He can, in some way or other, express his cheerfulness, and increase the general harmony. We remember a man who was asked to lead the congregation, but he answered, "I cannot *sing* a tune; but, if you like, I will whistle the Old Hundredth." What more could an organ have done?

Who comes seldom is welcome.

A warning against wearing out your welcome by making yourself too common. People value you the more for being scarce.

Who eats his fowl alone may saddle his horse alone.

We cannot expect people to rush forward to help us in our work if we never give them a share in our pleasures and luxuries.

Who eats till he is sick must fast till he is well.

Too many alternate between repletion and depletion. They are like the alderman of whom it was said, "His talent is in his jaws, and the more he grinds the more he gets. From the quantity he devours, it might be supposed that he had two stomachs, like a cow, were it not manifest that he is no ruminating animal."

Who falls to-day may rise to-morrow.

Waldemar, King of Denmark, when struggling for his country, was accustomed to say, "There is yet another day," meaning that he would try again, and yet hope to succeed.

Who fears makes cause for fear.

"Oh, Mr. Coachman," cried a timid traveller by the York Mail in the good old coaching days, "Is there any fear?" Jehu answered, "Plenty of fear, Madam, but no danger." But if Jehu had been afraid, there would have been danger enough.

Who felleth oaks must give great strokes.

The labour must be proportioned to the design. You cannot cut down a forest with a pair of scissors.

Who frets much because he hath little, will certainly have less.

Even if his property remains, it will bring less enjoyment, if it brings any. Fretting scrapes all the meat from the bone.

I would not fret, if I were you,
Till fretting brings you meat to stew.

Who gives his estate before he is dead,
Takes off his clothes before going to bed.

> Very unwise was King Lear, who did this. Wear your clothes till bedtime. Give away all you can spare, but retain the control of your property in your own hands, as long as you have hands.

Who gives not thanks to men, gives not thanks to God.

> He who is not grateful to his brother, whom he hath seen, how is he grateful to God whom he hath not seen? The least return we can make to benefactors is to be thankful.

Who gladdens not is not glad.

> For joy is pre-eminently contagious; and selfishness is its deadly foe. He who would shut the sunshine in, inevitably shuts it out.

Who goes softly goes safely.

Who halveth honey with a bear
Is like to get the smallest share.

> So to speak, the bear is sure to take the lion's share. He will be generous as to leaving you the bees and their stings, but your share of the honey will naturally stick to his paws.

" Who has drunk will drink."
I fear the charge is true ;
And this it is which makes me think
You'd better wear the blue.

Who has made no mistake has made nothing.

> So natural is it to our fallible minds to make mistakes which are almost unavoidable, that he who has never blundered must have never acted ; which, truth to tell, is the greatest blunder of all.

Who has never done thinking, never begins doing.

Who has no foes, has earned no friends.

> Usually we shall find that we may gauge our friends by our enemies. He who has warm opponents has warm advocates, and *vice versâ*. The energy of the man's personality, or its weakness, will be seen in its effects on those with whom he lives.

Who hath money to throw away,
Let him leave workmen alone all day.

> Wretchedly true in many cases. No master, no work. Talk of striking : it is more than striking to see how the pace quickens when the master is near !

Who has tasted a sour apple will have the more relish for a sweet one.

No doubt poverty endured makes wealth the more delicious when it comes; and he that has been long ill doubly enjoys health.

Who hunts two hares at once, catches none.

Divided aims ensure double disappointment.

Who is ill to his own, is ill to himself.

Especially in the case of wife and children: if a man does not make them comfortable, they will be no comfort to him.

Who is so deaf and blind as he
Who will not either hear or see?

Who judges others, condemns himself.

Who know don't talk; who talk don't know.

Frequently the case; though the rule has many exceptions.

Who knows where Crooked Lane will end?

It is easy to begin a tortuous policy; but to what will it lead you? It is easy to tell one lie, but very hard to tell *only* one lie.

Who laughs at crooked men had need walk very straight.

He invites criticism, and he deserves that it should be unmerciful. He strikes others, and therefore he ought to have it straight from the shoulder. His own measure should be returned into his bosom; and it should be "pressed down and running over."

Who lives at peace with God, and friend, and foe,
Shall rest in sleep when others do not so.

Who lives with a praying man may learn to pray.

He will, if that praying man acts as he prays, but not else.

Who loses cannot afford to laugh.

Poor man! he laughs on the other side of his face.

Who loves his son will chasten him; who hates him will pamper him.

The Chinese say that love will give the cudgel, and hate will cram with dainties. Let over-fond parents take note of this. Our Father in heaven does not err in this direction.

Who loves his work and knows to spare,
May live and flourish anywhere.

Who makes black white, will make white black.

He justifies your wrong-doing, and he will as readily defame your well-doing. The flatterer readily becomes a slanderer.

Who many do feed,
Save much they had need.

Who must needs follow fashion may one day go naked.

Things are looking that way already with ladies of the first quality, and hence a wag has said of them :—

"When dressed for the evening, the girls nowadays
Scarce an atom of dress on them leave.
Don't blame them; for what is an *evening* dress
But a dress that is suited to *Eve?*"

Who never tries, wins not the prize.

Who never warms, never burns.

Some cannot be excited, and therefore never rise to action. We know some awfully cool fellows who might act as refrigerators for a shipload of New Zealand mutton. They might sit in an oven for a month and never get melted.

Who nothing save, will nothing have.

Who reckons without his host must reckon again.

The host is sure to put down something which the guest forgets: he is not likely to abide by the guest's sole reckoning, and so the matter must be gone over again. Many come to conclusions without remembering all the main circumstances.

Who ripens fast, will seldom last.

Who rises late, must trot all day, and hardly overtake his business by night.

Most true. One has been made to feel it if the bed has held him too long in its embrace. Yet there are creatures who snore out verses like this :—

Up in the morning's not for me;
In the morning I am surly:
No fate can worse in winter be,
Than to rise in the morning early.

Who sees a pin and lets it lie,
May live to want it by-and-by.

Who sows beans, will reap beans.

> And it is the same with wild oats, and thistles. Our conduct brings its own reward or punishment.

Who steals a penny will steal a pound.

> If he can. He soon educates himself out of the roguery of taking paltry amounts, into the respectability of failing for thousands.

Who steals an egg would steal an ox.

Who strikes at mud will smear himself.

> If you assail an evil, you had better expect to be bespattered and evil entreated. It is part of the bargain in the case of every reformer. Don't take up the business if you can help it.

Who tells your fortune tells you lies ;
Who tells your faults has truthful eyes.

Who thinks himself singularly wise is a singular fool.

> Little harm will come of being stupid until the fellow thinks himself clever. Pretended wisdom is the worst of stupidity.

Who trifles with a loving heart,
Whip him at the tail of cart.

> Several parties have we known to whom this would apply. Jilting a loving girl is a crime for which flogging is too lenient a punishment. In love let us have sincerity. Say,
>
> > My hand and heart in one agree ;
> > I give my very self to thee.

Who trusts the morrow earneth sorrow.

> To-morrow is the tense of fools as to action, and the dream of the rash as to expectation. To postpone duty is to commit sin, and to make escape from it more difficult.
>
> > Let no man think he can repent too soon :
> > I found it midnight, ere I thought it noon.

Who undertakes very much will overtake very little.

> > Fools only make attempts beyond their skill :
> > A wise man's power's the limit of his will.

Who ventures to lend,
Loses money and friend.

Who wastes his time throws life away.

> " He liveth long who liveth well ;
>   All else is being flung away ;
> He liveth longest who can tell
>   Of true things truly done each day."

Who watches not catches not.

Many a golden chance goes by him unobserved.

Who weds a sot to get his cot,
Will lose the cot and keep the sot.

Thousands of times the little property has soon gone in drink, and the poor woman has had a drunken husband to keep all her life.

Who weds for dower resigns his power.

He sells himself to his rich wife, and is like a bull led by a ring in his nose. If she keeps my house up, she is likely to keep me down. The woman who buys a husband wastes her money.

Who will go far must not go fast.

Who will not be counselled cannot be helped.

As he refuses the wisdom of others, he has to learn it for himself when trouble overtakes him. The engine-driver who takes no notice of signals goes in for a smash. Yet many are angry at advice.

Who will not better the evil is an abettor of the evil.

By refusing to help a reform, he bolsters up the old wrong, and thus becomes a partaker in the evil deeds of the past by approving them, and in all similar deeds in the future by permitting them. Those who are not against sin are with it.

Who will not lend may come to borrow.

And when he comes to borrow, it will be of no use to come to those whom he refused his help. Who give no loan may want alone.

Who wills to fight will find a weapon.

Who work not the mill have not the meal.

That is a just rule, but it is not always carried out. Be a promoter of a company, then you may get the meal, and leave the mill to the shareholders, who will find it turn to *nil.*

Who would be great must first be little.

Sometimes it is greater to be little than to be great.

Who would deceive the devil must rise betimes.

Who would eat a good dinner, let him eat a good breakfast.

He had better get his food when he can. Moreover, he gets himself into condition by his breakfast, and will feel strong when dinner comes. We suspect that this is a proverb by which men of large appetite urge on their fellows, and excuse their own voracity. The old proverb is, "No breakfast, no man"; and if no man, there can be no dinner. No dinner, no stomach for the fight.

Who would have honey must put up with bees.

And in getting money, it would seem that men often put up with far worse things than stings. Many swallow much dirt while scraping up yellow dust. Let us hope that the lines are not true in which it is said:

"He who'd sit upon the woolsack, must be ne'er with conscience curst,
And for *wool* to fill the cushion, he must take to *fleecing* first."

But, certainly, in certain methods of amassing wealth, there is more to put up with than an honest man will endure.

Who would heal a wound must not handle it.

In settling quarrels say as little as possible. Don't go over the ground again and again. Enter not into particulars which are of an exasperating nature. As a rule leave the details alone.

Why dig up a mountain to catch a rat?

Why destroy a grand institution to destroy some minor evil?

Why go bare to deck an heir?

He will not thank you for it; and if he does, you will not be there to hear him. Use your money for yourself, and the poor. Let not your heir call you a fool for being so miserly.

Why live poor to die rich?

What is the use of dying rich? One told John Ploughman that a certain miser had left a million of money. "Ah!" said John, "I shall leave more than that behind me when I die; for I shall leave the whole world, and all that is in it." There is not much glory in having to leave more than your neighbours.

Why saddle your horse, if you will not ride?

> Why get an estate, and never enjoy it? Why get an education, and then do nothing with your learning?

Wickedness is great when great men are wicked.

> The poorer sort imitate them, and take great license from the kind of respectability which greatness lends to vice. It is bad enough in a private person to be vicious; but it would be worse in a peer, or a minister of state, or a magistrate, and worst of all in the chief of all.

Wilful makes woful, and such woe is the worst of woe.

Wilful people must have their own way.

> And that way will lead them into a churchyard, or a jail, or a county-court, or a workhouse, or a lunatic asylum.

Wilful pigs go forward if you pull them back.

> The more you say they shall not, the more they will. Invite them, and they will not come; refuse them admittance, and a regiment of soldiers could not keep them out.

Wilful waste makes woful want.

Will a black dog become a holy cow by merely going to Benares?

> Thus is the uselessness of merely outward religion illustrated among the Hindoos.

Will the headache be cured by changing the pillow?

Will to work, and work with a will.

> For in these days, wealth comes not by chance; but, as a rule,
>
> > Good striving
> > Brings thriving.

Willows are weak, but they bind other wood.

> So, many a gentle, tender woman is the bond of the family, and all feel that she holds them in loving union.

Wilt thou my true friend be?
Then love not mine, but me.

> Cupboard love is not worth keeping even in a cupboard. He loves me not who loves me for what I have, and not for what I am.

Win gold and wear it, is the motto of the vain man.
Win gold and share it, of the generous man.
Win gold and spare it, of the miser.
Win gold and spend it, of the profligate.
Win gold and lend it, of the broker.
Win gold and lose it, of the gambler.
Win gold and use it, of the wise man.

If you never win gold at all, you may be all the better man.
Better be a man *of* mettle than a man *with* metal !

Wind and tide for no man bide.

Windfalls are generally rotten.

Persons who are waiting for legacies, or unusual strokes of luck, are almost always deceived. Pick your fruit yourself, and don't wait in idleness for that which may never come.

Wine drowns more than the sea.

Alas, what wrecks it has caused ! Souls here are lost for ever.

Winking sets me thinking.

This old proverb makes me feel somewhat ill at ease in the presence of persons who have a knowing wink.

He that winks with one eye, and sees with the other,
I would not trust him, though he were my brother.

Winter finds out what summer lays up.

Then come forth the " poor frozen-out gardeners," or those who pretend to be such. They did not lay up a shilling in summer, and in winter they appeal to the pity of the provident.

Wisdom does not always speak Latin.

Words hard to be understood are marks of pedantry, and not of understanding. Friendship loves plain speech.

Not quibbling quirks, but simple speech,
True friends should deal in, each with each.

Wisdom is a good bargain, cost what it may.

Especially the heavenly wisdom which makes wise unto salvation.

Wisdom is the wealth of the wise.

Wisdom is better without an inheritance than an inheritance without wisdom.

Wisdom must be wooed ere it is won.

Wisdom never forces herself on men. If we use lock and bolt to keep her out, she will make no forcible entry. If an empty bottle is corked up, you may throw it into the sea, but it will not be filled thereby. Wisdom will only flow in where there is a clear entrance for it. Few men will ever be hanged for being too wise.

Wisdom spun too fine is folly.

Mere pedantry is not true learning, and prudishness is not prudence. A man may be so exactly right as to be practically wrong; so unspeakably wise as to be a marvellous fool.

Wise men change their minds; fools have none to change.

Wise men give good counsel, but wiser men take it.

It requires more true sense to be willing to be guided, than to act as a guide. Humility is a scarce grace, but it is the hall-mark of genuine wisdom. Take counsel, that thy counsel may be taken.

Wise men sue for offices, and blockheads get them.

So that the blockheads were 'cuter than the wise men. Is that so? Or is this the snarl of a disappointed candidate?

Wise mice keep away from the trap.

They do not go near it to investigate it, and see how far they can go into it without peril. Prudent men keep clear of the temptation, that it may not overcome them.

Wise words and lengthy seldom agree.

One has wittily and paradoxically said, "The smaller the calibre of the mind, the greater the *bore* of the perpetually open mouth." The wise man is like a dealer in diamonds—his goods go in small compass. Great thoughts seldom fill a great space.

Wish and wish; but who'll fill the dish?

The Chinese say, "Better go home, and make a net, than go down the river desiring to catch fishes." You cannot slake your thirst by wishing for lemonade; nor obtain salvation by wishing you had believed; nor grow in grace by wishing for edification.

Wish to be what you are, and you have what you wish.

Wishers and woulders are poor householders.

Wishes are very small fishes for our dishes, and might-have-beens are poor vegetables to eat with them.

Wit is folly unless a wise man hath the keeping of it.

It may be wit to enter a stable and steal a horse in fun, but it is wisdom to let it alone. Practical jokers are fools in bloom.

Wit must be bought if it cannot be taught.

Wit once bought is worth twice taught.

Because you have really learned it, and are never likely to forget it. No doubt the birch has been the tree of knowledge to many a boy, and trial has been the same to many a man.

Wit without wisdom is mustard without beef.

It is the flavouring with nothing to flavour. It is no joke to be always joking. When a jest cannot be digested it is sickening. Stale puns ought to be made punishable offences: he who deals in them is as bad as the seller of ancient mackerel.

With a staircase before you, you look for a rope to go down by.

Some persons never will follow the ordinary and easy plan of going to work, but must find out some out-of-the-way way. Why, even in going to heaven, the plain way of believing is often set aside that silly speculations may be tried.

With gold spectacles, men see strange things.

What makes all kinds of reasoning clear?
About five hundred pounds a year!
And all seem black was white before?
Why, something like five hundred more!

With great caution choose a wife:
Once you're wed, you're tied for life.

Happy will you be if you find a wife like the lady whose epitaph thus describes her:

She was——, but words are wanted to say what.
Think what a wife should be, and she was that.

With lands, houses, and gold,
Men are rarely too bold.

Capital is tender and conservative. He who has nothing to lose fears no risk; but he who has much to guard had rather not place himself in peril. "Throw stones, boys: I have no glass."

With morning prayer the day begin ;
With evening prayer the night shut in ;
With grateful thanks sit down to eat :
Thus much from Christian man is meet.

With seven nurses a child will be without eyes.

> Some serious omission or commission will injure the unhappy babe who has so many to look after it, and no one to be wholly responsible for it. With eight nurses it will have no head.

With shoes one can walk upon thorns.

> Being duly protected we can trample upon trouble. See how Paul would have our feet shod. Ephesians vi. 15.

With sour and sweet
We eat life's meat.

> Days change the flavouring, and the change is for our profit.

With tooth and nail
'Gainst debt prevail.

With truth at your back,
Though helpers you lack,
Yet fear no attack.

> But some, nowadays, will do anything but suffer for the truth. They must think the martyrs great fools ; for they don't think any doctrine is worth living for, much less dying for. We cannot call them all heterodox, and yet they are not orthodox : to us they are a paradox, and to many they are stumbling-blocks.

Without economy none can be rich ; but with economy few need be poor.

> Economy in the beginning of life, before marriage, is the only way of rising in the world. Economy is the price of comfort.

Without going you can get nowhere.

> This is a Chinese saying. It is self-evident ; and yet inactive and hesitating people may need to be reminded of it.

Without the doctor one dies a natural death.

Without the sun, what can be done !

> To ripen the fruits of the earth, or to give health to the sick, the sun's shining is of the first importance.

Wits are often unwittingly wise.

Such men fall upon good thoughts by accident, but they are not in the regular line of them. They flash now and then, but they do not burn with a steady light: they seem to be saving it up for special displays, as *Butler* says of one of his heroes : —

> " We grant, altho' he had much wit,
> He was very shy of using it,
> As being loth to wear it out,
> And, therefore, bore it not about,
> Unless on holidays or so,
> As men their best apparel do."

Woe to him who worries the weary.

Woe to the house where children are never chidden.

Woe will surely come. Unchecked, the youthful savages will tear their parents' hearts. Without rule, without peace.

Woes have come to courts and kings
Through neglect of trifling things.

Woman is the Sunday of man.

She helps his rest, his joy, his elevation, his sanctification. We do not quote this because the proverb is " Women must be praised " ; but because by experience we have found it true.

Woman, with all thy faults, I love thee still.

"But when is she still ? " cries the ungallant bachelor. The old rhyme is worth preserving : —

> " A woman once, as it is sung,
> Could speak so loud without a tongue,
> That they could hear her full a mile hence.
> A greater wonder I can tell :
> I knew a woman very well
> Who had a tongue, and yet kept silence."

I also know some of the quietest of mortals, and they are women. Still, it is a rare thing for a lady to be at a loss for words.

Women, on a sudden, are wiser than men.

They leap by instinct where men climb by reason.

Women talk less in February than in any other month.

Because it is the shortest month. This is quite as true of men ; but the women are not so ungenerous as to tell them of it.

Woo to win, and win to wed.

No man who is worthy of the name will act otherwise. Yet some like to play at wooing, and after a while cast off a tender heart as if it were an old glove.

> He who courts and runs away,
> May live to court another day ;
> But he who courts, and will not wed,
> May find himself in court instead.

Words are good when works follow.

Otherwise, " Words won't feed cats." Mere words become like the snow which fell last year, and has left no trace behind it.

Words are not work, as froth is not beer.

Words are very like the wind :
Faithful friend 'tis hard to find.

Words buy no wheat, but make much chaff.

Words are sometimes the signs of ideas, and sometimes of the want of them. When men talk for the sake of fine words, they are playing with the tools they ought to work with.

Words once spoken cannot be wiped out with a sponge.

Oh, that they could be ! Alas, they are spoken in a moment, but they may live through centuries. Our words diminish or increase the sum of human happiness throughout our own generation, and all the generations that are to follow.

Work as if thou'dst live for aye ;
Pray as if thou'dst die to-day.

Give both this world and the next its due. Work as if all depended on *you;* pray because all depends on God.

Work is a fine tonic.

It braces both soul and body, and helps us to cast off those nervous forebodings which haunt the inactive.

Work warms when coals are dear.

And the warmth is much healthier and cheaper, too, than that which comes through roasting yourself at a stove. Some people in waiting-rooms take up all the fire, and toast themselves so that you wish you could find a fork to take them off with.

Work when you work, and play when you play.

Do one thing or the other. It aggravates an employer to see a fellow fooling when he should be steadily toiling. He who gives in work a little more than his master can claim is seldom sent adrift. Employers know when a man is worth his money.

> He that to be obliging tries
> Is sure of work where'er he hies.

A mixture of work and play is poor stuff. It brings a workman into disrepute. You are not hired to be a merry-andrew.

Workmen are easier found than masters.

Hands you can get by the thousands, but heads are scarcer far. A man can always find a servant, but a servant cannot so soon find a master to employ him.

Worldly good is ebb and flood.

It is for ever changing, like the troubled sea, which cannot rest.

Worldly riches are like nuts.

Many clothes are torn in getting them, many a tooth is broken in cracking them, but never a belly filled with eating them. If you have wealth, use it as you would wish another to use it if you had none yourself. Call other folks in to have a crack with you when your basket is full of nuts.

Would you be thanked for feeding your own pigs?

We cannot expect gratitude for serving our own turn; yet some seem to look for it. Let them look. Who serves himself may pay himself. Let his own pigs grunt his lordship's praises.

**Would you live an angel's days?
Be holy, wise, and kind always.**

**Wouldst live in peace?
From gossip cease.**

But the regular gossip cannot cease. She is a fifth of November cracker, and, being once let off, she must fizz and crack till there's nothing left of her but a spent case. Poor dear!

Wouldst thou rule the world, first rule thyself.

This is true royalty. The ambition which makes us seek self-conquest is a virtue.

Wranglers are never in the wrong.

They will not hear reason. They are in too much heat of temper to consider that there are two sides to a question. Don't wrangle with them; there's no use in it: as well try to teach a pack of hounds to say the Shorter Catechism.

Wranglers never want words though they may want matter.

It is wonderful what a lot of grievances you can conjure up when you try, and what faults you can allege when you are in the humour. What is the use of it? It may be well to be Senior Wrangler at Cambridge, but I would neither wish to be senior nor junior in that line anywhere else, except it were at Oxford.

> Be not angry with each other ;
> Man is made to love his brother.

Wrinkled purses make wrinkled faces.

> A lonely penny in the purse,
> And need increasing worse and worse,
> Will make a man's face very blue,
> I know it well, and so may you.

Sayings of a more Spiritual Sort.

Wait for God's grace, for he waiteth to be gracious.

Watch against weariness *in* prayer, or you may soon be weary *of* prayer.

We are never right till we are right with God.

We are not saved by feeling, nor without feeling.

We are saved by faith, and not by feeling ; but being made alive unto God, we necessarily feel both joys and sorrows of a spiritual kind. He that does not feel does not live.

We are not to make our experience the rule of Scripture, but Scripture the rule of our experience.

We are undeserving, ill-deserving, hell-deserving sinners.

A confession often made in the prayers of good men a generation back, but seldom heard now. Why the omission ? Is it because the men of the present day are so much better and worthier than those of the past ? Is it not rather because they have a less vivid perception of the evil of sin and of their own guiltiness ? Not long since, one said frankly that he did not think himself bad enough to go to hell ; and there is no doubt that many are of the same opinion. They agree with the Duchess of Buckingham, who wrote to Lady Huntingdon that "it is monstrous to be told that you have a heart as sinful as the common wretches that crawl on the earth." But there is no hope of any being admitted to heaven who are not brought to acknowledge that they might justly be sent to hell.

We become happier than others, not by having more goods, but by doing more good.

We believe, but God gives us faith.

It is important to remember that we must ourselves believe. The Holy Spirit does not believe for us.

We burn our Master's candles ; let us mind our Master's work.

We cannot trust God too much, nor ourselves too little.

We fear men much, because we fear God little.

We fell by standing against God ; we shall stand by falling before him.

We know the true fold by the presence of the Great Shepherd.

> This is the test of a true Church. Where the Shepherd is, there is the chosen flock and the true fold. Whatever be the place of worship or the form of church government, if the Lord Jesus is there, no friend of his need be afraid to be with him.

We lie to God in prayer, if we do not rely on him after prayer.

> Prayer without faith is a kind of mockery.

We may pray to live, if we live to pray.

> For prayer is of the utmost value to the church and to the world, that we may desire to live to bless our age by its means.

We must be born twice, or we shall die twice.

We must be self-searchers, but not self-seekers.

We must believe to see, not see to believe.

> By faith realize the great goodness of the Lord, and do not wait to see what God will do before you believe his Word. Faith which depends upon sight is no faith at all.

We must not let crosses load us down, but we must lift them up and carry them.

We need to feel the storm that we may know the worth of the anchor.

> The storm-tossed Christian proves the staying power of faith. When the promise has been tried and proved, we value it.

We serve the devil if we serve not Christ.

> " The poet has put an awful truth into the lips of the father of lies, when he makes him say to Cain—
> ' He who does not bow to *him* has bow'd to *me*.' "

We work, not *for* life, but *from* life.

> I would not work my soul to save ;
> That work my Lord has done ;
> But I will work, like any slave,
> For love of God's dear Son.

Weak grace may *do* for God, but it must be *strong* grace to *die* for God.

"Have you grace enough to be burned at the stake?" was the question once put to Mr. Moody, who answered in the negative. "Do you not wish that you had?" "No, sir, for I do not need it. What I need just now is grace to live in Milwaukee three days and hold a convention."

Weave in faith, and God will find thread.

Weekly services neglected, make weakly Christians.

There is a proverb in Scotland, that "Mony ane will gang a mile tae hear a sang that winna gang a foot tae hear a sermon." A certain United Presbyterian Church in the North of England was the scene of two evening meetings in one week, viz., an evangelistic meeting and a concert, or service of song. A Scripture reader in connection with the congregation, while on her diurnal rounds, came in contact with a douce old Scotchman, a member of the church. "Now, David," queried the good woman, "are ye comin' up tae the meeting this week?" "Oh, ay," exclaimed the canny Scot, "I maun come tae the meeting: for I ken some o' the folk that's gaun to sing." "Tuts!" exclaimed his interrogator, "it's no the concert; it's the ither meeting I mean." "Oh!" sighed the devout Scot, "I dinna think that I can come; for you see I am sae tired at night that I can hardly stir aff my chair."

Well doth the good old proverb speak—
"As the Sunday, so the week."

What God's purpose plans, God's power performs.

What is anyone the better for ordinances, unless he be bettered by ordinances?

For in themselves, the outward forms are valueless: unless they are the channels of blessing, they are of no more use than old lead pipes when the water is cut off.

What the Papists cry up as the mother of devotion, that we cry down as the father of superstition.

Ignorance will smother true devotion. Know that you may worship. God asks not a blind faith; for such would only be the faith of blindness and darkness; and "God is light."

What we neither feel nor see,
We by faith believe to be.

"Faith is the substance of things hoped for, the evidence of things not seen."—Heb. xi. 1.

What we weave in time we must wear in eternity.

What we win with prayer we should wear with praise.

Whatsoever is not above the top of nature is below the bottom of grace.

> The work of grace, at its lowest degree, is above the highest effort of nature at its very best.

Wheat and tares may grow together, but they shall not remain together.

> The separation which cannot be wisely attempted by man will be perfectly accomplished by the Lord. What a mixture all our assemblies are! How true are *Herrick's* lines :—
>
> > " In holy meetings, there a man may be
> > One of the crowd, not of the company."

Wheat in a barn is better than chaff in a church.

> Just so. A few poor saints in the meanest room excel all the unconverted nobility and gentry of the district when assembled in the most magnificent cathedral.

When a saint at God's bidding can stand still, 'tis an evidence that he will soon go forward.

> Thus Israel, at the Red Sea, learned to stand still and see the salvation of God, and then came the word, " Go forward."

When Christians are rusty they're apt to turn crusty.

> Doing nothing, they growl at those who are workers.

When Christians dispute, worldlings deride.

> They cannot say, " See how these Christians love one another ! "

When clouds are heavy, blessings are near.

When God makes us his children, he makes us brothers.

When God wills, our ills are wells.

> He brings good out of evil ; and makes the bitter sweet.

When God would work, his tools are ready.

> In fact, he can use any tool : he can use *me*. The Lord's strength gets glory through our weakness.

When God's Word is opened, may our hearts be opened.

We read, "He opened to us the Scriptures"; and in the same chapter, "Then opened he their understanding."—Luke xxiv. 32, 45.

When mercy is rejected, judgment may be expected.

When once a man becomes a god to himself, he then becomes a devil to others.

He is so lifted up with pride that he plays the tyrant. Because Nebuchadnezzar was so proud, he threw those into a fiery furnace who would not obey his will. Good to yourself, evil to others.

When prayer leads the van, deliverance brings up the rear.

When the leaf falls,
To repentance it calls.

Or, "When leaves are falling, wisdom is calling."

When the sea is without waves, saints will be without trials.

This will come when they stand on the sea of glass, and not till then. Were we without trials, we might doubt our sonship; for "What son is there whom his father chasteneth not?"—Heb. xii. 7.

When the sun is set, we are all in the shade.

General calamity impoverishes all. When the Lord's Spirit leaves the church, we all suffer through his absence.

When the world is bitter, the Word is sweet.

When we are in Satan's hand, *he* is in God's hand.

God has a chain on the enemy, even when he gives him most latitude. He may rule as he wills, but the Lord overrules him.

When weeds are uprooted, good plants are in danger.

Hence the need of great care in discipline, lest in removing tares we destroy wheat. We need equal care in rebuking error, lest we destroy truth with falsehood.

When you rest, rest from sin.

It is the only true rest, for sin is a troubled sea. Those who allow themselves to enter sinful places, because they are taking a vacation, disgrace their vocation.

When you work, and when you play,
Call to mind the judgment-day.

Where can that soul stay, which stays not itself upon God?

Where death finds you, eternity binds you.

> Despite all that is said to the contrary, this is the plain teaching of the Scriptures of truth.

Where death leaves us, judgment finds us.

> All that men have done or said
> Lives when they themselves are dead.
>
> And when they are called to judgment they will find the things done in the body there to confound and to condemn them.

Where God becomes a donor, man becomes a debtor.

> Every gift of grace involves a debt of gratitude.

Where the Scripture hath no tongue to speak, we should have no ear to hear.

> If we are wise above what is written, we are presumptuously foolish. What the Lord does not reveal we should not wish to know. Beyond revelation all is speculation.

Where there's no repentance there's no religion.

While guile remains, guilt is not removed.

> With forgiveness of sin there comes honesty of mind. "Blessed is the man unto whom the Lord imputeth not iniquity, and in whose spirit there is no guile."—Ps. xxxii. 2.

While thou livest, pray; and as thou prayest, live.

Who has charge of souls cannot carry them in bundles.

> Each one will need a special treatment for its peculiar case.

Who has no thirst, has no business at the fountain.

> Hence our needs give us a right at the mercy-seat. "*No admission except on business*" is true of communion with God. None do come to God, and none *can* come to him, except on an errand of necessity. Necessity is the mother of supplication.

Who prays in grief, secures relief.

> And then he must take care to give glory to God for the gracious answer to prayer which has been vouchsafed to him.
>
> > Prayers and praises go in pairs:
> > They have praises who have prayers.

Whom free grace chooses, free grace cleanses.

Whom God calls, he qualifies.

> Hence we may be sure that a man is not called to an office for which he is utterly unfit. A being meant to fly has wings given it. If a man is meant for preaching he will have brain and tongue bestowed upon him.

Whom God will make, the devil cannot mar.

Woe be to him whose advocate becomes his accuser.

> When the Saviour shall witness against us, and our own conscience shall condemn us, how shall we escape?

Women were last at the cross and first at the sepulchre.

> " Not she with trait'rous kiss her Saviour stung,
> Not she denied him with unholy tongue ;
> She, while apostles shrank, could danger brave,
> Last at his cross, and earliest at his grave."

Worldlings make gold their god; saints find God their gold.

Worldly delights are winged delights.

> Soon do they fly away : why trust in them?

EARS know more than books.

Yielding is sometimes the best way of succeeding.

We may stoop and pick up victory. To yield a part for the sake of the whole is good economy. To yield one's right is often better than the right. We may gain by kindly giving way.

You a lady and I a lady, who's to clean the saucepans?

If everybody must be great, how will the common duties of life be performed? This is not a fit world for finery; yet people talk of their gentility.

> " Genteel it is to have soft hands,
> But not genteel to work on lands;
> Genteel it is to lie in bed,
> But not genteel to earn your bread."

You are not everybody in the world, and the man in the moon too.

But many a man talks as if he were cock of the walk, and king of the castle. He and his friends are all the plums in the pudding: if they were gone, the rest would be the commonest duff.

> In men this blunder still you find:
> All think their little set mankind.

You are rich if you want no more.

You break my head, and then bring me a plaster.

All very fine; but it would have been better if the wound had never been made. At the same time, if we have injured another accidentally, he ought not to resent our kindly endeavours to make amends. All we can say is :—

> " Take all in good part, whoever thou be,
> And wish me no worse than I wish unto thee."

You can break an egg without a sledge hammer.

Why speak so fiercely when a gentle word will do?

You *can* catch some old birds with chaff.

Though a proverb declares that you cannot, it is very often done. The very knowing are often very silly.

You can promise more in a minute that you can perform in a month.

You cannot call back yesterday.

You cannot climb a ladder by pushing others down.

Some seem to imagine that if they lower another in public estimation, they thereby rise themselves. They are much mistaken.

You cannot dig a well with a needle.

Adapt your means to your end.

You cannot draw a straight line with a crooked square.

False doctrine will not produce good living.

You cannot drink and whistle at the same time.

The child said, "I want to go home to dinner, and I want to stop here and sail my boat." Then he began to cry, because he could not have both his ways at once. We must not be so childish, but must give up one thing for another. Let us forego earth for heaven, and the praise of men for the glory of God.

You cannot eat your cake and have it too.

If the cake be eaten, it cannot be brought out to-morrow. If the food is saved, the children will not be fat and strong. We cannot have the thing in two forms. If you spend money discreetly, there is the pleasure; if you save it frugally, there is the interest.

You cannot fill a chest with grace, nor a heart with gold.

You cannot get more out of a bottle than you put in it.

That is an error. Besides what you put in, you can get out of it an aching head, a sick stomach, a lost situation, and perhaps a fine of five shillings, or a few days in prison.

You cannot have a good pennyworth of bad ware.

However many bad razors you buy, you can't shave. However many rotten apples you get for your money, you can't eat them. Yet cheapness is everything nowadays, and things are made to sell, for they say :—

> What is the worth of anything
> But how much money it will bring?

You cannot have a sandwich all of meat, nor a life all holiday.

You cannot have foreknowledge, but you should have forethought.

You cannot have two mornings in the same day.

> Nor can you expect to be youthful twice. Opportunities do not return. Use your morning lest you have cause for mourning.

You cannot know wine by the barrel.

> If men were honest you would, if you wanted to.

You cannot make good broth without meat.

> Solid matter is required for the making of a good sermon.

You cannot pull hard with a broken rope.

> Nor do much with a gospel in which you do not believe.

You cannot push a man far up a tree.

> He must exert himself and climb by his own efforts. We can do very little for one who does not help himself, and he deserves even less than we can do.

You cannot scold a man out of his sins.

> Let us try the gentler way, and see what can be done by prayerful, loving persuasion.
>
> > Let's find the sunny side of men,
> > Or be believers in it:
> > Wrath shuts the heart against the truth,
> > But love will surely win it.

You cannot swallow dates whole.

> The stone must be taken out, and the fruit masticated. So it is with what we hear: we must discern and divide.

You cannot work in iron with a wooden file.

> To deal with the sin of man you must have the solid truth of revelation, and of God's law, or you will labour for nothing.

You can't be lost on a straight road.

> I am not sure of this. Some seem to have the heavenly road right before their eyes, and they do not know it. Still the proverb is a good one, in one sense. Keep straight in the straight road.

You can't burn the faggot and have it.

To the same effect is the other proverb, "You can't keep a fire and keep the coal too."

You can't catch a cow in a cobweb.

Nor hold your heart to virtue by vows and promises made in your own strength. Nor alter facts by sophistical arguments.

You can't catch hares with unwilling hounds.

No hearts can be won by us unless we heartily desire it. Earnestness is in most things essential to success.

You can't draw a waggon with a hair.

Things must be proportionate and adequate.

You can't drive a nail into nothing.

Where there is no mind to retain your teaching, labour is lost.

You can't drown me in a spoonful of water.

I am able to bear what little you can inflict.

You can't earn your breakfast by lying in bed,
And if you won't work, you shall not be fed.

You can't expect pippins from a crabtree.

Nor figs from brambles : every man acts according to his nature.

You can't get good chickens from bad eggs.

When the design is bad, we may not hope for good results from it. Bad doctrine will not produce good lives.

You can't hang soft cheese on a hook, nor drive a nail of wax.

Some people are too limp for you to do anything with them.

You can't kick when your leg is off.

When you have lost your power it is idle to threaten.

You can't lay eggs, so don't cackle.

He that cannot help should not criticize.

You can't make a silk purse out of a sow's ear.

> Nor turn a boor into a gentleman.

You can't make pork pies out of pig iron.

You can't pass a rope through a needle's eye.

You can't shave a man's head in his absence.

You can't sing the savageness out of a bear.

You can't steer too far off danger.

You can't swim across the Thames by hanging on to a dog's tail.

> Nor can you attain great things by following mean means.

You can't tell a nut till you crack it.

> So the street-sellers say, "Try 'em before you buy 'em."
> "Prove all things; hold fast that which is good."—1 Thess. v. 21.

You can't turn charcoal into chalk by a thousand washings.

> A change of nature is needed both in men and charcoal; and only a miracle can change one or the other.

You carry fire in one hand, and water in the other.

> Blessing and cursing cannot both be kept;
> Fire in your right hand, water in your left.

You come a day after the fair.

You come of the McTakes, but not of the McGives.

> Always ready to absorb, but never willing to disperse. Who cares for you?

You drink out of the broad end of the funnel, and hold the little one to me.

You feed me with an empty spoon.

> You promise, and flatter, but you give me nothing.

You have debts, and make debts still;
If you've not lied, lie you will.

> Debtors make false promises, to put off pressure for payment. Debt is the death of truth; true men should hate it.

You have hit once, but don't always be shooting.

You spoke well once : don't be for ever speechifying. One venture has succeeded ; but do not become the slave of speculation.

You have kissed the Blarney Stone.

Though never in Ireland, some men have learned the art of gammoning, and laying on butter with a trowel.

You have less than you desire, but more than you deserve.

Therefore, find contentment in the consideration of free grace.

You have no more sense than a sucking turkey.

A cutting speech for a downright simpleton. Some have not the sense they were born with : you might pass them through a sieve, and never shake a dust of wit out of them.

You have run long on little ground.

How many talk without end, and all about nothing !

You may be right, but do not fight.

You may gape long before roast chicken will fly into your mouth.

Chance and expectation lead to nothing. Earn what you want.

You may grow good corn in a little field.

In a small sphere, with slender abilities, one may achieve very noble results.

You may hide the fire, but not the smoke.

Your action may not be seen, but the consequence will appear. You may be quiet yourself, but people will talk.

You may hold an eel so fast as to let it go.

You may judge a girl by her mother.

For the daughter is very apt to copy the mother, and she is very seldom an improvement upon her.

Now, young man, before you court her,
From the mother learn the daughter.

You may know a foolish woman by her finery.

The silly woman lives at the sign of " The Flowery Bonnet."

You *may* live, but you *must* die.

The proverb, "Young men may die, but old men must," has another shade of meaning. This applies to all alike: "It is appointed unto men once to die." Prepare for the necessity of death, and you will be prepared for the contingency of living. It would be a huge calamity if we were bound for ever to remain in this poor life.

> "I couldn't live for ever;
> I wouldn't if I could;
> But I needn't fret about it,
> For I couldn't if I would."

You may lose in an hour the work of a lifetime.

One false move throws away the game. A whole life-story may hinge upon the transactions of an hour.

You may milk a cow too often.

The most generous person may be worried into refusing to give at all. A man cannot always be giving. You may milk the cow oftener than is right, but you won't get any the more milk.

You may walk a long time behind a goose before you will pick up an ostrich feather.

And listen a long time to some talkers before you hear anything worth remembering.

You must contrive to bake with the flour you have.

If you cannot get all the materials you wish, you must work up those which are given you, and make the best of them. Be the flour what it may, let the bread-making be as good as good can be.

You must not throw your snails into your neighbour's garden.

You must put up with a great deal if you would put down a great deal.

The reformer must endure a world of misrepresentation, disappointment and enmity. You cannot vanquish "the armies of the aliens" without warfare and wounds. This work is for brave hearts only. "What man is there that is fearful and faint-hearted? let him go and return unto his house."—Deut. xx. 8.

You must spoil before you spin.

In learning any art we must expect some failures. Every speaker has his break-downs, as every potter has his broken pots.

You must take all the Bible or none.

It stands or falls together. He to whom it belongs will no more yield to its being divided, than the true mother, in Solomon's day, would consent to the dividing of the living child.

You mustn't tie up a hound with a string of sausages.

To try to check sin by a measure of indulgence in it is absurd.

You need iron nails to fight with a bear.

In such a conflict, hard must meet hard ; and as we are not thus fashioned, we shun the contest with hard, unfeeling men.

You need not jump over the house to open the window.

Do not exert yourself more than is needed to effect your purpose. To accept a great and useful truth, it is not needful to become an all-knowing philosopher, and solve the secret of the unconditioned and the absolute.

You need not provide frogs for the well you have dug.

Nor mice for your barley-mow. They will come naturally. Neither need you instruct young men in vices, nor girls in follies.

You need not teach a bull to bellow.

That which nature teaches of itself you need not inculcate.

You plough with an ox that will not miss a furrow.

A good, careful, painstaking worker shirks nothing.

You pour water into a sieve.

When you give to a spendthrift, or invest in speculative companies. In trying to help shiftless ne'er-do-wells it is much the same.

You trust a great weight to a slender thread.

Especially if you trust your soul to a priest, or risk eternity on an uncertain to-morrow.

You want a little licking into shape.

It was the belief of the older naturalists that bears lick their whelps into proper form while they are yet young and tender. This is a fable ; but it illustrates the duty of parents to fashion the crude mind ; and it also shows how Providence does, in very deed, " shape our ends, rough-hew them how we will."

You want better bread than wheaten.

And better milk than cows can give. Some are never satisfied.

You were put out of the oven for nipping the pies.

Hislop parallels this with the charge which a vulgar street boy brought against another:—"You was put out of the work'us for eating the number off your plate."

You will find critics to be as common as crickets.

Fellows who cannot write a line will criticize a poem. Once a critic was a good judge; but now he is simply an unmerciful fault-finder, two steps above a fool, but a great many below a wise man. Alas! that, in reference to Holy Scripture, we should be pestered with fellows who criticize things which they cannot understand.

> For truth is precious and divine;
> Too rich a pearl for carnal swine.

You will never please everybody.

Remember the fable of "The Old Man and his Ass." If you please God always, and your wife generally, be quite content.

You will not be loved yourself if you love none but yourself.

You would talk a horse's hind leg off.

Or chatter a cat to death, or beat a magpie into fits.

> A dearth of words we need not fear;
> But 'tis a task to learn to hear.

You'd do well in Lubberland, where they have half-a-crown a day for sleeping.

That is to say, you are a lazy fellow, not worth your salt.

You'll find it true,
The morning dew
Gives healthy hue.

It would be advisable to get up early and see if it be not so. It is due to the dew that we duly give it a fair trial.

You'll not put out the fire with tow.

Nor stay anger with provoking words.

You're in and out, like a dog at a fair.

Said of a person who seems to be everywhere, and especially where he is not wanted.

You're worse than a brute if you treat brutes cruelly.

None of my readers would do this himself; but it is also our duty never to let others do it without a vigorous protest.

Young idlers become old thieves.

Young people, like soft wax, soon take an impression.

" Ere your boy has reached to seven,
Teach him well the way to heaven ;
Better still the work will thrive,
If he learns before he's five."

Your choice of a wife will flavour your life.

Your dirty shoes are not welcome in my parlour.

You are welcome, but not those boots which spoil my carpets.

Your geese are not swans.

They are ordinary birds after all. Do not exaggerate, lest people should say, " He has a deal of thunder, and very little rain."

Your head should save your heels.

Your own legs are better than stilts.

If you depend upon yourself, you will do better than if you get help from others. It also means that the natural is better than the artificial. Let the speaker use his own voice, manner, and matter, and they will suit him far better than those he imitates.

Your shoes will not fit everybody.

Nor your ways, methods, and beliefs, suit all people. Do not try to force them upon others.

Your talk travels on, and on, and on; and yet it goes no further than all round the gooseberry bush.

Your wit will never worry you.

Very few need fret on that score.

Youth's too hot and bold ;
Age too weak and cold.

𝔖𝔞𝔶𝔦𝔫𝔤𝔰 𝔬𝔣 𝔞 𝔪𝔬𝔯𝔢 𝔖𝔭𝔦𝔯𝔦𝔱𝔲𝔞𝔩 𝔖𝔬𝔯𝔱.

Yokes are good for youthful shoulders.

> As with young bullock newly broke,
> Our neck must learn to bear the yoke.

You can be an honest man and not a Christian; but you cannot be a Christian and not be an honest man.

You cannot wrestle with God, and wrangle with your neighbour.

You have only one soul, give it to your one Saviour.

You may have much in little where others have little in much.

> A man's life consists not in what he possesses; fitness and content are all important.

> A little hearth best fits a little fire,
> A little chapel fits a little choir,
> My little bell best fits my little spire.

You must be divorced from the law to be married to Christ.

> Yet some would be both under law and gospel at the same time: but the double marriage is contrary both to law and gospel. If it be of works, it cannot be of grace.

Your trust is worthy when you trust the trust-worthy.

> Look well to the ground of your faith, that it be strong enough to bear up your soul.

> Little pillars, it is plain,
> Cannot heavy weights sustain.

EAL and discretion are like the two lions which supported the throne of Solomon.

They make a fine pair; but are poor things apart. Zeal without discretion is wildfire, and discretion without zeal is cowardice.

Zeal is fit only for wise men, but is mostly found in fools.

The more's the pity if so it be.

Zeal is like fire; it needs both feeding and watching.

It is a good servant, but a bad master. In the one case it is earnestness; in the other fanaticism.

Zeal pleaseth God, for zeal is the love of God in man.

Zeal without knowledge is a runaway horse.

Nobody knows where it will go, or what mischief it will do. In these dull times we are almost eager to run the risk. We are overdone with rocking-horse without life or progress.

Zeal without knowledge is fire without light, and knowledge without zeal is light without fire.

Zeal without knowledge is like haste to a man in the dark.

It leads to blunders and accidents.

Zeal without knowledge soon becomes cold.

There is nothing to feed its fires, and so it dies down, and is very hard to re-kindle.

Date Due

APR 1 7b			
JAN 23 '79			
DEC 5 '84			
APR 17 '85			
OCT 2 '85		–	
APR 23 '88			
MAY 11 '88			
	LINCOLN CHRISTIAN COLLEGE		